PRAISE FOR

OUT
in All Directions:

A Treasury of Gay and Lesbian America

❖ ❖ ❖

"PACKED WITH WONDERFUL ARTICLES, LISTS, PHOTOS, AND QUOTES."

—*Woman's Monthly*

"[A] SUPERB ADDITION TO THE FIELD OF GAY AND LESBIAN STUDIES...A MUST FOR THE COMPLETE LIBRARY. THIS IS ONE OF THOSE BOOKS YOU PORE OVER FOR HOURS."

—*Twn* **(FL)**

"ALMOST SCREAMED TO BE A BOARD GAME....THOUGH HUMOR AND ENTERTAINMENT PLAY A BIG PART IN THE VALUE OF THIS BOOK, THERE'S ALSO PLENTY OF MORE SOBER INFORMATION."

—*Echo Magazine*

"FASCINATING...PROVOCATIVE AND FUNNY."

—*Contax Guide* **(FL)**

in All Directions

A Treasury of Gay and Lesbian America

Edited by Lynn Witt,
Sherry Thomas, and Eric Marcus

A Time Warner Company

Warner Books, Inc., 1271 Avenue of the Americas,
New York, NY 10020
Visit our Web site at http://pathfinder.com/twep

A Time Warner Company

Printed in the United States of America
First Trade Printing: June 1997
10 9 8 7 6 5 4 3 2 1

Witt, Lynn.
Out in all directions: the almanac of gay and lesbian America / Lynn Witt, Sherry Thomas, and Eric Marcus.
p. cm.
ISBN 0-446-67237-8
1. Lesbians—United States—History. 2. Gay men—United States—History. 3. Lesbians—United States—Biography. 4. Gay men—United States—Biography. 5. Lesbians—United States—Social conditions. 6. Gay men—United States—Social conditions. 7. Gay liberation movement—United States—History. 8. Gay rights—United States—History. I. Thomas, Sherry. II. Marcus, Eric. III. Title.
HQ75.6.U5W57 1995
305.9'0664—dc20 95-3445
CIP

Book design by Wright Creative Associates, San Francisco, California.

All chapter opening photographs by Paula Keller, from the button collection of Jean Tretter.

This book is dedicated to

Beverly Remer
and
Clara Ann Simmons

for their unconditional love
and support

Acknowledgments

I have read hundreds of books in my lifetime, but until I wrote one myself, I'd never understood why some authors felt the need to include long lists of people in their acknowledgments. But the truth is, without all these people, no book would ever get published, not because the author didn't have great ideas, but because, especially in a nonfiction project such as this one, it takes more than vision to make a book.

Sherry, Eric, and I would like to thank the following volunteers and staff members who edited, typed, wrote letters, did research, proofread, fetched lunch, and helped out in other ways too numerous to mention: Al Baum, Megan Boler, Charlie Graham, Margaret Goins, Markham Hirt, Cullen Holliman, Jennifer Marshall (where are you?), Arwyn Moore, Ann Morse, Susan Regan, Joe Schubert, Jakki Spicer, Greg Walker, and most especially Steve Vezeris, to whom I owe more than can ever be repaid.

We need to thank the gay and lesbian booksellers and archivists around the country who shared with us their enormous wealth of knowledge, and provided contacts in communities and among people we might not otherwise have met. We would especially like to thank Sherry Emory at Charis Books in Atlanta; Jim Marks at *Lambda Book Report* in Washington, D.C.; Bill Walker at the Gay and Lesbian Historical Society of Northern California; Barbara Grier from Naiad Press; and Cal Gough from the

Gay and Lesbian Task Force of the American Library Association.

I would also like to thank Jennie McKnight for her dedication to the project and her help in reminding me of the complexity and diversity of the gay and lesbian community. Don Romesburg, our assistant editor, gets credit for coming up with the title. I would also like to thank Katherine Forrest for her friendship and encouragement on this project.

The editors thank Will Roscoe, Jewelle Gomez, Colin Robinson, Dennis Medina, and Alina Ever for helping us with the original conception of what later became the chapter on identity.

There are dozens of people around the country who took the time to meet with us and the project staff, either in person or by phone, and they all deserve our thanks: Bill Benemann, Faygele Ben Miriam, Carrie Barnett, Michael Bronski, Harneen Chernow, Paula Ettlebrick, Joan Garner, Michael Goff, Trevor Hailey, George Holdgrafer, John Howard, Arline Isaacson, Rupert Kinnard, Elizabeth Knowlton, Renée LaChance, Mev Miller, Sarah Petit, Howard Petric, Cynthia Scott, Brett Shingledecker, Linda Stamps, Sarah Schulman, David and Francis Stocks, and Caitlyn Sullivan.

We want to thank Colleen Kapklein, our editor at Warner Books, for shaping what you see here and for having the patience to see this project through. The staff at Wright Creative Associates, Inc., who had the task of taking 1,200 pages of manuscript and turning it into a very readable book, were a delight to work with, especially Liz Noteware and Jeffrey Whitten.

Finally, it goes without saying that without our agent, Loretta Barrett, there would have been no book at all. I want to acknowledge her friendship, support, and unwavering belief that made it possible for this ambitious fantasy to become a reality.

— LYNN WITT

Preface

Everyone always asks how *Out in All Directions* came to be published. People want to know: Who came up with the idea? How did we convince a mainstream publisher to take on such a book? Did we have an agent? Generally speaking, most authors of fiction write a book first and then, with or without the help of an agent, they try to get it published. Nonfiction writers usually start with a proposal and some sort of chapter outline, which they try to sell before completing the manuscript.

Out in All Directions, however, followed a somewhat different course on its way to publication. It was born one night in 1992 when Loretta Barrett, a New York literary agent, and Maureen Egan, editor-in-chief of Warner Books hardcover division, were having dinner. Loretta and Maureen had first met twenty-five years earlier, when they both worked at the same publishing company. As their careers progressed, they've stayed friends, getting together throughout the years to talk shop and catch up. That evening, they hit upon the idea of a gay and lesbian almanac—something they would both love to read.

Loretta immediately thought of Sherry Thomas, a writer she'd known for twenty years and whose work she'd edited in the 1970s, and gave her a call. Sherry had just begun work on a new job, so her initial impulse was to pass on the almanac. Loretta suggested instead that she think it over during the weekend. By Monday, an arrangement had been worked out whereby Lynn Witt, who was great at managing complex projects, would oversee the almanac and would be involved in the daily development of the book, while Sherry provided creative input and direction. A proposal was put together for Warner Books, complete with sample pages. Shortly thereafter, Eric Marcus, author of several books including *Making History: The Struggle for Gay and Lesbian Equal Rights, 1945–1990,* joined the creative collaboration.

Everyone took an active part in editing and shaping the final product, the scope of which is enormous. The ten chapters of the almanac cover more than 175 different topics; fifty-five contributors wrote over ninety original pieces, and 125 writers granted permission to reprint previously published works.

Each of the editors assumed a different role. In San Francisco, Sherry provided creative direction and "big picture" assessment, and she shared her contacts around the country. Her publishing background and guidance were invaluable to the book's completion. Lynn spent the first four months of this project traveling around the country soliciting contributors. Returning to San Francisco, she coordinated the day-to-day activities of the project, soliciting articles, organizing chapters, managing volunteers and paid staff, and writing introductions and other pieces as needed. In New York, meanwhile, Eric provided contacts for potential contributors, feedback on the structure and content of each chapter, and moral support.

Late in the project, Don Romesburg was brought in as an assistant editor. With his experience working on *Long Road to Freedom* and *Young, Gay and Proud,* he was just the boost we needed to get this book out on time.

The result is a book that we hope will amaze, astound, inspire, and inform everyone who picks it up.

— LYNN WITT, SHERRY THOMAS, AND ERIC MARCUS

Table of Contents

Introduction

The 1990s have brought a new era of visibility for lesbians and gay men. More and more public figures are coming out, from U.S. congressional representatives to Hollywood producers. There is an astonishing network of resources that has been created in the gay and lesbian community in the years since the Stonewall rebellion. Organizations that could not have been conceived of five years ago now flourish, in every arena from education to the trades. Colleges teach gay studies. More and more corporations and cities are offering domestic partnership benefits to their gay and lesbian employees. Gay people are openly present in boardrooms and schoolrooms, in churches and theaters, everywhere.

In short, there has never been a better time to show the world, both gay and nongay, the depth and breadth of the people, the history, and the communities that have been created by gay men and lesbians.

Traditional almanacs are full of information and advice, and so is this one. But charts and tables can only convey so much; what is lacking from traditional almanacs is the people behind the facts. As a rule, lesbians and gay men are missing from most general discussions of "who's who" and "what's what" in our society. What we have done here is present a broad picture of the myriad cultures and achievements of gay people in society at large; each page presents the reader with something new and interesting to ponder. Many of the pieces here were solicited specifically for this book. Others are reprints that fit well with the various themes of the chapters. In addition, we have included several dialogues from many of the gay computer bulletin boards that can be found on the Internet. This new medium seems to be the forum for some of our liveliest conversations.

The almanac is divided into ten chapters, any one of which could easily be a book unto itself. The first draft of the manuscript for this book ran 1,800 pages; there's clearly more to say than could possibly be included here.

The first chapter, "We Are Everywhere," features gay men and lesbians in a variety of mainstream venues, from local city council offices and scientific laboratories to hog farms and a high-school class reunion.

Both "inside" and "outside" views of gay and lesbian people in the media, from film and theater to television and the printed word, can be found in Chapter 2, "How We Are Seen, How We See Ourselves."

Gay people do have a past, but as Chapter 3, "Reinventing History," implies, it's not always obvious who we are or what we have done. We have rioted and we have written; we have organized and we have led battles. We have been closeted, and we have spoken out at the risk of losing all.

While gay people come from all economic, ethnic, religious, and social strata of society, we share the dilemma of being gay in a nongay world. In Chapter 4, "Finding Identity," we give voice to these individual explorations and to the continued examination of what it means to be "the other."

Beyond the individual is the community. Many of us come to the gay and lesbian community in search of family, in search of a home. We date; we have sex; some of us get married (sometimes to each other); and some of us have children. In Chapter 5, "Coming Together: Building Community," we explore the "familial" side of the gay community as well as the institutions we have built to sustain and document our lives.

We take both a serious and a lighthearted look at the "Myths and Facts" surrounding gay people in Chapter 6, from answers to commonly asked questions to tongue-in-cheek guidelines for spotting homosexuals.

Chapter 7, "Our Very Queer Lives," expands our view of who we are, talking among ourselves and exploring the range of people inside our communities and the complex cultures we have built.

In Chapter 8, "Ensuring Our Survival," we look at what it means to survive as a community, from being an AIDS buddy to working with allies such as P-FLAG to ensure our personal as well as our political future. But while remaining vigilant, we must remember at the same time not to take ourselves too seriously. From comics and gay bands to two-stepping and cruising (on the seas and in the bars), gay people know how to have fun. In Chapter 9, "Wanna Have Fun?" we present some of the ways in which lesbians and gay men let loose.

In the last chapter, "The Material World," we take a look at the work environment and some of the issues gay people face in their professional lives: deciding whether or not to come out in a job interview, facing the lavender glass ceiling, and choosing self-employment options, as well as other aspects of our economic lives. We also look at philanthropy as one way we can take responsibility for supporting our gay and lesbian institutions.

In every chapter we uncover history, illuminate gay and lesbian life, explode myths, and break new ground. The margins of the text contain hundreds of sidebars: quotes, little known facts ("Did you know..."), and other outrageous comments ("Can you believe it?"). Cartoons, photographs, and other graphics are also included to illustrate and inform the accompanying essays and articles. In addition, we've included a thorough index to help readers easily find the information they want.

As you read *Out in All Directions,* we hope that you will be entertained, informed, amused, and excited to discover the many rich facets of all that we call gay and lesbian.

A note about language

The phrase "gay men and lesbians" (or "lesbians and gay men") is used throughout the book whenever reference is made to the community as a whole. Other terms, however, such as "queer," "bi-identified," "lesbian-identified," "transgendered," and "homosexual," to name a few, are used liberally by some of the authors. If there is no monolithic gay and lesbian community (and the editors believe strongly that there isn't), then there can be no universal agreement on terms to describe that community. Here are just some examples of what we mean:

- The term "women" has often been used to mean "lesbian," as in "women's music" and "women's bookstores." While not all of the women involved are lesbians, it is safe to say that an overwhelming majority of them are.
- The first homosexual activists adopted the term "homophile" in the 1950s. While it's no longer in common use, some of those early activists still prefer this term. Later, many of us fought to get newspapers to replace the word "homosexual" with the word "gay," in the belief that "homosexual" placed too much emphasis on sex.
- As the word "gay" was gaining acceptance, it was becoming clear that most people equated "gay" with "male"; women were (once again) invisible. To counter this, the phrases "lesbian and gay" and "gay men and lesbians" and the like have become the standard for our organizations and newspapers.
- Some groups use the term "lesbian/gay/bisexual/transgender" (sometimes shortened to l/g/b/t) as a way of being overtly inclusive when dealing with the entire sexual minority community.
- For decades the term "queer" was used pejoratively. In recent years, thanks to groups like ACT UP and Queer Nation, many gay people have reclaimed "queer," using it to describe the many and sometimes outrageous facets of our gay selves and communities. "Queer" is sometimes used as shorthand for "l/g/b/t," and some people even use the word "queer" to describe those straight people who have a cutting-edge attitude toward their own sexuality.

Not all gay people are comfortable with all the terms used by society to describe them, but each person has a right to use the language that works best for him or her. Throughout the almanac, the reader will see these words and others; hopefully, all these terms convey the same thing: respect for ourselves as people who love people of the same sex.

A note about AIDS

There are many references in this book to AIDS, an epidemic few lesbians and gay men have not been personally affected by. We are not suggesting that gay men are the only people who get this disease. AIDS is certainly not the defining characteristic of our community, just as "gayness" is not the defining characteristic of the disease. However, given the dramatic and disproportionate impact of the AIDS epidemic on the lives of gay men, it is impossible—and undesirable—to write about the gay and lesbian community and culture without discussing AIDS.

FREEDOM
AGAINST THE BRIGGS INITIATIVE
1975
VOTE 84
Speak Out
1991
DC in 93
HOMOSEXUALS FOR PEACE
Gay Pride
NO GAY HOLOCAUST IN U.S.A.
street west
1976

CHAPTER 1

We Are Everywhere

"We are everywhere" is a statement that many lesbians and gay men have uttered in response to the oft heard "But I don't think I know anyone gay." But what does that mean, "We are everywhere"?

The truth is, lesbians and gay men are not always visible to each other, let alone to the nongay world. Despite common myths, most gay people cannot be picked out of a crowd. We cross all racial, class, ethnic, and religious lines. We are African Americans, Native Americans, Italian Americans, Asians, Latinos, Irish Americans, Buddhists, Catholics, Mormons, Japanese Americans, Chinese Americans, to name only a few. And we are in every family: We are mothers and daughters, fathers and sons, uncles and cousins.

There is an old joke that says that if all the gay people in this country were to stay home from work on the same day, business and government would cease to function; planes wouldn't fly; banks, schools, and grocery stores couldn't open; church pulpits would be empty; trains would stop running; and nobody would be able to get a decent haircut. This is not just because of our sheer numbers (see Chapter 6 for a discussion of those statistics), but also because even when we aren't visible, we are indeed everywhere: We are in every city and town, in every occupation, in every community.

It is invisibility that has led many people to dismiss the important contributions lesbians and gay men have made to society. This chapter is in large part about making the covert overt. It is one thing to know we are everywhere; it is another to become visible. In this chapter, we have focused on people who are prominent, whose names might be familiar to the reader not because they are gay, but because of their achievement or prominence in the world at large. (For another view of how gay people have made ourselves visible by creating our own institutions, see Chapter 5.)

For many gay people, the experience of finding ourselves has been a painful and rocky path; but many find coming out to be freeing. The thrill of discovering that someone like ourselves is gay is an almost giddy experience. In a world without role models, if you never see yourself, you have no idea of who you could become. Finally, that is changing. For young athletes today, sports figures like Greg Louganis (four-time Olympic gold medalist) and Martina Navratilova (the finest tennis player in the history of the sport) are the kinds of role models we wish we'd all had.

But just as important, both gay and straight people have their world expanded when they find out someone is gay. We all grow when we begin to recognize the diversity of lesbians and gay men, when we begin to see the whole picture of who gay people are, and when we understand the almost limitless possibilities of who we can become.

What we are attempting in this chapter is to break that invisibility, to present a wide range of out lesbians and gay men, a smorgasbord of who we are as lesbians and gay men. The examples here are not meant to be exhaustive—that would take several volumes. You'll notice that we've presented scientists but not psychologists, composers but not lawyers, dancers but not plumbers. This chapter represents only the tip of the iceberg of who we are.

DID YOU KNOW...

Jose Sarria, famous female impersonator, was the first openly gay person to campaign for public office, running for supervisor in San Francisco in 1961. While he was not successful, he did win nearly 7,000 votes. He ran, he said, not to win, but "to show gay people that we could do anything." Looking back years later, he added, "I don't know what I would have done if I had won!" It turns out that on the last day to file for candidacy, the "city fathers" discovered that there were fewer candidates than vacancies—which would have guaranteed Jose a spot on the board. By day's end, there were thirty-four candidates vying for the five vacant offices.

LESBIAN SURVIVAL HINT #211: WHEN THE TIME IS RIGHT TO COME OUT, YOU'LL KNOW.

(Rhonda Dicksion)

PINK POLITICS: GAY AND LESBIAN PUBLIC OFFICIALS

Social change happens in many ways, but gay and lesbian elected and appointed public officials are on the front lines of mainstream progress. While we must build coalitions with other groups in order to secure civil rights for all people, we must also stand up for ourselves. By running for public office, gay people demand inclusion in the democratic political process and they increase public awareness of gay struggles.

At the same time, it is important to recognize that gay and lesbian politicians, whether elected or appointed, do not necessarily represent only gay and lesbian issues. The contrary is often true; most gay people deal daily with the tension between being gay and having "gayness" define every aspect of what we do. While most out gay politicians are concerned about gay and lesbian civil rights, they are also concerned about the environment, education, health care, and taxes. When gay people are elected to office, they have been chosen by a constituency that is probably not overwhelmingly gay; they have been elected precisely because they bring all of who they are to the political table.

Today, out gay men and lesbians are running for public office in record numbers. According to the Gay and Lesbian Victory Fund, which provides support to gay candidates, in 1994 there were more than 150 gay people currently holding public office nationwide, either through appointment or direct election. More and more, gay candidates are being elected and appointed not only because they are gay, but also because gay people are no longer seen as one-issue candidates.

"There is a major difference between a friend [in office] and a gay person in office. It's not enough just to have friends represent us, no matter how good those friends may be. We must give people the chance to judge us by our own leaders, and our own legislators."

HARVEY MILK
MARCH 10, 1978

Harvey Milk

Sailor, Wall Street investment broker, hippie, and camera shop owner Harvey Milk went relatively unnoticed in his first two runs for the San Francisco Board of Supervisors. But in 1977, his successful bid brought him into the national media spotlight. The openly gay politician understood his role as a media darling: "I understand the responsibility of being gay," he said. "I was elected by the people of this district, but I also have a responsibility to gays—not just in this city, but elsewhere."

Harvey Milk in front of his Castro Street camera store, 1975. (Dan Nicoletta)

During his first year in office, he submitted and pushed through a gay-rights ordinance that moved to end antigay discrimination in jobs, housing, and public accommodations. Mayor George Moscone signed the policy into effect after Supervisor Dan White cast the only dissenting vote. Milk also took his show on the road, speaking to lesbian and gay organizations around the country. He was, and continues to be, an inspiration to gay people nationwide. Milk often told a story about a young boy from Altoona, Pennsylvania, who called him just to say "thank you" after hearing of Milk's election.

But his first year in public office was also to be his last. On November 27, 1978, politically conservative former supervisor Dan White gunned down both Mayor Moscone and Harvey Milk. The act of political vengeance shocked gays and straights alike. On the evening of the shooting, more than twenty-five thousand people carrying candles marched in silent vigil, and the memorial services two days later brought out thousands of people.

In May of the next year, when Dan White was found guilty only of manslaughter and sentenced to just seven years in prison, the city's lesbians and gay men erupted with rage. The White Night Riots brought three thousand angry gay people to city hall, where they caused an estimated million dollars in damage. Lesbian San Francisco State University Professor Sally Gearhart spoke to a crowd the next day, saying, "There is no way I will apologize for what happened last night. . . . Until we display our ungovernable rage at injustice, we won't get heard."

Harvey Milk was a kind man, an ambitious man, and a man of his people. His legacy lives on, detailed in both print and film. But more than that, he lives on as a symbol of the strength of our political convictions. His assassination serves as a historical reminder of the difficult opposition gay men and lesbians face demanding inclusion in the mainstream political process.

Gay and Lesbian Elected Officials

Out lesbians and gay men represent areas large and small—from Mayor Gene Ulrich of Bunceton, Missouri, population 321, to Carole Migden, the San Francisco supervisor elected at large in a city of 730,000. They've been elected in every region of the country—from Dallas, Texas, to Des Moines, Iowa, from Los Angeles to New York City, from Key West, Florida, to Burlington, Vermont, from Santa Fe, New Mexico, to Seattle, Washington, and many have been reelected time and time again.

DID YOU KNOW?

John Howell Park in Atlanta is the only public park in the country to be named for an openly gay man.

"When lesbians and gays choose to do public service and do it openly we can shift attitudes and change people's opinions," says Rochester, New York, Councilmember Tim Mains, who's been in office since 1985. History bears that out. West Hollywood, California, which has had three openly gay elected officials serving at one time, was one of the first cities in the nation to offer domestic partnership benefits to city employees. In fact, lesbian and gay elected officials, while working on issues as diverse as community preservation and a national health care plan, have pushed for lesbian and gay civil rights on several fronts. They've spoken out against antilesbian and antigay violence, helped pass state and local civil rights laws, organized successful campaigns to win domestic partnership benefits, and spearheaded efforts to fight ordinances undoing the gains of the lesbian and gay movement.

F I R S T S

Here are just a few of the firsts for known gay and lesbian elected officials.

1972

Nancy Wechsler and **Jerry DeGrieck** were elected to the Ann Arbor, Michigan, City Council as candidates from the Human Rights Party, though neither ran as openly gay. They both came out soon after in response to a homophobic incident at a local restaurant.

1974

Elaine Noble and **Kathy Kozachenko** were the first openly gay people elected to office—to the Massachusetts House of Representatives and the Ann Arbor, Michigan, City Council, respectively.

Allan Spear, a state senator in Minnesota, who had been elected in 1972, came out as an openly gay man.

1977

Steve Camara was the first openly gay person elected to a local school board, in Fall River, Massachusetts.

1980

Gene Ulrich was the first openly gay person to be elected mayor when he won the post in Bunceton, Missouri (population: 321). He has been reelected in every bid since.

1989

Albany, New York, Common Council member **Keith St. John** became the first openly gay African American elected official.

1990

Dale McCormick became the first openly lesbian state senator when she was elected to the office in Maine.

1991

Sherry D. Harris became the first out African American lesbian elected official when she won a seat on the Seattle City Council.

DID YOU KNOW...

On June 27, 1994, Deborah Batts was sworn in as the first openly gay federal district judge in the United States. She presides in Manhattan.

1994

San Francisco School Board member **Angie Fa** became the first Asian American lesbian or gay elected official.

Tom Duane of the New York City Council became the first openly HIV-positive candidate to be elected to office.

The same year saw the first statewide runs by lesbian and gay candidates—**Karen Burstein** for New York State attorney general and **Tony Miller** for California secretary of state.

And while there are still no openly gay or lesbian U.S. senators, there are three openly gay congressional representatives: **Gerry Studds** (D) and **Barney Frank** (D), both of Massachusetts, and **Steve Gunderson** (R) of Wisconsin.

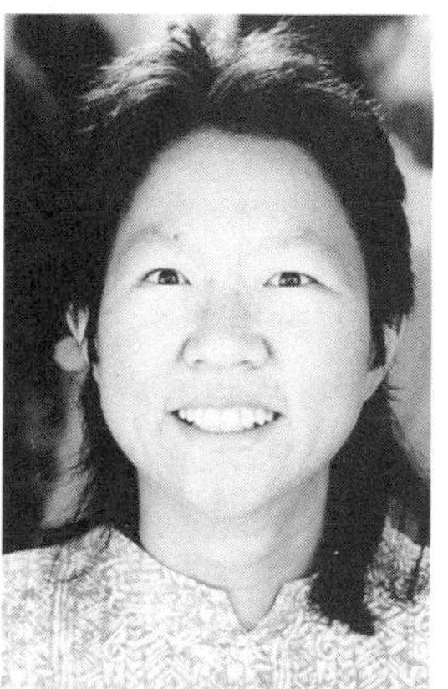

Angie Fa, elected member of the San Francisco School Board. (Rink Foto)

There is, of course, no "prototype" gay politician, just as there are no prototype gay people in any field. The individuals profiled on the following pages are representative examples of the more than 150 lesbians and gay men who have sought and won public office over the past twenty years.

STILL IN OFFICE AFTER ALL THIS TIME

Allan Spear, the Minnesota state senator originally elected in 1972 (and who came out in 1974), now in his sixth consecutive term, was elected Senate president in 1993.

Minnesota assembly member Karen Clark, elected in 1980, is still serving in 1995.

Elaine Noble

Although Kathy Kozachenko won election to the Ann Arbor, Michigan, City Council as an open lesbian in April 1974, it wasn't until Elaine Noble's race for the Massachusetts House of Representatives later that year that the nation's eyes really became focused on the possibility of an out lesbian serving in elected office. "She became the most highly publicized state legislator since Julian Bond," said *Ms.* magazine. Even the *New York Times* wrote an article about "the first avowed lesbian elected to state office."

Born in a Pennsylvania mining town, Noble put herself through Boston University by working as a cocktail waitress, then went on to get two graduate degrees, one in speech, the other in education. Noble also became active in her Fenway/Back Bay community, helping elderly people sign up for food stamps and get transportation to health clinics, organizing a neighborhood garbage cleanup, and fighting the conversion of a school playground into a Red Sox parking lot.

DID YOU KNOW...

As of 1994, openly lesbian and gay elected and appointed officials hold state or local offices in California, Colorado, Connecticut, Delaware, Florida, Illinois, Iowa, Louisiana, Maine, Maryland, Massachusetts, Michigan, Minnesota, Missouri, New Mexico, New Jersey, New York, North Carolina, Ohio, Oregon, Pennsylvania, Rhode Island, Texas, Utah, Vermont, Virginia, Washington, and Wisconsin. California has the most gay office holders, with thirty-five.

Offices range from mayor (Berkeley and Santa Monica, California; Melbourne, Iowa; Cambridge, Massachusetts; and Bunceton, Missouri) to state representative (Maine, Minnesota, Missouri, Texas, Vermont, Washington, and Wisconsin), and from police commissioner (Los Angeles) to public utility commissioner (Texas) to recreation and parks commissioner (Columbus, Ohio).

In 1973, she was appointed to the Governor's Commission on the Status of Women, and a year later, she ran for the Massachusetts State House, edging out her nearest opponent in a five-way Democratic primary by 169 votes—out of 1,231 cast. She then handily beat her Republican opponent with 59 percent of the vote.

"When I decided to run, it was because I'm the most qualified for this job," Noble told a *Newsday* reporter shortly after her election—a refrain that's been repeatedly echoed since by lesbian and gay candidates across the nation.

And despite slashed tires, obscene phone calls, and threats to campaign workers, "what enabled Miss Noble to win the district was a campaign that stressed her community work and the fact that she had met so many of the voters face to face," said the *New York Times.*

Noble served in the Massachusetts House until 1980, when she unsuccessfully ran for the U.S. Senate.

Sherry Harris

In 1991, Sherry D. Harris beat a twenty-four-year incumbent in the Seattle, Washington, City Council to become the first open African American lesbian elected to office anywhere in the United States. Harris, elected at large to represent Seattle's 525,000 residents, won with a whopping 70 percent of the vote. Like Elaine Noble, she attributes her victory to her history of community activism on issues including the environment, transportation, and economic development.

"In fact, when I began my campaign, it was a big question whether to be up front about my sexual orientation. I wasn't broadly known as a gay person, but we decided we could not NOT talk about it. Because then, in a big city like Seattle, there would be a whispering campaign. We didn't want my sexual orientation to be an issue in the race—we wanted to talk about real issues."

Harris notes that not having a "credential" in the gay community worked to her disadvantage. "They were really hard on me and made me prove myself to them," she says.

That's exactly what Harris has done. Not only does she chair the Council's Housing, Health, Human Services and Education Committee and serve as a member of both the Transportation and Utilities Committees, but she's also found the time to sponsor or co-sponsor more than a dozen gay-positive initiatives, and has helped raise more than a million dollars to fight antigay ordinances in Washington State.

Gerald Eugene Ulrich

Gerald Eugene Ulrich was one of only a handful of openly gay people to win office when, in 1980, he became mayor of Bunceton, Missouri (population: 321), in the heart of America's Bible Belt. He's been reelected in every election cycle since—including one tough campaign against an opponent "related to half the people in town," as Ulrich puts it. Ulrich won by a two-to-one margin.

Lesbian and gay elected officials from around the country gathered at Stonewall 25 to celebrate gay political visibility. (Gay and Lesbian Victory Fund)

"I just didn't think about it," says Ulrich of his sexual orientation. "Everyone in town knew me. They knew my parents. I grew up in this area."

"My lover and I have been together since 1972," Ulrich says. "We'd always gone to city and state functions together, so pretty much everybody in town knew about me."

Born to a farming family, Ulrich, a plant manager at a local rubber sponge factory, began his political life organizing a gay church for parishioners in central Missouri. But his life as mayor hasn't been that different from the life of any other mayor of a small town in America's heartland.

"I ran for office," Ulrich says, "to get some things done that weren't getting done by the old fogies here in town." Among his accomplishments: securing nearly a million dollars in state and federal grants for housing rehabilitation for the elderly, a new sewer system, parks, and a new town well. "People in this town judge me by my character and not my personal life—which is the way it should be," Ulrich declares.

Appointed Officials

One way to judge political power is to count how many people of a particular race, ethnicity, gender, religion, or any other category are appointed by elected officials. Judging by this standard, the political clout of lesbians and gay men has grown exponentially since Stephen Lachs and Mary Morgan were appointed to California municipal court judgeships by then-governor Edmund G. (Jerry) Brown, Jr., in 1981.

As of 1994, there were more than eighty lesbian or gay officials appointed to top local, state, or federal positions—and that's just counting the ones who've made themselves known to organizations like the Gay and Lesbian Victory Fund, an organization that raises funds for lesbian and gay political candidates. There are no doubt many more.

Roberta Achtenberg

Senator Jesse Helms of North Carolina got more than he bargained for when he took on Roberta Achtenberg, the San Francisco supervisor nominated to be assistant secretary for Fair Housing and Equal Opportunity at the U.S. Department of Housing and Urban Development. In an attempt to discredit Achtenberg, Helms decided to make an issue of Achtenberg's "outrageous" public behavior: She had actually kissed her life partner, Mary Morgan, at San Francisco's 1993 lesbian and gay pride parade. But

FEDERAL POLITICAL OFFICES HELD BY OUT LESBIANS AND GAY MEN, 1994

Though this compilation profiles only one year, it shows how pervasive our political presence is within the system. All positions are appointed.

DEPARTMENT OF INTERIOR
Assistant Deputy Secretary
Special Assistant to the Secretary
Special Assistant

DEPARTMENT OF COMMERCE
Assistant Secretary
Confidential Assistant to Assistant Secretary
Confidential Assistant to the General Counsel
Director of Interior Government Relations
Special Assistant to the Assistant Secretary
Special Assistant to the Secretary

DEPARTMENT OF HOUSING AND URBAN DEVELOPMENT
Assistant Secretary of Community Planning & Development on the Homeless
Assistant Secretary of Fair Housing
Commissioner of National Capital Planning
Deputy Assistant Secretary of Multi-Family Housing
Special Assistant to the Assistant Secretary
Special Assistant to the Secretary

DEPARTMENT OF HEALTH AND HUMAN SERVICES
Deputy General Counsel
Deputy Secretary for Public Affairs

dozens of senators rallied to her side, and Achtenberg became the first openly gay person to be confirmed by the U.S. Senate on May 24, 1993, by a margin of 58 to 31.

Achtenberg, who had served as a member of the San Francisco Board of Supervisors since January 1, 1991, is responsible for enforcing federal Fair Housing Law and for ensuring that HUD housing programs provide equal opportunity for all qualified Americans.

Prior to her election as supervisor, Achtenberg (who in 1992 became the first openly lesbian speaker at a Democratic National Convention) worked for fifteen years as a civil rights attorney. This included stints as the Executive Director of the National Center for Lesbian Rights and Director of the San Francisco Neighborhood Legal Assistance Foundation.

Paul Richard

Paul Richard, the deputy staff secretary at the Clinton White House, likes to tell a story about an interview the FBI had with Rob Keyes, Richard's partner of thirteen years. During the interview—part of the FBI's background investigation of Richard—the FBI asked Keyes whether Richard might be vulnerable to blackmail because of his sexual orientation. "The last time I was at the White House, Paul introduced me to the President as his spouse," Keyes told the FBI.

Richard, whose office manages all of the President's paperwork, is one of at least four openly gay appointed officials in the West Wing of the White House—the center of power for the executive branch. "As an African American and a gay man, I feel an obligation to make certain issues known to the President," Richard says.

Brought up in Washington, D.C., when the schools were still segregated and when African Americans wouldn't be seated at certain restaurants, Richard, a former lawyer in private practice, muses that "openly walking the corridors of power would have been inconceivable twenty-five years ago."

DEPARTMENT OF EDUCATION

Deputy Assistant Secretary of Special Education and Rehabilitation Services

Director of Special Education Programs

DEPARTMENT OF LABOR

Special Assistant of Labor

Special Assistant of Labor, Women's Bureau

Special Assistant to the Assistant Secretary

Presidential Personnel

Deputy Director of Information Services

Deputy Director Search Liaison

OTHER OFFICES

Correspondence Officer for Department of State, Department of Presidential Inquiries

Deputy Assistant Secretary of Internal Affairs

Deputy Staff Secretary to the President

Director of AIDS Prevention Center, the White House

General Counsel to General Services Administration

Office of Policy Development, Department of Justice

Senior Advisor for National AIDS Policy to the President

Senior Deputy Comptroller of the Currency

Senior Economist on Counsel of Economic Affairs

Special Assistant of Solid Waste, Environmental Protection Agency

Special Senior to the President

White House Liaison of Labor

DID YOU KNOW...

Inspired by the massive October 1979 March on Washington for Lesbian and Gay Rights, Melvin Boozer came out publicly. Already regarded as a "comer" in District of Columbia politics, Boozer, a young black professional, soon became president of the D.C. Gay Activists Alliance, a leading moderate voice among black gays nationally; in 1981 he became district director of the D.C. office of the National Gay Task Force. In 1980, he was an alternate delegate to the Democratic National Convention. That year, the seventy-five openly gay delegates and alternates placed Mel Boozer's name in nomination for vice president of the United States. As the first openly gay person to receive such a major party nomination Boozer had the opportunity to address the convention, after which he withdrew his nomination in favor of the party's official nominee. His work for gay rights and against racism continued until his death from AIDS-related causes in March 1987, at age forty-one.

Mary Morgan

In 1982, when Mary Morgan was appointed by Governor Jerry Brown to a judgeship in the San Francisco Municipal Court, to preside over both civil and criminal cases, she was worried. "Were people going to think of me as a judge? Or were they going to think of me as a lesbian?"

Most people gave her the respect she deserved, but one defense lawyer did write a note to the prosecuting attorney: "How can I get that bulldyke off my case?" Unbeknownst to the defense attorney, the prosecutor was gay—and promptly showed the note to Morgan. Despite this, Morgan avers, "I always felt good about the fact that a lot of people had gotten beyond the label of being a lesbian and focused on the fact that I was a very good judge."

By the time Morgan retired in 1993, she was Dean of the California Judicial College, responsible for training all the newly appointed judges in California.

— ANDREA BERNSTEIN

The information in this section was compiled with the assistance of the Gay and Lesbian Victory Fund, the national fundraising organization for lesbian and gay candidates for public office.

Gay Speakers Take the Floor

Gay men and lesbians in several cities first became visible in the Democratic Party as the 1972 presidential campaign geared up. Pro-gay resolutions passed in some state caucuses, and most Democratic presidential candidates made at least some effort to solicit the gay vote. At the Democratic National Convention, held in Miami Beach in August, five openly gay people were seated for the first time as delegates or alternates. Jim Foster, political head of San Francisco's Society for Individual Rights, or SIR, had written a strong gay rights position paper for Senator George McGovern, who, unfortunately, couldn't always remember whether he'd approved or even seen that statement.

While other gay people demonstrated in the park outside the convention, Jim Foster and Madeline Davis, of

Buffalo, New York's Mattachine Society of the Niagara Frontier, addressed those delegates who were still awake at five a.m.

"We do not come to you pleading for your understanding or begging for your tolerance," Foster said. "We come to you affirming our pride in our lifestyle, affirming the validity of our right to seek and maintain meaningful emotional relationships, and affirming our right to participate in the life of this country on an equal basis with every other citizen. . . .

"The kind of harassment, enticement, entrapment, brutality, discrimination, and injustice perpetrated against gay people is a shame to the concept of justice in this country. . . . [It is] ironic, in view of its valiant efforts to eradicate prejudice, discrimination, and abuse in matters of race, creed, and color, that the government has itself been a major and active promoter of the abuse our society directs against gay women and men."

He appealed for adoption of the gay rights plank, adding that whether or not it was adopted, "We are here. We will not be stilled. We will not go away until the ultimate goal of gay liberation is realized . . . [until] all people can live in the peace, freedom, and dignity of what they are."

Ms. Davis, whose gay folk song album, *Stonewall Nation*, had been released weeks earlier, said more briefly, "Twenty million gay Americans are the untouchables in our society. We have suffered the gamut of oppression, from being totally ignored to having our heads smashed and our blood spilled on the streets.

"Now we are coming out of our closets and onto the convention floor to tell you . . . and to tell all gay people throughout America, that we are here to put an end to our fears." Urging adoption of the gay rights plank, she said, "We must speak to the basic civil rights of all human beings. It is inherent in the American tradition that the private lives and lifestyles of the citizens should be both allowed and ensured, so long as they do not infringe on the rights of others. . . . You have before you a chance to reaffirm that tradition and that dream. . . .

"You have the opportunity to gain the votes of 20 million Americans who will hope to put a Democrat in the

DID YOU KNOW...

In 1993, after serving for two years as vice president of the San Francisco Board of Education, Tom Ammiano became the first openly gay school board president in the country.

White House. . . . I say to you that I am someone's neighbor, someone's sister, someone's daughter. A vote for this plank is a vote for all homosexual women and men across the country to peaceably live their own lives."

Despite the wee morning hour, it was a historic breakthrough, broadcast nationwide to an audience estimated by industry officials at a million. (More than 11 million heard Foster interviewed on NBC and CBS earlier.) Both speeches won loud applause, but the gay rights plank then lost by a voice vote. (A watered-down version passed four years later.)

Once he had the nomination wrapped up, George McGovern sought to distance himself from the gay men and lesbians, women's liberationists, peace activists, environmentalists, and counterculture people who'd won him the victory; later there was an angry confrontation in his office between gay activists who felt betrayed and the more "mainstream" gay people who still managed parts of McGovern's stumbling campaign.

—JIM KEPNER

OUT OF THE CLOSET, INTO THE NEWSROOM

Media shapes American society as much as it reflects it. From Washington politicians to Hollywood studios, from social movements to celebrities on trial, everyone has become keenly aware of the power of the media to influence attitudes and change public opinion.

Given the role media plays in our society, it is crucial to gay men and lesbians as a people that we have representation on the "inside." There have always been mainstream gay and lesbian journalists. But the pressure of being in an aggressive and competitive job market, as well as the homophobia within the industry, often keeps gay journalists in the closet. In the guise of "objectivity," their sexualities remain invisible both in the public eye and in the office.

More and more, individuals around the country have refused to remain silent. In the business of manufacturing images and presenting information, these openly gay and lesbian journalists are standing up and declaring that their identities are a relevant and essential part of who they are, not only privately, but publicly as well.

Out in the Media

• **Leroy Aarons**, *Oakland Tribune* executive editor in California. After coming out during a presentation of the first-ever survey of gay journalists at the American Society of Newspaper Editors, Aarons started the momentum that became the National Lesbian and Gay Journalists Association (NLGJA). He is currently president of the NLGJA.

• **Susan Baumgartner**, columnist for the *Moscow-Pullman Daily News* in Idaho. According to reports in gay publications at the time, Baumgartner was believed to be the first openly lesbian columnist for a rural daily newspaper when she came out in her column in October 1993.

• **Lily Eng**, *Philadelphia Inquirer* higher education reporter. Active in the Asian American Journalists Association, Eng was credited as being a leading force in having the National Lesbian and Gay Journalists Association invited to Unity, a historic national gathering of ethnic minority journalists, in Atlanta in 1994. She was also among those instrumental in making domestic partnership benefits available at the *Seattle Times.*

• **Steve Gendel**, CNBC reporter who disclosed his orientation during a network news report on Stonewall. According to *New York Newsday* of August 25, 1994: "CNBC producer and correspondent Steve Gendel has been openly gay for some time, but had never announced it in a news story until June, when he was narrating a *Today Show* report on the Stonewall riot. . . . 'Few will deny,' he intoned into the camera and out to millions of viewers, that the riot 'was a great catalyst for the American gay movement, allowing many of us who are gay, including myself, to come out of the closet and fight for acceptance.' With those words, Gendel became the first national TV correspondent to identify himself as gay during a network news story, breaking one of the most tenacious silences in broadcasting."

• **Lynda Moore**, network news anchor for ABC Radio. A lesbian-identified bisexual, Moore says she believes if not for her presence and that of a gay person with AIDS (PWA) editor, there would be much less attention paid to gay and lesbian issues at the network. She's been at ABC since 1980, and always out at work. She says if she hadn't covered events like the 1987 gay rights March on Washington, "then they wouldn't have been covered."

Juan Palomo, Texan columnist (Courtesy Houston Post)

• **Juan Palomo**, *Houston Post* columnist and editorial writer fired, then rehired, over coming out in print. Palomo wrote a column in July 1991 about a local Fourth of July gay-bashing murder. In the column, Palomo said people had a responsibility to speak out against such atrocities. His intended column concluded with Palomo saying he had a special responsibility to speak out because he himself was a gay man. His editors nixed that line (one expressing the fear, says Palomo, that the paper would lose subscribers). The *Houston Press*, an alternative weekly, found out, interviewed Palomo, and quoted him in its story about the deletion. This angered Palomo's editors. Other media outlets picked up the story, and Palomo was eventually fired for insisting on his right to speak to other reporters about the incident. The *Post* rehired Palomo within a week, after a national outcry from other media professionals. Palomo now writes his column, which he estimates addresses gay and lesbian issues about 10 percent of the time, as an openly gay man.

• **Tom Rolnicki**, executive director and editor of National Scholastic Press Association. Rolnicki, who has been involved with college and high school newspapers nationally for over a decade, says many of them are better on AIDS and gay issues than the mainstream commercial press is.

• **Jeffrey Schmalz**, *New York Times* AIDS reporter who died from complications of the disease in 1993. Some insiders say Schmalz had a profound effect on the *New York Times* (and, by extension, all the U.S. news media's) coverage of AIDS and gay issues. Schmalz, who began working at the *Times* as a copy boy at age eighteen and rose to become a deputy national editor, collapsed and suffered a seizure at his newsroom terminal in 1990. He was diagnosed with AIDS, and subsequently came out as a gay PWA to top editors at the paper. He returned to active reporting, covering the White House, gay politics, and AIDS. His last piece, "Whatever Happened to AIDS?" was published posthumously in the *New York Times Magazine* on November 26, 1993.

• **Andrew Sullivan**, editor-in-chief, the *New Republic.* When openly gay Briton Andrew Sullivan, at twenty-eight, was named editor of this conservative and influential national magazine in 1991, it caused quite a media stir. Sullivan, who began working at the *New Republic* four years before becoming editor, has written on such diverse topics as race wars in New York, the Catholic Church in America, and the rift between HIV-negative and HIV-positive people.

• **Helen Zia**, award-winning investigative reporter. Zia is a contributing editor and former executive editor of *Ms.* magazine, where she was the first Asian woman to head a major national magazine. Zia was instrumental in publicizing the Vincent Chin case in Detroit, as detailed in her award-winning documentary *Who Killed Vincent Chin?* Chin was beaten to death in 1982 by autoworkers who thought he was of Japanese ancestry and somehow responsible for hard times in the U.S. auto industry. At her request, Zia asked to be and was introduced as a lesbian before her keynote speech for the Asian American Journalists Association's national convention in 1990, broadcast live on C-SPAN.

— **ERIC JANSEN**

Linda Villarosa

Though she had been openly lesbian for years, Linda Villarosa, out African American lesbian and senior editor of *Essence Magazine,* broke new ground with "Coming Out," an article she wrote with her mother for the May 1991 Mother's Day issue of *Essence.* The decision did not come easily; it kept her up at night and gave her nightmares. But as Linda said in an interview with *Deneuve* magazine, "This was not something I wanted to do, but something I needed to do." Linda explained that writing "Coming Out" eradicated the pressures of hiding her personal life at work and in public. Most important, however, she was able to give voice and identity to a minority whom Linda says is invisible in our society. "There is a perpetuation of the stereotype, particularly in the black

DID YOU KNOW...

In 1991, *Essence Magazine* received more letters than ever before in its twenty-four-year history when readers responded to a Mother's Day article by senior editor Linda Villarosa and her mother, Clara, on Linda's coming out. "It was coming out in a big way," says Linda. The avalanche of responses were overwhelmingly positive, and prompted the Villarosas to follow "Coming Out" with a second article, "Readers Respond to Coming Out." For those articles, Linda received the Gay and Lesbian Alliance Against Defamation (GLAAD) Media Award.

Linda Villarosa, the openly lesbian editor of Essence Magazine, *was the first African American lesbian to head a major national magazine.*
(Essence Magazine)

community," she told *Deneuve*, "that there are no black lesbians . . . or that women who are gay are so unattractive and mannish—a bunch of people with bad haircuts. . . . Well, I wanted to challenge that stereotype."

"Coming Out" is Linda Villarosa's hope that black lesbians will gain a sense of entitlement to succeed in life as who they are without having to hide, and to serve as role models for young black lesbians and gays. "The best thing you can do in your life is to stop lying, be honest, be true to yourself and what is important in your life. I am very happy with how my life is going. And if I've helped a few other young women to come out and be honest with their lives, then that is great too."

Randy Shilts

Randy Shilts was probably the most widely recognized gay journalist in the mainstream media. His 1987 best-selling book, *And the Band Played On: Politics, People and the AIDS Epidemic*, details the early history of the AIDS epidemic and the indifferent, slow response to it by the federal government, the medical establishment, and by some gay organizations.

"He put AIDS on the front page," said prominent AIDS physician Dr. Marcus Conant in the *San Francisco Chronicle* report on Shilts's death from AIDS in February 1994. Shilts also wrote *The Mayor of Castro Street: The Life and Times of Harvey Milk* (1982), a biography of the gay San Francisco supervisor who was assassinated with Mayor George Moscone; and *Conduct Unbecoming: Lesbians and Gays in the U.S. Military* (1993).

Homophobia among editors, Shilts said, had kept him from finding full-time journalism work in Oregon, where he had attended the University of Oregon and was managing editor of the student newspaper. He came out while a student there and was active in gay politics in Eugene. It was only six years after his graduation, in 1981, that the *San Francisco Chronicle* hired Shilts, making him one of the first openly gay reporters for a major U.S. daily newspaper. In the six-year interim, Shilts was a correspondent for *The Advocate* and a reporter for television stations KQED in San Francisco and KTVU in Oakland, during which time he also wrote much of *The Mayor of Castro Street.*

Shilts said he didn't inquire about his HIV status until he had finished writing *And the Band Played On* because he didn't want this knowledge to affect his investigation. Similarly, he didn't publicize his illness until after *Conduct Unbecoming*, completed from his hospital bed, was published. Shilts told *The Advocate* he considered himself "more valuable to the gay movement as a journalist" than as "a professional AIDS patient."

Because of his frank reporting in the 1980s about gay bathhouses and their role in the spread of AIDS, and his stance later against "outing," Shilts was derided by some in the gay community, while others sung his praises.

Shilts himself seemed somewhat dismayed, writing in *Esquire* in 1989: "The bitter irony is, my role as an AIDS celebrity just gives me a more elevated promontory from which to watch the world make the same mistakes in the handling of the AIDS epidemic that I had hoped my work would help to change."

— **ERIC JANSEN**

Deb Price

Deb Price said she was "absolutely terrified" her sucessful journalism career might end when she proposed a weekly column on gay and lesbian topics for the *Detroit News*. But her editor and publisher liked the idea, and the column began in May 1992. It was quickly picked up nationally by *USA Today* and many of the eighty-three local Gannett newspapers, and has since been syndicated and is carried by other major publications.

Price says the positive reaction she received from early readers showed her how critical her columns are in small towns where gay people had no visibility.

In her columns, Price writes in a personal style about life with her partner (journalist Joyce Murdoch), religion, gays in the military, gay parents, and a wide range of other topics. She says her goal is to "bridge a gap between the gay and heterosexual communities, to get an open and honest dialogue started."

Formerly news editor of the *Detroit News* Washington, D.C., bureau, Price said it took her a while to get used to using "us" and "we" instead of "them" and "they." "No

DID YOU KNOW...

The National Lesbian and Gay Journalists Association is an organization that supports gay people in the media, pressing for gay inclusion in industry nondiscrimination statements, domestic partnership benefits, and accurate representations of gay men and lesbians in the media. As of 1994, the three-year-old organization had over eight hundred members nationwide.

one has been more liberated by this column than I have," says Price.

— ERIC JANSEN

Garrett Glaser

Garrett Glaser made history in 1992 when he became the first openly gay on-camera reporter to address the Radio and Television News Directors Association. Although certainly not the first openly gay man on television news, Glaser's presentation on a panel about newsroom diversity at the RTNDA's national conference immediately proclaimed his homosexuality to many of the most influential newsroom decision-makers in the country (news directors whom he might someday have to ask for a job).

Never closeted in his own newsrooms, Glaser's orientation became common knowledge to editors and reporters throughout Southern California when he became a director of the Gay & Lesbian Alliance Against Defamation/Los Angeles. At the time, he was a reporter for *Entertainment Tonight*, a national nightly covering Hollywood. He now covers media and entertainment for KNBC-TV in Los Angeles and, through syndication, is seen on other NBC stations nationally.

— ERIC JANSEN

DID YOU KNOW...

Dorothy Atchenson, an out lesbian, has been working on the editorial staff at *Playboy* magazine since 1990—and she loves it. Says Atchenson, "I don't get offended by what we do at *Playboy*. I've been really educated from my experience working here. Lesbians I meet think it's sort of interesting that I work at *Playboy*. Lesbians these days tend to be very pro-sex."

QUEERED SCIENCE

One can more easily prepare a list of gay scientists from almost any other country than the United States. For a variety of reasons, people in other countries who have gained high status in science feel less of a need to hide. In the United States, science is frequently wedded to the government and the military, both of which have traditionally been hostile to gay men and lesbians. Our society at large has never been particularly nurturing toward openly gay professionals and academics, either.

Still, there are great numbers of gay and lesbian scientists at the top of their fields, and the people we've included stand in the place of hundreds of others. There are also the geologists working for oil companies on the Alaskan Pipeline; horticulturists in the Midwest; and researchers in medical laboratories around the nation—a vast array of people across the scientific community count themselves as proud members of the gay family.

Gay and Lesbian Scientists

- **Dr. S. Josephine Baker** (1873–1952), pioneer public health specialist isolated "Typhoid Mary" and was listed in "American Men of Science." She dressed as a man and was the longtime lover of Australian-born novelist I. A. R. Wylie, who called her George.
- **Benjamin Banneker** (1731–1806), an African American gazetteer and astronomer, published *Banneker's Almanack* for the years 1792–1797, popularizing antislavery causes. He assisted Major Andrew Ellicott in a survey of what became the District of Columbia.
- **Rachel Carson** (1907–1964), marine biologist and author of the revolutionary *Sea Around Us* and *Silent Spring*, detailed the devastating overuse of insecticides that threatens the balance of nature and the future of life on earth. Carson was elected to the American Academy of Arts and Letters, and her pioneering work resulted in major environmental legislation.
- **George Washington Carver** (1864–1943), African American biochemist, agrobotanist, and teacher, born a slave, revolutionized the lagging Southern farm economy with his work on crop diversification, and his many farm-related inventions, while heading the Tuskeegee University research staff for half a century. He was openly gay and lived for years with his loving successor at Tuskeegee, Dr. Austin W. Curtis, Jr.
- **Charles Martin Hall** (1863–1914), one of the inventors of the electrolytic method of producing aluminum inexpensively. He left his fortune to Oberlin College and to his longtime companion.
- **Dean Hamer** (b. 1951), geneticist at the National Cancer Institute, who published the results of his two-year study on genetic links to homosexuality in the 1994 book *The Science of Desire: The Search for the Gay Gene and the Biology of Behavior,* co-authored with Peter Copeland.
- **Dr. Franklin P. Kameny** (b. 1925), Washington, D.C., Harvard-trained astronomer who fought his "security" dismissal from the U.S. Geodetic Survey—he had refused

to answer questions as to whether he was homosexual—and became a strident and effective fighter of civil service and military discrimination cases, winning many major decisions in the courts.

Kate Hutton, lesbian seismologist and spokeswoman for the California Institute of Technology during the 1994 Northridge Quake, on firm ground with her dog. (Bob Paz/Caltech)

• **Simon Levay** (b. 1943), controversial neurobiologist who in 1991 announced the discovery of smaller hypothalamus glands in gay men than in straight. His book, *The Sexual Brain*, details his theories.

• **Margaret Mead** (1901–1978) and her lover **Ruth Benedict** (1887–1948), influential anthropologists and social critics who revolutionized the way of looking at so-called "primitive" societies.

• **Maria Mitchell** (1818–1889), the first American woman astronomer, held the initial chair of astronomy at Vassar and became the first woman admitted to the American Academy of Arts and Sciences (1887).

• **Ellen Richards** (1842–1911), American chemist who helped establish the science of ecology and pushed for passage of the Pure Food and Drug Act.

• **Nicola Tesla** (1856–1943), Serbian-American scientist who invented the arc lamp and discovered the principle of the alternating current, wireless telegraphy, and other electrical breakthroughs. He worked first for Edison, then for Westinghouse.

— JIM KEPNER

KEEPING THE FAITH

For many gay people, organized religious institutions have not been exactly welcoming. Many mainstream religions openly condemn homosexuality; some of the more "open" institutions exhort their followers to "hate the sin but love the sinner." But for many lesbians and gay men who were raised with traditional religious or spiritual values, and for others looking for the deeper spiritual meanings of life, religious beliefs still hold an important place in their lives. And although many religious gay people have joined the growing number of "alternative" offshoots of traditional institutions, others have chosen to stay within the mainstream churches and synagogues of their upbringing, fighting for acceptance and change within the institution. And often, they have met with success. Not long ago, out lesbian rabbis or gay ministers could be found only in gay synagogues and churches. Today we can be found in most mainstream religious institutions as members, as lay leaders, and as officials.

DID YOU KNOW...

Alan Turing, the British mathematician who cracked the supposedly unbreakable German secret code during World War II, was tried and convicted of "gross indecency" in the 1950s. Because of his classified status with the British government, the court deemed his wartime achievements inadmissible, and he was forced to choose between prison and "organotherapy," an experimental hormone therapy. He opted for the latter, and the treatment caused him to grow breasts and become chemically depressed. In 1954, he committed suicide, abandoned by the country that he had played a critical role in saving less than a decade before.

Queers in the Church

In February 1994, mourners for gay San Francisco journalist Randy Shilts filled a large downtown church, their numbers swelling into the surrounding streets. As the memorial service began, a homophobic minister from Kansas arrived with several followers holding signs that condemned homosexuality and AIDS as a punishment from God. In the face of such blatant homophobia by antigay religious zealots, it would be natural to ask: Why would any self-respecting queer have anything to do with such a homophobic institution as the church?

Most lesbians and gay men who continue to work inside the structures of mainline churches often ask themselves that same question. And while some, for various reasons, have left the traditional church and organized specifically gay autonomous religious congregations, many gay and lesbian people of faith stay. They argue that lesbians and gay men have been an integral part of the church throughout its 2,000-year history and continue to find a sense of community and spirituality

Openly gay Lutheran minister Leo Treadway in his St. Paul, Minnesota, church. (MGM Photography)

that is life-giving while working within the structures to change its homophobia and injustice. In that struggle, gays and lesbians have found allies with justice-seeking communities in the church who share a history of working within racial justice, environmental, sanctuary, feminist, and abortion-rights movements, and now join the lesbian, gay, bisexual, and transgendered liberation movement.

One of the first places gay men and lesbians began pushing the church to change was in its policies on ordination. In the post-Stonewall 1970s, openly lesbian and gay candidates for ordination began pushing the churches to take a stand in support of lesbian and gay clergy. Most mainline churches voted to study the issue. Twenty-five years later many are still studying. While religious lesbian and gay support and advocacy organizations abound, most mainline denominations still refuse to ordain "self-avowed, practicing homosexuals."

— SELISSE BERRY

A History of Lesbian and Gay Ordination

• The **United Church of Christ** is one of the only mainline Protestant Christian denominations with a nondiscriminatory policy pertaining to sexual orientation. In 1972, Rev. Bill Johnson became the first out gay man to be ordained as a UCC clergyman.

• The **Unitarian Universalist Association** is not specifically Christian and also ordains lesbian and gay clergy. One of the denomination's largest churches, Arlington Street Unitarian Church in Boston, is led by out lesbian Rev. Kim Crawford.

• In 1978 the **Presbyterian Church** (USA) voted against the ordination of "unrepentant, self-avowed, practicing homosexuals" but did grandmother in lesbians and gay men who had been ordained prior to 1978. In 1992 out lesbian minister Rev. Jane Spahr was denied a position with the Downtown United Presbyterian Church in Rochester, New York, because of her sexuality.

• The **United Methodist Church** voted to prohibit the ordination of "self-avowed, practicing" lesbians and gay men in 1984.

DID YOU KNOW...

An overwhelming majority of the members of the University Congregational Church in Seattle voted in 1994 to let the Rev. Peter Ilgenfritz and his partner, David Shull, become the congregation's associate ministers. The pair, who met while at Yale Divinity School in 1986, are believed to be the first gay couple in the country to share a ministry at a nongay church.

• Instead of being a matter of policy, **Episcopal** ordination is left up to the local bishop. Few out lesbians and gay clergy serve as priests, even though Rev. Ellen Barrett was ordained as an Episcopal priest in 1977, the first open lesbian to achieve that status.

• In the **ELCA (Evangelical Lutheran Church in America)**, two San Francisco churches, St. Francis Lutheran and First United Lutheran, have been charged with heresy over the issue of an "irregular" ordination of gay and lesbian clergy—Reverends Jeff Johnson, Ruth Frost, and Phyllis Zilhart—and face expulsion from the denomination in 1995.

• Because of the ecclesiastical structure of the **American Baptist Church**, there is no national governing policy. The general denominational attitude is homophobic, although there are notable exceptions, including the 1991 call to lesbian clergy, by Rev. Nadean Bishop of University Baptist Church in Minneapolis.

• The **Roman Catholic Church** and the **Southern Baptist Church** still do not ordain women as clergy. The Southern Baptists have expelled from the denomination churches who advocate for lesbian and gay liberation, while the Catholic hierarchy refuses to allow Dignity (the lesbian and gay Catholic organization) to worship in Catholic parishes. While many closeted homosexuals serve as priests and pastors, these churches are in many ways the final frontier.

DID YOU KNOW...

In the Talmud, lesbianism is categorized as a misdemeanor, as opposed to the graver "crime" of male homosexuality. According to Maimonides, a woman who has had sex with another woman is still eligible to marry a Cohen (a member of the priestly class), or even (if married) to continue having sex with her own husband.

Toleration or Inclusion?

Despite most denominations' refusal to ordain lesbians and gay men as ministers, most denominations believe that while homosexuality is a "sin," homosexuals should be tolerated and treated with respect. The United Methodist Church's "Statement on Social Principles" regarding homosexuality reflects the general attitude shared by most mainline denominations:

"Homosexual persons no less than heterosexual persons are individuals of sacred worth. All persons need the ministry and guidance of the Church in their struggles for

"The Bible contains six admonishments to homosexuals and 362 to heterosexuals. This doesn't mean God doesn't love heterosexuals. It's just that they need more supervision."

LYNN LAVNER, SINGER/COMEDIAN

> **"In everything else, I was out front. In the open. But here's one piece of my life that wasn't at all. That'll kill you. You can deny something that is a basic part of you for only so long. . . . I enjoy gay friends. But equally, I enjoy straight friends. I really have tried to balance it. I don't want to be just in gay life."**
>
> **HENRY FINCH, FORMER PASTOR OF THE FIRST BAPTIST CHURCH OF CHARLESTON, SOUTH CAROLINA, AFTER BEING STRIPPED OF HIS POST FOR BEING OPENLY GAY**

human fulfillment, as well as the spiritual and emotional care of a fellowship which enables reconciling relationships with God, with others, and with self. Although we do not condone the practice of homosexuality and consider this practice incompatible with Christian teaching, we affirm that God's grace is available to all. We commit ourselves to be in ministry for and with all persons."

Not all individual churches agree with statements issued by denominations at a national level. Some churches disregard the tolerance and respect and are extremely homophobic. Others go beyond tolerance and embrace the lesbian and gay community. Many of the same churches that provided counseling for conscientious objectors during the Vietnam War, referred women to safe doctors before abortion was legal, and provided sanctuary to Central American refugees during the 1980s, have made a commitment to welcome people regardless of their sexuality. There are presently more than 350 individual churches that have voted to become "welcoming churches" for the lesbian and gay community across the country. In November 1992, the four oldest welcoming programs became linked in an ecumenical move to publish *Open Hands*, a quarterly journal of "resources for ministries affirming the diversity of human sexuality."

Each denomination has a different name for these welcoming programs including:

- Presbyterian: More Light Churches
- United Church of Christ/Disciples of Christ: Open and Affirming Congregations
- Methodist: Reconciling Congregations
- Lutheran: Reconciled in Christ
- Unitarian Universalist: UUA Welcoming Programs
- Brethren and Mennonite: Supportive Congregations
- American Baptist: Welcoming and Affirming Churches

Gay and lesbian people of faith have goals beyond being welcomed as worshipers and church leaders. They are not only interested in spirituality but are also interested in pushing the boundaries of misogynist and sex-negative theologies and strive to explore places where their spirituality and sexuality intersect. Much of the writing of lesbian and gay theologians and religious leaders has its roots in modern liberation theology. The basis of liberation theologies is that God stands on the side of the oppressed. Similar to Latin American, African American, Asian, and feminist liberation theologies, gay and lesbian liberation theologians contend that as an oppressed class of people, their very marginalization gives them a particular connection to the divine. Their work on earth—whether it involves tending to a lover with breast cancer or defending the rights of a gay father to keep his child—is sacred and holy work and is, in fact, being Christ in the world.

"After all is said and done, the choice for me is not whether or not I am a gay man, but whether or not I am honest with myself and others. It is a choice to take down the wall of silence I have built around an important and vital part of my life, to end the separation and isolation I have imposed upon myself all these years."

OTIS CHARLES, FORMER EPISCOPAL BISHOP OF UTAH AND DEAN OF THE EPISCOPAL DIVINITY SCHOOL IN CAMBRIDGE, MASSACHUSETTS, ON HIS REASONS FOR COMING OUT AT AGE SIXTY-SEVEN

Jane Spahr

Jane Adams Spahr grew up in a Presbyterian family in Pennsylvania. She loved the church and knew she wanted to become a minister. In 1974 Janie was ordained. Four years later, she came out as a lesbian and was forced to resign her position as associate minister of First Presbyterian Church in San Rafael, California.

In 1981 Janie became the founding director of the Ministry of Light, later renamed Spectrum, a community program for lesbian, gay, bisexual, and transgendered people. She stepped down in 1991 and became one of four co-pastors of Downtown Presbyterian Church in Rochester, New York.

Religious leader and ex–Presbyterian minister Jane Spahr (MGM Photography)

Despite endorsements from that church and its two supervising governing bodies, the Presbytery and the Synod, the appointment was overturned at the church's highest level. Spahr renewed her effort to work for the inclusion of Presbyterian lesbians and gay men. In her memoirs, *Travels of a Lesbian Evangelist*, Janie Spahr describes her work:

"I have met thousands of people who have shared their stories of the heart, asking difficult questions, crying, laughing, being angry, open, despondent, and hopeful. I have witnessed the most sacred moments . . . [from] a mother coming out to her son in Portland, Oregon, to several lesbian, gay, and bisexual seminarians who through tears say 'I know I have been called to this work. I don't want to lie about who I am, for it is a gift to be who I am.'"

— SELISSE BERRY

CONTEMPORARY OPENLY LESBIAN AND GAY RELIGIOUS LEADERS

Bishop Carl Bean, founder of the Unity Fellowship Church

Rev. Malcolm Boyd, Episcopal priest and writer

Rt. Rev. Otis Charles, retired Episcopal bishop of Utah

Rev. Johannes Willem DiMaria-Kuiper, minister

Beverly Wildung Harrison, Christian theologian

Rev. Carter Heyward, lesbian Episcopal priest and writer

Bernard Mayes, priest, journalist, and university dean

Rev. Renee McCoy, African-American minister and activist

Rev. Troy Perry, founder of the Metropolitan Community Churches

Rev. Dusty Pruitt, Metropolitan Community Church minister

Rev. Herman Verbeek, Catholic priest, Dutch member of European Parliament

FROM "THE OUT LIST" BY MARK HERTZOG

Gay and Lesbian Jews in Orthodox and Conservative Jewish Communities

Many orthodox and conservative Jewish communities continue to claim that Judaism cannot accept homosexuality as a viable way of life. Orthodox gay men and lesbians do not have the benefit of any codified tolerance or acceptance, as Reform Jews do. Homosexuality tends to be much more blatantly and publicly decried within orthodox communities, and the pressures toward marriage and child rearing tend to be much more pronounced.

Rabbis have at times echoed orthodox rabbi Abraham B. Hecht in stating that acceptance of homosexuality means "the institution of marriage will go out of style and children will become strange creatures—unwanted and unloved. Our country cannot afford the spread of this disease which is destroying the fabric of the traditional family unit."

Although some orthodox Jews have taken a slightly less virulent stance, their antigay message is still clear. Abraham Gross, while a spokesman for seven orthodox organizations that represent a thousand rabbis and a million and a half synagogue members, stated that "while we do not support the harassment of homosexuals, the Bible condemns the practice of homosexuality." It is rare that gay or lesbian orthodox Jews receive acceptance from their congregations or their families.

Gay and lesbian orthodox Jews often describe a disenchantment with Judaism accompanied by feelings of isolation and alienation, and eventual rejection of their Jewish identities. Others must hide their homosexuality in order to remain within the community, or to maintain their positions within their synagogues as rabbis, cantors, and educators. This hiding often hurts these individuals, as well as their congregations. For example, one lesbian rabbi writes (anonymously) about her perceived lack of emotional attachment: "It appears that I simply have no love life. In some very significant way, I become different from them. . . . I cannot communicate with them on an emotional level, because I cannot be honest with them about my own emotional life. I am impoverished and the people with whom I work are impoverished."

Another orthodox man has been married for twenty years, but finds male sexual partners "in the places frequented by many closeted homosexuals: bathhouses, porn flicks, and highway rest stops" once every six to eight weeks. When the guilt that these activities brought on became too much, he resolved to refrain from these encounters. However, after six to eight months, he became so irritable with his family that one of his children complained to a teacher. He decided that denying his homosexuality would not work. Although he believes strongly in obeying halacha (the Jewish law), this man feels that he has "to look away" when his sexuality is at issue. "To be happy, to be a good husband and father, I have to," he says. "And I am willing to pay the price."

There are a few organizations offering outlets to orthodox gay and lesbian Jews. Beth Simchat Torah in New York, the largest gay and lesbian synagogue in the U.S., has an orthodox minyan once a month. Additionally, David Belzer, an orthodox gay man, is a social worker in New York who works with other gay orthodox people. He and others meet regularly to talk about the complicated issues in their lives. These discussions give them, as one man puts it, "an outlet other than sex for feelings of frustration."

— JAKKI SPICER

DID YOU KNOW...

Pauline Newman, a Jewish lesbian, served as the International Ladies Garment Workers Union's first female organizer from 1909 until 1913, when she became a worker for the Joint Board of Sanitary Control. She and her longtime lover adopted a baby in 1923.

DID YOU KNOW...

The Supreme Rabbinical Court, a small group of orthodox halachic rabbis, issued a ruling that declared the lesbian contributors to *Nice Jewish Girls*, a Jewish lesbian anthology, "dead" and "non-Jews."

DID YOU KNOW...

Katherine Lee Bates, who composed "America the Beautiful," spent most of her adult life living with a lesbian lover.

"The homosexuality of so many composers [in the U.S.] is a tale that has at best been ignored and at worst expunged. And paradoxically, these very composers wrote many of this country's most accessible and enduring works."

THE NEW YORK TIMES, JUNE 19, 1994

THAT ARTISTIC FLAIR

Tennessee Williams once said that "homosexuals are indistinguishable from the straight man, except that they have more sensibility and they are more inclined to be good artists." To say that gay people have had an influence in the arts is an understatement. More than any other segment of the population, the arts community enjoys a large number of openly lesbian and gay members. Every gay person has her own theories about why that is; it can—and will—be eternally debated.

But for every artist who is out of the closet, there are hundreds of others who are not. Be it in music, fashion, visual arts, or dance, coming out is never easy. While the arts are in many ways more embracing of lesbians and gay men than other communities, there is still a great deal of homophobia and silence surrounding the subject of homosexuality.

Many mainstream performers fear that coming out will jeopardize their careers, narrow their creative possibilities, and lose them some of their fans. A handful are willing to take the risk, and those who have deserve applause, support, and admiration.

A Few American Gay Composers

- **Harold Arlen** (1905–1986), American songwriter who penned "Over the Rainbow" (with lyricist Yip Harburg), "Stormy Weather," "That Old Black Magic," "The Man That Got Away," "I Love a Parade," "Paper Moon," and at least 500 other popular songs and film scores.
- **Samuel Barber** (1910–1981), Pennsylvania-born composer best known for his *Adagio for Strings*, *Capricorn Concerto*, *Vanessa* (for which he won a Pulitzer in 1958), and *Piano Concerto #16* (for which he won the 1963 Pulitzer). His *Anthony and Cleopatra* opened the Met at Lincoln Center.
- **Mrs. A.H.A. Amy Beach** (1867–1944), composer and pianist whose major works include *Gaelic Symphony*, *Concerto for Piano and Orchestra*, *Quintet*, *Theme and Variations for Flute and String Quartet*, and

Improvisations for Piano. She wrote *Festival Jubilee* to dedicate the Women's Building at the Chicago World's Fair and *Panama Hymn* for the Panama-Pacific Exposition in San Francisco.

• **Leonard Bernstein** (1918–1990), dynamic, multi-faceted composer and conductor known for works as varied as *Peter and the Wolf, West Side Story, On the Town, Wonderful Town, Fancy Free, Candide,* and *Serenade for Violin and Strings*.

• **Marc Blitzstein** (1905–1964), left-leaning composer known mostly for *The Cradle Will Rock, The Airborne Symphony, Juno, Regina, Sacco and Vanzetti* and his Americanization of *The Threepenny Opera*.

• **John Cage** (b. 1912), avant-garde composer and inventor of unusual instruments, such as a piano with various noisemaking instruments between the strings. He was a longtime associate of choreographer Merce Cunningham. His best-known works are *I Ching, Europera, One, Imaginary Landscape,* and *Variations Four.*

• **Aaron Copland** (1900–1990), composer, concert organist, critic, author, and concert producer who encouraged "new music," Copland incorporated classical and popular or folk styles in *El Salon Mexico, Billy the Kid, Rodeo, Fanfare for the Common Man, Lincoln Portrait,* and *Appalachian Spring*. As "the Dean of American Music," he won a Pulitzer, a Guggenheim Fellowship, a Presidential Medal of Freedom, and an Oscar.

• **Henry Dixon Cowell** (1897–1965), pianist and composer who originated the concept of "tone clusters," as seen in *The Banshee, Aeolian Harp,* and *Rhythmicana.* His atonal *Quartet Romantic*, written in 1917 for two flutes, a violin, and a viola, each playing different rhythms, foreshadowed electronic music but didn't receive its world premiere for another sixty-one years.

• **Lehman Engel** (1911–1982), Broadway conductor of *Showboat, Carousel,* and *Guys and Dolls*, also composed music for *A Streetcar Named Desire* and various Martha Graham works.

• **Stephen Collins Foster** (1826–1864), self-taught composer of popular American songs "Old Folks at Home," "My Old Kentucky Home," "I Dream of Jeannie

DID YOU KNOW...

Brotherly collaborators Ira and George Gershwin, known later for the lyrics and music of *Porgy and Bess* and *Of Thee I Sing*, and for George's *Rhapsody in Blue*, took over management of New York City's gay Lafayette Baths just south of Cooper Union in 1916, when Ira was only twenty and George was known chiefly as a composer of popular songs.

DID YOU KNOW...

Harry Hay, a founder of the Mattachine Society and the Radical Faeries, believes that we can identify actual musical patterns in a composition that signal whether it was written by a gay man or lesbian. His research on minstrels of the Middle Ages and the Renaissance attempts to identify gay and lesbian performers and composers by isolating components of the music of known lesbians and gay men that are not found in the music of historically documented heterosexuals.

(with the Light Brown Hair)," "Oh, Suzanna," "Old Black Joe," and a number of Civil War songs.

• **Charles Tomlinson Griffes** (1884–1920), openly gay impressionist composer known as "The White Peacock" for his flamboyant manner and for one of his works of that name. He also wrote *The Pleasure Dome of Kubla Khan, The Kairn of London, Four Roman Sketches,* and *These Things Shall Be.*

• **Lou Harrison** (b. 1917), a composer and gay activist, was a student of Henry Cowell. Leontine Price premiered his opera *Rapunzel.* His other works include *Koncherto* for violin and percussion orchestra, *Symphony in G,* and *Invocation for the Health of All Beings.*

• **Robert Moran** (b. 1937), composed *The Desert of Roses* based on *Beauty and the Beast,* set in the post–Civil War period; *From the Towers of the Moon,* based on an ancient Japanese legend; and *The Juniper Tree,* co-written with Philip Glass from a bloody Brothers Grimm fairy tale.

• **Cole Porter** (1892–1964), Yale-bred American composer, lyricist, and performer who filled his wonderfully popular lyrics with gay lines. "I've Got You Under My Skin," "Love for Sale," and "Night and Day" are just a few of his better-known songs.

• **John Powell** (1882–1962), pianist and composer and lifetime companion of composer Daniel Gregory Mason (1873–1953). Powell's compositions include several that make much use of Negro folk themes—*Rhapsodie Negre, The Virginia Country Dances, Natchez on the Hill,* and *The Babe of Bethlehem*—and various concertos, songs, and chamber music.

• **Ned Rorem** (b. 1923), composer and author whose *Third Symphony* is a lament for his ex-lover, Claude. Rorem's written works hold more music-world gossip than most other published sources.

• **William Grant Still** (1895–1978), got his start as an arranger for W. C. Handy, Sophie Tucker, Paul Whitman, and Artie Shaw. He wrote the ballets *Sahdji* and *Lennox Avenue* and the operas *Troubled Island, A Bayou Legend,* and *Highway 1, U.S.A.* His first success came in 1931 with his *Afro-American Symphony.* In 1936 he became the first African American composer to lead a major symphony orchestra.

DID YOU KNOW...

In a move that killed his popularity, Civil War–era composer Stephen Foster ("I Dream of Jeannie") left his wife to live with handsome fellow composer George Cooper ("Sweet Genevieve"). Eventually impoverished in the Bowery, then the site of several gay taverns, he died in the Bellevue Hospital charity ward. His film biography (as usual) portrays him as quite heterosexual.

DID YOU KNOW...

The well-known fraternity song "Sweetheart of Sigma Chi" ("The girl of dreams is the sweetest girl of all girls") was originally written by Dudleigh Vernor with male pronouns for his lover at Albion College in Michigan; he reluctantly changed the gender in order to get the song published in 1912.

• **Billy Strayhorn** (1915–1967), songwriter, pianist, and recording director who collaborated with Duke Ellington (who generally got credit for Strayhorn's compositions) on "Take the A Train," "Lush Life," "Unforgettable," and "Satin Doll." Known as "Sweet Pea" by friends, he made no attempt to hide his gayness or to move out of the Duke's shadow.

• **Howard Swanson** (1907–1978), leading African American composer. Leontyne Price sang his *Night Song*, with words by Langston Hughes, at a White House performance. *Short Symphony* was his first major success, followed by several piano sonatas and chamber works.

• **Virgil Garnett Thomson** (1896–1989), critic and composer who collaborated with Gertrude Stein on *Four Saints in Three Acts* and set the story of Susan B. Anthony to music in *The Mother of Us All*. He also wrote several film scores, including *The Louisiana Story*.

— JIM KEPNER

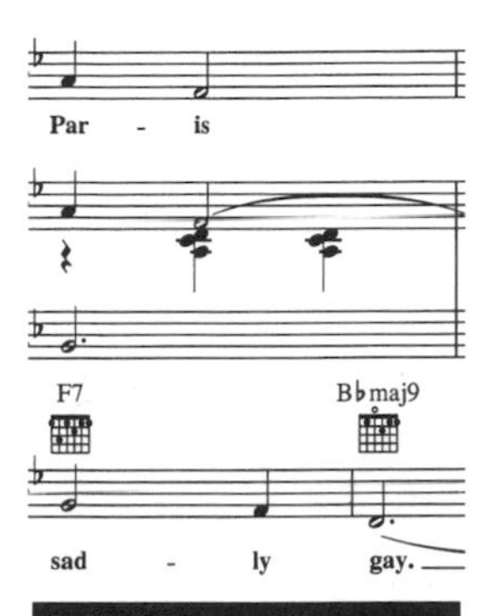

A GAY HEART

The song "I Left My Heart in San Francisco" was written by a gay man for his lover. It was written by Douglass Cross for George Corey, after they visited San Francisco in 1954.

Rock, Roll, and Riot Grrls

Warning: This list of lesbian, gay, and bisexual artists and bands that have at least one openly queer member will be forever incomplete, since to record the hundreds of local bands making queer-positive music today would require a whole separate book.

Marc Almond
Bratmobile
Adele Bertai
Betty
Billy Tipton Memorial Saxaphone Quartet
Book of Love
Breeders
Buzzcocks
Meryn Cadell
Coil
Ani DiFranco
Disappear Fear
Doubleplusgood
echobelly
Erasure
Melissa Etheridge
4 Non Blondes
Fifth Column
The Flirtations
Frankie Goes to Hollywood
Boy George
Girls in the Nose
The Gretchen Phillips Experience
Heavens to Betsy
Hole
Horse
Janis Ian

In 1995, lesbian rocker Melissa Etheridge won a Grammy for Best Female Rock Vocalist. (Courtesy Island Records)

Indigo Girls
Jane's Addiction
Elton John
Jose & Luis
k.d. lang
The Lucy Stoners
Luscious Jackson
Magnetic Fields
Maggie Moore
Malibu Barbie
Morrissey
Bob Mould
New Order
The Nylons
Pansy Division
Pet Shop Boys
Pussy Tourette
Queen
Toshi Reagon
Random Order
Ru Paul
Rumors of the Big Wave
Seven Year Bitch
Sexpod
Sister Double Happiness
Sister George
Jimmy Sommerville
Linda Smith
Doug Stevens and the Outband
Team Dresch
Thinking Fellers Union Local 282
Tribe 8
Vaginal Cream Davis
Y'all

— VICTORIA STARR

DID YOU KNOW...

John Williams, who composed scores for over fifty films—including *Jane Eyre, The Towering Inferno, Jaws, Star Wars,* and *Close Encounters of the Third Kind*—and was named conductor of the Boston Symphony in 1980, came out in a trade press ad in response to the homophobic Anita Bryant campaign.

Sylvester

Disco diva Sylvester topped the dance charts in the mid-1970s with the hit single "You Make Me Feel (Mighty Real)." But even before that, he had already become an icon of campiness, gay liberation, drag, and African American pride.

Born Sylvester James Hurd in 1948, he always knew that he was a queen. But it wasn't until his 1970 stage

DID YOU KNOW...

The Village People was one of the first gay groups to crack pop music's Top 40 and sell enough recordings to receive a coveted gold record, which they did in 1978. The group consisted of six gay male archetypes: the leatherman, the cop, the soldier, the construction worker, the cowboy, and the Indian. In its review of the group, *The New York Times* noted that the Village People's widespread success "attests to the continuing permeation of homosexual ideas into the mainstream."

Sylvester (Rink Foto)

debut with the Cockettes, a genderfucking drag troupe, that others began to sit up and take notice. By the next year, he was playing with his Hot New Band to packed houses on both coasts, and in 1972 came out with his first album, *Lights Out*. In 1977, his album *Step II* went gold, making him one of the first openly gay performers to enjoy such a mainstream musical success.

During the eighties, Sylvester's mainstream popularity waned, but he continued to perform for gay audiences both in the United States and abroad. Often he would play at AIDS benefits, supporting the communities that had supported him from the beginning. He died of AIDS-related causes in 1988 at the age of forty.

DID YOU KNOW...

The song "The Best of Times," by Jerry Herman, openly gay composer and lyricist of *Hello, Dolly!*, *Mame*, and *La Cage Aux Folles* and a confirmed Democrat, was played at the 1992 GOP convention (without his advance knowledge), right after Pat Buchanan's homophobic speech.

Gays in the Fashion Industry: What's Covered Up Is Revealing

Gianni Versace—the bearded, vivacious Italian designer who lives and works by the credo more is more—was sitting in his baroque studio in Milan almost two years ago, talking about how he bought a palatial home on Ocean Drive in that mecca of Florida hip, South Beach.

I will never forget that conversation.

"I was on the way to Cuba," he said, "and I stopped just for ten hours in Miami. I said to the driver, don't bring me to anything boring, just bring me to where the action is, where the young people go. He dropped me at News Cafe. After five minutes—five minutes!—I said to my boyfriend, Antonio, 'You can go to Cuba!' I stayed fifteen days and bought the house right away."

Such a multimillion-dollar impulse purchase is nothing in fashion. But a designer of Versace's international stature speaking openly about having a boyfriend . . . well, that's something that doesn't happen every day.

Though it's one of the worst-kept secrets in the world that the fashion industry is dominated by gay men, few designers talk to the press about their homosexuality or their relationships. And when they do take a journalist into their confidence, it's almost always off the record.

Speculation about who is gay and who isn't gay in fashion reached a fever pitch [in June 1994] with the publication of *Obsession,* the unauthorized biography of Calvin Klein by Steven Gaines and Sharon Churcher.

The authors, one of whom previously muckraked Halston, suggest that Klein, who is married to the former Kelly Rector and has a daughter from a previous marriage, is bisexual. They say he had an affair with the late designer Perry Ellis, often fell in love with straight men, spent summers in the Fire Island Pines on Long Island, and paid for sex with men, including porn stars. Published reports say Klein—through a channel of friendly entertainment moguls derisively called the Velvet Mafia—tried to have the book quashed for $5 million. The *New York Post* dedicated an entire column to the most tawdry of the "allegations."

Fashion insiders gave it one big yawn. Really, how shocking is it to learn that someone who designs dresses, sells cologne, and plasters Marky Mark in his underwear on bus shelters may be bisexual?

Sadly, Klein's sexuality—whatever it is—is being reported as an "allegation," right alongside tales of drug abuse, plastic surgery, and 1970s-era good-time debauchery [and] Klein was not commenting on any of it.

He has never been a tell-all type. When it comes to details about his personal life, Klein is as spare in interviews as he is in his design philosophy.

Not Versace. He has always been as colorful as his clothes and just as raucous. "I don't think a gay person has to be afraid," Versace said that day in Milan. "You don't have to go with a flag and say 'I'm this' or 'I'm that,' but I cannot be a liar.

"I'm more interested to know the real personality of a gay man or a straight man, not to know a gay man who wants to be straight or a 'straight' man who's gay. We are what we are. And, I don't think we're in bad company [with] all the creative persons who are gay."

Certainly, there are some very high-profile "out" gays in fashion. Isaac Mizrahi, Todd Oldham, John Bartlett, Marc Jacobs, and Jean-Paul Gaultier are among the few big names who have spoken freely in recent years. But for every star designer who is open about his homosexuality, there are many more gay and lesbian designers who don't say a word.

Klein has a right to privacy, I guess. And he has never hidden the fact that many of his closest friends—most notably David Geffen—are openly gay. But out gays find it puzzling and aggravating that an industry that prides itself on being on the vanguard of pop culture is lagging behind when it comes to the gay rights agenda.

Some suggest that designers don't talk about their sexuality for fear of losing customers. Mainstream designers, selling underwear and jeans to customers who may be less comfortable with anything-but-straight people, may have some cause to worry.

That's a good part of Klein's business. But in the world of high fashion—a world in which Klein is also very much a player—the risks seem negligible.

Designer Jacobs said several years ago during his tenure designing for the Perry Ellis company: "I'm not kidding myself about who fashion people are. Women love gay men. That's not an issue. . . . I can't imagine that a person who would say 'I'm not going to buy clothes from a designer who's gay' would want to buy my clothes."

Being out, Jacobs said, is "really about educating people. People can't really hate someone they know."

Still, he does not believe that out gays are "better homosexuals because we live our lives openly and they don't." For some designers, being out does not come so naturally. "I was very fortunate to grow up with people who encouraged whatever I did," Jacobs said. "I didn't grow up with rules. It was never about . . . this sexual preference is right and that sexual preference is wrong."

Jacobs continued: "It was just not something that was discussed in polite society. People put on that facade of being married or being straight or whatever. I just think it's a different time. The times have become more accepting of honesty. There are still many people left who come from a previous generation. But then there's this whole crop of people who wouldn't think of discussing it—not because they don't want to talk about it, but because it's just the way it is. It's a non-issue to them."

DID YOU KNOW...

On April 21, 1985, fashion celebrity Rudi Gernreich—who designed the first topless bathing suit and the "Thong" (and, who, unbeknownst to many, was one of the founders of the Mattachine Society)—died of cancer at the age of sixty-two. Despite a *New York Times* obituary stating that he lived alone and that "there are no survivors," Gernreich was in fact survived by his lover of thirty-one years, Dr. Oreste Pucciani.

Whether this controversy is a non-issue to Klein's customers remains to be seen.

— FRANK DECARO FROM NEWSDAY

DID YOU KNOW...

Both Liberace, in 1985, and Elton John, in 1975, have had the dubious honor of being gay men on Mr. Blackwell's annual list of Worst Dressed Women.

DID YOU KNOW...

Loie Fuller, a key figure in the development of modern dance who became famous in Paris toward the end of the nineteenth century, lived her life openly as a lesbian. While she was as much a maverick in art as she was in her personal life, she chose to focus her dances not on lesbian experiences but on the transformation of her body through sophisticated stage technologies that she often invented herself.

Robert Mapplethorpe

Controversial, shocking, and talented photographer Robert Mapplethorpe brought his stark and cold images of floral arrangements, leathermen, and shaved models to the forefront of the art world. During the late seventies and eighties, he enjoyed a level of success and critical acclaim rare for an artist who so explicitly represented homoeroticism, not to mention hardcore man-to-man S/M acts.

After a long struggle, Mapplethorpe died of AIDS-related causes in 1989, after documenting various stages of his illness with photographic self-portraits. Mapplethorpe's widest fame, however, came posthumously in 1989, when the Corcoran Gallery in Washington, D.C., canceled a traveling exhibit of his work after being pressured by politicians and the National Endowment for the Arts. The act cast a spotlight on the religious right and their attempts to censor art through preventing federal funding of projects that they deemed "obscene."

A Sampling of Contemporary Lesbian and Gay Visual Artists

Emily Anderson, photographer
Don Bachardy, artist
Alison Bechdel, cartoonist
Tom Bianchi, photographer
Joan E. Biren (JEB), photographer
Naylan Blake, artist
Angela Bocage, cartoonist and writer
Scott Burson, artist
Paul Cadmus, artist
Jerome Caja, artist
Craig Carver, artist
Christopher Ciccone, artist
Kate Connelly, artist
Janet Cooling, artist
Tee A. Corrine, artist
Betsy Damon, artist
Donelan, cartoonist
Jedd Garet, artist
David Hockney, painter
David Hutter, painter
Robert Indiana, artist
Phillip Johnson, architect
Kris Kovick, cartoonist and writer
David McDermott, artist
Peter McGough, artist

Duane Michaels, photographer
Richard Bruce Nugent, artist and writer
Erwin Olaf, photographer
Ross Paxton, artist
Jody Pinto, artist
Jill Posener, photographer
Benno Premsela, designer and early European gay movement leader
Herb Ritts, photographer
Larry Rivers, painter and sculptor
Carla Tardi, artist
Arthur Tress, photographer
Val Wilmer, photographer and writer
Millie Wilson, artist
Fran Winant, artist

— FROM "THE OUT LIST" BY MARK HERTZOG

Artists We Have Lost

Artists Who Have Died of AIDS-Related Causes, 1983–1994

While AIDS is not an exclusively gay disease, the gay community has suffered disproportionate losses. In the arts community, the losses are equally profound. Often these two worlds overlap. Many of the performers, celebrities, and creative people who have died from AIDS-related causes are gay, and though the following list is not exclusively gay, nor is it complete, it reflects the tragedy of a decade of the disease.

Poet, playwright, and performer Assotto Saint (Robert Giard)

1983
Paul Jacobs, 53, pianist and harpsichordist of the New York Philharmonic

1984
Michel Foucault, 57, postmodern French philosopher
Calvin Hampton, 42, composer
Robert Moore, 59, comic actor and director

1985
Rock Hudson, 59, movie star
Ricky Wilson, 32, guitar player of the B-52s

1986
Way Bandy, 45, makeup artist
Perry Ellis, 46, fashion designer

DID YOU KNOW?

AIDS activists were critical about Nureyev's silence about having AIDS, but fellow dancers respect his decision. Nureyev died at age 54. Cause of death was listed as a cardiac complication "following a cruel illness."

1987

Michael Bennett, 44, director, choreographer, and co-producer of *A Chorus Line*

Alan Buchsbaum, 51, architect and originator of High Tech style

Cal Culver, 43, actor, gay porn star

Choo-San Goh, 39, Washington Ballet choreographer

Fritz Holt, 46, co-producer of *La Cage Aux Folles*

Liberace, 67, flamboyant entertainer and pianist

Charles Ludlam, 44, actor-playwright-director, co-creator of *Vampire Lesbians of Sodom*

Willi Smith, 39, trendy designer

Sam Wagstaff, 65, museum curator and art collector

1988

Warren Casey, 53, lyricist and composer, co-wrote *Grease*

Robert Ferro, 46, novelist

Leonard Frey, 49, actor

Colin Higgins, 47, screenwriter and director of *Harold and Maude*

Anthony Holland, 60, member of Second City comedy troupe

John C. Holmes, 43, bisexual porn star

Gregory Huffman, 35, Joffrey Ballet leading dancer and teacher

Wilford Leach, 59, director of *The Mystery of Edwin Drood*

Paul Thek, 54, surrealist artist

Arnie Zane, 39, dancer and choreographer

Author Allen Barnett, a Lambda Literary Book Award winner (Robert Giard)

1989

Carlos Almaraz, 48, Chicano mural artist

Amanda Blake, 60, actress, Miss Kitty on *Gunsmoke*

Howard Brookner, 34, documentarian

Scott Burton, 50, public sculptor

Bruce Chatwin, 48, travel writer

James Crabe, 57, cinematographer for *Rocky* and *The Karate Kid*

Jeff Duncan, 59, co-founder of the Dance Theater Workshop

Peter Evans, 38, actor

Nathan Kolodoner, 38, director of Andre Emmerich Gallery

Robert Mapplethorpe, 42, photographer

Cookie Mueller, 40, art critic, actress

William Olander, 38, curator at New Museum of Contemporary Art

Jack Smith, 57, performance artist

Tim Wengerd, 44, Martha Graham leading dancer/choreographer

1990

Demian Acquavella, 32, dance and New York avant-garde celebrity

Reinaldo Arenas, 47, Cuban novelist

Ian Charleson, 40, actor, starred in *Chariots of Fire*
Robert Chesley, author of *Night Sweat*
Ethyl Eichelberger, 45, cross-dressing performance artist
Stuart Greenspan, 44, editor of *Art & Auction* magazine
Halston, 57, fashion designer
Keith Haring, 31, graffiti artist
Ian (Ernie) Horvath, 46, founder of Cleveland Ballet and Joeffrey Ballet soloist
Gregory Kolovakos, 38, director of literature program of the New York State Council on the Arts
Craig Russell, 42, female impersonator and entertainer
Vito Russo, 44, essayist and film critic
Bill Sherwood, 37, filmmaker, director of *Parting Glances*

DID YOU KNOW?

From 1981 to the present, more than 340,000 people in the United States have been diagnosed with AIDS. Of those, nearly three-fourths of them are either homosexual or bisexual men.

1991

Howard Ashman, 40, lyricist of Disney's *The Little Mermaid* and *Beauty and the Beast*
Allen Barnett, 36, short-story writer
Robert Bishop, 53, director of Museum of American Folk Art
Nicholas Dante, 49, coauthor of *A Chorus Line*
Brad Davis, 41, actor, star of *Midnight Express* and *The Normal Heart*
Tom Eyen, 50, writer of *Dreamgirls*
Robert Ferri, 42, architect
Herve Guibert, 36, autobiographical French novelist
Arturo Islas, 52, Chicano writer
Clifford Jahr, 54, writer known for entertainment interviews
Larry Kert, 60, singer/actor who played Tony in *West Side Story*
Freddie Mercury, 45, lead singer of Queen
Tony Richardson, 63, director of *Tom Jones*
Paul Russell, 43, principal dancer with the Dance Theater of Harlem and the San Francisco Ballet
Edward Stierle, 23, leading dancer with the Joffrey Ballet
Burton Taylor, 47, leading dancer with the Joffrey Ballet and *Dance Magazine* contributing editor

CAN YOU BELIEVE IT?

According to the National Institutes of Health, the number of AIDS cases diagnosed in 1982: 1,281. Number of those cases still living in 1992: 118.

1992

Gary Abrahams, 48, co-founder of Filmex Film Festival
Peter Allen, 48, songwriter and entertainer
A. J. Antoon, 47, stage director
David Carroll, 41, Broadway actor, star of *Grand Hotel*
Tina Chow, 41, fashion model and jewelry designer
Serge Daney, 48, French film critic
Melvin Dixon, 42, novelist
Jorge Donn, 45, dancer

Denholm Elliot, 70, actor
Gary Essert, 54, co-founder of Filmex
Vincent Fourcade, 58, interior designer
Paul Jabara, 44, songwriter of disco greats
Philipp Jung, 43, set designer
Scott McPherson, 33, playwright
Anthony Perkins, 60, actor
Leonard Raver, 65, organist for New York Philharmonic
Robert Reed, 59, father of *The Brady Bunch*
Larry Riley, 39, actor
Clovis Ruffin, 46, fashion designer
Clark Tippet, 37, choreographer with the American Ballet Theatre
Glenn White, 42, Joffrey Ballet teacher and principal dancer
John Wilson, 64, founding member of Joffrey Ballet
David Wojnarowicz, 37, mixed-media artist

Darrell Yates Rist, author and co-founder of the Gay and Lesbian Alliance Against Defamation (GLAAD) (Robert Giard)

1993

Emile Ardolino, 50, film director
Crawford Barton, 50, photographer
Marc Berman, 39, playwright
Anthony Bowles, 61, musical director
Gary DeLoatch, 40, dancer in Alvin Ailey American Dance Theater
Louis Falco, 50, choreographer
Bruce Ferden, 44, opera conductor
Christopher Gillis, 42, choreographer and leading dancer with Paul Taylor Dance Company
Kenneth Nelson, 63, star of *Boys in the Band*
Ruldolf Nureyev, 54, dancer
Kevin Oldham, 32, composer
Anthony Sabatino, 48, art director

1994

Michael Callen, 38, musician
Gary Claire, 32, public-television programer
Juan Gonzales, 51, painter
Derek Jarman, 52, filmmaker
Dack Rambo, 53, television actor
Marlon Riggs, 37, filmmaker
Tom Rund, 50, principal dancer in the San Francisco Ballet
David Steiger Wolfe, 40, choreographer

Bravo! Brava!

It is important to note that the lack of visibility of lesbians and gay men has kept all of us, gay and straight, from recognizing the enormous contributions and achievements made by gay people. One of the more traditional forms of recognition in our culture is the issuance of awards for outstanding merit in various arenas, from the Nobel Prize to the National Book Award.

To find every gay person who had ever won a significant mainstream award would be impossible, even if the issue of lesbian and gay invisibility weren't as far-reaching as it has been in our society. What we have presented here is an overview of the entire area of "mainstream awards," with an emphasis on literary awards. We are proud to be able to claim the winners on the next several pages as our own.

"Emily is sort of the sweetheart of America. It's interesting how scared people get talking about Emily's love for Sue [Gilbert] and the very idea that you may be able to call that lesbian love."

EMILY DICKINSON SCHOLAR MARTHA NELL SMITH

Gay/Lesbian/Bisexual Mainstream Award Winners

The following is a survey of documented gay, lesbian, and bisexual mainstream award winners. This list is categorized first by award, followed by some particularly high-profile or award-heavy individuals. The list is the tip of the iceberg and should be thought of only as the most basic indication of the number of gay and lesbian winners.

Gay and lesbian winners are accounted for as gay or lesbian in one or more of the following sources—*Encyclopedia of Homosexuality, Fireside Companion/ Book of Lists, Lesbian Lists, Alyson Almanac*—or are generally publicly known to be gay (e.g., Harvey Fierstein, Jean Genet). Winners with a * are generally thought to be homosexual based on well-known current biographies.

There are undoubtedly obvious oversights and omissions. The list should be thought of as a survey, rather than as a definitive list of gay and lesbian mainstream award winners through July 1994.

Emmy Award Winners

Leonard Bernstein: Best Musical Contribution to Television (1956, 1957, 1960–1961), Outstanding Achievement in the Field of Music, with the New York Philharmonic: (1959–1960, 1961–1962), Outstanding Individual Achievement in Entertainment (1964–1965), Outstanding Classical Music Program, with N.Y. Philharmonic (1975–1976)

Raymond Burr*: Best Actor in a Leading Role in a Drama Series (1958–1959)for *Perry Mason*

Truman Capote: Special Award (1966–1967)

Laurence Olivier: Outstanding Single Performance by an Actor in a Leading Role (1972) for *Long Day's Journey into Night,* Outstanding Lead Actor in a Special Program: Drama or Comedy (1974–1975), Outstanding Lead Actor in a Miniseries or Special (1984) for *King Lear,* Outstanding Supporting Actor in a Miniseries or Special (1982) for *Brideshead Revisited*

DID YOU KNOW...

In 1955, Lorraine Hansberry became the first black writer (and the youngest person) to win the New York Drama Critics Circle Award, for her play *A Raisin in the Sun.* She was also an early member of the New York chapter of the Daughters of Bilitis, the earliest lesbian organization in the United States, founded in 1955.

MacArthur Awards

John Ashbery, poet (1985)

Merce Cunningham*, dancer/choreographer (1985)

Thom Gunn, poet (1993)

Bill T. Jones, dancer/choreographer (1994)

Mark Morris, dancer/choreographer (1991)

Adrienne Rich, poet (1994)

May Swenson, poet (1987)

Paul Taylor, dancer/choreographer (1985)

Special Obie Awards (Off-Broadway Theater, New York)

(The list of gay Obie Winners could certainly fill a book.)

Charles Ludlam: for the *Ridiculous Theatre Company* (1969–1970), for *Professor Bedlam's Punch and Judy Show* (1974–1975), for *Derr Ring Gott Farblonjet* (1977–1978), Sustained Achievement Award (1986–1987)

Michael Bennett and the creators of *A Chorus Line* (1975–1976)

Harvey Fierstein: for*Torch Song Trilogy* (1981–1982)

Ethyl Eichelberger: for *Lucrezia Borgia* (1982–1983)

Ron Vawter: Sustained Excellence as a Performer (1984–1985)

Dance Magazine Annual Awards

Paul Taylor (1980)

Michael Bennett (1976)

Alvin Ailey (1977)

Rudolph Nureyev (1973)

Ted Shawn (1969)

Merce Cunningham* (1960)

Tony Awards

Tony Kushner: Best Play for *Perestroika* (1994), Best Play for *Millennium Approaches* (1993)

Stephen Spinella: Best Actor in a Play for *Perestroika (*1994), Best Supporting Actor in a Play for *Millennium Approaches* (1993)

Harvey Fierstein: Best Actor in a Play for *Torch Song Trilogy* (1983), Best Book of a Musical for *La Cage Aux Folles* (1984), Best Play for *Torch Song Trilogy* (1983)

Ian McKellen: Best Actor in a Play for *Amadeus* (1981)

B. D. Wong: Best Supporting Actor in a Play for *M. Butterfly* (1988)

Lily Tomlin*: Best Actress in a Play for *Search for Signs of Intelligent Life in the Universe* (1986), Special Award (1977)

Katherine Cornell: Best Actress in a Play for *Anthony and Cleopatra* (1948)

Tennessee Williams: Best Play for *Rose Tattoo* (1951)

Michael Bennett: Best Choreography for *Dreamgirls* (1982),Best Choreography for *Ballroom* (1979), Best Choreography for *A Chorus Line* (1976), Best Choreography for *Follies* (1972), Best Direction of a Musical for *A Chorus Line* (1976)

Leonard Bernstein*: Best Score for *Wonderful Town* (1953), Special Award (1959)

Edward Albee: Best Play for *Who's Afraid of Virginia Woolf?* (1963)

Cole Porter*: Best Score for *Kiss Me Kate* (1949)

Noel Coward*: Special Award (1970)

Marlene Dietrich*: Special Award (1968)

John Gielgud: Special Award (1959)

Eva Le Gallienne: Special Award (1964)

Tommy Tune: Best Actor in a Musical for *My One and Only* (1983), Best Supporting Actor in a Musical for *Seesaw* (1984),Best Choreography for *Will Rogers Follies* (1991), Best Choreography for *Grand Hotel* (1990), Best Choreography for *My One and Only* (1983), Best Choreography for *A Day in Hollywood/A Night in the Ukraine* (1980), Best Director of a Musical for *Will Rogers Follies* (1991), Best Director of a Musical for *Grand Hotel* (1990), Best Director of a Musical for *Nine* (1982)

> **"The time has come. You can feel it, in a hundred little ways year after year. It is so certain and inevitable, that the next century will be a time in which it is not simply safe, but commonplace, to be openly gay."**
>
> ANNA QUINDLEN OF THE NEW YORK TIMES, MARCH 1994, IN HER NATIONALLY SYNDICATED COLUMN.

Grammy Awards

k. d. lang: Best Vocal Performance, Country (Female) for "Absolute Torch and Twang," (1989), Best Vocal (Female) for "Constant Craving" (1989), Best Vocal Collaboration (with Roy Orbison) for "Crying" (1988)

Melissa Etheridge: Best Rock Vocalist (Female) for "Come to My Window" (1995), Best New Artist (1993), Best Vocal (Female) for "Come to My Window" (1995)

Culture Club (Boy George): Best New Artist (1983)

Indigo Girls: Best Contemporary Folk Recording (1989)

Janis Ian: Best Vocal (Female) for "At Seventeen," (1979)

Vladimir Horowitz*: Best Performance, Instrumental Soloist, Classical (15 times)

John Gielgud: Best Spoken Word for *Ages of Man* (1979)

Edward Albee: Best Spoken Word for *Who's Afraid of Virginia Woolf?* (1963)

Charles Laughton: Best Spoken Word for *The Story Teller: A Session with Charles Laughton* (1962)

Elton John: Best Vocal Performance, Group for "That's What Friends Are For," (1986), Best Male Pop Vocal for "Can You Feel the Love Tonight?" (1995)

In 1992, Paul Monette, the author of Becoming a Man: Half a Life, *became the first openly gay man to win the National Book Award in the award's forty-three-year history. (Carole Topalian)*

Nobel Prize

Andre Gide: Nobel Prize for Literature (1947)

Pulitzer Prize

Drama:

Tony Kushner: *Angels in America/Millennium Approaches* (1993)

Michael Bennett: *A Chorus Line* (1976)

Edward Albee: *A Delicate Balance* (1967), *Seascape* (1975), *Three Tall Women* (1994)

Tennessee Williams: *Cat on a Hot Tin Roof* (1955), *A Streetcar Named Desire* (1948)

Music:

Ned Rorem: *Air Music (Ten Etudes for Orchestra)* (1976)

Poetry:

John Ashbery: *Self-Portrait in a Convex Mirror* (1976)

Elizabeth Bishop: *North and South* (1956)

Richard Howard: *Untitled Subjects* (1970)

Amy Lowell: *What's O'Clock* (1926)

James Merrill: *Divine Comedies* (1977)

Marianne Moore: *Collected Poems* (1952)

Mary Oliver: *American Primitive* (1984)

James Schuyler: *The Morning of the Poem* (1981)

— COMPILED BY PHILLIP HORVITZ

DID YOU KNOW...

In the past decade, the North American ice-skating world has lost over forty of its top male athletes and coaches to AIDS-related deaths.

SPORTS ARE FOR SISSIES, TOO

Perhaps one of the most closeted worlds inhabited by lesbians and gay men is the world of sports. While gay politicians and gay people in other arenas are making great strides, gay and lesbian athletes are barely scratching at the closet door. Much of the sports world is a world of competition and domination, where brute strength is valued among men, and strong women are admired, as long as they're not too strong. Throw into this mixture homophobia ("sissies can't play sports," "she doesn't wear makeup on or off the field, she must be a dyke") and it is no wonder few professional athletes have come out publicly. Those who do face not only discrimination, but financial loss. For example, Martina Navratilova, an out lesbian and inarguably the best tennis player to ever hit the circuit, collects millions of dollars less in endorsements from sponsors than Chris Evert, who is not gay.

Imagine a world without homophobia, and then imagine that the sports items presented here were chosen from a database with thousands of entries. The pieces that follow are meant to give the reader a peek at what that world could look like, and the people here are the role models we all need.

People Who Have Come Out in Big-Name Athletics

Martina makes her point!
(© Carol L. Newsom)

- **Muffin Spencer-Devlin**, professional golfer
- **David Kopay**, former NFL running back
- **Glenn Burke,** an outfielder for the Los Angeles Dodgers and Oakland A's from 1976 to 1979 (and the only major league baseball player ever to come out)
- **Roy Simmons**, a former offensive tackle for the New York Giants
- **Bruce Hayes**, who won a gold medal swimming in the 800-meter freestyle relay at the 1984 Olympics
- **Bob Jackson-Paris**, former Mr. America and Mr. Universe
- **Justin Fashanu**, British soccer player
- **Dr. Tom Waddell**, Gay Games founder and Olympic decathlete
- **Dave Pallone**, former major league umpire
- **Ed Gallagher**, offensive lineman at University of Pittsburgh in the late seventies
- **Greg Louganis**, four-time Olympic gold medal diver
- **Matthew Hall**, a twenty-four-year-old figure skater on the Canadian national team, who came out while still active in his sport, the only professional or nationally ranked male athlete in North America to do so.
- **Martina Navratilova**, the best female tennis player the world has ever seen, who was the first gay person to come out while still on the circuit.

Greg Louganis
(Courtesy Random House)

"As a diver I was known for my strength and grace. One day, I'd like to be known as a person who made a difference beyond the world of diving."

GREG LOUGANIS

Greg Louganis

Growing up, Greg Louganis was called "retard" and "nigger" because of his dyslexia and dark complexion; he was also called a "sissy." Often harassed after school, he spent much of his childhood alone, seeking refuge in the rocky hills of his El Cajon, California, neighborhood. Diving saved him. "It was something that I could take pride in—and I was good at it," he says. "It was the one way I could respond to the people who called me names. I was terrible at fighting back with words or fists, but I could show them all by diving."

Louganis's artistry and skill earned him a silver medal in 10-meter platform diving at the 1976 Olympics in Montreal when he was only sixteen. In the years that followed, he won scores of national and international titles and awards, including a total of four Olympic gold medals in the 1984 and 1988 Olympics for both platform and springboard diving.

And if anyone ever had questions about Louganis's spirit, there was no doubt after the world watched him gash his head on the diving board during the preliminary round in three-meter springboard diving at the 1988 Olympics, only to see him return minutes later with stitches in his scalp to complete two more dives and qualify for the next day's final competition. Again, he took the gold medal. Resilience, perseverance, and breathtaking skill, combined with humility, warmth, and a sense of humor, have earned Louganis the admiration of people around the world.

For those who recognized Louganis as a gay person, his accomplishments had special meaning. Many young people wrote to Louganis expressing their appreciation. He also heard from those who were frustrated that he did not step forward and speak publicly about his sexual orientation. "I was always out to my family and friends," he says, "but I was never comfortable discussing that part of my life with the press or the general public. Keeping the secret was often painful. It was always the toughest for me when parents would bring their kids to meet me and say,

'I want to be just like you.' I always wondered if they'd still feel that way if they knew I was gay."

At Gay Games IV in June 1994, Greg took what he's called a "baby step" and came out publicly about being gay. Besides a videotaped welcome that was shown at the opening ceremonies in which he declared, "It's great to be out and proud," Greg gave two diving exhibitions. "Being a part of the Games," Greg said, "made me feel like a complete person for the first time in my life."

Eight months later, after finishing work on his autobiography and following a year of intensive psychotherapy, Greg took a much bigger step and came out about his HIV status, telling Barbara Walters in a *20/20* interview that he has AIDS. He also explained that he'd known he was HIV-positive since before the 1988 Olympics.

"I know there are people who wish I had come forward years ago," Greg explained to reporters at his first press conference, "but each of us has a journey in life, and I got to this point only when I was ready."

Greg's painfully honest autobiography [written with Eric Marcus], *Breaking the Surface*, was published by Random House in February 1995 and became an instant *New York Times* number one best-seller.

"I always wanted to make a difference beyond the world of diving," Greg said, "and by telling my story, perhaps I can prevent one teenager from becoming infected with HIV."

— ERIC MARCUS

"I have a lifelong aversion to athleticism. If God had intended us to be athletes, he would have given us jockstraps."

SIR IAN MCKELLEN, ENGLAND'S MOST FAMOUS OPENLY GAY ACTOR

I DIDN'T KNOW THERE WERE GAYS IN THE MILITARY

No place has been less welcoming of openly gay people than the U.S. military. While the militaries of other industrialized countries accept openly gay members, the U.S. government has adopted a "Don't Ask, Don't Tell" policy, which effectively keeps any openly gay person from serving.

Nonetheless, there are now and have always been people in the military who were gay, people who believe that serving their country is a cause worth fighting for. Many, though not all, of these men and women remained closeted throughout their careers. Those who have come out and struggled to change military policy deserve commendation for their strength, courage, and conviction.

Homophobia in the Military

Homophobia is often an underlying and unspoken form of hatred, but the military is one of few places where outright discrimination is sanctioned and where active persecution of gay men and lesbians occurs. For most of its history, the U.S. military has treated homosexuality as a behavioral problem, either discharging or jailing members who committed sodomy. In 1916 a revision of the Articles of War made sodomy a felony crime. A policy of not accepting gay men and lesbians as recruits and forcing them out of the service if they were later discovered was developed during World War II. In 1943, a policy was instituted that banned homosexuals from all branches of the service. This was due to contemporary psychiatric beliefs that homosexuals were mentally ill. The 1950s gave us McCarthyism and federal hiring rules that prevented the employment of known homosexuals.

Vietnam, the draft, and the civil rights movement meant more changes for the military. Sexual behavior and sex roles in society started to shift, and straight men attempted to evade the draft by pretending to be gay. The 1970s brought to the military a new dimension: an influx of women. From the 1970s to the 1990s, the admission of women as nearly equal members of the service has shaken the concept of going off and becoming a "man" through military experience. The struggle for change in the 1980s and into the 1990s centered on gays in the military, but despite the success of racial integration and the assimilation of women, homophobia is dying a hard, slow death.

Early in 1993, President Clinton, acting upon a campaign promise to end policy discrimination against gays in the military, publicly raised the issue for consideration by the military, both houses of Congress, and the media. The barrage of hateful and misinformed comments by Sen. Sam Nunn (D.-GA), chair of the Senate Armed

Services Committee, and Colin Powell (chairman of the Joint Chiefs of Staff) and others during the summer of 1993 gave the country an incredible chance to look at the roots of the rampant homophobia pervading the military—as well as a society as a whole—and its impact.

Gay community leaders tried to bring the debate into focus by placing the issue of gay civil rights almost exclusively in the language of equal rights. By doing so, the gay community missed an ideal opportunity to inform the public about the witch-hunts, coerced confessions, suicides, jail time, and waste of resources that the government has spent since World War II on ferreting out "suspected homosexuals." The Congressional hearings also failed to address the fact that women are three times more likely to be discharged for homosexuality than men.

The RAND Organization was commissioned by Clinton to study the impact of allowing gays and lesbians to serve as open homosexuals in the military. The report, withheld from Congress, stated that the readiness of our armed forces would not be compromised by allowing queers to serve. This was not the first of such studies. In 1956 a study on homosexuality in the Navy found that homosexuals posed no security risk but recommended nevertheless that nothing should be done until society moved forward on the issue of homosexuality. In 1989 a report from the Defense Personnel Security Research and Education Center found that gay people were not a threat to security or unit cohesiveness and cited the proven history of the military to accept change in integration and women. After being suppressed by then-President Bush, this report surfaced during the 1993 debate.

The problem of allowing gay men and lesbians to serve openly in the U.S. military is not a "gay" problem, it is the problem of straight men to accept that gay people are just like them when it comes to doing the job right. But despite President Clinton's initial backing of gay equality in the military, when the dust cleared, the oppressive and ambiguous "Don't Ask, Don't Tell, Don't Pursue" policy was enacted, and backed by the President.

Though a major defeat for gay equal rights activists, national gay political organizations, and lesbians and gay men serving in the military, perhaps we succeeded in some small way in teaching the country that gay people really do exist, and that we can and do serve our country honorably. The military is just a microcosm of the society as a whole—a society that is slowly coming to grips with the changes that have been developing for over two hundred years.

— JENNIFER FINLAY

Ten Lesbian and Gay Military Heroes

Revolutionary War (1776–1783)

• **Baron Frederich von Steuben**, known as the father of the United States Army, trained the Continental Army using consolidated drills, rules, and discipline.

• **Alexander Hamilton**, the first secretary of the United States Treasury, served as a colonel in the Continental Army and was assigned to help von Steuben at Valley Forge.

• **Gotthold Frederick Enslin**, a lieutenant in the Continental Army, was one of the first men to be discharged from the army for sodomy violations under the Articles of War.

Civil War (1861–1865)

• **Major General Patrick Ronayne Cleburne** was a Confederate hero, known as the "Stonewall Jackson of the West." He was killed in action November 30, 1864, at the Battle of Franklin, Tennessee.

• **The cross-dressing women of the Fifteenth Missouri Regiment.** Union General Philip Sheridan wrote of two women who passed as men and fought alongside the others. After nearly drowning, they were found to be women, discharged, and escorted behind friendly lines.

World War II (U.S. participation, 1941–1945)

• **WAC Sergeant Jonnie Phelps** served on General Eisenhower's staff after the war in Europe ended. Eisenhower asked her to provide a list of all lesbians in the WAC battalion. She said she would do it, but only if her name was at the top of the list. Eisenhower then chose not to use the list.

Korean War (1954–1956)

• **Navy Lieutenant (j.g.) Tom Dooley** wrote the book *Deliver Us from Evil*, about his participation in Operation Passage to Freedom (1954), in which the Navy helped deliver over 600,000 refugees from North to South Vietnam. Dishonorably discharged from the Navy in 1956, Dooley went on to set up medical aid for the indigenous people of Southeast Asia through MEDICO. President John F. Kennedy set up the Peace Corps with Dooley's accomplishments in mind.

Vietnam War (1959–1975)

• **Navy Lieutenant Armistead Maupin**, the popular author of the *Tales of the City* series, claims to have been the last American out of Cambodia by a toe.

• **Air Force Sergeant Leonard Matlovich**, earned a Bronze Star for valor as airman first class in 1966, and was given the Purple Heart for being wounded in action in 1969. He became the first openly gay man to be on the cover of a major newsmagazine *(Time)* in 1975.

Leonard Matlovich on a 1975 Time Magazine *cover (Alison Belcher)*

Operation Desert Storm (1990–1991)

Army reservist Donna Lynn Jackson. Under Operation Stop/Loss, a policy put in place during mobilization for the Persian Gulf, discharges for homosexuality were suspended if a unit was selected for deployment. Eventually she ended up on the cover of *On Our Backs.*

— JENNIFER FINLAY

CAN YOU BELIEVE IT?

Vice Admiral Joseph S. Donnell, the commander of the Navy's surface Atlantic Fleet, said of lesbian service personnel during testimony at the federal district court ruling reinstating Col. Margarethe Cammermeyer into the Washington State National Guard, "Experience has . . . shown that the stereotypical female homosexual in the Navy is hard-working, career-oriented, willing to put in long hours on the job, and among the command's top professionals."

Profiles of Early Challengers to the Antihomosexual Military Policy

• **Air Force Technical Sergeant Leonard Matlovich** was the son of an Air Force enlisted man born in 1943 on an Air Force base in Georgia. He challenged Air Force regulations against homosexuality through his appearance on the cover of *Time* magazine in 1975. He eventually won his case in 1980 but chose not to re-enlist and accepted a monetary settlement. Matlovich died in June 1988, from AIDS-related causes, after a life of controversial gay activism. Buried at Arlington National Cemetery, his epitaph reads, "They gave me a medal for killing two men, and a discharge for loving one."

• **Army Staff Sergeant Perry Watkins** grew up in Tacoma, Washington, with his mother and an Army sergeant stepfather. He was drafted in 1967 and inducted in 1968, even after stating that he was a homosexual. During his long career in the Army, he performed as Simone, a fabulous drag queen, and was always openly gay. In 1984 the Army tried to discharge him for a fourth time and succeeded. He filed suit and won, but only on an individual level. He was allowed to retire with the full benefits of a twenty-year veteran. He still resides in Tacoma and is very active in the gay community.

• **Army Reserve Sergeant Miriam Ben-Shalom** was a single lesbian mother and an Army reservist in Milwaukee. She saw Matlovich's photo on the cover of *Time* and asked her superiors why she wasn't discharged. This led to three court cases and eventually to the Supreme Court, which upheld the lower courts' decision to discharge Ben-Shalom in 1990. Ben-Shalom has made a career out of challenging the military's policy. During the Persian Gulf War, she proposed a gay and lesbian battalion. She also participated in a "freedom ride" during 1993 to publicize the unfairness of the antihomosexual policy.

— JENNIFER FINLAY

WE REALLY *ARE* EVERYWHERE

While we have attempted in this chapter to recognize the many ways in which gay men and lesbians are outstanding contributors to society, and to give the reader a taste of the limitless flavors of the phrase "We are everywhere," we have only touched on the diversity and vast experience of gay people in the world.

In this last section, we present an even more eclectic view of gay people, including lesbians and gay men in places where perhaps the reader wouldn't expect to find us. The individuals noted here range from Bayard Rustin, who was instrumental in organizing Martin Luther King's 1963 March on Washington, to the story of a hog farmer/politician in Minnesota. From the streets to the living rooms, from the classrooms to the boardrooms, gay people can be found everywhere. We're coming out of our closets, and society is slowly beginning to realize that we are here—and everywhere—to stay.

Bayard Rustin, African American Gay Hero

Bayard Rustin, a longtime African American civil rights and gay rights activist, organized the historic 1963 March on Washington. In 1987, he died at the age of 77, ending a life that spanned nearly the entire twentieth century.

In the course of a 1987 interview, he described how, in 1963 when his homosexuality was being used to discredit the civil rights effort, the movement's leaders readily stood behind him:

"Strom Thurmond stood in the Senate speaking for three-quarters of an hour on the fact that [I] was a homosexual, a draft dodger, and a communist. Newspapers all over the country came out with this front-page story. . . .

I went immediately to Mr. [A. Phillip] Randolph [the official March on Washington organizer], and we agreed he would make a statement for all the civil rights leaders which basically said, 'We have absolute confidence in Bayard Rustin's integrity and ability.' He read the statement to the labor leaders and the Jewish and Catholic and Protestant leaders involved in the march, and they all agreed to it."

African American community leader Bayard Rustin stands in front of a map detailing the 1963 March on Washington for Civil Rights. Rustin stepped down as the official organizer of the march when his homosexuality became a source of controversy. Nonetheless, he was a major player in the civil right movement of the 1950s and early 1960s, and continued to fight for the equal rights of people of color and gay people until his death in 1987. He was seventy-seven. (Bettmann Archives)

Later in the interview, Rustin compared the black struggle with that of gay men and lesbians:

"The gay movement is much simpler [than the civil rights movement]; it only seems harder. In the civil rights movement, we first had to gain equality under law. Then, as Martin Luther King once said, 'Now we have the right to go into the restaurant, but we don't have the money to buy the hotdog.' The economic uplift of blacks has been frustrated by every kind of technological development. . . . The homosexual struggle is only to fight prejudice under the law. It does not require billions of dollars for an economic program."

Dick Hanson

Dick Hanson was an openly gay hog farmer and political activist who lived in tiny Glenwood, Minnesota, with his life partner, Bert Henningson, from 1982 until his death from AIDS-related causes in 1987. Henningson died in May 1988, also of AIDS-related causes.

Hanson's political savvy and personal commitment to gay and lesbian rights, the farm movement, feminism, and AIDS education catapulted him into the spotlight of Democratic politics in Minnesota during the late 1980s. In a historic moment on May 5, 1987, two months before his death, Hanson addressed a special session of the Minnesota Senate, speaking to more than 250 people, including forty-five of the state's sixty-seven senators.

"My name is Dick Hanson and I have AIDS," he told the assembly. "But I am more than a statistic; I am a human being. I love and need to be loved. I live with hope and don't take it away from me."

Hanson and Henningson were the subjects of a Pulitzer Prize–winning series of articles called "AIDS in the Heartland" by *St. Paul Pioneer Press Dispatch* reporter Jacqui Banaszynski. The series chronicled the two men's struggle with AIDS from February 1987 until after Hanson's death. Banaszynski commented, "Dick and Bert were able to nudge people into rethinking attitudes, inherent and deep biases, because they were farmers born and raised in Minnesota. Readers couldn't as easily dismiss them as they could Castro Street gays. Their values are so similar to mainstream Minnesotans and Wisconsinites."

The two men's relationship exemplified their rural Midwest values. Henningson, a scholar who held a doctorate in agricultural history and economics, was an assistant professor of history at the University of Minnesota-Morris who met Hanson through their political activities. Upon Henningson's death, openly gay Minneapolis city council member Brian Coyle told *Equal Time*, a Minneapolis-

DID YOU KNOW...

In the early 1980s, a time capsule that had been buried at the first part of this century in California was opened. Among the items found was a book, inscribed with the words "Let it be known that I was a lover of my own sex." It was signed by the first woman to be admitted to the bar and permitted to practice law in the state.

based gay and lesbian newspaper, that he would remember Henningson and Hanson most for their love of one another.

"[Bert] and Dick loved one another passionately. They taught me a lot about gay love and courage," Coyle said.

Henningson himself wrote the epitaph for his and Hanson's panel on the AIDS Memorial Quilt: "Openly gay and at home on their family farm in Minnesota, their love ran deep as the prairie soil."

— CYNTHIA SCOTT

Homecoming Queer

The announcement of a ten-year high school reunion made this ex-cheerleader shake to the soles of her Converse high tops. Time flies? Ha. My panic-stricken reaction: It's only been ten years?

I went from kindergarten to high school with most of the same kids. Our parents met at the Alpha Beta and P.T.A. meetings, on the golf course or tennis courts, or at church. Presbyterians and Catholics. The first black kids came to town sometime during my high school years, and you could count them on one hand, not including your thumb. Gays? I thought they lived in nearby Laguna and were interior designers. I first heard of lesbians in fifth grade when Cindy Thompson ran up to me in recess, stroked my arm, and said "Lez-be friends." All the kids laughed. I didn't get it but laughed anyway. I went home and asked my babysitter what it meant.

My high school scenario mid-1970s: The most important thing was to be part of the "V-squad." The V-squad was a band of ever-changing most popular girls who were "V" as in virgin. Like a virgin didn't count. Mostly, we tried to go as far as we could without losing V-squad membership (round the bases but not hit home) or our boyfriends, football players and jocks. There were several social groups at school: sochies (socialites), jocks, nerds, druggies, and surf rats. Okay, I was a sochie, my boyfriend a jock—Most Valuable Player on the football team. I myself also qualified as a jock, being the only girl on the boys' water polo team. That presented a whole set of problems in itself: Pre-game pep talks in the locker room changed venue and, reluctantly, the coach made his talks a bit less spicy.

Getting dressed for high school was a two-hour ordeal: straightening and then curling the hair, changing outfits three times, calling to see what the other V-squaders were wearing. On game days we wore our cheerleading outfits and sipped soda cans filled with rum and Coke to give us that old school pep. Beach parties abounded. Beach Boys, Neil Young, Cat Stevens, our soundtrack; Mustangs and Cameros, our chariots; Mad Dog 20/20, our drink. I can't tell you how strict the social code was: Popularity was measured down to the color of one's lip gloss.

So you can see I was thrilled for the chance to get together with the old gang.

I offer public appreciation to my friends who weathered my apparel crises before the ordeal. It took hours of consultation to come up with linen trousers and a sequin-shell ensemble to highlight my flattop. My attempt to blend in was laughable as I arrived to find throngs of *Dynasty*-clad look-alikes in flower-print dresses and frosted, lacquered hair. I was not the sole female in pants; I was the only one with short hair. Any kind of short hair. No joke.

Now, several hometown friends had known of my coming out. My mother, who would have to face the aisle-to-aisle supermarket probings of small-town noseys, had balked at living with scads of inevitable town gossip. For the reunion, we compromised: I wasn't allowed to don a label reading "Lesbian" (a fashion complement I really hadn't thought of wearing); however, if the subject came up, I could answer truthfully.

Before-dinner chat ranged from the kids to husbands, and only once did I have the chance to offer my status. Mostly, I think people glanced to my left hand, assumed not married, and rabbited on to tell the names and ages of their offspring. Many people had to get close enough to see my name card and its senior picture to recognize me. "I can't believe it's you!" they said fondly, remembering the Farrah Fawcett hairdo.

I sat with some members of the V-squad, long defunct, and their hubbies. I mentioned the girlfriend, received

DID YOU KNOW...

Even "Ronald McDonald," the clown representing the well-known restaurant chain, has been portrayed by more than one gay man. But when one "Ronald," Bob Brandon, came out publicly in 1977, the McDonald's Corporation sought an injunction forbidding him from ever dressing as the corporate clown again, or from stating that "Ronald McDonald" is also a homosexual.

polite and seemingly accepting approval. As more alcohol was ingested, responses changed. "Rafkin, you always did make us open our narrow minds. I'm just not surprised." Then an ex cheer buddy asked me to dance. She kicked off her four-inch heels and bopped to a roaring Pointer Sisters tune. I'll be damned if she didn't flirt with me. My dancing was less relaxed than usual; still, raised eyebrows skirted the dance floor.

A Magnum P.I. look-alike surprised me with a hug and a kiss before I could recognize him as my very first ever boyfriend—fourteen years old and holding hands in a matinee, one kiss a day on the beach at sunset. Ah, romance. . . . Having told me he'd spent half of his high school years thinking of my breasts and how elusive I'd been with them, he seemed most unnerved by news of my girlfriend. I asked him for a dance for old times' sake—that is, if he wouldn't mind dancing with a queer. "As long as you're not one of those male kind who always try to grab my ass." I assured him I wasn't and wouldn't.

Early on I spotted the only other queer and later cornered him behind a fern. "Are you the other one in ten?" I asked nonchalantly, without a clue as to who he was. He looked startled, and I thought I might perhaps be in error. "You know, the other one in ten?"

"Um, yeah, I think, if I know what you mean," he stammered. "But you?"

We chatted, he wondering how I could tell he was one. (And we're talking obvious queer!) He conducts his life from a very small closet. Living at home, but not out to friends or family, on occasion he sneaks off to Laguna to hang out at a gay bar. Never been to San Francisco and couldn't imagine it. "A whole street of gay people, wow. . . ."

I thought about each one of us going to our high school reunions and coming out. Would this change people's attitudes? Would this change their hatred? I already live with their judgment, and this judgment is my own baggage. After all, everyone had been polite enough. Mr. First Boyfriend had even asked me sailing on his catamaran—no strings attached, he assured, glancing breastward.

Or had nothing changed in ten years? At the door, I glanced over my shoulder waiting for the knives to hit.

— LOUISE RAFKIN

It's Not Impossible to Be Queer in Idaho

"Well, the white purse has to go."

"But my mom just bought me this purse. If I stop using it, she'll get suspicious."

Lesa shrugged. "Well, no one's ever going to know you're gay if you carry that thing."

Lesa and I walked the streets of Moscow, Idaho. She is, as far as I know, the only other lesbian in Idaho, and she is teaching me how to be gay. I hide the white purse in the bottom drawer of my dresser. I get out my old backpack from college.

"Look! Did you see her?"

"Who? Where?"

"You've got to pay attention. You've got to keep your eyes open."

"Tell me again how it works."

"I don't know," Lesa says. "It's the way she walks. It's eye contact. It's a kind of electricity or chemistry."

Gaydar. I practice for weeks. Mostly, I pick out farm women. Boots. Blue jeans. Short, tousled hair. No makeup. I loiter nearby, hoping for some kind of return signal, but inevitably the kids show up and then the husband and they all go off together, clambering into a nearby pickup truck.

My first potluck. Surprise! Lesa is not the only lesbian in Idaho. There is a whole kitchen full of them and a dozen in the living room and even more out back drinking beer around the fire. I sit quietly in the corner with my plate of food, chewing with my mouth open, just looking and looking. Who could ever have believed there could be so many? Who could ever have believed they would all be so beautiful?

"Ida. . ."

". . . homos."

"Out in the middle of . . ."

". . . nowhere."

It's a couple years later. I've had my first long-term relationship. I've survived, barely, breaking up. I've come out to my sisters and my mom and my department chair.

Now I'm in Seattle for Gay Pride, marching with the Inland Northwest Gay People's Alliance. Our group starts small, about eight of us, but all along the parade route people rush to join us, all calling out their hometowns—Lewiston, Boise, Kendrick, Twin Falls—and add their voices, loud and proud, to our Ida-homo cheer. As we march on, spectators nudge each other and stare and smile at the cleverness of our chant. "Even in Idaho," they seem to be saying. "They even have queers in Idaho." Then they clap and whistle, proud of the pride of our tough little group.

It's challenging to be queer in Idaho. We have to drive two hours to get to the closest gay bar in Spokane, Washington. We get a copy of something like the *Washington Blade* and stare in wonder at the pages and pages of news and activities. Then we look at our four-page photocopied newsletter and wonder what the hell we're doing here. Some of us leave; just as many of you left your dull little hometowns for the action of D.C. But some of us are nonurban. Some of us have family here or good jobs or a kind of genetic dependency on wide, open spaces. So we stay and make the best of things.

Actually you are a part of the reason we can stay, the big communities in D.C., and San Francisco and New York City and Seattle. We read about the way you've banded together and the things you've accomplished, and we don't feel so alone. We feel like we're part of the big national gay community, and that solidarity gives us the courage to do what we can in our own little state.

We gossip about famous people who might be gay. We read the magazines and rent the movies. We pick up bits of the culture from friends who journey back from exciting places to visit us. Every other month or so, we rent the Moscow Community Center and gather together for a dance, all 100 to 150 of us who are out, who like to dance, who have just fallen in love and want to show off our partners. And for those few hours our world is gay. We are all crowded together in the same safe place and the energy of it makes the windows pulse and we soak up our combined gayness like sponges and carry it away until the next time and the next.

It's not easy to be queer in Idaho, but it's not impossible either. The exciting thing, I think, is that no matter where we live, no matter how old we are, if we're gay we somehow find a way to be gay, to come out, to join the revolution. Personal identity is a powerful thing, and all the Lon Mabons and Kelly Waltons and Samuel Woodwards in America won't be strong enough to make us disappear.
— SUSAN BAUMGARTNER

. . . One in Every Family

We *are* everywhere, including in the families of some well-known celebrities and public figures, gay-friendly and not so gay-friendly alike. Here is a list of just a few queer kin of famous folk.

- **Alexis Arquette**, younger brother of actresses Rosanna and Patricia Arquette.
- **Geraldine Barr** and **Ben Barr**, actor Roseanne's siblings.
- **Chastity Bono**, daughter of performer Cher and Republican U.S. representative Sonny Bono.
- **Betsy Brooks**, country-western star Garth Brooks's guitar-playing sister.
- **Cheryl Crane**, daughter of Hollywood movie goddess Lana Turner. Cheryl wrote about her experiences in her best-selling book *Detour: A Hollywood Story.*
- **Candace Gingrich**, 1995 National Coming Out Day spokesperson and half-sister of Newt Gingrich, the conservative representative from Georgia who is speaker of the House of the 104th Congress
- **Dave McPherson**, grandson of the founder of the Boy Scouts.
- **Dee Mossbacher**, physician and filmmaker daughter of former secretary of Commerce Robert Mossbacher.
- **Julia Pell**, daughter of Rhode Island senator Claiborne Pell. Julia says her father has been "very supportive" of her sexuality.
- **Ty Ross**, grandson of conservative political icon Barry Goldwater.
- **John Schlafly**, son of Phyllis Schlafly, leader of the antifeminist, conservative organization Concerned Women of America.

"It's terribly important that a public figure says 'I love my gay son.'"

IAN MACNEIL, SON OF ROBIN NACNEIL OF THE MACNEIL/LEHRER NEWS HOUR, ON HIS SUPPORTIVE FATHER

FORWARD

Stonewall 20
A GENERATION OF PRIDE
New York City Lesbian & Gay Pride Weekend
June 24-25, 1989

Pride

I.S.C.I.C.

GAY PRIDE WEEK

Ask me about
the

I'm not
gay my

CHAPTER 2

How We Are Seen, How We See Ourselves

Imagery and imagination are two variations on the same theme. They both come from the same root word (the Latin *imaginari*); imagery takes us outside of ourselves to look at the world around us; imagination takes us into ourselves to find and create our own internal visions. Without imagery, it is hard to have imagination. And without imagination, no one can create imagery. All of us, gay and straight, look both to the world around us and inside to discover who we are, and who we can become. But this discovery does not happen in a vacuum. In attempting to define ourselves for ourselves, we are strongly influenced by what we see in the media, on film, in newspapers and magazines, on television, and what we read or hear about ourselves or about people whom we perceive to be like us.

DID YOU KNOW...

The New York Times **did not start using the term "gay" in place of "homosexual" as an adjective until July 15, 1987, after negotiations with GLAAD, the Gay and Lesbian Alliance Against Defamation.**

For many years, the images of gay men and lesbians remained obscure. In novels, one had to "read between the lines" to find any gay presence at all; happy endings were not allowed for gay characters. The same was true for film and television: Most overtly gay characters (the early images were mostly of men) were either portrayed as evil or played for laughs. And while gay people have inherited this legacy of invisibility and negativism, there is more to the story. Over the past twenty-five years, as gay men and lesbians have become more active in creating our own imagery, there has been an enormous change in what we all see when we pick up a magazine or turn on the television.

The dual focus of this chapter is critical to fully understand what images of gay and lesbian people are available to us. It is important to look at how gay people have been and are currently portrayed in popular American culture; it is equally essential that we become aware of the myriad ways that we have created our own images for all to see. As gay and lesbian people, how we are seen and how we see ourselves—from television to theater to radio to the written word —profoundly affects every aspect of who we are.

?#!

DID YOU KNOW...

After bowing out of an on-screen gay kiss with Anthony Michael Hall in the 1993 film *Six Degrees of Separation*, actor/rapper Will Smith found himself in hot water with the gay community. In an otherwise well-conceived movie, Smith insisted on changing the camera angle so that, shot from behind his head, it was supposedly impossible to tell whether or not the two actually kissed. Instead, it was glaringly obvious that they hadn't. In a later *Advocate* interview, Smith said, "I would definitely like to have that moment back. Halfway is not the way to go. You either do it or you don't. You don't adjust the camera. . . . I wasn't mature enough to handle the homosexuality."

PROJECTED IMAGES: HOMOSEXUALITY AND FILM

Whether in large-scale Hollywood pictures or small independent movies, the visual imagery projected onto the big screen tells society a lot about what we think of ourselves and one another. The images we see in cinema are powerful; the larger-than-life portrayals are set to musical scores and carefully edited in order to create the most profound visual impact. Most of us have entire catalogues of memories based just on the images we have taken home from the movie theater.

But for lesbians and gay men, these images often leave much to be desired. When we aren't simply excluded, we're frequently portrayed in derogatory or superficial ways. Since the beginning of film, Hollywood has always had some representations of homosexuals and homosexuality. But the images have mostly been created by straight (or closeted) directors, screenwriters, producers, and actors. Just as Hollywood portrayals of women and people of color illuminate more about society's attitudes toward these marginalized people than they reflect reality, images of gay men and lesbians have for the most part been conjured out of homophobic or, at best, uninformed imaginations, having little to do with who we actually are.

Of course, there have also been overtly gay and lesbian filmmakers around for just over two decades who have been producing more accurate representations from within our communities. Their work, often seen only in festivals or on video, continues to be a source of inspiration, information, and strength for lesbians and gay men around the world.

More recently, as gay and lesbian filmmakers and videomakers have been able to produce their own movies in increasing numbers, new forms of film have been born. Whether or not one calls it "queer cinema," the new avant-garde has become the fascination of not only gay but also straight audiences in festivals and art movie houses across the nation.

AIDS, too, has been a major subject of gay male filmmaking over the past decade, and, in the last few years, has been the subject of several mainstream movies.

For better or worse, we have been seen by others and have seen ourselves on film. As we continue to gain visibility and access to the means of cinematic production, those images will expand to portray the diversity of gay and lesbian communities. Hopefully, those projected representations will give lesbians and gay men everywhere an ever-increasing source of empowerment and pride.

A Brief History of Lesbians and Gay Men in Mainstream Film

Until recently, dismissal and disinformation was Hollywood's modus operandi regarding homosexuality. Lesbian and gay characters were dismissed literally—the Production Code, the major studios' self-censorship mechanism, banned "sex perversion or any inference of it" from the 1930s into the 1960s—but also figuratively in the countless derisive portraits of sissy men, predatory lesbians, and psychopaths of both persuasions. The disinformation included the perpetuation of myths, long after they had been proven false, that lesbians and gays were mentally unbalanced, prone to criminality, incapable of moral behavior, and a general threat to society.

Lesbian and gay references in American films of the silent and early-sound eras occurred almost uniformly in comic circumstances, the laughs often hinging on reversals of gender and/or sex roles. The gags typically alluded to homosexuality without actually depicting homosexuals. Examples include the "sissy boy" title character of *Algie the Miner* (1912), whose adventures out west "make a man out of him"; a case of mistaken homosexual identity in Charlie Chaplin's *Behind the Screen* (1916); Fatty Arbuckle's flirtation with another man while dressed in a woman's bathing suit in *Fatty at Coney Island* (1917); Laurel and Hardy's extended clothes-changing routine in *Liberty* (1929); and lesbian-tinged role reversal in *A Florida Enchantment* (1914).

In the Arbuckle film, Fatty's flouting of gender and sexual norms eventually provokes violence; in this respect, the movies did mirror real life. What makes such

"The concept of the gentle man who chooses to love other men does not exist in American film except as slapstick comedy. Stan Laurel and Oliver Hardy had the perfect sissy-buddy relationship throughout their long career, and it is naive now, looking at their films, to assume that they were not aware of and did not consciously use this aspect of their screen relationship to enrich their comedy."

VITO RUSSO IN THE CELLULOID CLOSET: HOMOSEXUALITY IN THE MOVIES gags work, claimed the comic's mentor, Keystone Studios producer Mack Sennett, sounding a lot like Sigmund Freud, is the "exposure of repressed desire"—in Fatty's case homosexuality. Three-quarters of a century later, movies still trade on the taboo. Eddie Murphy gets a cheap laugh in *The Distinguished Gentleman* (1992) when he momentarily thinks a U.S. senator is "going homo" on him. Eddie's response is the same as in *Coney Island* and numerous other pictures: "'Cause if you are, I'm gonna have to whup you."

A Florida Enchantment's plot revolves around a special seed that turns women into men and vice versa. A woman who takes it becomes "mannish" and begins flirting with women, kissing them on the lips and dancing with them. The woman's behavior discombobulates everyone; *Florida* hints that one person's subversion of sex or gender roles leads to social chaos. Any claim *Florida* might make to being the "first" lesbian film is qualified: Its heroine's escapades turn out to be a "most horrible dream," reducing female homosexuality to a gag, same as with the men.

In the United States during the early Hollywood Production Code era, only wisps of lesbian sentiment—tux-wearing Marlene Dietrich's provocative kiss of a female bar patron in *Morocco* (1930), a fleeting reference to lesbianism in *Blood Money* (1933)—made it to the screen. More characteristic was the impulse toward deletion. *Maedchen in Uniform* (1931), from Germany, depicted the love between a young schoolgirl and her teacher. *Maedchen* made a direct connection between sexual and political repression just as the Nazis were coming to power. But when the drama played in New York, state censors removed lines of dialogue that made explicit *Maedchen*'s lesbian subplot. Greta Garbo's *Queen Christina* (1933) seeks men, not women as the real-life figure reputedly did. In *These Three* (1936), the first film version of *The Children's Hour*, what in Lillian Hellman's play was an accusation of lesbianism against two women evolved on the screen into a charge that one coveted the fiancé of the other. It is perhaps just as well that the treacherous Mrs. Danvers (Judith Anderson) is a lesbian only by implication in Alfred Hitchcock's *Rebecca* (1940).

Gay male references were equally "coded" in the 1940s. Director John Huston slipped three homosexuals—played by Peter Lorre, Elisha Cook, Jr., and Sydney Greenstreet—past code censors in *The Maltese Falcon* (1941), but did it so shrewdly that even most gays don't pick up on the last two. The hints are stronger in *Desert Fury* (1947), which features two gay gangsters on the lam. Alfred Hitchcock's *Rope* (1948), inspired by the Leopold-Loeb murder case of the 1920s, tiptoes around Code restrictions to allude to its leads' homosexuality. The gay connection was made slightly more clear in *Compulsion* (1959) and quite specific in *Swoon* (1992), also about the same case.

Faced with a declining box office in the wake of television, producers in the 1950s began to demand a relaxation of censorship to allow for more "adult" material. Since the studios were essentially censoring themselves, they, like Dorothy with her ruby slippers in *The Wizard of Oz*, had always had the power to get what they wanted. They simply didn't know how (or didn't dare) to use it.

The Production Code was revised in the early 1960s to allow depiction of "sex aberration" if treated with "care, discretion, and restraint." Unfortunately, little restraint was shown toward homosexuals: In films such as *Advise and Consent*, *Walk on the Wild Side*, and *The Children's Hour* (all 1962), they committed suicide, were murdered, or went to jail.

After the Code's demise in the late 1960s, the first pictures under the "alphabet" rating system, still in use today, tended to repeat old stereotypes. A pathologically spiteful lesbian couple is torn asunder by a third, conniving lesbian in *The Killing of Sister George* (1968). Lesbian vampires started popping up with increasing and more titillating frequency. Repressed homosexuals commit suicide and murder, respectively, in *The Sergeant* and *The Detective* (both 1968). Bitchy, self-loathing queens populate *The Boys in the Band* (1970) and *Some of My Best Friends Are . . .* (1971). "Homo Lesbo Themes at Peak: Deviate Theme Now Box Office," screamed a *Variety* headline in 1969, a telling indicator of the industry's level of sensitivity toward gays.

DID YOU KNOW...

The first dramatizations of lesbian and gay lives on film came from across the Atlantic, in European silents. The earliest example still extant is *The Wings* (1916), a Swedish film by gay director Mauritz Stiller, about a sculptor who falls in love with one of his male models. The story was also made as *Mikael* (1924) by Carl Dreyer in Germany, where five years earlier Richard Oswald had directed *Different from the Others* (1919), the first cinematic plea for tolerance of homosexuals. The Countess Geschwitz, who gives her all for the seductive Lulu in Austrian director G. W. Pabst's *Pandora's Box* (1928), is generally considered cinema's first lesbian, though a strong case could be made for characters in *My Lady of Whims* (1925) and *The Dangerous Hours* (1920), both U.S. productions.

Although censorship had slackened, producers found little financial incentive to buck audience expectations. Mainstream religion, psychology, and folklore had for years decreed gays perverse; the American Psychiatric Association's 1973 announcement that homosexuality was no longer a mental disorder did not immediately override a century of negative propaganda. Having found that audiences had no objection to sick and twisted gays, producers served them up in dozens of 1970s and 1980s flicks. More sensitive portraits were apparently not worth the monetary risk. Even into the 1990s, research found that a large portion of the American audience responded negatively to "positive" gay representation—and any overt sexual expression, even kissing.

The late 1970s and early 1980s saw a number of conflicting trends. *Cruising, Windows,* and *American Gigolo* (all 1980) presented lesbians and gays as perverted and/or criminal. The creators of *Cruising* and *Gigolo* maintained that their films weren't saying that all homosexuals were a threat. While this may have been true, it begged the question of the cumulative effects of such portraits. High-profile community protests of *Cruising* may have led to more benign projects, including *Making Love*, *Personal Best*, and *Victor/Victoria* (all 1982), but the boom in sunnier mainstream portraits many lesbian and gay critics predicted never panned out. Gratuitous fag jokes and downright slurs were far more common throughout the decade. On the other hand, the number of independent and art-house features—among them *Lianna* (1983), *Desert Hearts* (1985), *My Beautiful Laundrette* (1986), and *Parting Glances* (1986)—that attempted more complex representations steadily increased.

MAJOR GAY AND LESBIAN STEREOTYPES IN FILM

Gay Men:

Child molester
Neurotic
Promiscuous predator
Psychopath
Sissy
Sad young man

Lesbians:

Deceitful
Jealous
Just waiting for the right man
Predatory
Sexually immature
Hard-edged

— DANIEL MANGIN

Though most observers agreed that Hollywood continued to malign gays while simultaneously deleting more "positive" references—lesbian angles were downplayed or excised in *Switch, Fried Green Tomatoes*, and *LA Story* (all 1991)—how to deal with the problem was another matter. Many lesbians and gays debated the value of large-scale protests against *The Silence of the Lambs* (1991) and *Basic Instinct* (1992). *Silence* featured a killer with what one critic called "many gay signifiers," and three bisexual women and a lesbian are implicated in murder in *Basic Instinct.* Some accused the protesters of generating more interest in hateful portrayals; media strategists felt that although this might be true, going after big hits garnered more publicity for the notion that the malicious imagery was unfair.

It may only be coincidental that Tri-Star, which distributed *Instinct,* also financed the acclaimed AIDS drama *Philadelphia* (1993), by the same man (Jonathan Demme) who directed *The Silence of the Lambs.* What is worth noting is that the concept for *Philadelphia* had been kicking around Hollywood for several years but the "climate" had never quite been right for its production. Perhaps the protests did contribute to the change in atmosphere.

The girl is out there. Max (Guinevere Turner, left) finds love with Ely (V. S. Brodie, right) in Rose Troche's 1994 smash lesbian hit, Go Fish. *(Courtesy Samuel Goldwyn)*

As the cinema embarks on its second century, there is reason for optimism. The success of *Philadelphia* and *The Crying Game* (1992) may have persuaded major studios that under the right circumstances large-scale profits can be made on pictures with major gay themes or plots. While the creators of *Threesome* (1994), *Boys on the Side* (1995), and *Higher Learning* (1995) may have "played it safe" with their lesbian or gay characters, each was clearly well intentioned. On the independent scene, works that previously might have played only the gay film festival circuit began turning up at such prestigious showcases as the Sundance (Utah), New York, and Venice festivals. The "crossover" success of *Longtime Companion* (1990), *Paris Is Burning* (1991), *The Wedding Banquet* (1993), *Go Fish* (1994), and other films convinced independent distributors that the right projects could garner modest profits.

Even if the commercial cinema does become more consistently congenial toward lesbians and gays, the need for community-based works that reflect without compromise the full range of our lives and sexual expression will always remain. Hopefully, though, the gap between what the mainstream says about us and what we say and believe about ourselves will continue to close.

— DANIEL MANGIN

The Gay Psychokiller Hall of Fame

PRESTO CHANGE-O

Among the films in which lesbian or gay characters "turn straight" are:

The Third Sex (1957)
The Fox (1968)
Tell Me That You Love Me, Junie Moon (1970)
A Different Story (1978)
Personal Best (1982)

— DANIEL MANGIN

Rope (1948)
John Dall and Farley Granger kill a guy—just for the fun of it—who's about to get married. They smoke a cigarette afterward.

Reflections in a Golden Eye (1967)
Marlon Brando can't deal with being gay. He murders the object of his desire when he discovers the man loves Brando's wife.

The Detective (1968)
A repressed homosexual kills two gays, one of whom he picks up in a bar.

No Way to Treat a Lady (1968)
Rod Steiger and George Segal are both mama's boys. Segal finally works through it, but Steiger, who never cuts the apron strings, kills six middle-aged women.

The Laughing Policeman (1974)
A repressed homosexual becomes a serial killer.

Looking for Mr. Goodbar (1977)
Repressed Tom Berenger kills to prove his manhood.

Cruising (1980)
A repressed homosexual kills gays he picks up in bars and parks.

Deathtrap (1982)
A playwright and his gay lover knock off the playwright's high-strung wife to cash in on the inheritance, then kill each other.

The Boys Next Door (1985)
A repressed homosexual commits multiple murders, often after someone calls him queer.

No Way Out (1987)
A gay aide to the secretary of Defense kills to protect his boss.

The Phone Call (1991)
A "family man" accidentally calls and gets stalked by an employee of a phone-sex line in this gay *Fatal Attraction*.

The Silence of the Lambs (1991)
Was Jame Gumb gay, transsexual, or neither? He minced, had a fey voice, collected Nazi paraphernalia, had a male lover for ten years, thought he was a woman, and had a poodle named Precious.

— DANIEL MANGIN

The Screen's Nastiest Lesbian or Bisexual Women

Rebecca (1940)
Judith Anderson torments Joan Fontaine and tries to convince her to commit suicide.

Open City (1946)
Giovanna Galletti is Ingrid, the conniving Nazi lesbian who preys on the cravings of weak-willed, Resistance-era Italian women for furs and baubles.

Walk on the Wild Side (1962)
Barbara Stanwyck plays Jo, the predatory madam who won't let Capucine go straight.

From Russia with Love (1963)
Treacherous spy Lotte Lenya has the hots for pretty, blond Daniela Bianchi.

The Balcony (1963)
Hateful, sadistic Shelley Winters (in one of her three lesbian roles) has Lee Grant (in one of her two such roles) under her thumb.

The Killing of Sister George (1968)
Beryl Reid and Coral Browne do battle over Susannah York.

The Mafu Cage (1977)
Carol Kane and Lee Grant have an incestuous relationship. When her sister wants out, Kane kills Grant's boyfriend and later Grant herself.

Windows (1980)
Elizabeth Ashley pays a cabdriver to rape Talia Shire so Talia will (1) hate men and (2) need Ashley to comfort her.

Basic Instinct (1992)
Four lesbian or bisexual women have murder in their pasts and present in this controversial thriller.

Three of Hearts (1993)
Kelly Lynch pays stud-for-hire William Baldwin to seduce and then dump her girlfriend so that she'll (1) hate men and (2) need Lynch to comfort her.

— DANIEL MANGIN

DID YOU KNOW...

When Harold Lloyd played a female pitcher on an all-woman baseball team in *Spit-Ball Sadie* (1915), *Motion Picture News* called the scenes "repellent." The critics said the same thing about Jack Lemmon's performance in *Some Like It Hot* (1959) because Lemmon seemed to be enjoying his role too much. It was virtually the only female impersonation sustained throughout an entire film since the teens.

People Who Have Played Lesbian, Gay, or Bisexual Roles

Jane Alexander *(A Question of Love)*; F. Murray Abraham *(The Ritz)*; Kevin Bacon *(JFK)*; Antonio Banderas *(Law of Desire; Philadelphia)*; Alan Bates *(Butley; We Think the World of You)*; Tom Berenger *(Looking for Mr. Goodbar)*; Dirk Bogarde *(Victim*; *Death in Venice)*; Steve Buscemi *(Parting Glances; Miller's Crossing)*; Michael Caine *(Deathtrap)*; George Carlin *(The Prince of Tides)*; Cher *(Silkwood)*; Tim Curry *(The Rocky Horror Picture Show)*; Bruce Davison *(Longtime Companion);* Daniel

Day-Lewis *(My Beautiful Laundrette)*; Catherine Deneuve *(The Hunger)*; Peter Finch *(Sunday Bloody Sunday)*; Farley Granger *(Rope)*; Lee Grant *(The Balcony; The Mafu Cage)*; Tom Hanks *(Philadelphia)*;

Jane Alexander (left) and Gena Rowlands in ABC's 1978 movie A Question of Love

Mariel Hemingway *(Personal Best)*; Barbara Hershey *(In the Glitter Palace)*; John Hurt *(The Naked Civil Servant; Partners; Even Cowgirls Get the Blues)*; William Hurt *(Kiss of the Spider Woman)*; Jeremy Irons *(Brideshead Revisited)*; Tommy Lee Jones *(Cat on a Hot Tin Roof; JFK)*; Carol Kane *(The Mafu Cage)*; Alex Karras *(Victor/Victoria)*; Mitchell Lichtenstein *(Streamers; The Wedding Banquet)*; Shirley MacLaine *(The Children's Hour)*; Gary Oldman *(Prick Up Your Ears; We Think the World of You)*; Robert Preston *(Victor/Victoria)*; John Ratzenberger *(The Ritz)*; Christopher Reeve *(Deathtrap)*; Susan Sarandon *(The Hunger)*; Diana Scarwid *(In the Glitter Palace; Silkwood)*; Helen Shaver *(Desert Hearts)*; Rod Steiger *(The Sergeant; No Way to Treat a Lady)*; Elizabeth Taylor *(X, Y, & Zee)*; Meshach Taylor *(Mannequin)*; Meryl Streep *(Manhattan)*; Uma Thurman *(Henry and June; Even Cowgirls Get the Blues)*; Michael Warren *(Norman, Is That You?)*; Robert Webber *(10)*; Shelley Winters *(Mambo; The Balcony; Cleopatra Jones)*; Michael York *(Something for Everyone; Cabaret)*; Susannah York *(The Killing of Sister George; X,Y, & Zee)*.

DID YOU KNOW...

In *Sylvia Scarlett*, Katharine Hepburn "passes" as a young boy and is obviously attracted to Brian Aherne; the audience is meant to find her equally irresistible. In one scene Aherne tells Hepburn, "There's something that gives me a queer feeling every time I look at you."

DID YOU KNOW...

In 1970, *Midnight Cowboy* won the Academy Award as Best Picture, thereby becoming the first X-rated film (as well as the first film to feature an onscreen sexual encounter between two men) to do so. The film's gay director, John Schlesinger, also won a Best Director Oscar.

And I'd like to Thank. . .

Oscar Awards have been given to more than thirty-five openly lesbian, gay, and bisexual recipients and/or gay-themed films in the Academy's sixty-seven-year history:

1927–28

Artistic Quality of Production: *Sunrise* (director **F. W. Murnau**)
Best Actor: **Emil Jannings**, *The Last Command* and *The Way of All Flesh*
Best Actress: **Janet Gaynor**, *Seventh Heaven, Street Angels* and *Sunrise*

1932–33

Best Actor: **Charles Laughton**, *The Private Life of Henry VIII*

1934

Best Actress: **Claudette Colbert**, *It Happened One Night*

1940

Best Screenplay: **Donald Ogden Stewar**t, *The Philadelphia Story*

1948

Best Actor: **Laurence Olivier**, *Hamlet*

1949

Best Costume Design: **Edith Head** and **Gile Steele**, *The Heiress*

1950

Best Actress: **Judy Holiday**, *Born Yesterday*
Best Costume Design: **Edith Head** and **Charles LeMaire**, *All About Eve*

1953

Best Costume Design: **Edith Head**, *Roman Holiday*

1958

Best Costume Design: **Cecil Beaton**, *Gigi*

1959

Best Costume Design: **Orry-Kelly**, *Some Like It Hot*

1960

Best Costume Design: **Edith Head** and **Edward Stevenson,** *The Facts of Life*

1961

Best Supporting Actor: **George Chakiris**, *West Side Story*
Best Screenplay: **William Inge**, *Splendor in the Grass*
Best Costume Design: **Piero Gherardi**, *La Dolce Vita*

1963

Best Director: **Tony Richardson,** *Tom Jones*
Best Costume Design: **Piero Gherardi,** *8 1/2*

1964

Best Director: **George Cukor**, *My Fair Lady*
Best Costume Design: **Cecil Beaton,** *My Fair Lady*

1965

Best Screenplay: **Frederic Raphael**, *Darling*

1966

Best Costume Design: **Danilo Donati**, *Romeo and Juliet*

1969

Best Director: **John Schlesinger**, *Midnight Cowboy*

1981

Best Supporting Actor: **John Gielgud**, *Arthur*

1984

Best Documentary Feature: *The Times of Harvey Milk*

1985

Best Actor: **William Hurt**, *Kiss of the Spiderwoman*

1987

Best Director: **Bernardo Bertolucci**, *The Last Emperor*
Best Screenplay: **Bernardo Bertolucci** (with Mark People), *The Last Emperor*

1989

Best Documentary Feature: *Common Threads: Stories from the Quilt*

"I see American and European movies with gangs and people killing people, and nobody's complaining about that, but you play a gay character. . ."

PHILADELPHIA CO-STAR ANTONIO BANDERAS

DID YOU KNOW...

Threatened with a boycott by the Roman Catholic Church–led Legion of Decency, Hollywood agreed in 1934 not to depict homosexuality in movies.

1990
Best Song: **Howard Ashman**, *Little Mermaid*

1991
Best Song: **Howard Ashman**, *Beauty and the Beast*
Best Documentary Feature: **Deborah Chasnoff**, director, *Deadly Deception*

1994
Best Actor: **Tom Hanks**, *Philadelphia*
Best Song: **Bruce Springsteen**, *Philadelphia*

— DAVID EHRENSTEIN

Vito Russo, Movie Star

Vito Russo, author of the groundbreaking book *The Celluloid Closet: Homosexuality in the Movies*, died of AIDS in 1990 at the age of forty-four. His life and work have inspired two generations of lesbians and gay men to observe, question, and work to improve the images of us generated by media. He co-founded the media activist group Gay and Lesbian Alliance Against Defamation (GLAAD) and was an active member of ACT UP. His legacy also includes creating a foundation for many college-level courses in gay film in America and abroad.

Vito Russo stands in front of the Castro Theater in San Francisco prior to a 1981 sell-out show of his The Celluloid Closet *film and lecture on homosexuality in the movies. (Rink Foto)*

Russo's appreciation for the role film representations of lesbians and gay men could play in gay liberation began in the early 1970s while he was active in the Gay Activists Alliance. He would show camp classics to raise money for the GAA, inviting those in attendance to shout out queer comments. One of Vito's favorite moments was during a screening of *Night of the Living Dead*, when a lesbian in the back of the audience shouted out "Save me a breast!" Those early screenings turned into lectures on homosexuality in film, which led to his seminal text on the subject, *The Celluloid Closet.* A documentary based on the book is scheduled to come out in 1995.

Vito Russo is remembered by friends for his love of Judy Garland, his sense of camp, his honesty, ambition, and his ability to understand that both media representation and individual action are entirely political.

Important Figures in Lesbian/Gay Cinema

A short list of notable contributors to cinema. Obviously, this list is hardly exhaustive. There are many other lesbians and gay men involved in film production who deserve credit; some are mentioned at the end of the biographies.

Pratibha Parmar is a London-based filmmaker. (Jill Posener)

- **Kenneth Anger.** At just seventeen, Anger shot an erotic sailor-fantasy called *Fireworks* (1947). His vivid imagery contrasted markedly with censored Hollywood product. A major film artist who influenced George Lucas, Martin Scorsese, and others, Anger's output has been minimal but pivotal.
- **George Cukor.** Though publicly in the closet his entire career, this "A-list" director, as all Hollywood knew, was gay as a blade. Clark Gable reportedly had him fired from *Gone With the Wind* for this reason. Cukor's many hit films include *Dinner at Eight, The Women, The Philadelphia Story*, and the 1954 *A Star Is Born.* Interesting tidbit: Cukor directed *Two-Faced Woman,* Greta Garbo's last film. He died in 1976.
- **Donna Deitch.** She took seven years to scrape together the cash to make *Desert Hearts* (1985). It was worth the effort: The film just may be the most beloved lesbian film yet released. Deitch later directed the Oprah Winfrey TV-miniseries *The Women of Brewster Place* (1989), which featured two prominent lesbian characters.
- **Robert Epstein, Jeffrey Friedman.** These longtime companions collaborated on the Academy Award–winning AIDS documentary *Common Threads: Stories from the Quilt* (1989). Epstein had previously earned an Oscar for *The Times of Harvey Milk* (1984). Their latest work is a film version of Vito Russo's *The Celluloid Closet,* a history of gay people in film.

• **Rainer Werner Fassbinder.** The prolific "bad boy" of New German Cinema presented complex and difficult lesbian/gay/bi portraits. His legacy includes *The Bitter Tears of Petra Von Kant* (1972), *Fox and His Friends* (1975), and an adaptation of Jean Genet's *Querelle* (1982). He died in 1982.

• **Barbara Hammer.** *Dyketactics, Multiple Orgasm,* and *Doublestrength,* among the experimentalist's important 1970s works, unabashedly highlighted lesbian sensuality and sexuality in direct rebuttal to freakish mainstream depictions. Her first feature, *Nitrate Kisses,* released in 1993, examined censorship, erotic imagery, and lesbian/gay history.

• **Pratibha Parmar.** London-based Parmar transcends parochialism with works that also explore issues of race (*Krush*), disability (*Double the Trouble, Twice the Fun*), and women's rights (*Warrior Marks*, made with writer Alice Walker). A moving early work, *Flesh and Paper*, depicts the life of lesbian poet Suniti Namjoshi.

Marlon Riggs, filmmaker, is known best for Tongues Untied, *which examines the intersections of race, sexuality, and love. Riggs died from AIDS-related causes in 1994. (Courtesy Frameline)*

• **Marlon Riggs.** *Tongues Untied* (1989), this artist-activist's signature work, was an emphatic evocation of the beauty, conflict, and poetry of African American gay experience. Though it empowered many, *Tongues* ran afoul of PBS censors and members of Congress, and even became a cause célèbre during the 1992 Republican primary. Riggs's other works include *Color Adjustment,* about blacks on TV, and *No Regret,* about HIV-positive African Americans. He died in 1994.

• **Christine Vachon.** A director of some shorts, Vachon's major contribution to community cinema is as a producer. She's been connected with a number of "New Queer Cinema" projects, including *Poison* and *Swoon,* and she helped shepherd the 1994 lesbian mini-hit *Go Fish.* Most recently, she is working on a film adaptation of Martin Duberman's book *Stonewall.*

• **Andy Warhol.** Chiefly known as a visual artist and celebrity, Warhol's importance as a filmmaker cannot be overestimated. His form-oriented experiments called Hollywood conventions into question even as they borrowed from the same. Warhol's sixties films—*My Hustler, Blow Job, Haircut (No. 1),* and *Bike Boy*—are some of the queerest images ever committed to celluloid.

Other past and present lesbian/gay/bisexual film figures of note: Pedro Almodovar, Dorothy Arzner, Jean Cocteau, Arthur Bressan, Jr., James Broughton, Terence Davies, Dick Fontaine, Marcus Hu, Derek Jarman, Tom Kalin, George Kushar, Craig Lucas, Alla Nazimova, Ron Nyswaner, Ulrike Ottinger, Jan Oxenberg, Rosa Von Praunheim, Tony Richardson, Barry Sandler, Greta Schiller, John Schlesinger, Bill Sherwood, Monica Treut, John Waters, and James Whale.

— DANIEL MANGIN

Lesbian and Gay Documentaries

Documentaries have been an important part of gay and lesbian culture for over two decades. Both in film festivals and on video, documentaries provide tangible, accessible voices that represent a diverse variety of aspects of gay and lesbian life. This list covers some of the most enduring films.

Absolutely Positive (1989)
American Fabulous (1992)
Army of Lovers, or Revolt of the Perverts (1978)
Before Stonewall (1985)
A Bigger Splash (1974)
The Celluloid Closet (1995)
Changing Our Minds: The Story of Dr. Evelyn Hooker (1992)
Chicks in White Satin (1993)
Coming Out Under Fire (1994)
Complaints of a Dutiful Daughter (1994)
Common Threads: Stories from the Quilt (1989)
Daddy and the Muscle Academy (1992)
Damned in the USA (1992)
Desire (1989)
Erotikus: History of the Gay Movie (1975)
Forbidden Love (1993)
Gay U.S.A. (1977)
Home Movie (1971)
Improper Conduct (1984)
Last Call at Maud's (1992)
Life Is a Cucumber (1990)
Love Meetings (1964)
Nitrate Kisses (1992)

One Nation Under God (1993)
Out: Stories of Gay and Lesbian Youth (1994)
Paris Is Burning (1991)
Paul Cadmus: Enfant Terrible at 80 (1984)
Portrait of Jason (1967)
Positive (1990)
The Queen (1968)
Resident Alien (1991)
Sex Is . . . (1993)
Silence = Death (1990)
Silent Pioneers (1985)
Silverlake Life: The View from Here (1993)
Strip Jack Naked (Nighthawks II) (1991)
The Times of Harvey Milk (1984)
Voices from the Front (1992)
Whoever Says the Truth Shall Die (1985)
Word Is Out: Stories of Some of Our Lives (1977)

AIDS and the Cinema

AIDS Dramas

Philadelphia (1993) was Hollywood's belated acknowledgment of the AIDS epidemic, eight years after network television's *An Early Frost.* Previous independent features include *Buddies* (1985), *Parting Glances* (1986), *Longtime Companion* (1990), and *The Living End* (1992). In addition, Home Box Office produced the feature-length film adaptation of Randy Shilts's *And the Band Played On* in 1993.

AIDS Documentaries

Hundreds of films and tapes have explored AIDS and its medical, social, and personal repercussions. *Common Threads: Stories from the Quilt* (1990) won an Academy Award. *Absolutely Positive* (1989), *No Regrets* (1992), and *Living Proof* (1993) dealt with living with HIV. *Dying for Love* (1987) and *(In)Visible Women* chronicled the lives of women with AIDS. *Ojos Que No Ven* (1987) was one of the first AIDS-prevention videos developed for the Hispanic community. *Too Little, Too Late* (1987), which focused on families of people with AIDS, was the basis for the made-for-TV drama *Our Sons* (1991).

— DANIEL MANGIN

Film Notes and Quotable Quotes

"You are not a lesbian. This is a temporary thing."—Sylvia Miles to daughter Andrea Feldman in the tongue-in-cheek *Heat* (1972)

"We met at an automat off Times Square. . . . He paid for my ham and eggs" was one of several clues that the two gangsters in *Desert Fury* (1947) were gay.

"You're spoiling it for the rest of us," a discreet 1930s London gay bar owner tells the flamboyant Quentin Crisp in *The Naked Civil Servant* (1975). Replies Crisp, "You mean the way a consumptive with a cough spoils the fun of tuberculosis?"

"Every time a heterosexual actor puts on a dress, they give him a fucking Academy Award. I don't understand it. We spend our lives playing heterosexuals and nobody ever gives us any credit for the incredible job we've done."—Harvey Fierstein

"What made me think I could do this? I think I was out of my mind."—*Desert Hearts* (1985) director Donna Deitch on why she embarked on what turned out to be a seven-year project

Head Hollywood Code censor Joseph Breen found revisions to the *A Streetcar Named Desire* script that made more clear why Blanche's husband killed himself "completely unacceptable by reason of the fact that they inescapably suggest that the Grey boy is a sex pervert."

"The gay community simply has to accept the possibility that gay or bisexual people can be engaged in criminal activity."— *Basic Instinct* scriptwriter Joe Eszterhas

Mart Crowley conceived of *The Boys in the Band* as a cautionary tale about gay men's need not to "hate ourselves, so very, very much." He may have dramatized his characters' self-loathing all too well: Many gays so hate the film they perhaps miss his message. *The Boys in the Band* director William Friedkin went on to make the controversial *Cruising*.

DID YOU KNOW...

Although *The Children's Hour, Suddenly Last Summer, Tea and Sympathy, The Killing of Sister George,* and *Staircase* were all made into motion pictures, *Torch Song Trilogy*, in 1988, became the very first gay-affirmative play to make the transfer to celluloid.

"This is a not a gay story set in the straight world. This is a gay story set in the gay world, where the heterosexuals come in and sort of torture us!"—Harvey Fierstein on the difference between *Torch Song Trilogy* (1988) and earlier mainstream gay portrayals.

"The fear of homosexuality is found in movies more often than homosexuality itself."—Vito Russo in *The Celluloid Closet*

"Hollywood cinema, especially, needs to repress lesbianism in order to give free rein to its endless variations on heterosexuality."—Andrea Weiss in *Vampires and Violets: Lesbians in Film*

Robert Aldrich offered to remove lesbian love scenes from *The Killing of Sister George* (1968) to avoid an X rating. He was told the film would get an X anyway, because of its subject, lesbianism.

— **DANIEL MANGIN**

New Lesbian Cinema: More than a Casual Gesture

Lesbianism in the popular 1991 film *Fried Green Tomatoes* (based on a most admirable novel) was "completely cloaked." In my review of the movie, I also wrote, "For those in the know, Mary Stuart Masterson may be the cutest baby butch to hit the screen since Patricia Charbonneau in *Desert Hearts*."

In other words, the cumulative history of faux-lesbian representation in the movies has allowed us to stake our Sapphic claims where we can find them. Although lesbian film images are beginning to move out of the shadows, progress remains halting, due to both a lack of funding for independents and the intransigence of a studio system bent on recycling proven formula. Lesbian crowd-pleasers like *Personal Best* (1982) and *Desert Hearts* (1985) bubble up only occasionally, anomalies to the dictates of Hollywood's hegemonic machinery. But in the wake of *Claire of the Moon*, a 1992 romance that turned a surprisingly pretty profit, funding may be more readily available for enterprising lesbian filmmakers, and major studios may have caught the whiff of a trend.

Just as the so-called New Queer Cinema of the late 1980s and early 1990s showcased a wave of fresh work from gay male filmmakers (e.g., Tom Kalin, Christopher Munch, Todd Haynes), and a movement of vibrant African American cinema emerged in the aftermath of Spike Lee's success (from directors John Singleton, Julie Dash, Allen and Albert Hughes, and others), lesbians, too, on the cusp of the millennium, are developing a canon of our own. Not only are dyke filmmakers more willing than ever to push the lavender envelope, they're making aesthetic choices—sometimes born of economic necessity—that constitute an oppositional approach to the standard conventions of narrative moviemaking (and pay homage to pioneering lesbian predecessors like Barbara Hammer, Michelle Parkerson, and Ulrike Ottinger). Sure, mainstream movies will continue to offer up the occasional gesture, casual and otherwise, but the boldest lesbian work is coming from within our own ranks. Directors as diverse as Jennie Livingston, Cheryl Dunye, Jan Oxenberg, Midi Onodera, and Maria Maggenti have feature-length movies in the pipeline. And rumor has it that *Rubyfruit Jungle*, after many false starts, may finally make it to the silver screen.

"In queer discourses generally there is a worrying tendency to create an essentialist, so-called authentic, queer gaze. My personal style is determined by diverse aesthetic influences, from Indian cinema and cultural iconography to pop promos and seventies avant-garde films."

PRATIBHA PARMAR, LESBIAN FILMMAKER

Two films from 1994, *Go Fish* and *Fresh Kill*, are prime examples of the new wave of out-and-proud lesbian cinema, in which the kisses are passionate, the palette multicultural, and the politics knit seamlessly into the narrative. Rose Troche's *Go Fish* is a gentle romantic girl-meets-girl saga by and about the under-thirty set. Combining urban smarts with angsty intimacy, the movie spotlights a swath of contemporary youth culture familiar to anyone who lives (or sight-sees) in queer enclaves. The story centers on the courtship of aspiring writer Max (Guinevere Turner, who co-wrote the screenplay with Troche) and quiet, skittish Ely (V. S. Brodie). After a rocky introduction masterminded by Max's roommate, Max and Ely engage in regular date-type activities like dinner and a movie before progressing to more imaginative foreplay . . . nail clipping. If the climactic sex scene is more melty montage than cathartic cum shot, at least the day-after glimpse of a jubilant Ely strutting down the boulevard telegraphs a kind of lesbian-specific chutzpah rarely captured on celluloid.

Likewise, *Fresh Kill*, from director Shu Lea Cheang, weaves a bold, tender love story into a broader tale about environmental crises, global media monopolies, and living on the borderlands of race and gender. Shareen (Sarita Choudhury) and Claire (Erin McMurtry) are an interracial couple with a young daughter who become entangled in a surreal caper involving a kidnapping, contaminated sushi, and Staten Island's infamous landfill. More formally experimental than *Go Fish, Fresh Kill* jerks from stylized, cyberpunk set pieces to jangly Manhattan street scenes to graphic lesbian sex of considerable urgency and heat. As in *Go Fish,* nobody has to come out—all the key players are true-blue lesbians from the get-go. Both films break new ground, both in despectacularizing lesbian lives and in their renegade retro/pomo posturing. At once irreverent and respectful, *Go Fish* and *Fresh Kill* are more than just date movies; they are harbingers of terrific things to come in the arena of rebel filmmaking, lesbian and otherwise.

— **ELIZABETH PINCUS**

Queer Cinema

Who says what defines "new queer cinema"? Perhaps more important, who cares? For many of the filmmakers and videomakers who are being classified as "new queer," the label sends them scrambling to try to set themselves apart from the rest of the genre by explaining how their work diverges from what people consider "queer." So what makes a movie queer?

Queer cinema, with its influences in the works of Andy Warhol, Barbara Hammer, Derek Jarman, and Kenneth Anger (not to mention seventies television and MTV), began as a phenomenon in 1992, after producers Marcus Hu and Christine Vachon introduced *The Living End* and *Swoon* to the festival circuit. While arguably "queer" films were made prior to then, it was an article by B. Ruby Rich in the September 1992 issue of *Sight and Sound* that coined the phrase "New Queer Cinema," and by doing so invented a new genre.

Queer cinema is a pastiche of independent filmmaking, experimental approaches, gritty characters, low budgets, and innovative styles. Think of high school dropout Sadie Benning, whose raw and clever *Jollies* (1992) and *It Wasn't Love* (1993) were created using Fisher-Price Pixelvision for under twenty dollars apiece. Or *Poison* (1991) by Todd Haynes, which tells three stories about a boy killing his abusive father; explicit same-sex love conveyed through prison sex, humiliation, and violence; and flesh-dripping zombie-people as an AIDS metaphor.

Queer cinema is not politically correct, whatever that means. It breaks the boundaries that, in the quest for liberation and gay rights, many of us have inadvertently confined ourselves within. Rose Troche's *Go Fish* (1994), perhaps the most mainstream of the new queer films, attacks lesbian censorship of lesbians who sleep with men, explores "lesbian bed death," and acknowledges there are happy nonmonogamous dykes. In *The Living End* (1992), Gregg Araki unashamedly tells a road story of HIV-positive queer boys that involves murdering fagbashers, psychokiller lesbians, and loads of unsafe sex.

Queer cinema is also about an increased understanding of, appreciation for, and access to the means of production, including both film and video. The economic feasibility of video production allows greater diversity of expression, be it covertly political or a direct attack on issues of race, class, or gender in their intersections with sexuality. It's about having an ever-expanding base of gay, lesbian, and alternative film festivals that are looking for fresh new movies.

Unfortunately, it's also mostly about white boys. As author Cherry Smith says, "Perhaps 'queer' is saying, 'No, this film doesn't represent you, unless you're a young, hip, streetwise white boy, or a dyke who's a wannabe—tough shit.'" That is changing, as queers of color continue to gain access to media production, and film festivals welcome more low budget film and video works by people of color.

A TOTALLY SUBJECTIVE HANDFUL OF QUEER MOVIES

The Hours and Times (1991), Christopher Munch

Poison (1991), Todd Haynes

R.S.V.P. (1991), Laurie Lynd

Dry Kisses Only (1992), Kaucylia Brooke and Jane Cottis

Grapefruit (1992), Cecilia Dougherty

Krush and **Double the Trouble, Twice the Fun** (1992), Pratibha Parmar

L Is for the Way You Look (1992), Jean Carlomusto

The Living End (1992), Gregg Araki

The Meeting of Two Queens (1992), Cecilia Barriga

She Don't Fade and **Vanilla Sex** (1992), Cheryl Dunne

Swoon (1992), Tom Kalin

It Wasn't Love (1993), Sadie Benning

Fast Trip, Long Drop (1994), Greg Bordowitz

Fresh Kill (1994), Shu Lea Cheang

Go Fish (1994), Rose Troche

Postcards from America (1994), Steve McLean

Super 8 1/2 (1994), Bruce LaBruce

Totally F**d Up** (1994), Gregg Araki

Frisk (1995), Todd Verow

Most of all, though, it's about irreverence, pleasure, biting rage, overt eroticism, grittiness, and a refusal of clean and easy plots, characters, or endings. Perhaps that is the greatest virtue of queer cinema: Despite an ever-increasing pressure toward mainstreaming by many gay men and lesbians, these films get messy.

— DON ROMESBURG

Lesbian and Gay Film Festivals

Until recently, few mainstream films had positive or accurate portrayals of lesbians and gay men. Independent filmmakers, however, have been creating affirming, thought-provoking, and empowering movies from within the gay and lesbian communities for over two decades. Distribution and presentation of independent films can be a costly and difficult process, often far beyond the means of individual film- and videomakers. Gay and lesbian film festivals provide accessible forums for these artists and their movies. In addition, because many independent films are not feature length, it is more realistic to show them with a series of other films, and festivals organize and show shorts in groupings, often by subject matter. Finally, gay and lesbian film festivals are places where audiences and filmmakers alike can come together and share thoughts, exchange contacts, and enjoy a sense of community. Below is a list of festival cities in the United States:

DID YOU KNOW...

There are thirty-nine international gay and lesbian film festivals, screening everywhere from Cape Town, South Africa, to Turku, Finland, and from Budapest, Hungary, to South Victoria, Australia.

Albuquerque
Austin
Atlanta
Boston
Champaign (Ill.)
Chicago
Fresno
Hartford
Honolulu
Las Vegas
Long Beach
Los Angeles
Milwaukee
Minneapolis
Missoula (Mt.)
Mobile (Al.)
New York
Olympia (Wa.)
Pittsburgh
Portland (Me.)
Sacramento
Salt Lake City
San Antonio
San Diego
San Francisco
Santa Barbara
Santa Cruz
St. Louis
Tampa
Tallahassee
Washington

— DANIEL MANGIN

GAYS AND LESBIANS UNDER THE LIGHTS

One of the areas where gay men and lesbians have been most active and successful in creating our own space is in the theater. It has even been said that mainstream theater *is* gay male theater, partly due to the bohemian nature of the theater culture, and partly due to the large number of gay men involved in theater. The proof is in the pudding: Three of the plays nominated for Broadway's prestigious Tony Award in 1994 for Best Play were gay-themed. Lesbian representation in the mainstream has been more of a struggle, but there have been many successful lesbian theater companies and lesbian plays in the past twenty-five years.

While we still have a long way to go in bringing a diversity of lesbian and gay voices to the stage, we have come quite a distance. In a sense, theater is one of the few places where gay men have truly "arrived."

Lesbians and Gay Men on Stage: A Necessarily Incomplete History

"If it weren't for the Jews, the fags, and the gypsies, there wouldn't be any theatre."
—*Mel Brooks*

Up until roughly the 1960s, portrayals of lesbians and gay men on stage were rather rare, almost universally vague, and heavily "encoded." In the years that have followed, however, a shift has taken place, and the chief tension in lesbian and gay theatre across the last three decades has occurred not over whether homosexuality ought to be visible, but over how that which "doesn't show" should be made apparent.

Arguments can and frequently do still crop up over interpreting playwrights' "true" intentions for the characters or themes in their plays. Were George and Martha, for example, Edward Albee's warring, childless husband and wife in *Who's Afraid of Virginia Woolf?*, actually a barren male couple in "disguise"?—as more than a few scholars and critics have argued. Although he is openly gay, Albee vehemently rejects such an interpretation.

Daring to Speak Our Name

As theatre scholars point out, intentionally visible homosexuality did make its way onto American stages even during the early decades of this century. Kaier Curtin, in *We Can Always Call Them Bulgarians: The Emergence of Lesbians and Gay Men on the American Stage,* notes that the first lesbian character in an English-language play appeared in *The God of Vengeance* at Greenwich Village's Provincetown Theatre in 1922, a drama that was popular enough to move to Broadway's Apollo Theatre the next year. In 1926 *The Captive,* which premiered on Broadway, renewed the lesbian theme. Largely because of plays like these, theatrical depictions of "sex degeneracy or sex perversion" became illegal in New York State in 1927 under the Wales Padlock Law; in New York City, newspaper magnate William Randolph Hearst led a "public decency" campaign that resulted in even stricter limitations on Broadway stages. These laws were not repealed until 1967.

The God of Vengeance and *The Captive* were followed by the "homosexuality as dirty secret" school of theatre, as evidenced by *The Children's Hou*r (1934), *Tea and Sympathy* (1953), *Suddenly Last Summer* (1958), and even *A Streetcar Named Desire* (1947), in which the homosexual character, Blanche Dubois's young husband, whose suicide helps bring about her derangement, is never even seen. By the mid-1960s, explicitly homosexual, though still deranged, characters were much more likely to appear onstage, as in *The Killing of Sister George* (1965) and *Staircase* (1966).

But not all gay characters of the time were negative. An alternative, gay-centered voice was raising itself, albeit faintly. As early as 1961, the Caffe Cino playwrights had begun to produce club-style gay theatre for the Greenwich Village art crowd. The talents of gay playwrights Lanford Wilson, Robert Patrick, William Hoffman, and Doric Wilson, to name a few, were nurtured there. Cino's notable contemporaries included the Judson Poets' Theatre, where the openly gay Reverend Al Carmines wrote and produced early "rock operas," some dedicated to themes of gay liberation (such as *The Faggot,* which coincided with his 1973 sermon "We Are All Faggots").

The landmark gay theatre event of the era was the 1968 stage production of Mart Crowley's *Boys in the Band.* About *Boys,* nearly everything has been said: that it helped usher in Stonewall, that its outrageous depictions set gay lib back twenty years, that it is one of the most homophobic plays of all time, that it was one of the first plays to give genuine dimension to the lives of a variety of gay characters. Whatever one's opinion, *Boys in the Band* is a standard by which gay theatre was often measured in the two decades that came after, and it contributed to the boisterous new call for "positive" gay characters.

What was considered "positive" depended on who did the evaluating. Somewhat paradoxically, a great many gay plays of the 1970s—chiefly men's plays—represented aspects of gay life that mainstream theatre would have been pilloried for exploring. They included the loneliness that caused older men to turn to hustlers; the debauchery of innocents by urban gay life; the insularity of the gay ghetto; and the neurotic entanglements and complicated sexual victimizations that occurred among friends, partners, and frustrated would-be lovers.

But the mainstays of 1970s-style gay men's theatre were plays about relationships—or the unlikelihood of relationships. These nearly archetypal plays, basically lighthearted comedies about tricking, were generally set in the tasteful walk-ups/garden apartments/summer cottages of gay New York and typically showed gay men to be vain, fickle, and aesthetically sophisticated but emotionally shallow. Gay men were also screamingly witty, always ready with the clever put-down or the mordant bon mot. It was a renaissance of the "repartee play" that Oscar Wilde and Noel Coward would have envied (and which they doubtless helped inspire). The casts invariably included several handsome young men; at some point in the course of the play one of them (and maybe more) would have occasion to remove his shirt (and maybe more). Sexuality was the plays' currency. Far from tackling world-class issues, for most of its first two decades gay theatre was monopolized by white, urban, middle-class, male characters who only occasionally managed to find their way out of the bedroom.

Characteristic of the period are Doric Wilson's *A Perfect Relationship,* Robert Patrick's *T-Shirts,* Victor Bumbalo's *Kitchen Duty*, and Terry Miller's *Pines 79* (the quintessential Fire Island comedy). Reflecting on those years, journalist John F. Karr, then a staff member at San Francisco's Theatre Rhinoceros, quipped that Rhino's entire costume department in the 1970s consisted of a jockstrap and a flannel shirt.

Gay men's ambivalence regarding the intersection of physical and emotional intimacy found its counterpoint in a number of lesbian plays of the time, including the popular summer-cottage plays of Jane Chambers. These dramas, in which the heroines fall into committed coupledom at a pace approximately equal to the speed of sound, are perhaps as dated today as are men's sex farces. Nevertheless, their significance is that they represented the gay situation as many lesbians and gay men wanted it to be seen.

Politics and Art Size Each Other Up

"Positive" representation, though, had its own tensions. If lesbian and gay lives could be accurately described on stage, whom would we be willing to sanction as role models? Did the eternally single, alcoholic dyke (*A Late Snow*) or the long-coupled lesbian physician dedicated to AIDS work (*Falsettoland*) seem more "universal"? Were we more likely to admit that Emory, *Boys in the Band*'s "butterfly in heat," resembled someone we knew; or was Jed, Ken Talley's strong, silent (and very butch) lover in Lanford Wilson's *Fifth of July,* the fellow we'd like our parents to meet?

As early as the mid-1970s, lesbian and gay characters had begun to show up, without fanfare, in mainstream hits like Michael Cristofer's *Shadow Box* (1977), James Kirkwood's *P.S., Your Cat Is Dead* (1975), and even *A Chorus Line* (1976). Martin Sherman's *Bent* was a Broadway smash in 1979, and Jane Chambers's *Last Summer at Bluefish Cove* enjoyed a long and successful

Glines production during 1980 and 1981. *International Stud,* the first installment of what would become Harvey Fierstein's *Torch Song Trilogy*, appeared in 1978, and the second two parts followed in 1979. And George C. Wolfe's *The Colored Museum* (at The Public in 1986) featured Miss Roj, a fierce and prophetic "Snap Queen" who provides a dire yet dignified warning about "the life habits of a deteriorating society."

In large part, however, one of the major legacies of post-Stonewall liberation for the dramatic arts was the flourishing of not just gay and gay-inflected theatre but of lesbian and gay theaters as well. Gay and gay-friendly venues such as the La MaMa Experimental Theatre Club joined a growing number of American gay and lesbian companies, including Doric Wilson's The Other Side of Silence ("TOSOS," founded in 1974); The Glines (1976); Medusa's Revenge (1978); Ron Tavel and John Vacarro's Playhouse of the Ridiculous and, later, Charles Ludlam's Ridiculous Theatre Company; San Francisco's The Cockettes (1970–1972) and Angels of Light (roughly 1975–1980), and the Gay Men's Theatre Collective (which broke ground with its 1977 *Crimes Against Nature*). By the start of the 1980s, as many as two score lesbian and gay theatre companies were operating in the United States.

The Creation of a Theatre of AIDS

In the years since the health crisis began, literally hundreds of AIDS-themed plays have been produced across the country—a tribute both to theatre's ability to respond to contemporary concerns and to the struggle of artists to come to terms with the devastation of the disease.

Although gay and lesbian theatre was not the only tributary of an authentic "theatre of AIDS" that began to develop after 1984, the most enduring dramatic responses to AIDS have come from lesbian and gay playwrights. One of the earliest of these was *The A.I.D.S. Show* (1984), a collection of skits and monologues by fourteen writers that was produced at Theatre Rhinoceros. Particular recognition must go to Theatre Rhinoceros for its commitment to plays that explore the gay community's ongoing response to AIDS. Doug Holsclaw, a contributor to and co-director of *The A.I.D.S. Show,* later wrote *Life of the Party* (1986), one of the first plays to be, as Holsclaw put it, "blatant propaganda for safe sex." Leland Moss's *Quisbies* (1988), Robert Pitman's *Passing* (1989), Anthony Bruno's *Soul Survivor* (1989), Henry Mach's *Dirty Dreams of a Clean-Cut Kid* (1991), Holsclaw's *The Baddest of Boys* (1992), and James Carroll Pickett's *Queen of Angels* (1993) are only a few of the AIDS plays that have crossed Theatre Rhinoceros's stage.

DID YOU KNOW...

In the last two and a half decades more than 120 feminist and lesbian theatre companies were formed in the United States.

Robert Chesley's *Night Sweat* (1984) and *Jerker* (1986), first produced in San Francisco and Los Angeles, respectively, considered the expression and experience of gay male sexuality in the AIDS era. Harvey Fierstein contributed *Safe Sex* in 1987, a trio of one-acts that zeroed in on AIDS's impact on intimacy between gay men; and Lanford Wilson's *A Poster of the Cosmos* (1988) was a portrait of a man whose search for connection with his dying lover and for a way out of survival guilt leads him to expose himself deliberately to his lover's infected blood. Dystopian visions of a savage, totalitarian New York City, in which an unnamed plague has annihilated most of the population, were explored in Paul Selig's *Terminal Bar* (1985) and Alan Bowne's *Beirut* (1986).

Larry Kramer's *The Normal Heart,* which opened at The Public in 1985, and William Hoffman's *As Is,* which moved from Circle Repertory to Broadway just ten days later, are probably the best known examples of the "first generation" of AIDS plays. Kramer's personal contribution to the theatrical discourse on AIDS is huge, and his later *Just Say No* (1988) and *The Destiny of Me* (1992) remain major documents of an era.

No consideration of modern lesbian and gay and AIDS theatre would be complete without a respectful nod to Tony Kushner's *Angels in America,* a work so lavish and unprecedented that it almost immediately began to establish new standards. Although nearly six years passed between the time *Angels* was commissioned by San Francisco's now-defunct Eureka Theatre and the play's Broadway debut, *Angels* avoided aging in the manner of many AIDS plays. Indeed, *Angels* is a watershed not only in lesbian and gay theatre but in the American dramatic mainstream as well. Now that George C. Wolfe, an openly gay African American man who is largely responsible for bringing *Angels* to Broadway, is at the helm of New York's influential Public Theatre, a new kind of entrée into the world of "legitimate" theatre may become available to lesbian and gay dramatists.

Lesbian and Gay Theatre Learns a Queer Aesthetic

At the same time that AIDS was making its impact on the artistic world—and everywhere else—theatre was also being affected by the arrival of performance art as a popular, more-or-less legitimate, even mainstream dramatic product. For gay and lesbian theatre artists, accustomed as they often were to producing work in out-of-the-way, underfunded venues, performance art was almost made to order. It provided access to queer artists whose work had less often been seen (people of color and women, for example), and, because of spaces like the WOW Cafe in New York; Highways in Los Angeles; the Valencia Rose and its later incarnation, Josie's, in San Francisco; and others nationwide, small-venue, cabaret-type theatre made a kind of comeback—shades of Caffe Cino.

In a scene from Tony Kushner's award-winning Angels in America—Part I: Millennium Approaches, *the Angel (Lisa Bruneau, right) appears to Prior Walter (Garret Dillahunt, left) in a 1994 A.C.T. production in San Francisco.*

Perhaps most importantly, performance art provided, for the emerging "queer" arts community in particular, an immediate venue for the telling of the stories and myths not just of the individual but of the tribe. Although performance art sometimes furnished the opportunity for an entirely new echelon of artistic self-indulgence, it had the potential to command a degree of attention from the audience and, on the part of the artist, an intensity of purpose that made it extraordinary.

Indeed, performance art has done a great deal to expand the definition of lesbian, gay, and queer theatre. Among those literally creating today's avante-garde are artists like Kate Bornstein (whose popular shows, including *Hidden: A Gender*, *The Opposite Sex Is Neither,* and *Virtually Yours,* explore her experiences as a transsexual lesbian); Wayne Corbitt (who proclaims in his performance poem *Black Birds Boogie in the Black Moonlight* —a huge success at the Eighth Annual Gay and Lesbian Theatre Festival in Seattle in 1991—"What I am is a black, sadomasochistic queer with AIDS"); John Kelly (who "inhabits" characters as diverse as Maria Callas, Egon Schiele, Joni Mitchell, and Mona Lisa); and Holly Hughes (whose *Dress Suits to Hire, World Without End,* and *Clit Notes: Holly Hughes's One-Man Show* are a reflection on sexual identity that is so kaleidoscopic, instinctive, intimate, hilarious, and even perverse that audiences are stunned).

The Future Begins at Home

For many lesbian, gay, bisexual, and queer theatre artists, however, access and visibility remain significant obstacles. Blockades come from within the lesbian and gay community and from other segments of society as well. The internationally acclaimed gay troupe PomoAfro-Homos, for example, found themselves unwelcome at the National Black Theatre Festival in 1991 and again in 1993. And when Wayne Corbitt premiered his full-length, five-character play *Crying Holy* (1993)—the first staged play about gay life written by an openly gay African American man—*The Advocate* considered it "not newsworthy" enough to cover.

Many aspects of lesbian and gay life are still struggling to appear on stage. Lesbian theatre has demonstrated a certain unwillingness to look forcefully at sexuality (at lesbians who enjoy uncommitted sex or S/M or who sometimes sleep with men, for instance), although notable exceptions include the work of Holly Hughes and the collaborations of Peggy Shaw and Lois Weaver. Theatre by gay men, although it has often criticized "promiscuity," has seldom explored the ways in which white male privilege seriously compromises the meaning of "community" or questioned gay men's lack of interest in social issues that do not affect them directly. AIDS hasn't necessarily changed all that, although one of *Angels in America*'s many breakthroughs was its acknowledgment that some gay men do, in fact, turn tail and run when their lovers are diagnosed with AIDS. Still, there remains little in gay and lesbian drama to compare with works like *All My Sons* or *A Doll's House*—theatre's great morality plays.

If the 1980s heralded an opportunity for gay theatre not only to transcend pre-liberation images of psychotic dykes and pathetic queens, but to move beyond the static portrayals institutionalized by gay and lesbian playwrights themselves during the 1970s, lesbian and gay theatre in the 1990s continues to be molded (and occasionally immobilized) by conflicts between archetype and stereotype, between "otherness" and assimilation, between self-awareness and self-consciousness.

Although gay, lesbian, and even queer theatre cannot continue to be held hostage by the demand for "positive" images, the political and economic realities of our times also mean that the function of theatre in everyday life is changing in complicated ways. Lesbian and gay theatre is subject to all of the forces that are shaping theatre generally across the country; and that "general" theatre, in turn, is influenced (as it has always been) by the talents of gay and lesbian writers and by the extent to which gay life *is* American life. Such a cross-pollination is always in the process of yielding new crops, but certain continuities remain. Perhaps Emory from *Boys in the Band* still has a point today when he says that it "takes a fairy to make something pretty."

— **WENDELL RICKETTS**

DID YOU KNOW...

Of the "NEA Four," artists who were defunded by the National Endowment for the Arts in 1990 amid great controversy, all were performance artists and three of them—John Fleck, Holly Hughes, and Tim Miller—called themselves queer.

An Eclectic Collection of Lesbian and Gay Plays

1890s
1896 *A Florida Enchantment*

1896 *At St. Judas's*

1900s
1907 *The God of Vengeance*

1920s
1925 *Spring Cleaning*

1926 *The Captive*

1927 *The Drag*

1928 *Pleasureman*

1930s
1932 *Girls in Uniform*

1934 *The Children's Hour*

1937 *Wise Tomorrow*

1940s
1945 *Trio*

1946 *No Exit*

1947 *Now Barrabbas*

1950s
1953 *Something Unspoken*

1953 *Tea and Sympathy*

1954 *The Immoralist*

1955 *Cat on a Hot Tin Roof*

1958 *Suddenly Last Summer*

1960s
1960 *Aunt Edwina*

1965 *The Killing of Sister George*

1966 *Spitting Image*

1966 *Staircase*

1967 *Glamour, Glory and Gold: The Life of Nola Noonan, Goddess and Star*

1967 *When Queens Collide*

1968 *The Boys in the Band*

1969 *And Puppy Dog's Tails*

1969 *Fortune and Men's Eyes*

1970s

1971 *Steambath*
1972 *Coming Out!*
1972 *Norman, Is That You?*
1972 *Small Craft Warnings*
1973 *Camille* (the drag version)
1973 *The Faggot*
1973 *Prisons*
1973 *The Rocky Horror Show*
1973 *Tubstrip*
1975 *Boy Meets Boy*
1975 *A Chorus Line*
1975 *P.S., Your Cat Is Dead*
1975 *The Ritz*
1977 *Gemini*
1977 *The Shadow Box*
1977 *The West Street Gang*
1978 *Fifth of July*
1979 *Bent*

Charlotte (Michelle Agnew, right) talks with fellow lesbian bar patron Katherine (Ellen Gerstein) in a 1994 Celebration Theater (Los Angeles) production of Phyllis Nagy's Girl Bar.

1980s

1980 *Last Summer at Bluefish Cove*
1981 *Forty-Deuce*
1983 *Blue Is for Boys*
1983 *La Cage Aux Folles*
1983 *One* **
1983 *Torch Song Trilogy*
1983 *The Well of Horniness*
1984 *The A.I.D.S. Show* **
1984 *Night Sweat* **
1985 *As Is* **
1985 *Heart of the Scorpion*
1985 *The Normal Heart* **
1985 *Terminal Bar* **
1985 *Vampire Lesbians of Sodom*
1985 *Warren* **
1986 *Beirut* **
1986 *The Colored Museum*
1986 *Jerker* **
1987 *Burn This*
1987 *The Knife*
1987 *M. Butterfly*
1987 *Psycho Beach Party*
1987 *Safe Sex* **

1987 *Secret War*
1988 *Just Say No* **
1988 *A Poster of the Cosmos* **
1988 *Quisbies* **
1989 *Passing* **
1989 *Soul Survivor* **

1990s

1991 *Dirty Dreams of a Clean-Cut Kid* **
1992 *Angels in America* **
1992 *The Baddest of Boys* **
1992 *The Destiny of Me* **
1992 *Falsettos*
1992 *The Night Larry Kramer Kissed Me* **
1992 *Queens of Angels* **
1993 *Crying Holy* **
1993 *Jeffery* **
1993 *Kiss of the Spider Woman*
1993 *Twilight of the Golds*
1993 *Why We Have a Body*
1994 *Love! Valor! Compassion!*
1995 *Victor/Victoria*
1995 *Vita and Virginia*
(** denotes plays about AIDS)

?#!

CAN YOU BELIEVE IT?

In 1994, Bert and Ernie, *Sesame Street* muppet roomies, were accused by fundamentalist ministers as being a gay couple. Children's Television Workshop's response was: "Bert and Ernie do not portray a gay couple, and there are no plans for them to do so in the future."

FAGGOTS AND DYKES IN YOUR LIVING ROOM

Television—popular culture à la carte—reaches more people more profoundly (and, some would argue, more insidiously) than any other medium. It's no wonder that gay men and lesbians take an active interest in having accurate portrayals of themselves on the little screen.

Since the beginning of television, gay imagery, if not gay people, has been visible in one form or another. Drag was a staple of early television comedy, with Uncle Miltie as the reigning king (or queen) of drag. From the late sixties on, many shows had an occasional episode that dealt with lesbian or gay issues. By the mid-seventies, Jody, played by Billy Crystal on the situation comedy *Soap,* was an openly gay regular. By the nineties, our visibility has continued to increase, both on network and cable television.

But the battle for representation on mainstream television has been an uphill struggle. Accurate representations of gay men and lesbians are often met with great hostility by the religious fundamentalist right, who threaten to boycott companies that sponsor gay-friendly shows. For this reason, if a show makes a bold move and includes positive gay images, it may never be seen again. Such was the case with a 1990 *thirtysomething* episode that showed two gay men lying in bed together. For syndication purposes, the gay content was edited out, and the episode is noticeably missing from reruns.

In shaping the scope of what is "allowable" on TV, the significance of talk shows, however problematic, cannot be overstated. Ricki Lake had Bob and Rod Jackson-Paris on a Valentine's special. Phil Donahue has aired lesbians fighting for their right to keep their children. Sally Jesse Raphael had a show in which two gay men battled over whether or not one of them could "go straight." Such shows get people thinking—and talking—about a diversity of gay and lesbian issues.

We are on television, and hundreds of millions of viewers both nationally and internationally can now can enjoy seeing gay people in their very own living rooms on a near-daily basis.

DID YOU KNOW...

The queerest cast in television was that of *Bewitched*, which ran from 1964 to 1971. Among the gay cast members were one of the two men who played Darrin (Dick Sargent); one of the twins who played Tabitha, the daughter of Darrin and Samantha (Diane Murphy); Paul Lynde, who played Arthur, Samantha's trickster uncle; and, of course, Samantha's overbearing mother, Agnes Moorehead.

Gay Characters Who Weren't

For decades there have been certain characters who—to the lesbian or gay viewer—seem so overwhelmingly queer that the stated sexuality of the character is irrelevant. Oh, sure, they might say she's straight, but girlfriend, we know different! Here are just a few examples of claiming "straight" characters for ourselves:

Dr. Smith, villain, *Lost in Space*
All the men (**Gilligan,** the **Skipper** too, etc.), *Gilligan's Island*
Mr. French, butler/nanny, *Family Affair*
Jane Hathaway, no-nonsense secretary, *The Beverly Hillbillies*
Alice, super-butch housekeeper, *The Brady Bunch*
Oscar and **Felix,** butch/femme roommates, *The Odd Couple*
Buddy, tomboy, *Family*
Robin, boy wonder, *Batman*
Jo, the butch motorcycle chick, *The Facts of Life*
Darlene, sassy babe, *Roseanne*
Barney Fife, sissy lawman, and **Gomer Pyle**, sissy pumpboy and soldier, *The Andy Griffith Show*

Munroe, flamboyant neighbor, *Too Close for Comfort*
Brenda, Rhoda's world-weary sister, *Rhoda*
Sally Rogers, gal pal, *The Dick Van Dyke Show*
The Bionic Woman
Bea Arthur in any role

Phil Donahue's First Lesbian (And Eighteen Other Broadcasting Landmarks)

• ***Confidential File****, first appearance of a gay activist on a talk show, 1954, KTTV-TV, Los Angeles*
Talk show host Paul Coates devoted a half hour to "the problem" of homosexuality. Panelists included a psychiatrist, a vice squad cop, and "a homosexual." This gay man used a pseudonym, "Curtis White," and appeared only in silhouette. Despite these precautions, he told viewers, "I will probably lose my job as a result of the program." He described the homophile movement, and Coates showed movies of a Mattachine Society discussion group. The day after the show, "Curtis White" did, in fact, lose his job.

• **The Army-McCarthy Hearings**, *first national telecasts to address homosexuality as a social issue, 1954, various TV networks, live coverage*
Senator Joseph McCarthy included homosexuals on his list of "security threats" who he believed had infiltrated government. Both McCarthy and his opponents in the Army played fast and loose with accusations of homosexuality. For instance, McCarthy said there was an Army base that harbored homosexual soldiers. Several senators promptly announced that wherever the contaminated base might be, it was certainly not in their state. After McCarthy said he got his facts from "a little pixie," an Army lawyer took a jab at McCarthy's assistant, Roy Cohn, by quipping, "A pixie is a close relative of a fairy."

• ***The Rejected****, first nationally aired documentary about homosexuals, 1961, National Educational Television (NET)*
Almost forty public TV stations aired this one-hour documentary about gay men, produced in San Francisco by

KQED. Early in the show, a psychiatrist explained the Kinsey continuum of sexual orientation. Anthropologist Margaret Mead discussed sociological aspects of homosexuality. A doctor described the unusually high rates of venereal disease among gay men. Mattachine Society board members gave an insider's viewpoint. Of course, the show ignored lesbians.

• ***The Eleventh Hour:* "What Did She Mean by 'Good Luck'?"**, *first network TV drama about lesbianism, 1963, NBC*
The Eleventh Hour was a short-lived dramatic series about mental health professionals. One episode focused on Hallie Lambert, a childish, temperamental actress whose tantrums were causing dissent among the cast members of a play. Each time director Marya Stone suggested ways to improve Hallie's performance, the actress thought Marya hated her. The series' Freudian-therapist hero finally discovered that Hallie was in love with Marya and had channeled her denial and confusion into hostility. Aside from this neurotic mental patient, the era's only pseudo-lesbian TV character was a rifle-toting sniper in a 1962 episode of *The Asphalt Jungle.*

DID YOU KNOW...

One of the regular characters on ABC's *My So-Called Life*, a realistic drama about teen angst in the nineties, is bisexual half Latino, half African American Rickie Vasquez. He is played by openly gay Puerto Rican actor Wilson Cruz. Of the role, Cruz said in an *Advocate* interview, "There were some industry people who hinted that this might not be the best way to start my career. . . . Well, fine, so it's a risk. But what am I going to do? Turn down one of the best-written parts I've ever seen because it's a gay character? *Please!* Who better to play it than someone who's been there?"

• ***C.B.S. Reports:* "The Homosexuals,"** *first commercial network TV documentary about homosexuals, 1967, CBS*
During this documentary about gay men, Mike Wallace explained that "the homosexual" is "incapable of a fulfilling relationship with a woman or, for that matter, a man." Viewers saw police arrest a nineteen-year-old sailor for having sex in a men's room. Renowned psychiatrist Charles Socarides said that there are no happy homosexuals. A depressed gay man, hidden behind a potted palm, rambled about how mentally sick he was. Fortunately, the show was much less lurid than CBS's original 1964 outline for it.

• ***N.Y.P.D.* pilot/premiere: "Shakedown,"** *first gay-positive TV drama, 1967, ABC*
In this drama, detectives investigated an extortion ring whose members posed as cops to blackmail closeted gay men. One detective visited a homophile activist to see if

he had heard anything about the blackmailers. The activist was a successful businessman who traveled the country making gay-themed speeches; he was the first television character to say the words, "I'm homosexual." The story focused on a closeted gay construction worker whom the criminals were blackmailing. One regular character, a heterosexual black cop, made a strong case for coming out and drew parallels between antigay prejudice and racism.

• ***The Phil Donahue Show,*** *Phil's first lesbians, ca. 1968, WLWD, Dayton, Ohio*
Lilli Vincenz, longtime activist with the Mattachine Society of Washington, and Barbara Gittings, former editor of *The Ladder: A Lesbian Review*, traveled to Ohio around 1968 to appear on this early Donahue broadcast. Gittings recalls that Donahue asked excellent questions and that Vincenz exuded a wholesome, "all-American daughter" image throughout. Even so, she says, most of the studio audience were "hostile housewives" who made it clear they were unhappy to be in a room with two lesbians.

• ***The Corner Bar***, *first series with a gay regular character, 1972, ABC*
This sitcom's regulars were stock characters: a stereotyped Jew, a doddering drunkard, a flaming queen, and a two-dimensional bigot. Vincent Schiavelli played the gay character, flamboyant designer Peter Panama. With wrists flailing, Peter would lisp lines like (as the gang watched TV), "Couldn't we switch to Channel Six? Julia Child is stuffing a wild duck!" One week, he described a recent party he'd attended that was full of weirdos: all married couples. Like most of the few gay characters at the time, Peter was single.

• ***That Certain Summer***, *first TV depiction of a stable, same-gender couple; first network drama to focus on a gay parent; first gay-themed show to win an Emmy award, 1972, ABC*
The writers of this TV movie later recalled, "Given the realities of television, we assumed it would have to be written as a short story, or play, or a book." The story deals with a gay father trying to decide whether to come

out to his teenage son. ABC agreed to make the film only if the producers cast big-name stars. Hal Holbrook and Martin Sheen played the father and his lover, and Hope Lange played the father's ex-wife. The gay couple was likable, but the ending implied that there was little emotional support or warmth in their relationship. ABC deleted almost all touching between men in the film. The cuts led to some nonsensical dialogue—such as when Holbrook proclaimed "I don't like public displays," referring to two men who had walked past him *not* holding hands.

• ***Police Story:* "The Ripper,"** *first network drama rewritten with the consultation of gay activists, 1974, NBC*

The Gay Media Task Force and the National Gay Task Force began intensive negotiations with the major TV networks in 1973. Soon after, the producers of *Police Story* sent NBC a proposed script about an aging queen who butchered young gays who had rejected his advances. The script featured stereotypical, bitter lesbians and a florid gay man who "got that way" because of his mother. NBC told the producers to consult gay activists and draft a more balanced script. In the final version, the serial killer was an antigay psychopath who blamed the gay community for his son's death: the gay son had died with his lover in a car crash.

• ***Marcus Welby, M.D.:* "The Outrage,"** *first coordinated national gay campaign against a TV show, 1974, ABC*

This series was known for handling tough issues sensitively, so lesbian and gay activists were shocked when ABC approved this simplistic script about a male teacher who raped young boys. The activists pointed out that television's rare homosexuality-theme dramas tended to focus on false, harmful stereotypes. ABC refused to tone down the script, so gay groups pressured sponsors and stations. By the air date, most of the original sponsors had pulled their ads, and six stations had canceled the episode. Activists had good reasons to worry about TV: in the fall of 1974, every lesbian, gay, bisexual, or transvestite character on a TV drama was a violent criminal.

• ***Police Woman:* "Flowers of Evil,"** *TV's ultimate killer-dyke drama, 1974, NBC*

From 1962 to 1989, the lesbian guest characters on most drama series were dangerous criminals. This *Police Woman* first went further: it depicted a whole gang of deadly dykes who ran a nursing home. The women robbed, drugged, and occasionally killed the home's wealthy residents. Ringleader Mame was a scowling, swaggering, cursing ex-Marine who had short hair, wore men's shirts, and smoked little black cigarettes. "Flowers of Evil" and the controversial *Marcus Welby* episode have both been withdrawn from syndication. Curious individuals can view "Flowers of Evil" in New York at the Museum of Television and Radio.

• ***Cage Without a Key,*** *TV's first—and almost only—gay African American character, 1975, CBS*

This TV movie, a juvenile reformatory drama, broke ground in presenting a self-identified gay African American teenager: Tommy, a young lesbian who was stabbed to death near the film's end. She was a sympathetic character who befriended and protected the show's straight, white hero (Susan Dey). Other black gay characters on TV have included a male photographer in *Sins* (1986), the doomed lesbian couple in *The Women of Brewster Place* (1989), campy film critics Blaine and Antoine on *In Living Color* (1990–1994), and Andrew's brother on *Roc* (1991).

• ***Soap,*** *first successful sitcom with a gay regular character, 1977–1981, ABC*

Soap was not the first series with a gay male regular: *The Corner Bar* (1972), *Hot*l Baltimore* (1975), and *The Nancy Walker Show* (1976) preceded it. *Soap*, however, was a hit. Jody (Billy Crystal) was sweet, proud, nonstereotypical, and very out. Many isolated gay teenage viewers embraced him as a role model. Still, there were ambiguities. In early episodes, Jody said he had "always felt like a woman" and talked of having gender-reassignment surgery; by the final season, he was dating women, but still identified himself as gay. Some viewers complained that *Soap*'s writers didn't know a transsexual from a homosexual from a bisexual.

• ***St. Elsewhere:* "AIDS and Comfort,"** *first network drama to deal with AIDS, 1983, NBC*

A married, apparently straight city councilman was diagnosed with "the controversial disease AIDS," as one TV listing put it. His revelation of homosexuality jeopardized his political future and domestic life. As word spread that the hospital had an AIDS patient, participation in blood drives plummeted. By the time this first AIDS drama aired, AIDS had been in the news more than two years; the Centers for Disease Control had documented 3,000 cases in the U.S., of which 1,300 had been fatal. No other prime-time network drama was to address AIDS again until two years later, when CBS aired *Trapper John, M.D.:* "Friends and Lovers" and NBC presented the TV movie *An Early Frost.*

DID YOU KNOW...

From 1954 to 1959, only twelve gay-themed talk-show discussions aired on American television. Most ran locally in Los Angeles or New York. With few exceptions, the guests were ostensibly straight lawyers, psychotherapists, clergy, and vice-squad police. Openly gay people seldom had a chance to speak on the air.

• ***HeartBeat,*** *first series with a lesbian couple as regulars, 1988–89, ABC*

Wise, capable nurse-practitioner Marilyn McGrath (Gail Strickland) and her lover Patti, a caterer, were regulars on this sudsy medical drama. Their participation in the plot was casual, and their lesbianism was an accepted fact of life among Marilyn's co-workers. Marilyn and Patti were well-developed characters, generally convincing as a couple. Unlike the show's straight couples, however, they rarely touched: the writers contrived all manner of household tasks to keep their hands busy.

• ***L.A. Law,*** *first full, on-the-lips kiss between women on a network drama, 1991, NBC*

L.A. Law's famous "lesbian kiss" actually involved a straight character, Abby, and her bisexual friend, C.J. Reaction from gay and bisexual viewers, especially women, was favorable and strong. Phones buzzed. People mailed videotapes back and forth across the continent. Many had *L.A. Law* parties to watch and rewatch that nervous kiss. Since then, over 4,000 hours of prime-time network programming have passed, yet people still talk about this broadcast. The importance of this two-second kiss, even years later, says something powerful about the inadequate portrayal of lesbigay lives during the intervening years.

• ***Northern Exposure:* "The Wedding,"** *first same-gender union ceremony between recurring TV characters, 1994, CBS*

Eric and Rob's family, friends, and neighbors gathered to celebrate the two men's love in a wedding ceremony and banquet. The happy couple had appeared on the series off and on for several years. In this episode, they exchanged rings and vows, but no spit: CBS said they had to kiss off-camera. The same month, Fox-TV cut male-male kissing from a heterosexually sordid episode of *Melrose Place.* ABC, CBS, and NBC have shown lip-to-lip kisses between women (*Roseanne*, *Picket Fences*, *L.A. Law*), but kissing between men remains taboo.

• ***IKEA commercial,*** *first mainstream commercial about a gay couple, 1994, various stations*

Steve and Mitch—a comfy, white, middle-class, thirtysomething couple—told why they bought their first "serious dining room table" at an IKEA furniture store. Mitch explained that they chose a table with an expansion leaf because "a leaf means staying together, commitment." Countless straight viewers probably now think that table leaves have some special significance for gay couples. Right-wing groups, furious at the depiction of gay men as "normal," threatened to boycott. But most of the boycotters were nowhere near an IKEA store, so the threat had little impact. *New York Times* critic Frank Rich wrote of the commercial, "Certainly it makes me feel better about IKEA. But I still wouldn't let that dreary table anywhere near my house."

— STEVEN CAPSUTO

. . . And the Women Who Love Them

Talk Show Topics Through the Ages

Today, queer panels are what keep talk shows in business. In Februrary 1993 alone, more than a dozen nationally broadcast talk-show segments dealt with homosexuality. Almost all talk shows now let lesbians and gay men speak for themselves. Below is a small sampling of the ways in which radio and TV discussion shows have approached lesbian and gay lives.

1954

"Homosexuals and the Problem They Present" (*Confidential File*, KTTV-TV, Los Angeles)

1955

"Homosexuals Who Stalk and Molest Children" (*Confidential File*, syndicated TV)

1958

"Are Homosexuals Criminal?" (WTVS-TV, Detroit)

1959

"Should the Homosexual Marry?" (*Psychologically Speaking*, WEVD radio, New York)

1961

"How Normal Are Lesbians?" (*Psychologically Speaking,* WEVD radio, New York)

1962

"Society and the Homosexual" *(Argument,* KTTV-TV, Los Angeles)

National Convention of the Daughters of Bilitis. (*Paul Coates Interviews*, syndicated TV)

1966

Why are homosexuals picketing the U.S. government? (various local talk shows, Washington, D.C.)

1967

"Are Homosexuals Sick?" (*The David Susskind Show,* syndicated TV)

1970

Rev. Troy Perry and the Metropolitan Community Church. (*The Phil Donahue Show,* syndicated TV)

1971

"Should the State Recognize Homosexual Marriages?" (local broadcast, Minneapolis–St. Paul)

"Lesbians and Society" *(The David Susskind Show,* syndicated TV)

DID YOU KNOW...

In a 1993 *Advocate* interview, Amanda Bearse, a series regular on the Fox Network program *Married With Children*, was the first prime time series regular to ever come out. In the 1994 fall season, Harvey Fierstein became the first openly gay male actor to be a prime time regular (as a fashion designer on the short-lived CBS show *Daddy's Girls*.) Sandra Bernhard, a self-defined bisexual who plays a recurring lesbian character on the ABC program *Roseanne*, has also been public with her sexuality. In the spring of 1994, openly gay actors Dan Butler and Leslie Jordan became regular characters on NBC's *Frasier* and CBS's *Hearts Afire*, respectively.

PBS's The David Susskind Show *discusses "Gay Men and Lesbians in the Professions" in 1974. Guests included a professor, a registered nurse, an activist/journalist and a doctor.*

1973

"A Night at the Continental Baths" (*The Pat Collins Show*, WCBS-TV, New York)

1974

"Boy Prostitution" (*Tomorrow*, NBC-TV)
"Are Gays Going to Hell?" (*The Lou Gordon Show*, syndicated TV)

1975

"Gays and Military Service" (*Tomorrow*, NBC-TV)

1977

"The Threat of Militant Homosexuality" (*The 700 Club*, syndicated TV, Christian Broadcasting Network)

1980

"The Bisexual Couple." (*Donahue*, syndicated TV)
"Homosexual Prom Couple" (*Donahue*, syndicated TV)
"Lesbians Fighting to Stay in the Military" (*Speak Up, America*, NBC-TV)

1981

"The Question of Gay Rights" (*Firing Line*, PBS-TV)
"Gay Atheists" (*Donahue*, syndicated TV)

1982

"Lesbian Sperm Bank" (*Donahue*, syndicated TV)

1983

"Homosexuality Among Blacks" (*Tony Brown's Journal*, PBS-TV)

"Acquired Immune Deficiency Syndrome: AIDS." (*Donahue*, syndicated TV)

1984

"From Gay to Straight: Conversion Therapy" (*Donahue*, syndicated TV)
"Gay Characters on TV" (*Donahue*, syndicated TV)

1985

"Gay Senior Citizens" (*Donahue*, syndicated TV)
"Lesbian Nuns" (*Donahue*, syndicated TV)

1988

"Could Your Husband Be Gay?" (*Sally Jessy Raphael*, syndicated TV)
"National Coming Out Day" (*The Oprah Winfrey Show*, syndicated TV)

1989

"Teen Lesbians and Their Moms" (*Geraldo*, syndicated TV)
"When 'The Other Man' Is a Woman" (*Geraldo*, syndicated TV)
"Ex-Homosexuals and Their Wives" (*Donahue*, syndicated TV)
"They Got Me 'Cause I'm Gay" (*Sally Jessy Raphael*, syndicated TV)

Amanda Bearse

1990

"Pastors Playing with Perversion" (*The 700 Club*, syndicated TV/Christian Broadcasting Network)
"When Mom or Dad Is Gay" (*Geraldo*, syndicated TV)

1991

"When All Your Children Are Gay" (*The Oprah Winfrey Show*, syndicated TV)
"Lesbians and Gay Men Raising a Baby" (*Sally Jessy Raphael*, syndicated TV)
"Dumping Your Husband for Another Woman." (*The Oprah Winfrey Show*, syndicated TV)

1992

"Beautiful Women Who Are Lesbians" (*Sally Jessy Raphael*, syndicated TV)

1993

"Interracial Adoption and Homosexuality" (*Sally Jessy Raphael*, syndicated TV)

— STEVEN CAPSUTO

Gay Men, Lesbians, and the Cable TV Revolution

Gay and lesbian cable television shows have been around almost as long as cable television. The first known gay cable show was produced by the Gay Activists Alliance in 1971—a weekly call to arms in the infancy of the modern movement. Next came *Emerald City,* first produced in 1977 on Manhattan Cable's "leased access" Channel J by the late gay pioneer Frank O'Dowd. It was gay in the way that *After Dark* magazine was gay—covering gay-associated and campy entertainment news without being explicitly gay. O'Dowd was a roving entertainment reporter who featured such performers as Weyland Flowers and his catty marionette alter ego, Madame, drag star Divine, and local cabaret acts.

Following that, in the late 1970s, lesbian film critic Marcia Pally and the late film historian Vito Russo (of *The Celluloid Closet* fame), both activists, briefly took gay TV on the air with a weekly show on WNYC, a public station in New York. Lily Tomlin (as Mrs. Beadsley) was one of the featured guests of this short-lived show.

Cable TV pioneer Lou Maletta got his start producing male erotica (*Men and Films*) in 1982 in New York, but quickly recognized his obligation to incorporate short news segments, especially about the rapidly unfolding AIDS epidemic. Maletta now produces eight programs, some of which are seen in as many as twenty-two cities. He has sent crews to get the gay scoop on both the Democratic and Republican conventions since 1984. And his Gay Cable Network was the first gay electronic medium to secure White House press credentials. He is one of a growing number of producers that network their programming, including Gay Entertainment Television

(GET), which puts its shows up on satellite so that people with dishes can pull them in.

Another early pioneer was Butch Peaston, who produced the public access (and occasionally UHF) show *Out! In the 80's* (later changed to *Out! In the 90's*) from 1986 to 1993 live each Wednesday night in New York for an hour. Peaston brought an immediacy to gay television, allowing for call-ins and dialogue with the audience.

Today, many big cities—and some smaller ones—feature some gay and/or lesbian cable TV shows. Some still focus on entertainment and sexual matters. But the vast majority are produced by unpaid local activists with a desire to get the word out about what's going on within the local gay community and to spread gay news from the rest of the country, often culled from mainstream newspapers and gay publications, but also through original reporting.

Cable systems are obliged to make room on their access channels for all programs produced by community groups as long as "community standards" of obscenity are not violated. In the more conservative areas of the country, these standards have gotten some gay shows in trouble. On Manhattan Cable, the only restriction on content is a ban on showing insertive sex. That leaves a lot of things on Manhattan Cable that out-of-towners are shocked by, but programmers still have fights over the right to show such things as explicit safer sex demonstrations for educational purposes. In many other cities around the country, cable companies often exile gay programming to the wee hours of the morning even if the show is devoid of sexual content.

— **ANDY HUMM**

Make DYKE TV, Not War

Welcome to the 1990s. Amid the chaos of virulently homophobic amendments nationwide, President Clinton's flip-flop over queers in the military, and the firebombing of an HIV-positive lesbian activist's home in Tampa Bay, Florida, a ballsy, out and loud, four-inch-tall lesbian inside the television yells, "I want my *DYKE TV.*"

In April 1993, *DYKE TV* emerged from the ruins of New York City's AIDS-torn, ozone-challenged, ever-incestuous lesbian community. Now, every week gay girls across the country can turn themselves on—and learn a thing or two—in the comfort of their own homes.

It is, however, not the first lesbian cable show. In 1988, *Video Salon* in New Orleans and *Intergalactic Lesbian Video* in New Mexico jump-started their sapphic engines for a short ride and premiered half-hour monthly installments of lesbian cable programming. And now *DYKE TV*, the brainchild of executive producers Linda Chapman, Mary Patierno, and Ana Maria Simo, has taken this city's exceptionally diverse, political workhorse of a community by storm. The series follows a magazine format, covering both news and cultural events. In "Lesbian Health," one segment zeroed in on a half-nude dyke with a speculum in her vagina explaining the ins and outs of cervical self-exam. "The Arts" runs the gamut with filmmakers, performers, painters, and dancers. "Sports" has provided campy and inspiring investigations into local rugby fields, the beloved Brooklyn Women's Martial Arts, and the truly sweaty Gay Games IV. There's at least one in-depth news report at the beginning of each show and a "Calendar" segment at the tail end. However, the segment to tune in for is called "I Was a Lesbian Child," complete with old tomboy photos and amusing reminiscences.

DTV's historical moment was marked by both the in-your-face passion of the Lesbian Avengers, a movement formed to promote our visibility and survival, and the premiere of Manhattan Neighborhood Network's two new cable access channels in December 1992. *(DYKE TV* now airs on one of them.) In turn, the success of *DYKE TV* marks the birth of other cable shows, like *Girl/Girl TV* in Northampton, Massachusetts, and *Laughing Matters* in Cambridge.

Not including the endless in-kind services provided by a veritable legion of volunteers, four segments of *DYKE TV* cost $3,000 to $4,000 to produce. Seed money was planted by a few small foundations, but otherwise the series relies on homegrown strategies to raise cash: cocktail parties and pooled honorariums from university presentations. Furthermore, if you want to make your own dollars count, and, in Patierno's words, "to feel a part of it all," you can become a member with a quarterly newsletter. Or even better for both you and *DTV*, become a subscriber and get the quarterly "*Best of...*" tape mailed to you at home. Needless to say, Chapman verifies that the show functions on "pretty much of a shoestring."

Rest assured that media-starved girls-into-girls don't have to live in New York, Massachusetts, or Berlin (where the collectively produced *Läsbisch TV* presents similar fare) to catch dykes on TV. Having beat the bushes for local sponsorships, *DTV* currently airs on public access channels in seventeen cities from coast to coast. "People like the show and want it on in their own towns," says Patierno, so a small business or an individual woman donates $2,500 a year for tape stock, dubbing, and mailing of the weekly program. As for content, the producers are eager to dig their tripod legs in everyone's backyard. Chapman muses, "We definitely want to cover the scene in a bigger way than just Manhattan." Aiming to present the wider world of lesbians, they actively solicit volunteer stringers from around the country.

As the "Religious Right" perpetuates intolerance and hatred on their own crystal-clear transponders and satellites, we must fight for each minute of television airtime. We must learn from them, do as they do, work passionately to take over this nation, school district by school district, city by city, state by state, and channel by channel. To "Don't Ask, Don't Tell," our best response is "Make *DYKE TV*, not war."

— CATHERINE SAALFIELD

What's in a Name? Gay Cable TV Shows, Past and Present

The Barry Z Show (New York, NY)

Be Our Guest (New York, NY)

Being Gay Today (Sacramento, CA)

Between the Lines (Nashville, TN)

The Closet Case Show (New York, NY)

Coming Out! (Winnipeg, MB)

Dish (Los Angeles, CA)

Dishing It Up with T-Gala (Nashville, TN)

DYKE-TV (New York, NY)

Electric City (San Francisco, CA)
Gay & Lesbian News (Los Angeles, CA)
Gay Fairfax (VA)
The Gay 90's (Pittsburgh, PA)
Gay Perspectives (Rockville, MD)
Gay TV (Indianapolis, IN)
Gay USA (New York, NY, and nationally)
Gayblevision (Vancouver, BC)
GAZE-TV (Minneapolis, MN)
Good Morning, Gaymerica! (New York, NY)
Grass Roots (Madison, WI)
In the Dungeon (New York, NY)
In the Trenches (Madison, WI)
Inside/Out (New York, NY)
Inside/Outside the Beltway (Washington, DC)
Just for the Record (New Orleans, LA)
The Lambda Report (Denver, CO)
Latinos en Acción (New York, NY)
Lavender Lounge (San Francisco, CA)
LGTV (Lesbian/Gay Television) (Providence, RI)
Lovie TV (New York, NY)
Men for Men (New York, NY)
Network Q (national mail order)
Nothing to Hide (Madison, WI)
One in 10 People (Fairfax, VA)
Out! In the 90's (New York, NY)
Out on Wednesdays (New York, NY)
Outfront: Gay and Lesbian TV (Cincinnati, OH)
Outlook Video (Mountain View, CA)
Party Talk (New York, NY)
Pride Time (Boston, MA)
PRISM (Vancouver, BC)
Slightly Bent News (Portland, OR)
Spectrum News Report (Santa Ana, CA)
Stonewall Place After Dark (New York, NY)
Stonewall Union Lesbian/Gay Pride Report (Columbus, OH)
The 10% Show (Chicago, IL)
The Third Side (Washington, DC)
Thunder Gay Magazine (Thunder Bay, ON)
Tricks (Los Angeles, CA)
Two in Twenty (Because One in Ten Sounds Lonely) (Somerville, MA)
Way Out! (New York, NY)
Yellow on Thursday (Milwaukee, WI)

— ANDY HUMM

PBS Is *In the Life*

In the Life is the first regularly broadcast national gay and lesbian series on public television, carried on over sixty stations around the country. It's a fun, often lighthearted glimpse of gay and lesbian culture. Started in June 1992, the format of the program has evolved over time. Earlier shows were like the old Ed Sullivan variety show (hosted by Garrett Glaser or Kate Clinton), with a panoply of guests ranging from the singing group The Flirtations to actor David Drake, performing a scene from *The Night Larry Kramer Kissed Me.* Occasionally a show will be theme oriented, like the one that focused on gay and lesbian teens, hosted by comedian Karen Williams with co-hosts Ron Romanofsky and Paul Phillips of the singing duo Romanofsky and Phillips.

Advertising that it "bridges the gap between the straight and gay communities," the show has covered such topics as gay country-and-western life, presented sneak previews of films such as the smash lesbian film *Forbidden Love,* and provided coverage of both the 1993 March on Washington and the 1994 Stonewall 25 celebration in New York. Other notable guests over the years have been Lily Tomlin, Bob Hattoy, Tony Kushner, and Melissa Etheridge.

Although the program is sponsored by the Public Broadcasting System (PBS), it receives no funding from PBS or the Corporation for Public Broadcasting, relying on underwriting and donations from sympathetic foundations and private individuals.

THE LAVENDER AIRWAVES

Visibility is not only about being seen; it's also about being heard. Gay men and lesbians have taken to the airwaves around the country over the past several decades, spreading the words and music of our communities to anyone who could tune in. The gay radio movement has been moving slowly and steadily forward since the 1970s, struggling against high production costs, strict FCC regulations, and local homophobia.

Today there are radio programs for gay men, shows for lesbians, and co-sexual shows. There are news shows, talk shows, and women's music shows. Gay male radio can trace its roots as far back as Allen Ginsberg's reading of *Howl* on Berkeley's public radio station KPFA in the fifties. Growing out of lesbian-feminist separatism in the seventies, lesbian radio collectives brought out fresh new voices, many of which continue today.

Despite its continuing struggle with financial and censorship issues, gay and lesbian radio is here to stay as one of the most accessible ways to reach gay and lesbian communities in cities and suburbs around the country.

CAN YOU BELIEVE IT?

In Seattle during the early 1970s, there was a short-lived radio program called "Make No Mistake About It —It's the Faggot and the Dyke." When the "the dyke" repeatedly played the song "Every Woman Can Be a Lesbian" (from the Alix Dobkin album *Lavender Jane Loves Women*), the FCC attempted to pull the station's license on the grounds of "obscenity on the air." Apparently, the L-word airing more than six times in one hour greatly offended the FCC. At the hearing, the station retained control of its license, although "the dyke" was suspended from broadcasting for two years.

Out on the Radio

Memories are foggy and the tapes may no longer exist, but let's just say the first truly gay radio broadcast occurred whenever Allen Ginsberg first "Howled" on Pacifica Radio's KPFA in Berkeley, California, the nation's first successful noncommercial station. The language, rhythms, meaning, and in-your-face intensity of Ginsberg's Beat manifesto were quite unlike any message American radio had ever transmitted.

While Ginsberg's descent-into-hell imagery would resonate with a later generation of post-Stonewall out of the closet gay men, most of KPFA's early programs on same-sex love, such as the 1963 broadcast "Live and Let Live," stopped considerably short of proclaiming gayness a normal way of life, let alone echoing Ginsberg's belief that normality itself might be a form of madness.

For many years, the only toehold gay people had on the broadcast band was at those stations flying the banner of the Pacifica foundation. Created in 1946 by pacifist/journalist Lewis Hill to give Americans an alternative source of news and information from that provided by advertiser-backed corporate radio, Pacifica eventually grew into a looser network of five stations: KPFA (Berkeley), KPFK (Los Angeles), KPFT (Houston), WBAI (New York City), and WPFW (Washington, D.C.). Fortuitously, the five Pacifica stations served metropolitan areas with the largest concentrations of gay men and lesbians. Until the 1970s, virtually all of Pacifica's programs on gay subjects were under the aegis of the news, public affairs, or drama and literature department.

Many people are not aware that in 1964, a landmark decision by the Federal Communications Commission (FCC) upheld Pacifica's contention that the public was well served by gay-themed broadcasts "so long as the program is handled in good taste." However, an ominous foreshadowing of just how short the FCC leash on gay programs might turn out to be came in a separate statement by conservative Commissioner Robert E. Lee to the effect that "a microphone in a bordello, during slack hours, could give us similar information."

Beginnings

One of the earliest gay programs acknowledged its connection to Ginsberg by naming itself "Sunshine Gay Dreams" (later shortened simply to "Gay Dreams"). The program has served Philadelphia continuously since 1972 on WXPN-FM. For the remainder of the 1970s, it seemed that at least one new program sprang up every year: "Fruitpunch" (KPFA, 1973), "IMRU" (KPFK, 1975), "Wildc 'N Stein" (KPFT, 1975), "Just Before Dawn" (KCHU, Dallas, 1975). And in 1976, "The Gay Life" began on San Francisco's KSAN (now a country music station), one of the first gay programs to be regularly scheduled on a commercial station.

"Fruitpunch" began Monday night, June 4, 1973, under the bland title, "Gay Talk." Subscribers to the KPFA program guide, *The Folio,* were promised that "Gay Talk" would inform and educate straight and gay listeners alike, while showing gay men that they were not alone.

Former Fruitpuncher Philip Maldari recalls that the original collective members were recruited en masse one night at a gay coffeehouse in downtown Oakland. "Forty men from the East Bay were all asked if they would like to be on the radio," Maldari explains. "Everybody wanted to be a media star," says another ex-collective member, Christopher Lonc. "People wanted to read their own poetry and play their own music, but nobody wanted to edit tape or do the hard-core production work. Some people dropped out for political reasons. They thought there was very little support from the station—that we were on the air as a result of tokenism—a way for KPFA to show how liberal it was." By the end of the first year, that forty had dwindled down to a handful, which is the size of the collective today.

DID YOU KNOW...

The earliest known broadcast reference to homosexuality was in 1930, when Oregon politician Robert G. Duncan bought two hours of radio time per day on KVEP radio in Portland to blast the people he blamed for his recent defeat. The Federal Radio Commission (FRC) later deemed his comments "obscene, indecent, and profane." In one of the suspect remarks, Duncan accused a local newspaper of shielding "sodomites." In 1930, homosexuality was so taboo that one was not supposed to mention it on the air, even to condemn it.

— STEVEN CAPSUTO

The Jerker

For roughly the first twenty years, gay radio's howl was a barely audible whisper across the corridors of white noise emitted from America's more than 7,000 broadcast radio stations. On August 31, 1986, one gay broadcast burst through the white noise and became the focus of an intense debate about what is and is not fit for American ears.

That summer night, the Reverend Larry Poland was listening, he says, quite by accident to the weekly edition of KPFK's gay/lesbian program "IMRU (I Am, Are You?)." Reverend Poland, a Los Angeles area Christian fundamentalist minister, says he was deeply shocked and offended by what he heard. What Rev. Poland and thousands of Los Angeles listeners heard was excerpts from an AIDS-era safe-sex drama called *Jerker.* The late Robert Chesley, San Francisco playwright and author of *Jerker,* called his play "a pornographic elegy with redeeming social value." *Jerker* depicts the masturbatory fantasy relationship between two gay men whose sex lives have narrowed down, because of AIDS, to what can be described over the phone. Eventually one of the buddies reaches a disconnected phone—his discovery that his unseen friend has succumbed to the disease.

Reverend Poland complained the next day to the FCC that KPFK's broadcast of *Jerker* "did violence to me and my family. They potentially took away my control of being able to protect my children from learning about certain sexual practices at certain times in their lives." Playwright Chesley argued back that Poland and other would-be censors were asking the government to commit a far worse act of violence against the sexually informed members of the radio audience. "Prudery kills, on the radio or anywhere else. From the teenage girl who gets pregnant and takes her own life, to the young gay man who is still in the closet and doesn't understand the danger of AIDS, prudery kills. Nobody ever died from being offended by what they hear or see."

The broadcast of *Jerker* prompted the FCC to threaten to revoke the license of KPFK, and to set new guidelines considerably restricting the discussion of sexually sensitive issues by gay and lesbian broadcasters. Some observers noted a double standard invoked by the FCC, holding gay broadcasters to a more stringent set of language rules than those imposed on the commercial "shock jock" Howard Stern, for example.

Moving Ahead

As elsewhere in the competitive media world, gay radio has had its share of winners and losers. In Dallas, the program "Just Before Dawn," one of a handful of cosexually run shows, did not outlast the demise of its originating station, KCHU, and it was seven years before another gay and lesbian program had airtime in that city. The first attempt at a national gay radio network was in 1983 in San Francisco, and was called, appropriately, the National Gay Network. With the motto "National Gay Network: They Broke the Silence," NGN broadcast three times a week and was a source for both news and features to lesbians and gay men on several continents. Unfortunately, the two men who produced NGN, Tim O'Malley and Steve Lawson, found the financial and personal stress to be too great, and abandoned both their relationship and the show in late 1985.

Success

One major success story of the 1980s that has continued into the nasty 1990s is the Los Angeles–based nationally syndicated program "This Way Out." Greg Gordon and Lucia Chappelle are cohosts/producers of the satellite-distributed half-hour show. Gordon, who admits he was burned out and bored after ten years of volunteering for "IMRU," says that "This Way Out" is not aimed merely at the consumers of existing local gay programs around the country. "I want a program that is as entertaining and informative as possible, a program that will appeal to the scores of potential listeners who won't listen to public radio because of its pacing and content."

The heart of "This Way Out" consists of short reports from all over the world: the sounds of demonstrators in London protesting the antigay Clause 28, the story of a gay man protesting the ban on same-sex slow dancing at Disneyland, the latest on antigay organizing in Idaho. Both producers see their program as supplementing the already established gay programs, and hope to expand "This Way Out"'s coverage of international stories and people of color in the United States.

Growing Toward the Future

Gay radio never seems to stay put. Shows change program times, come in and out of existence, and change staff with a good deal of frequency. Still, many of the people who have been involved throughout the years remain involved today. As the gay men and lesbians who develop gay radio continue to learn from the successes and failures of themselves and others around the country, grass-roots foundations have been laid for the future. Gay radio may always be changing, but it is here to stay.

— DAVID LAMBLE

DID YOU KNOW...

In 1975, Frieda Werden, who later co-founded Women's International News Gathering Service with reporter and producer Katherine Davenport in Austin, Texas, produced what she believes was the first nationally syndicated multi-part series on homosexuality. "What's Normal?" was broadcast in 1975 in thirteen half-hour segments on the Longhorn Radio Network, based in Texas. Although only thirteen of Longhorn's nearly 600 commercial and non-profit affiliates aired "What's Normal?", Werden says it received more mail than any previous Longhorn series. To encourage letters, Werden offered a bibliography to every listener who wrote.

Dykes on the Air

Most radio programming produced for, about, and by lesbians grew out of the feminist movement of the 1970s. In those heady days of the women's liberation movement, women's radio collectives sprang up at community radio stations around the country.

Among the earliest was *Sophie's Parlor* Media Collective, which actually began as Radio Free Women at Georgetown University's radio station in Washington, D.C., in 1972. At that time, according to Moira Rankin in a 1992 interview with D.C.'s *Woman's Monthly*, "with all of the misogyny and homophobia, it was pretty courageous and audacious to go on the air with an all-woman production featuring women's music and women's issues with no men."

Rankin, a collective member from 1974 to 1985, went on to a successful career in public radio. In 1977, *Sophie's Parlor* moved to Pacifica network's WPFW, where it is still broadcast.

As on many feminist radio programs, lesbians and lesbianism were often included in both the music and public affairs segments. On one early *Sophie's Parlor* program, Ginny Berson and Meg Christian interviewed singer Cris Williamson. According to Berson, Cris was joking around and said something like, "I know—why don't you start a women's recording company?" "A lightbulb went off over my head," Berson said, and Olivia Records (and an entire movement) was conceived. The women of *Sophie's Parlor* also created a notorious public affairs special about lesbian nuns.

Frieda Werden, producer and co-founder of Women's International News Gathering Service (WINGS), says the mid-1970s saw "a wave of women's radio collectives. Some were mainly lesbian, some were not."

In 1976, the Feminist Radio Network formed in Washington, producing and distributing tapes nationally on women's issues. In 1979, FRN issued a catalog listing forty-nine women's programs throughout the U.S.; by 1985 the number had grown to eighty women's programs on forty-three stations.

While some stations aired women's news and information programs, "wimmin's music," says Werden, was especially important at the many stations that didn't allow any spoken-word feminist or lesbian programming. Women's music, although often very political, was not seen as threatening and more easily fit into many stations' formats.

In places where gay programs already existed, lesbians sometimes split from co-gender shows. Werden says that for men, radio was too often an ego thing. "Very rarely would you see men, even gay men, working in collectives," says Werden. Such a split occurred at WXPN in Philadelphia, where, according to "Gaydreams" producer Bert Wylen, "lesbian separatists invaded" and formed "Amazon Country," which "didn't want any male voices."

Helene Rosenbluth, producer of "Lesbian Sisters" at Pacifica's Los Angeles station, KPFK, from 1976 to 1986, said the rise of the women's movement "made it more difficult to work with gay men who were not working on sexist issues. Just because we were all gay, didn't mean we could all sit at the same table."

About producing "Lesbian Sisters," Rosenbluth says it was "incredible" to hear stories from listeners who said the program helped them come out. "They didn't feel crazy anymore, like they were the only ones. The power of radio is amazing."

Although most feminist programs started at noncommercial stations, the story's a little different in Boston. There, the firing of a female DJ at progressive commercial rock music station WBCM started a chain of events that Melanie Berzon says led to women's shows in the area.

Berzon, who now makes her living in public radio, says the DJ, Dinah Vapron, "got politicized and feminized" through the Boston women's movement. She started saying things and playing music management didn't like. The women's community mobilized around her firing in 1973, and demanded WBCM rehire Vapron and devote time to a women-run show. WBCM didn't rehire Vapron, but they conceded to the women's show, and the Red Tape Collective, made up of lesbians and straight women, was given an hour a week.

Today, both women's programs and specifically lesbian programs air locally and regionally at many stations, and WINGS continues to cover lesbian issues along with other women's issues in its internationally distributed programs. But WINGS producer Frieda Werden says women's airtime is diminishing overall at most stations, both commercial and noncommercial.

Helene Rosenbluth, former "Lesbian Sisters" producer, who continues to work in women's radio at KPFA in Berkeley, says it may be time to think of other, creative ways to work women's and lesbian and gay issues into existing mainstream programs.

"It's not the seventies anymore," says Rosenbluth. "The kinds of formats we loved to do back then aren't working anymore." At a National Lesbian and Gay Journalists conference in 1994, she suggested a need to "re-instill ourselves so that we're not just lesbian or gay broadcasters.

"You have to find out what they will air, not just what you like to do. If no one hears it, what good is it?"

— ERIC JANSEN

Gay Radio Programs from around the Country

"This Way Out," the Los Angeles–based gay and lesbian radio news and features program, broadcasts on more than forty stations across the United States, Canada, Europe, and Australia. Here is a list of some of the other major programs from around the country:

"Arts Magazine"
Mondays at 3 p.m.
WBAI 99.5 FM New York City

"Fresh Air/Fresh Fruit"
Thursdays at 7 p.m.
KFAI 90.3 FM Minneapolis/St. Paul

"Fruitpunch"
Wednesdays at 7 p.m.
KPFA 94.1 FM Berkeley, California
KFCF 88.1 FM Fresno, California

"Gay Dreams"
Sundays at 9 p.m.
WXPN 88.5 FM Philadelphia

"Gay Graffiti"
Thursdays at 7 p.m.
WRFG 89.3 FM Atlanta

"The Gay Show/Outlooks"
alternate Sundays at 7 p.m.
WBAI 99.5 FM New York City

"Ghosts in the Machine"
Wednesdays at 9:30 p.m.
WBAI 99.5 FM New York City

"Hibernia Beach"
Sundays at 7 a.m.
KITS 105.3 FM San Francsico

"House Fairy"
(call station for times)
WRAS 88.5 FM Atlanta

"IMRU"
(call station for times)
KPFK 90.7 FM Los Angeles

"Lavender Wimmin"
Thursdays at 6 p.m.
WUSH 90.1 FM Stony Brook, New York

"Radical Talk Show"
Saturdays at 5 p.m.
WIGO 1340 AM Atlanta

"Straight Jacket"
Mondays at 12 p.m.
KALX 90.7 FM Berkeley, California

"Wilde 'N Stein"
(call station for times)
KPFT 90.1 FM Houston

"Women's Forum"
(call station for times)
WRFG 89.3 FM Atlanta

— DAVID LAMBLE

THE WRITTEN WORD

Probably more than any other minority group, gay men and lesbians have looked to the written word for evidence of our existence. Lesbian and gay readers and scholars have spent untold efforts to discover if a particular favorite writer was homosexual, or to see if perhaps homosexuality has been "coded" into a story. Because lesbian and gay readers want and need to have our experiences and lives validated in the stories we read, we persist in trying to uncover the truth about authors whose sexualities have been "straightened up" by biographers and historians, as well as correct the distortions in the ways many stories about love and sex (among other things) have been interpreted by nongay critics and readers.

Of course, many difficult questions arise when we begin to investigate what writers who have lived in different historical and cultural contexts meant when they described love between men or love between women. Writers whose sexual orientation today we would describe as gay, lesbian, or bisexual have been a part of every literary form throughout history. From Albee, Alther, and Arenas, to Barnes, Baldwin, and Aphra Behn, from Sappho, Shakespeare, and Gertrude Stein, to Whitman, Wittig, and Woolf, the list goes across history, languages, nationalities, and colors, and includes poets, playwrights, and novelists. Just as gay authors have always existed, so too have gay characters and themes been present throughout literature, regardless of the sexual orientation of the writer. Carmilla, vampire and predecessor to Count Dracula, was a lesbian. Stephen Gordon became the most embattled butch in the English-speaking world in 1928 when *The Well of Loneliness* by Radclyffe Hall was banned in England (where it remained banned for thirty years). James Baldwin wrote some of the most powerful and enduring depictions of love between men. Virginia Woolf wrote *Orlando* (1928) for her beloved Vita Sackville West. And the novels of E. M. Forster and Edmund White have been regarded as homoerotic in tone and imagery.

Contemporary gay readers cannot only find images of ourselves in traditional literature, but we also live at a time when there has been an emergence of explicitly gay writing by and for gay and lesbian readers. We can move beyond proving that we exist to raise other questions about how we live and what shapes our experience.

Mainstream publishing houses now produce some gay and lesbian writing. For gay men, the struggle to be published in large houses is still difficult, but for lesbians it still is often impossible. Thanks to lesbian and gay presses, openly lesbian and gay male writers are published in larger numbers than ever before. Especially for lesbians, publishing from within the community provides access to audiences that may not otherwise be available. Never again will lesbian and gay readers be dependent on heterosexual writers for descriptions of our triumphs, pains, and joys.

Earliest American Gay and Lesbian Novels

Lesbians and gay men have been the subjects of fiction in all literary genres. In 1799, Charles Brockden Brown's novel *Ormond* was published, which contained the first known favorable description of lesbianism in American fiction. Other mid-17th century writers nibbled around the edges of homosexuality in their novels as well, and many of the poor-but-virtuous-boy-makes-good novels of Horatio Alger, Jr., have homocentric elements. In the 19th century, the poet Walt Whitman hints at homosexuality in his obscure temperance novel *Franklin Evans*.

The following list documents some of the earliest gay-themed novels, with an emphasis on books with positive lesbian and gay characters.

1800s

1870	*Joseph and His Friend* by Bayard Taylor
1887	*White Cockades* by E. I. Prime-Stevenson
1891	*Left to Themselves* by E. I. Prime-Stevenson
1894	*Marriage Below Zero* by Alfred J. Cohen

1900s

1908	*Imre* by Xavier Mayne (pen name of E. I. Prime-Stevenson)
1908	*The Intersexes* by E. I. Prime-Stevenson (nonfiction)

1920s

1928	*The Well of Loneliness* by Radclyffe Hall
1928	*Remembrance of Things Past* by Proust

1930s

1931	*The Loveliest of Friends* by Sheila G. Donisthorpe
1931	*Strange Brother* by Blair Niles
1931	*Twilight Men* by Andre Tellier
1933	*The Better Angel* by Forman Brown (pen name of Ralph Meeker)
1933	*Scarlet Pansy* by Lou Rand Hogan (pen name of Robert Sculley)
1933	*The Young and Evil* by Parker Tyler and Charles Henri Ford
1935	*We Too Are Drifting* by Gale Whilhelm
1937	*Either Is Love* by Elisabeth Craigin
1938	*Torchlight to Valhalla* by Gale Whilhelm
1939	*Diana* by Diana Fredericks

1940s

1941	*The Little Less* by Angela DuMaurier
1943	*Winter Solstice* by Elisabeth Craigin
1948	*The City and the Pillar* by Gore Vidal
1949	*Olivia* by Olivia (pen name of Dorothy Bussy)
1949	*Stranger in the Land* by Ward Thomas

1950s

1950	*Quatrefoil* by James Barr
1950	*Things as They Are* by Gertrude Stein
1951	*Divided Path* by Nial Kent (pen name of William Leroy Thomas)

1951 *Finistère* by Fritz Peters (pen name of Arthur Anderson Peters)
1952 *The Price of Salt* by Claire Morgan (pen name of Patricia Highsmith)
1955 *The Last Innocence* by Celia Bertin
1955 *Remembrance Way* by Jessie Rehder
1956 *The Hearth and the Strangeness* by N. Martin Kramer (pen name of Beatrice Ann Wright)
1958 *Rings of Glass* by Luise Rinser
1958 *The Wheel of Earth* by Helga Sandburg
1959 *Heroes and Orators* by Robert Phelps

— JIM KEPNER AND BARBARA GRIER

As the Twilight World Turns

Welcome to the post–*Well of Loneliness,* pre–*Rubyfruit Jungle* world of lesbian pulp fiction. For lesbians who came out during the fifties and early sixties, their first ties to the lesbian world were often the "Twilight Women" of these novels. This may also be true for women who came out much later. In December of 1986 as a student at the University of Michigan, I responded to my first notions of being a lesbian by going to the Undergraduate Library. There I stumbled upon a three-book series by Ann Bannon (of which *Women in the Shadows* is the middle). It was finals time and I spent a lot of hours in the library—but not studying. I never did check any of those books out, but I read them all. Here's a look at a few.

The Covers

One cannot help but wonder at the extravagantly melodramatic cover art and text which often has so little to do with the actual book that it could be readily exchanged from one book to another and be no less appropriate. The covers are almost universally sensationalized and some are downright homophobic—even if the book is not (like *Twilight Girl*). The lesbian world, according to these covers, is a twisted, twilight one, full of angst-ridden women who are trapped by the irresistible enticements of another woman. The covers reflect the perceptions of an intolerant

"Sophisticated, witty, attractive Val MacGregor was one of Inter-American's most popular stewardesses. . . . Then one day lovely, dark-haired Toni was assigned to be her co-stewardess. From their first moment of meeting Val sensed something oddly disturbing about the girl. Not until later did she realize what she was—and then it was much too late!"

FROM THE BACK COVER OF EDGE OF TWILIGHT

society toward lesbianisn—that is, that lesbians are sick people living in a dim, unhappy world who lure young innocents to join them in their pell-mell debauchery.

From a contemporary perspective, it seems the books were marketed this way for several potentially overlapping reasons. In order to avoid the wrath that might befall the publishers if they were perceived by the public to be printing novels sympathetic to lesbians, the covers made it appear that they were not. In addition, the buxom femmes obviously broadened the appeal of the books, making them marketable to straight men as well. Finally, the dissonance between covers and content illustrated the struggle for lesbians at the time. In some ways, the moralist covers took the guilt out of a "guilty pleasure" by simultaneously indulging in and disclaiming it.

But lesbians who picked their way through the verbal minefield of the covers often discovered stories that resonated with their own experience, perhaps for the first time in their lives.

The Books

The books themselves can be broken down into several broad categories:

• Stories where the woman accepts her lesbianism and at the end has hope of happiness. Examples include *The Twisted Year* and *Edge of Twilight*—that's right, popular stewardess Val MacGregor is a lesbian who is going to live happily ever after, finally.

• Stories where the woman accepts her lesbianism but faces a life brimming with tragedy, like *Twilight Girl.*

• Stories where the woman winds up with a man at the end (which some people might consider tragedy). But often these novels, like *Women in the Shadows*, have secondary characters who are lesbians and who are happy and who are not going to wind up with men.

• Stories written by men. While the covers may look sort of similar (though perhaps more sensationalized), the books themselves are quite different. First, male characters typically play a more significant role in the books written by men. Lesbians are almost uniformly nymphomaniacs and many are not particular at all whom they sleep with. There is also a peculiar male fear/fantasy dynamic. In the male-written books it is accepted as something of a truism that once a woman has had sex with another woman she will never go back to men. The men seem afraid that lesbians have some mysterious sexual tricks men cannot fathom, but this also makes these women the ultimate conquest, the ultimate test of virile manhood.

The Character

Most of the characters, and certainly the main characters, are not what was/is considered stereotypical. They are almost all "lovely" and "feminine," and so apparently "normal."

Twilight Girl does establish the butch/femme dynamic that was so much a part of the lesbian bar scene in the fifties and early sixties, though interestingly the very definitely butch main character is described on the cover as "a pretty teen-ager enticed into forbidden practices by older girls" and the girl pictured on the cover oozes femme.

Some of what is in these books may make us cringe—or chuckle—today, but for the fifties and sixties the books were daring. And they were a lifeline for lesbians struggling for some sort of definition of themselves.

They have earned their place as a treasured (albeit sometimes goofy) part of herstory, charting lesbians' burgeoning sense of identity and of community even in those still highly oppressive times. Someday, they will stand as a permanent record of what has turned out to be the crest of an enormously volatile time in the lesbian/gay rights struggle. They give a glimpse of pre-Stonewall life, with the promise of a more tolerant future butting against an intolerant present.

Plus, they're kind of fun.

— TERRI L. SMITH

Seeing Ourselves Where We Aren't—Putting Ourselves in the Picture

Overwhelmingly, the literature and novels available to most of us to read, the lyrics of the songs we listen to, the images that we see on the screen, large and small, are heterosexual. As a rule, gay and lesbian people are not in the picture. How, then, do we validate ourselves, create ourselves, learn to love and grow, when we do not see ourselves reflected back to us from the world at large? Among other strategies, we build communities, we create our own "families," we create our own images. We also "read between the lines," and underneath the text, trying to determine if an author or singer is gay. We look to see if perhaps there is some hidden theme, some other way to interpret what we see and read that would allow us to identify with the story being told. We seek out songs that have neutral genders ("we" and "you," not "he" and "her"). And we write our own books.

But when those strategies fail, or when we don't have access to gay and lesbian literature, we find other ways to put ourselves in the picture. This is easy to do with songs; it's pretty simple to change the gender in the lyrics, replacing "him" with "her," "he" with "she," even "man" with "woman." Doing this with literature, often called "guerilla reading," is a little more complicated.

Perhaps you are reading a book in which there is a romantic love triangle: two men love the same woman. If you are a gay man reading this book, you might put yourself in the role of the woman being fought over. You might put yourself in this story as male; on the other hand, you might choose to see yourself as female. Or you might go another route and look at the action between the two competitors as a story with its own homoerotic energy.

Or take a standard girl-meets-boy romance story. If you are a lesbian reading this, you might just close the book and decide to go for a walk instead. Or you might get inspired by the great writing and decide to overlook the fact that the two main characters are an opposite-sex couple, and imagine them as a same-sex couple instead. Or you might try more actively to put yourself in the picture by putting yourself in the role of the pursuer (or the pursued), and read all of the action from that perspective.

Still another approach to this literary dilemma would be to simply appropriate one or more of the characters, and build your own story. More than guerilla reading, this probably falls into the realm of fantasy. But who among us has not found a character in a novel whom we think about long after the book is finished, wondering what would have happened to him or her if the author continued the story? Or, feeling dissatisfied with the way the author has handled the story, how many times have we created our own homoerotic endings to heterosexual novels?

— LYNN WITT

"I see a lot of books by lesbian publishers coming through the cataloging stream at the Library of Congress, so I was not surprised to see a book called *South-East Fen Dyke Survey* on the book truck today. I was curious, however, to find out what sort of group the South-East Fen Dykes were. I supposed they were perhaps some sort of rural lesbian collective that staked out part of the Everglades as a commune. I was disappointed to discover that the book was all about drainage projects in rural England, and had nothing to do with lesbians. Too bad. A perfectly good name going to waste."

FROM AN ANONYMOUS GAY LIBRARIAN

Gays Men and Lesbians in Mainstream Mysteries

While gay and lesbian characters were once virtually nonexistent or relegated to the roles of murder victims in mainstream mystery novels, during the last fifteen years they have taken their place as integral figures in the genre—in mainstream books by well-known authors, as well as overtly gay-themed novels.

The use of gay and lesbian characters in mystery novels can be traced back to the nineteenth century. The earliest lesbian reference—and a major one at that—is in

Honore de Balzac's *La Fille aux Yeux d'Or/The Girl with the Golden Eyes (*1834), in which the title character loves both a young man and his half sister. Arguably, Charles Dickens's last, unfinished novel, *The Mystery of Edwin Drood* (1870), has a central gay character in John Jasper, who has a "womanish" devotion to his nephew, Edwin Drood. Drug use was often linked to homosexuality in early mystery novels, and here John Jasper is an opium addict. There is a strong possibility that had Dickens lived to finish out this novel, Jasper might have been shown to have murdered Edwin Drood out of jealousy over the boy's fixation with Rosa Bud.

While many consider the mystery novel a twentieth-century innovation, nineteenth-century writer Sir Arthur Conan Doyle gave us two of our first modern gay characters. The creator of Sherlock Holmes (a character whose relationship to Dr. Watson is open to interpretation) published *Round the Fire Stories* in 1909. One of the stories, "The Man with the Watches," concerns a young homosexual American who is led astray by an older gay man. When the young man is killed as a result of his brother's actions, the older man says to the sibling, "You loved your brother, I've no doubt; but you didn't love him a cent more than I loved him, though you'll say that I took a queer way to show it."

In a period when homosexuality could not be named as such, Doyle's work reflects a remarkable dialogue. It was not until 1930 that another gay character appeared on the scene—in Dashiell Hammett's *The Maltese Falcon.* Three of the figures in the novel—Joel Cairo, Casper Gutman, and his gangster sidekick Wilmer—are all presumed homosexual, but only the last is openly described as such with the use of the slang term "gunsel" (meaning catamite). A year earlier, British novelist Gladys Mitchell had introduced the first modern lesbian figure in the mystery genre in *Speedy Death.* The woman in question appears as a man named Everard Mountjoy, who is murdered in his/her bathtub. Mitchell's heroine, Beatrice Adela Lestrange Bradley, who appeared in some sixty-five novels, is able to identify "sexual perversion" as the theme behind the killing. "Not a pleasant subject," responds the chief constable, to which Mrs. Bradley replies, "I do not propose to discuss it"—end of topic!

Homosexuals as murder victims became a common theme in the next four or five decades—and if they were not victims, they were villains. British writer Richard Hull was the first to use a gay character as the narrator of a mystery novel with *The Murder of My Aunt* (1935), but unfortunately he is a "pansy boy" without a single redeeming quality and eventually, of course, he is killed off. The acerbic and witty tone of Hull's novel was recreated in the 1960s by George Baxt with a series of three outrageously gay mystery novels: *A Queer Kind of Death* (1966), *Swing Low, Sweet Harriet* (1967), and *Topsy & Evil* (1968). In *A Queer Kind of Death* a gay killer gets away with murder after promising to become the lover of the NYPD officer investigating the case.

Michael Nava, aside from being a prolific award-winning mystery-writer, cowrote (with Robert Dawidoff) Created Equal: Why Gay Rights Matter to America, *a nonfiction political work. (Tom Bianchi)*

Generally, the classic writers of the genre during this period steadfastly ignored gay and lesbian characters. In *Nemesis,* the last novel to feature Miss Marple (1971), Agatha Christie does introduce a lesbian murderess—and treats her harshly. Ngaio Marsh, who was positively homophobic, has gay characters in a number of her mystery novels; they are usually drug addicts with a fondness for dressing in female attire. Dorothy Sayers also had a number of lesbian minor characters.

By the 1970s, not only had gay characters started to become sympathetic, but also a number of openly gay authors had embraced the mystery genre. Nathan Aldyne (the pseudonym of Michael McDowell and Dennis Schuetz), Richard Stevenson (the pseudonym of Richard Lipez), and most important, Michael Nava, began to write novels with gay themes and gay characters that crossed the dividing line between gay and straight literature. Their heroes were gay but that did not mean that their readership was necessarily so. At the same time, Sarah Caudwell began a series of novels featuring a female lawyer who is sexually ambivalent. The new school of British mystery writers, led by P. D. James and Ruth Rendell, routinely introduced gays and lesbians as secondary, and sympathetic, characters in their novels.

In Reginald Hill's popular series of 1980s novels, he integrates a gay character in the form of Sergeant Wield, a closeted homosexual who fits no gay stereotype. Sergeant Wield is ugly, always ready for a fight, and while quiet about his private life around the police stations is not above admiring a young police cadet's bare chest in the locker room. The American equivalent of Wield is LAPD Sergeant Milo Sturgis, who works closely with straight child psychologist Dr. Alex Delaware in the novels of Jonathan Kellerman. As explained in Kellerman's first novel, *When the Bough Breaks* (1985), Sturgis "wasn't in the closet, neither did he flaunt it."

The most prominent of the gay private detectives is insurance investigator Dave Brandstetter, introduced by author Joseph Hansen in the 1970 novel *Fadeout.* Nine novels later, readers said good-bye to Brandstetter in *A Country of Old Men* (1991), which ends with his death from a massive heart attack. Yet again, here was no stereotypical gay character. Brandstetter was, like his creator, forty-seven when he made his first appearance; he has been involved in two long-term relationships in the course of the novels; he fends off somewhat implausible approaches from much younger men and expresses an active dislike for effeminate behavior. (This despite his first lover, recently deceased when the series begins, being "nelly," an interior decorator "one cut above a hairdresser.")

After more than a century of mystery writing, not only could gays and lesbians be identified as such, they could be depicted as no different from any other novel character. As novelist Hill points out, "It seems to me that any novelist whose picture of life does not contain homosexual characters is like a landscape painter whose trees are always oak or pine. It may be art but it surely isn't life!"

— **ANTHONY SLIDE**

Pulp and Circumstances

The Lesbian Love Affair with the Private Eye

I was hit with the detective fiction bug in the early 1980s, shortly after I moved to San Francisco. Like so many readers, I first walked those mean streets with Hammett, Chandler, and James M. Cain. In fact, I became obsessed with the Dashiell Hammett myth—I trekked San Francisco's fabled hills, haunted downtown neighborhoods, wandered moodily through fog-shrouded nights. I even went to work for Pinkerton's, Hammett's agency, to see what it was like to be a private eye. Finally, after almost ten years of immersion in the detective milieu, both literary and real, I was able to launch a series with my own fictional P.I., Nell Fury.

From the start, I knew Fury would be a lesbian. I was a lesbian, out of the closet, and political; I wanted the same for my protagonist. Not only was it natural to write from my experience, but I wanted to bring lesbian concerns front and center, and develop a series that would be funny, sexy, and contemporary. Fury is a dyke dick from the hard-boiled school of private eye novels, and—happily—she now shares the mean streets with a whole slew of feminist colleagues. The tough, autonomous female detective came of age in the eighties. I was adding my distinctly lesbian voice to a mix that included superstars like Sue Grafton and Sara Paretsky, as well as newcomers Patricia Cornwall, Barbara Neeley, Karen Kijewski, and many more.

Lesbian and gay detective fiction also made a big leap forward during this era. In the old days, mysteries that did mention us usually made being gay an indication of a character's pathology, or a twisted secret revealed in the unraveling of a perverse plot complication. Then came the groundbreaking efforts of authors such as Barbara Wilson, Joseph Hansen, and M. F. Beal. Suddenly, a spectrum of lesbian and gay characters—heroes and otherwise—began emerging. With Nell Fury, I hoped to introduce another edgy alternative to the standard male prototype. And I wasn't alone, especially among lesbians. A partial list of writers with their fingers on the pulse of lavender pulp includes Nikki Baker, Katherine V. Forrest, Jaye Maiman, J. M. Redmann, Sandra Scoppettone, and Mary Wings. Lesbian mystery fiction became the hottest queer genre since the heyday of the coming-out story.

But it didn't happen in isolation—the whole mystery field has diversified in recent years. In addition to lesbians and gay men, writers of color, both gay and straight, are contributing in increasing numbers. I believe mysteries are thriving these days precisely because of this phenomenon. It's certainly a factor in my love of the genre: as well as being accessible, lean, and deliciously trashy, detective fiction almost always deals with marginal characters. Those of us outside the mainstream can feel a keen affinity with the rebel P.I. bumping up against the status quo. Nell Fury, for example, is ambivalent about law and order. She's an agitator and an agent of change—albeit a pessimistic one—more than an enforcer of any rigid moral code.

As the mystery field continues to expand, along with genre fiction in general, lesbian and gay characters are no longer invisible and/or anathema. Yet progress continues to be slow. In writing about an outspoken lesbian private eye, I hope to validate the spylike experience of outsiders and provide another kind of fictional voice. Fury's lesbianism is at once matter-of-fact and uniquely relevant. Like me, she is both a part of and separate from the lonely, gritty, big-city tradition of her literary predecessors.

— ELIZABETH PINCUS

Early Gay and Lesbian Characters in Mystery Novels

- **Paquita Valdes** in *La Fille Aux Yeux d'Or/The Girl with the Golden Eyes* by Honore de Balzac (1834)
- **John Jasper** in *The Mystery of Edwin Drood* by Charles Dickens (1870)
- **Sparrow McCoy** in *Round the Fire Stories* by Sir Arthur Conan Doyle (1909)

• **Everard Mountjoy** in *Speedy Death* by Gladys Mitchell (1929)

• **Joel Cairo, Casper Gutman,** and **Wilmer** in *The Maltese Falcon* by Dashiell Hammett (1930)

• **Edward** in *The Murder of My Aunt* by Richard Hull (1934)

• **Peter Rigget** in *Flower for the Judge* by Margery Allingham (1936)

• **Anton Palook** and **Pavel Bunia** in *A Bullet in the Ballet* by Caryl Brahms S. J. Simon (1937)

• **Stephen Hawes** in *Serenade* by James M. Cain (1937)

• **Unidentified young man** in *Murder Among Friends* by Elizabeth Ferrars (1946)

• **Monica Brady** and **Ageline Small** in *Death of a Doll* by Hilda Lawrence (1947)

• **Charles Anthony Bruno** in *Strangers on a Train* by Patricia Highsmith (1949)

— **ANTHONY SLIDE**

Queer Aliens—Classic Gay and Lesbian Science Fiction Novels

Homosexuality has been a part of science fiction as long as there has been a genre. From derogatory images to positive representation, there have been thousands of science fiction books with gay and lesbian characters. During the seventies, science fiction in general enjoyed a publishing boom. It was during this time that homosexuality became a prominent and permanent theme in the science fiction universe. Below are just a handful of the many classics of the genre.

Einstein Intersection by Samuel R. Delaney (1967)
Moondust by Thomas Burnett Swann (1968)
Left Hand of Darkness by Ursula K. LeGuin (1969)
The Wild Boys by William S. Burroughs (1971)
The World Wreckers by Marion Zimmer Bradley (1971)
Breakfast in Ruins by Michael Moorcock (1972)
The Book of Skulls by Robert Silverberg (1972)
The English Assassin by Michael Moorcock (1972)
The Man Who Folded Himself by David Gerrold (1973)

334 by Thomas M. Disch (1974)
Earthwreck! by Thomas N. Scortia (1974)
Walk to the End of the World by Suzy McKee Charnas (1974)
Dhalgren by Samuel R. Delany (1975)
The Female Man by Joanna Russ (1975)
The Heritage of Hastur by Marion Zimmer Bradley (1975)
Imperial Earth by Arthur C. Clarke (1975)
Arslan by M. J. Engh (1976)
The Woman on the Edge of Time by Marge Piercy (1976)
The Forbidden Tower by Marion Zimmer Bradley (1977)
Gateway by Frederick Pohl (1977)
Moonstar Odyssey by David Gerrold (1977)
Chrome by George Nader (1978)
A Different Light by Elizabeh A. Lynn (1978)
Kalki by Gore Vidal (1978)
The Wanderground by Sally M. Gearhart (1978)
Benefits by Zoe Fairbairns (1979)
Blade Runner by William S. Burroughs (1979)
The Dancers of Arun by Elizabeth A. Lynn (1979)
Mindsong by Joan Cox (1979)
On Wings of Song by Thomas M. Disch (1979)
Project Lambda by Pell Wells (1979)
Retreat: As It Was! by Donna J. Young (1979)

— DON ROMESBURG

DID YOU KNOW...

The Minneapolis-based Womyn's Braille Press, founded by six blind lesbians in 1980, is the only organization in the United States dedicated to making feminist and lesbian literature available on tape and in Braille. The volunteer-run organization currently offers more than 800 book titles, periodicals, and pamphlets to its readership.

Words Make a Movement

There has been a great deal written lately heralding the coming of age of gay and lesbian writing. Although the "mainstream" is just now beginning to notice the market for this material, women's presses and women's bookstores have been hard at work for the last twenty-five years producing and selling books that feminists and lesbians want to read.

As former Spinsters Book Company publisher Sherry Thomas noted in *Publishers Weekly,* "This wave of the women's movement—the one that began in the early 1970s—was organized in its earliest days around writing. There was a whole network of newspapers, magazines,

Sasha Alyson, founder of Alyson Publications. (Robert Giard)

small publishers, bookstores and printing presses who would print our books (when the commercial printers refused this work). I can't find any other movement for social or cultural change in the country that's been as print-based. Publishing is integral to how women began to see themselves."

One of the central events in this movement was the 1976 Women in Print Movement Conference. The conference highlighted the aspirations and concerns of those women who had plunged into the third wave of feminism with enthusiasm, dedication, and a large dose of idealism, convinced that if women owned an independent press network, our words could not be suppressed.

In fact, the 1970s did see a great revival of feminism, and the vision of that time has given rise to a network of feminist bookstores (doing over $35 million in business annually), over forty women-owned publishing companies, and magazines and newspapers too numerous to count. We succeeded in making lesbian and feminist concerns visible.

Becoming Visible

While psychological treatises of lesbians or novels with lesbian characters have appeared in mainstream publishing for years, they generally presented a rather bleak picture of lesbian life, with suicides, or women seeing their true path and returning to men as the probable

"MAINSTREAM" QUEER AUTHORS WHO GOT THEIR START WITH THE GAY AND FEMINIST PRESSES

Dorothy Allison, National Book Award nominee (Firebrand Press)

Rita Mae Brown, novelist (Daughters, Inc.)

Larry Duplechan, novelist (Alyson Press)

Joseph Hansen, prolific mystery writer (One, Inc.)

Audre Lorde, poet and novelist (Spinsters)

Michael Nava, mystery writer (Alyson Press)

John Preston, erotic novelist (Alyson Press)

Sarah Schulman, novelist (Naiad)

Members of Kitchen Table/Women of Color Press (1981) included (from left to right) Barbara Smith, Audre Lorde, Cherríe Moraga, and hattie gossett. (©JEB)

outcomes. No tough dykes here; only passionate yet anguished women who struggled valiantly to overcome their attraction to other women.

Then came the revolution, at least it felt like that to lesbians who had remained securely in the closet. *Lesbian/Woman* by Del Martin and Phyllis Lyon appeared, lavender cover and all, touted as "Essential reading for all women!" by Bantam Books in 1972. And then *Lesbian Nation*, with a smiling, jeans-jacketed Jill Johnston proclaiming "until all women are lesbians, there will be no true political revolution," published by Simon and Schuster, 1973.

"In the beginning, it required small presses, gay newspapers and magazines, and mainstream houses all working together to launch gay and lesbian literature. As far as women's literature is concerned, the small presses have done virtually all of the work. Gay male fiction became more experimental in the 1980s. And presses like SeaHorse, Alyson, and Crossing Press brought out new writers whom the mainstream would not touch: Robert Gluck, Dennis Cooper, Brad Gooch—some of whom have since become mainstream. I still question the mainstream's ability to consistently find the cutting edge of gay and lesbian literature."

FELICE PICANO, A MEMBER OF THE VIOLET QUILL, A GAY MALE WRITERS' SALON FROM THE LATE SEVENTIES AND EARLY EIGHTIES

At this same time, the first of the feminist/lesbian presses were starting up, like Diana Press, Daughters, Inc., the Women's Press Collective, the Persephone Press, and others who believed that women's/lesbian voices would not be well-represented, if at all, by the mainstream, and that part of our empowerment was to determine what was published.

Over the past twenty years, the mainstream presses have continued to publish a few books here and there featuring lesbian protagonists, like *Don Juan in the Village*, or *After Delores*. However, the number of feminist/lesbian presses has grown to over forty in the United States, publishing hundreds of lesbian books a year, making it a challenge for all the dedicated readers to keep up. The 1990s have become the years of the queers, and mainstream publishers have "discovered" a new and literate market. Whether or not this fad continues, it is fair to assume that at some point women will once again have to rely on lesbian/feminist presses to supply the books they really want to read.

— **BETH DINGMAN**

Daughters, Inc.: Pioneer Publishers

The women's movement was reborn in the 1970s, and along with it came an avalanche of journals, newspapers, pamphlets, and books teaching women to take control of their bodies, their cars, their relationships, and their culture.

At the forefront of that movement was Daughters, Inc., founded by June Arnold and Parke Bowman in 1973 in Plainfield, Vermont. Working out of an old farmhouse, June and Parke, with the assistance of Bertha Harris, Jane Myers, Sam Stockwell, Martha Yates, Mary Dawson and others, made a lasting contribution to women's literature. Specializing in feminist and lesbian fiction, by 1978 Daughters had twenty-four titles in print, no small feat in the days when many printers would not handle lesbian material. Daughters' best known book was Rita Mae Brown's *Rubyfruit Jungle,* which became an instant success when it sold more than 70,000 copies. (*Rubyfruit* was later bought by the mass market publisher Bantam, where it continued to sell hotly for many years.)

Daughters was unique in other ways as well. "So far, every novel from Daughters has been without literary precedent," wrote Polly Joan and Andrea Chesman in *The Guide to Women's Publishing.* Books published by Daughters included *The Cook and the Carpenter* by June Arnold, *Confessions of a Cherubino* by Bertha Harris, and *Angel Dance* by M. F. Beal, as well as works by Joanna Russ, Monique Wittig, Elana Nachman, Blanche Boyd, and Charlotte Bunch. June dreamed of "building a feminist literature in which the power of women's words can reshape the language and the culture in which they are

CAN YOU BELIEVE IT?

In 1976, the first Women-In-Print conference was attended by one-hundred and twenty-seven women, representing seventy-three groups—feminist newspapers, journals/magazines, bookstores, book publishers, printers and distributors. While the conference was a watershed for the print movement, *The New York Times Magazine* article offered this sensationalist description of the event: The women "gathered together for the first time to chart their course and define their ultimate goal— not to become a unified underground women's press, but actually to lead a feminist takeover of the nation's media. The secret convention was held at a Campfire Girls camp near Omaha, Nebraska. They were, and are, serious. The only question is how they expect to succeed."

FEMINIST AND GAY MALE PRESSES STILL GOING STRONG TODAY

Feminist Press,
New York (1970)
Naiad Press,
Tallahassee, FL (1973)
Seal Press,
Seattle, WA (1975)
Down There Press,
San Francisco, CA (1975)
Volcano Press,
Volcano, CA (1976)
New Victoria Publishers,
Norwich, VT (1977)
Gay Sunshine Press,
San Francisco, CA (1977)
Spinsters, Ink,
Duluth, MI (1978)
Cleis Press,
Pittsburgh, PA (1980)
Alyson Press,
Boston, MA (1980)
Mother Courage,
Racine, WI (1981)
Kitchen Table Women of Color Press,
New York (1981)
Aunt Lute,
San Francisco, CA (1982)
Papier Maché,
Watsonville, CA (1984)
Firebrand Books,
Ithaca, NY (1984)
Clothespin Fever Press,
Los Angeles, CA (1985)
Calyx Press,
Corvalis, OR (1985)
Eighth Mountain Press,
Portland, OR (1985)
Paradigm Publishing,
San Diego, CA (1989)
Rising Tide Books,
Huntington, NY (1991)
Thirdside Press,
Chicago, IL (1991)
Madwoman Press,
Northboro, MA (1991)

— BETH DINGMAN

written." She and Parke were committed to making women culturally and economically independent, and were influential in organizing the first Women-In-Print conference, a watershed event in the feminist print movement, in 1976.

June died in 1985. And although Daughters died with her, the legacy she left continues in the more than forty feminist publishers alive and well today.

— BETH DINGMAN

Statement from the Second National Black Writers' Conference

The follow is a statement by Barbara Smith and Joseph Beam at the Second National Black Writers Conference at Medgar Evers College, New York, in 1998. It appeared in the journal *BLACK/OUT* in the fall of 1988, and was signed by many of the most prominent Black gay and lesbian writers of the 1980s.

We are Black lesbian and gay writers who are taking the opportunity of The Second National Black Writers Conference to go on record. We are well aware that despite our commitment to exploring gender roles and to challenging sexual, racial, and class oppression, work that has been essential to transforming the practice of African American literature in this era, the Black literary establishment systematically chooses to exclude us from the range of its activities. These include participation in conferences, invitations to submit work to journals, anthologies, serious and non-homophobic criticism of writing, positive depictions of lesbian and gay characters, inclusion in Black studies course curricula, and all levels of formal and informal mentoring and support. If we are sometimes included in token numbers, it is often amid heterosexist protest and homophobic attacks. Because we function with integrity, refuse to be closeted, and address lesbian and gay oppression as a political issue, our lives and work are made invisible.

In spite of effort to ghettoize and exclude us, we are part of a long and proud Black lesbian and gay literary tradition. The Harlem Renaissance could not have occurred if it had not been for its Black gay participants, among them: Countee Cullen, Langston Hughes, Wallace Thurman, Alain Locke, and R. Bruce Nugent. Historically, Black lesbian writers have been less easily identifiable, but recent research has documented that Alice Dunbar Nelson, Agelina Weld Grimke, and Lorraine Hansberry are also members of this tradition. James Baldwin, undoubtedly the best known African American writer, gave us many positive depictions of gay male relationships including those between Black men. Baldwin opened up new literary territory for an entire generation and served as a special role model for those of us who are lesbian and gay. Yet, since his death in December 1987, there has been a concerted effort to ignore the fact he was homosexual. The acknowledgment of our work as Black lesbian and gay writers necessitates a major revision of a currently homophobic and inaccurate Black literary history.

Black lesbian and gay men have always been here, as contributing family members in this country and before that in the Motherland of Africa; but, we have been frequently attacked as traitors to the race. Our existence is not what threatens the future of the race: instead the Black liberation struggle is imperiled by homophobic exclusion and emotional, physical, and sexual violence aimed at those of us who are lesbian and gay. Yet, we are alive, well, and living with dignity, carrying out the challenge of our difficult and much needed work.

Signed by: *Joseph Beam, Becky Birtha, Julie Blackwomon, Cheryl Clarke, Anita Cornwell, Doris Davenport, Alexis de Veaux, Jewelle Gomez, Craig G. Harris, Essex Hemphill, Issac Jackson, Cary Alan Johnson, Audre Lorde, Pat Parker, Michelle Parkerson, Philip Robinson, Assoto Saint, Barbara Smith, Lamont Steptoe, Evelyn C. White*

A Light-Hearted Look at Lesbian Novels and Their Love Scenes

In my reading of lesbian novels and short stories, I have encountered many attempts at The Love Scene, from abysmal to arousing. In general, they fall into four categories, which, for fun, I've classified as you might for a subspecies of plants: *Erotica dottica, Erotica botanica, Erotica naiad pressica,* and *Erotica explicita.*

Let me explain.

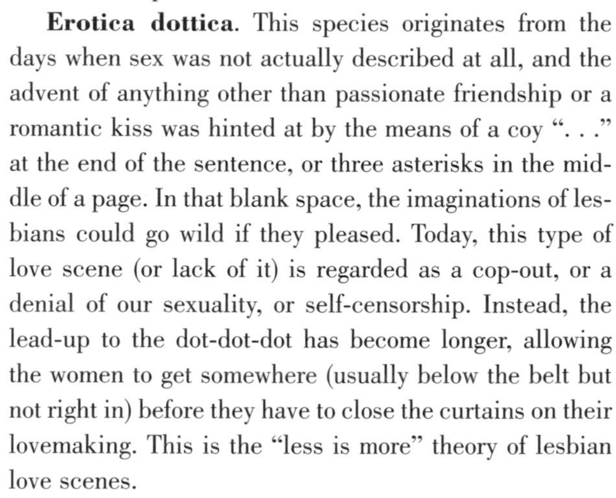

Erotica dottica. This species originates from the days when sex was not actually described at all, and the advent of anything other than passionate friendship or a romantic kiss was hinted at by the means of a coy ". . ." at the end of the sentence, or three asterisks in the middle of a page. In that blank space, the imaginations of lesbians could go wild if they pleased. Today, this type of love scene (or lack of it) is regarded as a cop-out, or a denial of our sexuality, or self-censorship. Instead, the lead-up to the dot-dot-dot has become longer, allowing the women to get somewhere (usually below the belt but not right in) before they have to close the curtains on their lovemaking. This is the "less is more" theory of lesbian love scenes.

DID YOU KNOW...

In 1994 there were sixty-five gay and lesbian newspapers in the United States, with an estimated combined readership of three million, according to the Queer Resources Directory (Internet). In addition, there are more than a dozen monthly and bimonthly magazines aimed at the gay and lesbian audience.

Of course, some authors can't do *Erotica dottica* very well at all. "Frances leaned over and kissed Caroline on the mouth," for example, is not the sort of sentence that should lead to a dot-dot-dot. This is selling the reader short. At the very least, Frances should continue kissing Caroline's longing nipples, trembling stomach, and be decisively making her way farther down to the aching warm wetness before any dots intrude.

Erotica botanica (rare). As a friend of mine says: "No petals, please!" *Erotica botanica* is the lesbian love scene where we are reminded constantly of our connection with the natural world and therefore the naturalness of our sexuality. Great in theory, but often overstated in practice: "Karen parted the dewy petals and sought out the rose bud within. Her fingers traced the ferny undergrowth to the wet cave of Bertha's desire . . ." is the sort of cosmic bush walk we usually get. All too often, the sensuality of nature is stuck on to lesbian bodies with the subtlety of metallic cones on to Madonna!

Erotica botanica is harder to find these days, as *Erotica naiad pressica* and *Erotica explicita* become more popular. Nowadays, we can name the rose, and most authors, running out of fresh fruit, flora, and fauna, have gratefully moved on to less limiting and more direct imagery. The moist velvet flowers of lesbiana are less likely to be found pressed between the covers of our favorite novels.

Erotica naiad pressica. These love scenes are the most common variety in lesbian light novels. They sneak into whodunits, historical romances, mysteries, love stories, and detective yarns.

Author and lesbian vampire creator Jewelle Gomez relaxes in Harlem in 1992. (Val Wilmer)

This is not, however, gratuitous sex. The characters are always on their way to a perfect orgasm (or two), but they stay in character while they come.

Erotica naiad pressica uses a join-the-dots description of sex to enable the author to describe every detail without actually using the Rude Words. This species of "soft core" love scenes usually indulges in one or two pages of stroking tongues, soft damp thighs, wet longing, eagerly sucked nipples, "feasting," arching bodies, and cries of passion before climaxing in a paragraph of orgasmic ecstasy. Watch out for chapters 5 and 10.

Isn't this *Erotica explicita*? No way! The effect aimed for is sensuous rather than straight-up sexy. There's a lot of bare skin, but no clitorises. Lots of orgasms (or, rather, shuddering releases) but no dildos or vibrators. In *Erotica naiad pressica,* you can slide urgent fingers into the exploding wetness, but you can't thrust hands up cunts. It's just not Nice!

Erotica explicita. Who cares about plot and character development? Let's fuck, baby!

Like all styles of love scenes, explicit sex can be written well or written appallingly. One book I've read lately (*Province Town*) had enough "throbbing wet holes" to make a geothermal wonderland, and enough "dripping hot pussies" to fill a cattery!

At least *Erotica explicita* gets around all those problems about what to call It. "Her clit was enflamed; her cunt was throbbing," Jewelle Gomez tells us in "White Flowers" (*Serious Pleasure*). Get the picture? In *Erotica explicita* you're allowed to say ass, fuck, fist, crack, slit, and clit. In fact, you should say them a lot. Everything is slippery or dripping, never silky. Hard is a great *Erotica explicita* word. You're allowed to be Politically Incorrect, too. That's almost an essential part of the genre.

You'll find most *Erotica explicita* in short stories or novels that might as well be a series of short stories—the plot is merely a rickety bridge to the next throbbing hole in which the reader can wallow. Great reading for a wet weekend!

— **BERYL PEARS**

Lambda Literary Award Winners

The "Lammys" began in 1988 when the *Lamba Book Report,* a gay and lesbian literary review, decided that lesbian and gay books deserved their own awards and commendations. During the first year, the ceremonies were held in Washington, D.C., with Armistead Maupin (*Tales of the City*) as emcee. Since that time the award has gone to some of the most honored books in the nation.

Lesbian Nonfiction

Lesbian Ethics by Sarah Hoagland (1988)
Really Reading Gertrude Stein edited by Judy Grahn (1989)
The Safe Sea of Women by Bonne Zimmerman (1990)
Cancer in Two Voices by Sandra Butler and Barbara Rosenblum (1991)
Eleanor Roosevelt by Blanche Wiesen Cook (1992)
Boots of Leather, Slippers of Gold by Elizabeth Kennedy and Madeline Davis (1993, Lesbian Studies)

Gay Men's Nonfiction

Borrowed Time by Paul Monette (1988)
In Search of Gay America by Neil Miller (1989)
Coming Out Under Fire by Alan Berube (1990)
Zuni Man-Woman by Will Roscoe (1991)
Becoming a Man by Paul Monette (1992)
Conduct Unbecoming by Randy Shilts (1993, Gay Men's Studies)

Lesbian Fiction

Trash by Dorothy Allison (1988)
The Bar Stories by Nisa Donnelly (1989)
Out of Time by Paula Martinac (1990)
Revolution of Little Girls by Blanche McCrary Boyd (1991) and *Gilda Stories* by Jewelle Gomez (1991, tie)
Running Fiercely Toward a High Thin Sound by Judith Katz (1992)
Written on the Body by Jeanette Winterson (1993)

DID YOU KNOW...

Time Warner gave up plans to publish a mainstream magazine aimed at gays and lesbians—because the publisher thought it wouldn't sell. "It's difficult to imagine taking on a magazine that would not make several million dollars annually in profits," the Time, Inc., Venture president told *The New York Times* in 1994.

Gay Men's Fiction

The Beautiful Room Is Empty by Edmund White (1988)
Eighty-Sixed by David B. Feinberg (1989)
The Body and Its Dangers by Allen Barnett (1990)
What the Dead Remember by Harlan Greene (1991)
Let the Dead Bury Their Dead by Randall Kenan (1992)
Living Upstairs by Joseph Hansen (1993)

AIDS (A Special Category)

Borrowed Time by Paul Monette (1988)
Reports from the Holocaust by Larry Kramer (1989)
The Way We Live Now edited by Elizabeth Osbourn (1990)
(no winners, 1991–1993)

Lesbian Mystery

(no winnner, 1988)
The Beverly Malibu by Katherine V. Forrest (1989)
Gaudi Afternoon by Barbara Wilson (1990) and
Ninth Life by Lauren Wright Douglas (1990, tie)
Murder by Tradition by Katherine V. Forrest (1991)
Two Bit Tango by Elizabeth Pincus (1992) and
Crazy for Loving by Jaye Maiman (1992, tie)
Divine Victim by Mary Wings (1993)

Gay Men's Mystery

Golden Boy by Michael Nava (1988)
Simple Suburban Murder by Mark Zubro (1989)
Howtown by Michael Nava (1990)
Country of Old Men: The Last Dave Brandsetter Mystery by Joseph Hansen (1991)
The Hidden Law by Michael Nava (1992)
Catilina's Riddle by Steven Saylor (1993)

Going Glossy

If 1993 was the year of the queer, then 1994 was definitely the year that gay went glossy. Never before in the history of lesbian and gay publishing had we seen anything like it. Suddenly, full-color covers, slick paper stock, bold graphics, and bar codes replaced the low-budget papers of yesteryear.

In the same way that gay literature has seen a tremendous boom in the 1990s, so too has the periodical industry. Where once gays and lesbians could turn only to their local newspapers, male porno mags, feminist rags, and the biweekly *Advocate* for queer content, suddenly, specialized mags were the norm. If you wanted travel info, there was *Our World.* If you were looking for hairy men, there was *Bear.* And just when you despaired of ever finding a stylish, well-written lesbian magazine, finally there was *Deneuve.*

While many people were caught off guard by the sudden glossy glut, they shouldn't have been. Magazines have always successfully captured the pulse of popular culture. Now that queer culture was coming into its own, there just didn't seem to be enough pages to contain it!

What else turned the tide toward gloss? For starters, the availability of desktop-publishing technology in the early 1990s meant that suddenly it was much easier to get into print. The queer 'zine explosion of 1990–93 was the immediate result, but "mainstream" gay magazine publishing picked up the slack a year or so later.

Not as obvious, but just as important, was the fact that more printers began accepting gay magazines.

QUEER 'ZINES

'Zines—those low-budget, self-published magazines often produced on photocopy machines—have been popular in the gay and lesbian movement for decades. By bringing the power of the press to people who have traditionally been denied it, 'zines have opened a world of communication, idea-sharing, networking, and community-building. Because so many gay men and lesbians can now produce a 'zine that meets their needs or reflects their interests, a whole new range of people are making their voices heard.

— KATHIE BERQUIST

Additionally, big advertisers finally began to realize the strength of an incredibly loyal market. Cautiously, large companies and their agencies have been increasing their presence in the gay glossies, even in titles like *POZ,* an HIV-positive lifestyle magazine, and *10 Percent,* which caters to the over thirty set. Of course, magazines like *Genre,* which combine a low level of overt sexuality and a sizable white, middle-class, male readership, pull in the most bucks.

Similarly, the willingness of chain bookstores and larger newsstands to carry gay titles—if they're professionally produced and "standard" size—has helped propel large numbers of specialty queer fetish mags like *Passport, Leather Journal, On Our Backs, Bulk Male,* and *Drummer* out of the sexual underground and onto the shelves of Tower, Barnes & Noble, and Waldenbooks stores everywhere. Amazing!

This glossy philosophy is not just an American phenomenon. Almost every European country now boasts at least a few glossies, albeit aimed primarily at men. Check out Italy's *Babilonia,* Germany's *Manner,* England's *Gay Times,* and Australia's *Outrage.* There are also some wonderful self-published lesbian glossies out there, the best

(Jill Posener)

of which are London's *Quim,* chock-full of photography and brimming over with dyke sexuality, and another young Brit upstart, *Diva.*

That being said, of course, there's no beating the American gay press for innovation. You can now find specialty gay magazines that celebrate everything from *The Big Ad,* a forum for obese men and their admirers, to *GirlJock,* a quarterly for athletic lesbians. And let's face it, there just hasn't ever been a publication like *OUT,* which has become the best-selling gay/lesbian magazine of all time. The phenomenal success of this New York–based publication, due as much to its own self-promotion as to the substance of its pages, gives hope to those for whom a magazine's panache is as important as its prose.

Witnessing the tremendous boom in gay glossies invites the inevitable question of market saturation. Can the gay community support such a spurt of new publications every few years? As queer bookstore shelves sag under the weight of new titles, publishers continue to duke it out for advertising revenue and subscribers. One thing remains certain, though. With both a rising number of titles and higher publishing standards as the new norm, the reader can only win.

— RACHEL PEPPER

DID YOU KNOW...

***Lesbian Connection* is a free bimonthly national newsletter by and for lesbians, started in 1974. Until 1995, it was produced in the same simple format it had been in at the start: A dozen or so pieces of paper stapled together, jam-packed with announcements, letters, news clippings, articles, and resources, all written by the readers. Even though the Elsie collective, as they call themselves, has gone somewhat high tech (they use computers instead of typewriters now), this grassroots precursor to today's 'zines still tags its suggested donation rate for subscription with the line "more if you can, less if you can't."**

Rachel Pepper's Top Ten Queer 'Zines of All Time

1. *Bimbox*

Without a doubt, the most influential queer 'zine ever published. Bitter, twisted, and absolutely awe-inspiring, this Toronto creation, scathingly penned by the infamous Johnny Noxzema and Ratboy, was pure genius.

2. *Homocore*

An institution in its own right, *Homocore* printed thousands of copies, most of which were distributed only by mail and a single San Francisco post office box. Isolated fag and dyke punk kids all across the planet networked through its pages and set the scene for the upcoming queer 'zine explosion.

3. *Hothead Paisan*

The cartoon adventures of Diane DiMassa's homicidal lesbian terrorist inspire a world-wide cult of followers.

4. *JD's*

This late 1980s creation, co-produced by artist/musician/filmmaker GB Jones and filmmaker/celebrity Bruce LaBruce, celebrated the underground queer punk aesthetic from the perspective of its juvenile delinquent namesake.

5. *Diseased Pariah News*

This 'zine took the author's experience with AIDS as its starting point and unapologetically presented itself at a time when there was little personal published information about AIDS. Alongside witty vendettas *DPN* provided safe sex information and useful columns like "Get Fat, Don't Die."

6. *Thing*

Chicago's famed African American gay 'zine boasted "big-name" writers like Essex Hemphill along with staff-written features on musicians, performers, and scenesters like Ru Paul long before they gained mainstream success.

7. *Frighten the Horses*

Biting political views, news, and great sexual stories.

8. *My Comrade/Sister*

Les Simpson's take on the New York club circuit from a drag perspective was snatched up coast-to-coast.

9. *Sister Nobody*

One of the first dyke 'zines to receive widespread distribution, *Sister Nobody* served as inspiration for a whole wave of wanna-be lesbian 'zinesters.

10. *Factsheet Five*

Published by 'zine guru Mike Gunderloy, *FF5* is not specifically a queer 'zine. Nonetheless, of the thousands of 'zines *FF5* reviewed each issue, there were always hundreds of gay titles listed. Distributed world-wide, this essential and much revered magazine ensures that queer 'zinesters, no matter where they live, can be part of the burgeoning 'zine revolution.

SMASH IMPERIALISM
LIBERATION FRONT
FEB. 16th.
GANGWAY
1918
1977
YOUR PURPLE STAR?
CHICAGO
Castaways M.C. Milwauke

CHAPTER 3

Reinventing History

What is gay history? Is it just when we discover that someone from the past had a long-term intimate relationship with someone of the same sex? Or is gay history simply the history of self-identified homosexuals? What do we make of Native American cultures that did not have concepts of homosexuality vs. heterosexuality? How do alternative interpretations of gender and sexuality fit into the picture?

Clear answers are hard to come by. Discovering that someone was intimate with others of the same sex does add to our history, but it does not make him or her "gay." "Gay" and "lesbian," like the word "homosexual," are terms that are fixed in a specific historical era, namely the 20th century. Unlike other minorities, for whom finding oneself in history is simply a matter of finding out a person's race or religion, gay people have to put together the pieces of a complex puzzle, often using suspicion and loose associations to discover the hidden lineage that is a part of our history.

J. C. Leyendecker, the commercial artist who came up with the Arrow Collar Man in the early twentieth century, was gay. His inspiration and model, Charles Beach, was his lover.

But the broader questions of what constitutes gay history and who decides it are more difficult to answer. In a sense, everything we do as lovers of our own sex is historical. What we remember about events and how we tell the stories of those events influences the very nature of history. In addition, everything that is done by others in reaction to same-sex intimacy, by politicians, religious leaders, and medical professionals, shapes the way that society views sexuality.

Gender can also be considered a part of gay history. Homosexual behavior, by both men and women, has often been characterized in the past as a gender transgression. In other words, gay men act "womanish" or "effeminate," while lesbians act "masculine" or "mannish." The ways a society defines gender affect the ways it defines sexuality. But what should we make of women who passed as men, drag queens, and Native American berdache? Are they part of a transgendered history or gay history? Or are the two histories inexorably intertwined?

In this chapter, we do not attempt to fully answer these questions. What we have done is create a mosaic of some of the aspects of American history we feel we can claim. From homosexual gathering places to political organizations, and from same-sex intimacy in the Old West to the medical "cures" that doctors have inflicted on queer people for over a century, one thing is certain: Gay people have a heritage and a history that is as multifaceted as our diverse contemporary culture.

DID YOU KNOW...

The first recorded evidence of homosexuality is found in Mesopotamia circa 3000 B.C., where artifacts depict men having sex with other men.

Claiming Our Own—Famous Names

When looking into the past, it's hard to say exactly who was or was not gay or lesbian. Depending on the era, culture, class, race, and gender of people, certain activities were considered within the realm of "normalcy," while other activities were considered "deviant." For example, before the late nineteenth century in the United States, concepts of same-sex love did not carry the same stigma they do today. What we can do is look at those who have loved their own sex throughout history, and celebrate that love, in whatever form it took. We don't necessarily have to label it as "gay." Here are some famous names from U.S. history who have been lovers of their own sex:

Horotio Alger (1832–1899), American success parable writer
Susan B. Anthony (1820–1906), suffragist and women's activist
Josephine Baker (1906–1975), jazz singer
James Baldwin (1924–1987), novelist
Djuna Barnes (1892–1982), modernist writer
Ruth Benedict (1887–1948), anthropologist and suffragist

Gladys Bentley (1907–1960), blues performer
James Buchanan (1791–1868), fifteenth President
Truman Capote (1924–1984), writer and wit
Willa Cather (1873–1947), novelist
Jane Chambers (1937–1983), playwright
Montgomery Clift (1920–1966), actor
Roy Cohn (1927–1986), Joseph McCarthy's lawyer
Hart Crane (1899–1932), poet
George Cukor (1899–1983), Hollywood director
Countee Cullen (1903–1946), Harlem Renaissance poet
James Dean (1931–1955), American icon and screen idol
Emily Dickinson (1830–1886), poet
Errol Flynn (1909–1989), swashbuckling actor
Stephen Foster (1826–1864), songwriter

That Montgomery Clift was a lover of his own sex is such an open Hollywood secret that calling someone "today's Montomgery Clift" in gossip columns is another way of saying an actor is gay. Here, a bare-chested Clift costarred in From Here to Eternity *in 1953. (Courtesy of Columbia Pictures)*

Paul Goodman (1911–1972), progressive writer
Alexander Hamilton (1755–1804), first secretary of the Treasury
Lorraine Hansbury (1930–1965), playwright
J. Edgar Hoover (1898–1972), FBI director
Rock Hudson (1925–1985), Hollywood heartthrob
Langston Hughes (1902–1967), Harlem Renaissance poet
Alberta Hunter (1898–1984), blues great
Christopher Isherwood (1904–1986), novelist
William Rufus King (1786–1853), Pierce's vice president
Liberace (1919–1987), flamboyant showman and pianist
Alain Locke (1886–1954), academic and writer
"Moms" Mabley (1897–1975), comic great
Margaret Mead (1901–1978), anthropologist
Herman Melville (1819–1891), novelist
Edna St. Vincent Millay (1892–1980), poet
Ramon Novarro (1899–1968), silent movie actor
Cole Porter (1893–1964), songwriter
Ma Rainey (1889–1939), blues performer

DID YOU KNOW...

In 1566, the Spanish military executed a Frenchman for homosexuality in St. Augustine, Florida. This is the earliest known case of punishment of homosexual activity in America.

Eleanor Roosevelt (1884–1962), activist and politician
Bayard Rustin (1912–1987), civil rights organizer and activist
Bessie Smith (1894–1937), blues icon
Gertrude Stein (1874–1946) , writer
"Big Bill" Tilden (1893–1953), tennis star
Rudolph Valentino (1895–1926), screen idol
Andy Warhol (1928–1987), pop artist
James Whale (1896–1957), classic horror film director
Walt Whitman (1819–1892), poet
Tennessee Williams (1911–1983), playwright

DID YOU KNOW...

On May 24, 1610, the state of Virginia created the first sodomy law in America. It called for the death penalty.

FRONTIER QUEERS

For the past decade, Jim Wilke has been doing pioneering research into the lives of gay men who were frontiersmen in the United States during the late nineteenth and early twentieth centuries. These were men who went west, either from the desire for adventure or the need to survive, men who worked the ranches, farmed the fields, or joined the army in search of independence and a different way of living from that offered in the cities of the East.

While today we use the term "gay" to describe these men, research has shown that they had no such language to describe themselves until sometime after the Civil War. Nonetheless, these men lived together and loved together, with a commitment beyond any notion of "situational homosexuality."

Frontier Comrades: Homosexuality in the American West

While filming *Red River* (1955), John Wayne's famous demand about Montgomery Clift—that director Howard Hawks "get that faggot off my set"—underscored a common belief that homosexuality had no place in the rough and tumble American West. Recent research, however, indicates that homosexuality was not only common, but may actually have thrived in the frontier.

Moreover, popular folklore which does acknowledge same-sex interactions in the frontier assumes that "situational homosexuality," the desire for sexual contact with members of the same sex in the absence of opposite sex partners, is the primary motivational force behind any existing homosexuality. Yet this does not account for urban homosexuality in Western cities, or homosexuality among Western women. It appears more likely that Westerners responded to a multitude of internal and external conditions that allowed them to alternately discover or redefine their emotional and sexual desire.

Historian Hubert Bancroft noted that during the 1850s California Gold Rush, "the requirements of mining life favored partnership . . . sacred like the marriage bonds, as illustrated by the softening of 'partner' into the familiar 'pard.' " In 1914, migrant California fieldworkers were recorded to have not only justified but idealized homosexually monogamous relationships. Larger groups of men in isolated mining, logging, or railroad construction camps appear to have been more gregarious. "Restlessness among the crew" of one Western mining camp brought over half of the camp's "brawny, ultra-masculine" men to seek sexual "relief" with each other. Similar conditions existed in Civilian Conservation Corp camps in Texas in the 1930s and a highway construction camp in California in the early 1950s.

Western cities such as San Francisco, Denver, Salt Lake City, and Chicago enjoyed highly developed homosexual urban subcultures which followed patterns established in Eastern cities. Several different "circles" within a city reflected divergent interests and pursuits. All provided a network of mutual support to those fortunate enough to be accepted into them. A San Francisco homosexual man wrote in 1911 that life could be "hard, for many crushing, but it is extremely interesting, and I am glad to have been given the opportunity to have lived it."

In the 1890s, a Colorado professor wrote that Denver's homosexual population included "five musicians, three teachers, three art dealers, one minister, one judge, two actors, one florist, and one woman's tailor." In California, an 1887 land boom led San Diego to build an elaborate Victorian house as an inducement for musician Jesse Owens Sharard and his male partner to move there and lend the city an air of cosmopolitan refinement. Similar

DID YOU KNOW...

According to historian Jonathan Katz in his book *Gay American History*, from the time that Alabama senator William Rufus De Vane King (a fifty-seven-year-old bachelor) met Pennsylvania senator James Buchanan in 1834, until King's appointment as U.S. minister to France, the two were inseparable. Their intimate relationship caused barbed comments in Washington. Andrew Jackson called King "Miss Nancy," and in a private letter in 1844, Aaron Brown referred to King as Buchanan's "better half" and (in jest) referred to Buchanan and King's "divorce."

social and artistic soirees were held in the 1880s in Southern California at the home of two San Juan Capistrano men.

There was probably no occupation in the West that did not have lesbian and gay participants. William Breakeridge worked as a Union Pacific brakeman before becoming a deputy sheriff at Tombstone, Arizona Territory, where he was known and accepted by many of the mining town's community. Stagecoach driver Charlie Parkhurst was discovered to be a woman only after her death in 1879, a fact which made much newspaper copy. The *San Francisco Call* remarked that "No doubt he was not like other men, indeed, it was generally said among his acquaintances that he was a hermaphrodite" and that "the discoveries of the successful concealment for protracted periods of the female sex are not infrequent." Oregon native Lucile Hart, a Stanford medical school graduate, is noted by historian Jonathan Katz to have dressed as a man in order to practice medicine and marry the woman she loved. Her own doctor wrote that "if society will but leave her alone, she will fill her niche in the world and leave it better for her bravery."

In the 1800s, sodomy laws were found in all states and territories, but were selectively enforced. In 1873, Lawrence G. Murphy, a civilian post trader at Fort Stanton, New Mexico, was charged with a "most unnatural" relationship with a local official in an effort to cancel his military contract. In El Paso, Texas, an 1896 charge of sodomy against Marcelo Alviar brought with it a bond set at $500, the same amount as for murder. The prohibitively expensive bond was punitive, and virtually guaranteed jail time or the loss of the defendant's life savings or property. This system of select enforcement was similarly applied to gambling houses, saloons, and brothels. Male prostitution existed in varying degrees, from an "elegantly furnished" 1882 Midwestern brothel to a particularly clandestine male street prostitution ring in San Francisco in 1902. Homosexuality in Western prisons was so common that in 1877, San Quentin director Dr. J. E. Pellham launched a crusade against it, advising solitary confinement as therapy.

DID YOU KNOW...

Train robber Bill Miner, the notorious "Grey Fox" who was "said to be a sodomite" by Pinkerton's Detective Agency, preferred as accomplices young men he met during periodic stays in prison.

Among Westerners there existed a gentleman's agreement that arose from the need to survive in the frontier. One part of this agreement was mutual respect, allowing one "the right to live the life and go the gait which seemed most pleasing to himself." Historian David Dary has written that cowboys "sought to live lives that were free from falsehood and hypocrisy." This frontier code of conduct allowed many people to enjoy open relationships that would have otherwise not been possible.

Two cowboys from the late nineteenth century pose in a manner traditionally used for portraits of husbands and wives. (©Jim Wilke)

On the open range, cowboys often developed strong and loyal relationships with each other. The dangers of stampedes and general rigors of the trail required absolute cooperation; a cowboy who could not be relied on found himself outcast. Loyalty was "one of the most notable characteristics of the cowboy," and devotion to one's "pard" was highly regarded. The cowboy expression that one was "in love" with someone could sometimes be taken literally. The *Texas Livestock Journal* remarked in 1882 that "if the inner history of friendships among the rough, and perhaps untutored cowboys could be written, it would be quite as unselfish and romantic as that as of Damon and [Patroclus]."

Many circumstances contributed to personal closeness on the ranch and trail. Cowboys frequently bedded in pairs with their "bunkie," and a ranch bunkhouse was occasionally called a "ram pasture." Many cowboys engaged in "mutual solace," a tender, expressive, and euphemistic term for sexual relations. Vulgar and explicit "ugly songs" describing phallic size, virility, and sodomy were sung around campfires. In 1920s Nevada, the "sixty-nine" sexual position was common enough among cowboys to warrant its own euphemism, "Swanson neuf."

Gay cowboys continue to be an intrinsic part of the West. In 1957, two Texas cowboys visiting the Mayflower Bar, an Oklahoma City gay bar, described their life as one where there are generally two or three gay cowboys to a ranch, who quietly recognize each other, keeping their identity a secret from the others. While many working horsemen and horsewomen maintain a quiet reticence associated with the broader aspects of ranching culture, the modern lesbian and gay civil rights movement has brought a growing number of openly gay and lesbian ranchers, as well as the creation of the International Gay Rodeo Association, with chapters around the United States and Canada.

— **JIM WILKE**

Things Were Hopping in Colorado in the Late 1800s

Trinidad restauranteur Charles "Frenchey" Vobaugh was a woman who passed as a man and, along with "his" wife, assumed the outward appearance of a heterosexual couple in order to remain married for thirty years. Colorado newspapers were full of successful lesbian and gay elopements. In 1889, the town of Emma was "rent from center to circumference" over the "sensational love affair between Miss Clara Dietrich, postmistress and general storekeeper, and Miss Ora Chatfield." Letters written between them caused the Denver papers to remark that the "love that existed between the two parties was of no ephemeral nature, but as strong as that of a strong man and his sweetheart." Despite attempts to separate them, the "lady lovers" successfully eloped. "If the case ever comes into court," wrote the Denver Times, "from a scientific standpoint alone it will attract widespread attention." In 1898, Boulder teamster W. H. Billings left his wife and sold his horses in order to run away with Charles Edwards, a saloon entertainer who played banjo and performed acrobatics. A Denver paper reported that Billings was "not happy unless he was trailing around the streets with Edwards" and that "if his home had any charms for him, said his wife, they had fled and all on account of a banjo player."

— JIM WILKE

She's Got Balls as Big as a Bull—Homosexuality in the Seventh Cavalry, 1868–1878

Reviews of military accounts during the frontier era reveal few instances of soldiers being prosecuted for sodomy. This was not because sodomy was rarely practiced; the military brass chose to disguise such situations rather than admit that they occurred within a military post. This allowed the military to prevent such charges from going on the public record, reflecting both contemporary prejudice and reticence upon the part of the military to acknowledge that such situations existed. In the 1890s, an infantryman was charged in private military correspondence with the "sin of Oscar Wilde"; however, he was publicly drummed out of the 24 Colored Infantry on unrelated charges.

Only when sodomy became publicly evident did the military find it necessary to enact an equally public response. The 1878 death of a Seventh Cavalry laundress caused a sensation that was telegraphed from New York to San Francisco. After ten years of loyal service with the Cavalry, Mrs. Corporal Noonan was discovered to be a man. Because she was a popular midwife, good cook, and nurse, the exposure of "her" identity revealed an extraordinary series of homosexual relationships among cavalrymen on one of the most well-known military posts, George Custer's Seventh Cavalry.

"She" was a New Mexican teamster that Seventh Cavalry Captain Lewis McClean Hamilton met on the streets of Leavenworth City, Kansas, in 1868. "Their recognition was mutual," a confidant later recalled. In order to have a relationship, Captain Hamilton brought her into his employ under the guise of a military laundress, appointing "her" to his company, Company A. Military laundresses served at the captain's prerogative, and the bullwhacker-turned-laundress faithfully followed Hamilton until his death eight months later in the Battle of Washita in November 1868.

After a hunt, (from left to right) Bloody Knife, General Custer, John Noonan, and Ludlow posed for a picture. Noonan was married to another man, who was passing as a woman. Mrs. Noonan washed Mrs. Custer's clothes. (South Dakota Historical Society, State Archives)

The bullet that pierced Hamilton's heart that morning left behind an unusual widow. Remarkably, "she" remained in military employ. Her resolve in the matter is admirable, for in addition to developing a growing reputation as a superb laundress, she became known as a sometime nurse, emergency midwife, excellent cook, and tailor. Elizabeth Bacon Custer, wife of Lieutenant General George Custer, employed her in the early 1870s. She recalled that "when she brought the linen home, it was fluted and frilled so daintily that I considered her a treasure. She always came at night, and when I went out to pay her she was very shy, and kept a veil pinned about the lower part of her face." All of these domestic skills contributed financially to the laundress's existing income and indicate that she was a very strong-willed and resourceful person. She was also very popular within the social worlds of military society. Mrs. Custer remembered her presence at military balls, wheeling about the barracks floor dressed in "pink tarletan and false curls, and not withstanding her height and colossal anatomy, she has constant partners."

Following Hamilton's death, the popular widow eventually married three more times. While the first two husbands deserted the Cavalry, her third and final marriage was successful and endured. With the transfer of the Seventh Cavalry to Fort Abraham Lincoln, Dakota Territory, in 1873, came Private John Noonan, Company L. His commitment to professional soldiering, an "excellent character," and subsequent rise from private to sergeant showed Noonan to have been a superb soldier. His reputation was further enhanced by assignments as orderly to the Custer command. In about 1874, "Colonel Tom's own man," as Mrs. Custer referred to Noonan, possessed sufficient merit to officially marry Mrs. Noonan. Noonan reenlisted in January 1877, and by the following year had again worked his way up to the rank of corporal.

When his wife died on October 30, 1878, Corporal Noonan was on escort duty over three hundred miles away. The success of her disguise had been thorough; the laundress who volunteered to prepare the body for burial was quite surprised, emerging from her duties shouting, "She's got balls as big as a bull, she's a man!" The news rapidly spread and the surrounding community was "plunged into a pleasurable curiosity to know the particulars." News of the "unnatural union and apparel" was telegraphed to newspapers from coast to coast. The accuracy of these sensational stories was confirmed by the official report of Post Surgeon W. D. Wolverton, who "found the body to be that of a fully developed male in all that makes the difference in sex, without any abnormal condition that would cause a doubt on the subject."

The enormous public attention paid to this matter led not only to Noonan's dishonorable discharge, but because of the public nature of his trespass against social convention and military "honor," it exacted an equally public

DID YOU KNOW...

Dr. Mary Edwards Walker, late-nineteenth- and early-twentieth-century physician and feminist, was called by her male enemies "the most distinguished sexual invert in the United States." She was actually not a lesbian, but an open cross-dresser. A qualified physician, she had to force her service on an unwilling federal government during the Civil War; she eventually won a Congressional Medal of Honor for her work. She also became the first woman in the United States permitted by Congress to dress in male attire. Eventually, the militant Dr. Walker moved out of step with her sister feminists because her taste in dress offended them. It was one thing to wear the men's trousers—but it was quite another to go whole hog as did Mary Walker. She affected shirt, bow tie, jacket, top hat, and cane.

punishment. Commanding Officer Sturgis wrote on November 23, 1878, that "if there is any law by which this man could be sent to the penitentiary I would respectfully suggest that it be called into requisition in his case." Military brass concurrred and Sturgis was "instructed to bring the case to attention of the U.S. District Attorney." However, Noonan committed suicide before prosecution could continue. He died in the Company stables at the age of thirty on November 30, 1878. His death was noted by a local newspaper to have "relieved the regiment of the odium which the man's presence had cast them."

While Mrs. Noonan had successfully eluded detection for some ten years, at least one officer was aware of her disguise. First Lieutenant Edward Settle Godfrey noted in 1868 that she was "tall and angular and had a coarse voice" and that "a stiff breeze whisked the veil off her face and revealed a bearded chin." Godfrey's suspicions were confirmed by Hamilton, who told him "the story of her employment." Until the news became public a decade later, Godfrey never spoke of the matter, believing discretion the better part of honor. The principles of decorum that ultimately destroyed Corporal Noonan had conversely served to protect his wife's identity prior to her death.

— JIM WILKE

DID YOU KNOW...

In 1702, Edward Hyde, Lord Cornbury, was appointed governor of New York by his cousin, Queen Anne. Cornbury dressed daily in women's clothes and commonly made appearances while in full dress and makeup. He posed in a low-necked dress for his official portrait, holding a fan and wearing a subtle swatch of lace in his hair. He remained governor until 1708. Eventually he returned to England, where he took a seat in the House of Lords.

PASSING AND CROSS-DRESSING

Gender roles are ingrained in society and affect nearly all facets of our lives. Depending on the culture, the historical era, and the geographic region of the world, everything from hairstyles and dress to career choices and marriage have had gender-specific "norms." For a variety of reasons, there have always been individuals who have transgressed those norms.

"Passing" is a specific kind of cross-dressing in which a person dons the attire, stance, walk, and attitudes of the opposite sex in order to pass as that sex. Women throughout history have successfully passed as men in order to gain access to the greater economic and political opportunities men have typically possessed. Some men and women have also passed to negotiate around social stigmas against same-sex love, and many passed in the nineteenth and early twentieth centuries in order to marry someone of their own gender.

Men who passed as women had many motives aside from access to same-sex intimacy. In a time before gender-reassignment operations (sex changes), passing as a woman was perhaps the closest one could come to "switching" gender, making passing men and women early pioneers of the transgender community. In addition, while men have historically had greater opportunities both politically and economically, the limitations of social expression in a dual-gendered society cuts both ways. From a very young age boys were, and still are, socialized to deny themselves access to certain kinds of activities (like playing with dolls and holding hands with other boys) and to define occupations in terms of gender (e.g., nurses are women and doctors are men). By passing as women, men could engage in activities that society would deem "unacceptable" for men.

In many traditional Native American cultures, cross dressing and transgressing gender norms was celebrated. Berdache, as French explorers called cross-gender Native Americans, were often seen as mystics and seers. Often, cross-gendered people were simply incorporated into the roles and activities of the opposite sex. Unlike most other people of the culture, many berdache had both sexual and emotional same-sex relationships.

By the twentieth century, much cross-dressing in the United States had less to do with passing than it did with identifying with lesbian and gay cultures. Butch and femme roles have enjoyed a resurgence in recent years, as lesbians have come to appreciate the distinctive pleasures and freedoms from gender expectations such roles can bring.

Drag, too, has its history. Entertainment drag was an important part of cabaret theater in the early and mid twentieth century, and continues in various forms today. We've compiled a list of some of the great drag performers of that era.

Clothes and attitude, it seems, do make the man (and, of course, the woman).

"When I was about twenty [in the 1860s] I decided that I was almost at the end of my rope. I had no money and a woman's wages were not enough to keep me alive. I looked around and saw men getting more money and more work, and more money for the same kind of work. I decided to become a man. It was simple. I just put on men's clothing and applied for a man's job. I got it and got good money for those times, so I stuck to it."

CHARLES WARNER, WHO PASSED AS A MAN IN SARATOGA SPRINGS, NEW YORK, FOR OVER SIXTY YEARS

The Man Who Lived Thirty Years as a Woman

In 1951, *Ebony* printed an article about Georgia Black, a man who had passed as a woman for thirty years in a small southern town. It is a rare glimpse into the life of a passing man who negotiated sexuality and gender to become the woman she truly wanted to be. Given the historical context of the piece, *Ebony,* while relying on popular notions of homosexuality, gives Georgia the dignity she deserved in a community that embraced her even after it was discovered she had been a he. Below is an abridged verison of that article.

CAN YOU BELIEVE IT?

Murray Hall passed for over twenty-five years as a man. During that time, she voted, married twice, and became a prominent New York politician in the 1880s and 1890s. She had breast cancer for years, and was near death when she finally confided in a doctor. The doctor neither cured her nor kept her secret, and she died amid public scandal.

By every law of society, Georgia Black should have died in disgrace and humiliation and been remembered as a sex pervert, a "fairy," and a "freak."

But when Georgia Black died in Sanford, Florida, four months ago, both the white and colored community alike paid its solemn tribute. A funeral cortege wound its way though the hushed crowded streets of the Negro section. And lining the sidewalks of the Dixie town that had once barred Jackie Robinson from its stadium, Negro and white mourners rubbed elbows, bowed heads, and shed genuine tears.

Exposure of Georgia Black as a man who had passed for a woman for thirty years was the tragic anti-climax to his death and revealed one of the most incredible stories in the history of sex abnormalities.

The exposure came about after County Physician Orville Barks of Sanford, Florida, found to his shocked amazement that the sick "woman" he was examining had all the physical characteristics of a man.

Black's decision to camouflage these characteristics and cross the sex line was made when, as a fifteen-year-old boy (then named George Cantey) on a farm near Galeyville, South Carolina, he rebelled against the grueling slavery of work in the fields and ran away to Charleston. There he became a house servant in a mansion where a homosexual—a male retainer at the mansion —invited him to become his "sweetheart." Illiterate, untutored, and insecure, having only a faint notion of right and wrong, the simple farm boy from the South Carolina hinterlands gracefully accepted. Black's "boyfriend" dressed him in women's clothes and coached him in feminine actions and mannerisms.

Under the schooling of this unidentified "boyfriend," the masquerade of Georgia Black became second nature. Even when his "lover" eventually forsook him, Georgia had become so accustomed to an unnatural way of life that he began looking for another man. In Winter Garden, Florida, Black met Alonzo Sabbe, at the time a seriously ill man. An unselfish, generous person, Georgia nursed Sabbe back to health. When he recovered, Sabbe asked Black to marry him.

It was during the marriage to Sabbe that Georgia adopted a "son," a fact that made her masquerade all the more convincing. The "son," a Pennsylvania steelworker, was devoted to his "mother," often sent her gifts and money, and was astounded to learn Black's true sex. Sabbe died shortly after the marriage and Georgia, now living in Sanford, married again.

Her second husband was Muster Black. The marriage took place in the home of Mrs. Joanna Moore, principal of Sanford's Negro elementary school. A prominent Negro minister officiated. Black, a World War I vet, died seven years after the marriage. As his "widow," Georgia collected a pension from the Veterans Association.

The reverence that friends and neighbors gave gentle Georgia Black in death was equaled only by the fierce loyalty townsfolk of both races accorded him during the last days of his life when sensational radio and newspaper publicity revealing his true sex spilled across the nation.

Dr. Orville Barks, the county physician who reported Black's secret, seemed somewhat regretful that he had become involved. A number of people bitterly condemned Barks for what they termed his "indiscreet" revelation.

Members of the St. James Methodist Church uttered approving "amens" each Sunday as Pastor Thomas Flowers asked their prayers for "our worthy Sister Black, who was even one of the most important leaders in our church." Succinctly, Sanford public opinion was divided

DID YOU KNOW...

According to historian Allan Bérubé, "Jeanne Bonnet grew up in San Francisco as a tomboy and in the 1870s, in her early twenties, was arrested dozens of times for wearing male attire. She visited local brothels as a male customer, and eventually organized French prostitutes in San Francisco into an all-woman gang whose members swore off prostitution, had nothing to do with men, and supported themselves by shoplifting. She traveled with a special friend, Blanche Buneau, whom the newspapers described as 'strangely and powerfully attached' to Jeanne. Her success at separating prostitutes from their pimps led to her murder in 1876."

into two classes: those who didn't believe Black had deceived them, and those who didn't care.

Mr. and Mrs. Walter Hand, who operate Sanford's Greyhound bus agency, were in the class of nonbelievers. Representative of the well-to-do whites who stoutly defended Black, the Hands said Georgia had done domestic work in their home for ten years. "Georgia is a perfectly wonderful person," Mrs. Hand declared. "I don't believe what they say about her."

Another wealthy Sanfordite, for whom Black did domestic work, said defiantly, "I don't care what Georgia Black was. She nursed members of our family through birth, sickness, and death. She was one of the best citizens in town."

DID YOU KNOW...

Current anti-cross-dressing laws in New York State originated as an attempt by the early state legislature to prevent militant farmers from committing acts of civil disobedience while dressed as Native Americans.

Black himself gave the impression of an amazing innocence of the double life he had led. In fact, despite all the evidence, official statements, and pictures, Georgia insisted that fate had intended him to be a female. Admitting that he had male organs, he dismissed them as "growths," and declared he had never had any emotional feeling for a woman.

"The doctor says he didn't see how I coulda married, but I don't pay no 'tention to that doctor. My husbands and me had a peaceful, lovely life," he stated.

A month before his death, as he lay in his bed, arms skin and bone, fingernails like thick encrustations of lime, sunken jaws sloping down to a chin covered with a light, white beard, Georgia told *Ebony* his story. His clear, dark eyes gave life to the wasted face, topped with coarse, heavy, black hair, fringed with white where the dye had faded. The final thing he said was:

"I never done nuthin' wrong in my life."

People in Sanford, where Black lived and died, loved and was loved, agree.

Berdache Roles in North American Tribes

We'wha (Zuni) (Courtesy of National Anthropological Archives, Smithsonian Institution)

Over 133 North American tribes have been documented to have berdache, or two-spirit, roles in their societies. Berdache were individuals with alternative gender roles, involving cross-gender behavior or same-sex relationships (for example, men who did traditional women's work or women who engaged in hunting and warfare). While some tribes gave no formal name to this behavior, an equal number formalized the two-spirited roles within their cultures. Listed below are several tribes from around North America with berdache roles:

Tribe	*Region*	*Male Role*	*Female Role*
Blackfeet	Plains	ake'skassi	sakwo'mapi akikwan
Cheyenne	Plains	heemaneh'	
Cocopa	Southwest	elha	warhameh
Dakota	Plains	wingkta wingkte	koskalaka
Klamath	Colombia Plateau	tw!inna'ek	tw!inna'ek
Kutenai	Columbia Plateau	kupalhke'tek	titqattek
Maricopa	Southwest	ilyaxai'	kwiraxame'
Mojave	Southwest	alyha	hwami
Northern Paiute	Great Basin	tuva'sa	moroni noho
Shoshoni	Great Basin	tubasa	nuwuduka waippu sungwe
Zuni	Southwest	lhamana	katsotse

Seven Famous Female Impersonators

From the beginning of the century through the 1930s, drag performers enjoyed a heyday in New York City everywhere from seedy dives to Broadway, and the popularity of female impersonation spread across the country. By the late 1930s, drag performance had been driven underground, primarily existing in gay clubs. There were, however, exceptions, such as T. C. Jones, who played on Broadway in *New Faces of 1956*. Jones always removed his wig at the close of a performance. Here are seven other famous female impersonators from history:

DID YOU KNOW?

Lavish costume and drag balls were popular in America from the 1820s through the 1930s, and were great social occasions in New York, Philadelphia, St. Louis, New Orleans, and Chicago. Dozens of enormous gay balls took place in Harlem and Greenwich Village each year from the 1860s through the 1930s. Society people, politicians, and flamboyant homosexuals rubbed shoulder pads at these events. The Vanderbilts were known to attend New York's Hamilton Lodge Ball, as was Mayor Jimmy Walker (sometimes in drag).

1. **Gene Malin** was a six-foot, 200-pound effeminate man who performed both in and out of drag costume. Briefly, in the late 1920s, he was the top earner of Broadway. By 1932, he had moved to a club in Hollywood bearing his name. A year later, Malin's career was cut tragically short when the twenty-five-year-old drove his automobile off a pier and drowned.

2. **Julian Eltinge** was active from the end of the nineteenth century through 1940. Though presumed to be homosexual, Eltinge went to extraordinary lengths to stress his heterosexuality, beating up stagehands, members of the public, and fellow vaudevillians who made any suggestive remarks about his sex life.

3. **Karyl Norman** billed himself as "The Creole Fashion Plate," but was known behind his back as "The Queer Old Fashion Plate." Milton Berle recalls that Norman was so used to wearing high heels that by the late 1920s, he found it impossible to put on male footwear.

4. **Bert Savoy** teamed up with another gay man, Jay Brennan, who appeared in male attire. Much of Mae West's personae was inspired by Savoy. On June 26, 1923, rumor has it that he and a friend were walking on Long Beach, Long Island, when a thunderstorm swept across the area. After a particularly strong clap of thunder, Savoy commented, "Mercy, ain't Miss God cutting up something awful?" Immediately, there was a lightning

bolt from the sky and both Savoy and his friend were instantly killed.

5. **Rae Bourbon** performed around the country from the 1930s through the 1960s. His raunchy behavior caused him to be ostracized from other female impersonators and frequently landed him in jail. In the mid-fifties, as a publicity stunt, he claimed to have had a sex change in Mexico performed by a Hungarian doctor. In 1968, he was accused of murder, and three years later, he died in a Texas jail hospital of a heart attack.

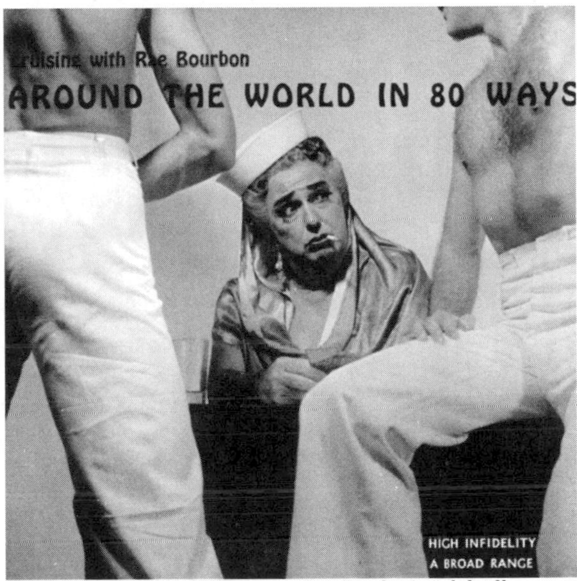

Around the World in 80 Ways *was Rae Bourbon's eighth album. Others included* You're Stepping on My Eyelashes, Hollywood Expose, *and* Let Me Tell You About My Operation. *(Collection of Don Romesburg)*

6. **Jose Sarria** gained fame for his many performances at the Black Cat on Montgomery Street in San Francisco, a popular bar for the city's gay and bohemian subcultures of the 1950s. His famous performances included his own parodies of grand operas like *Aida* and *Carmen.* Aside from his talents on the stage, he ran unsuccessfully for the Board of Supervisors in 1961, the first openly gay candidate in the nation. In 1966 he became the first Empress of San Francisco, beginning what continues today as the Imperial Court.

7. **Billy Jones** was perhaps Atlanta's (and the South's) most famous drag queen in the 1960s and 1970s. Beginning in 1961, he performed as Phyllis Killer at the Joy Lounge and as head of "Billy and the Beautiful Boys" at Club Centaur. He also hosted the Phyllis Killer Oscar Awards for seventeen years.

— **ANTHONY SLIDE**

Butch-Femme Relationships

Butch-femme relationships are a style of lesbian loving and self-presentation that can in America be traced back to the beginning of the twentieth century. Butches and femmes have separate sexual, emotional, and social identities outside of the relationship. Some butches believe they were born different from other women; others view their identity as socially constructed.

While no exact date has yet been established for the start of the usage of the terms "butch" and "femme," oral histories show their prevalence from the 1930s on. The butch-femme couple was particularly dominant in the United States, in both black and white lesbian communities, from the 1920s through the 1950s and early 1960s.

Because the complementarity of butch and femme is perceived differently by different women, no simple definition can be offered. When seen through outsiders' eyes, the butch appears simplistically "masculine," and the femme, "feminine," paralleling heterosexual categories. But butches and femmes transformed heterosexual attitude and dress into a unique lesbian language of sexuality and emotional bonding. Butch-femme relationships are based on an intense erotic attraction, with its own rituals of courtship, seduction, and offers of mutual protection. While the erotic connection is the basis for the relationship, and while butches often see themselves as the more aggressive partner, butch-femme relationships, when they work well, develop a nurturing balance between two different kinds of women, each encouraging the other's sexual-emotional identity. Couples often settle into domestic long-term relationships or engage in serial monogamy, a practice Liz Kennedy and Madeline Davis (authors of *Boots of Leather, Slippers of Gold*) trace back to the thirties, and one they view as a major lesbian contribution to an alternative for heterosexual marriage. In the fifties, butch-femme couples were a symbol of women's erotic autonomy, a visual statement of sexually and emotionally full lives that did not include men.

In the fifties, butch women, dressed in slacks and shirts and flashing pinky rings, announced their sexual expertise in a public style that often opened their lives to ridicule and assault. Many adopted men's clothes and wore "DA" haircuts. The butch woman took as her main goal in lovemaking the pleasure she could give her femme partner. This sense of dedication to her lover rather than to her own sexual fulfillment is one of the ways a butch is clearly distinct from the men she is assumed to be imitating.

(Andrea Natalie)

Before androgynous fashions became popular, many femmes were the breadwinners in their homes because they could get jobs open to traditional-looking women, but they confronted the same public scorn when appearing in public with their butch lovers. Contrary to gender stereotyping, many femmes were and are aggressive, strong women who take responsibility for actively seeking the sexual and social partner they desire.

Particularly in the fifties and sixties, the butch-femme community became the public face of lesbianism when its members formed bar communities across the country. In earlier decades, butch-femme communities were tightly knit, made up of couples who, in some cases, had longstanding relationships. Exhibiting traits of feminism before the seventies, butch-femme working-class women lived without the financial and social securities of the heterosexual world. Younger butches were often initiated into the community by older, more experienced women who passed on the rituals of dress, attitude, and erotic behavior.

Bars were the social background for many working-class butch-femme communities, and it was in their dimly lit interiors that butches and femmes could perfect their styles and find each other. In the fifties, sexual and social tension often erupted into fights and many butches felt they had to be tough to protect themselves and their women, not just in bars, but on the streets as well.

With the surge of lesbian feminism in the early seventies, butch-femme women were often ridiculed and ostracized because of their seeming adherence to heterosexual role playing. In the eighties, however, a new understanding of the historical and sexual-social importance of butch-femme women and communities began to emerge. Controversy still exists about the value of this lesbian way of loving and living, however. The American lesbian community is now marked by a wide range of relational styles: Butch-femme is just one of the ways to love, but the butch-femme community carries with it the heritage of being the first publicly visible lesbian community.

— **JOAN NESTLE, REPRINTED FROM** THE ENCYCLOPEDIA OF HOMOSEXUALITY

THE HARLEM RENAISSANCE

During the 1920s and early 1930's, what has come to be known as the Harlem Renaissance reshaped and celebrated African American culture. Often ignored, however, is the incredible contribution that the Harlem Renaissance has made to lesbian and gay community and culture.

Hopeful for social progress and new possibilities, many young and progressive African Americans flocked to Harlem, a mecca for these self-defined "New Negroes." Harlem became the worldwide center for African American jazz, literature, and the visual arts, and a place known for a bohemian, decadent nightlife.

It was within the arts and nightclub scenes of Harlem that lesbian and gay life was most openly explored and expressed. For African American and white homosexuals alike, Harlem provided a particular kind of freedom, and saw an early formation of a self-aware lesbian and gay community in the United States.

The Harlem Renaissance

Forming a Queer Consciousness Through the Blues

Many lesbians, gay men, and bisexuals, Black and white together, developed a tangible if tentative collective identity in New York during the 1920s and 1930s. The Harlem Renaissance, long celebrated in African American history for its rejuvenation of an oppressed people's culture, art, literature, and especially music, also served as a queer renaissance within a renaissance.

After World War I created a growth in industrial production in the northern United States, great numbers of Blacks migrated north from southern rural areas to fill factory jobs that were opening up for them. By the 1920s, large African American communities had formed in cities across the north, most notably in Detroit, Chicago, and Buffalo. Of these communities, however, New York's Harlem was by far the biggest and brightest, a subcity with Black residents in charge of every aspect of their community.

The 1920s and 1930s are also known as the Jazz Age. This music radiated the Harlem social sensibility regarding sex and sexuality. Some of the legends of the blues—Bessie Smith, Ethel Waters, Gladys Bentley, and Ma Rainey, to name a few—played integral roles in shaping Harlem's musical and sexual subcultures. These singers were not only long on talent and sass, they also lived openly bisexual and lesbian lives.

The whole of the Black experience in America—poverty, racism, love, hate, homesickness, and loneliness—is reflected in the blues, where life's too rough to limit one's possibilities for happiness. The blues, and the blues community, accepted sexuality in all its manifestations. The blues reflected a certain toleration for bi- and homosexuality in antiestablishment Harlem. Many blues artists took full advantage of this situation.

Gladys Bentley was perhaps the brassiest of her fellow blues singin' queers. Weighing 250 to 300 pounds, this dark, imposing woman with the masculine voice and white tuxedo lit up the famous Harry Hansberry's Clam House, where she often gigged as a featured performer. The smoky nightclub on 133rd Street got even smokier when Gladys was at the piano, belting out familiar tunes peppered with saucy, sometimes downright obscene, new lyrics. Bentley, who was bisexual, profited from her role as a "male impersonator" and played up the stereotypical "bull-diker" image people flocked to Harlem to see. Regular clubgoers and celebrities alike were her fans. The crowning jewel in her lesbianism came in the form of

DID YOU KNOW...

During a "pansy" craze in New York in the 1930s, straight couples would attend drag balls and flock to cabaret acts with female impersonators. According to George Chauncey in *Gay New York*, "If whites were intrigued by the 'primitivism' of black culture [in Harlem], heterosexuals were equally intrigued by the 'perversity' of gay culture."

a civil ceremony performed in New Jersey, where Bentley married another woman.

Known as the "Mother of the Blues," Ma Rainey was another Black lesbian singer with an attitude. In her famous song "Prove It On Me," Rainey sings:

Went out last night with a crowd of my friends,
They must have been women 'cause I don't like no men
They say I do it, ain't nobody caught me,
They sure got to prove it on me . . .

Prior to recording the song, Rainey proved it on herself in 1925 when she was arrested for throwing a dyke orgy at her flat, featuring some hot numbers from her all-female chorus. The incident also proved to be financially lucrative in light of the "scandal" that followed. "Prove It On Me," advertised with a picture of a squat, dark woman (a striking resemblance to Rainey herself), decked out in full male drag chatting up two femme flappers, skyrocketed record sales. Ma Rainey defended her lesbian experiences with a ferocity.

The avenues through which these extraordinary women plied their trade were not limited to Harlem's public nightspots. The blues, jazz, and dancing (as well as some fabulous bootleg booze) were regular fixtures at rent parties, private affairs to raise money for rent when times were tight. Rent parties were the ideal place for lesbians and gay men to mingle in relative safety, which they did with relish. Bessie Smith sang about one such party in "Gimme a Pigfoot and a Bottle of Beer." Harlem rent parties garnered a reputation well outside the city for their Babylonian abandon, as examples of the freer pathways to exploring sexual alternatives expressed in the music of the era.

Just as both queer men and women participated actively in rent parties, both male and female queerness was celebrated in the blues. Though the ladies grabbed a majority of the blues spotlights singing about each other, male singers got into the act as well, and thrived. Women and men sang about themselves and each other. George Hanna performed many a gender-bending tune, perhaps the most famous of which is "The Boy in the Boat," an ode to the joys of woman-to-woman encounters:

Lots of these dames had nothin' to do.
Uncle Sam thought he'd give 'em a fightin' chance.
Packed up all the men and sent 'em to France,
Sent 'em over there for the Germans to hunt,
Left all the women at home to try out all their new stunts.
You think I'm lyin', just ask Tack Ann
Took many a broad from many a man. . . .

"Freakish Blues" is another song in which George Hanna blurs the lines of sexual boundaries in much more explicit terms.

A cursory glance at some blues lyrics may not fill one with the greatest sense of queer positivity. "Sissy Man Blues," a song recorded by a variety of male vocalists, insists: "if you can't bring me a woman, bring me a sissy man." Ma Rainey wrote about her husband's homosexual exploits with a queer called "Miss Kate."

A deeper look reveals that though some songs poke fun at and even question some aspects of queerdom, none of them are written with any real contempt toward homosexuality. Rumored to have been initiated into "the Life" by friend and mentor Ma Rainey, singer Bessie Smith's lesbian pursuits were well documented, although she was married to a man. In addition, the women in her mid-1920s show "Harlem Frolics" were known for getting involved with each other. When it came to learning women-loving ways, Smith had a front-line education.

The blues pokes fun and questions most things, typically shrugging its shoulders in the end and saying, "Oh well, that's just the way it is." Blues singers are like that kid in grade school who pulled your ponytails but ran from you if you approached—they teased you if they thought you were groovy. The blues helped lesbians, gay men, and bisexuals not only accept themselves but turn around and make fun of themselves as well. There are few more distinctively queer characteristics or stronger gay weapons of modern life than an ironic sense of humor.

— **ARWYN MOORE**

DID YOU KNOW...

Bruce Nugent's "Smoke, Lilies, and Jade!" was the first published story on homosexual love written by an African American; it was published in the magazine *FIRE!* in 1926. The following is an excerpt:

"Alex turned in his doorway . . . up the stairs and the stranger waited for him to light the room . . . no need for words . . . they had always known each other . . . as they undressed by the blue dawn . . . Alex knew he had never seen a more perfect being . . . his body was all symmetry and music. . . . Alex called him Beauty. . . . Long they lay . . . blowing smoke and exchanging thoughts . . . and Alex swallowed with difficulty . . . he felt a glow of tremor . . . and they talked and . . . slept."

Langston Hughes at his typewriter in an undated photo. (Bettmann Archives)

Six Reasons Why Langston Hughes Couldn't Have Been Gay

Langston Hughes was widely regarded by contemporaries as gay. But his chief biographer, Arnold Rampersad, devotes much space to "proving" that Hughes wasn't, despite the poet's having shown no particular love interest in women, and the fact that he was often seen running around with effeminate and pretty young men. Rampersad's reasons:

1. Hughes couldn't have been gay because he was not effeminate.
2. Hughes couldn't have been gay because he didn't hate women.
3. Hughes couldn't have been gay because, even though most of his close friends were, he apparently didn't have sex with them, or admit to them if he was gay, though he admitted having sex once with a sailor.
4. He apparently didn't do the gay bar scene.
5. He wrote on gay themes only occasionally.
6. When Hughes shipped out in the Merchant Marine to the coast of Africa, and the white sailors brought two local boys on board for a gangbang, Hughes protested instead of joining the fun, as, Rampersad asserts, any gay man obviously would have done.

Convinced?

You make the call.

— JIM KEPNER

White Folks "Slumming" in Harlem

Accompanying the widespread popularity of Harlem's decadent parties, balls, and music came what historian Lillian Faderman calls the "sexual colonialism" of Harlem—white, largely middle-class heterosexuals, lesbians, and gay men streaming uptown to participate in what they perceived as Harlem's free-for-all atmosphere. In Harlem, they felt as though they could escape the restrictive societal norms imposed on them by colleagues and family. Homosexual experiences were the height of taboo, and they could have a taste of that as well in Harlem. The Cotton Club and the Clam House were heavily frequented by white thrill-seekers, anxious to titillate their repressed desires with bootleg liquor, marijuana dens, and peep shows.

For bi- and homosexual whites, however, Harlem represented more than just an exotic place where they could play all night and escape in the morning. Many felt as though they could, to a degree, relate to African Americans, likening their experiences with bigotry in mainstream society to the oppression of racism. A tenuous bond could be formed between the white queers and the Blacks of Harlem, as both sides knew the sting of prejudice. In Blair Niles's book *Strange Brother,* the author speaks through one of his characters: "In Harlem I found courage and joy and tolerance. I can be myself there. . . . They know all about me and I don't have to lie."

Without doubt, the white upper class exploited Harlem to a degree in those glory days. It is a compromise made by any area that relies somewhat on tourism for income. Wealthy white patrons introduced the Harlem Renaissance culture to the masses, resulting in varying levels of misrepresentation.

On the other hand, the whites who went to Harlem for sexual freedom were participants in Black queer culture. They danced in Black clubs, read Black literature, purchased Black art, and, perhaps above all, listened to Black music. With the aid of the blues, both white and Black lesbians, gay men, and bisexuals were able to develop a queer consciousness together, in part because the music and the performers they enjoyed provided the means to recognize and validate themselves with a homosexual identity more concrete than it had ever been before in American history.

— **ARWYN MOORE**

GATHERING PLACES

For well over half of the twentieth century, the constitutionally guaranteed right to associate freely was denied to lesbians and gay men. Lesbian and gay men who sought out public social interaction risked harassment, arrest, and the potential loss of family, friends, and careers.

DID YOU KNOW...

Over the course of 1892, police arrested eighteen men for engaging in oral sex in Washington, D.C.'s Lafayette Park.

Yet men who loved other men and women who loved other women did meet: More was at stake than simply having a drink at a local watering hole or finding sexual gratification in a public bathroom. Finding other homosexuals meant ending the isolation, if only for a short while, and discovering a community that validated one's sexuality. Because traditional gathering places were simply not accessible to them, these courageous gay people sought out, created, and discovered innovative new spaces to congregate for friendship, love, and sex.

This section explores the many places gay men and lesbians carved out as safe spaces of their own long before gay liberation. The variety of locales bears testimony to the innovation of gay men and lesbians in their time.

Cruising at the YMCA

Cruising at the YMCA has been celebrated in painting—as in a 1933 canvas *YMCA Locker Room* by Paul Cadmus—in literature—as in the 1920s gay novel *The Scarlet Pansy*—and in song—as in the popular 1970s Village People song "YMCA." The ambiguity and the campiness of the Village People's song speak to the gay male experience in America, but the song's lyrics also uncannily reflect the YMCA's 150-year-old mission to help urban young men help themselves. Talk of anonymous, public sex at the YMCA often provokes laughter partly because most people find the thought of men having sex with each other incongruous with the "C" in the Young Men's Christian Association. But the Christian mission of the YMCA and the presence of cruising there have evolved together for at least the last hundred years, maybe longer.

YMCA gyms, locker rooms, and dormitories offered public spaces where men had easy physical access to each other. The Christian reputation of the YMCA protected cruisers from the police harassment and gay-bashing that were a threat in other public urban spaces. The YMCA's pioneering work in American physical culture starting in the 1880s made the YMCA a place where male physical beauty could be openly contemplated. The Christian mission of the YMCA was not only a great cover for men in the closet, but it may also have been easier for men burdened with internalized homophobia to frequent a potential cruising area if that place was Christian. Finally, the images of the kinds of men at the YMCA—"clean-cut" youth, working-class men, and fresh farm boys—attracted men who were interested in connecting sexually with "real" (i.e., straight) men. The YMCA was often a first stop for young men moving from the country to the city, and the YMCA introduced many rural young men to the urban gay subculture.

Wayne Flottman grew up in southeastern Kansas and went to the YMCA for the first time in 1958 in Denver, Colorado. "I was somewhat naive about what went on there," he recalled, though his first night there he saw "some guy sitting in an open window totally nude," which led to his first YMCA sexual encounter. Martin Block recalled a "police friend" in the 1940s who went to the YMCA for sex because his fellow police officers never raided it. He knew a gay couple in the 1930s who had cruised at the YMCA in the 1890s. YMCA ministers and leaders also participated in the cruising scene. One ordained minister said he first heard about the sex scene at the YMCA from other seminarians in the 1950s. Donald Vining's diary confirmed what many gay men had long suspected: that YMCA desk staffs were often completely infiltrated by gay men. But being gay was not prerequisite for cruising at the Y. "Most of the men I had sex with [at the Y]," recalled one interviewee, "considered themselves completely straight."

Cruising at the YMCA has changed since the 1970s, transformed in part by the rise of the gay movement, in part by AIDS. But without a doubt, it played a key role in

DID YOU KNOW...

Since gay and lesbian people have often found each other by frequenting the local watering hole, homophobes in some communities have invented strange laws to keep us invisible. For example, in Virginia for many years it was illegal to serve alcohol to a homosexual, making gay bars difficult to operate. This predicament led to the establishment of speakeasies where lesbians or gay men would bring their own alcohol to a designated place and have dances or other social events.

the emergence of gay communities and identities in American cities, and in the memories of the many gay men for whom it lived up to its reputation as—in the words of gay author Sam Steward—"the biggest Christian whorehouse in the world."

– **JOHN D. WRATHALL**

Gay Beach, 1958

I hadn't gone near a gay beach for years when Marty and I drove out last summer to one of California's most famous. It was a long pleasant drive out the Boulevard and it seemed that quite a few others were going our way—a red convertible with two sunbaked blondes; two sporty lesbians in an MG; a carload of screaming queens. . . .

We arrived early. "Look at that!" Marty said with a sweep of his bronzed arm. "Doesn't the sight of that crowd thrill you? Right out in the open, hundreds of our people, peacefully enjoying themselves in public.

"I often lie awake nights wondering how long it'll take our group to become aware of itself—its strength and its rights. But I hardly ever appreciate just how many of us there really are except when I come here. Except for a few minutes on the Boulevard after the bars close, this is the only place where we ever form 'a crowd,' and there's something exciting about seeing homosexuals as a crowd. I can't explain how it stirs me, but I think beaches like this are a part of our liberation."

It was the largest crowd of homosexuals I'd ever seen. I stood around, looking at the remarkably handsome bodies, the colorful beach togs, the posturings, the camping.

The United States has hundreds of miles of fine public beaches. I guess homosexuals like to go swimming as much as anyone else, and there is something about the beach that makes one want to discard the mask and give up the defensive pretense that is second nature with most homosexuals. There must be six or eight million homosexuals in this country, so it's not surprising that here and there—one narrow sliver of Miami Beach, another in Santa Monica, Laguna Beach, Provincetown, the

"Indiana dunes," and a few spots like Fire Island—a few cramped areas have come to be known as "gay beach," "faggot's beach," "queer alley," "bitch beach," etc. But in all the learned claptrap I've read by so-called authorities on homosexuality, I don't recall any realistic description of a gay beach. The "authorities" prefer the clammy atmosphere of the bathhouse or the clandestine bar.

The July 1958 cover of ONE *magazine provided a rare glimpse at gay recreational life in the fifties. (San Francisco Gay and Lesbian Historical Society)*

Ronnie Chaise, an angel-faced, willowy young bank clerk I met at the beach that summer, exploded one Sunday when a husky married couple and two noisy kids settled down near us, looked around a bit, then muttering about "damned queers taking over the place," picked up baggage and brats and headed for a more moral beach. Ronnie had just come, slim and dripping, out of the water and was settling down on his towel when he heard them. "Well, go somewhere else if you don't want to be contaminated," he howled. "You've got fifty miles of beach around here and this is all we've got. So disappear!"

Later, I suggested that he'd offended them—hardly good public relations.

"*I* offended *them*? *They* offended *us*. Why always put the blame on this side? They started it. We weren't doing anything to spoil their day, except existing. Let them go somewhere else. This is our beach. It's small and crowded, but it's ours."

"What claim do we have to it?" I goaded him. "The cops and the papers don't think it's ours. And those people had just as much right here as we have."

"Rights, hell. You have the rights you earn. So we don't have a spelled-out legal title to this hundred yards of sand, but neither do heterosexuals have a title to the rest, or any right to chase us off here, like the police try to do every once in a while. They've taken squatter's rights on the rest and we've taken squatter's rights on this. And if they don't want us 'contaminating' the rest of their beaches, then they'd better leave us alone here.

"Nobody told those people they couldn't spend the day here. They objected to us and left. But there are plenty of other heteros around here who mind their own business, or maybe even enjoy our company.

"We've got to establish our right to have our own little corner, and when guys like that accidentally stumble into it, we have to see they act decent or get out fast, or we won't even have this. Now come on, let's go out and plunk in the water. I want to get cooled off. I didn't come out here to talk politics."

A really nelly one was camping it up in a large crowd of bikini-clad youths nearby. I knew one of them, Billy Forsing, and Ronnie wanted an introduction, so we went over and joined them. I didn't hit it off too well. Like an importunate reporter, more concerned with analyzing the beach than enjoying it, I asked the nelly one if he thought it gave a very good impression to make such a display in public.

"Well, get this one!" one of the others shrilled, and most of the bunch quickly flounced off for a swim, leaving Ronnie and me with Billy and George, the nelly one. He turned on me like an angry cat. "You're darned right I camp it up out here. Why not? It's about time these yokels learned to face the fact that we exist. I'm tired of hiding it. I work in a prissy office where half the guys in the place are really belles, but they'd all faint dead away if anyone dropped a bobby pin. I come out here to let my hair down, and I let it down good. Anybody else out here is here for the same reason, or else they've come to see the show. Show they want—show they'll get—from me, at least." With that, he upped and did a quick imitation of a strip teaser saucily showing her backside to the audience, and ran off to join his friends.

Then Ronnie and I took off for one of the gay bars facing the beach—and those bars are different from any other gay bars I've ever seen; they're really a sort of extension of the beach—and then wandered down for a

"If I don't know a patron, I give him a warm glass routine. . . . When I serve the stranger, I reach behind me and get him a warm glass. The whole bar buzzes. Those who saw the action tell those who didn't. . . . The act of giving the warm glass says, 'I don't know this person. No one is to talk to him until I have a chance to find who sent him.' If someone is so interested that he defies me and talks to him, he, the regular, has bought his last beer in my place."

HELEN P. BRANSON
IN GAY BAR

look at bicep-pumpers that were exhibiting their rippling muscles farther down the beach. And that place in itself is something to write about . . . some other time.

— FRANK GOLOVITZ EXCERPTED FROM ONE MAGAZINE, JULY 1958

Anatomy of a Raid, 1967

There was nothing very unusual about the Yukon—nothing to make it stand out from dozens of other small gay bars. As in any neighborhood place, most of the customers during the week were regulars who lived nearby. The bar usually wasn't jammed until Friday and Saturday nights and for the Sunday afternoon "beer bust." Even then, it took only about thirty-five people to make a mob in the Yukon. So, as I say, there was nothing unusual about the place—that is, not until that Friday night near the end of March 1966.

On that fateful Friday, I had picked up my lover, Larry, when he got off work. We went to the Yukon and drank beer for an hour or so. Several friends we hadn't seen for a while wandered in, and it looked like it was going to be a good fun night. We went to dinner and got

DID YOU KNOW...

The oldest, continuous gay bar in the United States is The Double Header in Seattle, founded in 1934. It is still run by the same (straight) family.

"Jane Jones," a Los Angeles women's bar, circa 1942. (Courtesy Paris Poirier)

back to the bar by about 10:30. By then the place was crowded, and there was a lot of laughing and joking around. There were several people I hadn't seen before, but that, too, was normal on a crowded night.

At one point, about 12:30 A.M., Tommy [the bartender] was passing by and stopped to talk to me. After we talked a few minutes, he looked over my shoulder toward the door. I turned and saw several uniformed policemen coming in. One of them, whom we later referred to as Hooknose, yanked the jukebox cord and ordered the lights turned up. The other, who chewed gum steadily, just stood around.

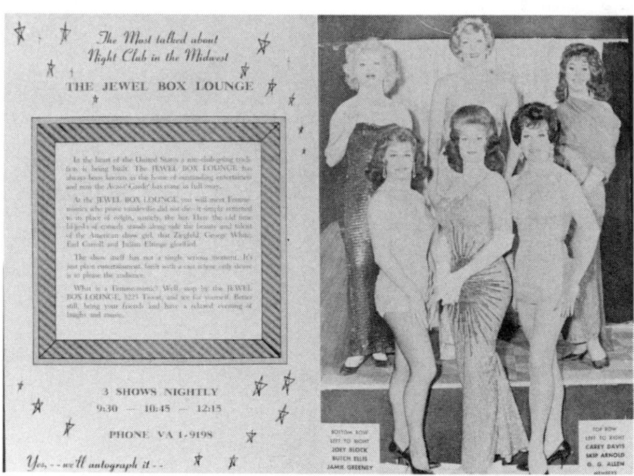

During the 1950s, the Jewel Box Lounge in Kansas City, Missouri, billed itself as "The Most Talked About Night Club in the Midwest." Drag performers, called "femme-mimics," performed musical and comedy numbers in classic cabaret style. (Courtesy of the Gerber/Hart Library and Archives, Chicago, IL)

Hooknose announced, "We're going to make a few arrests. Just stay where you are. Anyone who runs will be shot." No one ran. He went behind the bar, checked the license, then went about his fun task of picking victims.

I'm not sure where he started, but I think it was with two boys dressed in cowboy garb. He then picked George, who was standing at the bar to Larry's right. Each tap on the shoulder was punctuated with "You're under arrest." At one point he stopped to count on his fingers, seemingly figuring out how many people the cars outside could take. Then he went back to his grim business. He skipped over Larry. I felt the dreaded tap and turned. "You're under arrest."

Altogether they took twelve people that night—about a third of the patrons. At the Hollywood station, we assembled in a small room just inside the back door.

Gum Chewer, still chewing, advised us of our "rights." Then, as we passed through a door into the cell area, he pointed to each and said, "Lewd conduct." Then Gum Chewer called us out one at a time and talked to us for a minute or so. When my turn came, Gum Chewer pointed toward the cell. "See that boy in the blue shirt?" It was Lee; I've known him for years but never had sex with him. "You humped him," the Man said. I told him I didn't know what he was talking about.

That's pretty much the way it went for each one. Lee was accused of groping someone sitting next to him, and that guy was charged with rubbing legs with Lee. Tommy was supposed to have groped one of the "cowboys."

When I was booked, I answered the questions about name and address but balked at where I worked. "That's not necessary, is it?" I asked, not knowing what they were entitled to know. "You don't have to say a damn thing," he snapped back.

After that there was a lot of waiting in little rooms as the cops took mug shots and fingerprints of each person. I couldn't understand how some of the guys could joke around and laugh. I was worried about my job and personal matters that this arrest could make worse. One young Canadian boy was in a state of near-panic. He was so frightened that the cop trying to take his fingerprints was having a rough time. The cop threatened to knock him off his ass if he didn't relax, which just made things worse. The hassle went on for what seemed like a long time.

It was past 4 A.M. when I finally left the jail. I was irritated, tired, scared, and depressed. And I still am whenever I think about that night.

— DAVID S., AS TOLD TO DICK MICHAELS, EXCERPTED FROM THE ADVOCATE, JULY 1968

Rikki Streicher and the Lesbian Bar

When Rikki Streicher died in 1994 after a long struggle with cancer, San Francisco's mayor saw that the city flags flew at half-mast. As the founder and owner of Maud's Study, the longest-running women's bar in San Francisco, member of the board of directors of the Federation of Gay Games, and a local activist, Streicher had a profound effect on the lesbian

Rikki Streicher (Rink Foto, courtesy Mary Sager)

and gay communities not only in San Francisco, but nationally as well.

While her support of the Gay Games and lesbian and gay athletics was legendary, she is best known as the proprietor of Maud's and, later, of Amelia's, a popular women's dance club.

DID YOU KNOW...

Men have been gathering in bathhouses for sexual gratification and companionship for over a century. But exclusively gay bathhouses as we know them today did not exist until the 1950s. From the 1970s to the early 1980s, bathhouses enjoyed a boom, and by 1984 there were approximately 200 bathhouses in the United States.

Maud's, which opened in 1966 and quickly became a popular lesbian hangout in the Haight-Ashbury district, was in some ways typical of pre–gay liberation bars. More than just a bar, it was a safe place for lesbians to congregate, discuss their lives and issues of the day, play pool, and, of course, drink.

Gay and women's bars in the forties, fifties, and sixties were a central part of the lesbian community. For many lesbians, the bars were the only gathering place they had. The local women's bar was a home away from home, a group living room, and a community center. Patrons would have birthday, anniversary, and graduation parties at their favorite bar.

Unfortunately, there were very few exclusively lesbian bars, and most lesbians would gather at gay bars that were primarily patronized by gay men. Drag queens, sissies, and butch and femme women would all gather in the same places out of economic necessity, a sense of camaraderie, and a need for mutual protection.

In these bars, one might meet friends or sexual partners. Perhaps more significantly, the bars were a place where lesbians could celebrate their collective sexuality with each other and gay men. More than just being a place where men could love men and women could love women, the bars were an entire cultural underground that did not exist elsewhere. The lesbian and gay bar world was exciting, bohemian, and often a little grungy. Author Judy Grahn recalls entering a small, cramped gay bar in 1961 to the smell of both tobacco and marijuana smoke, and the sight of overflowing toilets.

Of course, going to a lesbian or gay bar before the late 1970s was not without significant risks. Police raids, harassment by men while walking to and from the bars, and risk of exposure were constant threats to lesbians who visited lesbian and gay watering holes. In many cities, men and women who were arrested during raids on gay bars would find their names and addresses printed in the local papers. Sometimes the police would even call the employers of those arrested and tell them the nature of the offense. Still, according to Phyllis Lyon in *Last Call at Maud's*, a documentary about Maud's and women's bar culture, "It was a lot of fun, in spite of the danger."

By the late 1970s and early 1980s, women's bars were giving way to a new generation of lesbian life. Many former bar regulars were becoming part of the Clean and Sober movement, and the younger crowd became attracted to the once-a-week "women's night" at larger, flashier gay discos. Neighborhood bars and places like Maud's found it increasingly difficult to make ends meet. As times have changed, exclusively lesbian bars are becoming an endangered species.

In 1989, Maud's Study closed its doors forever. For many San Francisco Bay Area lesbians, it was the end of an era. On closing, Rikki Streicher commented, "You can't go on forever. . . . Nothing does." Rikki Streicher, community leader, was sixty-eight when she died.

DID YOU KNOW...

The first homosexual-advocacy group in the United States was the Society for Human Rights, founded in 1924 by Henry Gerber. The Chicago organization lasted less than a year. In that time, they issued a mimeographed newsletter, "Friendship & Freedom." The group split after they were jailed when one member's wife reported them to a social worker, who called the police. Bailing out the nine members cost Gerber his life savings of two-hundred dollars, leaving him bitter that other homosexuals had failed to help him. The Gerber/Hart Library in Chicago is named in his honor.

EARLY ORGANIZATIONS

In the first half of the twentieth century, homosexual communities had virtually no organizations for political change. Ever since the 1950s, however, lesbians and gay men have experienced a continuous, dynamic, and growing political consciousness. Part of our understanding of ourselves as a body politic comes from the early organizations, whose members were not afraid to articulate the issues and debates around the need for social change. Generally, early organizations can be grouped into two distinct periods: homophile and gay liberation/lesbian-separatist.

Homophile organizations, born out of the efforts of gay men and lesbians during the fifties and sixties, were primarily interested in working from within the system to bring about changes in governmental laws and policies that oppressed gay people.

The three main national homophile organizations of the 1950s and 1960s were the Mattachine Society, ONE, Inc., and the Daughters of Bilitis. Gay liberation and lesbian-separatist groups came on the heels of the late sixties antiwar movement and the militant revolutionary movements of people of color. Rather than seeking to bring greater civil liberties to gay people through legislative change, gay liberation organizations sought to overhaul the entire governmental structure.

At the time of the Stonewall Riot in 1969, there were approximately four dozen gay political organizations. By the early seventies there were more than 400 such organizations around the country.

DID YOU KNOW...

One of the earliest gay and lesbian organizations was founded in San Francicso in 1965, by a group of people including Dorrwin Jones, Del Martin, and Phyllis Lyon. Called Citizens Alert, it was formed to report brutality against gays. The group remained active into the early 1970s.

The Mattachine Society

In 1950, a small group of leftist male homosexuals—including Harry Hay, Chuck Rowland and Bob Hull—formed the Mattachine Society in Los Angeles. The name means "little fool." Mattachines were male court jesters who dressed as women and performed songs and spiritual rites in thirteenth- and fourteenth-century Spain and France. Hay characterized the group as a "service and welfare organization devoted to the protection and improvement of society's androgynous minority." The society's charter called for "the solution of human sex behavior problems through various accepted techniques involving change of attitude and law."

In 1953, the organization was split by political differences and a conservative new camp forced out the original founders. The depoliticized group eventually folded in Los Angeles, but gained new members in San Francisco and elsewhere. The main publication of the group was *The Mattachine Review,* a monthly that began publication in 1955 and featured articles, book reviews, humor, fiction, criticism and opinion, news

Mattachine Society founder Harry Hay (right), with his lover, John Burnside, at the closing of the 1994 Gay Games in New York. (Dan Nicoletta)

reports, and commentary on legal, social, and cultural trends.

Although homosexual groups existed before this time, Mattachine was the first to establish a legally incorporated and long-lasting organization, and it represents the beginning of today's organized gay movement.

— EXCERPTED FROM "CIVIL RIGHTS/SOCIAL RITES: PRE-STONEWALL HOMOPHILE ORGANIZATIONS," FROM "100 YEARS BEFORE STONEWALL" EXHIBIT (UC BERKELEY, JUNE 1994)

"I can't tell you how deeply moved I am to be standing here in front of a hundred of my brothers and sisters determined at last to do something about the oppression we have suffered in silence for so many centuries. I look forward to the day when we will not gather behind closed doors, but will be out marching, arm-in-arm, singing militant songs, marching down all the main boulevards of America, and the world."

CHUCK ROWLAND, AT THE APRIL 1953 MATTACHINE SOCIETY REORGANIZING MEETING. AFTER THIS SPEECH, THE SHOCKED MEMBERSHIP REJECTED THE IDEOLOGY OF ITS MILITANT FOUNDERS AND VOTED OUT THE OLD GUARD.

ONE, Inc.

The founders of ONE, Inc., held their first meeting in Los Angeles in 1952 to "work for the betterment of the lives of homosexual men and women." The name was chosen from Thomas Carlyle's phrase "A mystic bond of brotherhood makes all men one." The group's goal was to "bring to light the lack of civil rights protections for the homosexual and to bring homosexuals and heterosexuals together in closer communication." Its endeavors included education, publishing, research, and social service.

The journal *One* was a leading voice in the homophile rights movement. It was sold to subscribers and from newsstands and contained articles, poetry, fiction, book reviews, and letters expressing "The Homosexual Viewpoint." The group successfully contested an attempt by the United States Post Office to declare their magazine obscene, thus securing the right of homosexuals to publish and mail homophile materials.

ONE Institute of Homophile Studies was formed in 1956 and began offering forums, public lectures, and classes. The organization maintained a large library of fiction, nonfiction, and periodicals, in several languages, devoted to homosexual questions. ONE also offered a book service that supplied books on homosexuality from publishers around the world.

— EXCERPTED FROM "CIVIL RIGHTS/SOCIAL RITES: PRE-STONEWALL HOMOPHILE ORGANIZATIONS," FROM "100 YEARS BEFORE STONEWALL" EXHIBIT (UC BERKELEY, JUNE 1994)

SIR (Society for Individual Rights)

DID YOU KNOW?

Since 1956, ONE, Inc. has held hundreds of "Homophile Studies" classes from its center in Los Angeles, fulfilling founder Dorr Legg's vision of a political organization for homosexuals that was also a place of learning and support.

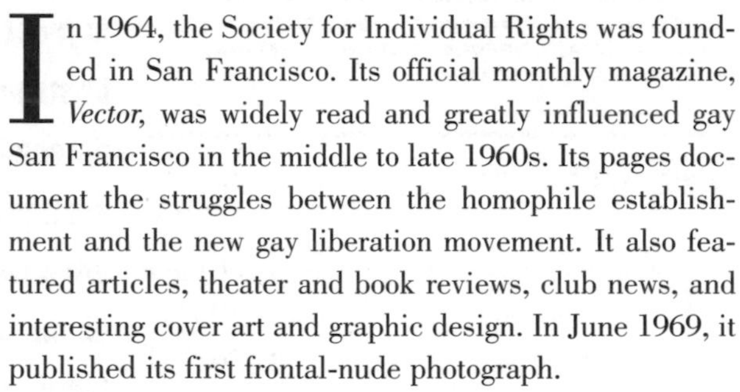

In 1964, the Society for Individual Rights was founded in San Francisco. Its official monthly magazine, *Vector*, was widely read and greatly influenced gay San Francisco in the middle to late 1960s. Its pages document the struggles between the homophile establishment and the new gay liberation movement. It also featured articles, theater and book reviews, club news, and interesting cover art and graphic design. In June 1969, it published its first frontal-nude photograph.

The group established a gay community center, providing for the first time a place where homosexuals could associate and organize beyond the bars and private homes. The SIR political committee hosted candidates' nights, and local politicians began to court gay voters. SIR also engaged in job counseling and legal referral, as well as organizing gay bowling.

— EXCERPTED FROM "CIVIL RIGHTS/SOCIAL RITES: PRE-STONEWALL HOMOPHILE ORGANIZATIONS," FROM "100 YEARS BEFORE STONEWALL" EXHIBIT (UC BERKELEY, JUNE 1994)

Daughters of Bilitis

The first national lesbian organization was established in September 1955 when a group of eight women, including Phyllis Lyon and Del Martin, met in San Francisco to form a club whose main purpose at the time was to offer lesbians a social alternative to the gay bar. In addition, they believed there was a need for a broad program of education for both lesbians and the public, as well as a need for legal reform and more adequate research than had yet taken place. The group called themselves the Daughters of Bilitis, from Pierre Louys's poem "Song of Bilitis," in which Bilitis is a lesbian on the isle of Lesbos with Sappho.

Daughters of Bilitis Founders Del Martin (left) and Phyllis Lyon during a moment of laughter in 1987. (© JEB)

In 1956 they started publishing a monthly magazine, *The Ladder*, which contained news items, fiction and poetry, book reviews, research reports, and political and social commentary. By 1958 chapters had been founded in Los Angeles and New York, and later in other cities. Other DOB activities included discussion groups, social events, research activity, and, later, participation with male homosexual groups and San Francisco's Council on Religion and the Homosexual in social, religious, and political activities.

— FROM "CIVIL RIGHTS/SOCIAL RITES: PRE-STONEWALL HOMOPHILE ORGANIZATIONS," FROM "100 YEARS BEFORE STONEWALL EXHIBIT" (UC BERKELEY, JUNE 1994)

Gay Liberation—(Way) Beyond Assimilation

Gay liberation was "born" in the late sixties. A series of protests against police harassment of gay people in Los Angeles, San Francisco, and New York culminated in June 1969 when, in the Stonewall Rebellion, gay people rioted for several nights against police oppression. During the next two years, gay liberation groups formed in dozens of cities. People met in bars, in classrooms, at people's houses, and in parks. Young queens and old bar dykes, lesbians and gay men who had been active in leftist politics since the Depression, lesbian factory workers living in small towns in the Midwest, and New Left dykes and fags who thought they had all the answers, came together and became the gay liberation movement.

Some of the lesbians and gay men of the early years of the movement had been inspired by the National Liberation Front of Vietnam and by revolutionary groups like the Black Panther Party. We did not demand an

DID YOU KNOW?

For four years, beginning in 1966, the North American Conference of Homophile Organizations (NACHO, pronounced NAY-CHO) met annually to socialize and strategize. At the first meeting, held in Kansas City, over thirty organizations were in attendance. By 1970, struggles between the older leaders and the young liberationists tore NACHO apart.

equal position within the fundamentally flawed American society. Rather, like the Black Liberation Movement, we demanded that straight society get its foot off our necks, so that we could create a world in which we would want to live. While the existing homophile civil rights organizations were asking that we be allowed to enter the armed forces, we were bringing gay liberation to the antiwar movement—whether the movement wanted it or not. Some Gay Liberation Front (GLF) activists took the position that all young men should claim to be gay to avoid the draft.

Gay people of color were central to the Stonewall Rebellion, and many people of color continued to participate in gay liberation despite insensitivity within the movement. In some cities, gay people of color formed separate groups. In 1971, Third World Gay Revolution began in New York; their sixteen-point program ends:

> *We want a new society—a revolutionary socialist society. We want liberation of humanity, free food, free shelter, free clothing, free transportation, free health care, free utilities, free education, free art for all. We want a society where the needs of the people come first. We believe that all people should share the labor and products of society, according to each one's needs and abilities, regardless of race, sex, age, or sexual preferences. We believe the land, technology, and the means of production belong to the people and must be shared by the people collectively for the liberation of all.*
>
> —*What We Want, What We Believe (1971)*

Gay liberation was also heavily influenced by the women's liberation movement. Most gay liberationists believe strongly that the roots of our oppression are tied to sexism, the systematic oppression of women, which is enforced through gender roles and the nuclear family. Throughout history, lesbians—the only women who are not tied into male approval and rewards—have always been active in the women's movement. In 1969 and 1970, we started to demand recognition and support.

Lesbians in the gay liberation movement often found the same sexism we had experienced from the straight left, and in the rest of our lives as well. Lesbians formed caucuses in some GLFs. In these caucuses and elsewhere, contradictions began to arise between gay-movement-identified lesbians (often calling themselves "gay women") and women's-movement-identified lesbians (often calling themselves "lesbian women"). However, as lesbians began to develop our own movement, history, and issues, those distinctions became less important. In cities as far apart as New York and Yellow Springs, Ohio, separate radical lesbian groups worked more or less closely with the men of the Gay Liberation Front. By 1973, lesbian separatist groups existed in most cities, although some lesbians remained in mixed groups.

Gay liberationists joined with other groups to march in a San Francisco counterculture demonstration in 1974. (Rink Foto)

In 1972, first in the lesbian journal *Spectre* and then in *Furies*, lesbians began to declare that we had to organize separately from both straight women and gay men in order to achieve liberation.

It is impossible to discuss here all of the events that made up the first wave of the gay liberation movement. We had demonstrations and mock weddings. We spoke in schools, churches, and parks. We had conferences and love-ins. We tried to get rid of racism, organized crime, and drink-pushing in lesbian and gay bars. We worked in collectives, ran free stores, set up health clinics, provided support for the Black Panther Party, and joined in the Revolutionary Peoples Constitutional Convention. There were dozens of underground papers, including *Body Politic, Gay Liberator, Lesbian Woman, Gay Sunshine, Come Out*, and the *Gay Community News*. We began radio shows and made movies and at least one group briefly took over a television station. We confronted the heterosexism of the left, psychiatry, the women's movement, and the church.

In the twenty-five years since Stonewall, many different lesbian and gay liberation voices have developed. But despite practical, strategic, and theoretical disagreements, certain common themes unite us: 1) Gay is *not* as good as straight—it is better. We bring to the world not only our love for people of the same sex, but also the cultures and strength we have developed in affirming and fighting for that love. We do not seek to assimilate or to imitate straight institutions like the nuclear family. 2) Gay people are not free in today's society. We are revolutionaries. We must create a society we want to live in. 3) Gay liberation is a broad movement. We can and must address all issues that impact our lives. We oppose war, poverty, environmental destruction, and the oppression of people based on race, sex, class, age, looks, physical ability, et cetera.

It is common to speak of the gay liberation movement as a historical period that the community has long since "outgrown" in favor of more assimilationist goals like joining the military or legalizing gay marriage. But as ACT UP, Queer Nation, and Lesbian Avengers have recently shown, our community is strongest when we are clearly and defiantly articulating a gay liberation vision. That vision, which puts our love at the center of our struggle, can never be denied.

— DEEG GOLD

The Gay Liberation Front—Revolutionary Queers

DO YOU THINK HOMOSEXUALS ARE REVOLTING? YOU BET YOUR SWEET ASS WE ARE!
We are going to make a place for ourselves in the revolutionary movement. We challenge the myths that are screwing up this society.
MEETING: Thursday, July 24, 6:30 P.M., at Alternate U—69 West 14th Street at Sixth Avenue.

—from the first GLF flier, 1969

Shortly after the Stonewall Riots in New York City, a group of young lesbians and gay men, frustrated by what they saw as milquetoast assimilation in the homophile movement, decided to break from business as usual. Influenced by the peace movement, the Black Panther Party, and the burgeoning women's movement, they formed the Gay Liberation Front (GLF).

At two meetings in the last weeks of July 1969, GLF was born. The start was bumpy, a sign of the turbulent nature of the revolutionaries involved. According to early GLF member Charles Pitts, at the second meeting "the chairmanship was constantly switched around because there was a rather sharp division in the meeting as to whether the purpose of the group should be self-enlightenment (as a kind of consciousness-raising-type thing) or integration immediately with other revolutionary or militant movements." By the end of the meeting, the group had developed a mission statement:

> *We are a revolutionary group of men and women formed with the realization that complete sexual liberation for all people cannot come about unless existing social institutions are abolished. We reject society's attempt to impose sexual roles and definitions of our nature. We are stepping outside these roles and simplistic myths. We are going to be who we are. At the same time, we are creating new social forms and relations, that is, relations based upon brotherhood, cooperation, human love, and uninhibited sexuality. Babylon has forced us to commit ourselves to one thing—revolution!*
>
> —*GLF Statement of Purpose, reprinted in* RAT, *August 12, 1969*

While many GLF members were either expatriates from Mattachine or members of Students for a Democratic Society (SDS) or other leftist groups, GLF represented more than just the radical gay left. As Donn Teal said in *The Gay Militants* (1971), "It appeals to a variety of young or young-minded American homosexuals whose sole common denominator was impatience."

As a result, the GLF organized a variety of events. From political actions and "zaps" to communal dinners, and from encounter-group consciousness-raising to gay and lesbian dances, the GLF had designs not on political reform, but on the creation of a whole new world: a world where "gay is good," sexism and racism were eradicated, and the military dismantled.

DID YOU KNOW...

In the 1950s, Jose Sarria, a fabulously political drag queen with a flair for biting humor, performed at San Francisco's Black Cat bar regularly on Sunday afternoons in revisionist operas that would comment on the injustices of the vice squad. At the end of the performance, he would lead his audiences of more than two hundred gay men in singing "God Save Us Nellie Queens" as undercover vice officers looked on.

Of course, theory and practice did not always coincide. Many of the GLF men, while progressive and outwardly supportive of women's liberation, were unable and/or unwilling to apply their beliefs to their actions. Many lesbians quickly became disenchanted with the GLF and began focusing more on lesbian-feminist organizations. And while there were a few people of color in GLF, the group was primarily white. By the end of 1969, the politics of the radical elements of the organization alienated more moderate members, who split off to form the Gay Activists Alliance.

But for many, the Gay Liberation Front, along with groups like the Committee for Homosexual Freedom (CHF), which had formed in the San Francisco Bay Area in the spring of 1969, served as the inspiration for a new generation of both personal and overtly political gay activism. Hundreds of gay liberation organizations sprang up in cities large and small. Gay and lesbian self-perceptions would never be the same.

— DON ROMESBURG

The Furies

In the early 1970s, lesbians were not chic. In fact, most people did not even know we existed. So it was revolutionary to say that women (as opposed to men) were primary, and that women-loving women—lesbians—could change the world. The Furies spoke and lived this understanding, and our impact moved beyond the short life of the collective (1971–1973) and the newspaper (1972–1973). The Furies put in print ideas that were previously unimaginable: "Women-identified Lesbianism is more than just a sexual preference, it is a political choice. It is political because relationships between men and women are essentially political, they involve power and dominance. Since the Lesbian actively rejects that relationship and chooses women, she defies the established political system." (Charlotte Bunch, "Lesbians in Revolt," *The Furies*, January 1972)

We named heterosexuality as the problem. We were radical and separatist. We were outlaws against the

Furies collective members in 1972 during a newsletter mailing gathering. (©JEB)

patriarchy. We understood lesbian life as feminist theory in action, including taking control of our bodies and exercising sexual self-determination. Because lesbian-feminists politicized lesbianism, we have been criticized for desexualizing lesbian identity. But we pushed lesbianism beyond being a question of either private sexual preference or equal civil rights into the realm of sexual politics and talk about sex. Later we would learn a lot more about the oppression, as well as the liberation, of openly claiming our sexuality as lesbians.

We were twelve white adults, ages eighteen to twenty-eight, and three children who lived and worked collectively in Washington, D.C. We said good-bye to the New Left and to gay liberation because they were male dominated, and to the women's movement because they were unwilling to make room for visible lesbians and lesbian issues. We hoped to create a political ideology based on our understanding of ourselves as lesbians and feminists, to build institutions to meet women's basic needs (like child care centers), and to change ourselves so we could stop oppressing others because of our own class and race privilege. Our rage at the way things were and our energy to transform them were both so burning hot that we knew we would succeed.

We did achieve our first goal. But the differences among us, primarily class, led to repeated painful conflicts that soon ended The Furies. In the next few years, former members went on to co-found Olivia Records, *Quest/a Feminist Quarterly,* Diana Press, Women in Distribution, and Moonforce Media, helping to break ground for the huge growth in lesbian and feminist business and culture that followed.

The Furies Collective: Ginny Berson, Joan E. Biren, Rita Mae Brown, Charlotte Bunch, Sharon Deevey, Helaine Harris, Susan Hathaway, Nancy Myron, Tasha Peterson, Coletta Reid, Lee Schwing, Jennifer Woodhul.

— JOAN E. BIREN

DID YOU KNOW...

San Francisco's preview to Stonewall was the 1965 New Year's Day charity drag ball for the Council on Religion and the Homosexual. As the night began, the police swarmed around California Hall, filmed people arriving at the event, and then attempted to enter the ballroom. They were stopped by two young lawyers guarding the door—Evander Smith and Herb Donaldson—who were arrested after telling the police that they could enter only with invitations or a warrant. The media recorded it as a night of shame for the police, and a judge ordered all charges dropped. It was a major victory in the struggle for civil rights.

EARLY DEMONSTRATIONS

Since the 1950s, gay men and lesbians have been acting up, acting out, and struggling for gay recognition and rights. It was not until the 1960s, however, that homophile groups and others began protesting against the injustices they faced in public arenas. The early demonstrations varied from peaceful picket lines and gay-ins in the mid-sixties to the famous Stonewall Riots of the first hours of June 28, 1969. By the early 1970s, protests included activist "zaps" and quick, media-savvy actions.

Stonewall holds a special place in gay mythology, as a symbol of the spirit of gay liberation when gay men and lesbians finally said, "Enough!" to the police brutality and the unjust treatment of us by society. Even before Stonewall, the gay movement was becoming more radicalized, inspired by the different revolutionary movements of the time. But it was Stonewall that gave gay liberationists the inspiration for immediate action.

Activism and demonstrations have continued to be an important part of gay and lesbian life, as we demand visibility in a society which, it seems, would often rather we just disappeared.

Seven Demonstrations Before Stonewall

1. The Cuban Labor Camp Protest (April 17, 1965): Craig Rodwell of the New York Mattachine Society (NYMS) and Jack Nichols of Mattachine Society,

Washington, D.C., staged protests in front of the United Nations and the White House after hearing that the Cuban government was putting known homosexuals into labor camps. Their picket signs read, "15 Million U.S. Homosexuals Protest Federal Treatment," and "Cuba's Government Persecutes Homosexuals. U.S. Government Beat Them to It."

Pickets protest the treatment of gay men and lesbians by the government. This photo was used as a cover for the October 1965 issue of The Ladder, *the first lesbian magazine in the United States. (Courtesy of Sherry Thomas)*

2. The Janus Sit-In (April and May 1965): After the manager of a Philadelphia restaurant refused to serve several women and men he thought were gay based on their "appearance," the Janus Society (a lesbian and gay organization) staged several sit-ins. At the first one, police arrested four people, including Clark Polak, Janus Society president.

3. The Government Protests of the Summer of 1965: To protest government treatment of homosexuals in military and government employment, members of the Eastern Conference of Homophile Organizations (ECHO) staged a series of picket lines at the Civil Service Commission building, the State Department, the Pentagon, the White House, and, on the Fourth of July, at Independence Hall in Philadelphia. Organizers excluded people who were underage or not dressed "properly" from marching. Seven men and three women picketed the White House in May; when ECHO groups protested in front of the White House again five months later, their numbers had risen to forty-five.

4. The Village Sip-Ins (April 1966): In New York City's Greenwich Village, after a flurry of gay bar close-downs and alcohol license revocations, Dick Leitsch, Craig Rodwell, and John Timmons of the New York Mattachine Society held "sip-ins" at Village bars to test the State Liquor Authority's policy against bars serving homosexuals. After being turned away from Julius, a gay bar, for being homosexual, they protested to the city's Human Rights Commission, and the policy was dismissed.

5. The Black Cat/New Faces Demonstration (January 1967): At New Year's Eve parties at the Black Cat and New Faces bars in the Silverlake district of Los Angeles, police conducted violent raids, seriously injuring several patrons and leaving a bartender in the hospital with a fractured skull and a ruptured spleen. Sixteen men were arrested and found guilty of lewd conduct. Soon after, several hundred gay men and women rallied on Sunset Boulevard in protest, and pickets marched in front of the Black Cat.

6. The Griffith Park Gay-In (March 1968): Griffith Park, in the middle of Los Angeles, was well known as a cruising area for men to have sex with each other. Police often would conduct sweeps of the area, entrapping and harassing gay men. On St. Patrick's Day, two drag queens who called themselves "The Princess" and "The Duchess" held a party at the park's Horseshoe Bend for all passers-by and area regulars. Over two hundred gay men ate cake, played volleyball (one report said the "Nells" played against the "Butches"), danced, and socialized. *The Advocate* called it Los Angeles's first major homosexual love-in.

7. The Patch Police Station Raid (August 1968): After police officers arrested two men and harassed the crowd at the Patch, a popular Los Angeles gay hotspot, bartender/activist Lee Glaze took to the stage and told the gay men there not to be intimidated. "It's not against the law to be a homosexual," he said, "and it's not a crime to be in a gay bar." To cheers and applause, he told a member of the audience, who owned a flower shop, that he would buy all his flowers, and then invited everyone to come with him to the police station to welcome out the two arrested. According to *The Advocate,* twenty-five patrons "marched into the waiting room carrying bouquets of gladioli, mums, daisies, carnations, and roses (but no pansies)." When the prisoners were released, they were showered with flowers and affection.

— **DON ROMESBURG**

Stonewall Revisited

The story of what really happened at Stonewall has yet to be distorted and embellished beyond the point of recognition, but it's well on its way. The myth gets a boost every time someone writes about how "heroic drag queens started a riot at the Stonewall Inn, which marked the beginning of the gay rights movement."

The Stonewall Inn was a nondescript two-story building at 53 Christopher Street, just off Sheridan Square in New York's Greenwich Village. You didn't just walk into the Stonewall, you had to be admitted. "You had to be identified by someone at the door who either assumed or knew you were of that life. I had worked at so many of the gay bars as a performer and hatcheck girl that I was often called to the door and asked, 'Do you know this person?' You see, at that time there was a lot of entrapment going on," said former hatcheck girl Dawn Hampton.

DID YOU KNOW...

In September 1970, Unidos, the first openly lesbian and gay Chicano/Chicana group in the United States, met for the first time, in Los Angeles. The group is still operating.

The Stonewall had a main bar, a dance floor, and a jukebox. There was another bar in back, with tables where people could sit. The late Morty Manford, who was a nineteen-year-old college student in 1969, recalled that the Stonewall was a dive. "It was my favorite place, but it was shabby, and the glasses they served the watered-down drinks in weren't particularly clean."

The Stonewall Inn attracted an eclectic crowd, from teenage college students like Morty Manford to conservatively dressed young men who stopped in with their dates after the theater or opera. There was also a sprinkling of young radicals, people like Ronnie Di Brienza, a twenty-six-year-old long-haired musician who didn't consider himself gay or straight: "I just consider myself a freak."

The Stonewall Inn was not a generally welcoming place for drag queens, although as Martin Duberman notes in *Stonewall*, "a few favored full-time transvestites, like Tiffany, Spanola Jerry, a hairdresser from Sheepshead Bay, and Tammy Novak . . . were allowed to enter Stonewall in drag."

The nightly crowd at the Stonewall Inn did include, however, quite a few men that Dick Leitsch described as the "fluffy sweater" type. "They were sissies, young effeminate guys, giggle girls." Leitsch, who was then executive director of the Mattachine Society, said you rarely saw people in full drag because "in those days you got busted for dressing up unless you were on your way to or from a licensed masquerade ball."

If men dressed as women were an uncommon sight, real women at the Stonewall Inn were rarer still. More often than not, when Dawn Hampton worked at the Stonewall she was the only woman there, yet she felt fully accepted. "A lot of the kids called me 'Mommie.'"

June 27, 1969, was not an average Friday night at the Stonewall Inn. Earlier that week, on Tuesday night, the police had raided the Stonewall "to gather evidence of illegal sale of alcohol."

As Ronnie Di Brienza later wrote in an article in *The East Village Other*: "On Wednesday and Thursday night, grumbling could be heard among the limp-wristed set. Predominantly, the theme was, 'this shit has got to stop!' . . . It used to be that a fag was happy to get slapped and chased home, as long as they didn't have to have their names splashed onto a court record. Now, times are a-changin'. Tuesday night was the last night for bullshit."

Morty Manford was at the Stonewall Inn when several plainclothes officers entered the bar around 2:00 A.M. on Saturday. "Whispers went around that the place was being raided. Suddenly, the lights were turned up, the doors were sealed, and all the patrons were held captive until the police decided what they were going to do. I was anxious, but I wasn't afraid. Everybody was anxious, not knowing whether we were going to be arrested or what was going to happen.

"It may have been ten or fifteen minutes later that we were all told to leave. We had to line up, and our identification was checked before we were freed. People who did not have identification or were underage and all transvestites were detained." Of the 200 people ejected from the Stonewall that night, 5 who were dressed as women were detained.

After being released from the bar, Morty watched and waited outside. "As some of the gays came out of the bar, they would take a bow, and their friends would cheer." It was a colorful scene, Morty recalled, but the tension began to grow. The crowd grew to more than 400 people.

Lucian Truscott IV, who was also at the Stonewall that night reporting for the *Village Voice,* wrote that the scene was initially festive: "Cheers would go up as favorites would emerge from the door, strike a pose, and swish by the detective with a 'Hello there, fella.' The stars were in their element. Wrists were limp, hair was primped, and reactions to the applause were classic. 'I gave them the gay power bit, and they loved it, girls.' 'Have you seen Maxine?' 'Where is my wife? I told her not to go far.'" Truscott reported that the mood changed once the paddy wagon arrived and three drag queens, the bartender, and the doorman were loaded inside. The crowd showered the police with boos and catcalls and "a cry went up to push the paddy wagon over, but it drove away before anything could happen. . . . The next person to come out was a dyke, and she put up a struggle." At this point Truscott reported that the police had trouble keeping "the dyke" in the patrol car. "Three times she slid out and tried to walk away. The last time a cop bodily heaved her in. The crowd shrieked, 'Police brutality!' 'Pigs!'"

The tension continued to rise. Truscott wrote: "Limp wrists were forgotten. Beer cans and bottles were heaved at the windows." Reporter Howard Smith retreated inside the bar along with Deputy Inspector Seymour Pine and the police officers who had conducted the raid. Once inside the bar, they bolted the heavy front door.

From his vantage point outside the bar, Morty remembered seeing someone throw a rock, which broke a window on the second floor of the Stonewall Inn building. "With the shattering of the glass, the crowd collectively exclaimed, 'Ooh.' It was a dramatic gesture of defiance. For me, there was a slight lancing of the festering wound of anger that had been building for so long over this kind of unfair harassment and prejudice. It wasn't my fault that many of the bars where I could meet other gay people were run by organized crime."

Inside the Stonewall, *Village Voice* reporter Howard Smith, who'd been accompanying the police, heard the shattering of glass, including at least one of the two large plate-glass windows on the first floor. The windows, which were painted black from the inside, were backed by plywood panels.

There was pounding at the door and people yelling. Smith wrote: "The door crashes open, beer cans and bottles hurtle in. . . . At that point the only uniformed cop among them gets hit with something under his eye. He hollers, and his hand comes away scarlet. . . . They are all suddenly furious. Three run out to see if they can scare the mob from the door. [Inspector Seymour] Pine leaps out into the crowd and drags a protester inside by the hair."

Di Brienza picks up the story: "A bunch of 'queens,' along with a few 'butch' members, grabbed a parking meter and began battering the entrance until the door swung open."

Inside, Smith and the police ducked as more debris was thrown in through the open door. In response, Smith wrote: "The detectives locate a fire hose, the idea being to ward off the madding crowd until reinforcements arrive." Lucian Truscott describes what happened next: "Several kids took the opportunity to cavort in the spray, and their momentary glee served to stave off what was rapidly becoming a full-scale attack."

Smith grew fearful as the tension escalated. "By now the mind's eye had forgotten the character of the mob; the sound filtering in doesn't suggest dancing faggots any more. It sounds like a powerful rage bent on vendetta. . . ." The crowd then heaved the uprooted parking meter through one of the plate-glass windows. The plywood behind the window gave.

Smith wrote: "It seems inevitable that the mob will pour in. A kind of tribal adrenaline rush bolsters all of us; they take out and check pistols. [Inspector] Pine places a few men on each side of the corridor leading away from the entrance. They aim unwavering at the door. . . . I hear, 'We'll shoot the first motherfucker that comes through the door!'" From outside the bar, Truscott recalled, "I heard several cries of, 'Let's get some gas.'"

A stream of liquid poured in through the broken window. Smith wrote: "A flaring match follows. Pine is not more than ten feet away [from the window]." Pine aimed his gun at the shadows framed by the window. But he didn't fire.

Smith wrote: "The sound of sirens coincides with the shoosh of flames where the lighter fluid was thrown. Later, Pine tells me he didn't shoot because he had heard the sirens in time and felt no need to kill someone if help was arriving. It was that close."

Reinforcements arrived, in the form of New York City's Tactical Police Force, and the streets were cleared in coordinated sweeps of the area. According to newspaper accounts in the days that followed, thirteen people were arrested that night and three police officers suffered minor injuries. No mention was made of civilian casualties.

The riot had ended by the time Vito Russo happened on the scene in front of the Stonewall, although people were still out on the sidewalks yelling at the police. He recalled, "I didn't get to see a lot of the hysteria that's been described in the press because I got there too late. I went to the little triangular park across the street and sat in a tree on a branch. I watched what was going on, but I didn't want to get involved. People were still throwing things, whatever they could find, mostly garbage. Then somebody came along and spray painted a message to the community on the front of Stonewall that this was our neighborhood, and we weren't going to let them take it away from us, that everybody should calm down and go home. But that's not the way it worked out, because there were constant confrontations for the next two nights."

Among gay people, both the organized gay community and those who remained on the sidelines, there was intense debate over how to respond to the riot. On one side were those who wanted the riots and mass protests to continue, and on the other were many who wanted an immediate end to the violence and public demonstrations. One fear among those who wanted peace restored was that the police would retaliate with increased bar raids, harassment, and arrests.

"It was inhumane, senseless bullshit. [The police] called us animals. We were the lowest scum of the Earth at that time. . . . Suddenly, the nickels, dimes, pennies, and quarters started flying. I threw quarters and pennies and whatnot. 'You already got the payoff, and here's some more!' To be there was so beautiful. It was so exciting. I said, 'Well, great, now it's my time. I'm out here being a revolutionary for everybody else, and now it's time to do my thing for my own people."

SYLVIA RIVERA,
DRAG QUEEN AT THE
STONEWALL RIOT

Saturday night, the crowds gathered once again in front of the Stonewall, and this time they included "onlookers, Eastsiders, and rough street people."

But the majority of the hundreds of people who crowded onto Christopher Street and jammed Sheridan Square were young gay men. And despite some nasty confrontations with the police, there was plenty of humor and camp left over from the previous night. As Lucian Truscott reported: "Friday night's crowd had returned and was being led in 'gay power' cheers by a group of gay cheerleaders. 'We are the Stonewall girls/We wear our hair in curls/We have no underwear/We show our pubic hairs!' . . . Hand-holding, kissing, and posing accented each of the cheers with a homosexual liberation that had appeared only fleetingly on the street before."

Not every gay person was thrilled with the very public displays of gay camp and freely expressed same-sex affection. As Truscott observed, "Older boys had strained looks on their faces and talked in concerned whispers as they watched the up-and-coming generation take being gay and flaunt it before the masses."

DID YOU KNOW?

At Columbia University in 1970, radical gay and lesbian activists exposed Kate Millet, an intellectual leader of the feminist movement, as a lesbian, causing many heterosexual feminists to reconsider their attitudes toward lesbians.

The violent challenge to police harassment and repression at the Stonewall Inn was more than enough to earn the riot a place in gay American history. For a variety of reasons, the riot was a key turning point in the gay rights struggle across the country. It led to a virtual explosion of activity and organizing, primarily among young people, in the months and years immediately following.

— ERIC MARCUS

Operation Liberation

In 1972, a handful of courageous Boston lesbians decided to "liberate" a local straight bar for all women by announcing their lesbian presence. Following is a narrative of that event.

We'd been thinking it would be a good idea to liberate a local bar for women to go to, something that would be different from the expensive institutionalized gay bars. Finally we picked this place that we had an idea was fairly hip, and about fifteen of us went over one Tuesday night. The trouble was, it turned out that our impressions had been slightly off; the clientele that night turned out to consist of a few couples and a number of single men, including some really tough-looking motorcycle gang–type characters. These last in particular really did not dig us at all: As we were dancing, they stood around threateningly, making comments like, "You're disgusting," and "What you need is some prick." Some of them aggressively asked us to dance. Then one of them poured some beer on one of us. She turned round and spilled the rest of his beer into his lap, and others of us came to her support and spilled beer on another guy, who, it turned out, hadn't actually been being offensive at all. Someone took out a gun and the atmosphere became fairly tense; a number of us decided to leave.

The rest stayed on, dancing in a rather nervous circle that kept being closed in on by three ugly-looking characters, who continued to make insulting comments. Then this woman who had been sitting at the bar and who seemed to have some official connection with the place went up to them and told them to stop harassing us, we weren't doing them any harm, and they left at her request. When we ourselves split half an hour later we went up and thanked her, and she spoke sympathetically about people who had no place to go. Also, the guy who had been the innocent victim of the beer-throwing came and spoke to us, saying he really admired our guts, and as we walked out the door the barman said, "See you again."

So the action was, in those terms, a success; it gave us some sense of our strength, as well as of our fears and weaknesses. We plan to go back there again and work toward making it a more comfortable place for us.

— **EXCERPTED FROM** LAVENDER VISION, **1972**

HOMOPHILE MAGAZINES

In many ways, the gay and lesbian movement has been as much about words as it has been about action. From the first typewritten newsletters in the 1940s to the glossies of today, gay men and women have used the printed word to communicate the ideas and aspirations of a people to a wider audience.

In 1947, a young secretary in Los Angeles, who took the name Lisa Ben, put her ideas about homosexuality down on paper in her own "magazine," *Vice Versa,* produced using carbon paper on her office typewriter. She was able to produce only ten copies of each edition. Ben was not part of an organized movement.

It was the burgeoning homophile movement in the early fifties that spawned what has been termed the "homophile press." These publications, whose circulation varied from 500 to 5,000, served to unite gay people and fledgling organizations across the country. Along with the organizations and bars, the presses were a critical part of the kinetic energy that shaped the early movement.

Vice Versa—in Explanation

Here are a few excerpts from *Vice Versa.*

Have you ever stopped to enumerate the many different publications to be found on the average newsstands? There are publications for a variety of races and creeds. A wide selection of fiction is available for those who like mysteries, westerns, science fiction, or romantic stories. For those who prefer fact to fiction, a variety of publications on politics, world affairs, economics, and sports are available. And newsstands fairly groan with the weight of hobby and miscellaneous publications devoted to subjects ranging from radio, engineering, gardening, home improvements, and sailing, to travel, fashions, and health.

Yet, there is one kind of publication that would, I am sure, have a great appeal to a definite group. Such a publication has never appeared on the stands. Newsstands carrying the crudest kind of magazines or pictorial pamphlets appealing to the vulgar would find themselves severely censured were they to display this other type of publication. Why? Because Society decrees it thus.

Hence the appearance of *Vice Versa*, a magazine dedicated, in all seriousness, to those of us who will never quite be able to adapt ourselves to the iron-bound rules of Convention. The circulation of this publication, under the circumstances, must be very limited, going only to those who, it is felt, will genuinely enjoy such a magazine. This little publication, at present free of charge, will be published whenever there is enough suitable material to warrant the appearance of another edition.

Perhaps even *Vice Versa* might be the forerunner of better magazines dedicated to the Third Sex that, in some future time, might take their rightful place on the newsstands beside other publications, to be available openly and without restriction to those who wish to read them.

• • • •

The following is a slightly altered version of a chain letter which has been tickling the funny-bones of quite a few people lately. Here it is adapted to apply to "us folks":

Dear Friend:

This chain letter was started in Hollywood in the hope of bringing relief and happiness to tired lesbians. Unlike most chain letters, this one does not cost you any money. Simply send a copy of this letter to five equally tired lesbian friends. Then bundle up your girl-friend and send her to the dyke at the top of the list.

When your name comes to the top of the list, you will receive 17,178 women. Have faith—do not break the chain. One butch broke it and got her own fluff back.

Sincerely,
Diana Frederics
"Tess" Wheeler
Tommy Williams
Radclyffe Hall
Beverly Shaw
Stephen Gordon

— LISA BEN (EXCERPTED FROM *VICE VERSA*, 1947)

"I, for one, am glad I am homosexual, glad to be spared the deadly monotonies of marital wranglings, or worse still the marshmallow puffiness of marital bliss. I consider myself fortunate in having seen through the deadly deceptions of the procreative cycle—devouring energies, talents, ambition, and individual achievement, all in the name of that great communal juggernaut The Family, before which Church and State so abjectly debase themselves."

ONE MAGAZINE, 1954

The Homophile Press

The Homophile Movement of the 1950s and 1960s spawned a handful of newsletters and magazines, with names like *Tangents, Citizens News, Vector, Town Talk, LCE News,* and the *P.R.I.D.E. Newsletter,* which later developed into *The Advocate.* The three major homophile magazines, however, were *One* magazine, which had an unapologetic voice about being gay; *The Ladder,* a monthly by and for lesbians; and the

Mattachine Review, the magazine affiliated with an early homophile group, the Mattachine Society. The organizations publishing these papers felt that homosexual rights had more to do with shaping the behavior of gay men and lesbians to better fit into society's restrictions and to keep from getting arrested and losing their jobs—than with changing public attitudes toward that behavior. Still, the fact that such organizations existed at all is commendable.

Homophile magazines provide an up-close-and-personal view of what it was like to be a "deviant" during those early days of the movement. For many gay men and lesbians, the magazines were a kind of survival manual, providing a lifeline to a community otherwise disparate. Articles addressed everything from what to do in case of a police raid to providing news on books being published about homosexuality, and from political essay to advice for the lovelorn.

Sometimes those categories overlapped. Many articles reflected a homophile appeal for "respectability." They criticized public sex as an act of self-hatred, and often attempted to dissuade people from going to homosexual bars. In one article, using the case of "Janet" the lonely lesbian who was dissatisfied with the "bar crowd," *One* pleaded for the establishment of lesbian social centers as an alternative to bars. Acknowledging the impracticability of a "lesbian center," the magazine nevertheless urged the Janets of the world to investigate the idea: "We hope for the sake of Janet—and all the Janets—that they try, for without some effort on their part, Janet and other homosexual women will never have the opportunity to meet the kind of people with whom they want to associate."

Just exactly what kind of people are those whom Janet wants to meet? According to *One,* they must look "safe." That is, they mustn't look too homosexual: "Look around you—at the girl with the close-cropped hair, fly-front pants, and oh so masculine voice and mannerisms (what's she trying to prove?) . . . at the boy with the rouged face, plucked eyebrows, and flailing arms (and he?); listen to some of the language and remarks; watch them on the streets and in the restaurants; listen to their voices, and watch the way they walk."

One also cautioned its readers, "In business, advertising is a great asset—in gay life it can be a thorn in your heart. . . . We don't have to broadcast! We know each other!"

The Ladder was especially nervous about lesbians who openly flaunted their sexuality. The magazine consistently admonished lesbians to cultivate "respectability," and that meant dressing and behaving in a manner "acceptable to society."

A vast majority of gay men and lesbians around the country weren't active in or in many cases even aware of the magazines and organizations. Many in the "bar culture" crowd and outside of the homophile movement saw the magazines as either too dogmatic and political or too conservative. The homophile movement was also distinctly white and middle class. Still, the homophile magazines are some of the few accounts we have by and for gay people at the time.

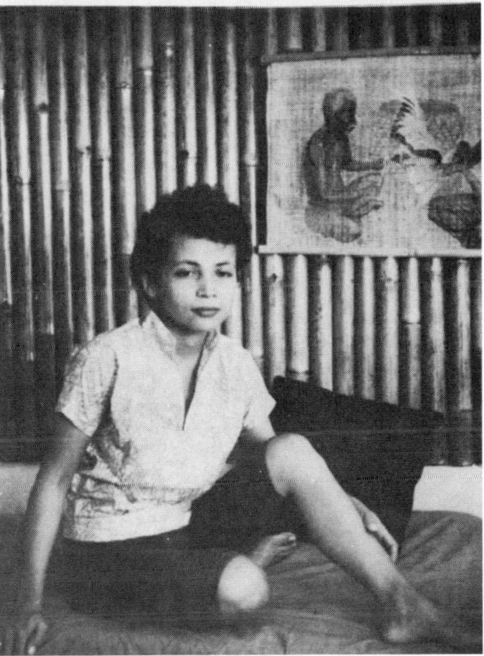

The October 1964 cover of The Ladder, *published by the Daughters of Bilitis. The first issue of* The Ladder *appeared in October 1956; the final issue appeared sixteen years later in the fall of 1972. (Courtesy of Sherry Thomas)*

Letters to the editor in particular are a rare record of how gay men and women of the era felt about and coped with being homosexual. Their feelings ran the gamut, from the positive: "In God's sight I feel sure that two people of the same sex are just as much married as a married man and woman if they pledge themselves to one another and are deeply in love"; to the not-so-positive: "Homosexuality is much more than just love between men: It's a rough and dirty road of shame and despair leading nowhere but to HELL. . . . I believe anyone wanting to be part of the Homophile Movement should at least be examined once by a psychiatrist or have had some treatment somewhere before he was twenty-one, for being homosexual."

The pages of these magazines chronicle the lives of gay men and women as they struggled to make a place for themselves in American society. Lesbian activist and author Joan Nestle offers a gentle interpretation of *The Ladder*'s anxiety about lesbian appearances: "The writing in *The Ladder* was bringing to the surface years of pain, opening a door on an intensely private experience, giving voice to an 'obscene' population in a decade of McCarthy witchhunts. To survive meant to take a public stance on societal cleanliness."

The homophile press withered as the more radical generation of gay and women's liberation spawned its own publications, which pioneered a politics of openness. Cautious and conservative as they may appear now, the homophile press nonetheless served as a forum for discussion and argument in the formative days of the gay and lesbian "community," and provided a place for homosexuals to begin to define their politics and culture.

— CYNTHIA SCOTT

Gay Liberation and Lesbian-Feminist Magazines and Newspapers

Along with the post-Stonewall explosion in gay organizations was an explosion in gay publishing. The following list represents just some of the gay liberation and lesbian-feminist periodicals founded between 1969 and 1972 (an asterisk denotes a lesbian-feminist periodical):

1969

Come Out (New York City)
Gay (New York City)
Gay Power (New York City)
Homosexual Renaissance (New York City)

1970

Feminary (Chapel Hill, NC) *
FREE (Fight Repression of Erotic Expression) Newsletter (Los Angeles)

Gay Dealer (Philadelphia)
Gay Flames (New York City)
Gay Liberator (Detroit)
Gay Sunshine (San Francisco)
Gay Youth's Gay Journal (New York City)
Sisters (San Francisco) *

1971
Fag Rag (San Francisco)
Focus (Boston) *
Gay Peoples Newsletter (Berkeley)
Gay Voice (Sacramento)
Lavender Vision (Boston)
Lavender Woman (Chicago) *
Lesbian Tide (Los Angeles) *
Mother (Stanford, CA) *
Spectre (Ann Arbor, MI) *

1972
Amazon Quarterly (Oakland, CA) *
Apostle (San Jose)
Echo of Sappho (Brooklyn) *
Faggotry (New York City)
The Furies (Washington, D.C.) *
Lesbians Fight Back (Philadelphia) *
New Life (Los Angeles)
Portcullis (Los Angeles) *
Tres Femmes (San Diego) *

DEVIANT MEDICINE

Beginning in the late nineteenth century, doctors in the United States seized upon European theories of the homosexual "deviant," drawing upon such German authors as Richard Krafft-Ebing and Karl Henrich Ulrichs. From that time forward, homosexuality was considered a disease by a considerable segment of the medical community. For decades to follow, homosexuals, both male and female, became the subjects of experimentation, stigmatization, and outright torture by the medical community.

It is often assumed that advancements in medicine create a better world for everyone; that discovering cures, identifying diseases, and locating psychological disorders is an impartial, unbiased

"At a time when those in the scientific and medical establishment regarded homosexuality as something to be cured . . . Baldwin believed that "everybody's journey is individual. If you fall in love with a boy, you fall in love with a boy. The fact that many Americans consider it a disease says more about them than it says about homosexuality."

FROM RANDALL KENAN'S JAMES BALDWIN

process toward a great, healthy society. No one knows better than lesbians and gay men how false this can be. In the last century, gay people have been accused by medical and psychological professionals of being psychopathic, hormonally imbalanced, sex-crazed, child-seducing, paranoid, masochistic, immature, and physically defective. Medicine, like all fields of study, is shaped in part by the biases of the people who study it, and the society in which they live. In this section, we illustrate both the ways in which doctors and psychologists have pathologized lesbians and gay men, and the success story of how we became "healthy" again.

Dr. Evelyn Hooker

Leading the Fight from Psychopathology to Liberation

"She never treated us like some strange tribe, so we told her things we never told anyone before."

—Christopher Isherwood on Dr. Evelyn Hooker

In post–World War II America, homosexuality was labeled a mental illness by the American psychiatric community, and believed by society in general to be a mental illness, psychopathology, criminal offense, and a sin. But, due largely to the efforts of Dr. Evelyn Hooker, that eventually changed.

"But what means the most to me, I think, is . . . if I went to a gay gathering of some kind, I was sure to have at least one person come up to me and say, 'I wanted to meet you because I wanted to tell you what you saved me from.' I'm thinking of a young woman who came up to me and said that when her parents discovered she was a lesbian, they put her in a psychiatric hospital. The standard procedure for treating homosexuals in that hospital was electroshock therapy. Her psychiatrist was familiar with my work, and he was able to keep them from giving it to her. She had tears streaming down her face as she told me this. I know that wherever I go, there are men and women for whom my little bit of work and my caring enough to do it has made an enormous difference in their lives."

DR. EVELYN HOOKER IN MAKING HISTORY

Dr. Hooker began her work in the late 1940s at the urging of a young gay man she had befriended in one of her courses and his friends. In 1953, she applied to the National Institute of Mental Health for a grant to study gay men. This was at the height of the McCarthy era, and homosexuals were one of the primary targets of the nation's hysteria. Therefore, just securing the government grant was a major accomplishment.

The final paper, presented to the American Psychological Association in 1956, was titled "The Adjustment of the Male Overt Homosexual." Her controversial and widely publicized findings were that gay men are as well adjusted as straight men.

It took another twenty years of work by Dr. Hooker and other psychologists, and the efforts of the early gay rights movement, but finally in 1973, the American Psychiatric Association dropped homosexuality from the *Diagnostic and Statistical Manual of Psychiatric Disorders,* its official list of mental diseases.

— FROM "100 YEARS BEFORE STONEWALL" EXHIBIT (UC BERKELEY, JUNE 1994)

CAN YOU BELIEVE IT?

Dr. H. C. Sharp of the Reformatory for Delinquent Boys in Jefferson, Indiana, performed several hundred vasectomies to remedy any number of deviant behaviors, including homosexuality, between 1899 and 1907. He claimed that the "patient becomes of a more sunny disposition, [and] advises his fellows to submit to the operation for their own good."

Thirteen Theories to "Cure" Homosexuality

Since the late nineteenth century doctors and religious leaders have been attempting to cure the desire for same-sex intimacy. The desire to "cure" homosexuality comes from societal discomfort with same-sex love rather than from any real pathology on the part of lesbians and gay men. Despite claims to the contrary, none of these "cures" work.

- **Prostitution Therapy** (late nineteenth century): Through sex with prostitutes, "inverted men" would experience co-gender sexual desire. Famous sexologist Havelock Ellis noted that "the treatment was usually interrupted by continual backsliding to homosexual practices, and sometimes this cure involved a venereal disorder."
- **Marriage Therapy** (late nineteenth century): When presented with the option of courting and marriage, the "deviant" would naturally go "straight." Dr. William

"The [homosexual] offender should be rendered incapable to a repetition of the offense, and the propagation of his kind should be inhibited in the interest of civilization and the well-being of future generations."

TEXAS DOCTOR F. C. DANIEL, ADVOCATE OF HOMOSEXUAL CASTRATION

Hammond, a New York medical researcher, prescribed a gay man "continuous association with virtuous women, and severe study of abstract studies (like math)."

- **Cauterization** (late nineteenth century): Dr. Hammond also suggested that homosexual patients be "cauterized [at] the nape of the neck and the lower dorsal and lumbar regions" every ten days.
- **Castration/Ovary Removal** (late nineteenth century): In a pre-Hitler world, the medical community did not consider castration particularly horrific. Aside from believing that removal of the testes would eliminate the sexual drive of the homosexual, many doctors also thought homosexuality to be hereditary.
- **Chastity** (late nineteenth century): If homosexuality could not be cured, then homosexuals had no moral choice but to remain chaste. Catholic doctor Marc-André Raffalovich confessed that "the tendencies of our time, particularly the prevalent contempt for religion, make chastity more difficult for everyone."
- **Hypnosis** (late nineteenth/early twentieth century): New Hampshire doctor John D. Quackenbos claimed that "unnatural passions for persons of the same sex"—like nymphomania, masturbation, and "gross impurity"—could be cured through hypnosis.
- **Aversion Therapy** (early to mid twentieth century): Reward heterosexual arousal and punish homosexual attraction, often through electric shock. In 1935, New York University's Dr. Louis Max said of a homosexual male patient that "intensities [of shock] considerably higher than those usually employed on human subjects definitely diminished the value of the stimulus for days after each experimental period."
- **Psychoanalysis** (early to mid twentieth century): With Freud came a whole new discussion of possible cures through a psychoanalytic approach. In the 1950s, Edmund Berger, M.D., spoke of homosexuality as a kind of "psychic masochism" in which the unconscious sets a person on a course of self-destruction. Find the cause, such as resentment toward a domineering mother, and you find the cure.

DID YOU KNOW...

Sigmund Freud did *not* consider homosexuality a mental illness. In responding to a worried mother, Freud wrote in 1935: "Homosexuality is assuredly no advantage, but it is nothing to be ashamed of, no vice, no degradation, it cannot be classified as an illness; we consider it to be a variation of the sexual development. Many highly respected individuals of ancient and modern times have been homosexuals, several of the greatest men among them (Plato, Michelangelo, Leonardo da Vinci, etc.). It is a great injustice to persecute homosexuality as a crime, and cruelty, too."

• **Radiation Treatment** (early to mid twentieth century): X-ray treatments were believed to reduce levels of promiscuous homosexual urges brought on by glandular hyperactivity. In 1933, New York doctor La Forest Potter lamented Oscar Wilde's being born too soon, because if he were still alive, "we could [have] subjected the overactive thymus to X-ray radiation, atrophied the gland, and suppressed the overactivity of its function."

• **Hormone Therapy** (mid twentieth century): If homosexual men are too effeminate and lesbians are too masculine, steroid treatments would theoretically butch up the boys and femme out the girls. Prolonged use also had effects such as sterility and cancer.

• **Lobotomy** (mid twentieth century): By cutting nerve fibers in the front of the brain, homosexual drives (indeed, most sexual and even emotional reaction capabilities) were eliminated. Lobotomies for homosexuality were performed until the 1950s in the U.S.

• **Psycho-Religious Therapy** (mid twentieth century): Religious doctors and therapists combined religious teachings with psychoanalysis to inspire heterosexuality. *Man on a Pendulum* (1955) written by rabbi/psychoanalyst Israel Gerber, is the "true story" of such a treatment.

• **Beauty Therapy** (mid twentieth century): All a butch lesbian needs is a good make-over. In *Is Homosexuality a Menace?* (1957), Dr. Arthur Guy Matthew tells of how he cured a lesbian by getting her hair "professionally coiffured," teaching her to apply cosmetics—"which she had never used in her life"—and hiring "a fashion expert (not a male homosexual) who selected the most elegant feminine styles for her to bring out the charm and beauty in her body."

— DON ROMESBURG

"Marriage is the worst of remedies [for the homosexual], sacrificing the peace and health of the children to the improbable cure."

TURN-OF-THE-CENTURY CONSERVATIVE CATHOLIC DOCTOR MARC-ANDRÉ RAFFALOVICH

DID YOU KNOW...

The American Psychiatric Association did not even add homosexuality to its list of mental disorders until 1952.

PLEASE DON'T FEED OR TEASE THE STRAIGHT PEOPLE

"One of 10 Be

JOE DALL

Style is being yourself, but on purpose.

Quentin Crisp

GAY DAWNING

QUAL TIME

les 1982

HERE,

Directed b

Paul Mo

CHAPTER 4

Finding Identity

One woman gave powerful testimony in the 1986 New York City hearings regarding passage of a citywide civil rights law, saying, "I am a university professor, a mother of two children, a first-generation Italian American, and a Catholic. By this time, you have begun to form a composite picture of the person that I am—I'm becoming the sum of various parts. When I add that I am also a lesbian, everything else I've told you now disappears and is forgotten. I have become a 'lesbian'—a single, solitary title. Nothing else is important in your perception of me as a person."

Faggot, dyke, queer, lesbian, gay, bulldagger, pansy, fairy: These labels don't begin to describe who we are. It is easily forgotten by nongay people that being gay or lesbian is only one part of who we are. For many of us, our sexual identity may not even be the most important part of ourselves. Identity is an evolving concept. Our identities are shaped in large part by the families and communities in which we are raised, the friends we seek out, and the communities we join when we become adults.

It is misleading to assume that there is one monolithic gay and lesbian community or that there is one kind of gay person. We all come to our gay and lesbian identities from different paths. We meet at our sexuality, but the paths leading up to and away from that sexuality are not necessarily shared. In response to being neither quite here nor there, we construct our own identities based on the qualities we wish to emulate from our multiple communities.

As a group, gay and lesbian Americans are as diverse as any population on earth. We are Latino, African American, disabled, people with AIDS, Jews, deaf, Native American, white, Asian American,

"There will always be someone begging you to isolate one piece of yourself, one segment of your identity above the others, and say, 'Here, this is who I am.' Resist that trivialization. I am not JUST a lesbian. I am not JUST a poet. I am not JUST a mother. Honor the complexity of your vision and yourselves."

AUDRE LORDE,
AUTHOR, POET,
AND ACTIVIST,
COMMENCEMENT SPEECH
AT OBERLIN COLLEGE,
MAY 29, 1989

young, middle-aged and old, and more. It is the merging of the rest of ourselves with our sexuality that creates our individual gay and lesbian identities.

In this chapter we present the voices of many different lesbians and gay men reflecting on their intersecting identities. Rather than trying to present a total picture of each group, the pieces here are presented in roughly alphabetical order by author, without regard to any category. Truth telling is not always simple, nor is it easy, yet it is essential if we are to become proud of who we are. The gay and lesbian people here talk about coming out and finding their own unique identities.

Heroes and Saints

The first place that I went to when I was coming out was the great Latino watering hole Circus Disco. Tried to get into Studio One but the doorman asked me for two I.D.'s. I gave him my driver's license and my JC Penny card but it wasn't good enough. Hey, what did I know? I was still wearing corduroys.

Circus Disco was the new world. Friday night, eleven-thirty. Yeah, I was *Born to Be Alive.* Two thousand people exactly like me. Well, maybe a little darker, but that was the only thing that separated me from the cha-cha boys in East Hollywood.

Where are my heroes? Where are my saints?
Where are my heroes? Where are my saints?

First night at Circus Disco and I order a Long Island Iced Tea, 'cause my brother told me it was the exotic drink, and it fucks you up real fast. The bartender looks at me with one of those gay-people-recognize-each-other looks. I try to act knowing and do it back. Earlier that year, I went to a straight bar on Melrose. When I asked for a screwdriver, the bartender asked me if I wanted a Phillips or a regular. I was never a good drunk.

Where are my heroes? Where are my saints?
Where are my heroes? Where are my saints?

The first guy I met at Circus Disco grabbed my ass in the bathroom, and I thought that was charming. In the middle of the dance floor, amidst all the *hoo-hoo, hoo-hoo,* to a thriving disco beat, he's slow dancing and sticking his tongue down my throat. He sticks a bottle of poppers up my nose and I get home at five-thirty the next morning.

Where are my heroes? Where are my saints?

Where are my heroes? Where are my saints?

Sitting outside Circus Disco with a 300-pound drag queen who's got me cornered in the patio listening to her life story, I think to myself, *One day I will become something and use this as an act.* At the time I was thinking less about performance art and more about Las Vegas.

Where are my heroes? Where are my saints?

Where are my heroes? Where are my saints?

A guy is beating the shit out of his lover in the parking lot of Circus Disco. Everybody is standing around them in a circle, but no one is stopping them. One of the guys is kicking and punching the other, who is lying on the ground in a fetal position. And the first guy's saying, "You want to cheat on me, bitch? You cheating on me, bitch? Get up, you goddamn faggot piece of shit!" It was the first time I saw us act like our parents. I try to move in, but the drag queen tells me to leave them alone. "That's a domestic thing, baby. Besides, that girl has AIDS. Don't get near that queen."

BETTER BLATANT
THAN LATENT

(Courtesy ACT UP)

Where are my heroes? Where are my saints?

Where are my heroes? Where are my saints?

I get home early and I'm shaken to tears. My mother asks me where I went. I tell her I went to see a movie at the Vista—an Italian film about a man who steals a bicycle. It was all I could think of. She says, "That made you cry?"

I swear, I'll never go back to Circus Disco. . . .

But at Woody's Hyperion! *Hoo-hoo, hoo-hoo.* I meet a guy there and his name is Rick Rascon and he's not like anyone else. No tight muscle shirt. No white Levi's. No colored stretch belt. He goes to UCLA and listens to Joni Mitchell. Is that too perfect or what? He comes home with me and we make love, but I'm thinking of him more like my brother. And I know we're gonna be friends for the rest of our lives.

Where are my heroes? Where are my saints?
Where are my heroes? Where are my saints?

Started working at an AIDS service center in South Central. But I gotta get out of here. 'Cause all of my boys. All of my dark-skinned boys. All of my cha-cha boys are dying on me. Sometimes I wish it was like the Circus Disco of my coming out. Two thousand square feet of my men. Boys like me. Who speak the languages of the border and of the *other*. The last time I drove down Santa Monica Boulevard and I passed by Circus Disco, hardly anybody was there.

Where are my heroes? Where are my saints?
Where are my heroes? Where are my saints?

— LUIS ALFARO

?#!

DID YOU KNOW...

According to a 1989 Department of Health and Human Services study, 28 percent of all high school dropouts are young gay men and lesbians.

Does It Matter?

My father asked if I am gay
I asked Does it matter?
He said No not really
I said Yes.
He said get out of my life
I guess it mattered.

My boss asked if I am gay
I asked Does it matter?
He said No not really
I told him Yes.
He said You're fired, faggot
I guess it mattered.

My friend asked if I am gay
I said Does it matter?
He said Not really
I told him Yes.

He said don't call me your friend
I guess it mattered.

My lover asked Do you love me?
I asked Does it matter?
He said Yes.
I told him I love you
He said Let me hold you in my arms
For the first time in my life something matters.

My God asked me Do you love yourself?
I said Does it matter?
He said Yes.
I said How can I love myself? I am Gay
He said That is what I made you
Nothing again will ever matter.

— AN ANONYMOUS HIGH SCHOOL STUDENT, FROM GROWING UP GAY/GROWING UP LESBIAN: A LITERARY ANTHOLOGY

DID YOU KNOW...

Founded in Los Angeles in 1980, Lesbianas Unidas is the oldest Latina lesbian organization in the United States. Among their many ongoing projects, they sponsor a support group designed specifically for Latina lesbians dealing with the effects of substance abuse, one of only a handful of such programs in the country.

Fear of Going Home: Homophobia

For the lesbian of color, the ultimate rebellion she can make against her native culture is through her sexual behavior. She goes against two moral prohibitions: sexuality and homosexuality. Being lesbian and raised Catholic, indoctrinated as straight, I *made the choice to be queer* (for some it is genetically inherent). It's an interesting path, one that continually slips in and out of the white, the Catholic, the Mexican, the indigenous, the instincts. In and out of my head. It makes for *loquería,* the crazies. It is a path of knowledge—one of knowing (and of learning) the history of the oppression of our *raza.* It is a way of balancing, of mitigating duality.

In a New England college where I taught, the presence of a few lesbians threw the more conservative heterosexual students and faculty into a panic. The two lesbian students and we two lesbian instructors met with them to discuss their fears. One of the students said, "I thought homophobia meant fear of going home after a residency."

And I thought, how apt. Fear of going home. And of not being taken in. We're afraid of being abandoned by the mother, the culture, *la Raza*, for being unacceptable, faulty, damaged. Most of us unconsciously believe that if we reveal this unacceptable aspect of the self our mother/culture/race will totally reject us. To avoid rejection, some of us conform to the values of the culture, push the unacceptable parts into the shadows. Which leaves only one fear—that we will be found out and that the Shadow-Beast will break out of its cage. Some of us take another

"Being the supreme crossers of cultures, homosexuals have strong bonds with the queer white, Black, Asian, Native American, Latino, and with the queer in Italy, Australia, and the rest of the planet. We come from all colors, all classes, all races, all time periods. Our role is to link people with each other—the Blacks with Jews with Indians with Asians with whites with extraterrestrials. It is to transfer ideas and information from one culture to another. Colored homosexuals have more knowledge of other cultures; have always been at the forefront (although sometimes in the closet) of all liberation struggles in this country; have suffered more injustices and have survived them despite all odds. Chicanos need to acknowledge the political and artistic contributions of their queer. People, listen to what your *jotería* is saying.

"The mestizo and the queer exist at this time and point on the evolutionary continuum for a purpose. We are a blending that proves that all blood is intricately woven together, and that we are spawned out of similar souls."

WRITER AND ACTIVIST
GLORIA ANZALDÚA
FROM BORDERLANDS/
LA FRONTERA

route. We try to make ourselves conscious of the Shadow-Beast, stare at the sexual lust and lust for power and destruction we see on its face, discern among its features the undershadow that the reigning order of heterosexual males project on our Beast. Yet still others of us take another step: We try to waken the Shadow-Beast inside us. Not many jump at the chance to confront the Shadow-Beast in the mirror without flinching at her lidless serpent eyes, her cold clammy moist hand dragging us underground, fangs bared and hissing. How does one put feathers on this particular serpent? But a few of us have been lucky—on the face of the Shadow-Beast we have seen not lust but tenderness; on its face we have uncovered the lie.

— GLORIA ANZALDÚA, FROM BORDERLANDS/LA FRONTERA

Poet and filmmaker James Broughton in 1988. (Robert Giard)

Reflections on a Birthday, a Bombshell, and a Parade

As older gay people, what are our major concerns? I don't think they include making a million dollars, earning world-class fame, building the next skyscraper, or writing a book that outsells the Bible. In no particular order I believe they include health, financial security, friendships, networking, and meaning.

Health comes first. Speaking for myself, I take very good care of my body. I see others doing the same thing, especially those accustomed to working out at a gym. I walk regularly at a quick, steady pace, up and down sharp inclines that make my heart beat faster. I swim passionately, with real verve and fervor. I love getting in the water, more so if it's the ocean. I am under the care of an excellent doctor and an excellent dentist, both of whom I visit faithfully.

In money matters many of us were Depression kids. I remember when my family lost everything in 1929 and the early 1930s. I became accustomed to frugality and occasional hunger. Those of us who shared this experience of limitation and loss naturally tend to be prudent and wise about money. We know it does not grow on trees. Also, we remember when a postage stamp cost three cents, there were hamburgers for a dime, and a kid got into a movie for a quarter. Believe me, this provides a conservative perspective on today's spiraling costs and easy-come, easy-go money.

Friendships are, I think, the most precious gifts in the world. Lesbians and gays know their value in a world that

"I would assure every man that it is never too late to be surprised by joy. The true love of my life came to me when I was sixty-one, an age when I was beginning to think it time to pull down the shades and fold up my fancies. Then unexpectedly, I was blessed with a psychic rebirth."

JAMES BROUGHTON, POET AND FILMMAKER

was often unfriendly. Many years ago an older gay couple, two men living in a longtime relationship, offered me friendship when I was beginning to come to terms with being gay. I desperately needed their understanding, support, experience, and presence in my life. They provided it unstintingly. I am forever grateful to them. Now I

Gay American Indians (GAI), founded in 1975 by Barbara Cameron (Lakota Sioux) and Randy Burns (Northern Paiute), has grown from a San Francisco social club into a national organization of a thousand Indian and non-Indian members. (Rink Foto)

have the opportunity to return their gift by offering my friendship to younger lesbians and gay men who need the same things they gave me. A corollary of friendship is networking. It's about the outreach and involvement of our lives. For example, there is community participation. Volunteerism. Dialogue with other people about matters of common concern. Being a part of decision making. Networking is the exact opposite of isolation and loneliness.

Meaning? It's as necessary to me as oxygen. Food, drink, sex, and money are not enough for me. I've got to come face-to-face with a new challenge. I need a fresh human need to meet. I yearn for an unexpected mountain to climb. I absolutely require a compelling reason to greet a new day with cheer and energy.

I find that many older lesbians and gay men I know feel the same way I do. Riding yesterday in the bright red convertible in the exciting Gay and Lesbian Pride Celebration parade, waving enthusiastically to thousands of people who lined the route, I felt happy about being gay *and* older. I am grateful for my life up to this moment: Being gay is a part of who I am in God's creation, and so a blessing. Being older is a new challenge, and a blessing.

— **MALCOLM BOYD, EXCERPTED FROM** LAMBDA GRAY

We Are Special

When the U.S. Supreme Court cited "millennia of moral teaching" in support of Georgia's sodomy law and when the Vatican declared homosexuality "intrinsically evil," they must not have been thinking of American history and American morals. Because, throughout America, for centuries before and after the arrival of Europeans, gay and lesbian American Indians were recognized and valued members of tribal communities. As Maurice Kenny declares, "We were special!"

Our tribes occupied every region of this continent, and our cultures were diverse and rich—from the hunters of the far North, to the trading people of the Northwest Coast, the farmers and city-builders of the Southwest, the hunters of the plains, and the great confederations of the Northeast.

Gay American Indians were a part of all these communities. We lived openly in our tribes. Our families and communities recognized us and encouraged us to develop our skills. In turn, we made special contributions to our communities.

French explorers used the word *berdache* to describe male Indians who specialized in the work of women and formed emotional and sexual relationships with other men. Many tribes had female berdaches, too—women who took on men's work and married other women. The History Project of Gay American Indians (GAI) has documented these alternative roles in over 135 North American tribes.

As artists, providers, and healers, our traditional gay ancestors had important responsibilities.

Women hunters and warriors brought food for their families and defended their communities, like the famous Kutenai woman warrior who became an intertribal courier

"In some Indian cultures, adolescents were given a choice between the basket or the bow—or other 'gender-specific' items. The person was then accepted and raised in the tradition of his or her choice without stigma."

CAYENNE WOODS (KIOWA)

and a prophet in the early 1800s, or Woman Chief of the Crow Indians, who achieved the third highest rank in her tribe. Among the Mohave, lesbian women became powerful shamans and medicine people.

Male berdaches specialized in the arts and crafts of their tribes and performed important social and religious roles. In California, we were often called upon to bury and mourn the dead, because such close contact with the spirit world was considered too dangerous for others. Among the Navajo, berdaches were healers and artists, while among the Plains Indians, we were famous for the valuable crafts we made.

Gay and lesbian American Indians today represent the continuity of this tradition. We are living in the spirit of our gay Indian ancestors. Much has changed in American Indian life, but we are still here, a part of our communities, struggling to face the realities of contemporary life.

Some of us continue to fill traditional roles in our tribal communities; others are artists, healers, mediators, and community organizers in urban areas; many of us are active in efforts to restore and preserve our cultural traditions.

Gay and lesbian Indians were special to a lot of tribes. We have roots here in North America.

— RANDY BURNS (NORTHERN PAIUTE, CO-FOUNDER, GAI, EXCERPTED FROM THE PREFACE OF LIVING THE TRADITION, ED. WILL ROSCOE

"It's taken more generations for us to get to where we're at now, but we've found a new tool now and that tool is speaking out."

ERNA PAHE (NAVAJO)

Fighting for Our Lives

From the first description of cases in the *New York Native* in the spring of 1981, there was never a question in my mind that I would get GRID. I retain a clear image of myself on a subway platform at rush hour, frozen in place, reading for the first time about a new, lethal, sexually transmitted disease that was affecting gay men. I remember feeling disoriented by the knowledge that life was going on all around me, oblivious to the fact that my world had just changed utterly and forever.

By late 1981, my doctor and I both knew that I had GRID. I was experiencing mysterious fevers, night sweats, fatigue, rashes, and relentless, debilitating diarrhea. I was losing weight and feeling more and more miserable.

In June 1982, I collapsed from dehydration and was admitted to the hospital with a high fever and violent, bloody diarrhea. When a doctor walked into my room and announced, with the satisfaction of Miss Marple, that I was now official, I was strangely relieved.

"Well, it's GRID all right," she said. "You have cryptosporidiosis. Before GRID, we didn't think cryptosporidiosis infected humans. It's a disease previously found only in livestock."

I tried to take in the fact that I had a disease of *cattle*!

"I'm afraid there is no known treatment..."

I thought I was prepared for this moment, but I felt myself beginning to go numb.

"All we can do is try to keep you hydrated and see what happens. Your body will either handle it or . . . it won't."

She smiled, not too optimistically, patted my leg, and left me alone to confront in earnest the very real possibility of my imminent death.

— **MICHAEL CALLEN, FROM** SURVIVING AIDS

Michael Callen, singer, songwriter, and AIDS activist. Callen died of AIDS-related causes in 1994. (Joel Sokolov)

Refug(e)e: Hiding out

All it takes is "Ahhlo, Quang?" for me to realize it's family calling. The sound of my name, spoken like it's supposed to be, massages from my temples to the back of my neck. I lean back, awash—it's my name, and yet it's been months since I've heard it right.

My great aunt Bà Cô is visiting my cousins for a week. My lover and I live nearby. Still, I manage excuses why I can't visit tonight. Over the phone, I hear my nephews and nieces screaming around.

Bà Cô commends me for being calmer when I was younger. She tells me the story of how quietly I held her hand throughout our escape from Vietnam in 1975; she recalls a panic—the time she momentarily lost my grasp in a crowded camp in Guam. She was able to retrace her steps to find me where we'd been separated; I'd stood in the same place, as instructed. She's told me this story only three times in my life, but I recount all the times I've

DID YOU KNOW...

In 1987, the first U.S. conference for lesbian and gay Asians and Pacific Islanders, called "Breaking the Silence: Beginning the Dialogue" attracted eighty-five participants to North Hollywood, California. The keynote speaker, Trinity Ordona, a Filipina lesbian, said "It is out of self-empowerment that comes collective empowerment. . . . We must break the silence to ourselves and shout our gayness so strongly that the social order to things changes to really include us."

thought of it, as a bond between me and her, and me and my family.

At another time in my life, it might have been easy to set things aside and go see Bà Cô. Things haven't been so simple since I came out. To start with, Bà Cô's older, from another time, another place. It would break her heart to see me, bright red-orange hair, pierced ears, and all. Easy solution, shave the head and take out the piercings.

Not so easy.

I choose to look the way I do because it makes me feel beautiful. And then there's the part about getting off on making people deal with me, as a freak. I have similar reasons for living my life out as a gay man. Being queer, living queer, I can make*it*find*it*explore*it*adore*it.* I choose *it* because living queer means breaking rule #1, so why stop there?

Before I see Bà Cô, I will probably cut my hair. Changing the way I look is not the biggest deal. I sometimes wear a hat in law school classes so the instructor won't single me out. They can see (when they're looking) I'm Asian, some may even guess I'm gay; in a situation where someone has so much power over me, being a freak is less a priority. So I concede, I change my look to be safe at times, to be anonymous at school. So of course I'll do it to spare Bà Cô. But these are acts of hiding, which I must endure and remember.

Coming out has caused much pain, cutting me away from my family. My parents and I dwell on nonsubjects, dancing around my sexuality on the rare occasions we speak on the phone. *Maybe it'd be better had I not told them.* I moved 3,000 miles away, a distance I desperately needed to start living on my own terms. Almost two decades before, my family fled from war, across the world to stake a new life. Survival was the goal, success our reward.

Now separation marks our dream-fulfilled, torn apart again. My parents fought to bring me to this country, for a chance at happiness, which I have by my terms found. *I —am in love/can turn to deep friendships/have [not lost] two wonderful sisters/find power from (in) my communities/take privilege from higher education.* And I can't share one bit of it with them.

"We are relatively uninformed about Asian American subcultures organized around sexuality. There are Asian American gay and lesbian social organizations, gay bars that are known for Asian clientele, conferences that have focused on Asian American lesbian and gay experiences, and electronic bulletin boards catering primarily to gay Asians, their friends, and their lovers."

DANA TAKAGI,
SOCIOLOGY PROFESSOR
AT UC SANTA CRUZ

I can lose the piercings and the hair, but the deception goes deeper. If Bà Cô asks about my life, I will focus on school, be ambiguous, lie. In this life, in my fight, coming out grants escape from bleakness, but the refuge(e) is not complete. There are new struggles and compromises. Every day, I come out of some closets, only to go back into others.

— QUANG H. DANG

"Gee, You Don't Seem like an Indian from the Reservation"

It is of particular importance to us as third world gay people to begin a serious interchange of sharing and educating ourselves about each other. We not only must struggle with racism and homophobia of straight white america, but must often struggle with homophobia that exists within our third world communities. Being third world doesn't always connote a political awareness or activism. I've met a number of third world and Native American lesbians who have said they're just into "being themselves," and that politics has no meaning in their lives. I agree that everyone is entitled to "be themselves," but in a society that denies respect and basic rights to people because of their ethnic background, I feel that individuals cannot idly sit by and allow themselves to be coopted by the dominant society. I don't know what moves a person to be politically active or attempt to raise the quality of life in our world. I only know what motivates my political responsibility . . . the death of Anna Mae Aquash—Native American freedom fighter—"mysteriously" murdered by a bullet in the head; Raymond Yellow Thunder—forced to dance naked in front of a white VFW club in Nebraska—murdered; Rita Silk-Nauni—imprisoned for life for defending her child; my dear friend Mani Lucas-Papago—shot in the back of the head outside of a gay bar in Phoenix. The list could go on and on. My Native American history, recent and past, moves me to continue as a political activist.

"The tradition of the gay Indian has always been a real special one, like someone who is touched by something special."

BETH BRANT (MOHAWK)

And in the white gay community there is rampant racism that is never adequately addressed or acknowledged.

My friend Chrystos from Menominee Nation gave a poetry reading in May 1980 at a Bay Area feminist bookstore. Her reading consisted of poems and journal entries in which she wrote honestly from her heart about the many "isms" and contradictions in most of our lives. Chrystos's bluntly revealing observations on her experiences with the white-lesbian-feminist community are similar to mine and are probably echoed by other lesbians of color.

Her honesty was courageous and should be representative of the kind of forum our community needs to openly discuss mutual racism. A few days following Chrystos's reading, a friend who was in the same bookstore overheard a white lesbian denounce Chrystos's reading as antilesbian and racist.

"I'm a weaver of social fabric. As I travel and relate the stories of different cultures that people have told me, I help to create a more direct link between cultures and among individuals. If we all realize how much we have in common, then the craziness of our world leaders will start to evaporate. . . . [As a child] I had to speak through the heterosexual mouth. I learned how to use pronouns and how not to use pronouns—'My friend and I went for a walk.' Things like that were chipping slowly away at my consciousness and making me become a revolutionary."

FLOATING EAGLE FEATHER, GAY NATIVE AMERICAN STORYTELLER

A few years ago, a white lesbian telephoned me requesting an interview, explaining that she was taking Native American courses at a local university, and that she needed data for her paper on gay Native Americans. I agreed to the interview with the idea I would be helping a "sister" and would also be able to educate her about Native American struggles. After we completed the interview, she began a diatribe on how sexist Native Americans are, followed by a questioning session in which I was to enlighten her mind about why Native Americans are so sexist. I attempted to rationally answer her inanely racist and insulting questions, although my inner response was to tell her to remove herself from my house. Later it became clear how I had been manipulated as a sounding board for her ugly and distorted views about Native Americans. Her arrogance and disrespect were characteristic of the racist white people in South Dakota. If I tried to point it out, I'm sure she would have vehemently denied her racism.

During the antigay Briggs Initiative scare in 1978, I was invited to speak at a rally to represent Native American solidarity against the initiative. The person who spoke prior to me expressed a pro-Bakke sentiment that the audience booed and hissed. His comments left the predominantly white audience angry and in disruption. A white lesbian stood up demanding that a third world person address the racist comments he had made. The MC, rather than taking responsibility for restoring order at the rally, realized that I was the next speaker and I was also T-H-I-R-D-W-O-R-L-D!! I refused to address the remarks of the previous speaker because of the attitudes of the MC and the white lesbian that only third world people are responsible for speaking out against racism. It is inappropriate for progressive or liberal white people to expect warriors in brown armor to eradicate racism. There must be co-responsibility from people of color and white people to equally work on this issue. It is not just MY responsibility to point out and educate about racist activities and beliefs.

Redman, redskin, savage, heathen, injun, american indian, first americans, indigenous people, natives, amerindian, native american, nigger, negro, black, wet back, greaser, mexican, spanish, latin, hispanic, chicano, chink, oriental, asian, disadvantaged, special interest group, minority, third world, fourth world, people of color, illegal aliens—oh yes about them, will the U.S. government recognize the Founding Fathers (you know, George Washington and all those guys) are this country's first illegal aliens?

We are named by others and we are named by ourselves.

— BARBARA CAMERON, EXCERPTED FROM THIS BRIDGE CALLED MY BACK

> **"The ways of the traditional Lakota are to accept things rather than to change them; to learn to work with things and try to live in peace with them. This does not mean total agreement with the gay lifestyle, but it does mean tolerance. In traditional values there is a definite place for gays. Even though this does little to shelter the modern gay lifestyle, it does give an important validity to homosexuality and, more importantly, a heritage to Indian gays."**
>
> — BEN THE DANCER, IN LIVING THE SPIRIT

One in a Million, but Rather Ordinary

There were about 200,000 disabled lesbians when I came out of my coma in 1981. AIDS was still "gay cancer," and lesbians were still "immune."

Now there are about one million disabled dykes, but back then lesbians evidently thought themselves immune to all other disabilities too, judging by their discomfort around me. Not to mention the exclusionism and the really thoughtless things that have been said to me. (One woman actually told me she'd never "let" anything happen to her eyes, since she was an artist!)

I can understand this immune-to-disability feeling, because I used to think the same thing. And I should have known better; after all, I taught disabled people. I should have realized, more than most people, that disability strikes anybody, anytime, anywhere.

But there I was, eating healthily, getting plenty of exercise, and never eating salt. I was hardly religious, but I figured that if you treated others with respect, you'd be left alone.

Wrong.

Even if you do everything "right," disability can still "get" you.

A lot of my negative experiences since 1981 can be laid at the feet of the [heterosexual] community at large. Like the institutions that abuse us, the maddening inaccessibility of mostly everything, the fact that we have exactly two states that pay for personal care assistants and that we usually live in ghettos, and the gruesome 60 to 90 percent unemployment rates. The list can go on, but it's much too depressing.

The unthinking continuation of physical and attitudinal barriers in gay communities is another way the discrimination occurs. The AIDS community in Boston took years to recognize the need for wheelchair accessibility. But if it weren't for gay men's acceptance of me, disability and all, I fully doubt I'd be here. I got invited by one of the sponsors of Woman of Color Press to a reading, but when I got there, no wheelchair seating section was to be found. Yet women of color have taught me how not to lash out at the practitioners of racism and exclusionism.

At the 1981 San Francisco Lesbian and Gay Freedom Day celebration, disabled lesbians and gay men enjoyed front row seating. This was the first year celebration organizers designated a specific area for the disabled. (Rink Foto)

It's hard not to feel isolated and alienated. Every time a disabled person suicides, OD's, or dies of a relatively minor disease, I wonder how much the isolation has to do with it.

There are times the lesbian/gay community just shines. Like the festivals, especially the 1993 March on Washington. But then there are some strange gaps. The 1987 March on Washington was completely nonhelpful to the average disabled person. Very few of the "alternative" magazines put themselves into accessible, affordable formats. None of the writers' colonies are accessible and Provincetown is just impossible.

A fairly newly disabled activist told me that the only way she keeps getting out is to focus on the good she's doing day to day.

And there is a lot of good happening to disabled people today. For years, we talked into the wind. We barely had a legal leg on which to stand or sit. Now, thanks to the Americans with Disabilities Act, the general population is finally hearing us. Sooner or later, the lesbian/gay communities will realize that AIDS is not their only disability, and that access isn't as hard and costly as people believe.

I know you can do it, I've seen you. Just try talking, signing, or writing to us. Be patient and it will be worth it. I promise.

— CARRIE DEARBORN

Ageful Equals Rageful

It's no accident that I am editing a newsletter for old lesbians and other women with the new title *We Are VISIBLE.*

Being invisible is one of many rages. First as an immigrant, then as working class, as a woman, as a wife, as a lesbian, and now as old.

Sometimes I say to my old friends, "And what to do with the rage?" and they nod, shrug, or laugh at my audacity.

In the seventies, when the women's movement was in full swing and I came out as a lesbian, one of my favorite statements was "I can be angry at anything you care to speak to me about!" All the pent-up rage of years of sitting on myself in so many aspects, shaping myself into the required image, holding in my stomach and my very being.

Older lesbians and gay men march with Seniors Active in a Gay Environment (SAGE) in the 1985 Christopher Street Parade in New York City. (Bettye Lane)

Eventually even the anger got stale and, like in so many of us, I tired of the struggle and wanted to love and be loved, to save myself and the planet in a less aggressive way. The system eagerly awaited to incorporate me while twelve-step and other programs enticed me with promises of peace and serenity.

But it's not working.

I've been sweating for twenty years—more, even. And why do I sweat? I am told it's MENopause. I have often talked myself into believing that it is connected with shame about my origins. Once, in my radical days, I researched the depletion of adrenaline due to women's constant fear and anxiety living in a patriarchy where she is constantly subjugated. At one time this gland produced and excreted estrogen, thus naturally replacing the estrogen which no longer came from the ovaries. But the research got lost somewhere in our efforts to take full responsibility for ourselves and quit blaming men. Am I sweating out my rage?

At the grand age of sixty-seven, I am still working a forty-hour-a-week job. I'd leave tomorrow if I had enough to live on. The reward for ten years' work is a pension of $650 a month—at the age of seventy. Guess I didn't plan my finances right, make the right investments, save more, work harder. So it's my fault, isn't it? Could this be a reason for my rage?

"Let this be a movement of brave old dykes led by brave old dykes. Age is a time of great wonder—a time when we have to hold, with a fine balance, contradictory truths in our heads and give them equal weight: Old is scary but very exciting; chaotic but self-integrating; narrowing yet wider; weaker yet stronger than ever before.

"It is we who must name the processes of our own aging. But just as we could not begin to say what it means to be a woman until we had confronted the distortions of sexism and homophobia, so we cannot explore our aging without examining and confronting ageism. It is the task that lies before us."

BARBARA MACDONALD,
OLD LESBIAN ACTIVIST

My work is with ordinary people, most of them living on what is called "welfare." In Canada, it's called pension, something a person deserves after working all their lives, received without the humiliation of reducing themselves to abject poverty. With that as a shadowy model, it's small wonder that many of us go into old age with the ogre of poverty as companion. That fear keeps me separate from my companion lover as we both work out time in different parts of the country. Rage!

I'm angry about the new age salve that attempts to mute out my rage. If only I would meditate more, do affirmations, practice yoga, give up chocolate and coffee, if only I would be a "real" vegetarian, grow my own vegetables, spend less, live in a cabin in the country. It's not that I don't believe in these and try to do and be them. It's that my rage is important too and I want to be valued in this new age.

It keeps me on my toes around all important feminist issues and I am grateful for it. I don't want it to be a contradiction to compassion and love. For me it is the yin yang of staying a healthy happy old lesbian. I use the ocean as my guide. One day she is so peaceful and calm I can see my face in her surface. The next she rages and roars with all the power she holds inside. That is how I am too.

— **VASHTE DOUBLEX, FROM** SINISTER WISDOM

Dreaming of Challah as the Goddess's Hair

I had a dream a few nights ago that I was at my sister's wedding. She got loads of praise; I was being completely ignored. Finally, about halfway through the ceremony, I stood up and said, "I'm part of this family, too. Is anyone ever going to *kvell* over me?" Then I felt awful, full of shame and regret for disrupting the wedding. I couldn't face myself, nor believe I had done it. I woke up shaking. I felt that as a lesbian/bisexual I was not a good enough Jew, I was disloyal to my family and my people. I believed the lie that a lesbian could not possibly be happy, and would have to be lonely and pitiful. Jews are big on family and blood relations (I was often told only to trust *mishpochah* [family]). As an unmarried woman, I would never become an adult member of my biological extended family.

I grew up mostly in New York with two immigrant parents, one who survived the Holocaust, the other one raised in England. My father and his family come from Transylvania. The Holocaust was the elephant in the living room—never talked about, always present. As a kid, I was hyperintellectual and overalert. I had many nightmares about being chased, murdered in my sleep, shot at, going into hiding. I've noticed a lot of us Jews have some survival-based paranoia. Having one-third of our people murdered in this century makes us a little edgy. Writing this article is terrifying. Exposure on such a large scale is the opposite of my childhood lessons. My father, sitting at the dinner table, said, "They can take everything away but they can't take away what's up here," tapping his temple. This is what I was taught: You have brains—use them, keep a low profile, never let anyone know where you come from, i.e., that you're a Jew.

Sometimes I feel a similar fear as a lesbian/bisexual woman. When I go to large gay parades or marches, I wonder if I'm the only one who's thinking *Wow, what an easy opportunity to drop a bomb and wipe us out. . . .* In different situations, I measure how out to be as a queer person (or as a Jew). My first day on a new job at a women's peace organization, I weighed heavily the pros and cons of placing a wall calendar above my desk. The theme of the calendar was peace and justice, and the month of April showed a picture of one dykey-looking woman leaning on another in the Greek Isles. All the other months featured sweet children's drawings and pictures of doves. I decided to hang the calendar. It cost me my job after the calendar roused the homophobic director. There are times I feel forced to prioritize myself as a Jew or as a gay person. If I'm in a multicultural group and there are no other Jews, but there are other lesbians, I will speak out as a Jew.

The two identities are completely intertwined, and I want to bring my full self everywhere. It's in the Jewish lesbian/bisexual community that I feel most at home. I sense that both Jews and queers have been forced by history and oppression to "take care of our own." I co-founded a Queer Minyan of lesbians, bisexuals, and gay men who meet monthly to celebrate Shabbat [Jewish Sabbath]. We sing "Hineh matov umanayim shevet ha*queer* gam yachad." It means "How good and sweet it is for us to be together." The original has *achim* [brothers]. Something about replacing the Hebrew word for brothers with the contemporary English word *queer* stirs a feeling in the group. We are a Jewish queer family with tremendous love and support for each other. It is a blessing to have a place where I can show myself freely.

I can pass as a non-Jew. I can also pass as a heterosexual. But every time I do, a part of me dies. At a meeting to plan a huge multicultural ritual honoring ancestors, one man turned to me and said, "Why would you want to keep being Jewish? Why not leave it behind with all the other patriarchal regressive belief systems?" And what my heart cried out was: I can't not be Jewish, just like I can't change my short square hands or my long thin feet or my skinny legs. I can't get over it by raising my consciousness or changing my diet. I am a Jew. It's the people I come from, it's my ethnicity, my culture, it's in my bones and my blood. It's the terror, the joy, the beauty, and the flavor of my thinking.

Non-Jews often reduce the Jewish people to the religion. But it is not only Judaism that makes me Jewish. It's the mix of culture and patterns, religion and stories. I identify with the long history of Jewish radicals, communists, socialists, and progressives in this country and elsewhere. People like Emma Goldman, Adrienne Rich, Karl Marx, Melanie Kaye/Kantrowitz, and Si Kahn. We have a proud history of Jewish culture separate from the religion. The Yiddishkeit culture of Eastern Europe was very rich and beautiful before it was destroyed by the Nazis. Now, fifty years later, lesbians in this country are among the most active in nourishing the remaining seeds of Yiddishkeit. I am a part of a very old, diverse, and multicultural people. We come from many countries, we speak many languages, we range in appearance from dark brown skin with kinky hair to light skinned with blond hair. We may have been unwelcome, on borrowed time, in the countries we found ourselves in, but we were deeply influenced by our surroundings. Since my immediate family came from Eastern Europe, the music and food and culture I grew up with was infused with this part of the world. (One example: I thought borsht [red beet soup] was a Jewish dish until a non-Jewish first-generation Russian friend of mine served it to me at a Christmas dinner!)

And in turn, as lesbians, we are reshaping what it means to be Jewish. I have a Jewish identity/spirituality that draws from parts of the religion and mixes in other spiritual traditions that speak to me as a woman and lesbian. I think of the priestesses in the Temple guarding the flame when I light my Shabbat candles. I dream of the Goddess's hair when I eat challah [ritual braided egg bread].

— **ALINA EVER**

Día de los Muertos

A few nights ago as I was getting out of my car at the top of my little hill in Los Angeles, I heard a terrible metal scream that sent shivers down my spine. It was a battle cry, a mother's wail, a dead man's laugh; the sound of a shotgun.

Having grown up in the Pico-Union district of downtown, I know all too well the sound of ammunition in the nighttime sky, but this one was so close that I jumped with the blast. A few seconds later I heard a car's leaping cry, like a dragster out of the gate at the speedway. A small Toyota raced by me with four homeboys. The two in the backseat were still holding their shotguns out of the car windows.

Later that night as I was working a pen toward paper, doing overtime on my poet duties, I decided to go down to my trusted 7-Eleven for one of those snacks that make me the last man on the totem pole at the gym. On the way down the hill I saw an ambulance and the coroner's truck at the site of where that bullet screamed and hit. It was the house on the block that makes everyone uncomfortable. The one the neighbors talk about when they mention "property values." The house where they park cars on the lawn. A Spanish bungalow blasting Sunday afternoon FM stations with a backyard keg. The house where beautiful brown-skinned shirtless boys with teardrop tattoos and shaved-head prison do's walk a fashion runway of "misfit." Daring each other to lower their baggy khakis and striped JC Penny boxers below the imaginary line of "acceptable." Somewhere down toward desire. Giving feisty chola girls and colored queer boys like me reason enough to still want to live in the bad neighborhoods where we grew up.

I watched the body bag, all zipped up and ready for the morgue, where a *veterana* chola mama will identify next-of-kin as shooting victim number "we've lost count, don't ask anymore." I pass a number of rod-iron-windowed houses where old ladies are peeking through the kitchen curtains for a glimpse of this week's tragedy. Heads nod at the corner while housewives go back inside to iron a *viejo's* clothes for the next day's commute. *Oprah said it would be like this.*

"Some queers like me come from or have sought social and cultural circumstances in which independent teachers . . . whom some call 'crazy wisdom masters,' are 'on the loose.' Their lives constantly challenge conventional wisdoms and ordinary morality, eccentrically assisting in the process of understanding the play and transience of psychohistorical structures and conventions rooted in history and in the psyches of individuals. Such eccentric teachings seem to empty the body and mind of crippling biographical and cultural baggage as a necessary prerequisite to the development of understandings which may lie outside ordinary human judgment, free of cultural blinders."

PITZER COLLEGE PROFESSOR LOURDES ARGUELLES, FROM "CRAZY WISDOM: MEMORIES OF A CUBAN QUEER" IN SISTERS, SEXPERTS AND QUEERS

I went off to 7-Eleven, standing there reading *Noticias del Mundo*, wondering what I could do. Feeling helpless, a bit traumatized, my urban dilemma started to feel like some bad movie-of-the-week and I decided to go home. As I was heading back up the hill I was convinced that I should drive by the shotgun house if only to confront my fears about this situation and its occupants. Let's not forget, they are my neighbors.

As I turned the corner I saw a faint glow of flickering firelight. I slowed down and saw a pool of dried blood. Over the traces of this once beating heart stood twelve candles in the shape of a cross. I was so moved by this image. By this reminder of what the living among us do. Someone was marking the loss. I knew I had to do something.

Two Cuban American men enjoy a dance at a Dade County, Florida, gay watering hole in 1977. (Bettye Lane)

The next morning, as I was fighting with the urban commuters for the first chance at the carpool lane, I slowed down at the bottom of the hill and saw the quiet candles flickering a small reminder of the previous night's event. Next to the candles and the pool of blood was a shopping cart and a small sign in modern-day Sanskrit, cholo writing, that spelled out the name *Eddie.* Inside the cart were a pile of clothes, pictures, a baseball cap, some hangers, and shoes. Eddie in a nutshell.

When I got to the corner, I did what my grandmother and I always did every summer in Tijuana at the announcement of a death in the *colonias,* I stopped at a flower shop and bought a small funeral wreath. I drove back and left it lying in front of the last drops of Eddie. I don't know if Eddie was an innocent drive-by victim or a violent motherfucker pissing on a territory he shouldn't have. I don't care. Back then, in Tijuana, buses fell over cliffs, jealous wives shot wandering husbands, a pack of coyotes stole away a child, cows fell on you. Whatever the reason, we were always there. To mark the passing. It was our responsibility. Our role.

In the queer community we mark the passing of our sisters and brothers because sometimes families don't. We put up pictures of our dead friends because sometimes we forget what they looked like before they got sick. We write about our dead artists because sometimes we forget what they did. We grieve openly in front of murals and altars of memory because we see how much we have lost. We say prayers for art works because that's what families tend to throw away first.

I started to make the documentation of queer Latino artists who had died of AIDS part of my art, because whole bodies of work became fragmented among collectors with no sense of what that work meant. This is what I give back to my community, my little hillside block. A sense of memory. The what-used-to-be of life.

That night on my way home I was amazed at what had happened to our blood-soaked Silver Lake corner. A transformation had taken place. Over thirty candles of various shapes and sizes were doing time illuminating the dead. Stacks of flowers piled on top of each other gave off shadows from candlelight. Little cards lay on the sidewalk. Someone had taken an old junior high picture of the dearly departed and made a large photocopy that hung over the shopping cart. This is what we give back to the community. The pictures left behind. The melted candles. The rituals. A history.

I saw an old lady walking home from the market with two bags of groceries, and she stopped at the corner. She kneeled down in front of the sidewalk altar and did a sign of the cross. She pulled a bead of rosaries out of her purse and draped them over the photocopy picture of that junior high school yearbook entry.

We remember you, *Eddie.* Whoever you are.

— **LUIS ALFARO**

Country Coming Out

I was living in the country, raising sheep, and publishing a magazine with other women in the community, gay and straight. We had done an early issue on sexuality, where all of us wrote rather intimate and exposing pieces. (Because of editorial decisions, the author's names did not appear on the pieces themselves.) I was quite proud of my involvement with the magazine, and had encouraged my entire family to get subscriptions to it. My parents were visiting when the sexuality issue came out.

One morning early, there was a knock on my door. There was my mother, holding the current issue, looking at me. "Sherry," she said in her Southern drawl. "Did you write this?" She pointed to the piece in which I had graphically described having sex with my lover, eleven years my senior.

"Yes, I did," I replied, trying not to sound tentative.

She looked at me. After several seconds, she asked, "All of this?"

What could I say? "Yes, all of it."

Another pause. "Well, let's not tell your father," she said with a gleam in her eye. "Let's see if he can figure it out."

— SHERRY

I Lost It at the Movies

My grandmother, Lydia, and my mother, Dolores, were both talking to me from their bathroom stalls in the Times Square movie theater. I was washing butter from my hands at the sink and didn't think it at all odd. The people in my family are always talking; conversation is a life force in our existence.

To be a lesbian was part of who I was, like being left-handed—even when I'd slept with men. When my great-grandmother asked me in the last days of her life if I would be marrying my college boyfriend I said yes, knowing I would not, knowing I was a lesbian.

It seemed a fact that needed no expression. Even my first encounter with the word "bulldagger" was not charged with emotional conflict. When I was a teen in the 1960s, my grandmother told a story about a particular building in our Boston neighborhood that had gone to seed. She described the building's past through the experience of a party she'd attended there thirty years before. The best part of the evening had been a woman she'd met and danced with. Lydia had been a professional dancer and singer on the black theater circuit; to dance with women was who she was. They'd danced, then the woman walked her home and asked her out. I heard the delicacy my grandmother searched for even in her retelling of how she'd explained to the "bulldagger," as she called her, that she liked her fine but she was more interested in men. I was struck with how careful my grandmother had been to make it clear to that woman (and in effect to me) that there was no offense taken in her attentions, that she just didn't "go that way," as they used to say. I was so happy at thirteen to have a word for what I knew myself to be. The word was mysterious and curious, as if from a new language that used some other alphabet which left nothing to cling to when touching its curves and crevices. But still, a word existed, and my grandmother was not flinching in using it. In fact, she'd smiled at the good heart and good looks of the bulldagger who'd liked her.

Once I had the knowledge of a word and a sense of its importance to me, I didn't feel the need to explain, confess, or define my identity as a lesbian. The process of reclaiming my ethnic identity in this country was already all-consuming. Later, of course, in moments of glorious self-righteousness, I did make declarations. But they were not usually ones I had to make. Mostly they were a testing of the waters.

I need not pretend to be other than who I was. But did I need to declare it? During the holidays when I brought home best friends or lovers my family always welcomed us warmly, clasping us to their magnificent bosoms. Yet there was always an element of silence in our neighborhood, and surprisingly enough in our family, that was disturbing to me.

If the idea of cathedral weddings and station wagons held no appeal for me, the concept of an extended family was certainly important. But my efforts were stunted by our inability to talk about the life I was creating for myself, for all of us. It felt all the more foolish because I thought I knew how my family would react. I was confident they would respond with their customary aplomb just as they had when I'd first had my hair cut as an Afro (which they hated) or when I brought home friends who were vegetarians (which they found curious). Somewhere deep inside I think I believed that neither my grandmother nor my mother would ever censure my choices. Neither had actually raised me; my great-grandmother had done that, and she had been a steely barricade against encroachment on our personal freedoms and she'd never disapproved out loud of anything I'd done.

But it was not enough to have an unabashed admiration for these women. It was one thing to have pride in how they'd so graciously survived in spite of the odds against them. It was something else to be standing in a Times Square movie theater faced with the chance to say "it" out loud and risk the loss of their brilliant and benevolent smiles.

My mother had started reading the graffiti written on the wall of the bathroom stall. We hooted at each of her dramatic renderings. Then she said (not breaking the rhythm, since we all know timing is everything), "Here's one I haven't seen before—'DYKES UNITE.'" There was that profound silence again, as if the frames of my life had ground to a halt. We were in a freeze-frame and options played themselves out in my head in rapid succession: Say nothing? Say something? Say what?

I laughed and said, "Yeah, but have you seen the rubber stamp on my desk at home?"

"No," said my mother with a slight bit of puzzlement. "What does it say?"

"I saw it," my grandmother called out from her stall. "It says: 'Lesbian Money'!"

"What?"

"Lesbian Money," Lydia repeated.

"I just stamp it on my big bills," I said tentatively, and we all screamed with laughter. The other woman at the sinks tried to pretend we didn't exist.

"I studied chests, arms, and thighs glistening with sweat, and the tricks light can play when reflecting off a mirrored ball. That was the beginning. The beginning of feeling that the word 'faggot' did not accurately name the man I was or the man I was aspiring to become. The beginning of thinking thoughts that started off with 'I have nothing to be ashamed of…' and 'I have a right to…' The beginning of discarding the silence and the shame. The beginning of seeing the truth through all of the lies."

CHARLES HARPE, FROM "AT 36" IN BROTHER TO BROTHER

DID YOU KNOW...

The first Annual Deaf Lesbian and Gay Awareness Week was held in May 1994. Taking place in the San Francisco Bay Area, the week-long celebration included workshops, readings from the first deaf gay and lesbian reader, *Eyes of Desire*, and a Deaf Queer Pride Party at the Deaf Gay and Lesbian Center. The center is the first national organization run by and for gay and lesbian deaf people, and not associated with a college or university.

Since then there has been little discussion. There have been some moments of awkwardness, usually in social situations where they feel uncertain. Although we have not explored the "it," the shift in our relationship is clear. When I go home it is with my lover and she is received as such. I was lucky. My family was as relieved as I to finally know who I was.

— **JEWELLE GOMEZ, EXCERPTED FROM** MAKING FACE, MAKING SOUL

Notes from a Diary: A Gay Deaf Man's Concern with Communication

September 19. Got rejected today at Christopher's —looked at myself in the mirror and liked what I saw. Must have been the fact that I was deaf that scared him off. So, what's new?

October 7. Met someone at the gym today in the strangest way—may be a perfect example of my situation of not being able to hear. His name's Stan, and he's from San Francisco. I was working out when I saw him and he noticed me. But after a few minutes at the machines, I noticed he wasn't looking at me anymore and that he was almost done. I beat him to the showers but he still ignored me. . . . I asked him if he'd lost a towel. He never answered my question about the missing towel. Instead, he looked at me and said quite clearly, "My God, you're deaf!" He told me he'd come up behind me while I was doing an exercise and spoken to me. I never answered him, so he put it off as New York snobbishness. Went to his hotel with him and had a marvelous time. Now I wonder how many times have people come up behind me and given up when I'd not responded? How many of them thought of the possibility I couldn't hear them?

December 3. Someone asked me what it was like to be deaf. I asked the person who said it what it was like to be hearing. He couldn't answer. I've never been able to hear, so how could I explain the difference?

December 4. Met some straight deaf people who were shocked when I told them I was gay. They disapprove for an obvious reason—I won't bring any deaf children into the world. But there are other people who will maintain the heritage of deaf culture. I don't have that "primitive urge" to maintain the "tribe" of deaf people for future generations. It's hard for me to identify with much of the deaf community—it's so varied—there are the differences along the lines of education, status, religion, race, and sexual preference. The gay community has exactly the same differences!

"In my research of deaf gay men, I've asked this question of them: Suppose there are two candidates running for president, the first one for rights of the handicapped and the second one supporting gay rights. All said they would rather vote for the one supporting the rights of the handicapped than the one for gay rights. Which means the deaf gay person is more concerned with deaf rights than with gay rights. This is also true of us in the deaf community. We think of ourselves as gay first, then deaf second; but in the hearing world, we think of our deafness first and our gayness second."

TOM KANE, DEAF GAY ACTIVIST
EXCERPTED FROM
"MEN IN PINK SPACESUITS,"
EYES OF DESIRE

January 3. Met a couple of deaf men from Washington, D.C. They were surprised I knew many hearing men, and they told me that I wasn't being fair. I shouldn't be socializing with anybody but deaf people. I'd rather look at it this way—my life is in the world, and I want to get involved with it as much as I can. For some deaf gay men, the world seems hostile because of the difficulty communicating. One man even accused me of showing off my ability to interact with the hearing world. I told him it wasn't easy at all, but I wasn't letting it prevent me from doing so. I relish the challenge.

— BRUCE HILBOK

I Am Your Sister: Black Women Organizing Across Sexualities

When I say I am a Black Lesbian, I mean I am a woman whose primary focus of loving, physical as well as emotional, is directed to women. It does not mean that I hate men. Far from it. The harshest attacks I have ever heard against Black men came from those women who are intimately bound to them and cannot free themselves from a subservient and silent position. I would never presume to speak about Black men the way I have heard some of my straight sisters talk about the men they are attached to. And of course, that concerns me, because it reflects a situation of noncommunication in the heterosexual Black community that is far more truly threatening than the existence of Black Lesbians.

What does this have to do with Black women organizing?

Kim Samsel (left) signs with Robin Ching in Baltimore, 1987. (©JEB)

I have heard it said—usually behind my back—that Black Lesbians are not normal. But what is normal in this deranged society by which we are all trapped? I remember, and so do many of you, when being Black was considered *not normal*, when they talked about us in whispers, tried to paint us, lynch us, bleach us, ignore us, pretend we did not exist. We called that racism.

I have heard it said that Black Lesbians are a threat to the Black family. But when 50 percent of children born to Black women are born out of wedlock, and 30 percent of all Black families are headed by women without husbands, we need to broaden and redefine what we mean by *family*.

I have heard it said that Black Lesbians will mean the death of the race. Yet Black Lesbians bear children in exactly the same way other women bear children, and a Lesbian household is simply another kind of family. Ask my son and daughter.

The terror of Black Lesbians is buried in that deep inner place where we have been taught to fear all difference—to kill it or ignore it. Be assured: Loving women is not a communicable disease. You don't catch it like the common cold. Yet the one accusation that seems to render even the most vocal straight Black woman totally silent and ineffective is the suggestion that she might be a Black *Lesbian*.

If someone says you're Russian and you know you're not, you don't collapse into stunned silence. Even if someone calls you a bigamist, or a childbeater, and you know you're not, you don't crumple into bits. You say it's not true and keep on printing the posters. But let anyone, particularly a Black man, accuse a straight Black woman of being a Black Lesbian, and right away that sister becomes immobilized, as if that is the most horrible thing she could be, and must at all costs be proven false. That is homophobia. It is a waste of woman energy, and it puts a terrible weapon into the hands of your enemies to be used against you to silence you, to keep you docile and in line. It also serves to keep us isolated and apart.

I have heard it said that Black Lesbians are not political, that we have not been and are not involved in the struggles of Black people. But when I taught Black and Puerto Rican students writing at City College in the SEEK program in the sixties, I was a Black Lesbian. I was a Black Lesbian when I helped organize and fight for the Black Studies Department of John Jay College. And because I was fifteen years younger then and less sure of myself, at one crucial moment, I yielded to pressures that said I should step back for a Black man even though I knew him to be a serious error of choice, and I did, and he was. But I was a Black Lesbian then.

When my girlfriends and I went out into the car one July Fourth night after fireworks with cans of white spray paint and our kids asleep in the backseat, one of us staying

DID YOU KNOW...

Thirteen-year-old writer Malkia Cyril attended the Second National Black Writers' Conference in March 1988. Accompanied by her mother, she had come especially to see Audre Lorde, the only black lesbian she knew—and a role model for her. Malkia took the microphone with Barbara Smith and Gail Lewis to share her happiness at discovering other black lesbians and role models. She later said, "I've been waiting for a long time so that I could see a positive lesbian role model for myself to follow. So I can continue the way I've been living, knowing it's okay... knowing that it's right."

behind to keep the motor running and watch the kids while the other two worked our way down the suburban New Jersey street, spraying white paint over the black jockey statues, and their little red jackets, too, we were Black Lesbians.

When I drove through the Mississippi Delta to Jackson in 1968 with a group of Black students from Toughaloo, another car full of redneck kids trying to bump us off the road all the way back into town, I was a Black Lesbian.

African American dykes marching together at the 1973 Christopher Street rally. (Bettye Lane)

When I weaned my daughter in 1963 to go to Washington in August to work in the coffee tents along with Lena Horne, making coffee for the marshals because that was what most Black women did in the 1963 March on Washington, I was a Black Lesbian.

When I taught a poetry workshop at Toughaloo, a small Black college in Mississippi, where white rowdies shot up the edge of the campus every night, and I felt the joy of seeing young Black poets find their voices and power through words in our mutual growth, I was a Black Lesbian. And there are strong Black poets today who date their growth and awareness from those workshops.

When Yoli and I cooked curried chicken and beans and rice and took our extra blankets and pillows up the hill to the striking students occupying buildings at City College in 1969, demanding open admissions and the right to an education, I was a Black Lesbian. When I walked through the midnight hallways of Lehman College that same year, carrying Midol and Kotex pads for the young Black radical women taking part in the action, and we tried to persuade them that their place in the revolution was not ten paces behind Black men, that spreading their legs to the guys on the tables in the cafeteria was not a revolutionary act no matter what the brothers said, I was a Black Lesbian. When I picketed for Welfare Mothers' Rights, and against the enforced sterilization of young Black girls, when I fought institutionalized racism in the New York City Schools, I was a Black Lesbian.

But you did not know it because we did not identify ourselves, so now, you can say that Black Lesbians and Gay men have nothing to do with the struggles of the Black Nation.

And I am not alone.

When you read the words of Langston Hughes you are reading the words of a Black Gay man. When you read the words of Alice Dunbar-Nelson and Angelina Weld Grimke, poets of the Harlem Renaissance, you are reading the words of Black Lesbians. When you listen to the life-affirming voices of Bessie Smith and Ma Rainey, you are hearing Black Lesbian women. When you see the plays and read the words of Lorraine Hansberry, you are reading the words of a woman who loved women deeply.

Today, Lesbians and Gay men are some of the most active and engaged members of Art Against Apartheid, a group that is making visible and immediate our cultural responsibilities against the tragedy of South Africa. We have organizations such as the National Coalition of Black Lesbians and Gays, Dykes Against Racism Everywhere, and Men of All Colors together, all of which are committed to and engaged in antiracist activity.

Homophobia and heterosexism mean you allow yourselves to be robbed of the sisterhood and strength of Black Lesbian women because you are afraid of being called a Lesbian yourself. Yet we share so many concerns as Black women, so much work to be done. The destruction of our Black children and the theft of young Black minds are joint urgencies. Black children shot down or doped up on the streets of our cities are priorities for all of us. The fact of Black women's blood flowing with grim regularity in the streets and living rooms of Black communities is not a Black Lesbian rumor. It is a sad statistical truth. The fact that there is a widening and dangerous lack of communication around our differences between Black women and men is not a Black Lesbian plot. It is a reality that is starkly clarified as we see our young people become more and more uncaring of each other. Young Black boys believing that they can define their manhood between a sixth-grade girl's legs, growing up believing that Black women and girls are the fitting target for their justifiable furies rather than the racist structure grinding us all into dust, these are not Black Lesbian myths. These are sad realities of Black communities today and of immediate concern to us all. We cannot afford to waste each other's energies in our common battles.

What does homophobia mean? It means that high-powered Black women are told it is not safe to attend a Conference on the Status of Women in Nairobi simply because we are Lesbians. It means that in a political action, you rob yourselves of the vital insight and energies of political women such as Betty Powell and Barbara Smith and Gwendolyn Rogers and Raymina Mays and Robin Christian and Yvonne Flowers. It means another instance of the divide-and-conquer routine.

How do we organize around our differences, neither denying them nor blowing them up out of proportion?

The first step is an effort of will on your part. Try to remember to keep certain facts in mind. Black Lesbians are not apolitical. We have been a part in every freedom struggle within this country. Black Lesbians are not a threat to the Black family. Many of us have families of our own. We are not white, and we are not a disease. We are women who love women. This does not mean we are going to assault your daughters in an alley on Nostrand Avenue. It does not mean we are about to attack you if we pay you a compliment on your dress. It does not mean we only think about sex, any more than you only think about sex.

Even if you *do* believe any of these stereotypes about Black Lesbians, begin to practice acting like you don't believe them. Just as racist stereotypes are the problem of the white people who believe them, so also are homophobic stereotypes the problem of the heterosexuals who believe them. In other words, those stereotypes are yours to solve, not mine, and they are a terrible and wasteful barrier to our working together. I am not your enemy. We do not have to become each other's unique experiences and insights in order to share what we have learned through our particular battles for survival as Black women.

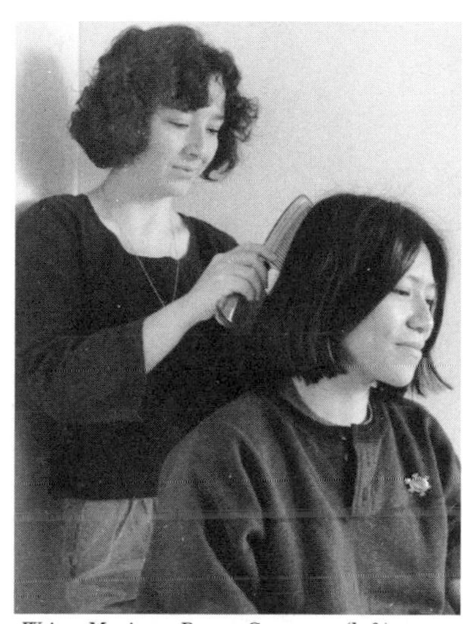

Writer Mariana Romo-Carmona (left) combs the hair of her lover, June Chan, 1988. (Robert Giard)

There was a poster in the 1960s that was very popular: HE'S NOT BLACK, HE'S MY BROTHER! It used to infuriate me because it implied that the two were mutually exclusive—*he* couldn't be both brother and Black. Well, I do not want to be tolerated, nor misnamed. I want to be recognized.

I am a Black Lesbian, and I am your sister.

— **AUDRE LORDE**

Friends of Dorothy

This past year I have attended three memorial services for black sisters or, as they used to say in the old days, "friends of Dorothy"—meaning that the women were lesbians. The services focused on esteeming these women, recognizing their intelligence, creativity, productivity, success, and their capacity to love. The women were recognized also as having had successful relationships, intimate and interpersonal, with other black women and their partners. One woman was out to her family and the world. The other two were not.

During the memorial services, several of us took turns telling herstory accounts about each of the women's lives, recognizing our personal sense of loss and the greater loss to the community, in that each had died relatively young without having achieved all her goals or impacted her society or the general community in a manner in which she would have preferred.

Some of their family members attended the special memorial services; each family preferred to have a funeral service in the church of choice in their community. I attended one of the funerals and experienced the entire service as a bad joke. No one acknowledged that the woman was also a lesbian in a fifteen-year relationship with a loving companion and friend—a woman, incidentally, not invited to attend the funeral.

I began to think about myself and the many other black lesbians who no doubt will live and die without ever having received special recognition or having been esteemed as persons by their own families. I began to think how I had for many years engaged in a rather collusive relationship with my family and many of my close friends. Many times I would fake an interest in their prearranged blind dates for me with men. I would often roll my eyes and wink when asked about my sex life or the current man in my life. It was easier for them to associate me with males, real or imagined, in order to suppress real concerns about my never bringing males home for family members to meet. We all played in the game, pretending I was like all the other black women in my family and the immediate community.

I did not feel comfortable coming out, and for a long time didn't even know how to come out. In my youth in the black community, an out lesbian was considered to be at the very bottom of the varying levels of low-life. I learned this lesson early when a woman in the community returned home after World War II and began to dress like a man and drive a taxicab. She was the pariah of the community and, even as children, we were warned not to go near her, talk to her, or accept any gifts from her. I don't remember much about this woman other than that she was always alone. I never recall seeing her with any other women or men.

When people outside my family asked why I wasn't married, family members would quite pridefully remind them that I was "too smart"—meaning too intelligent—to put up with a black man. Everybody would laugh, including me. When I was not in good financial standing, I would often be the butt of other family jokes about "funny people." Mine was the sad-funny laughter, because as a youth I was often reprimanded for being "too smart"—meaning too independent.

At thirty-five, I moved to California and began what I call learning how to love myself, share my closet, and be a lot more open and active in my community. I built significant bridges of friendship with the black and white women in my community. I gave new focus to my work; my self-esteem soared and I was on my way.

I created a family for myself—or, rather, a family of choice formed around me—and I was freed up to the extent that I no longer had to mentally look over my shoulder, wishing and wondering if I was loved and if I would reconnect with my family of origin in a newly productive manner. From age forty-five to fifty-five, I focused primarily on my lifestyle and role as a black lesbian in the black/white community.

I found that the black community often induced the same pain and anguish that I experienced in my family. I am strongly aware of the penalties the black community extracts from me. The community views me as a misfit because I am an assertive, self-directed, self-loving woman—traits seen by the black community as positive in heterosexual black women but viewed as male when exercised by me.

Those attitudes and ideas about lesbians are expressed in the negative behavior of heterosexual females and males. The mark of oppression lies heavy on my shoulders: homophobia on one side and racism on the other. At age sixty, I am mastering walking the middle line and have tempered my mettle to deal with the oppression on both sides of me.

I hope my story will serve as a source of empowerment to free other lesbians from the burden of the yoke I have borne for so long—free them to make friends, interact with their chosen community, expand themselves, and realize that we can create our own families. I hope more black lesbians will or already realize that relationships with relatives can be maintained without having to surrender one's identity or true sense of self.

— GREAR GREENE

Cost of Living Adjustment

A cover from insideOUT, a San Francisco–based magazine for lesbian, gay and bisexual youth. (insideOUT)

I was on the phone with my friend Jen, sitting in the kitchen with my mom while she made dinner. Jen and I were talking about girls, as usual, but I was being careful and letting her do most of the talking (not a problem for her!). Then Jen said, "Is your mom there?"

"Yeah," I said. "Why, you wanna chat with her?"

"No! But I think you should tell her right now."

"Right now? Just like that?"

"If you don't, I will," promised Jen ominously. "And you know I'll call her when your ass is out—"

"Okay, fine."

I looked over at my mom, who never listened to my conversations but always butted in. Without pausing to think, I said, "Mom, what would you do if I told you I was gonna start dating girls?"

She stopped what she was doing only long enough to smirk and reply, "What am I supposed to do? As long as it doesn't cost me any more money than your dating guys, it's fine with me."

— **ARWYN**

Coming Out for Love

My elder daughter has never shied away from pointing out the flaws she has seen in my arguments or my character. I have often been confused, sometimes to the point of anger, by her directness.

I remember one argument very clearly. She was sitting on the stairs leading up from the kitchen, tearful, fierce, and lovely. I remember I reached out suddenly, took both her hands and pulled her down to my level.

My first marriage failed in the next decade and my daughter's in the following one. We saw each other rarely after that.

About a year ago, we met on neutral ground, at a restaurant. My daughter told me about the delight she had found in dancing. She said she had fallen in love with a dancer. She said the dancer was a woman. She said the woman would come to the restaurant in a few minutes to meet me. And so she did, tall and slender, with a slow, wide smile and the grace of her art.

As the youngest child in a family of powerful people, I had learned the dodge of putting my emotions on hold when caught by surprise—by a parent's quick turn of mood, an older brother's trick.

I shook the young woman's hand and smiled. Then the three of us—our eyes bright with our separate anxieties—sat down and had tea.

But as I drove home, what I had suspended came crashing down. I found myself thinking of my own experiences with homosexuality: the schoolboy fumbling, the adult's fear of loving someone of the same sex, of being close to someone who did.

Yet I felt no fear in the restaurant and felt none now in the car. Shock, yes, wearing off. Worry over what my daughter and her dancer would suffer. Worry over what my daughter's two children might suffer.

Beyond that, something I would later call acceptance and, later still, respect. I could not forget how complete my daughter had seemed. The love and confidence so evident at that small table had been palpable and, yes, honorable.

Early last fall, these two women committed themselves to each other. My daughter invited her mother and younger sister to witness the ceremony. She did not invite me, and in time she wrote to explain why.

I had taught her how to be an accoutrement to a man's life, how to flirt with men and mistrust women. I had put down homosexuals.

"Now I am a homosexual," she wrote. "That doesn't make you a very safe person." And she ended by telling

"I came out on Mother's Day. My parents very quietly turned around, went inside the house, locked the door, and turned on the alarm. My mother thinks that if she finds me the right girlfriend, I'll still get married."

STUDENT BRANDAEN JONES, TWENTY-TWO

me that if I wanted her respect I could begin by admitting the degree to which I was homophobic and sexist.

I was mad—hurt and mad. But something kept me from firing off the attack letter that scrolled in my mind. Perhaps it was fear of the emptiness that would have followed: the end to our periodic attempts to find in each other what we needed to find.

I ended up talking out my anger with my second wife and then with a friend, a woman who has a lesbian daughter. Then I called another woman, a counselor in a nearby town, and, wincing a bit at the thought of the years already spent in therapy, went back to work on myself.

The official National Coming Out Day logo was created by Keith Haring. National Coming Out Day, every October 11, was first celebrated in 1988.

I have been with my daughter and her lover several times now, each time more free and open than the last. Not too long ago all of us — my second wife and I, my two daughters and their families—met and played in the dusk under oaks and maples, calling and laughing. That same night the Republicans were gathering in Houston.

For days I saw and heard a small group of extremists calling for their brand of cultural cleansing. They, the adherents of the repressive right, had a list of the enemies —and homosexuals were near the top. Their message was clear and ugly: We talk to God, and God says, "Get the gays."

Cults have been chanting similar chants in this country since Salem. But the hate show at Houston—and the antigay campaigns in states from Oregon to Maine—have taught me that the haters have not lost their talent for mining the seams of our least reputable fears. They obviously have not lost their staying power. I said to myself that now I had a strong reason to "come out" publicly against them.

With that thought, that phrase, I finally did get it. My elder daughter and her lover made no bones about their sexual preference. I was making bones, plenty of them. I was telling only my closest friends about the two women and then only in conspiratorial confidence.

I had fallen back on the safety, the old safety, of silence. If I were going to come out in the open against the repression, I first needed to come out of that safe closet of mine and talk about my own daughter.

I saw her again recently. There was some family furniture to divide up, and when she and her lover were ready to drive home, I asked her if I could say something in private to her.

We walked off into an old pasture and I asked her if she would mind my writing this piece.

She reached out suddenly, took both my hands and pulled me close to her. Close enough so that I could see the tears begin, the love.

— WILLIAM H. MACLEISH

Different Is Not Bad

Each day, as I skim through the newspaper and read the articles concerning homosexuals, and as I look at the editorials, I wonder what the big deal is. Why does it matter that I like members of my own sex?

There are a lot of answers to that question. We, as a sexual minority, face a lot of discrimination in everyday life. Probably the most prevalent source of this stems from the simple reason that we are different. Anything that is not mainstream and "generally accepted" is different, and therefore hated by many people. Most people have trouble adjusting to something that they're not used to. The other side of this is religion. Most religions deem homosexual and bisexual behavior as void of love, damaging to society, and wholly unacceptable.

Through all of this hate, disgust, and lack of knowledge, people are not really facing the issues at hand. Why does it really matter that I'm gay? I like other guys; I find

"The community of black gay men is very diverse. We are short, tall, average height. We are light-skinned, brown-skinned, dark-skinned, and every shade in between. We are tops, bottoms, versatile, fats, fems, teachers, lawyers, poets, doctors, filmmakers, computer analysts, and sailors."

WRITER CHARLES HARPE

companionship with another male very pleasurable. I do not harm other people in the process; quite the opposite. I can bring love and happiness to someone's life, and does it really matter that that person may be another male? Different is not bad, and such a relationship is most certainly filled with love.

Four young queers adorned in gay garb relax at the 1994 Christopher Street Parade in New York City. (Bettye Lane)

What is damaging to society is the refusal to deal with current issues. Religion teaches that all people are created equally, yet it discriminates on the basis of sexual orientation. Which is more damaging to society—persecuting people because they like members of their own sex and forcing them to feel isolated, guilty, and less than human (which directly affects society), or allowing people to be as they are, and accepting them for who they are? Not a very difficult question to answer.

In the process of dealing with my sexuality, I have discovered more about myself, and about other people. I look at the world and remark about its awesome beauty, and I laugh with other people and have fun spending time with them. I am no different from anyone else. I did not choose to be gay, but I don't want to change (assuming that I could). True, being straight in today's world is much easier than being gay. Yet, at the same time, I have learned much through my struggle to accept myself as I am, and I refuse to cover up my feelings, which are just as wonderful as those of heterosexuals. The bottom line is that it doesn't matter that I'm gay. It doesn't matter that someone else is gay. People are all equally capable of sharing love and friendship, regardless of who they share those feelings with. The ability of one person to bring happiness to someone else is truly amazing. Does it matter if both of them are male or female? As my best friend says, "So I like other guys; big deal."

Exactly.

— MICHAEL, AT SIXTEEN, EXCERPTED FROM GROWING UP GAY/GROWING UP LESBIAN

Reflections of a Gay Jew

It was the night of my Yiddish class at the Jewish Community Center. Heartsick from the recent break-up of a relationship, I didn't feel like leaving the house. But I forced myself to attend because it was a great class and I hoped it would distract me.

The teacher asked, "*Vos macht a Yid, Naphtali?*—How are you?" and wouldn't let me be when I said I was okay. He sensed my sadness and asked, "*Hastu tsuris?*—Have you got trouble?"

I reluctantly replied, "*Yaw*" in my newly rediscovered mother tongue. "*Der mann vos ich hub zich farleebten hub mich mehr nisht leeb:* The man I love doesn't love me."

A woman in her sixties raised her eyebrows. "*Far vos iz ehr nisht farleebt mit deer?:* Why doesn't he love you?" "*Vile ehr iz a nar,*" I simplified: "Because he's a fool."

Another classmate, a man about my age, asked, "*Oyb ehr iz a nar, far vos nus dee eem leeb?*: If he's a fool, why do you love him?" "*Ich bin oichet a nar,*" I replied with a shrug. "I'm also a fool."

The teacher postulated, "*Oyb ehr iz a nar oon dee bist a nar, es iz a giteh shidach!:* If he's a fool and you're a fool, it's a perfect match!"

— NAPHTALI OFFEN

"This was around 1967 or 1968. I was nineteen and in New York for the first time. I was just beginning to come to terms with my sexuality, and had just gone by myself to see the play *Boys in the Band* which had recently opened. Afterward, I knew that I wanted to meet other gay men, but I didn't know how or where. So I walked up and down Broadway whistling the theme from the play, hoping that someone would get the hint and talk to me. Unfortunately, no one did."

LONNIE

I Was Queer When Gay Meant Happy

1963—President Kennedy is assassinated. His photo appears on the front page of the Portland *Evening Express.* I kiss it and whisper, "I love you." I am seven years old.

1965—I am sent to the principal's office for making fun of a girl's hairstyle on the school bus. Even then I had a sense of fashion do's and don't's.

1968—Sex-segregated gym classes begin. My first time in a boys' locker room. The teacher shows us where to change into our gym uniforms. My friend Paul asks me if I know what happens in the showers. I don't but I don't admit to it. Boys learn how to square-dance with girls by first learning how to square-dance with other boys. In the locker room I can't take my eyes off the twelve-year-old cocks beginning to swell in snow-white Fruit of the Looms. My friend Alan has a locker next to mine, and his cock always seems to make a bigger lump than anyone else's.

1969—Judy Garland dies of an overdose and I'm sadder than when Jim Morrison, Janis Joplin, and Jimi Hendrix do the same.

1970—My hometown paper does a story on "gay liberationists" in New York City. I realize that there are other people like me—at least in NYC.

1971—I begin writing mash notes to the other ninth grade boys. I leave these notes in their lockers with my locker number listed if they want to write back. No one does, but on the school bus one guy says, "I bet you know all the words to 'Lola.'" I do. I realize for the first time that gay isn't good.

1971—I ride my bike to an art festival in Portland and am cruised by an older guy wearing a leather vest and blue jeans while I look at an "art" book of naked boys called *The Boy.* We don't speak and we don't have sex but I start to learn the silent language of cruising. Repeat whatever he does (e.g., tap your foot, rub your crotch, etc.). I get scared when he follows me to another store, and I ride my bike home exhilarated.

1971—Dr. David Reuben's *Everything You Always Wanted to Know About Sex (But Were Afraid to Ask)* becomes a best-seller. The idea of sticking light bulbs and Coke bottles up my bum and hairpins in my cock scares and excites me.

1972—I finally stick my fifteen-year-old cock through a glory hole in Bradlees and am sucked off by a guy. I have my first orgasm ever and have nothing to remember him by but his shoes visible beneath the cold, metal partition. The guy doesn't know it but he taught me what the end result of jerking off is (orgasm), that fifteen-year-olds are a hot commodity, that you can have sex almost anywhere and any time, and that silence is golden. I don't speak to a sex partner or have sex outside a bathroom for two years.

1974—I make my decision about where to go to college when I participate in an orgy in a tearoom in Providence, Rhode Island. In the fall, I enroll at Brown University.

1974—I meet my first boyfriend, a schoolteacher named Mike, in a tearoom at Brown. He fucks me every weekend using Vaseline Intensive Care hand lotion as lube. Condoms are still for straight guys who fuck girls who can't afford the pill, an IUD, or diaphragm.

1975—I become president of Gay Lib at Brown. There is only one female member.

1976—I attend my first gay liberation parade in Providence and come out to my family.

— REB

Yom Kippur Morning at Kehilla Community Synagogue

On the day of Yom Kippur we traditionally read the portion of Leviticus that includes the statement that a man lying with a man as with a woman is an abomination, which later goes on to pronounce the act as being punishable by death. I, like many of us, have spent years feeling furious about this portion and trying to either avoid it or dismiss it. It has always lent a bitter edge to Yom Kippur, because for many of us, part of what is especially powerful on this day is that we know that Jews all over the world and through the ages have gathered together to chant the same prayers and share the same feelings of tribal angst. I am also sadly and angrily aware that on this day, Jews all over the world have received reinforcement and even blessing for their hatred of those of us who are not heterosexual.

In the past few years, though, I have come to a new point with this *parsha.* While I know its original intent and how it has historically been used to justify hatred and violence toward my people—one of my peoples—this is how I read it at this point: It says, "Do not lie with a man as with a woman." In other words, if you are with a man, be with him, fully. If you are with a woman, be with her, fully. Do not pretend you are with someone else of another gender. Be present. As Audre Lorde said, do not look away as you come together. In this reading of the parsha, we are mandated to integrate our sexuality, however we define that for ourselves, with our spirituality and with the rest of our lives. And according to this *parsha,* to not do so is *to'evah,* usually translated in English as "abomination" but more accurately described as "that which leads us astray." So the *parsha* says that to not be our authentic selves, to not be fully present with one another, and to not bring our sexuality into the wholeness of our lives, leads us "astray," away from our truest and most aligned selves.

I don't necessarily expect that Jews all over the world are going to rush to embrace this new interpretation as the true meaning of this *parsha* each Yom Kippur. But then, I never expected to see Rabin and Arafat shake hands on the White House lawn. Anything is possible.

Meanwhile, I'd like to take a brief look at where the Jewish community as a whole is in relation to lesbian and gay issues. It wasn't that long ago that most of the community was dealing with the most basic issue of acknowledging our existence, admitting that yes, there are Jews who are lesbian and gay (though, of course, always in someone else's family). Most of the Jewish community has progressed along to "tolerance." Tolerance is characterized by the notion that lesbians and gay men should not be overtly discriminated against, and by the notion that we should be left alone. Tolerance is a lot better than overt persecution, but being left alone means exactly that —you are on your own, to be isolated, excluded, and as invisible as possible. Tolerance stops some of the overt oppression, but it does nothing to build community.

Parts of the Jewish community have moved along to deal with inclusion—encouraging us to be visible, acknowledging our relationships and families, valuing us as participants and leaders and role models. . . . And that's good. But it has still mostly operated on a kind of "Us/Them" paradigm. You are welcome here as long as you fit in with "Us," but don't challenge "Us" too much, don't try to change too many things, don't expect the dominant culture of "Our" institution to shift. Most of it is not conscious, and very little of it applies only to lesbians, gay men, bisexuals, and transgendered people. Many of us feel Outside at one point or another—we're too old, we're too young, we have visible or invisible disabilities, we don't know much about Judaism, we spent ten years practicing Buddhism, we didn't grow up as Jews. . . . Few or none of us feel totally secure, and there are many important stories to be listened to fully and respectfully.

— **ANDY/AVI ROSE**

You Dared Us to Dream That We Are Worth Wanting Each Other

January 30, 1989, Brooklyn

Dear Joe,

Night before last we dedicated the room in the Center named for Charles Angel. It was a wonderful, caring ceremony and I thought of you several times. Harold Robinson talked about how the room is important both as symbol and as substance. And we need both—equally. I guess that's a good way to remember you. To remember you as a metaphor, but not to forget the text, and to embrace all the humanity of your life, like an orisha—a flesh-and-blood hero. That sounds like a good African way to remember you.

It just dawned on me that you were the first man I knew with both ears pierced—way back when. I always wanted to, but only found the courage last summer, now that it's fashionable. So you never saw me with my two holes. I remember your Leroy mechanic shirt, too, when I met you. You were doing your "Black/Out" column in *Au Courant* then, and I was so excited to meet you. To me, your most important work was always those "Brother to Brother" essays. What they said was so simple, but so unsaid. There's nobody writing essays on the Black Gay Male experience, and that's so important. Your stuff went to the heart—and there's a new power in them for me each time I re-read them. If I had to pick your single most valuable gift, it would be the aphorism "Black men loving Black men is a revolutionary act." And it is! As simple as it seems, it is. And *that* is the challenge of your life and death. To make these words real. To really love each other. To love each other enough to care, to sacrifice, to risk, to "take care of our own when the night grows cold and silent."

Members of Other Countries, a groundbreaking New York literary collective of gay African American men, in 1987. (Robert Giard)

And now I realize that Black men loving Black men is truly "an autonomous agenda . . . not rooted in any particular sexual, political, or class affiliation, but in our mutual survival." That loving each other, more than politics or being out or marches or CD or legislation is what will "create the Black Gay community in which you have built your home." The ways in which we manifest that love must indeed be myriad.

"I dare *us* to dream that we are worth wanting each other," you wrote; dared yourself to dream: that we could "receive more of what we want from each other." You talked about giving "each other permission to dream and speak of those dreams," about friendships "not lost to anger, or silence."

You spoke, too, of breaking silence, of speaking and exorcising not only anger, but hurt. So in my love for you, I must also speak my anger and hurt, for "What legacy is to be found in our silence?" So I claim this *public* space to grieve, to explore *my* love and friendship; to say to *my* brother, "Man I loved you. I really, really loved you."

So you didn't write, as you once dreamed with me, "the last essay that would allow you to leave the planet." So you didn't find that relationship with another brother you spoke of so fiercely when we first met, with a spirit that dwindled in despair and resentment. And your biggest silence was you didn't talk about loving *yourself*. But you did enough, baby, you did more than enough. Thanks!

Our challenge now is to stand on the shoulders of your words and become the dream.

Brother to brother,

Love,
Colin

— **COLIN ROBINSON, EXCERPTED FROM** BROTHER TO BROTHER

Tomàs

I am an eighteen year-old gay Latino, and I'm HIV-positive. It makes me angry that if our society didn't make homosexuality such an awful thing, maybe I wouldn't have denied to myself that I was gay. Maybe I wouldn't have thought of the sex I began having with men at fifteen as something that never really happened. Maybe I wouldn't have thought that you had to be a gay man in San Francisco to get AIDS.

I didn't talk about AIDS or safe sex. I was afraid if I brought it up I'd be rejected by a sex partner. No one around me talked about it a lot.

The first time I tested, I was sixteen years old: My results came back negative. I hadn't been infected, so I figured that my sexual activities were okay, and I didn't change. I decided to again, one year later, because two of my friends were testing at the same time. I planned my second visit around my vacation, in the spring. I chose a family planning health clinic three cities away from suburbia and my home. I didn't want to run into anyone I knew.

I was afraid I might be positive, but I couldn't believe it when I was. I cried for a while and shouted, "Fuck, I can't even have my own kids!" After I calmed down, my counselor directed me to services for HIV-infected youth: a nurse practitioner, a support group, and a case manager. Again, I went to a neighboring county to use their services because I wanted to keep this anonymous from everyone I knew—especially my parents.

I don't have many gay friends, and those that I have (outside support groups) don't know I'm infected. I'm closed off from people because I'm afraid they'll reject me for having HIV. You'd think after living through the experience of growing up gay, that people would realize how hard it is to have HIV. But they don't, and they run away from you if you do. Most of my other gay or lesbian friendships have been formed through my support group for youth with HIV.

Surprisingly, some of my strongest support for being gay and having HIV has come from a place I never thought it would: high school. It had failed me before; the teachers never taught us about HIV. Now, however, I have two teachers that I talk to at least once a week.

My mother and two of my brothers know I am gay, and telling my mother truly helped me become in tune with my gayness. She has been very nurturing, and my coming out has made us closer. My father is from Guatemala, and he would reject me if he found out I was a *joto*.

I haven't told my family that I am HIV-infected. At a time when they are the people I need most, their own hate and prejudices would prevent them from helping one of their own.

The thing that really got me was when my best friend, who was twenty-one and just graduated from college, died of AIDS. I am still devastated. I truly don't know how I've handled all the cards some dealer has dealt me, but I learned through my friend that in any situation, no matter how many obstacles seem to be ahead of you, you should always try to make the most of any situation. My friend found out he was infected and had PCP in the space of few weeks. His life was turned upside down, but he still managed to maintain a 4.0 grade point average and graduate from college in three years.

I definitely think that being a teenager with this disease is different from being an adult. Does anyone really think that at seventeen I would have attained every skill that I needed to do better in life? Well, I sure hadn't. And because I had to learn fast, I lost out on my teenage years, which should have been fun. I wasn't prepared to figure out how to set goals, how to decide what to accomplish in my life.

I just passed my one-year milestone of learning I was HIV-infected. I didn't think much about it at the time; I was just happy to have lived that long. I wish more people would forget that stereotype—that once you test positive you die the next day.

I graduated from high school, and plan on transferring from junior college to a four-year university to focus on becoming a psychologist or public health worker. I hope to do something to improve the way American society thinks. HIV hasn't made me change my future plans, it has just made me concentrate on how to attain my goals. All in all, I somehow overcame the obstacles growing up in suburbia and going to school with so many close-minded, ignorant people. Now I can actually be my own self.

— ANONYMOUS

Stonewalled? A Journal

June 1. Most of the time I don't think of myself as being different. I don't say to myself as I go shopping, to the subway, to the movies, or to a meeting, "Here I am, a legally blind lesbian, going out in the world." My friends and most colleagues don't say, "Watch out! Move the furniture, lock away all the valuables; the blind lesbian's coming for dinner."

It's only when I run up against hatemongers that I come face-to-face with the fact that I am different;

unlike some in our society, I encounter discrimination, prejudice, ignorance, and well-meaning stupidity based not on my personality, but on disability and sexual orientation.

I know that when I'm identified only as a "blind lesbian," I sound like an exotic creature at the zoo or a guest on *Oprah.* And when you add the word writer . . . well, the *National Enquirer* comes to mind.

June 23. I never dreamed that in my lifetime gays and lesbians from so many different walks of life would be able to talk so openly about their lives; or that the media would cover this so positively.

But what, I think, about people with disabilities?

Despite some progress since the Americans with Disabilities Act (ADA) was passed, the media still barely know that we exist (other than as "superheroes" or "helpless victims"). The media acknowledge and chronicle the gay civil rights movement; for the most part, if it fell in their laps, they wouldn't grasp the fact that the disability rights movement exists.

I finally came to terms with my sexuality, thanks to some counseling and some friends who had the patience of Job, the wit of Woody Allen, and the common sense (but not, I'm sure, the mores) of June Cleaver. But I know that I was very lucky. What, I wonder as I skim through a newspaper story about the Gay Games, about disabled youths who are gay? Who's there for them? How do they learn about their history or themselves?

I've gotten much support from the disability rights movement. But what about the homophobia that exists in our movement?

And though I have gay friends and participate in some events in the gay community, I am aware of the prejudice against disabled people that exists among some lesbians and gays. I think of the inaccessible restaurants, stores, and other gay businesses that I've run up against.

When I was younger and first getting to know the gay community, I'd sometimes think when people saw only my blindness and nothing else about me, *I could come out but no one would see—they'll just think I got my cane out of the closet.*

June 26. I learned about Stonewall in the early 1980s. But the first time I found that I had rights [as a disabled person] was in 1981 when I attended some "504" training sessions. ["504" is the section of the Rehabilitation Act of 1973 that bars discrimination against people with disabilities in programs that get federal money.] Newton may have discovered gravity when the apple hit him on the head, but that was nothing compared to the headlines I felt when I learned that I didn't have to passively accept prejudice—that I had the legal right to fight against discrimination.

But I know that the "504" regulations and the ADA aren't enough; we need to fight much harder for our rights, for our lives, for our identity.

We need more than 2,000 ADAPT members [the ACT UP of the disability movement] to march on D.C. We need tens of hundreds of thousands—we need to march on the nation's capital.

We don't need an occasional disabled performance artist or a few disabled writers, actors, and comics. We need disability culture.

We need not just one or two movies or novels that deal openly and honestly with the disability experience. We need mountains of movies, numerous novels, oceans of operas and paintings and plays that depict our lives.

We need to hold fast to our dreams—to plan and work toward our Stonewall.

— **KATHI WOLFE**

On One Hand and the Other

On the one hand, Asian societies view homosexuality as a Western perversion, or (in the case of communist regimes) as a bourgeois Western perversion; this, despite the long tradition of homoerotic love in all Asian countries (e.g., the story of the emperor's 'cut sleeve' in ancient China, the elite Hwarang archers of traditional Korea, etc.). And ethnic communities in the United States often refuse to acknowledge the lesbian, gay, bisexual, and transgendered children of the Asian diaspora.

On the other hand, American society as a whole "construct" or imagines the Asian Pacific Islander as an exotic foreigner, as "orientalism" that sometimes can also manifest itself in the attitudes of gay white men to APIs. David Henry Hwang's Broadway hit play *M. Butterfly* depicted a latter-day Pinkerton deceived by self-generated illusions about his own Cio-Cio San, a pattern that all too well is replicated in the relationships between GWMs and APIs.

— JOURNALIST PAUL EE-NAM PARK HAGLAND, FROM "WHY ASIAN ONLY?" IN OUTLINES MAGAZINE

New Mexico APL

Let's see. Shall I tell you about when my mom disowned me? Ugh. It's a gory story—as all such stories are. Suffice it to say, my dad is a great peacemaker, and for this Asian family, the integrity of the family unit is very important. By the next summer, my mom was inviting me to lunches with the family again. In fact, a few years ago my parents (and most of my family) met my second lover, Ann, and my mom even took a liking to her. I tell you, after what I've been through with my mom, it was a distinct pleasure to see her sitting on the couch, chatting amiably with my lover about teaching (they're both teachers), ghosts, and other things.

For total acceptance by my family, though, I think Ann would have to learn Cantonese. Plus, of course, she'd have to somehow metamorphose into a Chinese person. They might accept that she and I are lovers, but that still doesn't stop my mom from making snide comments in Cantonese (when we're all, including Ann, sitting at the dinner table) about "that white one!" (Oh Goddess! Do you ever just get the feeling sometimes that our parents are just crazy?!?)

Ah, but back to New Mexico. Don't get me wrong, I really love this place—after fourteen years here, the deserts and mountains and open places have become a part of my being. Not to mention our unique mix of different peoples and cultures. Unfortunately, what New Mexico *doesn't* have is a lot of Asian queers. I could count all of us on two hands, and still not use all the fingers. I'm always looking around at dances or queer events, so I recognize two or three Asian-looking wimyn by sight now. About a year ago, I finally got up the courage to introduce myself to one of these wimyn at a dance. Now she and I and a couple of other (non-Asian) dykes get together regularly to play the Chinese "game of four winds," mah-jongg.

I am second-generation Chinese American. Thirty years ago, my parents met on the proverbial boat coming over to America. They have always spoken Cantonese at home. I can understand simple Cantonese like "it's time for dinner," but I cannot speak it. I love to hear the occasional Cantonese on TV or in movies, or even rarely people on the street or in a store. I can feel the language in my blood, feel the recognition from buried synapses formed long ago in my brain. Cantonese is my native language as much as any other, for it was the first language I heard. It was the language around which my neurons first structured themselves. They say that language shapes how we perceive our world. And so in that way, at least, a part of me—some of the most basic parts of who I am—will be forever Cantonese. I like that.

Two gay men pose together in 1994 as a part of the first authorized gay contingent to the annual Chinese New Year's Parade in San Francisco. (Rink Foto)

And so I continue to search. For a Cantonese dyke who can teach me the Cantonese word for lesbian, and help me open that buried Cantonese part of me. For more Asian queers, who can understand what it is to be slanty-eyed and short, to love someone of your own gender, and to have a crazy family that you love. Until then, I guess I'll just have to be the resident left-handed Asian dyke in New Mexico!

— **TZE-HEI YONG**

Lesbian & Gay Pride Week 1992
gaypride
LESBIAN & GAY PRIDE NYC 1989
YEARS
I Like Sober Gay Men
better gay than grumpy

CHAPTER 5

Coming Together: Building Community

When gay men and lesbians attempt to describe the world we inhabit with other gay people, the two most often used terms are "family" and "community." Many of us take an unofficial gay national anthem, "We Are Family," literally. If we want to know if someone is gay, we sometimes ask, "Is he family?" In the same way, the "gay and lesbian community" has become a commonly used expression meaning "all gay people." We use the terms family and community, because they give us a collective identity around which we can live, love, and organize.

As gay families, we come together out of love, friendship, and desire. We choose lovers, friends, partners, and sometimes children as a part of our lives; many of the bonds of these families we choose are as strong or stronger than our sometimes strained relationships with our biological families and families of origin. But we cannot deny that we are also deeply connected to our parents, siblings, and relatives. With our families of origin, the challenge is often to find out how to embrace our blood relatives—and how to help them to embrace us. In the first section of the chapter, we explore both kinds of gay families.

The concept of "family" is clear—but what is "community"? What does it mean to say we are part of the "gay and lesbian community"? During the 1970s and well into the 1980s, many lesbians worked politically and hung out socially primarily with other lesbians. Lesbian-feminism and lesbian separatism allowed lesbians to defy the sexism that many gay men, like men in general, embodied, and create organizations and communities of their own. Because of this, and because of the cultural differences between gay men and lesbians,

FIRSTS

On December 5, 1984, Berkeley became the first city in the United States to extend spousal benefits to gay city employees' live-in lovers. To qualify under the new program, applicants were required to fill out and submit an "affidavit of Domestic Partnership."

getting personal...

Now Accepting Applications
GWM, professional, 29, 6', 172 lbs., good shape, HIV-, fair-skinned blond. William Hurt type with receding hairline. Very well-educated preppy digs penny loafers, khaki, navy blue, and 100% cotton. Dress Republican —think Democrat. Now screening applications for personal sex slave/cabana boy (significant other). Must have stable employment and no personality disorder. All Republican looks give equal consideration. Prefer physically fit, HIV-, GWM (25–35), discreet, clean-cut, no drugs or criminal history, sharp dress and masculine —I didn't give up women to date girls. Ivy League alums and sensation-seeking personalities preferred. Must tolerate J. Crew, Gap, L.L. Bean, Nordstrom, and Abercrombie & Fitch. Hobbies: clinical psychology, psychiatry, medicine, law. Send resume/vitae with photo.

Clones Begone
I loathe clubs, but I finally went out with a friend to get her off my back (we don't have that kind of relationship) and I was appalled: cookie-cutter baby dyke clones by the dozen! What I want is a woman between 35–40 who's smart and secure enough to be herself; she's also attractive, slender, stable, sane, and possibly clean and sober. If you don't look like anyone else you know and you don't swap clothes with your buddies, call . . .

gay men spent most of their energies with other gay men. While there was always some overlap between the two communities, the issues of gender often kept them apart.

But in the late seventies the radical right began its attack on the rights of all gay men and lesbians, exemplified by California state senator John Briggs's attempt to forbid gay people from teaching in the public schools. A few years later, the AIDS epidemic hit the gay male community, leaving it devastated. By the mid-eighties, gay men and lesbians were beginning to work together for our very survival. Some gay men and lesbians of color found themselves less tied to their gendered communities than they were to their ethnic communities. In addition, younger gay people were finding more in common across gender than they found across generation within their own gender. In the 1990s, many of us have become allies in our quest to build a strong and vibrant community.

But a community is about more than political alliances and fighting a disease. It is about building institutions to take care of ourselves, from community centers to AIDS hospices. It is about joining together spiritually. For some rural gay men and lesbians, community is about discovering a shared joy in the land itself. Others have made music the center of their lives, coming together annually to celebrate each other with our own words and songs.

No matter what particular form it takes, that is the meaning of "community": celebrating ourselves together.

CREATING FAMILY

For gay men and lesbians, family is not necessarily limited to biological relatives. The idea of chosen, or created, families is not just a theoretical argument against the assumption that the nuclear family is the only ideal. While some gay people insist that the language of family still belongs to the straight world, more of us are starting to look at our relationships with our lovers and our friends as our family. We sometimes include our biological families in this definition; but unlike most straight people, our families often include our ex-lovers as well.

When mainstream society denies us formal recognitions of these created families, our anger is not theoretical, either. We care for loved ones with AIDS, but cannot provide them with our health insurance benefits in the same way that straight spouses can share their partner's health policies. We cannot automatically inherit should our partners die. For years, gay people routinely lost custody of children in court battles based solely on our orientation. Sometimes, as in the case of Karen Thompson and Sharon Kowalski, we can have our families forcibly broken apart by courts and biological relations.

Still, we continue to create powerful bonds. And whether we are making close friends, dating, involving ourselves in committed relationships, getting married, or having children, lesbians and gay men are redefining what it means to be a family, expanding our love and familial ties far beyond the tight constraints of the "traditional" family.

How We Meet

One of our editors went on-line and asked, "Where did you meet your most recent lover/boyfriend/girlfriend/trick?" Following are some of the responses that came back.

"In a laundromat. She was folding her underwear. I approached her because I recognized her from around town. After we talked for about half an hour, she informed me that she was looking for friends but wasn't 'into dating,' and would I like to come over for dinner sometime. That was over seven years ago. (P.S.: She's a great cook!")
— LYNN

"I met my girlfriend at a Girl Scout Camp in Orlando, Florida. She was the first new counselor I met, but she was walking the *back* trails reading *Jurassic Park*. My pickup line—"My name's Skippy, who the hell are you?" What can I say, it worked. Unfortunately, she was married at the time and I had never had any kind of experience with a woman. Luckily, it all worked out and we've been together almost a year and a half now. Oh, she was also my supervisor and we slept in the same tent. Made for some interesting nights. . . ."
— MARY

"I met my most recent significant other (I can't think of a better term for the relationship) in high school, during rehearsals for the fall musical. I was fifteen and very shy at the time; I had a crush on her but didn't have the guts to ask her out until another queer friend of ours outed her to me and fixed us up for the prom."
— SUSAN

getting personal...

Big Butch Daddy
Bearded, muscular, hairy, GWM, 6', 210 (50" chest, 18" arm), aggressive, physical, ex-military, into outdoors, travel, adventures. You are muscular, straight-acting, bear cub or boy, 18–35, any race, submissive or versatile, ready to live for your man. Bearded, hairy, ex-military, hunter, or outdoorsman a plus. I like wrestling, weights, hunting, camping, gold mining, and aggressive, physical men eager to bond—semper fi guys.

Beautiful Music
A loaf of bread, a jug of wine, and thou beside me, singing in the wilderness . . . a little pâté with the nice pain au levain and Veuve Cliqout would be nice. 47 y.o. GWF seeks companion to share life's simple pleasures.

Black And White
Is great color combination, but difficult to achieve without going to bars. So we try the ads...I did this before and met a fine man, but he turned out to be a flake, so here goes again. You: GBM, preferably under 35, shorter than I, bright, funny, professional, slim, sexy, and likes older GWM. Me: late 40s, 6', distinguished, slim, energetic, witty, traveled, graying at the temples, trim beard and 'stache. Active and popular member of the community, but lack that one special man. Are you out there?

getting personal...

Dynamic, Dapper Dyke
seeks sexy, sultry, sensual, sinister, seductive sister for volcanic eruptions and creative explorations into lesbianism.

HIV+ And Looking For Love
If you can't offer me love I'll take friendly sex, massage, horniness, and very good-natured fun. You must be over 40, HIV+ or able to deal with it, have varied interests. I am GWM, HIV+, trim, 5'6", 135#, mid-50s (of course I look and act younger) and want to meet you if you are interesting, reasonably attractive and looking for fun, support, and conversation.

Baby Kitten Seeks Leash
Submissive young kitten seeks dominant mistress for playful pawing and sexy scratching contests. Baby kitten: AF, 5'8", 126#, sexy, cute paws. Leash owner: playful, sexy, cute, fit, rough, friendly, dominant, sharp nails. Command me to sit on your lap, force me to snuggle with you on the sofa, make kitty earn her meal. If you think you can be my caregiver, then leave me a message and make me meow.

Topman, 56, Wants Monogamous
Long-term robust sessions with prudent, very mature kneeler. Simple, safe, discreet scenario.

"Mine is a little more unusual than most—the circus. A friend of mine knows some of the clowns in Ringling Brothers, and we wound up at a circus party. There was this cute li'l blonde thang, and we hit it off. He's in charge of training/caring for the two baby elephants Romeo and Juliet."
— JIM

"I met my partner last year at our tenth high school reunion. We both attended the residential high school, but lived in different dorms, and neither of us was 'out' during high school. A week later, I received a call from Mark, a classmate who lived about thirty-five miles away, whose only words to me the night of the reunion were: "Your name is Rob, right?" (No, I'm David). Mark is the first person I've ever dated. Three months later, I came out to my parents. Two months later, I bought a house and Mark moved in. And today (~1 year later) my parents, my two sisters and their boyfriends all came to our house for Thanksgiving. It sounds a little like a "Fairy Tale," doesn't it?"
— DAVID

"We met on Election Day in 1992. I was a judge of elections (Democrat, 'cause there's no real socialist party in this country). Anyway, I caught the Republican judge letting somebody vote twice. So I phoned the Election Board, who sent over some official people and a cop to arrest him. This cop and I dated for almost two years."
— IKOREN

"My lover and I met sixteen years ago at Harry's Back East, a now-defunct bar here in NYC. The meeting was due to our being the only two guys uninformed enough to be looking to get laid at eight o'clock on a Wednesday night."
— TNENNO

"I met my partner at Circuit City, a consumer electronics chain. We were both shopping for TVs. We started talking, I dropped copious hints about spending time in the City [San Francisco] and at "the river" [the Russian River], and he popped the question, "Do you want to go get some pizza?" That was January Fourth, 1989."
— MIKE

"The waiting room at your doctor's office can be an excellent meeting place. That cute guy isn't about to disappear into thin air like that sexy brown-haired boy you were dancing with at the Sound Factory Bar on Body Positive Sundays. . . . Do not, repeat, DO NOT try this at your therapist's office. . . . AIDS benefits are always jam-packed with wealthy and boring potential husbands."
— AUTHOR DAVID FEINBERG, IN POZ

Dating: Tips on Approval

In the dyke-dating realm, when a special someone new has entered your life, there are three major obstacles to overcome. They are: acceptance of your new sweetie from friends, family, and pets (and vice versa).

• **Friends.** They work in a funny way when evaluating a new date. The system is commonly referred to as "energy," i.e.: "We like her, she has good *energy*," or "I don't know, her *energy* just doesn't seem right for you."

In these cases, the word "energy" is usually being substituted for something more difficult to communicate. Your friend may find it more tactful to comment on a new date's "energy" than to say, flat out, something like: "She seems less psycho than your last girlfriend. She gains points with us for having a job." Or, "I don't think she's right for you because I wouldn't trust her as far as I could throw her."

If your friends comment on dream girl's "energy" in a positive way, take it as a good thing and let it rest. You probably don't want to know that they really mean: "Your last girlfriend was such an anal-retentive, uptight bitch. At least this one seems to know something about relaxation."

If, on the other hand, your friends think your hot momma doesn't have the right energy, this should be investigated a little further. Try to find out what they really mean. Maybe your friends see something that you, in your candy-heart haze, are missing. It could be that your friends know something that you don't. This doesn't mean you have to dump the apple of your eye like an overflowing ashtray. Just examine your friends' doubts and take them to heart. Sometimes a critical friend isn't always coming from the clearest of perspectives, either.

getting personal...

Lipstick Lesbians Are My Passion!
Androgynous soft butch seeks all lipstick lesbians for sexual exploration with no emotional ties. Respond to Lipstick . . .

Romantic & Sincere
Nice-looking, 51, GWM, HIV–, NS, 5'8", 158, clean-cut, personable, successful, masculine, loving, and fun. Not looking for someone to go to bed with, but someone to wake up with in the morning. Looking for special GWM (32–46), NS, educated, successful and nice. Someone who is comfortable with who he is. Must like to cuddle, be honest, know how to communicate and have a heart.

Princess With Moat
Fair femme top seeks dark butch bottom. Must be born in 1956 or '52. Be open-minded and aware. Please have manners and old money preferred. Light smokers and drinkers okay —no drugs or cats. Immaturity not accepted.

Gentle 60s WM Top Seeks
Soft 55-70s tender gentleman who is delectably affectionate and smooth. We are responsible, secure, intelligent, gracious, and devoid of drugs and disease. Comfortable and secure within our esoteric persona. Creative and exploring yet always considerate. All answered.

getting personal...

Go Fish

You: are f-e-m-a-l-e (don't laugh, you have to speak slowly and affirmatively for people—especially lesbians); have broader tastes in women than Venus-incarnate or similar pagan sex goddess; stable (can stand on two feet w/o falling down); think PC means "pretentious caca"; wonder why the 60s killed Janis instead of Jerry Garcia; read something besides Gloria Steinem and the personals; like blond jokes (even if you're blond); will still like me if I don't 2-step, wear work boots or fantasize about Madonna; are a little more substantial than "GF, br/bl, NS/ND, 30s, 5'5", 130# into long walks on the beach . . ."; truly know the meaning of "ex-girlfriend" (not the lesbian version); will wait 'til at least the third date to bring the wedding ring and are suspicious of all these beautiful people in the personals. Me, well I'm . . .

Bold Butch Babe

seeks androgynous dyke for spontaneous combustion. The meek shall not inherit this dyke. No LTRs. No glove, no love.

• **Family,** on the other hand, will usually not find it necessary to use so much tact. I have found there to be three common responses from family members on meeting the woman who is doing the nasty with their little girl. One response is the all-accepting, "I am open-minded and have no problem with my daughter's lesbianism, so welcome to the family—here, we got you an Easter basket." Another, which is maybe a little more common, is the "special friend" treatment, where the exact nature of your relationship is somewhat muted, and you are referred to as so-'n'-so's "friend." My own mom does this all the time. She'll say, "Kathie and her friend are going camping," or "Why don't you bring your *friend?*" As though I had only one. The third one is, "I can't see you, you're invisible."

If you want to win over someone's parents, don't stress out about it too much. Just keep in mind that, at least at first, public displays of affection may be a bit much for them to take. Also, call your sugar-blossom by her name instead of, say, Love Muffin. Otherwise, just relax and be yourself as you are when you are being *extremely polite* and *courteous.*

• **Finally, pets**. How your ray of sunshine's pets respond to you may, to her, be the most telling thing of all about your character. Whether it's true or not, many pet owners believe that their pets are, in fact, great judges of character. Therefore, it is essential you worm your way into the heart of Fido or Fluffy. Think Milkbones. Think Pounce. Whatever you do, just don't think, *Get this smelly bag of fleas away from me.*

So there it is. Friends, family, and pets: three acceptance obstacles we all must face. Oh, one last word of advice: whatever you do, make sure you have taken all the usual personal hygiene measures. Some first impressions never change.

— KATHIE BERQUIST

Dating Again

I have for the first time since my companion's death a real date, with a landscape architect whom I'm taking to a play. Tom, my date, is a nice-looking guy with a steady paycheck—every writer's fantasy. When he tells me he's reading a novel, I'm impressed and for a long minute bedeviled by stupid, involuntary fantasies of a partner, someone to fill this void in my life.

So it's after the play and he's driving us back to my car and the air is charged with possibility. Never good at leaving well enough alone, I break the silence by asking him what he's been reading, which turns out to be Stephen King, but that's OK, I don't hold it against him. "I'm an Anne Rice fan myself," I say. From *The Vampire Lestat* it's an easy non sequitur to complaining about the mess of blackberry briars my landlord calls a yard. "What you need is a landscape architect," Tom says.

"We'll both be old men before I can afford you," I say.

An awkward pause. Tom clears his throat. "There's something you ought to know," he says, but I know it already, I don't need to be told and I don't want to hear it. I cover his free hand with mine. "Next date," I say.

And now I'm homeward bound after a chaste peck on the cheek from Tom and all I can manage is a sad smile, but the next day when I tell this to a straight friend from the suburbs he looks at me as if I'm losing my mind. And maybe I am; or is this just the difference between those inside the epidemic and those looking on? What have I been brought to? "The lucky fellow," Elie Wiesel writes of the terrorist leader in *Dawn*. "At least he can cry. When a man weeps he knows that one day he will stop."

— **FENTON JOHNSON**

Lovers enjoy a quiet walk together in the country. (©JEB)

Twelve Tips for Meeting Other Young Queers

Too young for bars? Can't use the classifieds? Feel like you came out of the closet and stepped into a vacuum? Then this list is for you! Think of it as a starting point—and only take the risks you feel comfortable taking. We all come out at our own pace.

1. Visit your local lesbian/gay/bisexual community center. If you live in a big city, there will be a community center. Other towns may have organizations that provide activities for gay youth. Even if the activities don't interest you, some of the people might!

2. Hang out at progressive coffeehouses. Lots of queer youth frequent coffeehouses as alternatives to bars. You could even put up fliers advertising for young lesbians and gays to meet once a week or so at a certain café for conversation and a cup of joe.

Two young queers on the Christopher Street Pier in New York City. (Dan Nicoletta)

3. Volunteer at a gay youth talkline. While waiting for calls, you can get to know other talkline workers. You'll also be able to help other gay, lesbian, bi, and questioning youth with their own issues.

4. Wear a pink triangle or a queer T-shirt in public or at school. It pays to advertise!
5. Come out in one of your classes. If you figure one in ten are lesbian or gay, in a class of thirty, there are two or three of you. Maybe you'll start a trend!
6. Cruise down to a bookstore or library. If a library or bookstore has a gay/lesbian/bi section, chances are that other gay people will be stopping by. Ask them what they suggest or what they think of a book you've read. Be patient, though—you may be waiting for a while. Use the time to explore the world of queer writing.
7. Attend gay/lesbian/bi art openings, readings, and cultural events. You'll impress your teachers and parents with your maturity by seeking culture, and no one has to be the wiser about why you're seeking it with such enthusiasm!
8. Volunteer at a local AIDS organization. A lot of towns without explicitly gay organizations at least have AIDS support organizations. Even if you're just licking envelopes, you'll be doing the world and yourself a huge favor.
9. Join or start a queer teen group at school. Raise a few eyebrows, stir up some controversy, and get a date besides. What could be better?
10. Check out computer bulletin boards. Take a spin on the lavender information superhighway! America Online, for example, has many bulletin boards for queer and questioning youth.
11. Write a gay/lesbian pen pal service. Alyson Publications, in Boston, has one. Long-distance letters have the advantage of relative anonymity while allowing you to talk with someone who might be going through the same things you are.
12. Visit the lesbian/gay/bisexual group at the nearest college or university. Most college groups love to have active members from local high schools. You may not get dates, but you might find some great friends.
***BONUS FOR BABY DYKES**:* **Look into local women's bookstores and community centers.** Loads of lesbians participate in women's activities centered around feminist bookstores and community centers. Strut your stuff, sister, and use your woman-loving-woman sensibilities!
— DON ROMESBURG

DID YOU KNOW...

Gay and lesbian teens are taking same-sex dates to their high school proms in increasing numbers since Randy Rohl of Sioux Falls, South Dakota, and Aaron Fricke of Rock Port, Rhode Island, did it in the late 1970s and early 1980s. Alternative gay proms are emerging all over the country.

The 1994 "Live to Tell" prom in Los Angeles was the first-ever gay and lesbian prom in the country sanctioned by a public school district. In Minneapolis, District 202, a recreational and support center for lesbian, gay, bisexual, and transgendered youth, held the "Love Like Never Before '94" Prom in two parts. The first, for youth, was free. The second was a fund-raiser for the youth prom, attended by gay and lesbian adults who didn't have the chance to celebrate their same-sex love the first time around.

Stages of Gay Male Relationships

The stages, time periods, and characteristics listed below are from *The Male Couple: How Relationships Develop* by David P. McWhirter, M.D., and Andrew M. Mattison, M.S.W., Ph.D.

Blending: Stage One, the first year. Merging, limerence (falling in love), equalizing of partnership, and high sexual activity.

Nesting: Stage Two, the second and third years. Homemaking, finding compatibility, decline of limerence, and ambivalence.

Maintaining: Stage Three, the fourth and fifth years. Reappearance of the individual, taking risks, dealing with conflict, and establishing traditions.

Building: Stage Four, years six through ten. Collaborating, increasing productivity, establishing independence, and dependability of partners.

Releasing: Stage Five, years eleven through twenty. Trusting, merging of money and possessions, constricting, and taking each other for granted.

Renewing: Stage Six, beyond twenty years. Achieving security, shifting perspectives, restoring the partnership, and remembering.

Stages of Lesbian Relationships

The stages listed here are from *Lesbian Couples: Creating Healthy Relationships for the '90s* by D. Merilee Clunis and G. Dorsey Green.

Prerelationship stage: Stage One, the "getting to know you" or "dating" stage.

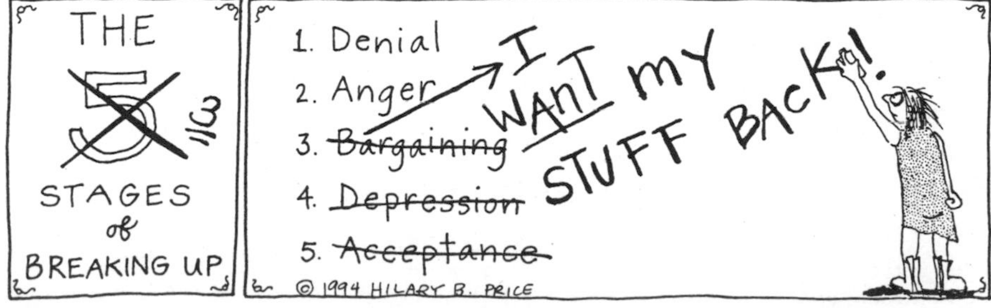

(Hilary Price)

Romance stage: Stage Two. A feeling of oneness, of being completely understood, accepted, loved, and appreciated. Also, lots of sex.

Conflict stage: Stage Three. Disappointment that the other isn't perfect, doesn't have enough time, and isn't perfect.

Acceptance stage: Stage Four. Stability, contentment, deep affection, and self-awareness.

Commitment stage: Stage Five. The decision to make choices about the relationship and be responsible for them, recognition about separate needs, and belief in the trustworthiness of the partner.

Collaboration: Stage Six. Focusing on shared goals and creating something outside of the couple—a political event, a baby, a business.

" 'The sex is a lot hotter in open relationships,' says my favorite fuck buddy. She recently told me she'll never hang out with me again if I'm in a monogamous relationship because I turn cranky and neurotic and my skin takes on a greenish hue. She insists that when I'm in an open relationship I'm 'more beautiful, fresher, certainly more fun, in a much better mood, and more alive.' And then she becomes attracted to me. She may be exaggerating, but that's always worked for her before. I know I feel more out, more open, friendlier, sexier, happier when I can relate to people on a variety of levels, when I'm not bound to discourage myself, distance people, and generally shut down. My favorite long-term relationship models all include periods of nonmonogamy, lots of flirtations, three-ways once in a while, and separate bedrooms, which almost never get used. I would rather feel exhilarated about the loves that constitute the fabric of my life than nostalgic for some tame ideal of what it means to be family."

WRITER CATHERINE SAALFIELD, IN SISTERS, SEXPERTS, AND QUEERS

Famous Long-Term Lesbian and Gay Couples

Mazo de la Roche and Caroline Clement: 75 years together
Edith Hamilton and Doris Fielding Reid: 60
Romaine Brooks and Natalie Barney: 53
Lady Eleanor Butler and Sarah Ponsonby: 53
Mary Woolley and Jeanette Marks: 52
Octave Thanet and Jane Crawford: 50
Mary Renault and Julie Mullard: 50
Gore Vidal and Howard Austen: 47
J. Edgar Hoover and Clyde Tolson: 44
Tiny Davis and Ruby Lucas: 44
Peter Pears and Benjamin Britten: 40
Rosa Bonheur and Natalie Micas: 40
Willa Cather and Edith Lewis: 40
H. D. (Hilda Doolittle) and Bryher: 40
Gertrude Stein and Alice B. Toklas: 39
W. H. Auden and Chester Kallman: 34
Christopher Isherwood and Don Bachardy: 32
Edward Carpenter and George Merrill: 30
Anna Cogswell Wood and Irene Leache: 30
Dame Ivy Compton-Burnett and Margaret Jourdain: 30
Sarah Orne Jewett and Annie Lewis: 30
W. Somerset Maugham and Gerald Haxton: 29
Sylvia Beach and Adrienne Monnier: 20
Charlotte Cushman and Emma Stebbins: 20
Maud Hunt Squire (Miss Furr) and Ethel Mars (Miss Skeene): 20

— **FROM INFORMATION PROVIDED BY PARTNERS TASK FORCE**

Longtime companions writer Christopher Isherwood (left) and artist Don Bachardy in 1976. (Mary Ellen Mark)

What to Answer When Your Mother Asks, "Why in the World Would You Want to Do That?"

Choose one or more of the following responses:

- "We've entered into a relationship that is too big and meaningful to deny."
- "It's a celebration of our lives together."

- "If Cousin Bernice can get married, why can't I?"
- "We're formalizing our relationship to the outside world."
- "We want to create an occasion to gather the diverse people who are important in both of our lives."
- "I'm expressing to my partner the ultimate in commitment and responsibility."
- "We're participating in an age-old tradition."
- "I'm making a political statement."
- "We want to raise a family, and we'd never consider having children unless we were married."
- "We're doing this to hurt you."

— TESS AYERS AND PAUL BROWN

Wedding Belles

So here it was. I knew the commitment was right; but I was scared. I also wondered how our families and friends would react to a gay wedding. Our friends were delighted. We agreed both sets of parents weren't ready for a marriage between two women. When we told my daughters we were planning a wedding ceremony, they reassured us they would be there, but they really didn't understand the concept behind it. My oldest daughter asked me why we felt we needed to do this.

"You love each other and are committed to each other already. Why do you need to go through all the planning and expense of a ceremony?"

I gathered my thoughts and tried to explain to her how it felt not to have the privilege of being able to marry legally the one you loved. Being legally married brought with it some very important benefits, and we, simply on the grounds of our sexual preference, were not able to enjoy those benefits that the straight world usually took for granted. A wedding ceremony is an avenue to share a commitment publicly with the one we love. I think she sort of understood.

Through all the picking out of a place to marry, a minister, the flowers, the cake, the invitations, and the DJ, I dragged my feet. I worried about what my daughters

NEWSPAPERS THAT LIST SAME-SEX WEDDING/UNION ANNOUNCEMENTS

Atlanta Journal Constitution (GA)
Austin-American Statesman (TX)
Brattleboro Reformer (VT)
El Paso Times (TX)
Everett Herald (WA)
Marin Independent Journal (CA)
Minnesota Star Tribune (MN)
The Northampton Gazette (MA)
Philadelphia Inquirer (PA)
Reno Gazette (NV)
San Jose Mercury News (CA)
The Salina Journal (KS)
Santa Cruz Sentinel (CA)
Seattle Times (WA)
Vancouver Sun (B.C., Canada)

DID YOU KNOW...

According to *This Way Out*, the international lesbian and gay radio magazine, there are six countries that allow citizens to sponsor the immigration of a same-sex partner of a different nationality. The six countries are Australia, Denmark, New Zealand, Norway, Sweden, and the Netherlands.

DID YOU KNOW...

On May 7, 1993, in response to a lawsuit filed by three same-sex couples against the state of Hawaii—whose constitutional marriage law does not specify gender—the Hawaii supreme court declared that the state must prove that prohibiting same-sex marriages does not violate the couples' constitutional rights.

would think of our gay friends and how they would react if someone kissed someone or danced with someone, not to mention when Bet and I kissed and danced together. We had never held each other or kissed in front of them. We were just happy they accepted our relationship. Now they would have to face it in its entirety, and I was a nervous wreck even thinking about it.

We had decided to get married at Ann Sather's Restaurant. We ordered our cake from the bakery down the street. All of the purchases and contracting of services were kept in the gay community or were with places that catered to the gay community. Each business went out of its way to make this day special and memorable and run smoothly.

Meanwhile the limo still had not arrived, and I was in a total panic. We waited a few minutes, and went to look for it. There it was, parked in front of the hotel. "Where have you been?" I whined. "Right here waiting for you. I was told you would be out front" was the driver's reply. I opened my mouth and then shut it and got into the limo. "Relax," said the driver. "They can't very well start without you."

Kate looked at me as I sat staring straight ahead. She opened the bottle of champagne sitting in front of us and

Geoffrey Etienne (left) and John Giacomazzi make the ceremonial first cut of the cake at their wedding. (George Olson)

tuned in some music on the radio. As we were coming out from lower Wacker onto Lake Shore Drive she said, "Look at that lake. Isn't that a beautiful sight for your wedding day?" What a good friend.

We pulled up in front of the restaurant to see two of my daughters waiting with a video camera. We got out of the limo and I tried not to think of what I would look like on videotape. I headed upstairs and back to see Lawrence and let him yell at me because I had wilted. I knew he would and he did. My best friend John was there. How very appropriate it seemed to have asked him to walk me down the aisle. Bet came to the back to see me, because she knew I would be nervous and because she loved me. I looked into her eyes and realized how very important this ceremony was, and why. God, how I loved this woman. . . .

She was standing there like petrified wood, not moving a muscle in her face. I wondered what she was thinking. I found out later she was trying not to cry. I looked at my daughters and all of our friends gathered on either side as we walked. I felt warmed by their love and very blessed. As I looked at my daughters I wondered why I had been so frightened for them to look at our lives and our friends. We were, after all, people like everyone else, with hopes, dreams, fears, desires, and love, lots of love.

The music stopped and the minister began. We exchanged the vows we had written, but not without a couple of tears and some laughs. The minister completed the union with his own words and a blessing. He pronounced us "partners in life" and we kissed. Why had I been so worried? All through the evening, my daughters took turns with the video camera. As Bet and I danced alone to the song we had picked for the first dance, she sang softly in my ear. We were in love and had just gotten married.

— **SHARON BRADSHAW**

CAN YOU BELIEVE IT?

In Boulder, Colorado, in March 1975, county clerk Clela Rorex issued a marriage license to two men. Over the next month, she issued five more licenses to same-sex couples. "I don't profess to be knowledgeable about homosexuality or even understand it," she said, "but it's not my business why people get married. No minority should be discriminated against." The Colorado attorney general later ruled that gay and lesbian marriages were illegal and ordered Ms. Rorex to stop issuing licenses to same-sex couples.

DID YOU KNOW...

The first lesbian couple in the United States to be given joint custody in the adoption of a child was Becky Smith and Annie Affleck in April 1986. With the help of the National Center for Lesbian Rights (then known as the Lesbian Rights Project), they adopted five-year-old Nan while living in Fremont (Alameda County), across the bay from San Francisco.

DID YOU KNOW...

Vermont and Massachusetts are the only states in the U.S. that have legalized same-sex second-parent adoption of children—allowing, for example, the lover of a gay man with a child to become a legal co-parent. According to the National Center for Lesbian Rights, nine other states plus the District of Columbia, including Alaska, California, Michigan, Minnesota, New York, New Jersey, Oregon, Texas, and Washington, have some counties or municipalities that also allow same-sex adoption.

Seven Bad Reasons to Get Married

- All of your friends say you bicker like an old married couple already.
- You need a new toaster oven.
- You think you look really great in a tuxedo and don't get enough chances to wear one.
- Since meeting last week, the two of you have not had a single disagreement.
- Both of you name *All About Eve* as your favorite movie of all time.
- She's the best two-step partner you've ever had.
- "Because I wanna."

— TESS AYERS AND PAUL BROWN

Where Did You Get it?

Many people would not have the nerve to ask "Where does your child come from?" when confronted by a gay or lesbian person with a child. Since we all know that same-sex does not produce offspring, "How did you do it?" might seem like a logical question to ask a gay parent. And while a simple "Why do you care?" can be a good retort for a parent who has no interest in continuing this dialogue, we've compiled a list of answers that may satisfy the curious.

- **I had this child/these children when I was married.** It's true: About 25 percent of all lesbians over forty today were heterosexually married at one time; many of those women had children. And while the number of gay men who were heterosexually married is somewhat lower, many of them had children as well.
- **I used artificial insemination.** Many lesbians have chosen this route to motherhood. Some have chosen to use unknown donors, choosing the donor from authorized sperm banks; others have used semen from "a friend of a friend." Still others opt for known donors, again using artificial insemination.
- **I had sex with a man.** Some lesbians do indeed have sex with men, especially for procreation.

• **I used a surrogate.** Unlike women, men don't have the option of getting pregnant. While expensive, some gay men have found this route to be the best alternative, allowing one of them to be the biological father, without having to share parenting with the birth mother.

• **I adopted her/him through a social services agency.** Although a few states expressly forbid gay people from adopting children, in many places around the country gay people are becoming parents in this way. In general, the older the child is, or if the child is disabled, or if the child has siblings whom you are willing to take,

(*Denise Ratliff*, Dykespeak)

Mommies Janine (left) and Josepha with their child, Patrick, in 1994. (Cathy Cade)

the less stringent the government agencies will be when considering who is a "fit" parent.

- **I adopted her/ him from another country.** For many lesbians and gay men who don't want to adopt older children, and who don't want to wait five years for a U.S.-born infant, second-country adoptions are becoming more common. The agencies representing these children are usually very open to single parents who want to adopt.

Caring for Each Other

A long year and then some since my companion died of AIDS, and it's a Friday, the birthday of Mark, an old friend whose companion of a decade has been dying-as-we-speak for the last two years. Early in the day I call and offer Mark these options: (1) coming to my place for lunch; (2) going out for lunch, my treat. He chooses coming to my place, which on this particular day carries some sad and delicious possibility of making love.

So, fine. I'm enthused at the excuse to leave work to spend a Friday afternoon with drop-dead-handsome Mark. We never talk of our companions, dying or dead, but we have established that it has been years since Mark has made love, and nearly as long for me. We've carefully avoided talk of the future, content with holding another person's commiserating hand. (The hand-holding has been mostly metaphorical, Mark being caught up in that man thing, and also, after two years of living-with-dying, very much into guarding his heart.)

So I go out and buy birthday candles and a couple of chocolate cupcakes and a book for a gift, and come home and wrap the book and set the table and stick the candles in the cupcakes and take a shower.

And I'm climbing from the shower and searching for a clean pair of Calvin Kleins when the phone rings and it's Mark, saying that his companion just got the results from his latest test and it's pneumocystis again, and his doctor has exhausted all drugs to treat it and doesn't know what to do, and Mark wants to spend the afternoon consoling his companion at this latest, grimmest turn of events.

So fine. I hang up, get dressed (the ragged old Fruit of the Looms will do) and eat my bowl of soup and one of the chocolate cupcakes and resign myself to resuming work, albeit without much enthusiasm.

And as I'm sitting down to my work the phone rings again, and it's Mark again, and the doctor has called back to say there's this one experimental drug he has remembered that he hasn't yet tried on Mark's companion and he's sending it over to start the treatment right away. And since for the moment Mark's companion is feeling OK, all things considered, and since it *is* Mark's birthday, maybe he *will* come over for lunch. So he does in fact come over, and I feed him soup and light the candles on the remaining cupcake. He carves it in two and gives me half, and in his gesture I understand what we both want: that short triumph over fate, over time and memory and circumstance that desire may bring at its best.

— **FENTON JOHNSON**

Southern Reflection

Carl, my friend Barbara, and I had lived together for a good part of a year in one of the two big houses that Carl and his friend Allan wanted to turn into a community. Carl's aunt, Elizabeth, had followed the two from Oregon and also became our friend. Elizabeth had helped raise Carl; he had helped bring her out as a lesbian, and they had marched together in San Francisco Pride parades under a banner that read, "Faggot Nephew, Dyke Aunt."

Carl was diagnosed with AIDS in December of 1985 after coming down with meningitis, and we made plans for the eighteen months the doctors figured he had to live. Carl and Allan decided to do as much care as possible at home. He went into the hospital and had a tube implanted in one of the veins near the heart so that friends could administer the medicine. That operation was hard for Carl, and he realized how much he hated having his body at the disposal of hospitals and tubes and machines.

Carl had built up a community—through teaching country dance and working against chemical dumps with his neighbors on the poor side of town, by working in the food co-op, and on gay and lesbian politics. He had more people wanting to spend time with him than he had time. From Christmas on, we began to take turns, bringing over his favorite dishes, reading to him, making tapes of his favorite music, helping with his medications. He wanted to finish work on a book he was writing about English country dance, and a team of dancers was helping to type, proof, and make notes on final revisions.

His case progressed quickly. He realized he would not get to see spring again. He went into the hospital on a Thursday in mid-January with a diagnosis of pneumocystis pneumonia. He began having allergic reactions to his medication. Elizabeth called me grief-stricken on Friday to say that Carl had decided to leave the hospital and refused any more medication. He had had enough.

I was caught by surprise. As I drove to Elizabeth's, I was very afraid and angry at Carl's decision. I soon began to realize, though, with Elizabeth's help, that the man knew how he wanted to die. Allan met with thirty of Carl's friends from Durham on Saturday night to explain Carl's decision and to tell us gently that the collective part of Carl's life was over—we would not see him again. He figured he'd have only a couple of days off the medication and was saving that time to spend with his own parents, Allan's family, Elizabeth, and Allan.

By Monday, Carl had said all his good-byes, except for Elizabeth and Allan, and he was still feeling pretty good. Allan and I laughed about the protocol, the manners of this unexpected time. "At what point do you allow the second string back in?" I joked, wanting to dart past Allan up the stairs. I wanted Carl to tell me what dying was like. But the respite did not last for long, and by Tuesday, Carl's breathing was very labored. On Wednesday morning, Allan told us that Carl had decided to take carefully measured doses of medication that evening—to finish taking death into his own hands. My friend Barb worked with the guys at Vale Street to lash a stretcher to carry Carl down the stairs. That night, ten of us gathered for a potluck, to keep watch in the other of the big white frame houses that were by now a gay men's community.

Up in Carl's room, Allan came to the last chapter of *Barchester Towers,* and they decided to stop reading. These two men, who had spent the last fifteen years of their lives as closest friends, listened for the last time to Bach's *Goldberg Variations*.

Word came to us that Carl had taken his first sleeping pills. We moved outside, walking and talking quietly below his window in a soft January night that did feel like spring. In ones and twos, we stepped in and out of the light from Carl's window that spilled on the grass and cobblestones, the window framing the spring flowers Allan had put there, translucent now before the light. Word finally came that Carl had taken a fatal dose of Seconal and Percodan.

Elizabeth and her partner, Elana, went into Carl's house to wait downstairs. Allan sat with Carl as he died, with some jerks and snorts, but peacefully. I was standing outside, and through the window I saw Allan enter the room and speak to Elizabeth and Elana, holding them one in each arm as they wept together. Seeing this grief from a distance, a pantomime framed by the windowsill, in their immediate loss—"Charlie's gone! Charlie's gone!" —this triptych of faggot lover, dyke aunt, and her friend were an image not of some "holy family," but of our gay and lesbian family in our love and grief.

— **MAB SEGREST**

"I was cleaning the garage and found one of his old shirts tossed in a corner. It still smelled like him — that light orange odor. I also found our old beach ball, but I could not let the air out — his breath was in it."

KENNETH MCCREARY, WRITER, FROM BROTHER TO BROTHER

EMBRACING FAMILY

Our society places great value on biological family. The phrase "blood is thicker than water" is more than a statement about chemical compounds. Blood ties, we are taught, are the strongest bonds. We have greater legal and social obligations and ties toward our blood families than we do toward any of our other families.

Most lesbians and gay men are born to and are raised by heterosexual parents, but for many of us, our blood relationships are a mixed bag. While more and more families today are learning to embrace their lesbian and gay relatives, there are still many people who are incredibly uncomfortable with the idea that homosexuality could be in *their* family. Even in the best families there is normally a period of adjustment from the time a gay relative comes out to the time when the rest of the family accepts it.

Still, our biological relations are a crucial part of our families. Some of us are close to our parents and siblings, some are distant, and others still never speak to them. But we all know we have them, and our parents had a lot to do with the shaping of our formative years.

Whether you are a gay person or a straight relative of a gay person, the challenge is to find a way to bring one another back into your life, your love, and your family. And it takes more than accepting each other's differences: Only through embracing who we are as individuals can we all be equal participants in our biological families.

Blood, Thick and Thin

"How can you say I don't love you? Why am I in America? . . . For you and your brother. . . . Daddy and I had to start all over." The veins in her forehead, blue and strong, overshadowed the testament of years of hard work that is her wrinkles.

"We don't hate you." Father, heretofore silent and standing by the door, decided to jump in. And as I learned when I was little, when Father jumps in, it's time to prepare yourself, especially when his voice, calm and patient, bears the shield of "rationality." The same rationality that is reflected in his glasses, distorting his eyes. "We are father and son. I never said I hated you."

"You are corrupting the world, and I am corrupting the world by having you," I quoted him—verbatim.

He said, shaking his head, "And to this day I still maintain what I said. I have to be honest: I still disapprove of this."

This being homosexuality.

The irony killed me. Almost everything I had done, I had been able to do because I am gay, because I had the burden of proof. And I had been too successful in proving that I was a good person, that this family needed me as much as I did them. This was why they were having such a hard time dealing with my sexuality, accepting it. It went against everything they knew about being gay. And now my own father was using the source of my strength against me.

Father and daughter march together in the 1979 Christopher Street parade. (Bettye Lane)

My parents' paradox—they hate queers, but they love me, *even though* I am gay—can be achieved by separating my gayness from my other identities, familial and cultural. This is easily done, since, for most Asian parents, being Asian and being gay are mutually exclusive. It is not only that homosexuality is a forbidden topic in most Asian communities. More significantly, there is not a need to talk about "it" because it is only a *problem* for white people: "it" is a white *disease*. For example, in Hong Kong, a Westernized colony where a gay community has become more visible in the last few years, the colloquial word for a gay man is simply *gay-loh* (gay fellow).

The concept that all queers are white is well corroborated by the media, where queers of color are nearly nonexistent. This is distressful for many Asian queers, especially those families where English is seldom or never spoken. To introduce dialogue will be difficult when homosexuality is not in one's verbal or conceptual lexicon. Even if it can be initiated, understanding would take tremendous time and effort.

The implication that homosexuality is a Western phenomenon reaches deeper into the lives of many queer Asians. To occupy an identity that tradition has not allowed room for is, for many Asian parents, to reject the validity of that tradition and, by extension, of the family whose foundation rests on that very tradition itself. If the language barrier has made coming out difficult, possible charges of betrayal and of disgraces to the family have kept many of us, as well as our parents, in the closet. After I came out to my parents, they immediately asked me not to repeat the revelation to other relatives, some of whom we lived with. We made sure our eyes were dry before we left my room that night. . . .

Before I came out to my parents, my silence about my sexuality had permeated the rest of our relationship, building a wall between us, making communication nearly impossible and conflicts inevitable. Many of us, though active in the gay community, remain closeted to our families.

However, that does not mean that a queer identity can never be developed among Asians. Tragically, the perceived conservatism of Asian communities has often led queer Asians to turn their backs on their ethnic and cultural identities. The separation is hereby complete, and the paradox preserved.

The paradox survives when we refuse to talk about being Asian and being gay at the same time, when one is abandoned for the sake of another. After many arguments, my father said to me eventually, "No matter what you do outside, you are still my son. You can always come home; you will always have a shelter." This was his compromise, his "acceptance." This is something I should feel good about, and I did.

And I did, until I remembered that this was essentially his philosophy about Ralph—our family dog. "If he runs away, he runs away. But as long as he stays with us, he is our responsibility." This compromise was not good enough. And it will never be, as long as my gayness is something I *do outside,* as long as our love for each other is only bound by blood, which, no matter how thick it is, cannot wash away twenty-some years of our lives.

— **ERIC C. WAT**

The Gift

Mother's Day passed and left me thinking about the mothers and daughters who didn't celebrate it. I think of the mother who let intolerance close her heart in pain and of the daughter who suffers from the rejection. I know the wall this mother builds is made of silence and fear and answers that are not accepted or searched for from within. I know this wall will separate her from her daughter to the end.

When my daughter's umbilical cord was cut I was fortunate to understand that it was merely a physical separation and that what would unite us later, stronger than a band of fleshy fibers, would be love, mutual respect, understanding, and acceptance. When I found out that my daughter was a lesbian I felt confusion and pain. I knew this was more than a word or a way of life. I knew how hard society is against this group of people. I knew they were discriminated against and even persecuted at times. I knew this because these attitudes are the ones that I had felt toward homosexuals all my life.

My first step was acceptance. I didn't think of trying to change her or offering to take her to a psychologist. I know my daughter well. When she chooses a path it is because she is convinced that it possesses her truth.

Little by little, without much desire but with great curiosity, I began to learn, to try to understand what it means to be a homosexual. I've only known my daughter's lesbian world. She is a feminist who embraces woman-related issues, including history, submission, and subjugation. She even fights for women's rights, including the right to abort, which I don't agree with.

She was one of the editors of *esto no tiene nombre* and is now the founder of *conmoción,* a new latina lesbian magazine. Her articles have been controversial. She is *atrevida,* daring in her choice of material. I don't like some of the things she writes about, like sadomasochism. But I admire her style of writing. And I like her way of delving into irreverent themes, as she does in her poem "the day I learned to pray" and her poem about women with beards. She even lets her own facial hair grow without shaving or bleaching it, which is something that people, including me, don't like to see or read about.

In other words, we have differences between us, some of them deep. I am Christian, and she is pagan. She doesn't accept God or Jesus. For me, Christianity is more than a belief. I live my religion. For me, a mother's love is like God's love, unconditional above all. I am proud of her and everything she has accomplished in her life, of what she is as a woman and as a person. She had the courage to step forward when many, out of fear, have stayed in the closet, and through *esto no tiene nombre* and *conmoción* she supports her community.

My daughter was born on an early Sunday on Mother's Day and God knows why she was given to me on such a special day. Since then I've been given fine, luxurious gifts, but none have ever equaled her.

— FAB, TATIANA DE LA TIERRA'S MOM

A Taste of Heaven

It was about this time last year that I came out to my grandmother. You see, it was Passover. And every year at this time I uproot myself from my comfortable lesbian household in Somerville, Massachusetts, drive four hours to New York, and make gefilte fish with my grandmother. The traveling, of course, is a real schlep. But to cook with my grandmother is to taste heaven.

I was chopping the fish. My grandmother was peeling carrots with a big knife. She looked down at her hands, so I knew it was time for "The Usual Boyfriend Question." For those of you unfamiliar with "The Usual Boyfriend Question," it is this: "Do you have a boyfriend?" It's a straightforward enough kind of a question, and my grandmother likes to ask it at least three times a year. Being basically a coward at heart, I respond thrice yearly with my "Usual Boyfriend Response": "No, but I have friends who are men." For some reason, I think this will satisfy her. And god forbid my grandmother should think I'm a man-hater! Sometimes, when I want to spice up my answer a bit, I remind her that in my life I have had a boyfriend. I neglect to mention that this was in February 1981. You see, I want my grandmother to think of me as "single." I want her to think I am currently unattached but could be swept at any moment into the world of soon-to-be-married. I want her to know that her dreams of our shopping trip to Fortunoff will not be shattered, that we will stroll down the aisle purchasing the kosher glass dishes with which I will begin my adult life.

Now, at twenty-five, I am proud to still make gefilte fish with my grandmother. Every year I brag to my friends about it. Many Jewish women my age are unschooled in gefilte fish preparation (to say nothing of stuffed cabbage, borscht, rugelach, kreplach, and tsimmes!). Some are too busy, or not interested. Others have forgone this time-honored art out of ethical consideration for the rights of fish. My grandmother, she also brags, to her friends and to her coworkers at the travel agency. As girls and young women before the advent of refrigeration, they shared bathtubs with whitefish and pike on their way to the slaughter. Now many can't be bothered. "You can buy it just as good in a jar," they say. "*Rokeach* is very nice." So my grandmother and I, we brag. But implicit in our bragging is our knowledge that we are part of a dying art, a dying tradition: Jewish grandmothers and their granddaughters making gefilte fish together in celebration of Passover, the season of our liberation.

I am chopping the fish. By this point I have given "The Usual Boyfriend Answer." I am not talking. Neither is my grandmother. Chatter is an important ingredient in our production of gefilte fish, and it is missing. While I chop I am thinking about my grandmother and how she loved me boisterously in my quiet, lonely childhood home. Her hands worked my small, awkward fingers around her knitting needles as I sat with her in my grandparents' La-Z-Boy recliner. One special time, she drove me to the corner of Blake Avenue and Alabama in East New York and told me the stories of her life as a young woman and her work in the family's chicken stall there. I think back to my life in Somerville and all that I have kept from her out of fear. I am thinking of broken bonds and lost worlds. I think it's time to tell my grandmother the truth.

I swallow (swallowing can be an important part of any coming-out declaration) and say, "What would you say if I said that I had a girlfriend?" To this my grandmother replies, "Do you think there's enough salt in the fish?"

DO YOU THINK THERE'S ENOUGH SALT IN THE FISH!?!!!

For this I have agonized over coming out for five years!!?!!

I wonder if my grandmother is going deaf. My grandfather, may he live and be well, is losing his hearing, but my grandmother? My grandmother goes on a lot of cruises for travel agents. She's a free spirit. She sits on a lounge chair on the deck of some Italian ocean liner and meets people. They converse, compare stories. All this goes on above tremendous engine noise and the crashing of waves against the hull. She hears. She's just not dealing with this.

Listen, it's not every day your oldest granddaughter tells you she's queer. I give her a few minutes. Eventually, my grandmother says, "*Do* you have a girlfriend?" I tell her I don't but that I do have them occasionally. She asks me a few questions about AIDS. She asks me about having children. She is skeptical, but still seems satisfied with my explanation of the current trend toward artificial insemination in the lesbian community. A little later I ask if she's upset that I am gay. She says, "No, but I think it's interesting that the first thing I said was 'Is there enough salt in the fish?'"

I'm glad I came out to my grandmother. I was lucky. She did not disown me, condemn me, and best of all, she did not die of a heart attack, a method successfully employed by some people's relatives to register disapproval. She said, "You're my granddaughter and I don't love you any less. I'm seventy-one years old, I've learned to accept a lot of things in my lifetime. This, too, I will accept." Afterwards, we went out for Chinese food and she told me things I never knew: about her belief in reincarnation and her marriage at an early age. We giggled a lot.

We have been able to move on, my grandmother and I. She seems satisfied knowing she may yet see her first great-grandchild. When and if I have a kid, it will be named for my great-grandmother Sarah, the gefilte fish maven. Since I came out to my grandmother, we have become bolder with each other. "OK, this gay movement, all right," she said to me at Yom Kippur. "But do you still have to dress like that?" You see, coming out can be a positive experience.

This year again I will schlep to New York and together my grandmother and I will make gefilte fish. I will chop, she will make sure I put in just the right amount of water; we will revel in each other's presence. Then we will bake *pesadich* spongecake from thirteen eggs, a little seltzer, and a shredded orange, and celebrate the other miracles of Passover.

— LIZ GALST

GATHERING TOGETHER

All of us, gay and straight, are searching for ways to connect to other people, to find ways to be rooted to this earth. For lesbians and gay men, we have formed a loosely collective community based simply on our same-sex desires and society's reaction to those desires. But within the lesbian and gay community-at-large, there are many different ways in which we have formed more tightly knit communities based on our interests, beliefs, and needs. We all belong to a variety of communities that intersect in a myriad of ways.

From houses of worship to music festivals to living sober conferences, lesbians and gay men have created our own gatherings as a way of bringing people together and celebrating our beliefs. The diversity of our communities of interest attests to the diversity of the individuals who are part of the gay and lesbian community. And appreciation for our many subcommunities can only strengthen our political and cultural body in the years to come.

GAY AND LESBIAN SPIRITUAL ORGANIZATIONS WITHIN MAJOR CHRISTIAN DENOMINATIONS

- Affirmation (Church of Jesus Christ of Latter-Day Saints—Mormons)
- Affirmation (United Methodists)
- American Baptists Concerned
- Dignity (Catholics)
- Evangelicals Concerned
- Integrity (Episcopalians)
- Integrity (Lutherans)
- Unitarians for Gay and Lesbian Concerns

The Universal Fellowship of Metropolitan Community Churches

"Calling people to new life through the liberating Gospel of Jesus Christ; Confronting the injustice of poverty, sexism, racism, and homophobia through Christian social

action; Creating a community of healing and reconciliation through faith, hope and love."
—MCC mission statement

The Metropolitcal Community Church was founded by the Rev. Troy Perry, a former Pentecostal minister who began preaching when he was thirteen and was ordained a Baptist minister two years later. By the time he was twenty-seven, Perry was defrocked because of his homosexuality. He was recovering from a suicide attempt when, fortified by the idea that "God cares" about all people, including gays and lesbians, he was inspired to found a church for gay people. Rev. Perry conducted the first MCC worship service on October 6, 1968, in the living room of his Los Angeles home. Eleven men and one woman participated in the first worship service.

MCC is open not only to gays and lesbians, but to all who identify with its mission. MCC ordained its first woman pastor in 1973, and it currently has the highest percentage of female clergy (43 percent) of any Christian church in the United States. MCC, while liberal on human rights and social issues, is theologically conservative.

The couple that prays together . . . at the 1979 Christopher Street Parade in New York. (Bettye Lane)

MCC has two sacraments, baptism and communion, as well as a number of traditionally recognized rites, including ordination. It also offers the rite of "Holy Union," the MCC's version of a same-sex couple's marriage ceremony.

MCC includes political and social activism in its mission, and it has participated in many human rights protests and campaigns. Most recently, MCC contributed to the effort to lift the ban on lesbians and gay men in the military, and in 1992 it asked the U.S. Defense Department to recognize its clergy as military chaplains.

Perry and his colleagues in MCC continue to preach their message that God loves gay people, and they continue to be involved in the everyday lives of gay men and lesbians in a way few other organizations are. "If you want to go to a church where you can't be openly gay, there are a thousand of those," he says. "But if you want to come to a church where you can honestly be yourself, we're it. No ifs, ands, or buts about it." As one attendee to the New York MCC sums up, "I come to MCC services weekly because it's important to me to have a place to worship in a context that's familiar. Since I grew up in an evangelical protestant church, the services are similar to what I experienced when I was young, but the MCC is also accepting of who I am as a lesbian, which is unlike any other church I've ever been to. This sense of continuity with familiar traditions and acceptance of the full me is what makes this my spiritual home and keeps me coming back."

— MATTHEW LORE

DID YOU KNOW...

As of May 1993, Metropolitan Community Church had more than 32,000 members and adherents in sixteen countries. Starting with one group of twelve in Los Angeles in 1968, MCC now has over 291 churches throughout the world, including 230 in the United States. The only states without a Metropolitan Community Church are Maine, North Dakota, Rhode Island, West Virginia, and Wyoming. There are members in every state.

Unity Fellowship Church

The Unity Fellowship Church was founded in 1985 in Los Angeles by Carl Bean, to serve African American gays and lesbians. In the 1970s, Bean was a successful gospel singer who recorded a hit album, *I Was Born This Way*, on the Motown label; it was a "gay liberation album," as he describes it, similar to the work of Sylvester and the Village People. Unity, which is unique among contemporary alternative gay churches in its emphasis of an Afrocentric worship style, has since grown to a national membership between 1,500 and 2,000, with congregations that gather every Sunday in New York City (established in 1992 with Rev. Zachary Jones as pastor); Detroit (established in 1989, overseen by Rev. Renee McCoy); and Washington, D.C. (established in 1993 under Rev. A. Rainer Cheeks). They all preach a message of self-acceptance and acceptance of others, embodied in Unity's central tenet: "God is love and love is for everyone." All Unity congregations are also involved with activist causes, including the Minority AIDS Project in Los Angeles and Breaking Ground in New York, an outreach program for gay, lesbian, and bisexual youth in Brooklyn.

— MATTHEW LORE

Gay and Lesbian Synagogues

Lee Hannah grew up in an Orthodox Jewish family and as a young girl wanted to be a rabbi. When her aspirations were crushed by her family and community "because she was a girl," she became angry at the invisibility of women in the orthodox culture. Although she had been "very Jewish" as a kid, as she approached adulthood and came out as a lesbian, she stopped identifying as Jewish.

Then, in 1990 she discovered Bet Havarim, Atlanta's Reconstructionist gay and lesbian synagogue. She started attending services and soon became a regular cantor for the congregation. She loves the questioning that is built into the Reconstructionist philosophy, the discussions—instead of sermons—at services, and the feminism that lives in the prayer books, the services, and in other members. In 1993, Lee's entire family came to hear her sing at High Holy Day services. Her father came on the *bimah* with her to play the violin for *Kol Nidre,* one of the Yom Kippur prayers, as she sang.

Bet Havarim is one of more than twenty-five gay and lesbian synagogues in the United States. Many Jewish gays and lesbians began to feel that to be Jewish as a gay or lesbian person was an important component of their identities.

The first gay and lesbian synagogues grew out of the Metropolitan Community Churches, nondenominational Protestant churches that served gay and lesbian communities. As there were no comparable Jewish establishments, Jews attended services at MCCs. Many Jews, however, felt a need to form a group more specifically tied to their own traditions, histories, and identities as Jews. Thus, in 1972, eight or twelve (depending on whom you ask) Jews approached the MCC leader in Los Angeles about forming a Jewish subgroup. He suggested, instead, that they form an independent synagogue focusing on the needs of the Jewish community.

The Metropolitan Community Temple, later to become BCC, or Beth Chayim Chadashim (which in Hebrew means "House of New Life"), grew quickly. When the Los Angeles BCC members approached the local offices of the United American Hebrew Congregations (UAHC), the umbrella organization for reform congregations in the U.S., they were "warmly greeted with assistance and support." This, however, caused a great deal of controversy and debate within the Reform Jewish community, from those who felt that homosexuality and Judaism were not compatible, to those who questioned the appropriateness of a "specialty synagogue" catering to a specific sector of society. Nonetheless, by the end of 1973, BCC was voted into full membership in the UAHC. As of 1992, there were ten "gay and lesbian outreach" synagogues affiliated with UAHC.

DID YOU KNOW...

The Reconstructionist Rabbinical College recently voted to explicitly state that sexual orientation would *not* be a factor in admitting rabbinical students. In addition, there are a number of openly gay and lesbian students in the Hebrew Union College, Reform Judaism's rabbinical college. Even some conservative rabbinical colleges have conceded quietly to the presence of gay students and graduates.

The Reform movement is not the only one to accept gay and lesbian outreach congregations. Bet Havarim, the gay and lesbian synagogue in Atlanta, is affiliated with the Reconstructionist movement, the newest and smallest of the Jewish denominations.

Bet Havarim had its beginnings in a group of gay and lesbian Jews who met socially in the late 1970s and early 1980s and then disbanded. However, in 1985, some of the former members decided that it was important to create an explicitly spiritual Jewish community.

The synagogue now boasts more than seventy families, a lesbian softball team (Burning Butches), and six committees, including Tzedakah (social action), and AIDSchaim, which provides emotional support and practical services to people with HIV.

Beyond Reform, Reconstructionist, Conservative, and Orthodox denominations of Judaism, there are alternatives. The Jewish Renewal and the Havurah movements have drawn in many lesbian, gay, bisexual, and transgender folks. Most services are held in members' homes without paid leaders. In the San Francisco Bay Area, Dyke Shabbos is a monthly gathering that has brought lesbians and bisexual Jewish women together for more than fifteen years. It is a safe place for women to come together, light the Sabbath candles, chant the blessings, sing songs, and reconnect with their Jewishness and with each other. Another group, Queer Minyan, grew out of the Jewish Renewal movement and meets monthly to celebrate Shabbat in an earth-centered, feminist, and particularly joyous queer way.

— JAKKI SPICER

The Radical Faeries: Queer Spirit Community

The Radical Faeries are a loosely affiliated group of men around the country who celebrate a kind of pagan spirituality. A central tenet of faerie lore is that there is no single definition of faerie. Faerie is a self-assumed identity—permeable, mutable, contradictory. Unfixed. Individual. So, no strict definitions here.

Some would place the starting of the faerie movement as a Labor Day weekend gathering in 1979 in Arizona. But I would say this was just one event, a festive blip, in a line going infinitely back, infinitely forward.

Whenever you have a society that constructs distinct gender behaviors—what it means to be a gal, what it means to be a guy—there will be a people who don't conform to those behaviors. Society never disregards this nonconformance. However, it can respond to the nonconformists in two ways. Society can vilify them, call them names, see them as corrupting decency, purity, and the glory of the reign of father ruler, father god. Or society can sanctify the nonconformists, call them names, see them as gifted edge walkers between the worlds of male and female, new and old, spirit shadow and spirit light.

The radical faeries lay claim to the role of sacred boundary crosser in this place and in this time. To be sure, faeries have their own boundaries, which are continually questioned and crossed. To be blunt, faeries are mostly gay men. The other boundary is geographic: North America. As such, faeries draw from the cultural traditions that come together on that part of the planet: europa, diaspora black, Native American, Hispanic, Asian.

The faeries are rife with contradictions and tensions, and can be exasperating. But there is a spirit in the faeries of withholding judgment and going on with the show. The intent is magical—transforming ourselves and the world through spirit. And that's how we're radical in the root sense of the word: *from the ground, from the earth, at the base where the matter is the most dense.*

• **Faerie 101:** You can't make a ballgown from a pattern for a three-piece suit.

Cultures live within the repetition of patterns. Since I believe that faerie-ness is fundamentally a matter of remaking culture, the best way to understand faeries is to look at the patterns we play with.

• **Circles:** Fundamentally, faeries are a group of people who have agreed to listen to each other. This listening, this talking, occurs in the most elemental of faerie forms —the circle. People *sit around.* A talisman is passed. Whoever has the talisman is listened to.

Harmodius and Hoti seriously "pose" in 1978. (Dan Nicoletta)

• **Gatherings:** A lived experience of communal faerie culture; usually over several days; usually in the country. Faeries conceptualize gatherings in many different ways. Some see them as performance, or a healing rite, or a tribal meeting, or a vacation. Aside from contributing to the pool for running the gathering, money is not used; food, clothing, shelter is freely given and taken; abundance reigns. Time becomes a matter of riding the rhythm of the day. Faeries relax, and smile more. They touch each other a lot.

• **Sanctuary:** Faeries are far from real estate mavens. Land cannot be owned, *really.* However, land *can* become a focused repository of faerie culture and energy. As of this writing, there are four faerie sanctuaries:

Short Mountain in Tennessee, Kawashaway in Minnesota, Amber Fox in Ontario, and Wolf Creek in Oregon. But then, there are many other faerie sanctuaries: city apartments, small farms, a knoll in the park. It's all in the living.

• **Ritual:** There is no single faerie spirituality. I have been at gatherings with Catholic priests, staunch agnostics, and pagan witches. However, there is a faerie spiritual urge, which is to unite queerness with the sacred.

That is, we are sacred because we are queer.

Most gatherings include at least one group ritual. Not every faerie believes rituals to be central to the gathering experience; many faeries don't even go. It is true that faerie rituals usually follow a neopagan formula: a circle is cast, energy is raised through chanting and dancing, excess energy is "earthed," the circle is reopened. But no matter how many ceremonial magick queens get together, faerie rituals always get gate crashed by the trickster spirits of Anar-she and X-hilaration. A chant is spontaneously changed; a dance breaks out; a new goddess is named. Every faerie communes with the sacred as an ontological fact. We don't need a recognized priesthood or a tradition to guide us.

• **Drag:** You can call "yoo-hoo" and "hey girl" to death, but the surest way to get a group of faeries together is to empty out a big plastic garbage bag of fabulous thrift store finds. Changing drag, changing self presentation, changing self: a faerie putting together a new outfit—paisley scarf, metallic blouse, prized skirt—is not demonstrating conformity, not dressing for the office. She is exploring a new dimension to herself, dancing the edge between male and female, the alleged sacred and supposed profane, the lavender fantastic and the lavender present. She is *being* fabulous.

A FAERIE SPELL

The faeries come together within a queer context of other strands of oppositional North American culture that are woven, cut, sewn and accessorized. As a witch, I would like to name those strands and braid them together into a sacred lavender cord:

Anarchism. For a movement toward decentralism and small communities where the individual is prized. Nondogmatic, leaderless.

Feminism. For a value of women and womanly qualities and stance against the patriarchy.

Antiracism. For an appreciation of the value of diversity and the excitement of many cultural traditions.

Gay Liberation. For an exploration of the radical potential of gay identity.

Hippies. For spontaneous mass cultural transformation, communalism, and good drag.

Neopaganism. For new forms of ritual and a realization of the immanent spirit.

Ecology. For a respect for nature.

Men's Movement. For men coming together and examining the conditions of their lives.

At the end of this cord I would tie a sacred, ancient, and heavy stone bead. The bead would be the weight of a pendulum swinging across time, connecting me to the sissy priests and shamans of the past and the future. The bead would be a condensation of energy, a source of knowledge and power; a faerie bead.

• **Hissing:** Snakes shed their skin like faeries shed their drag. Snakes crawl on the ground, close to the mother, like faeries value the state of being grounded, close to the mother. Snakes hiss like faeries hiss: to say we're near. *Sssssssssss.*

— MARK LEGER/TRIXIE GLAMOURAMA

Gay Spirit Visions Comes to the North Carolina Mountains

What do gay men do when they find traditional avenues of spiritual expression closed? That's the question explored at the Celebrating Gay Spirit Visions Conference, an annual (fall) gathering of gay men near Highlands, North Carolina.

The first conference occurred in 1990. The opening Heart Circle, where everyone gathers around to say who they are, why they've come, and what's in their heart, can be a breathtakingly intimate introduction to other gay men's dreams and desires. Other weekend activities include keynote speakers, workshops, a Saturday night talent show, a gift-giving ritual, a Closing Circle, and lots of smiling, hugging, crying, dancing, spirit-filled gay men.

For some, the Gay Spirit Visions Conference has become a touchstone for an entire year's worth of spiritual growth. For others, the process clarifies what true spirituality is. "The conference has taught me what to expect from anything that claims to be a spiritual process—it must give me a chance to create who I am, and my existence as a gay man is an integral part of that," says organizer Martin Isganitis.

— AL COTTON

Lesbians on Land: A Tribe of Womyn

The year was 1981 and I was lucky enough to be traveling with a lover across country in a blue VW van. There were so many women's land communities that we could travel a day in almost any direction and be on womyn's land by night. We stopped at Dragon

Wimmin's land. We met Rue, Dark Artemis Silverowl, and a woman who made the largest labyrises I ever saw. They were weapons, not jewelry. That summed up the spirit of the time. No men allowed. This was safe womyn space, where you could go out late at night under the moon without danger—except for chiggers.

The Women's land movement in this country gathered strength in the 1970s and 1980s. Oregon might well have been the matrix out of which the movement sprang. There were several significant forces at work. Land was available and affordable. Early on there was *Womanspirit* magazine and later the Women's Writers' Group, Gourmet Eating Society, and Chorus. *Womanspirit,* founded by Ruth and Jean Mountaingrove, spread the word that it was possible for women to live on the land. For ten years they nurtured the magazine as a forum on spirituality as well as a network between different land spaces. Nearby in Southern Oregon there were many different parcels of land with women on them living collectively: Cabbage Lane (1972), Womanshare (1974), and Fishpond, OWL (1976), Fly Away Home, Rainbow's End (1974), and Rainbow's Other End. Further north there was WHO (1972) and We'Moon Healing Ground.

We thought of ourselves as a large tribe. When a new wimmin came onto the land, one of the first things that she shared was what other land she had been to, news of who was still living there, what wimmin had moved where, who was being lovers with who, a genealogy passed on in our oral tradition. Wimmin were always on the road moving between enclaves.

You say to us: if this is a tribe, why do you never stay still? You say if this is a tribe what is the given language? What is its name and who belongs?

Any woman belonged who stayed through a winter, helped put up a roof, put in a garden, and lasted through the meetings. We built permanent structures. We became strong and competent, and with each new skill, we proved to ourselves we could live outside the system.

Every community had its unique style and the ways of organizing were myriad, but collectivity and consensus were widespread as well as, ironically, the fierce spirit of independence. Women attempted to share money, space, decision making, and labor in nonhierarchical, noncapitalist ways. However, few had skills in negotiating, and energy was often consumed in long, painstaking meetings.

Liz on OWL Farm in 1977. (©JEB)

For some women, the experience of living on the land day to day allowed them to participate in a natural cycle quite different from city life. One governed by the sun. The moon. The seasons. Time, like the space of silence that rose up from the land, stretched out on all sides of you instead of pushing at your back. Women learned how to find their own rhythm and to perceive themselves differently in this landscape. They learned to look within. To open like a vessel, receptive to transformation. They were able to invite spirit when they were cold to the bone, only to find the bones themselves transmuted. There was indeed magic.

Then there was the land itself: what we gave to it, what it taught us. We are not a land-based people. We forfeited that when the matriarchy lost power, when the cities propelled men into power. So where did this deep-rooted affinity for the land come from? It was about reclaiming an ancient bond. It was about community; it was about home. It was about the need to caretake the land and recover balance. It was about separatism, but given the ways that word can be abused, see it as a need for safe, womyn-only land, places to heal. Most of all, there was an intrinsic relationship between being a lesbian, living on land, and connecting to one's spirituality. Jean Moutaingrove of Rootworks envisioned it as a "natural sanctuary, an outdoor temple" (*Womanspirit,* Spring Equinox, 1981). Our circles and rituals were life-affirming. They brought the vision of gynocracy deep into the core of our being where our sexuality, the land, and the goddess melded into a psychic wellspring that strengthened and healed us.

It is necessary to place the land movement in context as a primarily white wimmin phenomenon. I met many women of color on the land, but by and large white wimmin had the money and the privilege to leave the cities. Even at ARF, surrounded by the richness of Indian and Hispanic culture, womyn were overwhelmingly white. One notable exception was the women of Arco Iris in Arkansas, who created their land community as a survival camp for native womyn of color and their children. They had been called there by their visions to create a place for spirituality and healing.

Many have left the land, relating to cities and technology as the times demand. Few people are still doing what they did fifteen years ago; change is imperative. Some left because they felt isolated; others felt a growing need for multicultural communities formed out of diversity, of the need to include disenfranchised and differently abled women. Of the need to bring ecological awareness into the cities in terms of recycling, growing our own organic foods, sharing resources, preserving land. Womyn work actively to take back food production, protect endangered animals and the earth, exchange seeds, heal with herbs. The "wanderground" shifts, but our sacred connection to the earth, the process of affirmation and renewal, continues.

Although the land communities have dwindled in number, many are still active today. Many womyn continue to live in a parallel universe outside the system, moving in a circle outside the norm, still working for change. The womyn of Oregon and Colorado have helped defeat homophobic legislation. Womyn who never lived on land honor wimmin and natural cycles by producing moon calendars with images of womoon that stir the psyche. We give stones to wimmin we love.

— **SANDIA BEAR**

HOW MANY WAYS CAN YOU SPELL WOMAN?

women
womyn
wimmin
wimyn
womon
wymmyn
wimon
womoon
wombmoon

Wimmin's Lands

There were communities everywhere, including Alaska and Hawaii. Here's a partial list of the many land groups that have existed; the * indicate active ones. *Maize* magazine is the best source of current information.

Arizona: Amazon Acres*, White Rocks*, Sister Homelands on Earth*, Saguaroland Sisterland*, Adobe Land*
Arkansas: Maude's, Arco Iris*, Whypperwillow Wymin
British Columbia: Spinstervale*, Sky Ranch*
California: Heraseed, Wicca Mountain, Tai Farm, Trillium, Lavender Hill (which started as older lesbian land), Deepdish*, Moon Shadow*
Florida: Pagoda*, Barbara Deming's place in the Keys
Georgia: A Full Circle*
Kentucky: Spiral Land*
Louisiana: Women's World*
Maine: Gathering Ground, Wombland*, Coventry*
Maryland: Heathcote Community
Minnesota: North Minnesota*, Harmony Hill Farm*
Mississippi: Silver Circle
Missouri: Gathering Root Farm
New Mexico: Outland*, ARF*
New York: The Women's Art Colony*, Beechtree* in the Catskills
North Carolina: A Full Circle*
Ohio: Wise Heart*, the Susan B. Anthony Memorial Unrest*
Oregon: Riverland*
Tennessee: Okra Ridge
Vermont: Redbird, Howl*
Virginia: Dixie's Crystal Ridge*
Wisconsin: Raven's Hollow*, Lunar Circle Farm*, Doe Farm*

— SANDIA BEAR

Women's Music

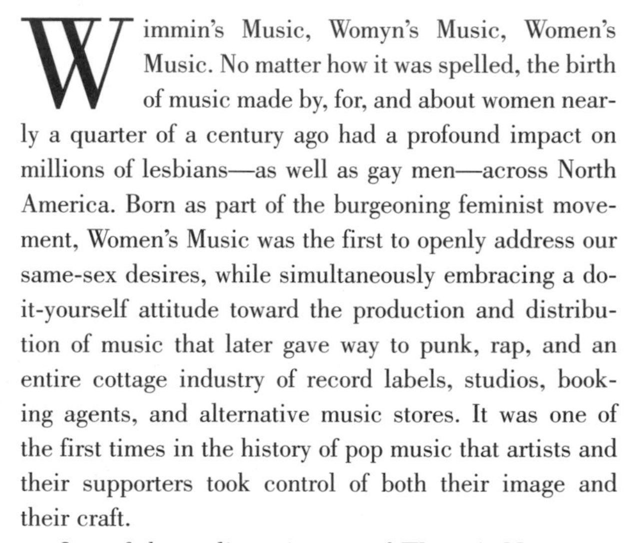

Wimmin's Music, Womyn's Music, Women's Music. No matter how it was spelled, the birth of music made by, for, and about women nearly a quarter of a century ago had a profound impact on millions of lesbians—as well as gay men—across North America. Born as part of the burgeoning feminist movement, Women's Music was the first to openly address our same-sex desires, while simultaneously embracing a do-it-yourself attitude toward the production and distribution of music that later gave way to punk, rap, and an entire cottage industry of record labels, studios, booking agents, and alternative music stores. It was one of the first times in the history of pop music that artists and their supporters took control of both their image and their craft.

One of the earliest pioneers of Women's Music was Holly Near, a well-known civil rights activist and folk musician who, in 1972, founded Redwood Records to celebrate and document the birth of feminism. In the years that followed, Redwood gained a reputation for recording songs of struggle and resistance, releasing music by such landmark artists as Sweet Honey in the Rock, Ferron, Faith Nolan, Teresa Trull, and Ronnie Gilbert.

Shortly thereafter, lesbian-specific records began surfacing in women's bookstores and on the jukeboxes of a handful of lesbian and gay bars around the country. Most popular accounts trace this music back to Alix Dobkin, who began performing women-only concerts in 1972 (often working with Kay Gardner under the moniker Lavendar Jane). Against the better judgment of a friend who warned her she would never get a record deal until she learned to conform to the rules of the mainstream music industry, Alix Dobkin released *Lavender Jane Loves Women* in 1973. The same year, Maxine Feldman of Los Angeles and Madeline Davis of Buffalo had both recorded 45-rpm discs that were circulating throughout the gay community. Feldman's 45 included "Angry Atthis," a song that expressed anger at not being able to

DID YOU KNOW...

June Millington, founder of Fabulous Records, cofounded the Institute for Musical Arts with Ann Hackler in 1987. IMA is a nonprofit, multiracial, multicultural arts organization that offers training and support for women—particularly women of color—pursuing careers in music. Classes, performances, studio recording, and apprenticeships provide students with knowledge and expertise in every aspect of the music industry.

hold her lover's hand in public and was produced by Harrison & Tyler Productions (who themselves were a feminist comedy team). Of the original printing of 1,000 records pressed, 500 were sold in first month. Davis's release, which featured the cut "Stonewall Nation," also sold out its first 500 copies, predominantly through mail order.

Then came Olivia Records, which sprung from a five-woman separatist collective based in Washington, D.C. Like most of the early players in the Women's Music scene, none of these women knew anything about music production or distribution. Nevertheless, they raised a few thousand lesbian dollars and, by 1974, had released the first split single, with "Lady" by Meg Christian on one side and "If It Weren't for the Music" by Chris Williamson on the other. The record sold for $1.50, (plus $.30 shipping and handling), the proceeds of which went toward setting up the company's own recording studio, run entirely by women. Then, on November 4, 1974, Olivia finished producing their first full album, *Meg Christian: I Know You Know.*

(Jill Posener)

It wasn't long before the rise in lesbian musicians and recordings gave way to an expanding national network of women's coffeehouses, cabarets, and festivals that created touring opportunities for these artists to reach a rapidly growing lesbian audience. The National Women's Music Festival in Champaign, Illinois, and the Amazon Music Project in Santa Cruz were just two of the earliest weekend-long festivals to attract women looking for gay-friendly and culturally enriching weekend getaways. Of course, producing these festivals required women with technical expertise—or at least the willingness to learn—and soon all-women production teams like the D.C.-based Roadwork and the San Francisco Bay Area's Women in Production were specializing in staging, lighting, and sound. For those in smaller cities and towns, Women's Soul Publishing, based in Milwaukee, Wisconsin, published a pamphlet called "Producing Concerts," with tips on the costs of production, along with some "how to's" on publicity, security, and sound production.

By 1975 Women's Music had hit the ground running. Both Olivia and Redwood were releasing up to a dozen records a year, and Women's Music bins had even begun to appear in a number of mainstream record stores. This was the year that Chris Williamson recorded her seminal album *The Changer and the Changed*, a record that remains one of the most well-known of the Women's Music scene and which has sold more than 250,000 copies to date.

Now Lady Slipper, a North Carolina–based mail-order distributor that began in 1976 with thirteen Women's Music titles, has grown to offer nearly two thousand recordings by women artists. Although by the 1990s both Olivia and Redwood have grown away from Women's Music and into other aspects of pop culture, there are still dozens of records being produced every year by veteran Women's Music artists as well as newer, openly gay artists who are breaking new ground both in and outside of the mainstream music industry.

In its heyday, Women's Music created a cultural environment where lesbians and other women could learn the business of making music. In addition, many credit it with being one of the first musical genres to aggressively challenge the racism, sexism, and homophobia of the mainstream music industry. It was the first to raise the issues of child care and provide signing for the hearing-impaired at concerts. And while many of the artists, producers, and promoters have since moved on to other types of work, there's no denying that without them there would be no k.d. lang, no Melissa Etheridge, or any other proud lesbian voices gracing the covers of music magazines and MTV.

— VICTORIA STARR

"I was so totally amazed and shocked to see SO many lesbians in the SAME place. It was certainly a feast for these baby-dyke eyes. Very powerful and moving and affirming. I still love 'women's music' and have all of Olivia's recordings, even though it's no longer 'fashionable.' I always felt and still feel a real sense of power and community when I attend a women's concert."

JULIA, THIRTY-ONE-YEAR-OLD FROM SANTA CRUZ, CALIFORNIA

Women's Music Festivals

More than twenty women's music and culture festivals are held annually in the U.S., with the oldest festivals—the National Women's Music Festival and the Michigan Womyn's Music Festival—celebrating their twentieth anniversaries in 1995.

Festivals have become the primary way to see live performances of women's music and culture. While the number of women's production companies who regularly organize concerts has dwindled to a handful, thousands of women (and some men) make the annual pilgrimage to a festival in their communities or around the world.

At their most basic, the festivals are a celebration of lesbian culture and heritage, with lesbians being the vast majority of organizers, workers, performers, and attendees. Most of the festivals are for women only; however, those held on college campuses, such as the National Women's Music Festival and Wimminfest, are open to men.

Women who want to attend a festival but can't deal with the mosquitoes that outdoor festivals promise opt for the more cushy indoor festivals, whereas other "festiegoers" plan their annual vacations around working "on the land," often in the nude. The festivals have two major things in common. One is to provide a nurturing place for women who come for a rest from their lives at home. Many women speak of the exhilaration they feel in being surrounded by lesbian energy, by being able to walk alone at night with no worry of being physically attacked. The second is to be a breeding ground for dyke drama. The Michigan Festival is mythic for the number of relationships that break up or begin in its week span.

"[Women's music concerts] were my first introduction to the lesbian community at large. Of course, I'd seen dozens of women at the bars, but the concerts gave me my first education on the scope of lesbian experience. I couldn't possibly overemphasize the transforming nature of being in the midst of that many lesbians—it was my first experience with being an insider to something!! I was seeing lesbians from all walks of life for the first time—women of color, older women, disabled women, professionals in expensive evening-wear (it of course sounds funny to say now, but my only intro to lesbian life before the concerts had been young, white, working-class dykes in jeans) and on and on. I got to see that the group lesbians comprised many different kinds of people."

AMY, THIRTY-FOUR-YEAR-OLD TEXAN

Michigan Womyn's Music Festival

More than seven thousand women make their way to the festival-owned square mile of Michigan woods and meadows each year, coming from all over the U.S., Canada, and many other countries.

What makes Michigan unique is the number of participants, but also its emphasis on diversity and quality. Michigan is the role model when it comes to being "politically correct" and genuinely sensitive to everyone's differences. Compared to other festivals, Michigan has the largest percentage of women of color and disabled women who come as workers and festiegoers. The festival is often on the cutting edge of issues in the lesbian community, such as Michigan's policy of admitting only "women-born-as-women," sparking protests in recent years from male-to-female transsexuals and their supporters.

A Day Stage crowd at the Michigan Womyn's festival cheers the performers on. (©JEB)

One of Michigan's appeals lies in its risk-taking approach of booking upcoming artists who stretch the boundaries of what's been considered "women's music." State-of-the-art sound and light systems provide a high quality listening experience. Participation in creating lesbian culture is encouraged with hundreds of workshops, a craftswomyn's bazaar and craft workshops, a country-and-western dance stage, and spontaneous drumming circles.

With participants from every age bracket and walk of life (not to mention the communal showers), Michigan is lesbian nirvana and the right wing's largest lesbian nightmare.

— KAREN HESTER

Women's Music/Cultural Festivals

There are dozens of women's music and cultural festivals around the country each year. Rather than list addresses and phone numbers, we suggest you check with women's bookstore nearest you for the most current contact numbers.

Camp Dyke
Memorial Day Weekend
Santa Cruz, California

Campfest
Memorial Day Weekend
Franklinville, New Jersey

East Coast Lesbians Festival
Labor Day Weekend
(location varies)

Gulf Coast Women's Festival
early April
Gulfport, Mississippi

Hawaii Fest
mid-February
Oahu

Michigan Womyn's Music Festival
second week of August
Hart, Michigan

National Women's Music Festival
early June
Bloomington, Indiana

Northampton Lesbian Festival
late July
Northampton, Massachusetts

Ohio Lesbian Festival
early September
Columbus, Ohio

Pacific Northwest Women's Music and Cultural Jamboree
early June
Bellingham, Washington

Rhythmfest
Labor Day Weekend
North Carolina Mountains

Sisterspace Pocono Weekend
early September
Pennsylvania Poconos

Virginia Women's Music Festival
early May
Virginia

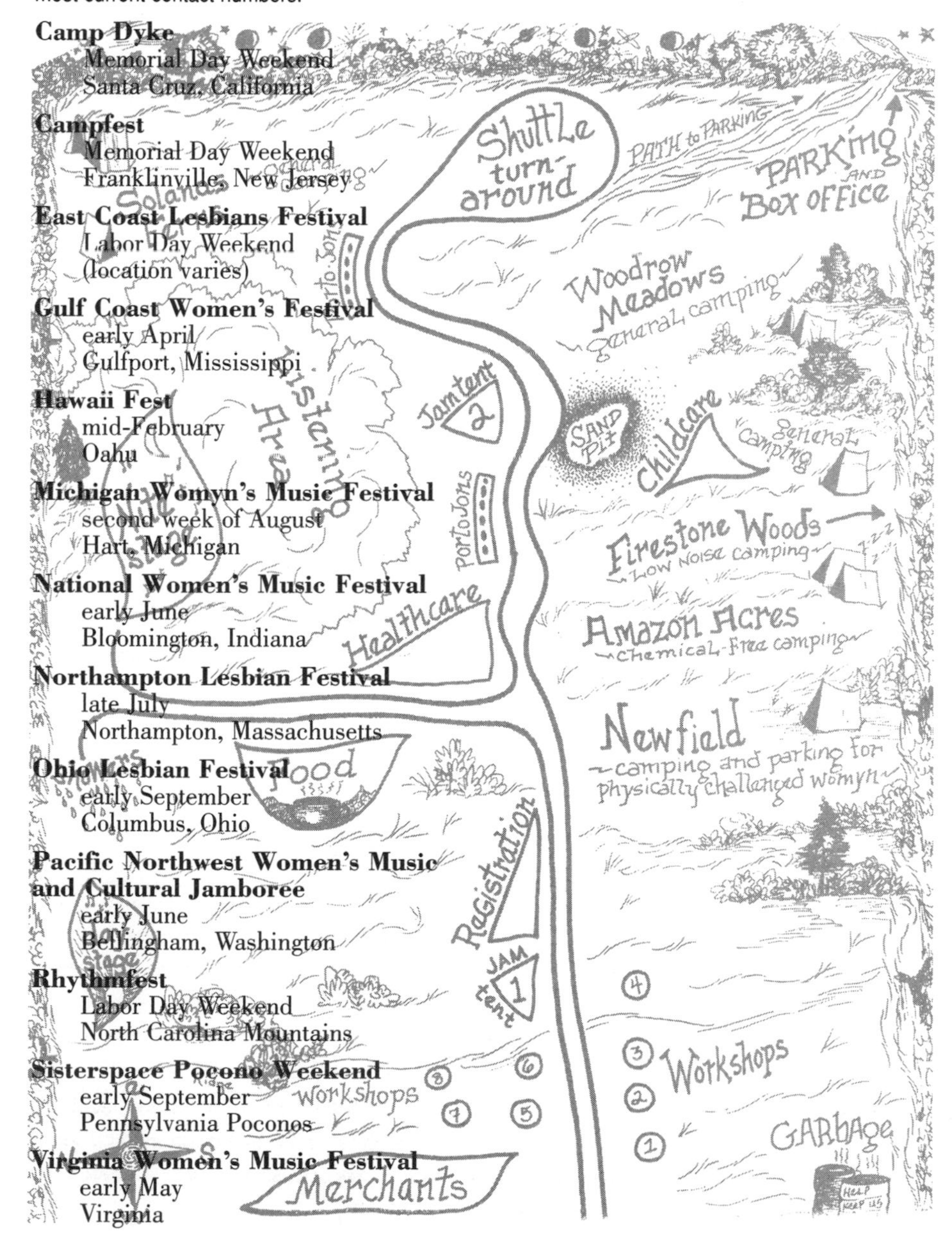

West Coast Women's Music and Comedy Festival
Labor Day Weekend
Yosemite, California

Wild Western Women's Weekend
Labor Day Weekend
Virginia

Wiminfest
Memorial Day Weekend
Albuquerque, New Mexico

The Roots of Feminist Men's Music

Although political lesbian music blossomed and flourished in the seventies, openly gay men were only beginning to record their topical songs at the end of the decade. One forerunner stands out. Steve Grossman released *Caravan Tonight* on the Mercury label in 1973. A bit ahead of its time in its male-to-male romanticism, it was overlooked as most gay men found themselves transfixed by the disco beat.

Ironically, it took a heterosexual man, Willie Sordillo, to jump-start what was coined "feminist men's music" when he invited fourteen men in August 1978 to Cambridge, Massachusetts, to record *Walls to Roses* on the Folkways label. Gay artists Charlie Murphy, Chris Tanner, Blackberri, George Fulginiti-Shakar, and Kenny Arkin made their debut recordings on this album.

A year later, Tom Wilson Weinberg of Philadelphia independently released *Gay Name Game,* on his own Aboveground Records label, and he released *All-American Boy* in 1982. The National Conferences on Men and Masculinity in Los Angeles (1979) and Ann Arbor (1983) also became focal points for this new musical niche. These small gatherings of feminist men applauded what they saw as an emerging men's culture—nurturing, supporting, and decidedly nonviolent.

The early eighties saw album releases by many of the new gay men's music mainstays—for example, Charlie Murphy with *Catch the Fire* and Blackberri with *Finally.* Good Fairy and Bea B. Queen, the names of their own record labels, reflected the gay spirit of the time. George Fulginiti-Shakar brought his own gay sensibility to the topical folk group Bright Morning Star's initial recording, *Arisin.* Charlie Murphy went on to form his own Seattle-based band, Rumors of the Big Wave, which released *Burning Times* in 1993 on the EarthBeat label.

The Flirtations, 1994 (Courtesy Creative Management Services)

Longtime political performer Bill Folk came out, recorded and released the single "We Are Here" as the theme song for Phoenix's first gay pride rally in 1981. Performing throughout the eighties, he released his first CD, *Looking for Mr. Right,* in 1991 on his own Bright Moon label.

Newcomers Pilshaw & Sklamberg (Elliot and Lorin) and Romanovsky & Phillips (Ron and Paul), with law firm–like monikers, began performing in Los Angeles and San Francisco concurrently. The short-lived duo of Pilshaw & Sklamberg released *Bending the Rules* on cassette in 1982. Another solo artist living in Los Angeles, LeRoy Dysart, released *We Are Everywhere* on his own label the same year.

After their initial 1983 cassette recording, *In the Outfield,* Romanovsky & Phillips began touring nationwide and establishing a network of concert producers, smaller in scale but not unlike the women's music circuit. This prolific, enduring, and entertaining duo released six albums on their Fresh Fruit label, including *I Thought You'd Be Taller* (1984), *Trouble in Paradise* (1986), *Emotional Rollercoaster* (1989), *Be Political, Not Polite* (1991), *Brave Boys* (1994), *Let's Flaunt It* (1995), as well as Romanovsky's solo album, *Hopeful Romantic* (1992).

They also released a posthumous collection of recordings by Joe Bracco, *True to Myself,* in 1992.

In 1986, Elliot Pilshaw moved to New York City and with Jon Arterton founded The Flirtations. The original members (sans Pilshaw), consisting of Arterton, Michael Callen, T. J. Myers, Aurelio Font, and Cliff Townsend, released their first recording, *The Flirtations,* in 1990. This high-energy a cappella quintet took the gay community by storm. Appearances on *Donahue* and in the film *Philadelphia* gave them exposure to a broader audience. Jimmy Rutland replaced Myers after his death from AIDS in 1990. Their second recording, *Live: Out on the Road,* was released in 1992.

WELL-KNOWN GAY LOCALITIES

West Hollywood (44.6%)
Northampton (18.1.%)
Palm Springs (25.0%)
Provincetown (24.7%)
Oakland (16.5%)
Takoma Park, MD (17.1%)

Michael Callen, although an integral part of The Flirtations, also had a prolific songwriting career of his own. As an eloquent and outspoken person with AIDS, he released *Purple Heart* in 1988. In the year prior to his death in late 1993, he recorded more than sixty songs to be released on CD in 1995.

Prolific songwriter Fred Small recorded "Everything Possible" on his third album, *No Limit,* released in 1986 on Rounder Records, which later became The Flirtations's signature song. His songs "Scott and Jamie" (about gay adoption) and "The Marine's Lament" (about gays in the military), recorded on subsequent CDs, positioned Small as a heterosexual man who continues to unabashedly write and sing gay-positive material.

NOTORIOUSLY UNGAY LOCALITIES

Cobb County, GA (4.5%)
Colorado Springs, CO (3.0%)
Jones County, MI (6.1%); (special note: all of the 293 unmarried same-sex partner households in the county are women)
Fairfax County, VA (7.0%)

— THE WASHINGTON BLADE

In 1990, Willie Sordillo brought together the songs of fifteen artists, both gay and straight, to record a compilation CD titled *Feeding the Flame: Songs by Men to End AIDS* on the Flying Fish label.

The newest kids on the block in this genre, Sons & Lovers, were formed by Elliot Pilshaw in 1993. The members of this New York–-based five-man a cappella group —Pilshaw, John Whitley, Bob Stern, Ken Browne, and Deian McBryde—released a cassette of the same name in 1994.

— JOHN PAUL

PHYSICAL COMMUNITY/ VIRTUAL COMMUNITY

Gay men and lesbians are in every town and city, in the country and in the suburbs. We are a part of the fabric of American communities. But we have also built our own communities. Many of us live or work in gay neighborhoods in large cities; towns like Northampton, Massachusetts, with a substantial lesbian population, are referred to in the media as "gay meccas." From Fire Island to the Florida Keys, gay resorts flourish. Living together, or at least visiting often, is a way of building community.

But getting away or living in a gay district are not options for most gay people. There is, however, an alternative: virtual community. The global computer revolution has spawned the creation of on-line gay and lesbian bulletin boards. These bulletin board systems allow people to connect across continents and oceans. Entire conferences are dedicated to particular topics of interest to queers, from deaf lesbian and gay chat lines to the gay librarians' network. (Many a romance has begun on-line, too.)

Community is whatever we want it to be, whether it is virtual or in person, and lesbians and gay men are building themselves homes.

DID YOU KNOW...

A heterosexual couple in San Diego's Azalea Park district are passing out fliers as part of a campaign to aggressively attract gay men and lesbians into the neighborhood to "boost declining property values." They marched in San Diego's 1993 Pride Parade carrying a banner reading "Gays Welcome—Azalea Park" and handed out literature at the festival following the march.

There's a There There Now: Gay and Lesbian Communities in the U.S.

When Gertrude Stein said "There is no there there," she was referring to Oakland, California. But one might almost say the same thing about gay and lesbian communities in the United States. Can they really be defined by geographical boundary, or are they more ephemeral—"community" only in the sense of a group of people linked by common cause and beliefs? For all our numbers and increasingly visible presence in society, do we gay men and lesbians have any place to call our own?

Say "gay neighborhood" and what place immediately comes to mind? Many would name San Francisco's Castro district. Others might point to West Hollywood, the first self-proclaimed "gay city." New York's Greenwich Village has a long tradition of being home to bohemians and homosexuals. These are the gay meccas. Boystowns. These and others are bustling neighborhoods with a large gay population, gay-owned businesses and restaurants, bars and discos. This is where you'll find the gay bookstores and coffeehouses where you can sit for an hour or two and spot the next fashion trend.

Gay neighborhoods differ from straight ones in that here gay people don't have to pretend to pass for straight. They can see their lives reflected in a positive way: people who look like them, merchandise aimed at them, books and magazines with images of lesbians and gay men on the covers in shop windows. On these streets you'll see men holding hands, greeting friends, stopping to sign a petition soliciting support for a local ordinance or a candidate actively courting the gay vote.

Often absent from these gay neighborhoods, however, are large numbers of lesbians (or large numbers of gay people of color). Sure, you can go over the hill from the Castro and dip into Noe Valley, a very gay-friendly neighborhood, and see lesbians. Or drive south from West Hollywood to Long Beach, home to a sizable lesbian population. But there are few lesbian equivalents of West Hollywood's Santa Monica Boulevard, the strip where most of the action is.

Of course, there are exceptions, even to boystowns. Take Northampton, Massachusetts. Dubbed "Lesbianville, U.S.A." by *Newsweek* magazine, Northampton falls under many lesbians' definition of an oasis because of its active and visible lesbian population, which is estimated at around 3,000 in a town of 30,000. And that number has increased after the run on the town caused by a huge media stir in 1992, when Northampton was the subject of a segment on ABC's newsmagazine *20/20*. The town was also featured in *Newsweek*'s cover story on lesbians, not to mention a *National Enquirer* "exposé." One longtime resident, owner of the Tin Roof Bed and Breakfast, personally knows at least twenty lesbian couples who, attracted by national attention, stayed at her B&B and have since moved to the area. Many others heard about Northampton and dropped everything to live in a town where lesbians are accepted. The town newspaper prints announcements of lesbian commitment ceremonies alongside those of heterosexual marriages. It is not uncommon to see women holding hands as they walk down Main Street.

A group of women in Kansas City, Missouri, are trying a different idea. In 1990 two women had a vision of forming a deliberate community of lesbians called Womontown. Through word of mouth, and by placing announcements in such publications as *Lesbian Connection*, they have attracted women from other states as well as locally. They have encouraged them to buy homes or to rent in this mostly low-income inner city neighborhood to create a safe space for lesbians. Unlike most gay male neighborhoods, Womontown has attempted to define itself politically and ideologically. Residents have monthly Womontown meetings at which they discuss problems or issues related to the neighborhood. It's the kind of neighborhood where people help each other.

Reaction of the old timers (mostly nongay) in the neighborhood is mostly positive. Landlords and old people welcome the women. The other group most affected has been drug dealers, the majority of whom have been forced out of the neighborhood by increased police presence as well as private security patrols, results of active lesbian involvement in the neighborhood.

Of course, not all gay men and lesbians live in or near major metropolitan areas. Many gay people live in rural areas not just because they were born there, but because that kind of life appeals to them. Surprisingly, many of them are out. One section of a small town in northern California is affectionately referred to by its neighbors as "Amazon Ridge" because of the large numbers of lesbians living there. Other gay men and lesbians are living in places like rural Idaho and Oregon, where virulent antigay initiatives have compelled many to come out of the closet, educating their neighbors and putting to rest the false belief that the townspeople don't know any gay people.

And then there are the resorts: Provincetown, Massachusetts, the Russian River area of northern California, Cherry Grove on New York's Fire Island, and

GAY NEIGHBORHOODS AROUND THE COUNTRY

In many large cities, there are neighborhoods where gay people live, own businesses, or just hang out. Each has its own local designation; some are included on city maps; others must be found by word of mouth. Here are a few around the country:

Back Bay, Boston
Boystown, Chicago
Capitol Hill, Seattle
Capitol Hill, Denver
The Castro, San Francisco
Chelsea, New York City
Clintonville, Columbus, OH (lesbian)
Delmar Loop, St. Louis
Dupont Circle, Washington, D.C.
Greenwich Village, New York City
Highland Park, Detroit
Jamaica Plain, Boston (lesbian)
Little Five Points, Atlanta
Montrose, Houston
Mt. Vernon, Baltimore
Newtown, Chicago
Northampton, MA
Northwest, Portland, OR
Oak Lawn, Dallas
Park Slope, Brooklyn
Provincetown, MA
Silverlake, Los Angeles
South Beach, Miami
The backside of the French Quarter, New Orleans
Victorian Village, Columbus, OH
West Hollywood, Los Angeles
Winter Park, Orlando

Key West, Florida, are among the towns that provide gay and lesbian oases year round. Palm Springs in southern California, Rehoboth Beach in Delaware, and Saugatuck, Michigan, have also become summertime gay meccas.

Whether it's a vacation spot in P-town, a home in Womontown, or a stroll down Castro Street, gay and lesbian communities provide residents and visitors alike the opportunity to spend time in a safe environment, a place where they can be comfortable showing affection to their lovers and partners, where they know they will be accepted for who they are, and where they don't have to hide. Until this is possible in all areas of America's towns and cities, individual gay neighborhoods will flourish as highly visible pockets of gay and lesbian culture, places of work, play, and celebration.

— ELISABETH NONAS

The Queer Global Village: Come Out, Log On, Drop in

Queer people have staked out the electronic frontier since the early days of on-line communication. In 1984, Tom Jennings, a queer anarchist, created FidoNet, the first software that allowed bulletin boards around the world to intercommunicate through a large distributed network. In 1986, Bill Essex founded San Francisco's Fog City BBS in San Francisco, one of the first to cater to a gay male clientele. In 1991, Ron Buckmire created the Queer Resources Directory (QRD), now the world's largest electronic library of gay and lesbian resources on the Internet. Another gay man, David Casti, manages QRD along with many other queer-related Internet services. Also in 1991, a lesbian forum host known as Quirk started the Gay and Lesbian Community Forum (GLCF) on America Online, a fast-growing commercial service. She has grown the Forum into the densest concentration of gay and lesbian on-line activity today. In the GLCF you will find special-interest groups, including cat lovers, bisexuals, S/M aficionados, science fiction fans, Twelve Steppers, and transsexuals, just to name a few.

Gay and lesbian resources can also be found on other commercial on-line services, including CompuServe, GEnie, the WELL, and ATT Personalink, and the newest ones: Interchange, eWorld, and Microsoft Network. Clearly, there's a distinctive queer market on-line already —and there will be plenty more where they came from.

These commercial on-line services are tiny in relation to the Internet, which is a vast, decentralized network of computer networks growing at a furious clip. Because the Internet is worldwide, it has enormous potential to help queer people communicate and organize on many fronts around the globe. On the Internet you can find, in addition to the Queer Resources Directory, newsgroups (areas for discussing information) and mail lists (areas for sending and receiving mail on specific topics), such as GayNet, soc.motss (social members of the same sex), and alt. (alternative) sublists catering to every sexual and social subculture imaginable.

In the days of slow modems and local bulletin boards, the first on-line experience available was cruising for companionship or sex. Most early personal computer users were men, and it's not surprising that homosexual communication services emerged—and flourished. Gay men were able to meet each other through the relative safety of electronic chat and cruising. Communicating by personal computer offers true anonymity; as on citizen's band radios, one can use a "handle," or assumed name. Handles allow people to reach out and experiment with gender and sexual orientation whether from inside the closet or out. A woman might pretend to be a man to avoid on-line harassment; closeted or questioning gay men and lesbians can present themselves as straight in order to more comfortably explore virtual gay areas; young men can pretend to be older to avoid chicken hawks; and anyone might create fantasy identities with which to engage others on-line. No matter which persona you're wearing, interacting on-line is the way to feel connected, part of the larger queer community. The hunger for community, along with intense media attention on the "information superhighway," is an important factor in the recent explosion of queer on-line traffic.

The cost of owning a simple computer and modem setup has fallen drastically, from over $3,500 in 1989 to under $1,000 in 1995. While ultraconservatives prefer broadcast media ("one-to-many" communications), so that their message will not be challenged, queers are using on-line networks to create, publish, and disseminate "many-to-many" communications. Unlike with traditional broadcasting, recipients can respond, modify, or disagree—in other words, participate in the process of creating and publishing news and information.

Though this participation can be anarchic because it is "many-to-many," it's also revolutionary in its power to involve people directly and to subvert the traditional media institutions, which regularly ignore queer people. Electronic traffic has other powerful benefits, too: it's easy, fast, and cheap to create, publish, file, update, append, and centralize data of all kinds. And data can then be disseminated, copied, and forwarded at a moment's notice.

The benefits of electronic information flow are the gospel that Digital Queers (DQ), a San Francisco–based, nonprofit national association of computer professionals, is preaching to queer organizations—national, state, and local—who want to get on-line and stay there. Since its inception in 1992, through workshops, consultations, and news stories, DQ has fostered a vision of an "electronic town square" of national, state, local and community services, information resources, and meeting areas.

In addition, this virtual town square could contain a queer shopping mall to give everyone access to the goods and services that only lesbian and gay urbanites have in the real world. The space would also allow people to meet friends and learn about organizations they would not ordinarily find in their own hometowns.

Such a vision is particularly important to queers who live in far-flung outposts, away from traditional gay urban enclaves. In rural states like Utah, Wyoming, and Idaho, where queers are hundreds of miles apart, on-line services can help bring a community together without the need for travel.

In his book *Stranger at the Gate*, Mel White quotes a supporter of Beverly LaHaye (pillar of the archconservative Concerned Women of America), warning about the power of such "digital queers": "Gay activists . . . will outlast you . . . they have long memories . . . [and] are hooked up by computers." Outlast? We plan to. Hooked up? We all will be. As multiple electronic town squares spring up around the world, they become part of a larger entity—a queer global village. Eventually, this village will make a global queer and queer-friendly community that is more resilient, diverse, and productive than all the one-to-many homophobes who preach intolerance. So start now: come out, log on, drop in. As DQ's popular T-shirt says, "We're here, we're queer, we have e-mail!"

— KAREN WICKRE AND TOM RIELLY

Notes on Queer 'N' Asian Virtual Sex

It is not surprising that with the advent of the information superhighway, more and more folks are discovering the sexual underground within the virtual community in cyberspace.

Like the stereotypical computer nerd, I have sat in front of my computer, pressed some keys, and connected to a remote computer, perhaps twice daily, if not more often. But unlike the desexualized computer nerd, I have used the computer to connect to a Bulletin Board System (BBS) with a significant number of gay Asian members and used it to meet others for affection, romance, love, and sex for several years. In fact, as I write, I have logged on to this board more than 1,680 times, out of more than 600,000 calls made by everyone to the board since its creation in September 1991. How many sexual partners I have met will remain a state secret. Of the 1,088 BBSers registered, some 88 (or 8 percent) identify as Asian gay or bisexual men.

DID YOU KNOW...

By 1995, there were more than 2,000 on-line computer networks tailored to gay, lesbian, and bisexual participants, and available to users in North America, Australia, and Europe. Here are a sample of the Bulletin Board Systems in the U.S. and Canada:

Rainbow Connection (Alberta, Canada)
Torch Song (Alabama)
Leather Connection (Louisiana)
Infinite Diversity (Alabama)
Lavender Ranch (Arizona)
Butch's Board (California)
MEAT Market (Utah)
Men for Men (Florida)
Stonewall West (California)
Lambda Zone (Illinois)
Queen of Hearts (Florida)
Amazon's (New Jersey)
Gay Bytes (Nevada)
Bear's Cave (New York)
Gay Blade (Ontario, Canada)
Pink Triangle (Texas)

Initially this just seemed like the computerized, electronic version of placing or responding to a personal ad, as I had several times before. But as time went on, it dawned on me that this was something entirely different, with a potential for creativity (and mischief) largely untapped by myself and most of the others (I presumed) on the BBS. . . . With instantaneous communication now available, dating—and fulfilling our sexual desires—is much more immediately realizable.

One reason BBSing is so fascinating is that the on-line environment truly allows one to continually reinvent one's identity, including sexual. For once you are in total control of your sexual identity, or identities, or at least what you decide to show the outside world.

Ethnicity or race is another characteristic that can be changed, almost at will. If being Vietnamese today is not what you want to be, you could pick some other category. One BBSer from Taiwan even picked "Caucasian," and found out lots more people wanted to chat with him than when he was "Chinese," a recognition that the electronic environment does not screen out racist sentiments.

Given the prevalence of Asians in computer-based careers, one would not be surprised to find BBS's to be the places where gay or bisexual Asians gain entry into the sexual communities that now span the globe. . . . BBSers, then, challenge prevailing notions of Asian males as asexual. They provide Asians and Pacific Islanders (APIs) an anonymous forum for sexually explicit dialogue and for exploring their sexualities. On these boards, APIs are truly "breaking the silence" about taboo sexualities. In the process, APIs are empowered to voice our own forbidden desires and to reconstruct our own sexual identities.

— **DANIEL C. TSANG**

BUILDING FOUNDATIONS

Writer Fenton Johnson has said that "community is simply people caring for each other." Lesbians and gay men, together and separately, have joined together to take care of each other in a multitude of ways. In many cities and towns, we have created gay and lesbian community centers to provide a way of finding each other, and to provide a physical space for other groups in our communities to get together.

We have also created our own social services agencies, providing counseling and referrals for numerous groups, from people dealing with AIDS to young people looking for a safe place to meet other young gay people. These institutions are at the very core of how we take care of each other.

Another important way that gay people take care of each other is by preserving our culture. Without the gay and lesbian archives and libraries around the country, we would quickly lose the underpinnings and foundations of our movement.

Caring for ourselves means respecting ourselves. And respecting ourselves means taking care of our own, and taking care that we not lose our history.

DID YOU KNOW...

The Lesbian Resource Center in Seattle is the oldest independent social services agency in the U.S. exclusively for lesbians. It was founded on March 5, 1971.

Community Centers

The Engine of Lesbian and Gay Liberation

Lesbian and gay community centers provide something for nearly everyone. By facilitating a wide range of political, cultural, and social service programs, they serve different functions for different constituents within our communities. Unlike single-issue lesbian and gay organizations—such as social service providers or political action committees—community centers can bring together the many disparate elements of gay culture, providing newcomers with access to a complex community.

The lesbian and gay community centers movement began in 1966 with the Society for Individual Rights community center in San Francisco, followed by the development of other centers in California and upstate

New York in 1971. Currently dozens of lesbian and gay community centers serve gay people in urban, rural, and suburban settings. Community centers often function as the engine of lesbian and gay liberation in the communities they serve. By providing the physical space to nuture political consciousness and develop organizations for social change, lesbian and gay community centers can *drive* the development of a community without *directing* it.

When the New York Center opened its doors in 1983, sixty lesbian and gay groups met at the Center; now more than 400 hold regular meetings there. A number of national lesbian and gay organizations got their start at the Center, including ACT UP, Gay and Lesbian Alliance Against Defamation, and Queer Nation. The Center's structure facilitates an organic organizing process. Imagine the following scenario: a few like-minded individuals come together to start a new political or social group. The Center's newsletter, which is mailed monthly to 40,000 New York households, lists the meeting times of the nascent organization free of charge. At the given date, interested members of the community arrive at the Center for the meeting. With minimal effort and expense, a new organization is born.

"A friend of mine told me, and I think he's right, that it is the lonely young queens who become the lonely old queens. Many elderly people are too busy with activities to worry about being lonely."

GEORGE ROOSEN, SEVENTY, HEAD OF SAN FRANCISCO'S CHAPTER OF GAY AND LESBIAN OUTREACH TO ELDERS

In addition, the New York Center offers more than two dozen of its own social-service, cultural, civic, and recreational programs and acts as landlord to four other lesbian and gay agencies. Someone who comes to the Center seeking substance abuse counseling may be exposed to political and social organizations like the Gay and Lesbian Independent Democrats, Men of All Colors Together, or the Lesbian Avengers, while someone else coming to join CyberQueers, a group for computer professionals, may discover HIV-related health services or programs for elderly lesbians and gay men.

The Gay, Lesbian and Bisexual Community *Services* Center of Colorado

During the many waves of immigration to the United States, settlement houses were established in cities like New York and Chicago to provide safe havens and services to the arriving immigrants. Lesbian and gay community centers can function in the tradition of these settlement houses, providing services and orienting lesbian and gay people to their newly adopted culture.

Lesbian and gay community centers are some of the most valuable institutions within our communities. More than a room of our own, community centers are the engine of our movement, providing the opportunity for our culture to flourish and our different communities to evolve.

— RICHARD D. BURNS, EXECUTIVE DIRECTOR, LESBIAN AND GAY COMMUNITY SERVICES CENTER, NEW YORK

DID YOU KNOW...

Duluth, Minnesota, is home to both a gay men's center and a lesbian center. The Aurora Lesbian Center, founded in 1988, serves as a drop-in center, with discussion groups, films, and a support group for lesbian mothers. In September 1990, it hosted the first annual Northern Lights Womyn's Music Festival, the only such event in Minnesota. Aurora also sponsored a one-and-a-half-year dialogue educating area churches about lesbian and gay issues. The Northland Gay Men's Center, founded in 1992, is a drop-in center about twenty hours a week, offering a monthly Tuesday night discussion group for gay and bisexual men. The Center was instrumental in securing a place for gay men and lesbians in Duluth's St. Patrick Day Parade, and marched on Duluth's city hall in 1993 the day Minnesota's law protecting gay men and lesbians from discrimination took effect.

Events at New York Gay and Lesbian Community Services Center: November 1993

- a speech by Dennis deLeon, Commissioner/Chair of the NYC Commission on Human Rights and board member for the Latino Commission on AIDS, Housing Works, and the Latino Coalition for Fair Media
- a reading by contributors to *Sojourner: Black Gay Voices in the Age of AIDS*, published by the collective Other Countries
- lesbian movie night, featuring three films on the subject of female hysteria
- an exhibit at the National Museum & Archive of Lesbian & Gay History (housed at the community center) called "Out on the Island: 60 Years of Lesbian & Gay Life on Fire Island"
- orientations (including one specifically for lesbians) that provide an introduction to New York's lesbian and gay communities, including speakers, representatives, and literature from dozens of groups
- a forum on the importance of wills for lesbians and gay men in which experts discuss wills, insurance, and bequests
- several meetings involving the center's family project for lesbian and gay parents and their children and those considering parenthood
- a drag variety show produced by the Imperial Court of NY
- a lecture on how to find a therapist

• a series of workshops on starting and running your own business

• Asian Lesbians of the East Coast Annual Cross-dressing Party

• a wrestling exhibition presented by Metro Gay Wrestling Alliance

• a meeting to discuss how to prepare for and enter the physique competition of the Gay Games

• Body Positive Social: a get-together for HIV-postive people

• panel discussion by lesbians of various ages on "Lesbian Chic": the pros and cons of increased visibility for our politics and our relationships within the community and outside it

DID YOU KNOW...

The lesbian and gay AA Living Sober conference in San Francisco is the first and oldest gathering in the country. The first conference, in 1976, registered 192 people; it continues as an annual event. The largest one to date in San Francisco has had 5,218 partcipants. Annual Living Sober conferences sponsored by the lesbian and gay members of Alcoholics Anonymous happen in Denver, Houston, Los Angeles, New York, Palm Springs, San Jose, San Diego, San Francisco, Seattle, and Vancouver.

Living Sober

When I first got sober in 1978, I thought I was the only gay alcoholic in the world. Or maybe the first one to do something about it. I soon discovered that there were about five gay-identified Alcoholics Anonymous meetings in San Francisco. I didn't attend any of them for a long time, because the only time I was "comfortable" with gay men was when I was drunk. I was absolutely terrified of them sober. I didn't know why.

After a year or so of sobriety I ventured into a gay meeting and discovered that I was at home. These were the VIPs in my life. These were the people whom I had abused emotionally and physically during my alcoholic career. They had been mutually destructive relationships. On some conscious level I realized that if I were to become a happy and healthy gay man, I needed the men in that room to teach me how to love myself and them "without orgasm." The journey into intimacy, friendship, and solidarity that began that very evening has continued for more than fifteen years. My life today is richer, happier, and more productive than I could ever have imagined.

What I didn't know at the time was that I didn't know how "to do" life. I didn't know how to ask for help and to continue asking for help. And I didn't know that I didn't know that. That is a working definition of classical denial. The solution is to not take the next drink. The insights can only come if "the brain has drained and the body has dried out."

AA has a saying that "service is its own reward." One can never adequately imagine the payoffs from community service. I worked on the San Francisco Living Sober conference for many years. The conference was the "playground" for me to learn how to socialize again, discover my own racism, sexism, and homophobia, develop confidence and new competencies, learn collaborative management, find a sense of humor, learn to love and be loved for the first time, and above all, to be a proud gay man. The Twelve Steps of AA are there for personal recovery, and the Twelve Traditions exist as guidelines to help the group in its recovery process.

Many gifts have come to me in my sobriety—being conscious on a daily basis, happy and fulfilling relationships, international traveling, new business adventures, graduate school, the opportunity to serve the lesbian and gay community professionally. I will savor for the rest of my life the joy of mentoring lesbians and gay men as they come alive for the first time and move from isolation into community, from despair into hope.

To be a brother and companion to those in our community living with AIDS has been a blessing I never anticipated. To experience the heroic courage of those who die clean and sober, sharing the hope and joys of lives taken out of season, touches me more deeply than I can say. As my brothers have taught me how to love and be loved, they are also teaching me how to live and how to die.

Wherever I go in this country I meet recovering lesbians and gay men who have turned their lives around. They are deeply committed to their families, extended families, neighborhood, and community. They are in every profession and way of life. They bring to their daily activities a perspective that only enriches the people they serve. I am proud of them and they are proud of me.

— ANONYMOUS

GRAY & GAY

There are several social service organizations around the country dedicated to the specific needs of older gay men and lesbians.

SAGE (Senior Action in a Gay Environment), New York: Goals are to increase the visibility of gay and lesbian seniors and help improve the image of all seniors in the media; to outreach and locate gay and lesbian seniors who are homebound and isolated.

GLOE (Gay and Lesbian Outreach to Elders), San Francisco: Programs are run by older people doing whatever they want to do.

Metropolitan Retirees, Washington, D.C.: Sponsors events from museum trips to parties.

Retired Gays and Lesbians of Northern Virginia: Members enjoy services, including day trips out of town, and "practical assistance in matters of transportation, in-home convalescent care, a sympathetic ear, and 'just being there' for our fellow members."

Lesbian and Gay Youth Programs

One hundred and seventy programs in the United States and Canada address issues for gay young people. Following are some of the most exciting programs around the country:

- **District 202,** in Minneapolis, is a youth center with projects including a print-making workshop, two-step lessons, and annual lesbian and gay proms.
- **Hetrick-Martin Institute** (HMI) in New York City provides some of the most extensive services around, including the Harvey Milk School for lesbian, gay, bisexual, and transgendered youth. HMI also puts out *You Are Not Alone*, an annual directory of gay youth organizations in the United States and Canada, and has an outreach program for homeless and street youth.
- San Francisco's **Lambda Youth Recreation and Information Center** sponsors a young women's basketball team in a local league, holds an annual young women's health conference, has young gay men's programs that fuse photography and creative writing with HIV awareness, and developed Proactive Youth, a job-training program with computer and résumé classes, conflict resolution, and group-facilitation skills.

GAY YOUTH HIT THE AIRWAVES

The following Public Service Announcement (PSA) ran on Seattle area radio stations in August 1993.

SOUND	COPY
Sounds of a school hallway at break (hustle and bustle, lockers shutting, conversations, bell ringing, etc.) The girls are teenagers.	Girl #1: You won't believe what I just heard!
	Girl #2: What?
	Girl #3: This better be good!
	Girl #1: Heather is taking Ashley to the prom!
	Girl #2: No way!
#1 approaches # 2 and #3.	Girl #3: You're joking!
	Girl #1: I swear!
	Girl #2: But I thought she was dating Brenda!
	Girl #3: Yeah, I thought so too.
After Girl #3 delivers her last line, quickly fade their now-unintelligible conversation and ambient sounds under the announcer and music. *Music beat: upbeat, funky* *This spot emphasizes fun and feel should be lighthearted.*	Announcer: This conversation could happen in your school; after all, one in ten teenagers is gay. If you're the one and you want to meet others just like you and have some fun, visit Lambert, the Gay Youth Center. It's a big old house where you can watch movies, listen to music, have something to eat, and a lot more. If you don't feel comfortable visiting Lambert House yet, you can get a list of activities and programs by calling the Gay/Lesbian Youth Info Line. It's prerecorded, so no one will ever know you called. Just look under "Gay" in the white pages. This message is brought to you with pride by the Pride Foundation.

• **Lambert House** in Seattle reaches out to lesbian, gay, bisexual, transgender, and questioning youth all over the Pacific Northwest, with HIV education and support for homeless youth, a "crash pad" for gay young people who need a place to sleep, and a twenty-four-hour events line.

• **Project 10** and the **Eagles Center**, in Los Angeles, have an alternative high school for gay and lesbian students, including a gay youth prom.

DID YOU KNOW...

The Harvey Milk School, a city-funded high school for gay and lesbian teenagers in New York City, held its first classes in a Greenwich Village church on April 1, 1985. At that time the school had an enrollment of twenty students, mostly openly gay and lesbian youths who had been beaten up, threatened, harassed, or repeatedly abused at other schools, often to the point where they had stopped attending classes altogether. "At least here," observed one grateful student, "we can be ourselves." Today, many gay and lesbian students use HMS as an educational place of transition.

Special Collections of Gay and Lesbian Materials

Preserving our culture is the primary mission of many of the private archives around the country. Some public institutions, such as the New York Public Library, maintain gay and lesbian collections. Similarly, many colleges and universities have been actively soliciting archive materials from prominent gay and lesbian writers and activists. But the archives listed below, run primarily with gay and lesbian volunteers and on low budgets, serve to maintain and preserve our local gay history. Some, such as the Quatrefoil Library in St. Paul and the Henry Gerber/Pearl Hart Library and Archives in Chicago, act as lending libraries as well. These institutions deserve our on-going support and patronage.

Atlanta Gay and Lesbian Thang, Atlanta, GA

Blanche M. Baker Memorial Library, ONE, Inc., Los Angeles, CA

Dallas Gay/Lesbian Historic Archives, Dallas, TX

Gay Alliance of the Genesee Valley Library, Rochester, NY

Gay & Lesbian Historical Society of Northern California, San Francisco, CA

Gay & Lesbian Archives of Washington, D.C.

Gay & Lesiban Archives of Philadelphia, PA

Happy Foundation, San Antonio, TX

Harvey Milk Archives, San Francisco, CA

Henry Gerber/Pearl Hart Library, Chicago, IL

Homosexual Information Center Library, Bossier City, LA

DID YOU KNOW...
The Gay and Lesbian Center in San Francisco's New Main Library, named for gay philanthropist James C. Hormel, makes it the first public library to have a separate collection of gay and lesbian materials. The initial 7,000 volumes are from the private collection of lesbian publishers Barbara Grier and Donna McBride. In addition, the collection contains the papers and archival materials of Randy Shilts, filmmakers Rob Epstein and Peter Adair, as well as thousands of books published each year by both the independent and mainstream presses. Thanks to the successful fund-raising efforts of the gay and lesbian community around the country, an endowment has been created to support and maintain the collection, providing a permanent legacy of gay culture for generations to come.

International Gay & Lesbian Archives, West Hollywood, CA

June Mazar Lesbian Collection, West Hollywood, CA

Kentucky Gay & Lesbian Archives, Louisville, KY

Lesbian Herstory Archive, Brooklyn, NY

Lesbian/Gay Archives of San Diego, CA

Metropolitan Community Church (MCC) Library, Houston, TX

National Museum of Lesbian and Gay History, New York, NY

Northeast Ohio Lesbian/Gay Archives, Cleveland, OH

Quatrefoil Library, St. Paul, MN

Southeastern Lesbian Archives Atlanta Lesbian Feminist Alliance Library, Atlanta, GA

Stonewall Library, Fort Lauderdale, FL

Women's Library, Fayetteville, AR

Women's Movement Archives and Library, Cambridge, MA

Lesbian and Gay Studies

The growth of lesbian and gay studies has been explosive over the last decade, and the scope and breadth of the work produced is astonishing. Hundreds of books and articles have appeared on various aspects of lesbian and gay history, politics, and culture—work that has transformed our own sense of who we are and has begun to convey to a larger audience the challenging specialness of our lives.

Soon after Stonewall, lesbian and gay scholars made an effort to bring gay liberation and feminist perspectives to bear on their research and writing when they founded the Gay Academic Union (GAU) in March 1973. Professors, writers, students, and librarians like Martin Duberman, Bertha Harris, Karla Jay, John D'Emilio, Jonathan Ned Katz, and Barbara Gittings were among those who banded together. Three hundred people attended the first GAU conference on November 23 and 24, 1973.

The rapid growth of women's studies program in the 1970s provided a safe space for lesbian studies—that is, courses with lesbian content and themes. Lesbian feminism presented lesbianism as an alternative model for female identity. Some of the major contributions to lesbian studies—such as Lillian Faderman's history of romantic friendship among women, *Surpassing the Love of Men*—were written in this tradition. Most significantly, women's studies programs often created a safe place for lesbians to come out and familiarize themselves with lesbian culture. But as women's studies programs came under attack from conservatives and budget cutbacks, the lesbian content of women's studies courses was downplayed or eliminated. Many lesbian professors found themselves shut out of tenure track positions.

One of the first major challenges to cultural feminism grew out of the passionate and bitter controversy provoked by the feminist antipornography movement in the late seventies and early eighties. Underlying the "sex wars," as the debate was called, were differences among lesbians and feminists about the political priority of a woman's identity as a woman over a woman's identity as a sexual person. New ideas about the social construction of sexual norms and behavior were an outgrowth of this debate.

DID YOU KNOW...

In the spring of 1989, San Francisco City College established the first Gay and Lesbian Studies department in the United States. The program got its start in 1972 when an English department instructor launched one of the first gay literature courses in the country.

Another intellectual development of the eighties that made a major contribution to lesbian and gay studies was the publication of *This Bridge Called My Back*, which included work by Audre Lorde, Cherríe Moraga, Barbara Smith, and Gloria Anzaldúa, among others. In that powerful collection of essays, poetry, and personal narratives, as well as in several other books—*Sister Outsider* (1984) by Audre Lorde, *Home Girls* (1983) edited by Barbara Smith, *Borderlands* (1987) by Gloria Anzaldúa, *Loving in the War Years* (1983) by Cherríe Moraga—these women of color proposed a new way of thinking about cultural identity and difference. They criticized the impulse, widely prevalent among cultural feminists, that emphasized the essential similiarities of all women rather than the differences of race and sexuality that existed among women. The exploration by these writers of the overlapping identities of gender, race, and sexuality also implies criticism of "universalistic" conceptions of the making of the homosexual identity.

Since 1986 there has been a new wave of efforts to establish lesbian and gay studies as a legitimate academic subject—research centers, graduate seminars, undergraduate courses, publishing programs have been started at a number of institutions. In 1986 Martin Duberman and John Boswell initiated a new trend of faculty leadership when they brought together a group of scholars from both generations to start a Center for Lesbian and Gay Studies at Yale. While that original group split up over differences regarding the participation of women, minorities, and independent scholars, many other groups are in the process of setting up different types of academic programs that could eventually become the basis for officially recognized lesbian and gay studies. Boswell and a group of junior faculty and graduate students at Yale have put on three annual lesbian and gay studies conferences. Duberman, Esther Newton, and George Chauncey, all of whom had originally met with the Yale group, started the Committee for Lesbian and Gay Studies at the City University of New York, which established the Center for Lesbian and Gay Studies (CLAGS) in 1991.

DID YOU KNOW...

CLAGS (Center for Lesbian and Gay Studies), established at the City University of New York in 1991, was the first university-affiliated research center in the U.S. devoted to the exclusive study of lesbian and gay themes. CLAGS serves as a national clearinghouse for scholarly research on multicultural, multiracial, and feminist perspectives on gay and lesbian lives.

Lesbian and gay studies are under way at Yale University, the City University of New York, City College of San Francisco, New York University, Columbia University, Duke University, University of California at Santa Cruz and Berkeley, and many other institutions. At many of these institutions undergraduate and graduate courses with lesbian or gay themes are offered by regular departments of literature, sociology, and history. Publishers like Routledge, Columbia University Press, New York University Press, and the University of Minnesota Press have begun to publish dozens of books in lesbian and gay or queer studies. In 1994, a new academic journal devoted exclusively to lesbian and gay studies was started—*GLQ,* edited by Carolyn Dinshaw and David Halperin.

For several years now lesbian and gay studies has been increasingly defined by work done in literary theory and cultural studies. More recently, this body of work is categorized as "queer theory" and stresses analysis of the representations of homosexuality in literature, film, and popular culture. Queer theory represents a new paradigm of cultural studies indebted to the work of theorists like Michel Foucault, Jacques Lacan, Jacques Derrida, and Roland Barthes. It differs from writing and research done by earlier generations of scholars in lesbian and gay studies in its emphasis on the close analysis of texts, popular culture, and the media. The earlier generation had focuses on historical, social, and anthropological analysis of documents, movements, and social structures—supplemented by the recovery of lost and forgotten authors, historical figures, and early political activities.

The second wave is a group of scholars whose work has become identified as "queer theory" or queer studies. Judith Butler, Eve Sedgewick, David Halperin, Sue Ellen Case, Michael Warner, Michele Aina Barale, Cindy Patton, Diana Fuss, and Douglas Crimp are representatives of this second wave. These two groups of scholars come to their writing and research with radically different approaches to their work. Many of the first-wave scholars have been influenced by work in social history and anthropology, while the second wave has been heavily influenced by literary and cultural criticism.

— JEFFREY ESCOFFIER

DID YOU KNOW...

The Institute for Gay and Lesbian Education (IGLE) is an education institution in Los Angeles, founded in 1992 by Simon LeVay and Chris Patrouch. Courses and lecture series are offered on a variety of subjects of general interest, and of particular interest to gay people. IGLE seeks to break down institutionalization and cultural barriers that divide our community and separate us from society at large. Sample class offerings include *Gay Sensibilities in Film; Writing the First Novel;* and *Psychological Development for Men.* In 1994, the Harvey Milk Institute was formed in San Francisco. While HMI is a similar program, its curriculum is more eclectic. In 1996, HMI sponsored a symposium on the *Queer Beats,* as well as offering classes ranging from *French for the Queer Traveler* to *Basic Tax Information for Self-Employed People.*

OMOPHOB
is incompatible with
MILITARY SERVICE
IDS
TRADING
FEARS
FOR FACTS
© K. Haring 88
A GUIDE FOR TEENS
Consumer
Reports
Books
Someone you
care about i
Lesbian or
JUST
PATRO
BY
of the
Facts...

CHAPTER 6

Myths and Facts

An unnamed member of the U.S. Congress, when asked recently by Daniel Zingale of the Human Rights Campaign Fund if he would support a bill guaranteeing the right of all gay men and lesbians to work without fear of being fired simply for being gay, replied that he thought it was a good law. "But," he said, "I don't think I have any gay people in my district. After all, I haven't heard about this issue from any of my constituents."

This not atypical response was based on several common myths about gay men and lesbians, the biggest ones being that there aren't very many gay people in the world, and that all gay people are "out" and obvious to spot. (By the congressman's statement, it is clear that another myth was operating too: the myth that all gay people have a "gay agenda" and are politically organized.)

LESBIAN SURVIVAL HINT #216: YOU CAN TELL A LOT ABOUT A WOMAN BY WHERE SHE PUTS HER HIPS.
(Rhonda Dicksion)

Despite all the science and research that has been done, myths about lesbians and gay men persist. When people subscribe to these myths, a productive dialogue about gay people is nearly impossible. On a recent television talk show addressing gay parenting, for example, a homophobic fundamentalist was placed on the panel, supposedly for "balance." Instead of being able to discuss the complex legal, moral, and social issues surrounding gay parenting, the lesbian and gay panelists spent almost the entire hour debating with the fundamentalist panelist about whether gay people are child molesters and want to have kids to "turn" them gay.

If straight people hold beliefs about gay people that are not necessarily based on fact, the same is true for many lesbians and gay men about each other. Even within the lesbian and gay community, there is a lot of confusion and debate surrounding many questions.

In this chapter we have tackled a number of tricky issues in an attempt to explain some facts and discuss some of the more common misperceptions about gay men and lesbians. The public dialogue about gay people and politics will not progress beyond myth-dispelling until we can move past these misperceptions.

The Most Common Myths about Gay Men and Lesbians

DID YOU KNOW...

In 1992, Ann Landers asked in her daily column for gay people to let her know whether or not they were happy with their orientation. A total of 75,875 lesbians and gays responded to her survey. By a margin of 30 to 1, gay people said that they were happy to be gay.

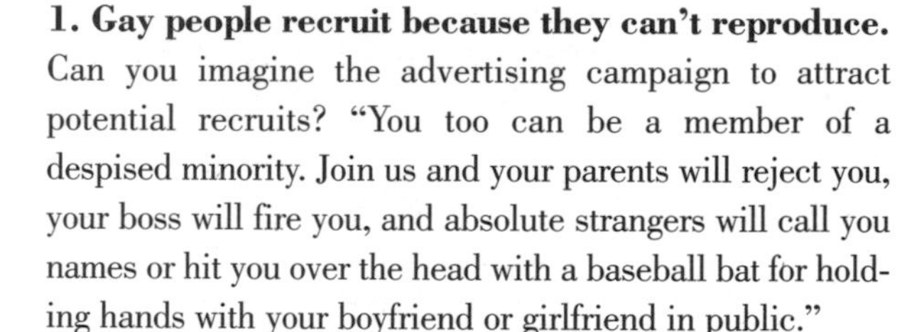

1. Gay people recruit because they can't reproduce.

Can you imagine the advertising campaign to attract potential recruits? "You too can be a member of a despised minority. Join us and your parents will reject you, your boss will fire you, and absolute strangers will call you names or hit you over the head with a baseball bat for holding hands with your boyfriend or girlfriend in public."

This is a multipart myth. First, gay people can reproduce and do, but their children are no more likely to be gay or lesbian than the children of heterosexual parents. Second, the recruit myth suggests that homosexuals seduce unsuspecting heterosexuals into becoming gay. Even if gay people wanted to recruit, they can't make a heterosexual person a homosexual. It doesn't work that way.

At best, gay and lesbian people can serve as positive role models for those who are struggling with their gay and lesbian identities. We can show by example that you can be homosexual and lead a full and happy life—at least as happy as anyone else's. But despite what some people may claim, gay and lesbian people do not recruit heterosexual children or adults.

2. Homosexuality is caused by a distant father and dominant mother.

We have Freud to thank for this myth. He came up with the theory that homosexuality in men results from having a passive, indifferent, or hostile father and a strong mother. But this flawed theory can't explain families in which passive, indifferent fathers and strong mothers raise heterosexual children, or families in which strong fathers and passive mothers raise homosexual children. And what about a family in which the parents are both dominant? Does that mean the kids will be bisexual?

Bottom line: The personalities or power dynamics of mothers and fathers have no impact on whether a child is heterosexual, homosexual, or bisexual.

3. Gay people are by nature predatory child molesters.

This hateful myth just won't go away, when the truth is that the most likely person to molest children is a heterosexual male, and his most likely victim is a female child who is a member of his own family. Men who molest prepubescent boys almost always identify as heterosexual and are heterosexual in their adult relationships.

It would be nice to say that there are no child molesters who are gay. That would be a lie—but gay people are no more likely than heterosexuals to sexually abuse children. In fact, according to a study conducted in the early 1990s by Children's Hospital in Denver, Colorado, gay people are far *less* likely than heterosexuals to molest children: During a one-year period, only one of 387 cases of suspected child molestation there involved a gay perpetrator.

4. Women become lesbians because they've had bad experiences with men.

If every woman who had a bad experience with a man became a lesbian, there wouldn't be a heterosexual woman left on the planet.

5. Gay men want to be women and lesbians want to be men.

There are indeed men who wish to be women and women who wish to be men, but this has nothing to do with sexual orientation. These are conflicts regarding gender. Most gay and lesbian people, like most heterosexual people, are perfectly content to keep the male or female bodies they were born with.

6. Gay and lesbian people don't have lasting, loving, couple relationships.

Lasting, loving relationships are tough for heterosexuals.

> **"Girls who put out are tramps. Girls who don't are ladies. This is, however, a rather archaic usage of the word. Should one of you boys happen upon a girl who doesn't put out, do not jump to the conclusion that you have found a lady. What you have probably found is a lesbian."**
>
> FRAN LEBOWITZ, CULTURAL CRITIC

Just look at the divorce statistics. And heterosexuals generally have the support of their families, communities, and the state. Against all odds, many gay and lesbian people have found lasting and loving relationships. Unfortunately, because gay people remain largely hidden, there are no accurate statistics on the number of gay and lesbian couples or the average length of these relationships.

7. Gay men hate women. Lesbians hate men.

As a blanket statement, this is simply untrue, though some gay men hate women and some lesbians hate men, just as some heterosexual men hate women and some heterosexual women hate men. Let's not forget that some gay people hate heterosexuals, and more than a few heterosexuals hate gay people. And, of course, some people hate everyone. Hate is, after all, an equal opportunity emotion.

Not all gay people are rich, white, or male, despite the myth to the contrary. Here, Gay American Indians (GAI) and AIDS activists joined together in 1985 to protest the lack of federal funding for AIDS programs and Native American health care. (Rink Foto)

8. Gay people are all rich and all white.

This relatively new myth is an unfortunate conclusion drawn from misleading marketing studies of the "gay community" that suggest all gay men are affluent, urban, white, and well-educated, drive nice cars, and drink expensive designer coffee. Compared to the older myth that all gay men are child molesters, this is quite an improvement, but it's still way off the mark. How many times do we have to say it? Gay people are both male and female, come from all walks of life, all racial, ethnic, and religious groups, all parts of the nation, and all socioeconomic groups.

9. Gay men are extremely promiscuous.

If you believe what some people say about gay men, you would think that all gay men have had a thousand or more sexual partners by the time they're thirty. Some very sexually active men—straight and gay—have had a thousand or more sexual partners by the time they're thirty, but most single gay men feel lucky to have a date on a Saturday night.

10. Lesbians "have a thing" for cats. Gay men have good fashion sense.
This may look like two myths, but it's really one. The myth is that what is true about one gay person is true for all. It's not. The truth is, some lesbians love cats, and some lesbians hate cats. No scientific survey has ever been conducted to establish whether or not lesbians own more cats per capita than any other group of people, but you can bet that it's only a matter of time before one of those new gay marketing companies starts one.

When it comes to gay men and fashion, how do you explain Elton John and Liberace? They are proof that not all gay men have good fashion sense. Of course, plenty of gay men do indeed have better fashion sense than many straight men, but the reverse is also true.

— ERIC MARCUS

"I'm not even interested in all lesbians, much less all women. Why would I be interested in someone who isn't even sexually interested in women, much less in me? That seems kind of counterproductive."

ALICIA LUCKSTEAD, IN THE WASHINGTON BLADE, EXPLAINING THAT SHE IS NOT ATTRACTED TO STRAIGHT WOMEN

The Prevalence of Sexual Inversion (1901)

Concerning the wide prevalence of sexual inversion, and of homosexual phenomena generally, there can be no manner of doubt. In Berlin, [Albert] Moll states that he has himself seen between six hundred and seven hundred homosexual persons, and heard of some two hundred and fifty to three hundred others. I have much evidence as to this frequency both in England and the United States. In England, concerning which I can naturally speak with most assurance, its manifestations are well-marked for those whose eyes have been opened. . . . Among the professional and most cultured element of the middle class in England there must be a distinct percentage of inverts, which may sometimes be as much as 5 percent, though such estimates must always be hazardous. Among women of the same class the percentage seems to be at least double—though here the phenomena are less definite and deepseated."

— HAVELOCK ELLIS, IN PSYCHOLOGY OF SEX

Urnings Are Not Rare

Contrary to the general impression, one of the first points that emerges from this study is that 'Urnings,' or Uranians [from *Uranos,* 'heaven'; the idea being that the Uranian love was of a higher order than the ordinary attachment] are by no means so very rare, but that they form, beneath the surface of society, a large class. It remains difficult, however, to get an exact statement of their numbers, and this for more than one reason: partly because, owing to the want of any general understanding of their case, these folk tend to conceal their true feelings from all but their own kind, and indeed often deliberately act in such a manner as to lead the world astray (whence it arises that a normal man living in a certain society will often refuse to believe that there is a single Urning in the circle of his acquaintance, while one of the latter, or one that understands the nature, living in the same society, can count perhaps a score or more) and partly because it is indubitable that the numbers do vary very greatly, not only in different countries but even in different classes in the same country. The consequence of all this being that we have estimates differing widely from each other. Dr. Grabowsky, a well-known writer in Germany, quotes figures (which we think must be exaggerated) as high as one man in every 22, while Dr. Albert Moll gives estimates varying from one to every 50 to as low as one in every 500.

— EDWARD CARPENTER IN THE INTERMEDIATE SEX (1908)

?#!

DID YOU KNOW...

The U.S. government completed its first-ever attempt to enumerate the number of gay and lesbian couples in the nation as part of its 1990 census. Data suggests that there are 145,130 such couples heading households in this country. California had 25 percent of all those responding; Massachusetts 6.6 percent; New York 5.8 percent; Minnesota 5.1 percent; and Georgia and Washington, 5 percent each. States with the smallest percentages were Wyoming (0.6 percent), South Dakota (0.6 percent), and Idaho (1.7 percent).

Where Do They Get Those Numbers?

Any lesbian or gay man in America today, if asked how many gay people there are, would probably respond almost automatically with "10 percent." This 10 percent figure, which is so often quoted, is apparently a misinterpretation of the data presented in Alfred Kinsey's two reports: *Sexual Behavior in the Human Male*, published in 1948, and *Sexual Behavior in the Human Female*, published in 1953.

In fact, Kinsey never actually stated that 10 percent of the population was actively homosexual. Drawing from a pool of approximately 6,000 male Americans, Kinsey and his staff found that 37 percent of the male population had had some homosexual contact after adolescence, 13 percent had been more homosexual than heterosexual for at least three years between adolescence and age fifty-five, and 4 percent were exclusively homosexual after adolescence. Among the 6,000 American women studied, 13 percent had some homosexual contact after adolescence, and, compared with the male subjects, "there were only about a half to a third as many of the females who were, in any age period, primarily or exclusively homosexual." In other words, approximately 2 percent of women were exclusively homosexual.

In 1993, the Alan Guttmacher Institute published a

GENESIS OF A GAY FACTOID

Kinsey did not say that 10 percent of American men and women were *actively* homosexual, but he did invite that impression by ambiguous wording. "Kinsey was trying to show that homosexuality wasn't rare and perverse and so he was sometimes imprecise by not always making a clear distinction between active and cumulative incidence," says Paul Gebhard, Kinsey's co-author and successor. The 10 percent figure became famous in 1977 after the National Gay Task Force requested an update from the Kinsey Institute on the incidence of homosexuals in the United States. Gebhard replied with a memo that read, in part:

"In the 1948 and 1953 studies, it was stated that 13 percent of the male and 7 percent of the female population had more homosexual than heterosexual experience or psychological response for at least three years between the ages of sixteen and fifty-five, for a combined percentage of 10 percent for the total population. These figures have been criticized for including psychological response along with overt experience. However, I have been recently reworking the 1938 to 1963 data to include only 'experience' (defined as deliberate physical contact intended by at least one of the participants to produce sexual arousal).

"Tabulations based on these criteria indicate that 13.95 percent of males and 4.25 percent of females, or a combined average of 9.13 percent of the total population, had either extensive (21 or more partners or 52 or more experiences) or more than incidental (5–20 partners or 21–50 experiences) homosexual experience. I wish to point out that although the Institute did interview members of homosexual groups and organizations as part of its research, all such persons were excluded from the above tabulation."

— **PHILIP NOBILE,** VILLAGE VOICE, **JUNE 1, 1993**

study conducted by the Battelle Human Affairs Research Center in Seattle which was based on face-to-face interviews in 1991 with 3,321 men, ages twenty through thirty-nine. The study concluded that 1 percent identified themselves as homosexual. Tom W. Smith, who directs the General Social Survey at the University of Chicago, said that the new findings are in line with a series of surveys of sexual practices done in each of the last four years by researchers at the University of Chicago and with recently published reports from Britain, France, and Denmark.

The Battelle study has several obvious problems. Among them are the fact that the age group sampled (twenty to thirty-nine) leaves out a lot of sexually active people; all the respondents were male, which omits more than half of the U.S. population; and the studies were face-to-face. Many gay people will not admit their sexuality to a total stranger.

THE CONFUSING COUNT

How many gay people are there? One in 100? One in 10? There are no clear answers. For years, gay activists clung to figures from studies Alfred Kinsey conducted in the 1940s and 1950s that suggested 10 percent of Americans are homosexual. But those numbers—based on interviews with the institutional populations of schools, hospitals, and prisons—have been considered less reliable in recent years. Yet finding studies with more definitive numbers hasn't been easy. A look at some of those studies:

Alfred Kinsey (1940s and 1950s) 10%
National Opinion Research Center (1988–91)
Men having sex exclusively with men in past year 2%
Women having sex exclusively with women in past year. . . . 0.7%
Men and women who had engaged in homosexual activity during adult lives 5–6%
Alan Guttmacher Institute (1993)
The study was limited to men between the ages of 20 and 39.
Adult men who have engaged in homosexual sex.. . . . . 2%
Adult men who think of themselves as exclusively homosexual 1%
The Janus Report on Sexual Behavior (1993)
Study drew from a non-random national sample of adults
Women who identified themselves as homosexual 2%
Men who identified themselves as homosexual 4%

—THE KANSAS CITY STAR, MARCH 20, 1994

Voter Research & Surveys conducted a survey of voters on Election Day 1992 for the four television networks, and found that 3 percent of men and 2 percent of women who voted that day said that they were gay, lesbian, or bisexual.

Murray Edelman, director of the company, estimated that because people are reluctant to identify themselves as gay or lesbian the actual homosexual vote was slightly higher, at around 4 percent of the total.

In February 1992, the Campaign for Women's Health and the American Medical Women's Association released the results of a survey of 1,000 women chosen by random and conducted by telephone. The overall purpose of the survey was to gather information about women's health needs. Only one question dealt with sexuality: "Have your sexual partners been mainly men, women, or both?" Twenty women said they had sex with women exclusively, and another twenty said that they had sexual partners of both sexes. The total, forty, represents 4 percent of the women surveyed. Yankelovich Partners, who have been tracking consumer values and attitudes since 1971, included a question about sexual identity in its most recent Yankelovich Monitor survey, the results of which were released in June 1994. The result among the 2,503 people participating in the 1993 study was that 5.7 percent, or 143, described themselves as "gay/homosexual/lesbian," which was one of fifty-two questions on personal topics. *Out* magazine editor Michael Goff was quoted in *The New York Times* as saying about this survey, "That almost 6 percent of the people say they're gay is incredibly important," because "it's the first real hard study done by a gold-standard research company" to indicate what percentage of the population identifies itself as gay or lesbian.

In 1994, when a University of Chicago survey team asked 3,432 men and women between the ages of eighteen and fifty-nine about their sexual behavior, 10.2 percent of the men and 2.1 percent of the women in the country's top twelve largest cities acknowledged having had sex with someone of the same sex in the year preceding the survey. Asked about their entire adulthood, 16.4 percent of the men and 6.2 percent of the women said they had had at least one sexual partner of their own sex.

THE U.S. CENSUS: THE GOVERNMENT TRIES TO COUNT

In the 1990 Census, the U.S. government tried in a roundabout way to determine the number of gay men and lesbians living as couples in the country by including questions regarding the number and sex of any unmarried adults living in the household. The breakdown of the unmarried couples living together in the largest twenty cities follows.

1. San Francisco (35.4%)
2. Washington, D.C. (18.9%)
3. Boston (16.2%)
4. Los Angeles (9.6%)
5. San Diego (9.3%)
6. New York (8.9%)
7. Chicago (8.6%)
8. Dallas (8.5%)
9. Houston (7.4%)
10. San Jose (6.8%)
11. Columbus (6.6%)
12. Philadelphia (6.3%)
13. Baltimore (6.2%)
14. Phoenix (5.0%)
15. Indianapolis (5.0%)
16. San Antonio (4.1%)
17. Milwaukee (4.1%)
18. Jacksonville (4.0%)
19. Detroit (3.5%)
20. Memphis (3.2%)

In rural areas, the figures drop considerably: Only 1 percent of men and 0.6 percent of women reported same-sex sexual behavior in the past year. For their entire adulthoods, the figures were 1.5 percent for women and 2.8 percent for men. Again, it is important to keep in mind that these surveys were face-to-face in respondents' homes. These questions were part of a much larger survey on the sexual behavior of Americans; 20 percent of the sample group refused to participate in the survey at all. It can be assumed that many gay men and lesbians, especially in rural areas, self-selected out of the survey, skewing the statistics even further. On the other hand, it is great to see the large number of gay people willing to be honest about their sex lives.

Despite all the studies, all the numbers, and all the graphs, we think Kinsey came closest to speaking the truth when he said, "The number of persons in the world who are homosexual and the number who are heterosexual is unanswerable."

"Homophobia is based on prejudice, not science, and science has little to do with the power to eradicate it."

DR. DEAN HAMER, WHOSE 1993 STUDY LINKED MALE HOMOSEXUALITY TO A STRETCH OF DNA ON THE X CHROMOSOME

ARE YOU BORN THAT WAY?

Since the medical-scientific community began studying homosexuality in the late nineteenth century, there has been speculation as to whether homosexuality is biological, psychological, or both. Often the debate has centered around whether or not gay people were born "that way." Arguments of "nature" vs. "nurture" have been staples of opponents to gay rights, who talk about the "lifestyle choice" of homosexuals as a way of trying to invalidate demands for civil rights.

Biological research into the origins of homosexuality has taken a new turn in recent years. Both Dean Hamer and Simon LeVay are openly gay scientists who have done research with the hopes that their findings will assist gay rights causes. A study of female twins in 1993 found that nearly 50 percent of identical twin sisters of lesbians are lesbian themselves. Psychologist J. Michael Bailey, who conducted the study, argues that it shows a genetic link in female homosexuality. But all three scientists are quick to acknowledge that biology is not the only cause. Most scientists, like most gay people, feel that the discussion of sexuality should not be based on the "either/or" dichotomy of "nature" vs. "nurture"; rather, we should be looking at how both factors influence our development as sexual beings.

Gay rights activists have mixed feelings about this new science of "homosexual biology." Many feel that people who are reluctant to support gay men and lesbians will become more sympathetic to gay rights if they believe being gay is not a choice. Parents of gay people will be able to reject the whole question of whether it was their "fault" and focus on embracing their children more readily. People who are struggling with their own homosexuality will be more able to appreciate that their sexual feelings are natural.

Other gay men and lesbians argue that trying to find liberation through science is about as likely as the eradication of racism in this country during our lifetimes. Science, like everything else, is shaped by the attitudes and values of the societies in which research is conducted. If society is homophobic, then the discovery that homosexuality is genetic will be used against gay people; opponents of gay men and lesbians will simply declare that homosexuality is a genetic disease and should be eradicated.

Still others say that the entire discussion of causes should be moot anyway. This philosophy holds that gay liberation is about individual rights; as long as gay men and lesbians aren't harming anyone, the biological (or nonbiological) basis of homosexuality is irrelevant. Simon LeVay concurs with this point, saying in a 1993 *Advocate* interview, "I don't think that gay rights should depend on proving that we can't help being gay. We should have equal rights even if we are gay out of sheer wanton perversity."

The issue of biology is complex. And whether or not science is the answer, the research into the causes of homosexuality will continue. The struggle will be to try to change public biases against lesbians and gay men before technology creates a means of eradicating the "nature" part of the equation.

DID YOU KNOW...

A 1973 study that appeared in the academic journal *Male and Female Homosexuality* found that most gay males realize their orientation by age sixteen and most females by age nineteen.

LESBIAN SURVIVAL HINT #169:
CHANCES ARE YOUR ANTHROPOLOGY TEACHER ONLY SHOWED YOU A PORTION OF THE WHOLE DIAGRAM.

(Rhonda Dicksion)

The Sex That Is Not One

In 1908, when Edward Carpenter expanded the same-sex chapter of his most popular book, *Love's Coming of Age* (1897), into the book The Intermediate Sex, it quickly became one of the most widely read books on the subject of homosexuality. Along with Havelock Ellis, Carpenter was considered one of the foremost authorities on homosexuality in the English-speaking world. Unlike Ellis, Carpenter was homosexual, and lived in a life-long partnership with George Merrill. In the excerpt below, Carpenter details the theories of Austrian doctor Karl Heinrich Ulrichs as an early scientific explanation of homosexuality:

More than thirty years ago . . . an Austrian writer, K.H. Ulrichs, drew attention in a series of pamphlets (*Memnon, Ara Spei, Inclusa,* etc.) to the existence of a class of people who strongly illustrate the above remarks [about homosexuality]. . . . He pointed out that there were people born in such a position—as it were on the dividing line between the sexes—that while belonging distinctly to one sex as far as their bodies are concerned they may be said to belong *mentally* and *emotionally* to the other; that there were men, for instance, who might be described as of feminine soul enclosed in a male body (*anima muliebris in corpe virili inclusa*), or in other cases, women whose definition would be just the reverse. And he maintained that this doubleness of nature was to a great extent proved by the special direction of their love-sentiment. For in such cases, as indeed might be expected, the (apparently) masculine person instead of forming a love-union with a female tended to contract romantic friendships with

"A survey conducted among 200 girls who had been riding horses male fashion showed that nearly all of them received pleasant sexual sensations due to the continuous bounce and friction established between the saddle pommel and their clitoris. Many of the riders admitted that they especially became fond of horseback riding for that reason alone. Several declared that it started them on the road to homosexuality because males no longer were desirous to them."

DR. ARTHUR GUY MATHEWS, FROM IS HOMOSEXUALITY A MENACE? (1959)

one of his own sex; while the apparently feminine would, instead of marrying in the usual way, devote herself to the love of another feminine.

People of this kind (i.e., having this special variation of the love-sentiment) he called Urnings; and though we are not obliged to accept his theory about the crosswise connexion between "soul" and "body," since at best these words are somewhat vague and indefinite; yet his work was important because it was one of the first attempts, in modern times, to recognise the existence of what might be called an Intermediate Sex, and to give at any rate *some* explanation of it.

— **EDWARD CARPENTER,** THE INTERMEDIATE SEX (1908)

It's in the Jeans: Biology, Culture, and the Struggle for Gay Liberation

The July 1993 release of a study that links male homosexuality to an area on the X chromosome met with mixed reactions from gay rights advocates. The Human Rights Campaign Fund, the Washington-based gay lobby, welcomed the findings and said, "We believe it will help increase support for gay and lesbian rights" *(New York Times,* July 16, 1993). Others were less enthusiastic. Many gays are suspicious of attempts to find the cause(s) of homosexuality, because historically the search for a cause has been part of the search for a "cure." Antigay forces, on the other hand, have decried the recent research as "pro-gay" and contend that the "hypothesis of recruitment" and the "traditional psychological model of disturbed families producing more homosexuals" should be given greater attention (*Wall Street Journal,* August 12, 1993). A 1991 study by Simon LeVay that found differences in the size of the hypothalamus of gay and straight men met with a similar reception. Researchers, meanwhile, have found themselves in the spotlight on a politically "hot" issue that has been exploited by the right wing in distinctly nonscientific ways. And women, as usual, have been ignored; both studies have dealt exclusively with men.

For all of the uproar, however, the biological research on sexual orientation is still inconclusive, and in any case it is unlikely to affect either the lives of gay people or the opinions of those who hate them.

The most recent study, conducted by Dr. Dean Hamer of the National Cancer Institute and published in the July 1993 issue of *Science,* found that more than 75 percent of a group of pairs of gay brothers had inherited identical DNA markers on a particular region of the X chromosome, suggesting that same-sex attraction may have some hereditary disposition. But even those who consider this finding interesting or significant are quick to acknowledge that sexual orientation is a complex, multi-dimensional phenomenon whose determinants are, at best, partially genetic. Hamer's study did not isolate a "gay gene," and it is still a matter of total speculation as to how likely carriers of a "gay gene"—or, more likely, genes—would be to become gay as a result of such a genetic makeup. Moreover, the study has been criticized for omitting a control experiment checking for the presence of the genetic markers among heterosexual brothers. The results have not yet been replicated, and the small number of cases involved in the study (forty) is further reason for a cautionary reading of the results. Nevertheless, Hamer's study has generally won acclaim and will certainly encourage similar research.

Gay proponents of biological research on sexual orientation argue that discovering a biological cause of homosexuality would strengthen the case for legal protections against discrimination. A crucial part of equal-protection law is built on the concept of an "immutable characteristic." If sexual orientation were considered an immutable characteristic, like race or gender, efforts to decriminalize homosexual sex, outlaw discrimination, and legalize marriage would have improved chances of enactment. That a biological basis for homosexuality could help the legal case for gay rights is indisputable, but it is important to note that such a basis is neither a necessary nor a sufficient argument for legal protections. Religion is constitutionally protected and considered an "immutable" characteristic in this context, and yet there is clearly no biological basis for religion. In addition, legal victories have been won for gays on the basis of immutability despite the lack of conclusive biological evidence.

More instructive than the success of the immutable characteristic argument sans biological determinants, however, is the historical failure of biological differences to inspire tolerance and equal treatment. As the experience of African Americans should make abundantly clear, hereditary difference is no guard against oppression. The argument that skin color was an illegal (and immoral) basis for discrimination gained purchase only after decades of calculated legal struggles and a considerable popular mobilization on its behalf. (The same can be said for gender differences, of course—and both are battles that are still far from over.) The lesson is an important one: Unless Americans are persuaded that homophobia is wrong, no amount of biological evidence will suffice to dismantle legal discrimination against gays and lesbians. The argument of biological difference can be a tool gay activists can use to help their cause, but without a movement that challenges heterosexist norms, it is ultimately useless.

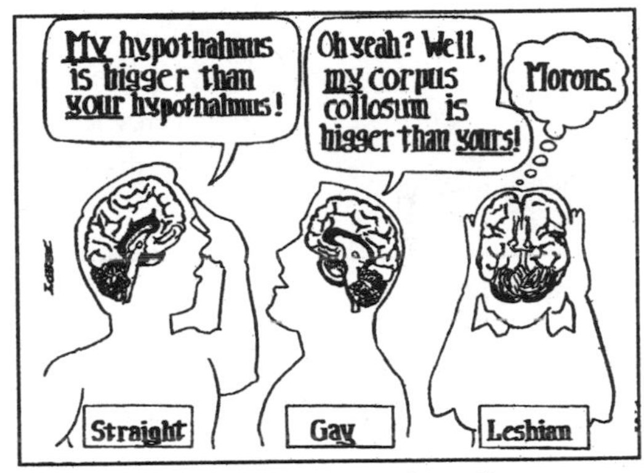

(Brady, courtesy of the San Francisco Sentinel*)*

The focus on legal advances is, of course, only part of the broader goal of overcoming ignorance and hatred for gay people. Supporters of biological research hope that demonstrating that sexual orientation is not chosen will compel bigots to see gays in a different light. However, religious intolerance of lesbians and gays—which provides much of the fuel that feeds the current antigay hate —already acknowledges the immutability of sexual orientation (or its possibility, at least). The argument of many antigay Christians has long been that one may not be able to help having homosexual feelings, but one definitely has the capacity and obligation to resist acting on them and to learn to adapt to heterosexual habits. In biblical jargon, this is known as "loving the sinner, hating the sin." The religious argument against homosexuality is not based in a distinction of whether the behavior is voluntary or not, and hence biological evidence that it is inborn or hereditary will not lessen the prejudice of those who consider it immoral.

Discovering a biological basis for homosexuality is at best a two-edged sword. Far from helping erode prejudice, grounding difference in biology has a long and horrible history as the basis of persecution. People of color, Jews, the disabled, and the mentally ill have all suffered unspeakable crimes in the name of racial or genetic inferiority. The very premise of Nazi anti-Semitism was the claim that Jews were a biological threat to German racial purity. Indeed, biological difference is typically used not to demonstrate that people are similar despite genetic variations, but rather to argue that people are morally different because they are biologically predisposed to certain behaviors. (Abnormal sexual appetites in particular have frequently been ascribed to biological or genetic predispositions—for instance, in the racist image of black men as sexual predators.) There is no reason for gay people to expect a more enlightened interpretation than others have been subjected to throughout history. Lest readers should consider this an unnecessarily dark and pessimistic view, I offer the *London Daily Mail* headline reporting on the Hamer study as a possible omen of what the future could hold: "Abortion Hope After 'Gay Gene' Findings" (*New York Times,* August 2, 1993).

> **"The next time someone asks you 'Hey, how do you get to be a homosexual anyway?' tell them, 'Homosexuals are chosen first on talent—then interview—then the swimsuit and evening gown competition pretty much gets rid of the rest of them.'"**
>
> COMIC KAREN WILLIAMS, AT THE 1993 MARCH ON WASHINGTON

Enthusiasts of biological research are at heart interested in showing that sexual orientation is not a matter of choice. The importance of demonstrating the involuntary nature of homosexuality lies in its usefulness for the strategy of appealing to a common humanity as a basis for tolerance and acceptance. Gay people are people like everybody else, except they happen to be gay. This approach has unmistakable echoes of the assimilationism of the homophile movement of the 1950s and 1960s, and risks limiting the gay rights agenda in similar ways. While asserting that our human similarities are more important than our sexual differences—which is certainly true—it runs the risk of undercutting our claim to the *right* to be different.

An overemphasis on the biological determinants of sexual orientation leaves gays and lesbians more vulnerable to cultural intolerances. Someone might argue, for instance, that basic vanilla sex and traditional relationships between same-sex couples is okay (because homosexual inclination is involuntary) but that cross-dressing is unacceptable, or that butch women and effeminate men should alter their behavior. Someone might say that S/M or cruising are immoral behaviors. Earrings, pierced nipples, pink triangles, short hair, and black leather would all be open to the argument that since predilections toward them are not biologically determined, they need not be tolerated. But the fact is that if all these things were taken away from gay people, a very large part of what makes being gay fun and expressive would be gone. And that is because fighting for the right to be gay means fighting for the right to act gay, whatever that means to the individual.

"I might as well say it now. I think that gay people are special. To a friend who also has a gay son, I say, 'Gay people are more creative, spirited, and have a zest for life.' She disagrees and says that gay people are just like everyone else. They work, pay taxes, and rear children. I agree, but these qualities come from the father's genetic material. I'm convinced that my son's leather jacket with all the political stickers, his earrings, and his backwards red baseball cap come from me, the X chromosome only a mother can supply."

LAURA SIEGAL OF P-FLAG IN AN OPINION PIECE, "A VERY SPECIAL X CHROMOSOME," IN THE SAN FRANCISCO EXAMINER

Gay people are not essentially a biological minority but a cultural minority. Moreover, the source of most people's prejudice against gays is not the (mistaken) view that homosexuality is chosen; therefore the struggle against homophobia cannot be advanced by demonstrating that it is not chosen. Rather, the source of bias is a complex field of cultural/ideological beliefs (expectations about gender roles, including appropriate sexual-object choice for each gender, religious teachings, general hang-ups about sex, and so on) and thus the terrain of struggle for gays and lesbians must also be cultural.

Coming out has been the quintessential gay political act since the Stonewall Riots. It is at once an act of individual liberation from a life of lying and hiding, and a challenge to social norms. But the battle against the closet is a cultural battle; the closet has no biological meaning. Clearly, there is no biological basis compelling people to come out, and yet the right to be out is at the very core of the struggle for gay rights.

A misdirected emphasis on biological determinants in fact undercuts our claim as a cultural minority. If gayness is focused on biology instead of culture, then people are more likely to question whether we should dress distinctly, socialize together, have gay neighborhoods, and so on. They can say—and some have—there is no such thing as gay culture. In truth, of course, there not only is gay culture (many gay cultures, some more visible than others) but it is the existence of gay culture and the community it sustains that has made the daily life of gay people better. We need our community centers, our networks, our newspapers and magazines, our traditions, our trademarks. Our claim to them, however, has nothing to do with our genes.

Gay people are born into a diaspora; in addition to the deaf and disabled, we are the only minority whose biological parents do not necessarily share our minority status. Our collective identity and survival depends on the ability to transmit our culture to each new generation. Randy Shilts has said that a biological explanation "would reduce being gay to something like being left-handed, which is in fact all that it is" (*New York Times,* August 2, 1993). Apart from the fact that left-handed people until recently were routinely forced to switch, making this a very unfortunate choice of analogy, Shilts is simply wrong. It's much more in the jeans—and the bandannas in the back pockets, the matching boots, and the pose—than in the genes.

— DOROTHEE BENZ

Born Republican

The startling discovery that affiliation with the Republican party is genetically determined was announced by scientists in the current issue of the journal *Nurture.* Reports of the gene that codes for political conservatism, discovered after a long study of quintuplets in Orange County, California, has sent shock waves through the medical, political, and golfing communities.

Psychologists and psychoanalysts have long believed that Republicans' unnatural and frequently unconstitutional tendencies result from unhealthy family life—a remarkably high percentage of Republicans had authoritative, domineering fathers and emotionally distant mothers who didn't teach them how to be kind and gentle. But biologists have long suspected that conservatism is inherited. "After all," said one author of the *Nurture* article, "it's quite common for a Republican to have a brother or a sister who is a Republican."

The finding has been greeted with relief by parents and friends of Republicans, who have tended to blame themselves for the political views of otherwise lovable people—their children, friends, and unindicted co-conspirators.

One mother, a longtime Democrat, clasped her hands in ecstasy on hearing of the findings. "I just knew it was genetic," she said, seated beside her two sons, both avowed Republicans. "I just knew that nobody would actually choose that lifestyle!" When asked what the Republican lifestyle was, she said, "Well, you can just tell from watching TV, like at the convention in Houston: the loud outfits, the flaming xenophobia, the flamboyant demagogy—you know."

Both sons said they had suspected their Republicanism from an early age but did not confirm it until they were in college, when they became convinced it wasn't just a phase they were going through.

Despite the near-certainty the medical community holds towards Republicanism's genetic origins, troubling issues remain. The *Nurture* article offered no response to the suggestion that the startlingly high incidence of Republicanism among siblings could result from the fact that they share not only genes but also psychological and emotional attitudes, being the products of the same parents and family dynamics.

And it remains to be explained why so many avowed Democrats are known to vote Republican occasionally—or at least to fantasize about doing so. Polls show that three out of five Democrats admit to having had a Republican experience. In well-adjusted people, however, this experimentation rarely outlasts adolescence.

Surprisingly, some Republican activists hail the findings as a step forward, rather than an invitation to more conservophobia. They argue that since Republicans didn't "choose" their unwholesome lifestyle any more than someone "chooses" to have a ski-jump nose, they shouldn't be denied civil rights to which normal people are entitled.

Other Republicans, recalling ninteenth-century scientific studies that "proved" the mental inferiority of blacks, find the frenzied search for the biological cause of Republicanism pointless, if not downright sinister.

But for most real Americans, the discovery opens a window on a brighter tomorrow. In a few years, gene therapy could eradicate Republicanism altogether.

If conservatism is not the result of sheer orneriness (as many suspect) but is something Republicans can't help and probably don't even like, there's no reason why we shouldn't tolerate Republicans in the military or even high elected office—provided they don't flaunt their political beliefs.

— **DANIEL MENDELSOHN**

MYTH MAKING AND UNMAKING

Both inside and outside of the lesbian and gay community, gay people are dogged by myths and stereotypes and misinformation. While many of us can dismiss them as ridiculous, we still find ourselves in situations where these myths have harmful effects. To the informed and gay or gay-friendly, the myths are obviously based in ignorance, hate, and misunderstanding. But to a great many Americans, these myths continue to surface—in conversations around the office cooler, in books and magazines, in our church and military, and in our own families—and are assumed to be true.

Lies and stereotypes about gay men and lesbians give people false impressions of gay men and lesbians as individuals and as a community. Sometimes nongay people act upon these assumptions, lashing out against gay people with discriminatory legislation, restrictive sexual laws, harassment, and physical violence. For many gay people, part of coming out is shedding the internalized homophobia we feel in a society that nurtures these myths as facts.

The Degradation of Love—How Homosexuals and Lesbians Have Sex

The lesbian (female homosexual), since she cannot have intercourse with another female, can only offer herself as a mechanical device for the performance of masturbation. She usually excites her female partner by a variety of devious and often degrading techniques. She will kiss and fondle passionately in a masculine role, extending manipulations from the mouth to the breasts, ultimately exciting the victims to the peak of a sex climax through abnormal contacts with the clitoris. In all cases, the lesbian uses her mouth in a variety of unnatural acts. The female who is held captive by the lesbian soon becomes a mental and physical wreck, who suffers from the pangs of hell and remorse, but like a drug addict she is unable to ward off the repeated advances made toward her by the octopus-like creature who continually saps her strength, the lesbian.

The male who is held captive by a male homosexual suffers mentally and physically equally as much as the female victim. In addition to being mentally and physically destroyed, he loses all control of willpower, dignity, and sense of self-preservation, and often becomes involved with sadistic, cruel, possessive, jealous maniacs who would destroy him completely if he tried to shrug them off.

Quite often, homosexuals accommodate each other in a variety of sex-deviating roles, but usually, they seduce normals who are in mental conflict, or alcoholics, drug addicts, and others who have an outright fear of sexual intercourse. The lesbian believes that she is a substitute for a male, and the male homosexual believes he is a female substitute. Both will claim to be superior in performance than what they are substituting for. This is the common sales talk given to those they are attempting to seduce.

— DR. ARTHUR GUY MATHEWS, IN *IS HOMOSEXUALITY A MENACE?* (1959)

The Most Frequently Asked Questions about Gay Men and Lesbians

1. Is it a choice?

Life would be simple if this were a one-word answer, but like all human sexuality, being gay is more complicated than that. So here goes. . . Just as heterosexual people don't choose their feelings of sexual attraction, gay and lesbian people don't choose theirs. All of us become aware of our feelings of sexual attraction as we grow, whether those feelings are for someone of the same sex, the opposite sex, or both sexes. For almost all people who lead a gay or lesbian life, the only real choice is between suppressing these feelings of same-sex attraction—pretending to be asexual or heterosexual—and choosing to live the full emotional and physical life of a gay man or lesbian.

There are exceptions. While most people who live a gay or lesbian life don't have a true choice between a homosexual life or a heterosexual life, there are men and women who have feelings of sexual attraction to both sexes and for that reason have the option of choosing a same-sex partner over an opposite-sex partner.

2. Can you be seduced into being gay?

This question assumes that you can turn a heterosexual person into a homosexual person through seduction. You can't. A heterosexual person can't be seduced into being a gay man or a lesbian any more than you can seduce a gay man or lesbian into being a heterosexual. Plenty have tried. Virtually all have failed.

3. How do you know if you're gay or lesbian?
The key to knowing whether you're heterosexual, homosexual, or bisexual is to pay attention to your feelings of attraction. In other words, if you look at or think about or have consistent fantasies about being with someone of the same sex, then there's a good chance you're gay or lesbian. If you have feelings of sexual attraction for both men and women, then you may be bisexual.

The challenge for many gay, lesbian, and bisexual people is being honest with themselves about what they're feeling, because society is, in general, so unaccepting.

4. Is there a cure for homosexuality?
At one time, homosexuality was thought of as a disease and/or mental illness. In that context, you could talk about treatment and cures and not be laughed out of the annual meeting of the American Psychiatric Association. Today, the only people who speak of trying to cure homosexuals are in need of treatment and/or reeducation themselves.

5. Isn't it sinful and immoral? (Or, Isn't it against God and the Bible?)
Some people consider homosexuality to be sinful and immoral. Other people consider homosexuality to be without sin and perfectly moral. Fortunately, in our society religion and morality are a matter of personal choice.

Some people like to quote Jesus on the subject of homosexuality, but despite what anyone says, it's a subject he never addressed.

6. What do gay people do in bed?
There's no mystery about what gay and lesbian people do to stimulate each other sexually, because what gay and lesbian people do is essentially what heterosexual people do. Generally, people do what makes them feel good. That means looking at each other, talking to each other, kissing, holding hands, massaging each other, holding each other, licking each other; in short, stimulating each other in some way that makes you feel aroused. Of course, some things feel better than others, because some parts of the body are more naturally sensitive, like nipples, breasts, buttocks, the clitoris, the penis, the anus, lips, and for some people, that tender spot on the back of the neck or behind

the knee. People use all kinds of things to stimulate the parts that feel good, including fingers, hands, the tongue, the mouth, the penis, toes — you name it, people use it.

7. Who plays the husband? Who plays the wife?
Why does anyone have to play any role? In gay and lesbian relationships, couples have the same household chores and tasks on a day-to-day basis and have to make the same kinds of decisions as do heterosexual couples. How those tasks are done and how those decisions are made is not intrinsically dependent on gender, so men aren't limited to doing stereotypically masculine things, like fixing the car and making the final decisions. And women aren't limited to stereotypically feminine things, like cooking and cleaning and deferring to their husbands.

Plenty of heterosexual couples still play out traditional gender roles, as do some homosexual couples. But in general, for homosexual couples, who prepares dinner is based more on who has more time or is better at making dinner than who is more masculine or feminine.

8. What is the "gay lifestyle"?
There is no such thing as a gay lifestyle, just as there is no such thing as a heterosexual lifestyle. The fact is, gay and lesbian people, like heterosexual people, live in a variety of ways, from fast-lane urban single life to suburban split-level family life, to everything in between and beyond.

(P. S. Mueller)

9. Do gay people raise gay children?
You cannot, repeat, *cannot* intentionally raise a child to be gay any more than you can intentionally raise a child to be heterosexual. From everything that is known, a parent cannot affect a child's sexual orientation, other than helping a child to feel comfortable with who he or she is.

10. How do gay people identify each other?
Unless you meet in a setting where you know for sure that everyone is gay, you have to look for clues. The ability to identify and sort through clues is sometimes referred to as "gaydar" (as in, "gay radar").

Sometimes it's easy to tell, and sometimes it's not. For example, if someone is wearing a button or jewelry that indicates support for gay causes, then you don't even need gaydar to figure out that this person is in all likelihood gay. Another clue might be if a man or woman's style of clothing or haircut conforms to what's popular among gay and lesbian people. Or if a man or woman exhibits some of the characteristics that are stereotypically associated with homosexuals—but that doesn't always work. Not all effeminate men are gay, and not all masculine women are lesbians. Most gay and lesbian people aren't stereotypically anything, which can make it difficult to positively identify who is what.

In the end, answering this question comes down to a simple but wholly inadequate answer: You can just tell. Sometimes.

— ERIC MARCUS

If Gays Have No Choice, Why Are They So Hated?

Gay men and lesbians come in all shapes, sizes, and ideologies. Often voices that run counter to the majority of openly gay people are silenced or dismissed. But in many ways, these voices, however problematic, need to be acknowledged as a part of the multidimensional community in which we live. It is an important part of breaking down the myths that have haunted our communities for generations. The letter below reflects just such a voice.

Dear Ann Landers:

It amazes me that I am actually writing to you. Mine is a story I am sure you have heard before. I am a homosexual, and nobody knows it. I am the typical "boy next door." My friends and family would be shocked if they knew the truth.

My longtime companion died recently of AIDS, and I feel very much alone. Both my friend and I worked for very conservative business firms, and the disclosure of our sexual orientation would have meant professional suicide. I am trying hard to accept my loss, and I hope someday that I will be able to feel good again.

I guess the reason I am writing is to plead for a little understanding and compassion. I watch the news and read the papers every day and wonder why homosexuals are so despised. Do these haters actually believe we had a choice? Why would anyone choose to be a constant object of ridicule and hate?

If I could be "normal," I would grab that option in a heartbeat. But a series of failed heterosexual relationships and the pain they inflicted on the women I became involved with have taught me that I really have no right to try to be straight.

I simply do not understand how people who profess to care about their fellow man can spend so much time and energy perpetuating a climate of hate directed at a segment of society that has no choice.

I'm not particularly comfortable with the image some flamboyant homosexuals project. It makes it difficult for those of us who choose not to go public, but perhaps bizarre behavior is their response to rejection. I just wish we could all learn to live together and be a little nicer to one another.

— *J.C. in Chicago*

Dear J.C.: Thank you for a letter that just might open the door a crack. It never ceases to amaze me that in this day and age, so many people fail to understand that homosexuality is not a lifestyle that is chosen. That "choice" was made at birth. Maybe one day, those haters will understand this.

CAN YOU BELIEVE IT?

In 1994, two male flamingos at the Rotterdam Zoo in the Netherlands got the nesting urge and set up a same-sex co-habitation. After the two repeatedly sought to steal eggs from female flamingos to hatch them as their own, the zookeepers decided to provide them with a fertilized egg. The proud parents successfully hatched their own little chick, and remained faithfully by the side of the baby flamingo for a while. However, six months later, one of the two gay birds turned straight and found a female mate.

Gay Sheep Come out of the Closet

Eight percent of the male sheep at the United States Department of Agriculture's Sheep Experimental Station in Dubois, Idaho, are gay, officials confirmed in late November 1988.

"These animals are homosexual. They are responding physically to how they are," explained Anne Perkins, a doctoral student at the station who is completing her dissertation on "Reproductive Behavior in Rams."

"It's a very interesting model and we can learn a great deal about homosexuality from it," Perkins said. "They are not morally or culturally or ethically behaving like humans. These sheep are just doing what their bodies are telling them to do."

Homosexuality among animals is "nothing real unique," according to Perkins, who said gay sex has been observed in sixty-three distinct mammalian species. "It's not considered aberrant in farm animals at all," she said.

The gay sheep, like some gay men, practice anal intercourse, according to Perkins, although some achieve orgasm simply by rubbing their penis around another male sheep's tail.

There is, however, a serious social problem currently in gay sheep culture in that most gay sheep, Perkins said, only want to be on top.

"The difficulty for homosexual sheep is that it's difficult to find another male who will stand still," Perkins explained. "If there is a ram that is hurt or caught in a fence, then they can mount him, but otherwise there are so few receivers that it becomes difficult for homosexuals to express themselves."

Lesbian sheep, meanwhile, are apparently wrestling with a major "invisibility" problem in the gay sheep world, a difficulty that has plagued human lesbians too.

"It's very difficult to look at the possibility of lesbian sheep," Perkins explained, "because if you are a female sheep, what you do to solicit sex is stand still. You don't mount. So it's very rare that a female sheep would mount another female sheep."

"Maybe there is a female sheep out there really wanting another female," Perkins speculated, "but there's just no way for us to know it."

— **REX WOCKNER**

...EVEN EDUCATED FLEAS DO IT

One of the biggest arguments used by opponents of gay rights and of governmental funding for lesbian and gay services, art, and education is that homosexuality is unnatural. Natural law is based on a lot of different factors, but one of the primary, and most obvious, definitions of "natural" is "that which is done in nature." In other words, if the animal kingdom does it, then it reflects the natural state of affairs. Here is a partial list of other animals that commit the "crime" of same-sex coupling:

antelope
bees
butterflies
cats
cattle
cimicid bugs
cockroaches
coreid bugs
corixid bugs
dogs
dolphins
donkeys
elephants
field crickets
flamingoes
fleas
fruit flies
geckos
goats
green lizards
guinea pigs
gulls
hamsters
horses
hyenas
killer whales
lions
marten
mice
monkeys
moths
octopi
naucorid bugs
pentatomid bugs
pigs
porcupines
porpoises
rabbits
raccoons
rats
sheep
stallions
wasps

A Reverse Questionnaire

- What do you think caused your heterosexuality?
- When and how did you decide you were heterosexual?
- Is it possible that heterosexuality is just a phase you may grow out of?
- Is it possible your heterosexuality stems from a neurotic fear of others of the same sex?
- If you've never slept with someone of the same sex, is it possible that all you need is a good same-sex lover?
- To whom have you disclosed your heterosexual tendencies? How did they react?
- Why do heterosexuals place so much emphasis on sex?
- Why do heterosexuals feel compelled to seduce others into their lifestyle?
- Why do you insist on flaunting your heterosexuality? Why can't you just be who you are and keep quiet about it?
- Studies show that more than 95 percent of child molesters are heterosexual. Do you consider it safe to expose your children to heterosexual teachers?
- With all the social support marriage receives, the divorce rate is still 50 percent. Why are there so few stable relationships among heterosexuals?
- Heterosexuals are noted for adhering to narrowly restricted, stereotyped sex roles. Why do you cling to such an unhealthy form of role playing?
- Looking at the news media, there seem to be so few happy heterosexuals.
- Techniques have been developed that might enable you to change. Have you considered aversion therapy?
- Why do you make a point of attributing heterosexuality to famous people? Is it to justify your own heterosexuality?
- Considering the menace of hunger and overpopulation, can the human race survive if everyone were heterosexual like yourself?
- The group with the fastest-growing number of AIDS cases is heterosexual. Shouldn't we prohibit sex between heterosexuals?

— DEVELOPED BY MARTIN ROCHLIN, PH.D.

"Homosexuality is God's way of ensuring that the truly gifted aren't burdened with children."

COMPOSER AND LYRICIST SAM AUSTIN, 1988

When You Meet Gay and Lesbian People: Hints for the Heterosexual

1. Do not run screaming from the room. This is rude.
2. If you must back away, do so slowly and with discretion.
3. Do not assume they are attracted to you.
4. Do not assume they are *not* attracted to you.
5. Do not expect them to be as excited about meeting a heterosexual as you may be about meeting a gay person.
6. Do not immediately start talking about your boy-/girl-friend or husband/wife in order to make it clear that you are straight.
7. Do not ask them how they got that way. Instead, ask yourself how you got the way you are.
8. Do not assume they are dying to talk about being gay.
9. Do not expect them to refrain from talking about being gay.
10. Do not trivialize their experience by assuming it is a bed-room issue only. They are gay twenty-four hours a day.

CAN YOU SPOT THE HOMOSEXUAL?

The idea that all gay men and lesbians are easy to spot is a myth. Gay people are not an explicitly visual minority. Unlike being a person of color, being gay does not automatically provide visual clues. Many gay people can blend into the folds of mainstream society—if they choose to. For people uncomfortable with homosexuality, a "hidden" minority is incredibly threatening. And for those who wrongly believe in a "Gay Agenda," or who think that gay people are going to try seduce them or their children, hidden homosexuals could be lurking on every bus and park bench.

Of course, many gay people would love to have a surefire way to tell who *is* and who is *not.* Even a gay person with sophisticated "gaydar" (the ability to detect gayness) will fail sometimes. (*What about that rancher with her cowboy boots and no-nonsense look?*) So while sometimes "you can just tell" by looking, the reality is that you can never be quite sure.

"Somebody was asking me. Said he thought Richard Nixon was obviously homosexual. I said: 'Why do you think that?' He said: 'You know, that funny, uncoordinated way he moves.' I said: 'Yeah, like Nureyev.'"

WRITER AND WIT GORE VIDAL, 1970

For over a century, people have tried to establish rules for what a homosexual looks like and how he or she acts. Any code for identifying gay people tells much more about the assumptions of the individuals responsible for creating the rules than it does about gay people. We've included here some classics of the "how to tell" genre, as well as some more contemporary approaches.

How to Tell If Your Son Is Gay, According to the *Weekly World News*

1. Clothing style: Watch for feminine touches in your son's clothing. Soft, clingy fabrics and pale, girlish colors are definite warning signals.

2. Reading: A boy who hangs out indoors and reads instead of playing ball with the other guys most likely has problems. Certain periodicals—like *Playboy*—are okay, but if your son is reading something romantic, like *Gone With the Wind,* he's probably teetering on the verge of homosexuality.

3. Friends: Watch out if your son is bringing home "buddies" who wear earrings, tight T-shirts, or heavy perfumes. And, of course, if he's hanging out with male flight attendants and people like that, it's a good indication that he's running with a homo crowd.

4. Hobbies: All red-blooded males enjoy sports like hockey and basketball. If your kid doesn't like sports, or chooses hobbies like knitting or flower-arranging, he needs help!

(Hilary Price)

5. Music: Normal kids like rock music, or country and western tunes. They don't listen to classical pieces or recordings of Liberace.

6. Dating: After the age of eleven or so, boys learn to worship members of the opposite sex. If your son usually hangs out with guys and avoids dating, have a little talk with him.

"You don't have to despair if your son shows some — or even all—of these signs," says South African sociology professor Dr. James Packer. "But you must take action immediately. I advise getting the boy into some red-blooded sports programs."

— DOROTHY STEELE IN THE WORLD WEEKLY NEWS, A GROCERY STORE TABLOID, DECEMBER 12, 1992

> **One Houston mother recalls, "When my son came home and told me he was gay, I said, 'But how can that be? You're a terrible dresser and you always have holes in your socks.' Every gay man I knew was always a snappy dresser."**
>
> FROM A P-FLAG NEWSLETTER

How to Recognize Homosexuals

While most knowledgeable people who have counseled in this field agree that there is no positive way to tell whether or not a person is overtly homosexual, listed are some ways to tell a homosexual. Normal men may demonstrate a few of these tendencies, while homosexuals will usually demonstrate most of the listed characteristics.

1. demonstrations of pouting—petulance
2. short interest spans—shifting moods
3. a taste for unconventional clothing
4. attraction to bright colors, tight clothing, and special boots
5. attraction to ornaments and gadgets
6. swaying hips
7. striking unusual poses
8. flirting with the eyelids (fluttering)
9. tripping gait and swaggering shoulders
10. certain types of chronic alcoholism
11. insane jealousy
12. a tendency to lie and deceive
13. overly emotional
14. withdrawn—a tendency to want to be alone
15. delicate physique or overly muscular

16. broad hips
17. soft, pale skin
18. a limp wrist
19. prettiness effected by make-up
20. special hair styles and artful combing
21. too much deodorant or toiletry
22. gushy, flowery conversation, i.e., "wild," "mad," etc.
23. shrillness of voice, lisping or a tendency to falsetto
24. a dislike for belts, garters, laced shoes, ties, hats, gloves
25. a compulsion to move around, walk, hustle

— FROM HOPE FOR HOMOSEXUALS: TEEN CHALLENGE (1964)

CAN YOU BELIEVE IT?

According to Dr. Arthur Guy Mathews, in *Is Homosexuality a Menace?* (1959), bisexuality is a sport for the rich and idle. He says that "bisexuality is common among women who have too much money on their hands and not enough to do at home. Such types usually go in a crowd to places where lesbians work or patronize. In time, they are induced by a lesbian to give homosexuality a try. In some cases, like men, they attribute such behavior to a state of frigidity, also blaming their spouses for a complete lack of sex attention. It may be true in some cases, but it is more likely a case of idleness leading to mischievous conduct."

Newly Misinterpreted

On October 31, 1969, *Time* magazine ran a seven-page feature story on "The Homosexual: Newly Visible, Newly Understood," and offered its readers a field guide to the various "homosexual types":

The Blatant Homosexual: This is the eunuch-like caricature of femininity that most people associate with homosexuality. . . . He may be the catty hairdresser or the lisping, limp-wristed interior decorator. His lesbian counterpart is the "butch."

The Secret Lifer: Their wrists are rigid, their s's well-formed; they prefer subdued clothes and close-cropped hair. . . . They fake enjoyment when their boss throws a stag party with nude movies.

The Desperate: Members of this group are likely to haunt public toilets ("tearooms") or Turkish baths. They may be pathologically driven to sex.

The Adjusted: They lead relatively conventional lives. . . . Often they try to settle down with a regular lover, and although these liaisons are generally short-lived among men, some develop into so-called "gay marriages."

The Bisexual: Men and women who have a definite preference for their own sex but engage in occasional activity with the opposite sex and enjoy it.

The Situational-experimental: A man who engages in homosexual acts without any deep homosexual motivation. . . . In prisons and occasionally the armed forces, men frequently turn to homosexual contacts in order to reassert their masculinity and recapture a feeling of dominance.

Just What Is the Much-Feared Gay Lifestyle?

In 1994, a political struggle between antigay forces led by a fundamentalist housewife, gay activists, and Apple Computer ensued in Williamson County, Texas, over whether or not to grant a $750,000 tax break to Apple Computer Company. The issue was not the $80 million that Apple wanted to spend on a new factory, nor was it the 700 jobs with which it would provide the county. Local homophobes were afraid that the gay-friendly company's employee benefits policy that includes same-sex partners would attract "the wrong element" to their community. After a heated debate, the commissioners voted in favor of the tax break. Vicki Torres wrote this article in response to the attitudes of the antigay people of Williamson County.

"*What is the gay lifestyle?*" To me, that makes as much sense as talking about the black lifestyle or the Latino lifestyle or even the white lifestyle. In fact, try making a generalization about whites and you'll get all sorts of resistance along the lines of "How dare you assume this or that about me!"

We know it's not PC (politically correct) to assume that all blacks like Motown or all Latinos eat tacos, but the religious right still wants to impress everyone with the idea that all gay men and lesbians like drag, Barbra Streisand, and promiscuous sex.

For me, the responses would be: occasionally, only when she sings "Somewhere;" and I really try not to.

In truth, the idea of a gay lifestyle probably rears its head in the life of every gay person, especially those who previously considered themselves straight.

"OK, now I'm a lesbian," I thought years ago as I stared at the mirror trying to perceive the difference in myself.

Nope, it was still me looking back out: long, unruly hair, slightly crooked nose, and brown eyes. Same old me, just a different gender in bed.

I looked around at the gay women I was meeting at the time and they all seemed to be driving Datsuns. Aha! I thought, the lesbian car, an idea quickly abandoned once I got on the freeway.

I tried wimmin's music, lesbian bars, and lesbian separatist philosophies, and found that I preferred Brahms, a glass of wine in a small, quiet restaurant (straight or gay), and mainstream liberal political thought. And I still considered myself a lesbian.

During the heyday of the 1970s, San Francisco's Handball Express "Red Hanky Party" (above) brought in large crowds to dance the night away. While this may be what many people mean when they talk about the "gay lifestyle," this is just one of many types of gay "lifestyles." (Rink Foto)

But even if every queer finally concludes that there is no definitive gay male or lesbian lifestyle, others still think so. A few years ago, a straight woman rejected me as a lover, in part, she said, because she couldn't commit to the gay lifestyle.

Darn! I thought to myself as I looked around my apartment at the gay couch, gay stereo, gay dining room table, and gay cupboards filled with my gay coffee, gay pasta, and gay apples. They had given me away!

More recently, my father, in his always well-intentioned but slightly skewed way, tried to reassure me that he "accepted" poor, abnormal gays like myself and felt sorry for us. Yes, well, pity is the proper response to a populace portrayed as emotionally unstable, suicidal, drug- or alcohol-addicted, lonely, sex-driven, abused, maligned, desperate.

But, as one sharp-eyed straight friend said to me recently, a Mexican American man who has been dealt his share of prejudice in the world, "You haven't had it so bad as a lesbian, have you, Vicki?"

The truth is, no, I haven't.

(But then, that just might be because as a woman, never mind a lesbian, my behavior, like that of children, generates extreme indifference from a society in which men are considered the real people, the real movers and shakers. Thus, apathy provides freedom.)

There are advantages to being a queer woman. Lesbians learn and acquire independence, and don't need the acceptance of men because you don't really have to depend on them for anything, exposure to a wide spectrum of thought within the small populace that comprises lesbians, a sense of community, and a commitment to working for social justice.

That, finally, may be the true gay lifestyle, and why others find us so objectionable. Independent people not in thrall to others and able to define life for themselves are always scary to those bound and gagged by their own fetters.

To live one's life in freedom and self-responsibility is a terrifying prospect because it means questioning the basic assumptions of day-to-day life. Most people are not up to it. And like the Texas housewife, they fear freedom so much, they will try everything in their power to stamp out a force that, historically, will never die. It's a losing fight.

— VICKI TORRES

Black Gay & Proud
PREVENT AID
KNOWLEDGE
THE PATH
PREVENTION
PROTECT YOURSELF
MAIATF 612-870-1723
QUEER NATION
I S&M
OSEXUALS
ORT OF
& GA
IS LE
Gay Youth of N.Y.
Gay & Catholic

CHAPTER 7

Our Very Queer Lives

Queer. The word has many different meanings: Different. Odd. Strange. Out of place. We use *queer* to describe things that make us uncomfortable, things that don't quite fit into the world as we have defined it. While many people, gay and straight, can and do accept much of what is lesbian and gay, there are some aspects of our lives that are controversial, that make people uncomfortable. There are certainly aspects to being gay that are difficult for many of us to understand and embrace. Curious is another definition of the word *queer.* And much of what is queer is also what piques our curiosity. This chapter is a nonthreatening look at both aspects of queer as it relates to the gay community, sort of a "Queer 101."

"I think it's okay that you're gay, but why do you have to flaunt it?" is a comment most gay people have heard many times. Gay parades and marches are one way that gay and lesbian people make their presence felt publicly, and that makes many nongay people uncomfortable. It's intellectually easy to accept that your cousin who lives in New Jersey is gay; it's another thing when 200,000 gay people are marching through the center of town. But for those marching, there is no comparable experience. Having spent most of our lives in the minority, these events offer gay people a once-a-year opportunity to feel safe on the streets, surrounded by "our own kind."

Gay or straight, the subject of sexuality also makes many people uncomfortable. People who challenge traditional conventions of gender—drag queens, leather dykes, bisexuals, transgendered people, lesbians into butch/femme—are all in some way toying with society's long-held views of what makes a person masculine or feminine.

These are hard concepts to get a handle on. At the same time, we are all curious about those whose identities are different from our own.

If the topic of sexuality makes people nervous, then the topic of sex can send them out the door. It's hard for some people to accept, but, yes, Virginia, gay people do have sex. In the push to gain acceptance, discussions of sex are often neglected; forgotten is that for many of the Stonewall-era gay activists, "gay liberation" was seen in part as a movement for "sexual liberation." For many gay and lesbian people, this is still primary. In this section we talk about many aspects of sex and the community, including leather, gay porn, and lesbian erotica.

Finally, despite the notion that gay and lesbian people are "just like everyone else," we have developed our own styles and ways of dressing. These "codes," along with the "gaydar" most gay people appear to have been born with, have evolved over time to help us find each other. Some of the icons, fashions, and symbols of our movement are found at the end of this chapter.

. . . As a Three-dollar Bill

The heart of *queer* is basic: It's recognizing one's own uniqueness in society and celebrating it. Queer is understanding that it is our *differences* that make life exciting, that allow us to grow as a community, that challenge us to better appreciate those around us. Queers understand that while it is sometimes difficult and frustrating, difference is an opportunity for progress, not simply a thing to "get over." It is through the differences that we can discover our common ground, and create a safe place for everyone to express their opinions, passions, and concerns.

QUEER LIBERATION NOT GAY ASSIMILATION

Good point

This seems to be something that the "gay-not-queer" crowd overlooks. They see difference as a problem to be solved or ignored. One of the arguments against recognition of lesbians and gay men has been that being gay is a "bedroom issue," that is, that our sexuality has nothing to do with the larger political world. Difference, to gay-not-queers, is a bedroom issue, as if it has nothing to do with political struggle or even cooperation between communities in day-today life. They talk a lot about emphasizing similarities rather than focusing on difference, as if the two things are mutually exclusive. The "gay-not-queer" world pictures difference as five people screaming at each other in different languages, with no one listening to or understanding anyone else. Queer vision recognizes that only through listening to these different languages can we build a common vocabulary.

Being queer means being comfortable with having a spotlight, even a bull's-eye, directly on one's chest where it cannot be ignored. If you accept the responsibility of being queer, you can't (and won't) be stock for the soup in the fantasy "melting pot" of America. We're queer as hell, and frankly, that's a relief. We want to be different. We love being different—and it's a privilege we're not willing to give up. Not for "equal rights," or "acceptance," or to make being queer more palatable to the homophobic tongue.

"It's a lot easier to see the center from the margins than it is to see the margins from the center."

OVERHEARD AT A LESBIAN, GAY, AND BISEXUAL STUDENT UNION MEETING AT THE CLAREMONT COLLEGES, CLAREMONT, CALIFORNIA

And the reality is, even if some people don't want to be "different," we *are* different, because the heterosexual world, which holds the power, sees us as such. As long as one is gay, lesbian, bisexual, and/or transgendered, one is "queer." Gay men, lesbians, bisexuals, transgendered people, and everything in between cannot afford to blend into anything.

Gay-not-queers seek to deny people they consider "controversial" access to our movement. Yet within the "gay and lesbian" community, there *are* bisexuals and transgendered people. Many queers are ostracized or made invisible by their biological families. How dare any gay man or lesbian propose that we kick out or conceal the members of our family who don't easily fit under the arbitrary umbrella of gay/lesbian?

Key

Being queer isn't about eliminating our insecurities about difference but the hostility toward it. Queers recognize that while acceptance of difference is not always comfortable, it is a valuable tool through which we can enrich and strengthen ourselves both individually and as a community.

— ARWYN MOORE AND DON ROMESBURG

What's in a Name?

I don't think *queer* is a fundamentally bad word. Queer is a fine word to describe things that are odd, out of the ordinary, or strange. Queer also has a history and confrontational quality about it that makes it ideal for militant political slogans like "We're here, we're queer, get used to it," and for the name of out-front groups like Queer Nation and Queer Action.

Two men take an out and proud walk together in New York City (1981). (Bettye Lane)

Some gay and lesbian people also find queer a fun and playful word to use among friends the same way they use *fag* and *dyke*. And I can hardly object to those homosexual men and women who choose to identify themselves as queer and align themselves with the latest wave of a forty-five-year-old gay rights movement. But queer is not my word. Not because I'm an old fogey who can't get with the new program and the latest language. Queer is not my word because it does not define who I am or represent what I believe in.

One of the claims I've heard made for queer is that it's an inclusive word, embracing all kinds of people. It eliminates the need for naming a long list of groups to describe our movement, as in "gay, lesbian, bisexual, transgender, transvestite," and so forth. But as a gay man, I'm not all those things. I'm a man who feels sexually attracted to people of the same gender.

As a gay man, I don't want to be grouped under the all-encompassing umbrella of queer. I'm not even all that comfortable being grouped with bisexuals, let alone transsexuals, transvestites, and queer straights. Not because I have anything against these groups or don't support their quests for equal rights, acceptance, and understanding—in fact, I do—but because we have different lives, face different challenges, and don't necessarily share the same aspirations.

I have no desire to set myself apart from the mainstream or to carve a new path. Of course, as a gay man, I'm different from someone who grew up straight. And it's important to recognize that difference and understand how that difference affects who I am. But I'd rather emphasize what I have in common with other people than focus on the differences. The last thing I want to do is institutionalize that difference by defining myself with a word and a political philosophy that set me outside the mainstream.

My approach to gay rights does not lead to revolutionary change in attitudes toward gay people, and it can be frustratingly slow. But it leads to the kind of evolutionary change that I believe will one day make it possible for gay men and lesbians to live without fear of rejection and discrimination, a day when we are no longer considered "the other" or "odd" or "queer."

— **ERIC MARCUS**

EXPLORING GENDER

From the moment a child is born, people begin asking, "Is it a boy or a girl?" That child is then raised to become a heterosexual woman or man. These two genders, which many people understand as set in stone as the only two genders, are determined in a variety of ways. From the time a child is born, society will aggressively regulate its journey toward a gendered self.

In the hospital, we can tell whether the child has a penis (which would indicate "boy") or a vagina (which would indicate "girl"). The boy is wrapped in a blue swath, while the girl is wrapped in pink. These colors are the first step toward the social aspects of gender. But gender is much more than just biology. Once the child comes home from the hospital, parents and society begin training it to believe that girls are soft, emotional, and sensitive while boys are aggressive, tough, and rational. Girls are encouraged to desire lacy things and dolls and boys are supposed to like sports and trucks. As the child grows older, the rules of desire extend to sexual attraction, and boys are understood to be sexually attracted to girls and vice versa.

But many people fail to fall into these two genders, a strict two-piece set of "male" and "female" biology, behavior, and desire. For those people, these definitions are limitations, or, as JoAnn Loulan puts it, a "gender jail." For those of us who grow up to be homosexual, bisexual, or transgendered, our journey toward a gendered self is a confusing and ambiguous road.

Loulan explains, "Many lesbians grow up identifying not as boys, but *with* boys. These girls want to do what the boys do and dress as the boys dress. And while these girls know that they aren't actually boys, they only see two alternatives: male or female. If they are not girls, they must be boys. But they are not boys. From the time of that realization, as painful and alienating as it is, these young lesbians become gender outlaws. Residing in the netherlands of neither-nor, they begin to explore what it means to be something else entirely. In doing so, they create new genders.

Many gay and transgendered men also grow up with a sense of being a "neither-nor." Some gay men respond to this ambiguity by attempting to diminish the difference between their sense of gendered self and the societal sense of "male." They try to resolve the issue by accepting most of the "rules," by being "masculine" and rational, but with a twist: They like to sleep with other men. As Loulan says, "The real issue of gender is about who has sex with who and how: who puts what appendage into what orifice." Even while trying to accommodate the gender norms, these men inadvertently create yet another gender. Other gay men play with gender in a variety of ways, from drag to leather to hypermasculinity.

So what is gender? "Gender" is defined in *Webster's Dictionary* as a colloquial or informal word used to describe one's sex. But the words are anything but informal. The proscribed choices are two: "male" or "female." Loulan says that this feminine/masculine paradigm literally stops us from being able to describe who we are: "What if, instead of two genders, there are more? What if there are endless ways of being female, and infinite ways of being male?"

The reality is that most people, including many lesbians and gay men, are threatened by the possible worlds Loulan's questions suggest. Few things, after all, make people more uncomfortable than being unable to discern the gender of a person we're talking with, either face-to-face or on the phone. It's even more upsetting when men *become* women and women *become* men. Transsexuals are truly on the gender front lines. People hate transsexuals because they are confusing to those of us that feel we are safe within gender limits. Even in on-line computer conversations, one of the first things people want to know is: "Male or female?"

Perhaps, as Loulan says, "Homophobia can really be looked at as genderphobia."

She continues, "Imagine a world in which you get to choose whatever you want to wear. You get to choose however you want to play, and what you do for work. You don't worry about who you are having sex with or who you want to marry. All of the concerns about homosexuality, bisexuality, transsexuality, and heterosexuality are gone. A world where gender is seen as a combination of genetics, choice, and culture, and is ultimately irrelevant."

Truly, love (and hate) is a many-gendered thing. In this section, we explore the idea that, within a galaxy of gendered selves, "male" and "female" are not the only stars. And to wonder, as Loulan does, whether "in our scramble to prove that we are women and men, we stumble right past our opportunity to claim more honest gender identities." To do that, we may need to move beyond the discussion of male/female altogether.

Would You Still Be Gay . . .

. . . if you were of the other sex? That is, if you are a lesbian, would you be a gay man if you were a male? Conversely, if you are a gay man, do you think that you would be a lesbian if you were female? One of the editors ran across this discussion on Gaynet, one of the Internet gay bulletin boards. This thread had garnered more than thirty-five responses. Here are some of those responses:

If I were a woman I wouldn't *be* me, so I can't even attempt to guess at *anything* about this not-me female, much less her sexuality. Well, OK—I do think she'd wear *faaabulous* shoes, whatever *that* means. . . .

Rod, San Francisco

• • • •

Forget about the shoes—I would be a *whore*.

Greg

• • • •

Ahah! A chance, once again, to tell the tale of an acquaintance of some years ago:

I was at a dance club in 1965 and this beautiful person walked in with some dykes. After ogling what I thought was a beautiful young man, I was politely informed that she was not. She was a mechanic and a lesbian (which immediately stirred my suppressed bi side).

I lost track of this person till a number of years later when I met *him* tending bar. Since he now had a rather nice moustache, I was puzzled. He told me of his gender problems since a very young age and his change from female to male. I (very stupidly) asked why he was tending bar in a gay bar and he said, "because I'm gay, of course."

Over the years, we discussed many things, including intimacies of the operations (not that that matters). One of the things that we both discussed often was the curious fact that, as a woman, he enjoyed the company of women and as a male, males.

The sum of all this?? I somehow feel that homosexual is homosexual and has little to do with being transexual or with the person's sex.

Doug, still fascinated by the whole concept

P.S. I *definitely* would be a lesbian if I were female. No question about that at all. I have pondered this question since the mid 60s and have often wished (I don't know why) I *were* female just so I *could* be.

• • • •

I adore women, and that's about the sum of it.

Melinda, Ithaca, New York

• • • •

I honestly don't know. I would think I would be attracted to men no matter what. I certainly know that, if I woke up female tomorrow (god forbid), I'd still be attracted to men. No doubt about that.

Trey/Nothing Wrong With Being Female, But I'm Happy To Be Male –Asheville, OR

• • • •

About 25 years ago I figured out that if I had been born a man I would have been gay. While this might be due to a failure of imagination (I simply can't imagine not finding men attractive) I suspect it is something deeper.

Emily

• • • •

Hmm, this is a real brain twister. Well, I suppose I still wouldn't be able to shop, or color coordinate my clothing, or know how to cook. So nothing would change.

I guess I'd have to do just what I do now. Even though I'd be a woman, I'd have to marry a gay man to cook, clean, tell me what to wear, and be there with a shoulder to cry on.

Face it, not many straight men would be able to meet my needs. :)

Chuck, Berkeley, CA

• • • •

What fascinates me is that someone could actually think that sexual preference could actually change when gender changes.

Do you mean if I was born a man or I became a man? If I were to wake up tomorrow and *gasp* discovered I had a dick that was actually attached (perish the thought) I would still adore women lesbians in particular. (Though, I guess it would be hard to get a date in my circle of friends.) I would probably become a <insert favorite term for str8 man who hangs out with dykes>. I think that if I were born male I would be a str8 male.

But sitting here thinking about it, I wouldn't want to be anything but a lesbian. I think, given a choice, I would choose dyke every time.

It is not just about loving women per se. It is about *women* loving women.

Sammie, Athens, GA

• • • •

If I had a sex change, and had the choice of having a straight man or a lesbian woman as a partner, I think I would be most unlikely to put up with the sort of nonsense that straight men dish out in general (and not only to women). Call me a possible-worlds political lesbian, if you wish.

Keith, Toronto

• • • •

OGod yes, I *definitely* would be a lesbian if I were female. Anything rather than straight men (but I would be into strap-ons).

Dylan, Bellingham, WA

Myths/Realities of Bisexuality

Sexuality runs along a continuum. It is not a static "thing" but rather a process that can flow, changing throughout our lifetime. Bisexuality falls along this continuum. As Boston bisexual activist Robyn Ochs says, bisexuality is the "potential for being sexually and/or romantically involved with members of either gender."

MYTH: Bisexuals are promiscuous/swingers.
TRUTH: Bisexual people have a range of sexual behaviors. Some have multiple partners; some have one partner; some go through partnerless periods. Promiscuity is no more prevalent in the bisexual population than in other groups of people.

MYTH: Bisexuals are equally attracted to both sexes.
TRUTH: Bisexuals tend to favor either the same or the opposite sex, while recognizing their attraction to both genders.

MYTH: Bisexual means having concurrent lovers of both genders.
TRUTH: Bisexual simply means the *potential* for involvement with either gender. This may mean sexually, emotionally, in reality, or fantasy. Some bisexual people may have concurrent lovers; others may relate to different genders at various time periods. Most bisexuals do not need to see both genders in order to feel fulfilled.

MYTH: Bisexuals cannot be monogamous.
TRUTH: Bisexuality is a sexual orientation. It is independent of a lifestyle of monogamy or nonmonogamy. Bisexuals are as capable as anyone of making a long-term monogamous commitment to a partner they love. Bisexuals live a variety of lifestyles, as do gays and heterosexuals.

MYTH: Bisexuals are denying their lesbianism or gayness.
TRUTH: Bisexuality is a legitimate sexual orientation that incorporates gayness. Most bisexuals consider themselves part of the generic term "gay." Many are quite active in the gay community, both socially and politically. Some of us use terms such as "bisexual lesbian" to increase our visibility on both issues.

MYTH: Bisexuals are in "transition."
TRUTH: Some people go through a transitional period of bisexuality on their way to adopting a lesbian/gay or heterosexual identity. For many others, bisexuality remains a long-term orientation. Indeed, we are finding that homosexuality may be a transitional phase in the coming-out process for bisexual people.

MYTH: Bisexuals spread AIDS to lesbian and heterosexual communities.
TRUTH: This myth legitimizes discrimination against bisexuals. The label "bisexual" simply refers to sexual orientation. It says nothing about sexual behavior. AIDS occurs in people of all sexual orientations. AIDS is contracted through unsafe sexual practices, shared needles, and contaminated blood transfusions. Sexual orientation does not "cause" AIDS.

MYTH: Bisexuals are confused about their sexuality.
TRUTH: It is natural for both bisexuals and gays to go through a period of confusion in the coming-out process. When you are an oppressed people and are constantly told that you don't exist, confusion is an appropriate reaction until you come out to yourself and find a supportive environment.

MYTH: Bisexuals can hide in the heterosexual community when the going gets tough.
TRUTH: To "pass" for straight and deny your bisexuality is just as painful and damaging for a bisexual as it is for someone gay. Bisexuals are not heterosexual and we do not identify as heterosexual.

MYTH: Bisexuals are not gay.
TRUTH: We are part of the generic definition of gay. Nongays lump us all together. Bisexuals have lost their jobs and suffer the same legal discrimination as other gays.

MYTH: Bisexual women will dump you for a man.
TRUTH: Women who are uncomfortable or confused about their same-sex attraction may use the bisexual label. True bisexuals acknowledge both their same-sex and opposite-sex attraction. Both bisexuals and gays are capable of going back into the closet. People who are

unable to make commitments may use a person of either gender to leave a relationship.

It is important to remember that bisexual, gay, lesbian, and heterosexual are labels created by a homophobic, biphobic, heterosexist society to separate and alienate us from each other. We are all unique; we don't fit into neat little categories. We sometimes need to use these labels for political reasons and to increase our visibilities. Our sexual esteem is facilitated by acknowledging and accepting the differences and seeing the beauty in our diversity.

— DANAHY SHARONROSE

Bisexuality: Beyond the Walls of Gender

I am bisexual. I am a lesbian. I am a bi-identified lesbian. I am a lesbian-identified bisexual. I am a lesbian who has sex with men. I am confused. I am all these things, given the day of the week and who wants to know.

A large part of this society's social relation problem is its constant need to pigeonhole people. I thought I would escape that when I took refuge in the world of gay men and lesbians, who understand the repressive, limiting categories of the heterosexual world and would not impose their own. On the contrary. Gay men and lesbians have generated more categories among themselves than you can keep track of. Regarding bisexuality, however, the gay community often practices discrimination by omission. "Bisexuality" isn't even considered a legitimate category; it's some strange limbo between straight and gay that eventually has to dissolve into one or the other.

It's as though the same school of thought on bisexuality exists among gay men and lesbians as exists among many heterosexuals toward gay men and lesbians—that our sexuality is a *choice.* I sense resentment from gay people who believe I can "pass" as straight and therefore have no claim to the gay community. Like people are saying, If you all can sleep with either men or women, why not just pick one, so you can either take your proper place among us, or be cast back into the abyss of heterosexuality?

If that's the case, I'd rather be part of the queer community than the gay community. A distinct difference exists between the two. "Gay" is a sexuality, while "queer" is a sensibility. I know many gay people who are *not* queer. Queer is defined as outside the mainstream, anti–status quo, mentioning nothing about sexuality or emotionality. It is a willingness to be open to things that others shy away from, including but not exclusively same-gender sex. Even very hip straight people (emphasis on *very*) can have certain queer sensibilities, though they may never be gay. Gay men and lesbians who choose to embrace the outsider identity as a means of unity and empowerment ought to think about that. A friend of mine once said, "I don't know *what* a queer is, but I know we're not like everyone else."

Westernized society has socialized us, straight and gay alike, to pair ourselves with *genders,* as opposed to personalities and spiritualities. We commit the fallacy of defining sexualities in terms of the sex act, because it is the easiest level to grasp. What is a woman who has sex with men but falls in love only with other women? What is a man who finds himself attracted to a male-to-female transsexual? The labels we attach reveal how we prioritize two definitions of sexuality: sex then emotion, or emotion then sex? The emotional and spiritual connections are often disregarded in place of who people have sex with. For me, bisexuality reaches beyond the physical, beyond the genital, where the walls of gender fade into the all-inclusive "human species."

— ARWYN MOORE

Modern Day Butch/Femme

While rooted in the past, butch/femme is not a thing of the past. Today, many lesbians are reclaiming their "butch" and "femme" selves and are finding that, among other things, these roles add an erotic dynamic to their relationships. But even the definition of butch/femme changes over time. And if we had fifteen words for genders, who knows how we would define our sexuality? So what is this thing called butch/femme?

Here is some of what butch/femme is not:

- Butch/femme is not about who is "top" and who is "bottom."
- Butch/femme is not about being male and female.
- Butch/femme is not about playing husband and wife.
- Butch/femme is not about who earns the money and who spends it.
- Butch/femme is not about who makes love to whom.
- Butch/femme is not about who makes the decisions and who doesn't.
- Butch/femme is not about passing for straight.
- Butch/femme is not about imitating heterosexual relationships.

The harder task comes in trying to define exactly what butch/femme *is*. Can straight women be butch? Can men be femme? Didn't we all fight for years to eliminate rules (and roles) altogether? Does everyone fall into one category or the other?

Here is some of what butch/femme is:

- Butch/femme is about clothes and image.
- Butch/femme is about self-perception.
- Butch/femme is about redefining what it means to be a woman.
- Butch/femme is about femininity and masculinity.
- Butch/femme is about sexual dynamics.
- Butch/femme is about role playing.
- Butch/femme is about gender.

Joan Nestle, who defines herself as "a femme who came out in the 1950s," attempts in *The Persistent Desire* to define butch/femme:

> *In the most basic terms, butch-femme means a way of looking, loving, and living that can be expressed by individuals, couples, or a community. . . . Butch-femme relationships, as I experienced them, were complex erotic and social statements, not phony heterosexual replicas. They were filled deeply with the language of stance, dress, gesture, love, courage, and autonomy.*

From a more recent perspective, here are two women on butch/femme from "Debate #1" in *The Lesbian Erotic Dance* by JoAnn Loulan:

Part of identifying as butch stems from a desire to defend, protect, and defy the traditional feminine stereotype. All of these verbs imply a reaction to the world. Being butch to me to a large degree means reacting to the world. A large part of identifying as femme stems from a desire to create, empathize, and become the woman (femininity and all) inside us. Therefore identifying as femme is more of an initial action—not passive at all.

There are also women who identify with one role and are perceived to be the other. These lesbians are often referred to as butchy/femmes or femmy/butches.

I was putting on a new toilet seat—should be easy, right—just two screws—of course not. So I'm under the toilet trying to get these goddamned fucking corroded screws loose. My young son is watching all this. I say, "It's sure a bitch being butch." He looks at me in confusion and says, "Mom, I thought your girlfriend was butch."

—from Debate #2 in The Lesbian Erotic Dance

(Jane Caminos)

Of course, for every lesbian who says she relates to the terms "butch" and "femme" there is another who claims "androgynous" as her self-description. And while self-definition is the most essential part of claiming our lesbian selves, even those who don't identify themselves as butch or femme do have clear ideas about others. When Joanne Loulan talks to lesbians around the country, she will often get a woman to come on stage who says she is neither, and "let the audience decide." And a roomful of lesbians, often 200 or more, who have never laid eyes on the woman, will always overwhelmingly choose one label or the other, before the woman has even opened her mouth.

— LYNN WITT

The Transsexual Mythtique

Transsexuals are a diverse group. For some, it's important to disconnect totally from their past and lead a new life, telling practically no one. And then there are those who consider themselves neither gender, or a blend, regardless of the degree of their physical transition. Just as it's important to have one's sexual orientation acknowledged and accepted by the outside world, it is appreciated when one addresses a transsexual and refers to him or her with the pronoun of the gender presented by that person.

MYTH: Transsexuals just need to learn to be comfortable with the bodies they were born into.
TRUTH: Many of us spend years in therapy trying to adjust to the bodies we're in. Sometimes we try to hide traces of our transgender issues by overcompensating the behavior of our *assigned* gender. By the time we start taking steps to change our bodies, this is literally the last resort. Few people question getting a facelift or breast implants to make a person feel more comfortable, but when gender is involved there's a double standard. Physical adjustments aside, learning how to live in a role for which we haven't been trained is challenging. Imagine going to a foreign country where you don't know the language but you've got to act as if you do.

MYTH: FTMs (female-to-male transsexuals) become men to gain male privilege.
TRUTH: I have come across many people who are confused about why a man would become a woman, but at the same time think they know why a woman would become a man. It is often assumed that it has to do with having access to the opportunities that men have, like getting a better job. Historically, when women "passed" as men, it's possibly true that they wanted more opportunity, but has anyone considered that maybe they also felt their true gender identity was male? It takes a lot more than just wanting a better job to cross over and live in a new gender role.

MYTH: Transsexuals can't deal with their true homosexuality, so they change gender to lead heterosexual lives.
TRUTH: Gender identity and sexual orientation are separate issues. About half of MTFs (male-to-females) end up as lesbians, and among FTMs, there are more and more now identifying themselves as bisexual or gay. Some MTFs were gay men and now find themselves interested in women, and there are quite a number of FTMs who were lesbians and now identify as gay men. When going through a gender change, sexuality can be very fluid, and you never really know how you're going to turn out.

MYTH: There are many more male-to-females than female-to-males.
TRUTH: Current statistics say it's about 50/50.

MYTH: There is an increasing number of FTMs because there is no room in the lesbian community to be "butch."
TRUTH: I have never heard of any FTM who made his change because of acceptance—or lack of it—from an outside community. It's what goes on inside, how one feels in one's body, and whom one sees in the mirror.

MYTH: The gender change happens when you have the "operation."
TRUTH: "Have you had the operation yet?" is the classic "talk-show" line—as if you go to sleep a man, have an operation, and suddenly wake up as a woman. It takes about five years to get comfortable living as the new gender. Internally, the transition is ongoing. For most transsexuals the change really starts when they realize they need to change their body. The biggest changes are psychological. Within a three-month period, I had between fifty and seventy-five dreams about a gender change. Finally it sunk in that I needed to do something about it. Starting hormones triggers the most dramatic physical and emotional changes that take place during the first year. If you can imagine, your body has been receiving a certain set of signals for most of your life and then suddenly it starts getting a whole new set of messages. It takes time to shift gears. The next step might be surgery. Some transsexuals, for a variety of different reasons, don't have surgery. For those of us who do, it might consist of a

series of surgeries, (i.e., for FTMs, chest and then genital) several years apart.

MYTH: Masculinity and femininity can be expressed through whatever body one is in.
TRUTH: I often wonder why it is that we ascribe "male" to one set of behaviors and "female" to another. Ultimately I believe we have access to all of it. For transsexuals, however, it's a *visceral* experience along with the compelling desire to change the body to more closely reflect the psyche. For some, it is absolutely *necessary* to transform completely on a physical level. For others, not. There are many possiblities and ways to express gender. I feel it's important that we find what works for us as individuals and, at the same time, respect the choices that others make for themselves.

— DAVID HARRISON

"Prohibido la entrada a hombres vestidos de mujer porque carecemos de un baño para personas de tercer sex." ("Men dressed as women are prohibited because we don't have a bathroom for persons of the third sex.")

SIGN AT THE FLAMINGO NIGHTCLUB IN REDWOOD CITY, CALIFORNIA, WHICH IS POPULAR WITH LATINOS

You're Strange and We're Wonderful

The Relationship Between the Gay/Lesbian and Transgender Communities

The alliance between the gay/lesbian and transgender communities is characterized by suspicion and misunderstanding on both sides. In many ways, it is the age-old story of an enfranchised group overlooking the needs of and actively excluding a less empowered group.

Of course, a considerable number of gay men and lesbians are sensitive toward transgendered persons and our plight. But others do not see and are often totally unaware of the larger transgender community, which is separate and distinct from the gay community. They don't understand the diversity of the transgender community, and they certainly give little or no thought to the advantages of working together. Consequently, they rarely think of transgendered persons when affirming their own rights to serve in the military, to love whomever they please, and to work in discrimination-free settings.

But there is much more going on than mere indifference. There is a pervasive distrust of, antagonism toward, and even hatred of transgendered persons. A few gay men and lesbians seem determined to mandate us out of existence. They deliberately misuse pronouns, force transsexual persons out of gay and lesbian events, and on more than one occasion have been physically violent toward transsexual persons.

If the levels of understanding and attitudes of many gay men and lesbians toward transgendered persons can be characterized as ignorant, indifferent, embarrassed, or hostile, it becomes puzzling how and why the gay community has accepted transgender behavior to the extent that it has. Female impersonation is frequent at bars and parties, and many valued members of the community have gender presentations that vary far from the usual gender stereotypes. But acceptance of the idea of trangender is partial and sometimes grudging, resulting from ignorance by the gay/lesbian community that many in their community are transgendered.

This has resulted in what I call Gay Imperialism, in which the accomplishments and the very identities of transgendered persons are collapsed into the gay community. Perhaps the most obvious example of this is Billy Tipton.

Tipton was an accomplished jazz musician, a husband, and father of two adopted sons. After his death in 1989, it was revealed that he was biologically a woman. Marjorie Garber has written elegantly about Tipton in her book *Vested Interests.* She points out that the facts of Tipton's life make no sense except when looked at in a transgendered light. His life was much more than a means to express himself via his music, and much more than a way to live a lesbian relationship. Neither his wife nor his sons were aware that he did not have male genitalia. He was a husband and a father to them and a man to his neighbors and fellow musicians; he was a woman only to the press and the gay/lesbian community, both of which claimed him and exploited him after he was conveniently dead.

Gay scholars have similarly exploited transgendered persons, even while specifically writing about them. In books about transgendered two-spirited American Indians, some scholars look at their subjects through gay-colored spectacles. It's true that the sexual orientation of many and perhaps even most two-spirit people was to those of the same biological sex, but the two-spirit people are also, with equal if not greater profundity, transgendered. Gay scholars have interpreted two-spirit people from a gay perspective, even as heterosexual anthropologists have interpreted homosexual behavior in various cultures from their own point of view.

With its newly found voice, the transgender community will no longer tolerate such colonization by the gay community. People like Billy Tipton, Radclyffe Hall, and Joan of Arc are being reclaimed as transgendered—queer, but not gay. And it's clear that it is a reclamation and not a revision, for they were stolen from the transgendered community. And make no mistake: The murmur of today will be a roar tomorrow.

The gay/lesbian and transgender communities have much to learn from each other. The transgender community is eager for discourse. It has much to learn about politics, self-discovery, and self-acceptance from the gay/lesbian community. And the gay/lesbian community must come to understand that the voices of transgendered persons will forever after be in their ears.

It's a marvelous opportunity for both communities. Here's hoping that the cannons will be pointed outward, toward those who would deny "queers"—all of them, transgendered or gay—the right to live, and not inward, toward those who are more like us than we care to think.

— DALLAS DENNY

"When you think of a bombshell, you think of Monroe or Mansfield, you don't think of a 300-pound man. People like to be shocked."

DIVINE, ACTOR AND BLOND BOMBSHELL

The Politics of Drag

The radical drag underground. The Wigstock generation. Drag post-*moderne*. Whatever it's called, there is a new generation of drag performers who have no desire to coddle their audience with the umpteenth rendition of Marilyn. Spurred on by both homophobia and AIDSphobia, this drag is fresh, fierce, and fighting mad.

But not all drag performers see false eyelash to false eyelash on the activist power of donning a dress. There are those performers, both male and female, who use cross-gender guise to bring attention to their political forum and those who do it strictly for entertainment value.

The late great Divine terrorizes and enthralls his 1978 audience at the Trocadero in San Francisco. (Dan Nicoletta)

While Atlanta drag performer Lurleen and Los Angeles drag Vaginal Creme Davis are out on the front lines, involved in groups such as ACT UP, and giving benefit performances for the fight against AIDS, others, such as John Epperson as Lypsinka, see their roles simply as entertainers.

"AIDS has forced gay people to think about who we are and what our relationship with straight society really is," says the strawberry-blond Lurleen. "It's hard to be an apolitical person these days. I'm no strident Marxist, but when there is a reactionary government in power, it's kind of hard to get up onstage and lip-synch Barbra and then say, 'Drink up, everybody.'"

Lypsinka, who hopes to cross over from the stage into mainstream network television, disagrees. "Some people opt to do that [be political]. I don't. I set out to entertain."

The disagreements over style and form between Lypsinka, Lurleen, Vaginal Creme Davis, and legions of other drag queens—politics versus entertainment—are not new.

CAN YOU BELIEVE IT?

In 1974, Tommie Temple, a female impersonator, was fired from his job as show director and star of the Jewel Box Lounge for being gay. The Kansas City liquor ordinance said that a bar could not employ a homosexual.

The Judy Garlands of the drag queen world became the unquestioned norm during the heady disco days of the 1970s and 1980s, when drag bars blossomed throughout the country. Although there were several drag troupes, such as the Sisters of Perpetual Indulgence and the Cockettes in San Francisco, who maintained a high profile at parades and demonstrations, it was not until the late 1980s and the acceleration of the AIDS crisis that drag embraced a political message.

DID YOU KNOW...

Magnolia, a/k/a Tommy Keene, reigned over drag queens in West Alabama and Northeast Mississippi in the late 1980s and early 1990s, performing regularly at Michael's, the gay bar in Tuscaloosa, Alabama, owned by and named after her stepfather. Her mother, Mary Ann, once joined Magnolia on stage for a lip-synched rendition of "Mama, He's Crazy," by the mother/daughter country-western duo Naomi and Winona Judd. Magnolia and fellow drag queens Princess DeShaye and Coco Chanel traveled and performed throughout the region, accompanied by their hairstylist Grant LaTondress.

Clearly, today's drag artists have a lot more on their minds than tight wigs. "[Political] drag is absolutely, unquestionably experiencing a comeback," claims Martin Worman, aka Philthee Ritz, one of the original members of the Cockettes. "The Cockettes didn't have a dogma. Now drag has an edge and a conscience because of AIDS."

"The difference between old-line drag and new drag is that those performers took *themselves* seriously," continues Lurleen. "That's tedious in any form of self-expression. What we do reflects the mentality of our generation. We approach serious causes with humor and react to what's going on in our culture and society."

The setting for this rebirth can probably be traced to the Pyramid Club in Manhattan's East Village, where acts like the band Now Explosion and performers such as Hapi Phace, Tabboo!, and the late Ethyl Eichelberger honed their considerable talents in front of an audience that included New York's intellectual and social elite.

"Now drag is about trying new things," explains New York drag figurehead Lady Bunny. "It isn't limited to lip-synching. There is a new generation of queers whose icons aren't Barbra, Judy, and Eartha." Instead, blaxploitation films, 1970s sitcoms, glitter-rock bands, or parodies of other drags are now de rigueur inspirations.

"Drag adds an element of fun to politics so that it's not all Maoist uniforms and being glum and gray," says the platform-heeled Lurleen. "Hopefully it makes thinking about politics more palatable."

Lypsinka, whose lightning-paced lip-synch revue *I Could Go On Lip-Synching!* has had tremendous financial success on both coasts, says that although he has performed at AIDS and gay-related fund-raisers, he sees himself as "not political at all."

"It's easier to digest Lypsinka's kind of performance," explains self-styled "blacktress" Vaginal Creme Davis. "It's safer, and people aren't challenged. But when people see an African American in this feminized role, they realize that there's a whole spectrum of being out there and that the black experience or the queer experience is not just limited to one aspect."

Of course, drag performance is not strictly the domain of men. San Francisco is also home to Leigh Crow, whose character, Elvis Herselvis, puts an ironic spin on Elvis impersonators, discussing the King's drug problem and making copious references to "little girls in white cotton panties."

Shelly Mars's male characters have a somewhat harder edge. The New York performer's best-known character is Martin, a leering, cigar-chomping man in a baggy suit who performs a striptease and fondles his dick. By the end of the performance, Martin transforms into a woman and the idea comes full circle.

Leigh Crow, performer and drag king extraordinaire, as her alter-ego, Elvis Herselvis. (Rink Foto)

Mars's newest male character, Peter, is a person with AIDS who is slightly psychotic from medication and dementia. Modeled after people she met through ACT UP and friends who have died of the disease, Peter elicits very powerful reactions from her audience.

"It's a scary thing to do," says Mars. "You never know what kind of response you are going to get. Some people think that since I am portraying an insane character, I am making fun of him or saying all people with AIDS are this way. That narrow-mindedness comes from their own denial."

Beyond the politics and the divisions it engenders, there is a common thread running through the drag community: the desire to get audiences thinking about their own sexuality.

"We challenge gender roles," explains Glennda Orgasm of the New York public-access cable program *The Brenda and Glennda Show.* "And even though it's a campy parody, it goes beyond that. A lot of gay men are bothered by their own femininity. Like 'I'm gay, but I'm not feminine, I'm not a fag. I'm a man, even though I like to suck cock.' Seeing a drag queen confronts all those fears. That's why we do drag."

"I hate that when they call me a transvestite. If I were a transvestite, I'd be sitting here with a little crocodile handbag and a polka-dot bow. Those are my work clothes. That's how I make people laugh."

DIVINE, DRAG LEGEND

"I understand the objection to drag from gays within the system who are working on gay and lesbian issues that way," says Lurleen, "and yet I think that's wrong. The issue is diversity and tolerance for people who are different and not just people who are different 'our way.' All oppressed people have something in common and need to work together."

— JEFFREY HILBERT

Get Her!—Wisdom from Great Drag Queens

Famed drag queen Miss Kitty, a/k/a Dan Jones (Dan Nicoletta)

"I speak for the individual. For anyone out there who's ever had a dream and has had to listen to 'Honey, you can't do that.' 'We don't allow blacks here.' 'We don't allow fags here.' 'We don't allow women in this bar.' I am a giant 'Fuck you' to bigotry. Buddha, Krishna, Jesus, and now RuPaul. I'm about the politics of the soul. I transcend the gay community. I speak to everyone with pain in their heart."

—RUPAUL, SUPERMODEL OF THE WORLD

"I mean, how political can a piece of clothing be?"

— GENDER, TAP-DANCING QUEER DRAG QUEEN

"The cross-dressers, to put it bluntly, we're the ones who had the balls to say, Look—I'm gay!"

— JOSE SARRIA, FEMALE IMPERSONATOR AND LONG-TIME PERFORMER/ACTIVIST

"I kind of see drag queens as the suffragettes of the gay community. . . . I think the root of that problem really is various people saying, 'I am ashamed of who I am and I don't want anyone to remind me of what I am.'

'Cause I can remember when I first came out of the closet, I hated camp men."
— BOY GEORGE, POP QUEEN

"No matter what they say on *Oprah* or *Donahue,* I have never met a female impersonator who wasn't gay. I met one guy who is married, but that's a crock. I think those who are saying they are not and thinking that it will get them further are just wasting their time."
— DRAG QUEEN POISON WATERS, 1992 QUEEN OF LA FEMME MAGNIFIQUE, THE WESTERN UNITED STATES PAGEANT TO FIND "THE MOST BEAUTIFUL FEMALE IMPERSONATOR"

DID YOU KNOW...

Wigstock, an annual drag celebration, attracts thousands of participants and spectators to Tompkins Square Park in Manhattan's East Village every Labor Day. It was created in 1984 by New York–based Atlanta drag queen Lady Bunny in hopes of bringing "the drags of the New York club world into daylight." The tenth anniversary festival in 1994 saw performances from the likes of Lypsinka and RuPaul.

Behind the Mask

For African American men, masculinity is a complicated issue: How do you define being a man in a society that doesn't see you as one?

If you are homosexual as well, this issue is even more complex. All our cultural and social mores are based on heterosexual manhood. Furthermore, in the media—gay and straight—being gay is a white thing. I always believed, though, that I had society's laws licked, that my being out challenged the notion that African Americans can't be homosexual. It seemed so simple. But then I met Sydney.

Sydney is a six-foot-two, 225-pound nineteen-year-old with dimples for days, and Hershey's chocolate skin. He is also a B-boy. That's right—a ruffneck. There's no such thing as a *gay* B-boy, you say? Sorry, but not all African American gay men walk the runway like RuPaul. Some of us appear on MTV and BET, rhymin' and harmonizin' up a storm. Of course, you can't tell these homeboys are gay since they don't "look" or "act" like it. Being banjie is the perfect disguise for an African American gay —or bisexual—male: Who would ever think that one of these hip-hop-lovin', crazy crotch-grabbin', droopy-jean-wearin', forty-ounce-guzzlin' brothers is a faggot? Yes, some wear a mask and wear it well.

But the mask slowly came off Sydney as he and I got to know each other. I was apprehensive at first. We have almost nothing in common (he worships Snoop Doggy Dogg; I love Rachelle Ferrell). He's a bit too egotistical (he religiously wears a cap announcing I'M 2 SEXY 4

MYSELF). And he says the *f* word so much, you'd think it was his middle name. But a friend pushed me to give Sydney, who pursued me for two months after ringing up my groceries at the local supermarket, a chance. "You don't know," my friend argued. "He might surprise you."

Well, he did. After a month Sydney and I became "a couple." He'd drop by almost every day after school or work—sometimes with a rose or a bouquet of flowers—and I'd help him with his homework. We'd watch TV or play Scrabble or Trivial Pursuit (he'd usually win). Or we'd "max" in each other's arms (which is a sight, since I'm six inches shorter and ninety pounds lighter) as he read me one of his poems (he wants to be a writer). Sometimes, though, he'd just cry on my shoulder—which he'd never do in front of his homies—because of the confusion he felt about his sexual orientation. He is a sweet, sensitive young man who, like most gay men, was brainwashed into believing he should be ashamed of who he is.

He was surprised when I told him his literary heroes—Langston Hughes and James Baldwin—were gay. He was shocked when I didn't want to "get busy" with him on our first date. And he was even more bewildered when I refused to be "the woman" (as if his hand being attached to his penis 24–7 meant he was "the man"). Being around a gay man who respected himself and did not subscribe to a moronic machismo culture that brands women "bitches" and "hos" and homosexuals "punks" made him more comfortable talking about his sexuality. He let his guard down and let the real him come out.

As my relationship with Sydney blooms, I am filled with hope and love—but also anger. Our society's warped ideas about masculinity have young men like him in limbo. Some commit suicide because they believe no one understands or cares; Sydney admitted he contemplated doing it once. Others adopt archaic sexual codes that force them to play roles. Sydney is beginning to see that acting "hard" doesn't make him a real man, nor will it change who he is.

Through him I've learned that as long as there is heterosexism, it isn't enough to open only my own closet door. I must make sure others know they can too, especially the next generation. If we don't serve as role models for young lesbians and gays, who will? How can they value their true selves if they believe that wearing a mask will make their lives easier? As Dr. Martin Luther King, Jr., once said, "Silence is betrayal." And what bigger crime is there but to betray yourself?

— **JAMES EARL HARDY**

DIRTY TALK

Lesbians and gay men have taken great pains to convince everyone, including ourselves, that our movement is not just about sex. Of course it isn't. We have a thriving movement for civil rights, a myriad of cultural experiences and discoveries, and day-to-day life that goes on outside of our bedrooms. But sometimes we forget that, while our movement is not *only* about sex, sex *is* an integral part of our lives, our loves, and our political struggles.

AIDS has changed the ways we relate to our bodies and sex. For many gay men during the eighties, AIDS made sex terrifying, a forbidden pleasure that could mean death. Since that time, most of us have adjusted to sex in the era of AIDS, accepting responsibility for protecting ourselves and others. Still, though, far too many of us are ignoring the warnings and having unsafe sex. And since the onslaught of the epidemic, an entire generation of gay men and lesbians have come to sexual maturity.

Lesbians, too, have experienced a revolution in sexual thought and deed. During the eighties, lesbians came out of the closet about leather sex, S/M, dildos, and pornography. In addition, while methods of HIV transmission via lesbian sex are still hotly debated, lesbians are discovering latex, cellophane wrap, and other ways of decreasing the risk of AIDS.

Sex has become so *serious.* But what we are learning now as a people is that serious does not have to mean bad, nor does it have to mean we can't have fun. Sex is a crucial part of our sexuality. This section explores several different ways in which sex, far from equaling death, equals laughter, liberation, and life.

Sex and Stonewall

As a gay man living an openly gay life before Stonewall, the effects of the Riots in my life were immediate. The excitement of insurrection was palpable; my friends and myself, already connected to progressive leftist political groups, were elated: this was our revolution. I began going to Gay Liberation Front meetings in Manhattan two weeks later (and am still going to political meetings twenty-five years later). I had understood that feminist writings had some meaning for me, but now I had a real, vibrant context for specifically gay political theorizing—a way to think and analyze how gay men lived their lives.

But more than any of this, Stonewall meant sex. It is not as though gay men did not have sex before the Riots; they did, and much of the sex was good, nurturing, exciting. But after Stonewall sex was different. Not only was there less guilt and less anxiety, but the promise of Stonewall was, in a very real way, the promise of sex: free sex, better sex, lots of sex, sex at home and sex in the streets. As Tony Kushner writes in *Angels in America: Perestroika*, sex after Stonewall was the "Praxis, True Praxis. True Theory married to Actual Life." This sexual energy fueled the movement. It filled us with fervor and desire—not only for one another, but to change the world.

The advent of AIDS changed all that. Suddenly sex had become something that enslaved rather than liberated, something that was not only dirty but, in the original meaning of the word, *dreadful.* Once we'd realized that AIDS could be spread by sexual transmission—a process that took several years—it was clear that we had to change some of our behaviors. But behavior was not the only thing that began changing. Homophobic social critics began labeling *all* gay male sex as dangerous. Early safe-sex guidelines preyed upon gay men's uncertainties and proscribed all kinds of behaviors—especially the more socially unacceptable activities such as S/M—as life-threatening. Promiscuity—whether safe or not—was condemned as unhealthy and regressive; monogamy was now to become the norm. Some gay psychologists proclaimed that AIDS would shift gay men's behaviors from an "adolescent" stage of sleeping around to the more "mature" stage of monogamous coupledom. It was perhaps inevitable that early attempts to promote responsible behavior dovetailed with the most homophobic, antisex attitudes in our culture, and in many ways "safe sex" came to mean less sex, fewer partners, and less sexual experimentation. The sexual promises of Stonewall seemed to have ended, betrayed by reality and disease, fear and loathing.

But in recent years it has become clear that our more traditional ideas about safe-sex education have not been completely successful. Some have argued that they have, indeed, failed as we have seen gay male seroconversion rates in cities such as San Francisco once again rise. The political right has argued that this is because gay male sexuality is intrinsically disordered. Some AIDS educators have suggested that the epidemic has caused many gay men to have a death wish. Others have argued that it is simply human nature to act irresponsibly. I would like to posit another response.

The problem with our conceptualization of "safe sex" is—and has always been—that it did not value sex enough. Sexual desire has become something to fear and to contain. Sex with one person was better than sex with ten, sex at home was better than sex at the baths, sex with love was superior to sex for sex's sake: Sex was being seen as a luxury, a bonus, to good health—not as a necessity for it. It's no wonder that safe sex based upon these precepts would be a failure. It ignored the reality that sexuality is a powerful force in our lives, that desire itself can be nurturing, that sex—in any number of manifestations—is an affirmation of who we are as queers living in the world. Of course, we have to be responsible in our sexual behavior, but that is quite a different matter from restraining our sexual desire or curtailing our sexual lives because of fear or dread.

The promise of sex that Stonewall delivered in 1969 is still with us today and its message is as important—if not more important—than ever. If we are going to get

> **"One strain of 1970s gay liberationist rhetoric proclaimed that sex was inherently liberating; by a curiously naive calculus, it seemed to follow that *more* sex was *more* liberating. In other words, I should consider myself more liberated if I'd had a thousand sex partners than if I'd only had five hundred."**
>
> MICHAEL CALLEN, SINGER, SONGWRITER, AND AIDS ACTIVIST

through the AIDS crisis, if we are truly going to love and respect ourselves as gay men, if we are going to grow and thrive in this homophobic world we are going to have to learn—once again—how to love and embrace our sexuality in all of its forms, all of its desires, all of its manifestations. If we can begin doing this, the liberating promise of Stonewall will set us free again today.

— MICHAEL BRONSKI

A History of Sex-Positive Lesbian Erotica

DID YOU KNOW...

***Safe Is Desire*, released in 1993 by the Fatale line of erotic videos, was the first full-length safer-sex video for lesbians.**

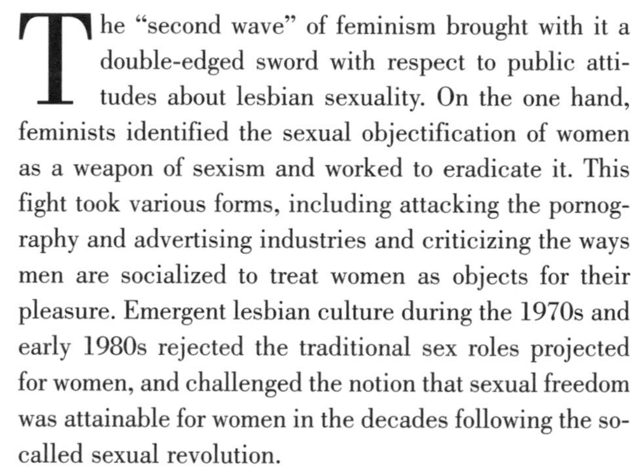

The "second wave" of feminism brought with it a double-edged sword with respect to public attitudes about lesbian sexuality. On the one hand, feminists identified the sexual objectification of women as a weapon of sexism and worked to eradicate it. This fight took various forms, including attacking the pornography and advertising industries and criticizing the ways men are socialized to treat women as objects for their pleasure. Emergent lesbian culture during the 1970s and early 1980s rejected the traditional sex roles projected for women, and challenged the notion that sexual freedom was attainable for women in the decades following the so-called sexual revolution.

On the other hand, rejecting the ways women have been sexualized by the dominant culture did not automatically give women positive images of ourselves as sexual. For example, many of the fashions lesbians adopted kept us from appearing sexually available not only to men, but to each other as well. Carrying out the agenda of women's liberation in our own sex lives was challenging.

DID YOU KNOW...

Approximately 675 new gay porn releases came out in 1994, including both higher-profile "major studio" releases as well as the products put out by the rapidly proliferating "fetish" and "specialty" mail-order companies. Since "hard core" was legalized in the early 1970s, an estimated 4,000 feature-length products have been put out.

Lesbian-feminists resisted being defined by the mainstream as primarily sexual beings. At the same time, lesbians *were* having sex and regarding those experiences as an integral part of lesbian identity. There was a tension among some lesbians between those who wanted more public representations of lesbian sexuality and those who argued that these representations perpetuated sexist oppression.

In response to the need for more explicit and radical forms of lesbian sexual expression, in the 1980s a "sex-positive" movement for lesbians emerged. In just a little over a decade, the United States and British lesbian communities have seen a burgeoning in the publication, production, and distribution of lesbian erotic materials, sexual performances by and for women, and stores or catalogues that sell "sex toys."

Nowhere was this emergence of the sex-positive movement more prominent than in San Francisco. It started with a big bang in 1984, when Blush Productions created venues for live erotic dancing for women at places like the now defunct Baybrick Inn. In women-only, safe spaces—a radical change from the male-owned clubs attended primarily by men—evenings were marked by a fevered, ecstatic, tangibly sexual energy and excitement that was surely a first. The dancers and the audience spanned a range of lesbian identities—butch, femme, and everything in between—in all manner of attire from lace to leather, from uniform to street clothes.

Today the sex-positive community has as many diverse components and variations as one can imagine. Sex-positive describes lesbians who are reclaiming sexuality as an aspect of creative, spiritual, political, and loving expression long denied to women globally. Publications range from mild erotica and depictions of nudity to erotic stories and poems and videotapes of women's fantasies by and for women. Groups range from

"The real dilemma of women's sexuality and AIDS is fear, stigma, humiliation, and estrangement. The goal is to feel close, sexy, and passionate—and turn on and dig yourself."

LESBIAN SEXPERT SUSIE BRIGHT, IN SUSIE SEXPERT'S LESBIAN SEX WORLD

(Jill Posener)

DID YOU KNOW...

In the industry, porn actors are usually referred to as either "models" or "talent." They are normally paid by the sex scene (or "commercial scene"). They are never paid before completing a scene (commonly understood to require an on-camera ejaculation) and signing an elaborate model release providing iron-clad proof of legal age. The mean average pay today is about $600 per scene, with the range approximately $150–$1,400. There are a significant number of "top stars" who can work as often as they like and expect to always get at least $800. There are a small handful of "superstars" like Ryan Idol and Jeff Stryker who can demand greater one-time fees for a project. Idol was rumored to have landed $15,000 for his most recent flick.

— IDOL COUNTRY FOR HIS VIDEO

women's workshops on "Creative Explorations of Intimacy With Your Long-Term Lover" to "Tantric Sexuality for Lesbians" to "Bondage 101" and "Making Safe Sex Fun."

Sexually explicit publications created by and for lesbians began to appear on the market during the 1980s. A pioneer in this field was the lesbian-feminist S/M organization Samois, which produced the forty-five-page booklet *What Color Is Your Handkerchief? A Lesbian S/M Sexuality Reader* in 1979, followed by *Coming to Power* in 1981. *On Our Backs* was first published in 1984, about the same time as *Outrageous Women* and *Bad Attitude* came out of the East Coast. The year 1985 hailed the first lesbian erotic video, *Private Pleasures* and *Shadows,* followed in 1986 by *Erotic in Nature*, a representation of quiet and sensual lesbian-lovemaking in the summer trees. In 1987, lesbian-made and sexually explicit videos began to proliferate, including *Rites of Passion,* by Annie Sprinkle and Veronica Vera, and *Burlezk Live,* a lesbian striptease filmed at one of the Baybrick cabarets. Since the early 1980s, there has been a rapid increase in the number of magazines and books with all varieties of pornography and erotica. Even sex clubs—establishments open only to members and guests, safe sex only, alcohol and drugs not permitted—and the occasional sex party have been available to women in San Francisco off and on since 1978.

Thanks to the pioneering work of lesbians—Susie Bright, JoAnn Loulan, and Pat Califia—writing about forms and expressions of lesbian sexuality, lesbians in the 1990s are exposed to a wider range of possible sexual personae. The increased visual and written representations of lesbians as sexual beings and a cultural atmosphere that values sexual discussion and experience are some of the great fruits of the struggle for sexual freedom.

— MEGAN BOLER

Gay Male Porn—Look Back in Swagger

Zak Spears (left) and Tyler Scott, from the 1993 Hot House production, On the Mark. *(Hot House Entertainment)*

Gay porn is the gay community's perennial ugly duckling. All the same, it's the most popular fowl in many gay households—more common than even the Thanksgiving turkey. Hardcore gay pornography is watched by a very large number of gay men. Even a lifelong conscientious objector to filmed carnality is likely to have at least a passing familiarity with some of the icons of the medium. In gay circles, exchanging frank viewpoints on Jeff Stryker's money-making member beats idle chitchat about the weather most any old day.

There are three basic positions gay men tend to take when talking about the sex-vid biz. And please—no snappy comebacks to that statement that begins "the first is hanging upside down in a full-body harness . . ." if you don't mind! The first and perhaps the most common school of opining goes something like this: "Gay porn is just plain tacky and an embarrassment to our community. The production values in those videos are so shoddy! Surely as a group we can do better than this . . ." The second goes more like "Porn is a worthy pastime—but artistically expendable. It's something to be kept by the VCR and watched now and then—but not if *Murphy Brown* is on."

The third is along the lines of "Porn is its own art form, a valuable cultural tool, and a lot of fun." In just the past couple of years, a small but growing number of perhaps more academically inclined individuals have begun to scrutinize porn video with less concern for its current artistic shortcomings and more attention devoted to its cultural potential. Because when you strip away the prudishness and societal stereotypes with which many of us have been preconditioned into approaching the subject of

pornography, it can be argued that by the very nature of its explicitness, gay porn is well suited to portraying what it is that defines us as a group: who we choose to love and the way we go about engineering it. Mainstream Hollywood movies can (and occasionally even have) depicted our lives with vibrancy and insight. But Hollywood can never get the entire picture.

In the nineties, gay porn has infiltrated the American cultural mainstream more than ever. Whether it's gay performers speaking out candidly on any number of daytime talk shows or the naked lusciousness that is porn boy Joey Stefano popping up in Madonna's highly publicized *Sex* book, gay porn has obviously made its presence known across a broad range of folks who, a decade ago, would hardly have admitted to stopping in a bookstore and perusing the jacket notes on a copy of *The Joy of Gay Sex.*

An episode of the hit Canadian comedy series *The Kids in the Hall* summed up the lively public debate on the subject of gay smut when openly gay troop member Scot Thompson in a monologue featuring his flip and flouncy "queen" character, Buddy Cole, said, "On the topic of 'Freedom of Choice'. . . The idea of persecuting gay porn is redundant. Gay life is porn. Nobody's being exploited. What you see up on that screen are the community standards."

— DAVE KINNICK

DAVE KINNICK'S TOP TEN LIST OF GAY XXX VIDEOS

Best Friends, 1985, TCS Studio. Directed by Mark Reynolds.

The Bigger the Better, 1984, Firstplace Video. Directed by Matt Sterling.

Carnival in Rio, 1989, Sarava Video. Directed by Kristen Bjorn.

Cousins, 1983, Laguna-Pacific Ltd. Directed by William Higgins.

Getting Even, 1986, Videomo/French Art. Directed by J. D. Cadinot

Honorable Discharge, 1993, All Worlds Video. Directed by Jerry Douglas.

Pleasure Beach, 1984, HIS Video. Directed by Arthur J. Bresnan, Jr.

Sizing Up, 1984, Huge Video. Directed by Matt Sterling.

Two Handfuls, 1986, Bijou Video. Directed by John Travis.

The Young & the Hung, 1985, Laguna-Pacific Ltd. Directed by William Higgins.

LEATHER AND LOVE

The gay and lesbian community is nothing if not complex. Millions of people with perhaps nothing more in common than an attraction to members of their own sex are lumped together as a community, wrongly assumed by many nongay people to have one set of shared values and goals. When it comes to sex, not everyone likes or wants the same thing. In the gay and lesbian world, there are a number of people, men and women, who find their identity and sexual fulfillment within the S/M and leather world.

Leather is about sex, costume, and erotic exploration. It is also about community, trust, and communication. The leather community has long taken care of its own; it was one of the first groups to insist that gay men and lesbians practice safe sex. Many early fund-raisers for AIDS causes were sponsored by the leather community, and among the responsibilities of the Mr. and Ms. International Leather titleholders each year is the promotion of AIDS and safe-sex awareness.

The Spiritual Side of Radical Sexuality

In the loose confederation of organizations, circles, causes, and individuals that make up the gay and lesbian community, few groups are more prone to misunderstanding by their fellow travelers than leatherfolk. The black-clad clan is as diverse as any other faction within the gay world, yet is narrowly viewed by many as a barely tolerable relic from homosexuality's shadowing past.

Image-conscious critics see queers in black leather as a serious problem for a movement wanting to assimilate into society. The leather community's confrontative public posture and its unapologetic advocacy of taboo erotic practices appear radical—even subversive—by mainstream standards. As a result, leatherfolk are often scapegoated by other gays as a reason for society's dislike and distancing of homosexuals. Few such critics, however, would admit that the underlying reason for their prejudice toward the leather lifestyle is their own internalized homophobia and fear of difference. Leatherfolk, by their very nature, hold up a disquieting mirror.

What those outside the leather domain often fail to see is that through boldly exploring their bodies, many radical sensualists are nurturing spiritual growth within themselves. They've discovered that the S/M ritual helps to clear out the psychic basement, that deep inner place where troubling and fearful things are kept hidden. Long-held feelings of inferiority or low self-esteem, grief and loss, familial rejection and abandonment often come to the surface during S/M rituals. Rather than keep a tight lid on the psyche's dark contents, these extreme sensual acts undo memories of the past and thus provide passage from the unconscious underworld to the aboveworld of self-realization and, ultimately, emotional healing.

"WHAT S/M MEANS TO ME"

Samois was a lesbian S/M support group that started in San Francisco in the late 1970s. For several years, the group produced a monthly newsletter, which included the advice column "Ask Aunt Sadie." The following is an anonymous sample from this column, suggested to us for this book by Aunt Sadie herself.

Dear Aunt Sadie:

Here is "What S/M Means to Me" with gratuitous *pun*ishment, compliments of the Phantom Punster:

Sadism and Masochism

Sensual and Mutual (the basics)

Simply Magnificent

Sensory Memory

Sensual Magic

Sexual Magic

South of Market (San Francisco leather area)

Sex Maniac

Southern Methodist

Send Money

Sue Me

Service Manual

SM is the last word in feminiSM

Whether acknowledged or not, many urbanized gay men become attracted to radical sexuality because it offers some form of masculine initiation, the kind of rites of passage found in indigenous cultures around the world but usually lacking in their own. The process of masculine initiation traditionally begins with a rite of submission, followed by a period of containment, and then by a further rite of liberation — a psychological journey well known to leather practitioners.

Men, gay and straight, find their worth and define their manliness through trials of endurance. They must expose their limits, submit to fiery tests, in order to grow spiritually. It is the hero's obligation to meet these rites of passage with faith intact, for they balance the eternal conflict between the claims of the ego and the soul. As any seasoned leatherman knows, one of the indispensable conditions of a successful S/M scene is the ability of the initiate to submit fully to the experience. A blackening must occur before any new light can dawn.

During the past decade, leatherfolk have been especially hard at work in strengthening the cultural ties that bind their community—in creating a new tribal identity. This collective effort has encompassed the preservation of the past (leathermen in major cities were among the first to fall from AIDS and also the first to rally against it), as well as a more profound articulation of radical sexuality's spiritual implications—its potential for curing the wounds of the soul. For some leatherfolk, the definition of the term "S/M" has evolved in recent years from connoting sadomasochism, to implying sensuality and mutuality, to meaning "sex magic." They see radical sexuality as an empowering, soul-making process—not the witless, pathological acting out of inner demons as some would claim.

Still, the idea that radical sexuality has spiritual value is a difficult one for most people to grasp. Even some leatherfolk reject the thought as well, confusing spirituality with religiosity and its condemning institutions. Few, however, would dismiss the transcendent moments of cathartic release they've experienced through intense erotic play. The enhanced physical, visual, and aural sensations of radical sex ritual allow for a transportation of self, or awareness of self, beyond normal everyday references.

It is not unusual to find leatherfolk who are members of the clergy or the New Age movement, or who have explored psychoanalysis or various recovery programs—spiritually seeking individuals who are in some way seriously committed to personal and social change. By gaining the psychological insight made available to them through radical sexual practices, leatherfolk now stand among the gay community's most consistently aware, socially responsible, and politically motivated members.

— **MARK THOMPSON**

Truth Is an Absolute Essential

Since the late 1970s, lesbians have been actively engaged in sharing their experiences and knowledge about the leather scene with other interested women. Support groups and safe-sex play groups have formed from San Francisco to New York. In the following excerpt from *Coming to Power,* "Juicy Lucy" provides us some insight into the lesbian S/M world.

Truth is an absolute essential. To build valid trust requires some ability to risk and some common sense. Since S/M is consensual there's always some talking, before and after, so that you both (or all) know what's going on. It's a lot easier to trust a dyke when you've told her what you don't want so you know she won't accidentally cross your boundaries. It's important to agree on a safe word, something you could say that would automatically stop the action. . . . I've found that I use the safe word much more often because my emotional boundaries are being crossed rather than because my physical boundaries are being crossed. Again, everyone's experience is unique to her. . . .

Gabrielle Antolovich, an Australian native currently residing in San Jose, after being crowned International Ms. Leather in 1990. (Rick Gerharter)

The main issues are to talk through it openly and make sure you agree, trust each other (and if you don't trust her, either find someone else or examine your own blocks, whichever is relevant), agree on a safe word, and get all the pleasure and joy there is between you in that situation. S/M is basically about good times. It's a part of who I am to analyze and have to understand everything . . . Ultimately I wouldn't have been interested in S/M, whatever its healing value, if it hadn't been such a good time.

LEATHER QUEENS AND KINGS

Chuck Renslow and Dom Orejudos, founders of the Mr. International Leather title and owners of Chicago's famous Gold Coast Leather Bar, created the competition as an outgrowth of the Mr. Gold Coast contest, held in 1972. The first Mr. International Leather Contest was held in March 1979 in Chicago. Ten primarily local contestants competed for the title, with David Kloff of San Francisco winning. Nearly two decades later, crowds of thousands watch up to sixty contestants from around the world vie for the honor. Four days of activities surround what is referred to as the "Academy Awards of Leatherdom."

In 1987, San Francisco began holding the Ms. International Leather competition. There were already contestants from all around the United States. Hundreds of leather dykes cheered Judy Tallwing McCarthy of Portland, Oregon, in her victory. The competition has continued to thrive in the years since.

Titleholders have been active in helping local organizations around the country raise hundreds of thousands of dollars to fight AIDS. In addition, both Mr. and Ms. International Leather have been aggressive in their promotion of safer sex and condom usage.

GAYSPEAK/GAYDRESS

From language to fashion, gay people use words and clothing to stake out a place, both within our community and in society at large. The combination of words and symbols we adopt allows each of us to express our own unique senses of self.

Language is often used to help us determine who we think we are. Some of us call ourselves "gay," others use "queer"; some use "dyke," others prefer "lesbian"; some find the term "faggot" offensive and some use it with pride—syndicated newspaper advice columnist Dan Savage prefers to be addressed as "Hey Faggot!" We've taken a look at some of the origins of these word issues.

While drag queens are the extreme example, all clothes make a statement. What we wear reflects not only the popular culture of the times in which we live, but also provides a way for us to claim our own identity, and to help us recognize other lesbians and gay men. Over the decades, these fashions, as well as the symbols and icons of the lesbian and gay cultural world, have continued to evolve. In this section, we've captured some of the more universal icons in mid-evolution and organized them by decade.

Gayspeak vs. Phobespeak

Gay people and homophobes are constantly struggling against one another to define the language of sexuality and politics. In the same way that the religious right uses "pro-life" (implying their opponents are "anti-life") while reproductive rights activists use "pro-choice," in an attempt to sway the media and public toward their causes, gay men and lesbians have a language that is often at odds with the language used by homophobes to describe the same thing. Below are some examples of "Gayspeak vs. Phobespeak":

Gayspeak	***Phobespeak***
Lesbian and Gay Movement	Gay Agenda
Gay man	Sodomite
Gay men and lesbians	Perverts, Deviants
Queers	Queers
Gay people	Homosexuals
Equal rights	Special rights
White, heterosexual, procreative, dogmatically Christian, patriarchal ideology that seeks to legislate aggressive discrimination against single parents, women, people of color, and gay people	Family values
Sexuality	Gay lifestyle choice
Sex	Sodomy
People with AIDS	Plague victims
Feminist	Feminazi

DID YOU KNOW...

According to George Chauncey, Jr., author of *Gay New York*, the phrase "coming out" used to mean coming *into* gay life, such as having a debut party, as opposed to coming out of hiding. "Coming out of the closet" didn't have its present meaning until after 1966.

True Confessions of a Queer Banana

Names, the identities we give ourselves.

Over the years, due to direct political action, and social and economic shifts, the words that we use to describe ourselves have been rescued from derogatory usage of the mainstream. We are dykes. We are queers. We are fags. Many of us have found strength, support, and love through our sexual identity. But we are by no means a homogeneous community. We are split by sexual practice, gender, politics, race, culture, class, food preferences.

I am a queer banana. I say this with a need to reclaim a definition that has haunted me since childhood. An insult, an accusation that one is in disguise, a traitor—yellow on the outside and white on the inside. I don't see how watching *The Brady Bunch* or going to an Osmond Brothers concert could make me a traitor. I am of Japanese descent but I am third-generation Canadian.

SPEAKING IN CODE

It's not always a good idea to announce that someone else is "queer"—in a workplace, for example, where everyone may not already know. It is times like these that have given rise to some of the code words and phrases that are used by gay men and lesbians to identify other gay people without coming out and saying "she's a dyke" or "he's gay, too."

Friend of Dorothy
Member of the tribe
Member of the family
Sings in the choir
Walking the lavender path
In the same church
A sister
A brother

Many of my Asian-American friends have other terms to define themselves. Nip-anese. Chink-ese. OY-IN (Outwardly Yellow, Inwardly Neutral). But somehow the term "queer banana" (or bana) is one that I feel most at home with. It is simple, direct, and visually striking.

How we decide to name ourselves and what term we end up feeling comfortable with is not without its problems. In a world of constant change and evolutionary wordplay, the real intent and meaning of these self-described names is sometimes lost. I call myself a "queer banana," but I know how this can be used against me. I know how this term can be misinterpreted and how by naming my identity I am still open to misunderstanding. The context and history of this term are personal, and I would never use "queer banana" to describe someone else. I believe it is important to encourage the continual process of self-examination and self-definition. Today I may be a "queer banana" but tomorrow I may not be. But whichever way I decide to describe myself, the meaning will be one of my choosing and my design.

— **MIDI ONODERA**

What's in a Color?

"Our color is purple, or lavender. No one knows why this is, it just is."

—Judy Grahn's first lover, quoted in Another Mother Tongue: Gay Words, Gay Worlds.

How did the colors purple and lavender come to be associated with lesbians and gay men? Judy Grahn, the poet and author, has done much research into the question and uncovered a number of interesting facts:

- **Violets,** which are related to pansies, were worn in England in the 1500s by men and women to indicate that they did not intend to marry.
- In Greek mythology, **Narcissus** scorned the love of women, fell in love with his own image, and eventually died. In his place grew a purple flower surrounded by white leaves (the narcissus).

DID YOU KNOW...

The collective noun for a group of lesbians is simply "a world of lesbians."

• In another Greek myth, the maid **Persephone,** daughter of Demeter, was gathering flowers with twenty-three other young women, when she reached for a brilliant purple narcissus and the earth opened and she was swept into the spiritworld. She became a queen of the Underworld and lifelong companion to the crone goddess Hekate.

• The **hyacinth** is another purple flower named for the love between two men, the Greek sun god Apollo and the youth Hyacinthus, of whom Apollo was "passionately fond."

• The Greek lesbian poet **Sappho** has been described as violet-haired. The fragments of her poetry that remain make seven references to the color purple, five to violets or violet-colored, and two to purple hyacinth.

• One hundred years after Sappho, purple appeared in a poem by the Greek poet **Anacreon,** in what is the oldest known poem to explicitly record the use of the word "Lesbian" as a reference to a woman who loves other women, and not just a resident of Lesbos.

• A name for one purple Greek dye from the ancient cities of Sidon and Tyre was **Paideros,** which also meant "boy-lover."

• In **medieval times**, purple was worn by court jesters, wise men and women, astrologers, and soothsayers.

• The Yoruba religion of West Africa, known also as *Macumba,* worships a powerful trilogy of goddesses including **Oya,** who appears wearing men's clothing and weapons and whose special color is purple.

• Native American tradition includes the Caddo Indian story of a **gay shaman** who had the bewitching powers of a sorcerer; his life was protected by the presence of a purple spot on his left little finger.

• Another more contemporary theory is that lavender, which is created by **combining pink and blue** (the traditional colors used in American society for distinguishing girls and boys at birth), represents the merging of the male and female, and it is a perfect symbol for a group of people who do not fit traditional gender expectations.

HOW GAY IS GAY?

There are several theories about the origin of the word "gay." Researcher John Boswell traces the use of the word as a noun back to the eleventh century. In his book *Same-Sex Unions in Pre-Modern Europe,* he writes that it comes from the Portuguese *gai,* which meant "love outside marriage" until its use focused to mean homosexual. Many writers believe, however, that the term was originally an adjective, as in "gay club," and that its use as a noun emerged after World War II. Others theorize that the word derives from the Greek name Gaia, goddess of the earth.

Then there is the definition of gay seen on the Internet: "Gay is the feeling you get when all of the straight people leave the room."

The origin of "lesbian" is clear: It derives from the name Lesbos, the small Greek island that was home to the famous woman-loving-woman poet Sappho.

DID YOU KNOW...

The pink triangle, the most widely recognized of all gay symbols, was derived from Nazi death camps. Gay men were forced to wear pink triangles to mark them, as Jews wore yellow Stars of David. The gay power movement adopted the triangle to turn a symbol of degradation into one of pride. Lesbians, who were not singled out in the camps, were sometimes arrested as prostitutes and forced to wear the black triangle worn by those branded criminals.

DID YOU KNOW...

The labrys, a symbol adopted by many in the lesbian community, is a Greek double-bladed ax thought to have been wielded by the legendary Amazon warriors in battle.

Symbolically Queer — Gay and Lesbian Icons of the 1970s, 1980s, and 1990s

Being gay is so much more than sex—there are a gigantic number of people, places, and things that are quintessentially gay and lesbian. Here are just a few era-specific examples:

Gay Male 1970s
Sylvester
San Francisco
discos
Crisco
Charles Pierce
amyl nitrate (poppers)
bathhouses
Casey Donovan
Bette Midler
"Gay Is Good"

Lesbian 1970s
double women's symbol
labyris
"Woman-identified-woman"
gym teachers
Sappho
menstrual sponges
collectives
lesbian separatism
Meg Christian
softball

Gay Male 1980s
"safe sex"
Sisters of Perpetual Indulgence
Boy George
phone sex
Harvey Fierstein
"Clean and Sober"
j-o parties
Madonna
"Silence = Death"
radical faeries

Lesbian 1980s
leatherdykes
Lily Tomlin
tattoos
Desert Hearts
On Our Backs
Tracy Chapman
Twelve-Step meetings
Clit Club
Olivia Cruises
Cagney and Lacey

Gay Male 1990s
"safer sex"
Queer Nation
Calvin Klein ads
virtual sex
pride paraphernalia
Sandra Bernhard
body piercing
sex clubs
RuPaul
Genre

Lesbian 1990s
Sandra Bernhard
Melissa Etheridge
Deneuve
riot grrls
body piercing
strap-ons
dental dams
butch/femme
Lesbian Avengers
Dorothy Allison

History of the Rainbow Flag

A highlight of the 1994 Stonewall 25 March in New York City was the thirty-foot wide and mile-long Rainbow Flag, carried by close to 10,000 people. Designed by flag expert Gilbert Baker out of thousands of pounds of material, the flag was the centerpiece of the "Raise the Rainbow" project.

Baker is credited as being the creator of the original Rainbow Flag. The artist proposed the design to the 1978 San Francisco Gay Freedom Day Parade organizing committee in response to their request for a symbol that could be used every year. Thirty volunteers hand-dyed and hand-stitched the two huge flags for the 1978 parade.

The first rainbow design had eight horizontal stripes, from top to bottom: hot pink for sex, red for life, orange for healing, yellow for sun, green for serenity with nature, turquoise for art, indigo for harmony, and violet for spirit. For the 1979 parade, due to production constraints, hot pink and turquoise stripes were dropped and royal blue replaced the indigo stripe. Thus, the current six-striped flag (red, orange, yellow, green, blue, and violet) was created and adopted.

— STEVE VEZERIS

DID YOU KNOW...

A variant to the Rainbow Flag was proposed in response to the AIDS crisis. A San Francisco group designed a "Victory Over AIDS" flag—a Rainbow Flag with a black stripe at the bottom. While dying of AIDS, Sergeant Leonard Matlovich, the much-decorated Vietnam veteran, proposed that when a cure for AIDS was found, the black stripes should be removed from all the flags and should be ceremoniously burned in Washington, D.C.

Fashion Is Such a Drag—The Clothes We Wear

Lesbian and gay styles and fashions have changed a lot over the past thirty years. Here are some of the popular looks from each decade:

Gay Men 1970s

"clone" look
tight, short cutoff jeans
flannel shirts
hanky codes
tight muscle shirts
genderfuck
long hair, mustaches
one earring (right ear)
Tony Llamas boots
crystals

Lesbians 1970s

flannel shirts
one earring
Birkenstocks
handkerchief tied around the neck
hiking boots
overalls
braless
men's vests
crystals

DID YOU KNOW...

In the early 1970s, the Los Angeles gay community created a flag with a simple lavender lambda on a plain white field, which they hoped would catch on throughout the country. Widespread appeal was limited, unfortunately, as some saw the lambda as an exclusively male symbol.

Gay Men 1980s
Izod shirts
khaki pants
black leather jackets
short, groomed hair
five o'clock shadow
Speedos
tight running shorts
cable-knit sweaters
ACT UP T-shirts
Levis 501s

Lesbians 1980s
Crew shirts, collar up
ear cuffs
black leather jackets
STLB hair
(short top, long back)
rattail with ribbons
bolo ties
peroxide-blond hair
running shoes
sports jacket
(sleeves rolled up)
lipstick

Gay Men 1990s
multiple body piercings
Gap clothes
shaved head
white T-shirts
60s/70s secondhand clothes
shaved bodies
baggy jeans
pride paraphernalia
Calvin Klein underwear
multiple tattoos

Lesbians 1990s
multiple body piercings
wallet with chain attached
shaved head
white T-shirts
overalls
shaved legs
baggy jeans
pride paraphernalia
Doc Martens
multiple tattoos

DID YOU KNOW...

In 1993, Mattel came out with Earring Magic Ken, a Ken doll sporting an earring, a large ring on a necklace, and a mesh lavender shirt with matching purple vest. The doll instantly became a camp classic, with gay men nationwide running to toy stores to buy it. Mattel denied any intention to create a gay Ken.

If I Simply Wanted Status, I'd Wear Calvin Klein

I have never been a slave to fashion, so it was simply rash of me to think I could boldly wear my fireball-red FAG CLUB T-shirt in public and not be confronted. I had purchased the T-shirt in San Francisco without any hesitation whatsoever. In fact, I purchased two T-shirts: the red athletic T and the black crewneck, both bearing FAG CLUB prominently displayed in bold white letters stacked across the front. Mind you, the day I wore that T-shirt all over Washington, D.C., I was truly voguing. I was featuring heavy transgression in a town of government secrets, political intrigue, and kinky sex.

The confrontation did not occur downtown or on the bus or subway as I thought it might. I was in my neighborhood, Mt. Pleasant, when it happened. People I had encountered on the buses and downtown sidewalks didn't challenge me. They were surprised by the T-shirt, as indicated by the number of double takes it received.

What with ripped jeans, black belts, a beaded necklace, a long-sleeve T-shirt, and a backwards baseball cap, these men sport the latest in gay fashions during the Gay Pride parade in 1993. (Rink Foto)

The red was tinted with a little orange and was very eye-catching in the summer sun. By the time I returned to Mt. Pleasant later that afternoon, I had completely forgotten I was wearing it. I had never flaunted my sexuality so immediately to so many. I had never communicated my sexual identity so intentionally as I did by choosing to wear that FAG CLUB T-shirt in public.

I needed to get a few things for dinner before going home, so I stopped at the supermarket a few blocks from my apartment. As the market doors swooshed behind me and I passed through the entrance turnstile, a young boy screamed out, "Look, everybody, there's a faggot in the store!" You would have thought people were supposed to start diving to the floor.

I stopped only for an instant to look over my shoulder to see whom he was calling out. Seeing no one behind me, when I looked ahead again I realized everyone was looking at me. I then remembered I was wearing FAG CLUB emblazoned on my chest like the name Superhero.

I immediately stepped forward in full control of my location and my presence of mind. I know this scene must have looked very funny, but I was determined to keep my composure. There were little bursts of laughter here and there but nothing too serious. I glided down the aisles, completing my short grocery list and avoiding direct eye contact, until I reached the checkout line. The clerk looked at my T-shirt and smiled. I smiled back at her, then she turned and began ringing my groceries.

"Most gay bashers will be wearing what gay people had on four years earlier —only in polyester with a Penney's label."

PLAYWRIGHT PAUL RUDNICK IN THE WASHINGTON POST, APRIL 25, 1993

Just then, the young boy who had shouted "There's a faggot in the store!" came up to me from the exit of the checkout line. He was a curly-haired, ten-year-old Black boy.

"Hey, mister, I have a cousin like you. He's gay, too."

He continued approaching until he was standing beside me. I looked into his face and saw no fear, no hatred, no disgust.

"Did you get that in Washington?" he asked, pointing to my T-shirt. "My cousin would like one of those."

He was not the least bit shy in telling me this. He looked me directly in the eye, waiting for my response.

"No, I didn't get this in Washington," I told him. "I got it in San Francisco. You can get them there."

"I thought so," he said. "I didn't think you could get a T-shirt like that in D.C. I like it. See you!" Then he turned and left.

I stood there momentarily disarmed by his candor and only a little self-conscious about my interaction with him. How we appeared to the others watching us did not cross my mind. But then I thought, if I simply wanted status I could wear Calvin Klein and strike a pose. That's safe.

— ESSEX HEMPHILL

"[Gay people] pick up on things faster than straight mainstream America does. They don't pick up on it, I believe, any faster than street kids or trendy kids of any sexual orientation. I think gay kids borrow from homeboys and trendies borrow from gay people."

FRANK DECARO, NEW YORK NEWSDAY COLUMNIST, IN THE WASHINGTON POST, APRIL 25, 1993

The Minefield of Lesbian Fashion

"Wrong," Jackie said, shaking her head. We had just worked out. I was putting on my sneakers, white Nikes over black-and-white wool argyle socks.

"No dress socks with tennis shoes," she said. "And your socks have to be lighter than your shoes. And with sports shoes, the socks have to be cotton."

I sat frozen to the bench. Hadn't I read years of *Glamour* magazine's "Do's and Don't's"? And hadn't I winced at the photos of girls in the wrong coats, carrying the wrong bags, layering the wrong sweaters, those photos of slight girls on windy New York streets with black brick-like bars slapped over their faces to save them from what could only be acute embarrassment?

But here I was, a lesbian voted "Best Dressed" of the 1976 Senior Class of San Clemente High School, IN THE WRONG SOCKS.

(Alison Bechdel)

I had slipped. The black-and-white photo—a black slash across my face—the caption: "Dress socks with sport shoes? DON'T."

"But, Jackie," I pleaded. "These are warm. And besides, they tie the white of the sneakers into the black of my jeans . . ."

"Forget it, girlfriend," Jackie said like the New York dyke that she is. "Get yourself to the Gap."

The minefield of lesbian fashion.

It's treacherous. A constantly shifting battlefield demanding changing strategies and perspectives.

When I came out in the early eighties, I was living in Auckland, New Zealand. I dressed with care, having no one to ask, no cross reference. How I wished I was back in high school with the old gang so I would call a pal: What are you wearing? I was in my late-punk stage, long curly hair, a stripe of red—geranium red—over one temple. After many changes of clothes, I set this coif against a torn T-shirt that featured black bombers silhouetted against a paint-spattered backdrop. My miniskirt: red, black, and green. Finally, red pumps. Pointy, sixties retro. Inch-high heels. Lipstick to match. My roommates at the time—straight girls not unsympathetic to my experimentation—approved enthusiastically. "You look hot," Julie said. (I should have been suspicious of such support.)

I visited my first lesbian bar with much näiveté:

At our entrance it seemed as if everything stopped. Everyone turned and stared. My date (a misnomer, I soon found out) disappeared into the dark, and I was left standing against the wall feeling like I did in the seventh grade at my first dance when I had finally convinced my mother to let me shave my legs and wear "hose," only to find the other girls in hip-hugger corduroy trousers.

So here I was again, the only one in a dress, not to mention makeup. The swarms of jeans-clad, sweatshirted, army-booted dykes circled with some disdain before a brave butch soul asked me to dance. Okay, sure we got together, but not for a few weeks and not until I had cut my hair, purchased black jeans, hightops, and a motorcycle jacket.

A year or so later, gals started wearing a spot of eyeliner—an especially nice complement to leather and studs—and pretty much all you saw on anyone was black highlighted by glints of metal. Not long after, I moved myself stateside, to San Francisco, where the range of lesbo fashion sent me reeling. I marched into my first dyke bar in black regalia only to find myself amidst—what? Straight girls? Nope, femmes! Beautiful Latina women in clothes from Macy's and long fingernails—at least on most fingers . . . And a gang of softball dykes, who looked like they leapt out of an L.L. Bean catalogue. You even saw older gals in polyester pantsuits with butches in men's trousers. Young punks in long underwear leashed—often literally—to girlfriends in little more than rags and safety pins. Gads! Anything was possible. What was a young dyke to do?

I'm not such a young dyke anymore, but still my fashion dilemmas haven't been solved. And in some ways they get more complicated. I think the hows and whats of dyke dressing are always mitigated by bigger issues:

Where do you live? How out are you? Do you want people to know you're a dyke? Are you dressing as a dyke among dykes or a dyke among straights? Fashion has to do with political choices; what's out or in has to do with one's own out-ness or in-ness, and where the political climate is swaying.

My little town is so queer that many of these questions become twisted. Provincetown is a place where anyone can be anything and there is certainly one of everything. I can dress completely "straight" here—in fact, I now look more "mainstream" than I ever have, because no one assumes heterosexuality. Many of us locals have long hair, wear dresses and makeup. And when the gal *turistas* descend in droves, we're always amazed at how "dykey" they look. Everywhere there are music festival T-shirts and Girbaud jeans and high-top sneakers. There are jock couples in matching neon shorts and schoolteachers from the Midwest in khaki safari pants. Is there anything wrong with a lesbo look? No. And I can guess that in their hometowns such dressing is a clue to others, an underground code. The short-back-and-sides haircut of the bus driver is a message to the short-back-and-sides secretary. But here in Queersville not much of this seems necessary.

"Every man should own at least one dress—and so should lesbians."

LESBIAN ACTIVIST JANE ADAMS SPAHR

My final digression: I have this unbelievable Polaroid picture dated on its curling edge July 1969. I was ten years old in this picture, taken at a summer camp carnival. I had decided I wanted to be "half-girl" and "half-boy" for the occasion. On the left side, I am a girl: I've got a skirt fastened on one leg and a pink polyester shell that shows just the bud of a breast. My long blond hair is wavy and loose, and the red lipstick is carefully portioned over half of each lip. On the other side I've done the boy thing: a black vest, tight jeans, a single cowboy boot, my hair slicked back tight against my head. Both sides of me, girl and boy, are grinning wide.

In some ways I've spanned both sides of that early view of what I now see as my nascent lesbianism. I do the boy thing, I do the girl thing, I even do the cowboy thing. But, according to Jackie, and I'm apt to trust her, I still wear the wrong socks.

— LOUISE RAFKIN

STANDING OUT IN A CROWD

Most gay and lesbian people spend the majority of their time surrounded by nongay people—in the grocery store, at work, waiting for the bus. Gay pride marches and parades, which are both political endeavors and joyous celebrations, give lesbian and gay people an opportunity to be truly visible to each other and the nongay world.

Marches give gay people a way to publicly express the pride most of us try to feel on a daily basis. On the street, with thousands of other gay people, we can smile and sing, march and proclaim ourselves, and let ourselves feel joy in being gay.

CAN YOU BELIEVE IT?

Jesse Helms, from his tirade after seeing video clips of past San Francisco lesbian and gay pride parades: "I wish every American could have seen it."

Gay and lesbian parades also serve to remind the nongay population that we are an important, vital part of society, from the smallest midwestern town to the largest cities in the country.

Lesbians and gay men also feel safety and freedom walking down the street with thousands of other people just like us. For one day, we don't have to look over our shoulders before we grab our lover's hand or kiss our partner in public. We get to take up space, proclaim our politics and our love, and remind ourselves (and the public at large) that we deserve this freedom.

And most of all, marches are fun! When else do you get to cruise men and women openly, shout slogans at right-wing fanatics, and take over the whole damned street?

Why Have a Gay Pride Parade?

It was asked more in fun than with envy, more in joking than with malice, but it struck a chord with me. I had casually mentioned to a couple of my straight friends that the Gay Pride Parade was coming up and I was looking forward to it.

"What about Straight Pride Day?" the female of the couple asked with a grin.

"Every day is Straight Pride Day," I answered, also grinning. "This culture celebrates it with gay abandon." She laughed.

"When do we get our parade?" demanded her male counterpart.

"Turn the television on," I said. "There's your parade." We all laughed and went about our business, but the brief exchange kept coming back to me through the week. The more I thought about it, the more serious it became.

Why have a Gay Pride Parade? It's a question many straight people might be asking. Gay people, I believe, inherently, intuitively know why we have a parade. We have a Gay Pride Parade because in 1969 a bunch of queers at the Stonewall Inn fought back. We have a Gay Pride Parade so that at least for one day in a year we can walk down the streets of where we live and show our numbers for all the world to see. We have a Gay Pride Parade to celebrate our defeat of The Closet, to have a day when we can proclaim, without reservation, who we are and who we love.

So when do the straight people get their own parade?

When straight people are prevented from marrying the people they choose to marry, precluded from enjoying tax benefits available to married people, then they should have a parade. When straight people are barred from serving their country in the military, then they should have a parade. When straight people are routinely fired from their jobs because of whom they love or live with, then they should have a parade. When straight people are blocked from holding sensitive jobs in the government merely because of their sexual orientation, then they should have a parade. When straight people are forbidden to raise their own children or adopt, then they should have a parade. When straight people are beaten, harassed, and shot at for holding hands in public then I'll be marching there with them.

A man who lives in my neighborhood was shot on our street two years ago by a carload of young thugs because he was bidding a male companion farewell with an embrace. The Human Rights Commissioner of my city publicly intimated that the men were "asking for it" through engaging in "provocative behavior" by embracing to say good-bye. That's why I'll be at the Gay Pride Parade. Unless we stand together, march together, care together, no one will do it for us. We gay and lesbian people are on our own and we must depend on each other.

DID YOU KNOW...

Washington, D.C., is home to Black Lesbian and Gay Pride Day at the end of May each year. Ernest Hopkins, Theodore Kirkland, and Wellmore Cook founded the event in 1991 as a fund-raiser for AIDS service organizations and for outreach in the African American community. The first year the event lasted one day, with just over 1,000 people attending. By 1994, nearly 8,000 people from around the United States and the world came to a week-long celebration marked by a film festival, several large parties, and a fair on Banneker Field across from Howard University. For the fourth annual event, D.C. mayor Sharon Pratt Kelly officially proclaimed May 29 Black Gay and Lesbian Pride Day. The young tradition has already raised tens of thousands of dollars for AIDS organizations.

So when some well-meaning, or not so well-meaning, straight acquaintance of yours questions the need for a Gay Pride Parade, educate the poor soul. I'm picking up the phone to call my two friends now.

— DAVID NAVA

DID YOU KNOW...

On June 28, 1970, a gay pride parade up New York's Sixth Avenue drew an estimated 10,000 gay men and lesbians to celebrate the first anniversary of the Stonewall Riots. "It serves notice on every politician in the state and nation," said one participant, "that homosexuals are not going to hide anymore." Marchers chanted slogans of "Two, four, six, eight! Gay is just as good as straight!" and "Out of the closets! Into the streets!" One woman carried a sign reading "Homosexuality is not a four-letter word," while another held aloft a placard reading "Hi, Mom!" A dachshund trotting with its owner had a sign tied to its back: "Me Too!" The parade culminated in a "gay-in" at Central Park, where couples leisurely held hands, kissed, and smoked pot.

Where Do I Belong in this Parade, Anyway?

Deciding which contingent to march with at the annual gay pride parade in your city can be as difficult for many lesbians as deciding what to bring to the next potluck. Louise Rafkin has provided some helpful hints for the gals.

Lesbians in Limbo: I think this contingent has a huge potential, and could very well be one of the largest groups in the parade. We would, of course, have various limbo ropes with loud limbo music playing, and a large banner reading "How Low Can We Go?" Marchers would be expected to periodically try a little limbo-ing. What? You don't remember how to limbo? Simple: Bend back at a precarious angle and waggle your hips mucho. Hop, hop, hop. This would be hard on the calves and tush, I'd imagine, but if those queens can sashay that strip in five-inch spikes, us gals should at least be able to dip our hips. Starting practicing now. There are several subsets to the Limbo group:

Relationship Limbo: For those gals who don't know quite where they stand. Half in or half out? Are we lovers or are we friends? Break-up or break-through? And what about all the friends of these women? The ones who say to each other, "Are they really broken up or are they at it again?" Limbo-land definitely.

Career Limbo: I always watch the parade on the lookout for a career. There are all the helping groups, teachers, lawyers, lesbian and gay this-and-that-ers. You'd think I could have found a career by now. (I'll admit: I was awfully tempted by firefighting—something about the ambience . . .) Anyway, I'm still considering dental hygiene and dog grooming (although I'm allergic), but in the meantime, I'm definitely in career limbo. I think this group should bring dress-up clothes for various professions, and while marching, we could swap horror stories about our old jobs while changing outfits and trying on new hats—so to speak. On to other groups . . .

Lesbian Homeowners: Yes, I might march with this group, although really I've only paid for a doorknob or two. This group could pull wagons filled with various do-it-yourself books—while simultaneously pulling their hair. Our clothes would be wet (from the floods) and paint-spattered, and several marchers could have bandages on their limbs from misusing "simple" home fix-it tools. Calculators and small bits of paper with various figures figured various ways (and then crossed over) could float from our pockets. On several occasions I've joined the Living Sober crowd, and it's always been great. But this year as I watched them party-past, I thought of a new group:

(Denise Ratliff)

Living Emotionally Sober: This might well be a smaller group than the Living Sober mass, and my pal Rita even thought it might be one of those groups you can only walk in for part of the parade—is anyone really emotionally sober for the length of time it takes to walk an entire parade route? We thought perhaps small, still emotionally sober children could carry the banner. Or perhaps—

though the animal rights folks would never stand for it—dogs could lead this group. I've known some very emotionally sober dogs, but then, what about those Irish setters? Anyway, kids and canines aside, next year I hope to at least be in the group momentarily. . . .

Lesbians for the preservation of the California Desert Tortoise: Yes, my first love is tortoises. Rita suggested that I might march with my beloved pets next year, but then added that the parade perhaps already goes on too long. Perhaps me and my four-legged friends could start a day before. . . .

Co-Gay: This is an idea for a general section of the parade. My pal Babs offered this as a theme to encourage more straight folks to march. It also umbrellas all the dandy groups already marching, like Parents and Friends, etc. Also, a section for straight best friends who have to hear all your life's dish and traumas.

— LOUISE RAFKIN

DID YOU KNOW...

Beginning in 1965, four years prior to the Stonewall Riots, several homophile organizations staged an annual demonstration on July Fourth in front of Independence Hall in Philadelphia. Called "The Annual Reminder," the fifth demonstration took place just a few days after the New York riots. Later that fall, the organizers decided to move the 1970 event to New York to commemorate the anniversary of Stonewall, and the tradition of annual gay pride marches began.

Marching for Power: The Gay and Lesbian Marches on Washington and Stonewall 25

In 1979, more than 100,000 gay men and lesbians came to Washington, D.C., from around the country and around the world to take part in the first of several historic marches for lesbian and gay rights. Though well attended, there was little mainstream media coverage of the event, and the major news weeklies simply ignored it.

In 1987, gay people again took to the streets of the nation's capital, in much greater numbers. The nearly half-a-million participants came from every state, as well as many countries. And while there was significant mainstream media coverage of the march in several mainstream newspapers, much of the national press, including the major weekly magazines, ignored the event.

Six years later, in April 1993, the hotels and hostels of Washington, D.C., and the surrounding areas were again booked as an estimated one million people came to march for gay, lesbian, and bisexual rights. Many gay people felt that after twelve years of Ronald Reagan and George Bush they finally had a friend in the White House in Bill Clinton. This time the media had caught on. CNN

Hundreds of thousands of gay people gathered in Washington, D.C., for the 1987 March on Washington for Lesbian and Gay Rights. (Marc Geller)

provided live coverage of all six hours of the march and the rally on the Mall. Both ABC and NBC broadcast their morning television shows live from Washington. Almost every major daily newspaper in the country headlined the march the following day. And the national weekly news magazines each devoted at least one major column in their Monday editions to the issues being addressed by the marchers.

The Stonewall 25 commemoration in June 1994 attracted an estimated total of 1.1 million people from eighty-four countries and all fifty states. Unfortunately, media coverage for Stonewall 25 was significantly less than that for the March on Washington the previous year.

Impressions of the March

Tom's favorite sign in the march was a simple one saying "Gay Dentist." My own sign said "Country Faggot" on one side, and on the other, "Homophobia and Nuclear Power—Two Things We Can Do Without." My "Country Faggot" sign won me many smiles. A guy came over to me to shake my hand and confide that he was a "city faggot." A few country dykes waved. I wasn't the only one at the march concerned about nuclear power. The issue was mentioned several times by speakers, and one of the largest and prettiest banners was New York's "Dykes Opposed to Nuclear Technology," or DONT. It was fun running into my Vermont friends, Vicki, Lynn, and Jeremiah. I had just seen them at the big demonstration two weeks before in southern Vermont, where we protested the Vermont Yankee nuclear power plant.

Two women come out of the crowd to show their pride at the 1987 March on Washington. (©JEB)

My neighbor Denis had a sign saying "Sex Is Fun," and he won many smiles with that one. The prize-winning T-shirt (which appeared in a UPI photo) said "I don't molest children and I don't do windows."

I loved Robin Tyler. She was funny, radical, friendly, intelligent, pro-sex. Everyone (especially the dykes) laughed at Robin's comments about the irony of gathering at the foot of the Washington Monument. Another favorite line from Robin Tyler's rap was "Anita Bryant is to Christianity what painting by numbers is to art."

— ALLEN YOUNG

When I First Saw Audre Lorde

I reclined on the grass among the sea of faces. We were all smiling. A good many of them were trying to spot people they knew. Once again I felt alone. I knew that few of them could really understand how isolating and threatening it is for a person of color to be so surrounded. But by now I was full of adrenaline that was shooting through us all and the joy that filled the air.

I relaxed, listening to speeches, scanning the crowd, simply taking everyone in. I saw black faces scattered in the groupings, but no one I knew. Until I spotted Audre Lorde. She was standing several yards away from me, tall above those seated on the ground. I'd been reading her work since the 1960s but had only seen her from a distance at readings. She was unmistakable, though—the brightly colored African-print cap on her head, her penetrating eyes. I started to wave, as if I really knew her, and continued to watch as she talked to someone sitting below her. Then she looked over and caught my gaze. She winked conspiratorially, as if she knew I needed to make that connection with another Black lesbian. The wink was both flirtatious and sisterly. It opened up a dialogue between us that lasted for more than a decade.

— JEWELLE GOMEZ

Gay, Gifted, and Black, There Ain't No Turning Back

Suddenly, a feeling which seemed so contrary to everything this march was about struck me. I was feeling very much alone, and very lonely. In the midst of hundreds of thousands of lesbians and gays, I was ensconced in solitude. I felt like I wanted to bring my late lover Marc back, wipe the Kaposi's lesions from his face, breathe new life into his contaminated lungs, and see the optimism of his smile once again. . . .

A Black queen from Baltimore with a bandaged foot and a cane had joined me and my friends. He pointed out the men he wanted to duck, suck, fuck—without even the vaguest allusions to latex—in the middle of Jesse Jackson's speech. I shushed him, wondering why he'd even come out (pardon the pun) and realized that, of course, it was because to him, this was the hottest cruising spot in the mid-Atlantic, and little else.

While Jesse encouraged us all to join together in a unified fight against the injustices of AIDS and lesbian/gay discrimination, I felt the absence of another's arms, envisioned the static poses of so many who should have marched but opted to look on instead and listened to the Baltimore queen. Our challenge of consciousness raising is not limited to the heterosexually impaired, but extends into our own ranks as well. So come on.

— CRAIG G. HARRIS

Remembrances

At the Congressional Cemetery, the ashes of Harvey Milk were interred near the graves of Dolly Madison, Matthew Brady, John Phillip Sousa, and J. Edgar Hoover.

Along with Harvey's ashes, his friends buried a photograph, a piece of his ponytail, and several other mementos. They joked that this was not a time capsule to be dug up at a later date.

Despite the humor, the interment was a solemn occasion, and many were moved to tears. Said activist Morris Knight of Los Angeles, "Never again will we allow members of our community to die in anonymity. . . . We will be there to say, 'Goodbye, brother. Goodbye sister.'"

On Sunday, by far the most moving aspect was the Names Quilt. The *Washington Post*, in a front-page article Saturday, called it "the emotional focal point; and most dramatic symbol of the march." It certainly was that.

At sunset, beset by October's bone-chilling winds, we retreated to the subway to shout a few final slogans and wave farewell to fellow marchers disappearing up the escalators.

— MIKE HIPPLER

The 1993 March on Washington

The train from New York to Washington on Friday evening was practically taken over by people going to the March. The few heterosexuals were keeping their heads low and were generally quite uncomfortable. I savored every minute of this rare reversal of roles. When we reached Washington, the train station was full of gay people. For someone like me who grew up in

India loving trains and train stations, it was especially delightful. Can you imagine Victoria Terminus in Bombay suddenly becoming completely gay?

Most cheers were elicited by the gay soldiers who have become the new heroes of the movement because of the public and bitter fight going on to lift the ban on homosexuals serving in the armed forces. All twenty-five of us marched behind the SALGA (South Asian Lesbian & Gay Association) banner and were cheered all the way by onlookers. Our contingent was part of the larger Asian-Pacific Islander contingent, which chanted, "We are Queer, we are Asian, we are all across the nation."

— **NIRAJ**

The Starting Gate

We just started walking — through P-FLAG, Kentucky, and the S/M Leather contingents, not knowing who was who until we got past them and turned around to read their placards. By the time we got to the starting gate and the group we were in at the moment started to move as a unit, we were with Colorado, so we stayed with them to the Mall. We screamed "SHAME!" at the few fundamentalist protesters. We listened to Martina and a host of other speakers, and by the time we were ready to go, we both felt truly empowered: We owe it to ourselves and each other to fight the status quo until we win our rights.

I wish I could say that I came home and came out in a big way: becoming an activist and anarchist, shucking my job, piercing my ears, wearing Doc Martens, and telling the Establishment to shove it. But I didn't. I'm still in the same job, same suit and tie. But I'm continuing to come out in many smaller ways. I have gotten more involved in the community. My dates and relationships are no longer androgynous and anonymous—they're now male and have names. Friends who are PWAs are no longer afflicted with some unknown or undiagnosed illness—they're now fighting AIDS, and we discuss the symptoms and treatments openly and honestly. I have begun to pick my fights.

— **STEVE VEZERIS**

Stonewall 25—A Celebration

Yes, I went to the Stonewall commemoration and saw more queers in one place than I'd ever seen before. There had never been anything like this magnificent outpouring of pride and freedom. It was such a powerful demonstration of strength, so beautiful and liberating; we would never be turned back! It was 1970. And all the same could be said for Stonewall 25 in 1994.

In 1970, there were "only" 10,000 of us—but imagine 10,000 self-declared queers marching up Sixth Avenue in 1970!—a ragtag band of homo hippies, freaks, and radicals from the oddest fringe of society, carrying hand-made picket signs, announcing a year of networking and organizing, inviting others to join us in a new struggle. The media did their best to ignore us.

Now in 1994 we are over a million, celebrating a quarter century of accomplishments that in 1970 nobody expected we would live to see. The New York City Library displayed a wonderful history of the Gay Movement from Stonewall to today, announced by a great lavender triangle on a banner out front. Hotel marquees welcomed gay athletes and Stonewall marchers. Reporters from all over were eagerly interviewing participants. Gay Games, International Gay and Lesbian Association, Leather-S/M-Fetish Conference, a reunion of the Gay Liberation Front, religious services and dance parties—Queerness in all its varieties flourished beyond human reckoning.

— JACK FERTIG

Stonewall 25 Radical

Months before the events came to pass, stories were flying that both the Gay Games and Stonewall 25 were almost completely controlled, if not completely staffed, by rich, conservative white boys. One of them—who worked at the Gay Games, in fact—had fired a friend of mine, a Black lesbian, for what amounted to "insubordination." And, in this year, when lesbians and gay men were to come to this city from all over the world, somebody had the colossally arrogant idea of holding three huge benefit dances aboard the U.S.S. *Intrepid,* a battleship from which 9,000 bombing runs were staged during the Viet Nam War. So I felt I had to find whatever radical aspect remained of Stonewall 25 and the Gay Games. I think what I've found this week, in terms of modern queer radicalism, is that Power concedes nothing without a really good marketing strategy.

All 1.1 million of us have somehow understood that we would be allowed—but only for a few days—to be visible, because we've essentially given society an image of us that it could trust. I reflect on how there's really not much difference between the "commercial" and the "radical" queers, after all—except, of course, in political viewpoints; very little really shocks or outrages either side anymore—even the prospect of an oncoming police state. I think of what my friend Michael Bronski had said the day before in a panel on the Gay Liberation Front: "People keep asking, 'Isn't it *nice* to see so many same-sex couples here, so many open queers?' But we don't ask why we can't have this all the time." Now *that's* radical.

— **SUSIE DAY**

Bring
Sharon
Home
forces...
lift
the
ban
I AM
WHAT
I AM
A SIN
A SICKNESS
HOMOPHOBI
ANTI-FAMILY
A CRIME
Women
THE
QUILT.
STRIDES IN
REPORT
VIOLENC
GAY AND LESBIAN COMMUNITY

CHAPTER 8

Ensuring Our Survival

Despite attempts by antigay bigots who claim that lesbians and gay men have some diabolical "gay agenda," there is no such thing. It is clear that gay men and lesbians are a diverse group of people. We are Democrats and Republicans, socialists and anarchists, voters and nonvoters, radicals and conservatives; in short, we cross all political lines.

What gay men and lesbians *do* have in common is the desire to see a change in American society that will allow us all, gay and straight, to be treated with dignity and respect. But while we may all share this goal, we do not necessarily agree on the steps to achieve it. We only agree that steps must be taken, that our very survival depends not on sitting back and hoping for change, but on each of us being involved in creating the world we want to live in.

Lesbians and gay men stage a die-in at the 1979 March on Washington for Lesbian and Gay Civil Rights. (Bettye Lane)

From the early days of the homophile movement to the more current focus on gay and lesbian civil rights, gay people have been joining together to create associations and institutions whose mission is to secure equal rights, encourage self-love, and increase gay and lesbian visibility. We have organized political action committees, spoken at rallies, gone to law school, and committed civil disobedience to make ourselves heard. We have learned to examine the strategies of those who oppose basic rights for gay people; we have lobbied for the passage of laws that will protect us.

Gay and lesbian activists have also taken to the streets. We have blocked bridges and shut down federal buildings to make our point. And we have suffered defeat on more than one occasion with the passing of antigay initiatives, and we have lost the very visible "gays in the military" issue, at least for the time being.

At the same time, we have learned to work with other movements, to learn from them, and to build bridges with allies. We have learned that some of our best allies are the people with whom we grew up, our parents and siblings, our neighbors and teachers.

Above all, we have learned firsthand that the personal is political. Being political in our daily lives is as simple as being out of the closet and encouraging our friends and parents to come out, too. It is remembering our dead, caring for each other, realizing that daily actions, even small actions, can make a difference.

For gay men and lesbians to thrive as a people, we must continue to stand up for ourselves, to speak out, to act up when acting up is called for, to write to our politicians when writing is called for, to hold someone's hand when hand holding is all we can do. We must support our communities' efforts with time, with money, and with our hearts. Only then can we be sure that we are doing everything we can to ensure our own survival.

Urvashi Vaid's 1993 March on Washington Speech

Urvashi Vaid, a longtime political activist and former executive director of the National Gay and Lesbian Task Force, gave this speech in front of hundreds of thousands of lesbians, gay men, bisexuals and straights in Washington, D.C.

With hearts full of hope and an abiding faith in justice, we have come to Washington to speak to America. We have come to speak the truth of our lives and silence the liars. We have come to challenge the cowardly Congress to end its paralysis on moral leadership. We have come to defend our honor and win our equality. But most of all, we have come, in peace and with courage to say to America that this day marks the return from exile of the gay and lesbian people.

We are banished no more. We wander the wilderness of despair no more. We are afraid no more. This day marks the end of the power of fear, which has defined our lives. For on this day, with love in our hearts, we have come to reach out to all America to build a bridge of understanding and progress, a majestic bridge as solid as steel, a bridge to a land where no one suffers prejudice because of their sexual orientation, their race, their gender, their religion, or their human difference.

I've been asked by the March organizers to speak about the Far Right, which threatens the construction of this bridge—about the extremist Right, which has targeted every one of us; about the supremacist Right, which seeks to redefine the very meaning of democracy. Language itself fails in this task, for to call our opponents the Right states a profound untruth.

They are wrong. They are wrong. They are wrong. They are wrong spiritually, they are wrong morally, and they are wrong politically.

The Christian supremacists are wrong spiritually when they demonize us and reduce the complexity and beauty of our spirit into a freak show. They are wrong spiritually because if we are the untouchables of American society, then we are, indeed, as Mahatma Gandhi said, its children of god. And as god's children, we know that the gods of our understanding, the gods of goodness and love and righteousness, march with us today.

The supremacists who lead the antigay crusade are wrong morally. They are wrong because justice is moral, and prejudice is evil. Because truth is moral and the lie of the closet is the real sin. Because their claim of morality is a subterfuge, a strategy that hides their true aim, which is much more secular.

These supremacist leaders, Bill Bennett and Pat Robertson, Lou Sheldon and Pat Buchanan, Phyllis Schlafly and Ralph Reed, Bill Kristol and R. J. Rushdoony—these supremacist leaders don't care about morality. They care about power. They seek social control. And their goal is the reconstruction of American democracy into American theocracy.

Which brings me to my final point. We who are gathered here today must work together to prove the religious supremacists wrong politically. We cannot, we must not, and we will not let them seize our democratic system. Today, we—lesbians, gays, bisexuals—are the targets of a war declared against us in the name of God. This is a war about values. On one side are the values we march for today: the values of democracy and pluralism. On the other side are those who want to turn the Christian Church into the government, those whose value is monotheism.

We believe in democracy—in many voices coexisting in peace, in people of all faiths living under a common civil framework known as the U.S. Constitution.

Our opponents believe in monotheism—one way (theirs), one god (theirs), one law (Old Testament), one nation supreme (the Christian and white one).

Democracy battles monotheism today in the school board fights across this country. Democracy fights monotheism in the antigay city ordinance campaigns from Lewiston, Maine, to Tampa, Florida. Democracy fights theocracy in antigay statewide campaigns from the state of Washington to Michigan, Arizona to Florida, Ohio to Idaho. We won the antigay measure in Oregon, but today thirty-three counties and municipalities face local versions of that antigay measure. We lost a big fight in Colorado, but thanks to the hard work of gay and straight allies, the Boycott Colorado movement is working, the boycott continues, and we will overturn that initiative and win our equality. We must work together to ensure that we do not lose this war of ideas and values.

My fellow activists, we must prove the fanatical Right politically wrong. This is our challenge. How will we defeat the supremacists? By marching from Washington into action at home. I challenge every one of you—straight or gay—who can hear my voice to join the national gay and lesbian movement. Join NGLTF to Fight the Right. We must match their power—member for member, voice for voice, vote for vote. I challenge every one of you to get involved in your state gay rights group, and if none exists, start one, so that by 1996 we will have fifty state organizations working for freedom and democracy. I challenge each of us to volunteer our time to our political movement. Volunteer for the hotline, the community center, the local political group. Because with our small actions, we make an impact on history itself. And I also challenge our straight allies—liberals and libertarians, independents and conservatives, Republicans and radicals—I challenge and invite you—America—to open your eyes and face us without fear and apprehension.

The gay rights movement is not a party. It is not a lifestyle. It is not a hairstyle or a fad or a fringe or a sickness. It is not about sin or salvation. The gay rights movement is an integral part of the American promise of freedom. We are the descendants of a proud tradition of people asserting their dignity.

It is fitting that the Holocaust Museum was dedicated the same weekend as this March. For not only were gay people persecuted by the Nazi state, but we are indebted to the struggle of the Jewish people against bigotry and intolerance.

It is fitting that the NAACP Board unanimously endorsed this March and stands with us today, because we are indebted to the African American struggle for freedom, and we are committed to ending racism. It is fitting that feminist leaders speak loudly for us today, for we are indebted to the women's movement and committed to ending the subjugation of women.

When all of us who believe in freedom and diversity, when we see this gathering today, we see beauty. When monotheists see this gathering they see the millennium. Well, perhaps the monotheists are right about one thing after all. We do represent a millennial moment—we are gathered here today to call for the end of the world as we know it.

We call for the end of bigotry as we know it. The end of racism as we know it. The end of child abuse in the family as we know it. The end of domestic violence and hate violence as we know it. The end of sexism as we know it. The end of homophobia as we know it. We stand for freedom as we have yet to know it. And we will not be denied.

GETTING IT TOGETHER—LESBIAN AND GAY POLITICAL ORGANIZATIONS

Lesbians and gay men in the United States have been gathering together to form groups for political change for over four decades. In the last twenty years, however, the number of organizations has been growing exponentially. From grass-roots activist groups with a handful of people and a one-year life span to national mainstream associations that have endured over time, the gay community is constantly becoming more sophisticated and complex in its political organizing.

Unfortunately, our enemies are also becoming more savvy as well, learning to couch their messages of hate in euphemistic terms. Lesbians and gay men are now heavily involved in a fight for our very right to be full participants in American democracy.

In this section, we have included a look at both the diversity of organizations within our own communities and some of the major homophobic organizations working against us.

"AIDS is a test of who we are as a people. When future generations ask what we did in the war, we have to be able to tell them that we were out here fighting. And we have to leave a legacy to the generations of people that come after us. Remember that someday the AIDS crisis will be over. And when that day has come and gone there will be people alive on this earth—gay people and straight people, Black people and white people, men and women—who will hear the story that once there was a terrible disease, and that a brave group of people stood up and fought and in some cases died so that others might live and be free."

VITO RUSSO, IN 1987

National Lesbian and Gay and AIDS Political Organizations

There are thousands of lesbian, gay, bisexual, and transgender political organizations around the country, with ideologies as diverse as the community itself. There are queer radicals and gay Republicans; there are huge Washington, D.C.–based political action committees and five-member guerrilla theater street activist groups; there are gay and lesbian labor, pro-choice, big business, and, yes, even pro-life organizations. Listed below are leading national lesbian and gay and AIDS organizations. For current phone numbers and addresses of these groups, call the National Gay and Lesbian Task Force in Washington, D.C., check out the resource listings in the *Washington Blade*, contact your local gay and lesbian community center, or access the Queer Resources Directory on-line.

DID YOU KNOW...

In 1987, the first U.S. conference for lesbian and gay Asians and Pacific Islanders, called "Breaking the Silence: Beginning the Dialogue," attracted eighty-five participants to North Hollywood, California. The keynote speaker, Trinity Ordona, a Filipina lesbian, said, "It is out of self-empowerment that comes collective empowerment. . . . We must break the silence to ourselves and shout our gayness so strongly that the social order of things changes to really include us."

AIDS Action Council (AAC) [1986]
Based in Washington, D.C., AAC devotes its energy solely to lobbying at the national level for AIDS program funding and research monies.

AIDS Coalition to Unleash Power (ACT UP) [1987]
ACT UP is a national coalition of local affiliates devoted to media savvy radical actions demanding government and corporate response to the AIDS pandemic.

American Federation of Veterans (AFV) [1994]
AFV is an alliance for equality of rights for lesbian and gay veterans that honors those who have served, lobbies for furtherance of care, and calls for a removal of the ban on lesbians and gays in the military.

Asian and Pacific Islander Lesbian and Bisexual Women's Network (APLBN) [1988]
Founded originally as the Asian Pacific Lesbian Network, the coalition umbrella organization of regional groups and individuals has remained dedicated to providing a bottom-up structure that fosters grass-roots

development of Asian and Pacific Islander Lesbians and Bisexual Women around the country.

Bisexual Resource Center
(BRC) [1991]
The Boston-based BRC provides information, resources, and support for bisexuals and serves as a clearinghouse for bisexual organizations nationally.

The Black Gay and Lesbian Leadership Forum
(BGLLF) [1988]
The BGLLF provides networking and support for lesbian and gay African American individuals and organizations nationwide. In addition, BGLLF holds an annual award ceremony to honor African American lesbians and gay men in politics, AIDS service, letters, and lesbian community service.

The Gay and Lesbian Alliance Against Defamation (GLAAD) is the main gay media watchdog group in the country. (GLAAD)

The Campaign to End Homophobia
[1986]
This Boston–based network of people works to end homophobia through education. It plans conferences, provides educational resources, and assists in networking for lesbians and gay men.

Children of Lesbians and Gays Everywhere
(COLAGE) [1992]
This San Francisco–based organization provides support and services for children ages twelve and up of lesbian and gay parents.

Gay and Lesbian Alliance Against Defamation
(GLAAD) [1985]
GLAAD monitors media portrayals of gay concerns and responds whenever negative or positive images are used in newspapers, television, radio, or film. There are chapters throughout the country.

Gay and Lesbian Americans (GLA) [1994]
A demonstration-focused non-partisan coalition for lesbian and gay grass-roots advocacy, GLA assists activists

committed to civil rights for lesbian, gay, bisexual, and transgender people and people with AIDS.

The Gay and Lesbian Arabic Society (GLAS) [1990]
Based in Washington, D.C., GLAS is open to gays and lesbians of Arabic descent and their supporters. Through networking, support, and visibility, GLAS works to make known the issues of lesbian and gay Middle Easterners.

Gays and Lesbians for Individual Liberty (GLIL) [1993]
GLIL is an organization for gay and lesbian libertarians committed to political philosophies for lesbian, gay, and bisexual individual liberty, including market liberalism, anarcho-capitalist, objectivist, and classical libertarianism.

Gay and Lesbian Parents Coalition International (GLPCI) [1987]
Providing information, advocacy, and support of lesbian, gay, and bisexual parents and children in eight countries through eighty-five local chapters.

The Gay and Lesbian Victory Fund [1991]
The Victory Fund raises money for openly gay candidates who support a national gay civil rights bill, are pro-choice, and aggressively seek increased AIDS funding. The candidates must also be viable.

Human Rights Campaign Fund (HRCF) [1980]
The largest lesbian and gay political action committee (PAC) in Washington, D.C., HRCF is dedicated to the election of gay and gay-friendly politicians at local, state, and national levels. In addition, the HRCF lobbies for gay-related legislation in Congress.

International Gay and Lesbian Human Rights Commission (IGLHRC) [1992]
Through press releases and letter-writing campaigns, this San Francisco–based organization is essentially a gay Amnesty International.

International Gay and Lesbian Youth Organization (IGLYO) [1993]
Devoted to ending discrimination against lesbian, gay, and bisexual youth worldwide, IGLYO also fights for gay

DID YOU KNOW...

According the International Lesbian and Gay Association (ILGA), there are ten countries that recognize homosexuals as a distinct social class subject to persecution in their home countries and are thus eligible for asylum: Austria, Australia, Canada, Denmark, Germany, Finland, The Netherlands, New Zealand, Sweden, and the United States.

TOP TEN LESBIAN AVENGER QUALITIES

(in descending order)

10. Compassion
9. Leadership
8. No big ego
7. Informed
6. Fearlessness
5. Righteous anger
4. Fighting spirit
3. Pro sex
2. Good dancer
1. Access to resources (Xerox machines)

— FROM THE LESBIAN AVENGER "DYKE MANIFESTO" BROADSHEET, 1993

youth emancipation and equal opportunity in a variety of areas.

International Lesbian and Gay Association (ILGA) [1987]
In 1993, ILGA, an umbrella association for lesbian and gay organizations worldwide, became the first gay organization to be granted membership status in the United Nations.

Lambda Legal Defense and Education Fund (LLDEF) [1973]
LLDEF is the oldest extant gay national political or legal advocacy group in the United States. At its founding, the LLDEF was called the Lambda Legal Defense Fund, but later added education and outreach programs.

Lavender Family Resource Network (LFRN) [1974]
Originally founded as the Lesbian Mothers National Defense Fund, this Seattle-based advocacy and legal education organization is the oldest in the country. In 1993, the name was changed to reflect representation of gay male parents as well.

Lesbian Avengers [1992]
The Lesbian Avengers were founded in New York City, devoted to radical queer activism. Six dykes began the movement which, in three years, has already gained over 25,000 members nationally.

LLEGO [1987]
The national organization for Latino/a lesbian and gay activists. LLEGO lends advocacy, leadership, and technical assistance to local Latino/a groups from around the country in addition to organizing forums, conferences, seminars, and national gatherings.

Log Cabin Federation (LCF) [1990]
With nearly 8,000 members, the LCF is the largest organization for lesbian and gay Republicans in the country. With a national office in Washington, D.C., it provides information and advocacy for lesbian and gay individual rights.

National Association for People With AIDS (NAPWA) [1983]
NAPWA is a Washington, D.C.–based organization devoted to being a national voice for Americans infected and affected by HIV disease. It provides information services, treatment development partnership, technical assistance, and public policy and education.

National Center for Lesbian Rights (NCLR) [1977]
Based both in San Francisco and New York, the NCLR seeks equality for lesbians through impact litigation, community judicial education, and the distribution of resource publications.

National Coalition for Black Lesbians and Gays (NCBLG) [1979]
As the first national organization to address the needs and concerns of African American lesbians and gay men, NCBLG has been a political and service/support organization, holding national conferences for black lesbians and gay men as well as hosting the AIDS in the Black Community Conference beginning in 1986.

The National Gay and Lesbian Task Force (NGLTF) [1973]
By focusing on local issues, the second-oldest and still-strong gay advocacy and lobbying group has been devoted to grass-roots lesbian and gay struggles for more than two decades. In 1986, the National Gay Task Force changed its name to include lesbians in the title.

National Institute for Gays, Lesbians, Bisexuals, and Transgender Concerns in Education (NIGLBTCE) [1994]
Provides information and referral for organizations, schools, and individuals, working to create a safe learning environment for gay, lesbian, bisexual, and transgender youth.

National Lesbian and Gay Health Association (NLGHA) [1994]
The association is dedicated to enhancing the quality of health care for lesbians and gay men through education, policy development, advocacy, and the facilitation of

health care delivery. Headquartered in Washington, D.C., the NLGHA represents a network of 20,000 lesbian and gay health care providers around the country.

National Lesbian and Gay Journalists Association (NLGJA) [1991]
The NLGJA serves as a networking and advocacy organization for people in print, radio, and television journalism.

Parents, Family, and Friends of Lesbians and Gays (P-FLAG) [first support group in 1972; organization founded 1982]
Started as a support organization for parents of lesbians and gay men, P-FLAG now boasts over 300 chapters, a quarterly newsletter, and extensive networking for more political organizing.

Queer Nation [1990]
Considered the screaming child of ACT UP, Queer Nation was born in response to a pipe bomb which exploded in Uncle Charlie's, a New York City gay bar. Known for fliers, flamboyance, and neon stickers, the organization took demonstration to a new level, invading suburban shopping malls and staging impromptu fashion shows.

Rural Alliance Network (RAN) [1994]
RAN serves isolated, diffuse, and noninteractive gay and lesbian communities. With a progressive philosophy, RAN networks with rural, suburban, Native American, and nonurbanized individuals and organizations nationwide.

South Asian Lesbian and Gay Association (SALGA)
A national lesbian, gay, and bisexual social and political organization for people descending from Afghanistan, Bangladesh, Bhutan, Burma, Guiana, India, Kenya, Nepal, Pakistan, Sri Lanka, South Africa, Tibet, Trinidad and Tobago, or Uganda.

"We're seeing more and more participation of drag queens on the front lines of the movement. Who could ever calculate how much money has been raised by queens for the AIDS epidemic?"

ROBERT BRAY, FORMER NATIONAL GAY AND LESBIAN TASK FORCE DIRECTOR

Created Equal

In the fall of 1991, California governor Pete Wilson vetoed a bill that would have banned job discrimination on the basis of sexual orientation. During the two weeks of demonstrations in Los Angeles and Sacramento that followed, a placard that appeared at several of the demonstrations read, "Thank you, Rosa Parks."

This invocation of Rosa Parks, the African American woman who would not move to the back of the bus, makes a point that lesbians and gay men need to remember: The struggle for our civil rights is based, first and foremost, on our status as U.S. citizens. American civic mythology holds that all citizens are entitled to "life, liberty, and the pursuit of happiness," and to equal protection under the law. That concept is our most powerful argument against the radical right's insistence that gay men and lesbians should be consigned to second-class citizenship, which is based solely on selective interpretations of the Bible and on old-fashioned prejudice.

In our book *Created Equal,* Professor Robert Dawidoff and I seek to remind our readers of the basic American rights that are *due* all American citizens, including its gay and lesbian ones.

The right to personal freedom and privacy means, in the context of our struggle as lesbians and gay men, that Americans are entitled to make choices about their personal lives and intimate relationships without fearing that government will punish them for those choices. This constitutionally protected right is denied gay men and lesbians wherever our sexual practices are criminalized by sodomy law. In addition, political and judicial officials at every level of government use sexual orientation to justify discrimination in virtually every sphere of public life, from employment to child custody.

The Fourteenth Amendment of the Constitution promises equal protection under the law. In its simplest form, this means that one class of citizens cannot be discriminated against simply on the basis of prejudice against them. The state cannot deprive citizens of their

DID YOU KNOW...

While there had been earlier attempts to organize the Latino gay and lesbian community, El Primer Encuentro (The First Encounter) was the first national conference of gay and lesbian Latinos ever held in the U.S. Sponsored by LLEGO (the National Latino Lesbian and Gay Organization) in May 1992, over 250 participants from around the country attended this historic "encounter."

rights without a compelling reason, and theoretically, the burden is on the state to articulate that reason. Yet, over and over, we see lesbians and gay men routinely denied our rights for no other reason than the hostility of the majority. The denial of these rights strips us of our citizenship in a way that is profoundly out of keeping with constitutional guarantees of both liberty and equal protection.

At every point, and in every debate, we must remind our fellow citizens that what is at stake is not "special rights" for homosexuals but the ordinary rights to which all Americans are entitled. We must also remind them that the radical, religious right is a profoundly antidemocratic force because it espouses the idea that a handful of self-appointed religious leaders know better than the average citizen how best he or she should lead his or her life. The radical right wants to diminish everyone's enjoyment of personal liberty—not just lesbians and gay men. It seeks to overthrow constitutional guarantees of equal citizenship and substitute in their place a narrow, religious morality that is not shared by the majority. It would erase the First Amendment's separation of church and state, which the founders wisely erected precisely to protect citizens against the imposition of religious absolutism in public life.

Our point is a simple one: In America, individuals, not government, should get to decide how best to lead their lives. Government exists to protect those decisions, not to dictate them. If America is to remain faithful to this principle, then it must include the decisions that its gay and lesbian citizens make about our lives. The cause of lesbians and gay men is, finally, everyone's cause, because a genuine commitment to individual freedom does not pick and choose among individuals but embraces all of them.

— MICHAEL NAVA

HATE-CRIME LAWS— THE GOOD & THE BAD

By including antigay violence in hate-crime legislation, attacks that are made on the basis of homophobia are penalized with the same severity as racist, antisemetic, and misogynist violence. We've compiled a list of states that make the grade and those that have taken active steps to not include gay people:

States That *Include* Antigay Violence in Hate-Crime Legislation:

California, Connecticut, District of Columbia, Florida, Illinois, Iowa, Minnesota, Nevada, New Hampshire, New Jersey, Oregon, Vermont, Washington, Wisconsin

States That *Actively Exclude* Antigay Violence from Hate-Crime Legislation:

Colorado, Idaho, Maryland, Massachusetts, Michigan, Missouri, Montana, New York, North Carolina, North Dakota, Ohio, Oklahoma, Pennsylvania, Rhode Island, South Dakota, Tennessee, West Virginia

Who Cares about Sodomy Laws, Anyway?

Gay and lesbian people seem to be winning the war against sodomy laws. Prior to 1962, all fifty states in this country outlawed sodomy, some for same-sex couples only, most for both same-sex and opposite-sex couples, married or unmarried, partners consenting or not. The antisodomy laws of this country are the progeny of English common law, imported by colonists anxious for freedom of religion but not of sexual expression.

Today, twenty-two states retain laws to regulate, control, and constrain sexual behavior between consenting adults. Twenty-eight states and the District of Columbia have abandoned antisodomy laws, through either outright legislative repeal, state court rulings, or the cumbersome process of recodifying the state penal code. We've been so successful in fighting antisodomy laws that it's difficult to get people interested in the continuing project of

DID YOU KNOW...

In 1993, there were 1,813 antigay incidents nationally, a 14 percent decrease from the 2,103 such incidents in 1992. It was the first annual drop in five years. However, in Los Angeles that same year, gay men supplanted African Americans as the primary target of hate crimes.

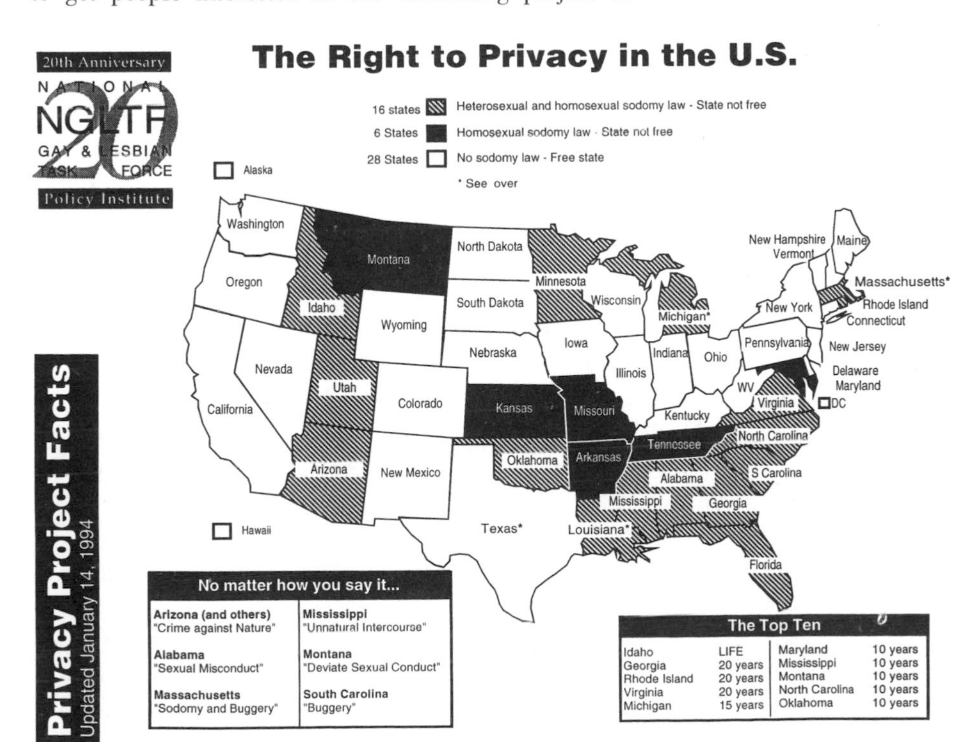

repealing the rest of such laws. Who cares about sodomy laws, anyway?

If you're one of the hapless homos caught in the act, you care a lot. Actual prosecutions against heterosexuals are so rare that the sodomy laws now seem to have been enacted for the persecution of same-sex couples only. Maryland, Tennessee, Arkansas, Missouri, Kansas, Texas, and Montana criminalize only same-sex behavior. As for the remaining fifteen "unfree" states, we must surmise from their records of prosecutions that the authorities have long since lost interest in what adult heterosexual sex criminals do in private.

DID YOU KNOW...

In March 1994, the Immigration and Naturalization Service (INS) granted asylum to a gay man from Coahuila, Mexico, living in San Francisco who said he was harassed in his homeland because of his sexual orientation. The decision marked the first time the INS had accepted an asylum application based on a claim of antigay persecution. INS spokesman Duke Austin said the decision sets no precedent and does not mean that all gays and lesbians from Mexico are automatically eligible for asylum.

Only the U.S. military maintains active and enthusiastic interest in the sexual behavior of both straight and gay/lesbian/bisexual service members. But in the case of prosecutions of straight service members, these are most often pursued when the system of rank and command has been threatened by sexual fraternization between members of the different military castes. By contrast, all branches of the military, new regulations notwithstanding, pursue with vigor same-sex violations of the military's antisex laws, regardless of the sucker and suckee's relative ranks.

Still, gay and lesbian civilian sexual scofflaws don't stand much chance of being arrested, but it *does* still happen. Michael Hardwick, the most celebrated U.S. sodomite of modern times, thanks to the Supreme Court, was caught in the act because of an unfortunate fluke. A guest in his Atlanta home on a fateful summer day in 1983 allowed a police officer to enter his house and, unannounced, proceed into Hardwick's bedroom, where he was engaged in fellatio with another man. We can well imagine that if Michael had been "Marsha" Hardwick, the police officer would have closed the door with an embarrassed clearing of his throat, requesting through the shut door that Marsha get dressed and come speak with him.

Then there is the sad tale from 1986 of the two men caught sucking *al fresco* late one night in their automobile in a deserted parking lot at East Tennessee State University in Johnson City, Tennessee. The officer who made the arrest claimed that one of the men frantically pulled up his pants as the officer approached the car, meaning, of course, that "an act too terrible to be named" was under way. The two men were prosecuted mercilessly by the county district attorney and found guilty. Punishment for one included being banned from the campus of ETSU; the other, an ETSU student, was expelled from school as a convicted felon. But one wonders why the arresting officer, the D.A., and the judge, all of whom surely had engaged in the time-honored practice of "parking," were incapable of perceiving the incident as the innocent act it was—two people, stark naked with no place to go.

CAN YOU BELIEVE IT?

According to a study from Northeastern University, 85 percent of all hate crimes are committed by young men in their early or mid-teens.

To the cops, the prosecutors, the judges, the attorneys general, and the U.S. Supreme Court, as well as to most of straight America, homosexual people are guilty criminals, not innocent lovers. Straight people have sexual freedom and sexual privilege. An unlucky few gay/lesbian people can and will be prosecuted for precisely these same "crimes" committed by the privileged hets. As for the rest of us unprosecuted sex criminals, sodomy laws harshly remind us that our sexuality is unnatural, immoral, perverse, and, in twenty-two states, against the law.

But in 1994, as I write this essay, sodomy laws are being transfused with new energy and new life to justify antigay public policy decisions. In a very sinister and dangerous trend, the religiously based right-wing organizations in this country are calling upon sodomy laws

"We have a freedom legacy as Southerners. We also have the challenge of creating our own indigenous movement as Southern dykes and faggots. Everybody can't move to San Francisco from Durham or Atlanta or Richmond or New Orleans. Everybody can't move to Durham from Pittsboro, Atlanta from Brunswick, Richmond from Lynchburg, or New Orleans from Shreveport or Monroe. When we started organizing for a Pride Parade in 1986, fundamentalists yelled we were trying to make Durham the 'San Francisco of the South.' While this has a certain appeal, I also know what I want from a Southern freedom movement is not to create more refugee centers, but to keep us from being run out of our homes—wherever they are."

LESBIAN ACTIVIST MAB SEGREST

to support their efforts to erase us from culture, society, and politics.

In Mississippi, two lesbians who purchased a plot of land on which they intended to establish a women's retreat center were recently targeted to be driven out of town by a church-based group that claims, among other things, the women are in violation of the state sodomy law.

In Kentucky, right-wing legislators have attempted to reverse a state court decision striking down that state's sodomy law in the belief that homosexuals are sinners and, as such, should be considered criminals.

In North Carolina, legislators have attempted to ban public school discussion of any behavior that is illegal in the state, a clear attempt to limit positive speech about gay and lesbian people.

And in Virginia, a lesbian mother has lost custody of her young son because the judge declared her an unfit mother on account of the Virginia sodomy law. This lesbian mother is not the first to suffer this fate, nor will she be the last.

The extremist right wing wants desperately to enforce the twenty-two unfree states' sodomy laws as the earthly long, strong arm of God's law. They will likewise press for the recriminalization of same-sex sodomy in the twenty-eight free states and the District of Columbia. In the coming years, gay and lesbian organizers will increasingly find themselves struggling against a backlash of sexual repression, fighting a fight we thought we had already won in more than two dozen states. Gird your loins, gayfolk, the sodomy wars are just heating up!

— SUE HYDE

CAN YOU BELIEVE IT?

Richard Creede and Raymond Paul had lived together for twenty years. In many ways they were like any other suburban couple: They owned a home and a car together, shared both a joint checking account and a dog. But when they went to purchase a family burial plot in the municipal cemetery in Hempstead, Long Island, they were told that two unrelated men could not be buried in a single plot with a shared headstone—it would violate town law. Only after they sought legal advice from Lamda Legal Defense and Education Fund, and agreed to sign an affidavit swearing that no one but themselves would occupy the grave, did the city relent.

Why We Need to Find Legal Ways to Protect Our Relationships: A True Story

In 1976, Sharon Kowalski had returned to college, attending classes at St. Cloud State University in Minnesota. One of her instructors was Karen Thompson. The two hit it off, but it wasn't until several months later that they acknowledged their mutual attraction. (Neither had had a previous relationship with a woman.)

Eventually, they became lovers. They also bought a house together. Karen recalls that Sharon's family treated her "just like one of them." The Kowalskis gave Karen presents at Christmas. Both women felt that Sharon's family tacitly approved of the relationship between the two women, although neither woman had explicitly announced to either family its nature.

Sharon Kowalski (left) and Karen Thompson (right) during an occupational therapy session in 1994. (Courtesy Karen Thompson)

On a cold winter afternoon in November of 1983, a drunk driver hit Sharon as she was driving her four-year-old niece and seven-year-old nephew back to Sharon's sister's house. Sharon suffered a severe brain stem injury, leaving her unable to talk or care for herself. (Her nephew sustained minor injuries in the accident; her niece was killed.)

At first, Sharon's parents welcomed Karen's assistance in their daughter's rehabilitation. Every moment that she wasn't teaching, Karen spent with Sharon, helping her in the arduous fight to regain basic life-skills. But several weeks after the accident, the Kowalskis stopped welcoming her. Given the circumstances and their history, Karen felt that this was an appropriate time to tell Sharon's parents about their relationship. She didn't expect them to be pleased, but she doubted that it would come as a surprise.

As it became clear that Sharon would not recover quickly, her father filed to become Sharon's legal guardian. Immediately upon being granted guardianship, he issued orders barring Karen from visiting his daughter. (Of course, if Karen and Sharon had been legally married, he never could have done that.) Even when the medical staff pointed out to him that Sharon's recovery seemed to go better with Karen around, he refused to allow Karen access to his daughter. Sharon herself could not speak and was too severely injured to express her own desires. Soon her father was refusing to allow any of Sharon's friends to visit.

CAN YOU BELIEVE IT?

Falsely insinuating that someone is gay constitutes slander in Missouri—so ruled that state's Supreme Court in the summer of 1993. Remarks that "clearly insinuate" that a straight person is "a homosexual" should be considered defamatory because it "is still viewed with disfavor, if not outright contempt, by a sizable proportion of our population." Also, noted the Court, "deviant sexual intercourse" is a crime in Missouri.

Karen refused to accept Donald Kowalski's edicts. Eventually, as Sharon became able to communicate using a keyboard, she expressed her desire to be with Karen. Over the next several years, Karen fought in court for her right to visit Sharon and eventually succeeded in having Sharon's father removed from guardianship. Finally, in 1992, nine years after the accident, Karen herself was appointed as Sharon's legal guardian, the first time that a gay or lesbian partner had been so appointed.

Karen has since built a wheelchair-accessible house not far from where she and Sharon used to live. While Sharon remains severely disabled, she is responsive and happy most of the time. Minnesota pays for her homecare, respite care when Karen has to leave town, and daycare so that Sharon can be out of the house for eight hours a day, five days a week. She is doing better than Karen ever dared hope.

DID YOU KNOW...

• Eight states have civil rights laws that include forbidding discrimination that is based on sexual orientation: California (1992), Connecticut (1991), Hawaii (1991), Massachusetts (1989), Minnesota (1993), New Jersey (1992), Vermont (1992), Wisconsin (1982).

• Eighteen states have executive orders banning discrimination based on sexual orientation. At least eighty-seven cities or counties have civil rights ordinances that include forbidding discrimination based on sexual orientation. And at least thirty-nine cities and counties have council or mayoral proclamations banning discrimination in public employment based on sexual orientation.

How Can Gay and Lesbian Couples Protect Themselves?

If you are in a committed couple relationship, you have probably thought about how to protect your rights (and your home) if one of you dies or becomes incapacitated. Here are some things that you can do on your own, without a lawyer; however, you might want to consult an attorney, depending on your particular circumstances.

Durable power of attorney: Give your partner durable power of attorney for both health care and finance. While not every state and jurisdiction will always honor these documents, they are the best bet for making clear your intentions. These forms are printed in *The Power of Attorney Book*, published by Nolo Press.

Wills: Make your intentions clear in your will to ensure that your wishes are followed after your death. Update your will on a yearly basis. While yearly updating might seem burdensome, it will make it harder for an unsympathetic family member to challenge your will if there is ongoing evidence of your intentions.

Register as a family: If you are a California resident, you can register with the Secretary of State's office as a family. While this does not provide you any benefits, it does signal your intentions and put you and your partner on paper as a bona fide family.

Domestic partnerships: Sign up as domestic partners at work, in your city or state, wherever it is offered. Most city, state, and county domestic partnerships allow unmarried partners the right to visit their spouse in the hospital and allow time off for bereavement when a partner dies; some go as far as to provide health care and survivor's benefits for government workers. The private companies that offer domestic partnership benefits do so in order to provide their employees' partners with health care benefits. To top it off, you might even get a certificate you can put on your wall for all to see.

Own things in common: One of the best ways to make sure you don't lose your home if your partner dies is to own things in joint tenancy with the right of survivorship: houses and cars, bank accounts, summer homes, stock portfolios, etc. While many couples may choose not to merge their finances, it is important that you make these decisions consciously.

CAN YOU BELIEVE IT?

"These two guys that got killed wouldn't have been killed if they hadn't been cruising the streets picking up teenage boys. . . . Some murder victims are less innocent in their deaths than others. In those cases a defendant is unlikely to deserve a maximum sentence. . . . I put prostitutes and gays at about the same level. If these boys had picked up two prostitutes and taken them to the woods and killed them, I'd consider that a similar case."

— JACK HAMPTON, TEXAS DISTRICT COURT JUDGE

(M. Wuerker, courtesy of the National Gay and Lesbian Task Force)

Groups That Promote Hatred and Homophobia Under the Guise of "Family Values"

You can do a lot to change the way people think by educating them to the hateful agenda behind organizations that hide beneath the innocuous banner of "family values."

American Family Association—Promotes their agenda through court actions; also targets the media/entertainment industry. Concerns include homosexuality, pornography, profanity, "anti-Christian bigotry," liberal media. 600,000 members, 640 local chapters. (Head: Donald Wildmon)

DID YOU KNOW...

In 1993, Minnesota became the first (and only) state whose antidiscrimination laws forbid not only discrimination against gay men and lesbians, but also discrimination against bisexuals and transgendered people.

Concerned Women of America—Antigay, antiabortion, "pro-family" agenda via grass-roots organizing and congressional lobbying. 600,000 members, 800 U.S. chapters. (Head: Beverly LaHaye)

Eagle Forum—A women's organization powerful in national and Republican party politics, thanks to Phyllis Schlafly, founder. Mother of a gay man, she opposes AIDS education, sex education, daycare, family leave, abortion rights, the ERA, and NEA funding. 80,000 members. (Head: Phyllis Schlafly)

Family Research Council—Lobbies against gay, lesbian, and bisexual civil rights, reproductive freedom, government-funded health care, child care, and equal protection laws for women in the workplace. (Head: Gary Bauer)

Focus on the Family—Employs almost 1,000 people, with 1,550 radio stations worldwide. A leader in the passage of Colorado's Amendment 2 to disallow equal rights for gay men, lesbians, and bisexuals. Conducts seminars nationally to involve fundamentalists in the political process. (Head: James Dobson)

Traditional Values Coalition—Opposes gay rights, reproductive freedom, teaching evolution, and sex education except abstinence. Helped repeal gay and lesbian rights in Irvine and Concord, California. Advocates AIDS quarantine. 25,000 churches nationally. (Head: Rev. Lou Sheldon)

Operation Rescue—Nationally known for violent shutdowns of abortion clinics, vandalizing property, terrorizing women and health care providers through stalking, harassment, and other intimidation tactics. Trains activists. Added gay rights to agenda when President Clinton proposed to lift the military ban. 35,000+ members. (Head: Randall Terry)

National Association of Christian Educators/ Citizens for Excellence in Education—Goal is to bring public education under Christian control. Priority is disruption of public schools via attacks on curricula, text books, and school boards. 1,250 chapters. (Head: Dr. Robert L. Simonds)

— COMPILED BY P-FLAG

DID YOU KNOW...

In 1993, the Massachusetts Board of Education adopted, unanimously, the nation's first state educational policy prohibiting discrimination against gay elementary and secondary students.

Statement on Family Values

The Federation of Parents, Family, and Friends of Lesbians and Gays represents thousands of families throughout the United States and eleven other countries. One of our primary objectives is to maintain families through loving relationships. We challenge any concept of traditional family values that excludes our gay, lesbian, and bisexual loved ones.

Homosexual and bisexual persons are important and vital members of society. They function in leadership roles at every level of public life, and as responsible and caring individuals in their private lives. They are your doctor, nurse, teacher, minister, lawyer, salesclerk, union leader, chief executive officer, auto mechanic, political representative, star athlete, and office colleague. They are your, and our, children, brothers, sisters, nieces, nephews, uncles, aunts, and cherished friends.

With all of our children, heterosexual and homosexual alike, we share values that include personal integrity

"It may be an academically interesting puzzle as to why we are gay. . . but it is much more interesting and important to find out why people are homophobic."

PITZER COLLEGE PROFESSOR PETER NARDI OF GLAAD/LA

and responsibility, adherence to the work ethic and to religious values, compassion for those in need, and commitment to healthy and mutually respectful family relationships.

Gay, lesbian, and bisexual persons are beloved and cherished members of millions of families. They create their own families, and instill in their own children the same values of integrity, work, responsibility, religion, and compassion.

We love, respect, and support our gay, lesbian, and bisexual children. We denounce and will strongly resist any effort to label them as less than the responsible citizens and caring family members we know them to be.

— P-FLAG BOARD OF DIRECTORS

DID YOU KNOW...

In response to the homophobic right-wing video *The Gay Agenda*, which was distributed in Congress during the 1993 gays in the military debate, lesbian activist Dee Mosbacher created *Straight from the Heart*, a video about the parents of lesbian and gay children. She sends it to local and state officials whenever an antigay ballot initiative is being considered. The film was nominated for an Oscar in 1994.

OUT IN THE STREETS

For three decades, lesbians and gay men have been demonstrating, marching, and stirring up trouble to bring about visibility, public awareness of our issues, protest, and liberation. During the seventies, most gay protests were localized, and many lesbians and gay men were more active in other progressive movements than we were in gay liberation.

But as community organization and communication became more sophisticated, we began organizing nationally around issues that concerned us as gay people. The onslaught of AIDS further revealed the need for national organizations and coalitions for protest and change. In a very real way, political actions are about reminding ourselves and others—the same way we did at Stonewall—that lesbian and gay people are unwilling to be stepped on or have our rights compromised.

We have had both triumphs and setbacks in our movement. In this section, we explore both. While styles and agendas for queer political actions have changed over time, one thing has remained constant—there has always been a significant number of lesbians and gay men who find creative ways to act up in the face of adversity.

Great Lesbian and Gay and AIDS Actions of the Last Twenty Years

A gay family in 1978 protests the Proposition 6, the so-called Briggs Initiative, which attempted to ban lesbian and gay teachers from public positions on the grounds that gay people were "immoral." The initiative failed. (Rink Foto)

Coors Beer Boycott (1975)
The gay community targeted the Coors Brewery, owned by the legendary right-wing Coors family, for boycott in 1975 when it was revealed that among the company's many unfair labor practices was an employee questionnaire that requested information about the employee's sexual behavior, including their sexual orientation. The gay community focused its organizing efforts in bars, where much of the beer bought by gay consumers was sold. The Coors boycott, which had been a coalition effort between labor and gay activists, lost much of its momentum in 1987 when the AFL-CIO settled with Coors. The boycott was successful both because it had a large impact on the company's profits, and because it resulted in major corporate policy changes at Coors. Unfortunately, Coors profits are still at the disposal of the Coors family, which continues to fund antigay and antilabor causes.

Florida Orange Juice "Gaycott" (1977)
When gay men and lesbians called a boycott of Florida orange juice in response to the homophobic preachings of Anita Bryant, then the official spokesperson for the Florida Citrus Commission, the first nationwide organized gay act of resistance began. Bryant and her religious hate organization "Save Our Children" launched an attack on the gay community when Dade County passed an ordinance banning discrimination on the basis of sexual orientation. Although Bryant and her group were successful in getting the ordinance repealed, the nationwide boycott of Florida juice was effective, and in 1980, the Citrus Commission dropped Bryant as its spokesperson.

(History repeated itself in 1994, when right-wing homophobic mouthpiece and juice spokesperson Rush Limbaugh was canned after the targets of his hate rhetoric pressured the Citrus Commission.)

Briggs Initiative (1978)
Anita Bryant's antigay backlash was taken up in 1978 in California by state Senator John Briggs, whose ballot measure Proposition 6, known commonly as the "Briggs Initiative," would have banned gay and lesbian teachers from working in public schools. Opposition to the initiative came from around the country, and some of the most brave, creative, and exhaustive grass-roots activism grew up in response to Briggs. For several months before the vote, activists literally crisscrossed the state, stopping in the tiniest of towns and rural communities in search of gay and lesbian voters whom they hoped to enlist in the organized network of Briggs opponents. In an electoral victory that gave a shot of strength to gays and lesbians coast to coast, the Briggs Initiative went down to defeat by a vote of three-to-two.

In the wake of the Bowers v. Hardwick, a woman protests with her gay sisters and brothers during a 1987 Sandra Day O'Connor speech in San Francisco. (Rink)

White Night Riots—San Francisco (1979)
When homophobic former supervisor Dan White assassinated San Francisco's mayor George Moscone and openly gay supervisor (and beloved community leader) Harvey Milk in the fall of 1978, the city's gay community was shocked and grief-stricken. When White was convicted of manslaughter instead of murder a year later, the community erupted in violent outrage. On May 21, several thousand protesters gathered at City Hall, and their anger soon led to property destruction and combat with police. Several police cruisers were overturned and torched, City Hall itself was damaged, and scores of rioters were arrested. Milk is remembered annually in San Francisco the Sunday after Thanksgiving with a candlelight march from the gay-identified Castro Distict to City Hall.

Moral Majority/
Democratic National Convention (1984)

When the Democrats met in San Francisco in 1984, the Moral Majority (then the most visible of the religious right organizations concerned with domestic issues like homosexuality and the disappearance of the nuclear family) showed up for a convention of its own. Gay and lesbian activists didn't take too kindly to fire-and-brimstone folk coming to the "Gay Mecca" and preaching about our sin and abomination. Three days of anti–Moral Majority actions culminated in a kiss-in in the midst of the convention itself.

ACT UP/NY on Wall Street (1987)

Responding to the woefully inadequate government, public health, and medical response to AIDS, activists founded the AIDS Coalition to Unleash Power (ACT UP) in 1987. In its first action, ACT UP, which would spawn a nationwide network of chapters in other cities, took on Wall Street. Protesting the lack of promising drug treatments for HIV and the exorbitant price of the only drug then available, AZT, the media savvy and intense demonstrators rallied to the call "No Business as Usual." This historic protest marked the beginning of the AIDS activist movement, and eventually led to changes in the Food and Drug Administration's drug-approval process as well as a lowering of the retail cost of AZT.

Supreme Court Civil Disobedience,
March on Washington (1987)

In 1986, the Supreme Court handed down one of the most explicitly homophobic decisions of all time. In *Bowers v. Hardwick,* Georgia's sodomy law was upheld by the nation's highest court, sending a clear signal to all gay people that it is legal for state governments to criminalize our physical relationships. As a result, when over half a million lesbians and gay men converged on Washington, D.C., in October 1987 for the largest gay rally in history, many of the activists attending the march organized a civil disobedience for the next day at the Supreme Court. Protesting the *Hardwick* decision, approximately 800 lesbians and gay men and their supporters were arrested in the massive nonviolent civil disobedience. It was the largest number of people ever to be arrested at the Supreme Court, and the largest number of arrests for a public demonstration in D.C. since the Vietnam War.

DID YOU KNOW...

The first action of the Lesbian Avengers was swooping down on a public elementary school in Queens, wearing T-shirts stating "I was a lesbian child," and handing out lavender balloons reading "Ask About Lesbian Lives" to the kids.

Texans March for Rights (1989)
As gay men and lesbians sought greater space and freedom in mainstream culture in the 1980s, many took up the battle for legislative action that banned discrimination against us. Hundreds of local activists fought for city and county protections, while larger and organized networks went for state legislation. In what was the largest march on the state capital in the history of Texas, more than 20,000 lesbians and gay men marched in Austin in April 1989 for passage of a state bill protecting gay Texans from discrimination.

Stop the Church (1989)
In what may be one of the most controversial demonstrations by gay, lesbian, reproductive rights, and AIDS activists, more than 4,000 protesters held a demonstration at St. Patrick's Cathedral in New York, including a disruption of Sunday Mass. In a unique coalition, the groups ACT UP and WHAM (Women's Health Action Mobilization) called for the protest, which focused on the policies of the Catholic Church and the public statements of New York's Cardinal John O'Connor about AIDS and abortion. (O'Connor, a member of former President Reagan's national panel on HIV, was an outspoken opponent of AIDS education and prevention efforts.) The most controversial aspects of the action included people chaining themselves to church pews and staging die-ins inside and outside of the church. One protester attempted to interrupt communion by stating that the Church's policies on abortion and safe sex constituted murder.

ACT UP Meets Burroughs Wellcome (1990)
In May of 1990, ACT UP staged a mass demonstration at the National Institutes of Health in Maryland to protest the failure of deeper research into AIDS treatments, and demand open clinical trials of new treatments for all people infected with HIV. As a result of ACT UP's rabble-rousing, Burroughs Wellcome, Inc., cut the exorbitant price of AZT by 20 percent.

Queer Nation/Atlanta and the Cracker Barrel Boycott (1991)
The Atlanta chapter of Queer Nation, an activist organization whose explicitly gay and non-assimilationist politics are modeled after ACT UP's, spearheaded what became a nationwide boycott of the Cracker Barrel restaurant chain, based on the company's 1990 employment policy stating that employees could be fired for being gay. Over a period of three years, Queer Nation/Atlanta and a coalition of lesbian, gay, feminist, and union organizations waged direct actions, sit-ins, and media events designed to draw public attention to the homophobic policies of Cracker Barrel.

Lesbian Avengers Dyke March (1993)
The Lesbian Avengers, a direct-action group formed in 1992 by lesbians who were inspired by ACT UP/Queer Nation and years of progressive organizing, quickly became the fastest-growing political lesbian organization in the country. On April 24, 1993, the night before the March on Washington for Gay, Lesbian, and Bi Rights, the Lesbian Avengers led 20,000 lesbians on the Dyke March down Pennsylvania Avenue. It was the largest-ever lesbian march, inspiring subsequent dyke marches in cities around the country.

"Rare Cancer Seen in 41 Homosexuals"

OUTBREAK OCCURS AMONG MEN IN NEW YORK AND CALIFORNIA—8 DIED INSIDE 2 YEARS

Doctors in New York and California have diagnosed among homosexual men 41 cases of a rare and often rapidly fatal form of cancer. Eight of the victims died less than 24 months after the diagnosis was made.

This article in *The New York Times* from July 3, 1981, helped to change the shape of modern medicine and public health by reporting a rare cancer and infections of the human immune system found in forty-one homosexual men. This was the first public notice given to the disease that became known as HIV and AIDS, originally called GRID (Gay Related Immune Disease).

As a response to this article and after consultation with several local health experts, an effort led by author and activist Larry Kramer resulted in the mobilization of community resources to raise funds to fight the disease, which led to the eventual establishment of the Gay Men's Health Crisis—New York's response to the epidemic. No one at that time could guess at the eventual magnitude of the disease.

At the same time, similar programs were growing in San Francisco (the Kaposi's Sarcoma Research and Education Foundation, later to become the San Francisco AIDS Foundation) and in Los Angeles (AIDS Project Los Angeles). These three major organizations have provided support and served as models for AIDS education, case management, public policy, and the development of volunteer services throughout the world.

As a result of efforts in these three major metropolitan areas and elsewhere across the country, the way U.S. society views terminal illness has been radically changed. People with AIDS are probably the most well-versed patients as to medical treatments, drug protocols, and experimental drugs. The same knowledge and advocacy used in treating AIDS victims—including hospices and visiting home nurses—is pouring over into other medical areas as a model for dealing with any patient with a terminal illness.

There has been an amazing response to the epidemic by gay men and lesbians. Families and friends have worked together tirelessly to meet the demanding needs of caring for a person with AIDS. Through the many organizations that have sprung up in large cities, in smaller towns, and in rural areas, patient care has been at the forefront of the agenda.

Because the disease involves minority and outcast elements of society, the road to funding and implementation has been slow. Government inaction during the epidemic has been continuously criticized by the affected communities. With limited funding, cooperative efforts have become popular as a means of providing services to ensure a minimum level of support.

Another of the innovative approaches to caring for the person with AIDS (PWA) is the "buddy system," created by GMHC. It entails linking a PWA with an individual who can help handle household chores as well as assist the PWA in obtaining medical treatment. The buddies concept has spread to virtually every other caregiving organization—not only those dealing with AIDS. As a team, the pair can face more effectively the emotional highs and lows of medical treatment, as well as the daily emotional needs of the caregiver and the person with AIDS. In many parts of the country, groups have sprung up to provide emotional and practical support for patients, in addition to meeting their direct medical needs. These include food banks and hot-meal delivery services like Project Open Hand in San Francisco.

— **GREG WALKER**

My Buddy Died Today

I'm an AIDS buddy, and my buddy died today. He was not rich. He was not famous. He was not handsome. But he was smart, and he was brave. He taught me about bravery. He went into the hospital three weeks ago because he was throwing up blood. Then he was told his Kaposi's Sarcoma had spread throughout his body. He knew he was dying. He told me it was okay to die. He was ready. He worried about his lover of fifteen years. He worried about me. Odd: I thought that he was dying, but he was worried about us. I talked about getting him out of bed and into the sunshine. His lover talked about getting him home again. He smiled, but I think he knew better than we. He never did get into the sunshine or home again.

Yesterday, when I got to the hospital, he was having another fit of throwing up blood. Over and over and over again. The doctor said he had a tumor, and there was nothing he could do. We didn't talk much, but held hands. It was the only time I felt he was really afraid. When I would remove my hand to go clean the pan he was spitting in, he would reach for me and pull me back to him. Then they told me I must wear rubber gloves. They were right—after all it was blood he was spitting—but I hated those gloves. Holding hands with a glove is just not the same. Then he quieted down and began to sleep. I left.

Just after 6 a.m. this morning, the phone rang. I think I knew already what the message was. He had just died. It was time, and yet it's never time. His lover kept saying, "But I always thought we were going to grow old together."

— **PHILLIP WESLEY**

The Beginning of Acting Up

On March 10, 1987, Larry Kramer gave a speech at the Gay and Lesbian Community Center in New York calling for the gay community to become more active and angry in its political response to government inaction in the AIDS epidemic. The speech was a furious indictment of the medical industry, the government, and the existing AIDS organizations, including New York's Gay Men's Health Crisis (GMHC), which Kramer had helped found five years before. Below is an excerpt from that call to arms, which became the impetus for the AIDS Coalition to Unleash Power (ACT UP).

The AIDS Coalition to Unleash Power (ACT UP) coined what became a central cry for lesbian, gay, and AIDS activists: SILENCE = DEATH. (ACT UP Golden Gate)

We must immediately rethink the structure of our community, and that is why I have invited you here tonight: to seek your input and advice, in the hope that we can come out of tonight with some definite and active ideas. Do we want to reactivate the old AIDS Network? Do we want to start a new organization devoted solely to political actions?

I want to talk to you about power. We are all in awe of power, of those who have it, and we always bemoan the fact that we don't have it. Power is little pieces of paper on the floor. No one picks them up. Ten people walk by and no one picks up the piece of paper on the floor. The eleventh person walks by and is tired of looking at it, and so he bends down and picks it up. The next day he does the same thing. And soon he's in charge of picking up the paper. And he's got a lot of pieces of paper that he's picked up. Now, think of those pieces of paper as standing for responsibility. This man or woman who is picking up the pieces of paper is, by being responsible, acquiring more and more power. He doesn't necessarily want it, but he's tired of seeing the floor littered. All power is the willingness to accept responsibility. But we live in a city and a country where no one is willing to pick up pieces of paper. Where no one wants any responsibility. . . .

It's our fault, boys and girls. It's our fault. Two thousand Catholics can walk through the corridors of Albany. The American Foundation for AIDS Research has on its board Elizabeth Taylor, Warren Beatty, Leonard Bernstein, Woody Allen, Barbra Streisand, Michael Sovern [the president of Columbia University], a veritable *Who's Who;* why can't they get a meeting with the President, their former acting buddy? Why don't we think like that?

Well, until we all bend over and pick up all those little pieces of paper, I don't have to tell you what's going to happen.

— **LARRY KRAMER**

Surviving AIDS

The PWA self-empowerment movement was born when a dozen of us met for the first time at a historic AIDS conference held in Denver in 1983. Once we were in the same room, we discovered that we had similar complaints: No one was listening to us or taking us seriously.

We drafted the founding manifesto of the people with AIDS self-empowerment movement, which became known as The Denver Principles. Bobbi Campbell and I wrote the first draft on the back of some old handbills.

Our opening statement made clear our resolve to fight back against the powerful forces that were trying to dehumanize us.

The Denver Principles

We condemn attempts to label us as "victims," which implies defeat, and we are only occasionally "patients," which implies passivity, helplessness, and dependence upon the care of others. We are "people with AIDS."

We recommend that health care professionals:
Who are gay, come out, especially to their patients who have AIDS. Always clearly identify and discuss the theory they favor as to the cause of AIDS, since this bias affects the treatment and advice they give. Get in touch with their feeling (fears, anxieties, hopes, etc.) about AIDS; do not simply deal with AIDS intellectually.

Take a thorough personal inventory and identify and examine their own agendas around AIDS.

Treat people with AIDS as whole people and address psychosocial as well as biophysical issues. Address the question of sexuality in people with AIDS specifically, sensitively, and with information about gay male sexuality in general and the sexuality of people with AIDS in particular.

We recommend that all people:
Support us in our struggle against those who would fire us from our jobs, evict us from our homes, refuse to touch us, separate us from our loved ones, our community or our peers, since there is no evidence that AIDS can spread by casual social contact.

Do not scapegoat people with AIDS, blame us for the epidemic, or generalize about our lifestyles.

We recommend that people with AIDS:
Form caucuses to choose their own representatives, to deal with the media, to choose their own agenda, and to plan their own strategies.

Be involved at every level of decision-making and specifically serve on the boards of directors of provider organizations.

Be included in all AIDS forums with equal credibility as other participants, to share their own experiences and knowledge.

Substitute low-risk behaviors for those that could endanger themselves or their partners, and we feel that people with AIDS have an ethical responsibility to inform potential sexual partners of their health status.

People with AIDS have the right:
To as full and satisfying sexual and emotional lives as anyone else. To quality medical treatment and quality social service provision, without discrimination of any form, including sexual orientation, gender, diagnosis, economic status, age, or race.

To full explanations of all medical procedures and risks, to choose or refuse their treatment modalities, to refuse or participate in research without jeopardizing their treatment, and to make informed decisions about their lives.

To privacy, to confidentiality of medical records, to human respect, and to choose who their significant others are.

To die and live in dignity.
— MICHAEL CALLEN AND BOBBI CAMPBELL

Myths about HIV for Gay or Bisexual Men

Myth: HIV is not the cause of AIDS.
Fact: Sometimes it's easy to confuse what we don't know about the treatment of AIDS with what we do know about what causes it and how it's transmitted. HIV is clearly the virus associated with the breakdown in the immune system called AIDS. Some scientists have proposed that a lifestyle that includes "promiscuous" sex and lots of drug use is responsible for AIDS. Mistrust the medical establishment all you want, but be careful not to confuse homophobia with science.

Myth: Because there are so many "gray areas" of risk, like the risk of oral sex, it's impossible to know what's safe and what isn't.
Fact: The fact is that there really is no "medium" ground of risk behaviors. Unprotected anal sex is considered to be a high risk for HIV infection (or reinfection). Sucking, like most other behaviors, except when blood or semen can get into the bloodstream, has a minimal to low risk of HIV infection. (Some people have become infected through sucking, though it seems to happen rarely.) To

make oral sex safer, (1) avoid getting cum (or blood) in your mouth; (2) avoid brushing or flossing just before sucking; (3) if you have cuts, sores, or bleeding gums, wait till they've healed, or use a condom. (Oral sex can lead to other sexually transmitted diseases that can have serious consequences, especially for HIV-positive individuals.)

Myth: Condoms are the only way to reduce risk for HIV infection or reinfection.
Fact: While latex condoms with lots of water-based lube are an effective way to make anal sex safer, many men are reducing their risk by choosing less risky behaviors and by making sure that blood or semen doesn't have an entry into the bloodstream—through a cut, lesion, sore, or extremely chapped or abraded skin.

Myth: Getting tested regularly is one way to prevent HIV.
Fact: Testing doesn't prevent HIV. For some, testing can confirm that safe sex really does work. Testing, however, which can reduce fear, doesn't in itself reduce risk. Unfortunately, some men may see a negative test result as a green light to continue unsafe behaviors. It's not fate that keeps someone uninfected. It's a belief that we can control our fate by making well-informed choices every time we have sex.

Myth: Most gay men will eventually become HIV-positive.
Fact: Though it's estimated that in some cities up to fifty percent of gay men may already be HIV-positive, the majority were infected *before* we had good information about preventing HIV. With the information we have today, the rate of new infections has remained low. But for those who have recently become positive, lack of knowledge doesn't seem to be the problem. It's feelings of giving up . . . of fatalism, inevitability, or of low self-esteem that seem to cause men to lapse into unsafe sex. We need to find ways to let HIV-negative men know how important it is to stay negative and stay healthy.

Myth: If I'm HIV-positive, there's not much I can do but sit and wait.
Fact: False! It's important for HIV-positive people to

(1) get emotional support; (2) get good medical care; and (3) keep healthy habits. Emotional support is especially helpful in the first few months after getting test results. If you're like most, you may have no symptoms of HIV, but it's important to know your medical options and to find ways of keeping your immune system healthy—with a balanced diet, plenty of sleep, and regular exercise.

— COMPILED BY WAYNE BLACKENSHIP OF THE SAN FRANCISCO AIDS FOUNDATION

Lesbians and AIDS: Myths and Facts

Myth: Lesbians are at high risk for AIDS and HIV infection because they are homosexual.
Fact: Lesbians, like gay men, are attracted to members of their own sex. However, their sexual activities are often very different from those of gay men. For example, there is no penis and therefore no semen (which has a high concentration of HIV if the man is infected) in woman-to-woman sex. Most lesbians who are infected with HIV contract it from injecting drugs or from sex with men, not from genital sex with other women. While some women who call themselves lesbians have sex with men—straight, gay, or bisexual—other lesbians wouldn't even fantasize about it. The risk of HIV infection via woman-to-woman sex is lower than the risk for either men or women who have most of their sexual encounters with men.

Myth: Lesbians have no risk of AIDS because they do not have sex with men.
Fact: HIV is transmitted by specific behaviors: vaginal and anal sex with men, injection drug use, exposure to blood (both menstrual and other blood) during sex, use of sex toys such as dildos or other objects that are put into the vagina. No matter how a woman labels herself, if she does any of these things, she can transmit or receive the virus if she or her partner is infected.

Myth: Although lesbians can get infected with HIV via shared needles or sex with men, sex with another woman is safe.

"Lesbians are not an isolated community; there are lesbians who shoot drugs and share needles, there are lesbians who have been married, who have babies, who are in prisons, who have sex for money, who get raped. When examining the AIDS epidemic, it becomes obvious that stereotypes are useless; it's not who you are that puts you at risk, it's what you do."

ZOE LEONARD, AUTHOR OF LESBIANS IN THE AIDS CRISIS

Fact: No! No! No! There are documented cases of lesbians being infected with HIV via a female partner. Blood has high concentrations of HIV, and if a woman is exposed anally or vaginally to the blood of an infected partner, she could become infected.

Myth: Menstrual blood is different from other blood and does not carry the HIV virus
Fact: Menstrual blood is basically the same as other blood, except that it contains extra cells from the lining of the uterus. Menstrual blood does contain HIV if the menstruating woman is infected.

Myth: There is enough research on women and HIV/AIDS that we can tell pretty much what HIV and AIDS in lesbians is like.
Fact: The research agenda on women and AIDS lags far behind that on men, whether the issue is transmission or treatment. For the first decade of the epidemic it was almost impossible for women of childbearing age to enter treatment studies, and most of the studies of the "natural" course of the illness have been on men. Also, when women have been studied, most of the research has been on maternal transmission—to a fetus or an infant—and not on the effects of the illness on women themselves. For all these reasons, the limited research on women and HIV has even more limited value for understanding HIV in lesbians. Much more research is needed to understand the illness and its treatment in women—whether they are straight or lesbian.

Myth: Lesbian safe sex means using a dental dam.
Fact: Completely safe sex between lesbians involves either two women who are both HIV-negative or two women who have sex in such a way that no virus could be passed from one to another. Safe strategies include monogamy between two HIV-negative partners; mouth-to-mouth kissing; using new condoms on sex toys each time they are used; protection from blood—via dental dams, plastic wrap, or other barriers; and, if needles or any other sharp objects are used—for drug injection, piercing, or other activity—being certain that they are sterile (cleaned with bleach) or not sharing them with the partner.

Myth: Donor insemination is safer than getting pregnant via vaginal intercourse.
Fact: Donor insemination is only safe if the donor has been tested and found negative, then donates the sperm and has it frozen until he is retested in six months and is still found to be negative for the virus (which can take up to six months to appear in an antibody test). All licensed sperm banks are required to test donors for HIV and to freeze and hold sperm to make sure it is safe.

— NANCY E. STOLLER

BRIDGES: ALLIES AND COALITIONS

The lesbian and gay community has made a lot of advances in visibility, civil liberties, and political organization in the last twenty-five years. We have also learned through hard lessons that for the most part we have to depend on ourselves to make change happen. But we have come to appreciate that we cannot achieve equality or liberation without some help. As Mahatma Gandhi said, "None of us are free until all of us are free."

Coalition politics have been a valuable tool for all oppressed minorities; lesbians and gay men are no exception. By teaming up with other groups that share common grievances and challenges, we have been able to make inroads into many areas in which we might have otherwise not succeeded. Our boycotts have always relied on the cooperation of labor, communities of color, mainstream politicians, and businesses. In addition, lesbian and gay organizations have been able to lend support to others in their struggles.

On a more individual level, many lesbians and gay men value the acceptance and support of straight family members and friends. Through the families we have, both straight and gay, we find love, belonging, and advocacy of our political causes. Parents, Family, and Friends of Lesbians and Gays (P-FLAG) is a very important group devoted to organizing and affirming our personal allies.

The gay and lesbian community does not exist in a vacuum. This section explores the many bridges we have built with a variety of other communities in our lives.

An Injury to One . . .

Howard Wallace played a pioneer role in the early 1970s as the first trade union activist to come out and fight publicly for gay rights within the labor movement. He also led the Adolph Coors and Shell Oil boycotts of that decade, and gave a stirring speech about coalition building at the 1979 March on Washington. He wrote the following piece in 1994 for the progressive magazine *Crossroads.*

Since I gave my speech at the 1979 March on Washington, the lesbian and gay labor movement has made a lot of progress. A lot more unionists have come out of the closet and many are playing important roles in their unions. We are now at a significant turning point.

With each wave of attacks against us, we attract new throngs of activists. The lesbian/gay movement has tremendous ability to revitalize itself—look at how we've come back from the AIDS crisis. In terms of regular day-in, day-out activism, we probably have more people involved today than most other social and economic movements.

There have been steady advances by working-class gays and lesbians, and gays and lesbians of color. But they haven't had a huge amount of organized political expression. The main thing over the last several years has been the development of networks among different groups of lesbians and gays of color.

There has also been a steady increase of network-building within the labor movement. There has always been a significant level of working-class participation in the lesbian/gay movement. A lot of ordinary working people have taken part. And now we are starting to find more organizational expression. For instance, we are getting ready to launch a national organization of lesbian and gay trade unionists. It's been a long time coming. Yet because many local networks are already in place, we will begin with a measure of clout. I don't believe there is a single major union that we can't exert some influence upon. When I came out, I was all by myself as an openly gay union activist for several years. Now it is quite different.

DID YOU KNOW...

The late Cesar Chavez, president of the United Farm Workers, spoke to the nearly half a million gay people at the 1987 March on Washington, acknowledging the impact gay support had had on UFW boycotts and pledging ongoing labor support for gay and lesbian rights.

Yet pressure to be in the closet at work remains as one of the big plagues of lesbians and gays. One of our great challenges is to liberate the workplace. All workers have a stake in this fight for freedom of expression. The assertion of our political, sexual, and cultural identity at work raises the question of the workplace being *our* place, not just the employers' place; *our* domain, not just the employers'.

There are also lesbians and gays organizing at work in other forms than unions, through lesbian and gay employee associations and groups such as Digital Queers and High Tech Gays. We can build alliances with them, around issues such as job protection and domestic partners. But, of course, you don't have any *real* job protection without a union contract.

In certain centers, economic and class issues have receded in today's era of the so-called "identity" issues. There is a constant ebb and flow—people get involved through all different issues as part of their overall political awakening. Among lesbian and gay people, there is a deep well of distrust of society's dominant institutions. Of course, you find lesbians and gays who are conservative —gay Republicans and so on. But in general we have a profound skepticism about U.S. institutions. Even when people start to get satisfied with the gains they've made, they know in their bones that the gains are precarious. This produces waves of alarm over Pat Buchanan–style attacks, and consequently new waves of activism—often with innovative and unorthodox approaches, and a cutting edge of militancy. The ultraright offensive, then, has forced a polarization that is profoundly politicizing our community.

And again we may be at a turning point. The networks among lesbians and gays of color are growing. The lesbian and gay movement has been able to build broader alliances with other powerful forces—for example, in the African American movement—despite areas of obvious conflict. Lesbian and gay labor networks are cropping up in more and more cities—it's not just San Francisco, New York, and Boston anymore.

Overall, we're in a better position to cooperate with other groups in the fight for social change. We're in a position to find common ground with the recently formed Asian Pacific Labor Alliance, the Coalition of Black Trade Unions, the Coalition of Labor Unions Women, the Latin American Council for Labor Advancement, the A. Philip Randolph Institute, and other forces that have special concerns and can influence the labor movement.

The Civil Rights Resolution passed by the AFL-CIO in 1993 included an important new provision calling for affiliated unions to become involved in coalitions fighting against the antigay ballot measures that are now emerging in more than twenty states. It provides a big opportunity if we seize it to involve unions in our coalitions against the ultraright. It's up to us to publicize this resolution, to use it to build a grass-roots movement, and to maintain the fight to hold all labor leadership accountable to this official position.

Altogether, we are in a better position than ever to express our own identity and perspective as part of working-class life. We can provide a large portion of the fresh imagination and energy that the labor movement desperately needs—that the entire progressive movement desperately needs.

— **HOWARD WALLACE**

Fishnets, Not Bomber Jets

"Fishnets, not bomber jets/Bring the troops home!" It was so nice to hear a change from aging lefty slogans at the march against the Gulf War in the winter of 1991–1992. The strong presence of Queer Nation and ACT UP was energizing and, at an otherwise straight progressive event, they linked insufficient AIDS spending with military buildup and the fierce homophobia of the military. They brought visibility.

Lesbians and gays have been a part of each and every progressive movement for hundreds of years. The women's movement has been peopled by lesbians for a long time, and their work makes sure women's issues consistently include lesbian issues as part of women's rights. The presence of and pressure from lesbians in the international women's movement has made it a very real possibility that lesbian rights will be on the agenda of the 1995 United Nations World Conference on Women in Beijing. Says longtime feminist, leftist, and Queer Nation activist Sushawn Robb, "Because of strong lesbian involvement in the women's movement, our visibility is inevitable [and] anything that makes [our issues] visible is an assistance to breaking down isolation."

Lesbian, gay, and bisexual political power has been, and continues to be, strengthened by coalitions with progressive groups. Observes lesbian labor organizer Angie Fa, "There have been dramatic changes inside the labor movement. Today, it's possible to get all sorts of straight people in top leadership positions to support gay and lesbian civil rights. People who five, ten, or twenty years ago wouldn't go near the issue, have worked hard." The presence of lesbians and gays in the labor movement, and left organizations supporting it, pushes labor to deal with gay and lesbian issues, making domestic partnership and job discrimination on the basis of sexual orientation or AIDS part of union organizing and contract demands.

Without explicit political pressure, however, lesbian and gay work in progressive institutions often gets little credit. Argues longtime lesbian and antiracism organizer Pat Norman, "We have to come out and be courageous. And after we come out we have to stay out." This has been true, and sucessful, in international solidarity movements: Queers for Cuba traveled to Cuba, in violation of the travel ban, in order to both challenge the U.S. embargo against Cuba and, by refusing to be closeted, come in solidarity with Cuban gays

During the Gulf War, Queer Nation in San Francisco joined with other progressives in protesting Desert Storm. (Marc Geller)

and lesbians in order to challenge the homophobia in the Cuban state and people. The work of out lesbians and gays for freedom in South Africa, by organizers both in South Africa and around the world, led to the outlawing of discrimination based on sexual orientation in the new South African constitution. The international power of the gay rights movement is increased by allying with other international progressive movements, and ensuring in their success an obligation to gay rights.

To fight the increasing presence of the religious right, progressive coalitions are crucial. In the right-wing propaganda film *Gay Rights—Special Rights*, the religious right specifically pits the black community and gays and lesbians against each other by portraying lesbians and gays as rich whites appropriating the language of civil rights. It is a tactical move by the religious right to ply the black community (whose rights they have never been interested in) with their antigay agenda. The success of this tactic lies in the rollback of civil rights since the sixties, and the very real lack of gains in the black community. An increased presence of out gays and lesbians in the fight against racism is crucial to counter this divisive maneuver, especially since the disporportianate spread of AIDS in both communities makes a common fight vital.

The fact is that gay rights is inextricably linked with civil rights of people of color, workers' rights, and women's rights. "We are everywhere" means that the possibilities and challenges of the struggle for gay rights are as diverse as the communities that make up gays and lesbians as a whole. Progressive gays and lesbians bring back to the queer community resources for recognizing that diversity and building it into a strength, as well as bringing gay rights into the agendas of progressives. As activist Kenya Briggs argues, "It is important to be involved in civil rights movements for everybody—it just makes our fight that much stronger."

— MICHAEL GREER

I Was a Teenage Draft Dodger

Until his death from AIDS-related causes in 1994, Tede Mathews was a longtime activist in both the peace movement and the gay print movement. He also served as a liaison between gay and straight Latinos in San Francisco. The following is an excerpt from a series of Lesbians and Gays Against Intervention (LaGAI) "We Like Our Queers Out of Uniform" pamphlets handed out beginning in 1989 to protest the military and its role in oppressing other countries around the world. This excerpt picks up after Tede has been arrested for draft dodging in 1970 and jailed overnight.

So I was out on the streets again, thanks to the Quakers who fronted my bail money. The FBI and the State of Florida wanted to extradite me back to the Sunshine State, so they could have a show trial. My lawyer finally worked out an agreement that they would drop all charges against me if I would go through another physical and comply with the results. I readily agreed and soon I was on the South Boston bus on my way to the army base. I can safely wager that the South Boston Army Base had not seen the likes of me before. After removing 90 percent of my body hair (use your imagination as to what hair I left), I put on my best black lace garter belt and fishnet hose with matching panties. Over that I wore a fetching coral crepe pantsuit, my black fur coat (what becomes a legend most?), and every rhinestone I could borrow. To add to the effect, I applied long fake fingernails and had my hair done up like a Dolly Parton wig.

Tede Mathews

As I sashayed into the waiting room full of fresh cannon fodder, all eyes were upon me. The prudent military decided to put me through my physical alone. After a lavish striptease, I teetered about on my lavender pumps, refusing to go barefoot unless the Army replaced my fishnets. Finally, I was led to a bench in the hallway to wait my turn with the psychiatrist. I could see into the changing room, and it was full of men taking their clothes off. To ensure my classification, I flew into the room and took hold of a very shocked young man's "member." I blurted out that it was the most beautiful cock in God's creation, and could I please kiss it? Before my blushing suitor could respond, two burly MPs carried me into the psychiatrist's office.

Suffice to say that the poor shrink had trouble maintaining his composure. He was the last act in my performance piece, and I planned to leave that army base in a blaze of glory. I flirted with him shamelessly. When he asked me if I had ever had homosexual fantasies, I laughed out loud and exclaimed, "Dahling, I *am* a homosexual fantasy!" With that, the curtain dropped and I was escorted back to my drag and shown to the bus stop.

Thus ended my divorce from Uncle Sam.

— TEDE MATHEWS

Gay Liberation Movements

Huey Newton was one of the early organizers of the Black Panther Party. The Panthers sprang from their Oakland, California, base in the sixties to become a major black radical movement. Despite the schools and health clinics they ran and all their anti-poverty work (clothing, feeding, and housing in the African American ghettoes of several large American cities), the Panthers were treated by the media and government as pathological and violent. Newton presented the speech below on August 15, 1970.

DID YOU KNOW...

In 1974, Rep. Bella Abzug (D-NY), introduced H.R. 14752, proposing that the categories of "sex, sexual orientation, and marital status" be added to the 1964 civil rights act. It was the first time gay civil rights legislation was proposed at the federal level.

During the past few years strong movements have developed among women and among homosexuals seeking their liberation. There has been some uncertainty about how to relate to these movements.

Whatever your personal opinions and your insecurities about homosexuality and the various liberation movements among homosexuals and women (and I speak of the homosexuals and women as oppressed groups), we should try to unite with them in a revolutionary fashion. I say "whatever your insecurities are" because as we very well know, sometimes our first instinct is to want to hit a homosexual in the mouth, and want a woman to be quiet. We want to hit a homosexual in the mouth because we are afraid we might be homosexual; and we want to hit the woman or shut her up because we are afraid that she might castrate us, or take the nuts that we might not have to start with.

We must gain security in ourselves and therefore have respect and feelings for all oppressed people. We must not use the racist attitude that the White racists use against our people because they are Black and poor. Many times the poorest White person is the most racist because he is afraid he might lose something, or discover something that he does not have. So you're some kind of threat to him. This kind of psychology is in operation when we view oppressed people and we are angry with them because of their particular kind of behavior, or their particular kind of deviation from the established norm.

Remember, we have not established a revolutionary value system; we are only in the process of establishing it. I do not remember our ever constituting any value that said that a revolutionary must say offensive things toward homosexuals, or that a revolutionary should make sure that women do not speak out about their own particular kind of oppression. As a matter of fact, it is just the opposite: We say that we recognize the women's right to be free. We have not said much about the homosexual at all, but we must relate to the homosexual movement because it is a real thing. And I know through reading, and through my life experience and observations, that homosexuals are not given freedom and liberty by anyone in the society. They might be the most oppressed people in the society.

And what made them homosexual? Perhaps it's a phenomenon that I don't understand entirely. Some people say that it is the decadence of capitalism. I don't know if that is the case; I rather doubt it. But whatever the case is, we know that homosexuality is a fact that exists, and we must understand it in its purest form: That is, a person should have the freedom to use his body in whatever way he wants.

That is not endorsing things in homosexuality that we wouldn't view as revolutionary. But there is nothing to say that a homosexual cannot also be a revolutionary. And maybe I'm now injecting some of my prejudice by saying that "even a homosexual can be a revolutionary." Quite the contrary, maybe a homosexual could be the most revolutionary.

When we have revolutionary conferences, rallies, and demonstrations, there should be full participation of the gay liberation movement and the women's liberation movement. Some groups might be more revolutionary than others. We should not use the actions of a few to say that they are all reactionary or counterrevolutionary, because they are not.

We should deal with the factions just as we deal with any other group or party that claims to be revolutionary. We should try to judge, somehow, whether they are operating in a sincere revolutionary fashion and from a really oppressed situation. (And we will grant that if they are women, they are probably oppressed.) If they do things that are unrevolutionary or counterrevolutionary, then criticize that action. If we feel that a group in spirit means to be revolutionary in practice, but they make mistakes in interpretation of the revolutionary philosophy, or they do not understand the dialectics of the social forces in operation, we should criticize that and not criticize them because they are women trying to be free. And the same is true for homosexuals. We should never say a whole movement is dishonest when in fact they are trying to be honest. They are just making honest mistakes. Friends are allowed to make mistakes. The enemy is not allowed to make mistakes because his whole existence is a mistake, and we suffer from it. But the women's liberation front and the gay liberation front are our friends, they are potential allies, and *we need as many allies as possible.*

We should be ready and willing to discuss the insecurities that many people have about

"The conservative movement is founded on the simple tenet that people have the right to live life as they please, as long as they don't hurt anyone else in the process. No one has ever shown me how being gay or lesbian harms anyone. . . . Last year [1993], many who opposed lifting the ban on gays in the military gave lip service to the American ideal that employment opportunities should be based on skill and performance. In civilian life, they'd never condone discrimination. Well, now's their chance to put up or shut up."

CONSERVATIVE LEADER
AND FORMER REPUBLICAN
SEN. BARRY GOLDWATER

homosexuality. When I say "insecurities," I mean the fear that they are some kind of threat to our manhood. I can understand this fear. Because of the long conditioning process which builds insecurity in the American male, homosexuality might produce certain hang-ups in us. I have hang-ups myself about male homosexuality. But on the other hand, I have no hang-up about female homosexuality. And that is a phenomenon in itself. I think it is probably because male homosexuality is a threat to me and female homosexuality is not.

We should be careful about using those terms that might turn our friends off. The terms "faggot" and "punk" should be deleted from our vocabulary, and especially we should not attach names normally designed for homosexuals to men who are enemies of the people, such as Nixon or Mitchell. Homosexuals are not enemies of the people.

We should try to form a working coalition with the gay liberation and women's liberation groups. We must always handle social forces in the most appropriate manner.

— **HUEY NEWTON**

Reflections on Homophobia

Antigay propaganda sounds less like antiblack rhetoric than like classical anti-Jewish rhetoric: Both evoke the image of the small, cliquish minority that nevertheless commands disproportionate and sinister worldly influence. More broadly, attitudes toward homosexuals are bound up with sexism and the attitudes toward gender that feminism, with impressive, though only partial, success, asks us to reexamine.

That doesn't mean that the race analogy is without merit, or that there are no relevant points of comparison. Just as blacks have historically been represented as sexually uncontrollable beasts, ready to pounce on an unwilling victim with little provocation, a similar vision of the predatory homosexual has been insinuated, often quite subtly, into the defense of the ban on gays in the military. . . . What makes the race analogy complicated is that gays, as demographic composites, do indeed "have it better" than blacks—and yet in many ways contemporary homophobia is more virulent than contemporary racism. According to one monitoring group, one in four gay men has been physically assaulted as a result of his perceived sexual orientation; about 50 percent have been threatened with violence. (For lesbians, the incidence is lower but still disturbing.) A moral consensus now exists in this country that discriminating against blacks as teachers, priests, or tenants is simply wrong. (That doesn't mean it doesn't happen.) For much of the country, however, the moral legitimacy of homosexuals, as homosexuals, remains very much in question.

— **HENRY LOUIS GATES, JR., IN "REFLECTIONS: BLACKLASH?"** NEW YORKER **(MAY 17, 1993)**

Things Straight People Can Do for Gay People

Every lesbian and gay man has family and friends who are straight. Some of our straight peers want to help us in the struggle for our rights and freedom, but they don't know how, feel awkward asking, or think that they do not have the time. Gay men and lesbians cannot win our fight alone. Here are some things straight people can do to help their gay loved ones:

- Come out at home, at work, at school, and in your place of worship as the family or friend of someone gay.
- Join Parents, Family, and Friends of Lesbians and Gays (P-FLAG).
- Donate time or money at least once a year to a lesbian/gay political organization.
- Vote only for gay-friendly candidates who explicitly support lesbian and gay equal rights.

• Educate yourself about AIDS and the issues surrounding it.

• Hug, kiss, hold hands, and dance in public with lesbian and gay friends.

• Wearing a red ribbon is a nice thought, but AIDS organizations need more than your support. They need money and volunteers. Consider it tithing.

• Speak out at your local school board, PTA, and library council about the need for recognition and support of lesbian and gay youth in our public institutions.

• Put a "Straight But Not Narrow" bumper sticker on your car.

• If you think people are being homophobic, let them know how you feel. It's about time they started feeling more uncomfortable and self-conscious about expressing their hate than we sometimes do expressing our love.

• See lesbian- and gay-themed movies. Read lesbian- and gay-themed books and magazines. Lesbians and gay men are saturated by heterosexual culture. Exploring in the other direction takes more effort than simply having gay friends.

• Become involved in lesbian and gay petition drives and demonstrations, identifying yourself as straight friends of lesbians and gay men.

— DON ROMESBURG

"My son came out and all I got was this lousy T-shirt"

SEEN AT THE 1993 P-FLAG CONVENTION IN NEW ORLEANS

Chief Kisses Officer in Public — P-FLAG's True Blue Family

P-FLAG (Parents, Family, and Friends of Lesbians and Gays) is an international organization keeping families together and offering support, advocacy, and networking for the family and friends of lesbians and gay men. Of all organizations, P-FLAG has done the most to bridge the gap between gay people and their straight family and friends.

Portland, Oregon, P-FLAG's favorite father-daughter team delivered a joint "thank you" to the organization in an emotional highlight of the 1994 annual Northwest regional conference.

Retiring police chief Tom Potter and his lesbian daughter, police officer Katie Potter, drew a prolonged standing ovation when they appeared together before P-FLAGers at the Portland meeting. The event was proclaimed in a banner headline in the local newspaper, *The Oregonian,* over an extended story illustrated by a picture of the chief kissing his daughter in front of the host chapter's huge P-FLAG banner.

Both publicly and privately, the Potters told the conference, P-FLAG has given them important support.

Publicly, Potter often came under fire for his open support of his lesbian daughter and the lesbian and gay community. In particular, he was severely faulted for participating in uniform in gay pride parades.

A Baltimore gay man and his supportive mother march together in the 1976 Christopher Street March in New York City. (Bettye Lane)

But the chief said he had sworn to fight "racism, sexism, and homophobia." He wore his uniform in the marches, he said, to send a deliberate message that his police bureau welcomed gay and lesbian recruits.

"Some officers felt I was tarnishing the badge," he said. "I felt I was burnishing it."

Privately, P-FLAG was instrumental in gaining Katie the understanding and support of her mother, who is divorced from Tom. In particular, her mother has strong religious misgivings about Katie's orientation, but was helped by meeting with P-FLAG members of similar religious background. Two years ago, with Tom, Katie, and Katie's nongay siblings, she cooperated with a reporter-photographer in preparation of a major feature in *The Oregonian.*

"This has not been easy for my mother," Katie told the P-FLAG conference. "I'm forever indebted to P-FLAG and my father for helping me develop a relationship with my mother."

— **EXCERPTED FROM** THE PFLAGPOLE, **WINTER 1994**

THE PERSONAL IS THE POLITICAL

Many people assume that "politics" means things like election campaigns, protest marches, *Crossfire* analysis, debates, and coalition work. But for lesbians and gay men, simply living openly as gay is a political act. Holding hands with our lovers in public is a political act. Mourning our dead is a political act. Requesting lesbian and gay literature in public libraries, or even our local bookstores, is a political act. Living queer *is* living political.

Even so, we all sometimes need to be reminded how we can make change happen in our lives and in our society. In this section, there are many suggestions for action, for lesbians and gay men, for people with AIDS, for people of faith. Some activism takes a lot of time, effort, and money; but there are a lot of things we can all do every day that strengthen personal pride and public appreciation of gay people everywhere. In addition, because you're never too young to empower yourself and make a difference, we've included some of the great gay and lesbian youth heroes of our time.

The Politics of Silence

Someone whose sister is a novelist asked me last week whether art should be political or not.

I said, "Is she political?"

And he said, "No, she's an artist."

That's not something I agree with. It is not enough to be an artist. If you live in cataclysmic times, if the lightning rod of history hits you, then all art is political, and all art that is not consciously so still partakes of politics, if only to run away.

Robin Lane Fox, a historian of religion, says most people believe the Christian world was a fait accompli, that it was a force of circumstance, a historical inevitability. But in fact, until Constantine converted to

Christianity in 313, it was a battle between pagans and Christians. The pagans were an urban, sophisticated class. They had their mysteries, and they had their gods. So one of the things the early popes did was destroy the pagan texts, and Mr. Fox was able to reconstruct part of the pagan world by going through cemeteries reading the gravestones. If you destroy the record, you destroy the truth.

I've learned in my adult life that the will to silence the truth is always and everywhere as strong as the truth itself, and so it is a necessary fight we will always be in: those of us who struggle to understand our truths and those who try to erase them. The first Nazi book burning, I would have you remember, was a gay and lesbian archive.

I would like to draw a distinction between homophobia and homo-ignorance. There's much more homo-ignorance than there is homophobia, I think, and though it's difficult for us as a people, as a tribe, to hear the hate spewed at us, we know it's better for that hate to be public than for it to be secret. When I speak of the politics of silence, I don't just speak of the silence of gay and lesbian people for 1,500 years, those rare exceptions like Whitman or Michelangelo notwithstanding. I speak of a silence that is tied up with our lack of self-esteem.

Sometimes I think that the ones who hate us can't stand the fact that we have won out over oppression. They can't stand to see us leading happy and productive lives. Many of the right-wing pundits and preachers clearly chose not to be gay or lesbian. For them being "straight" was a lifestyle choice, to use their jargon. With a white-knuckled grip they have clung to "traditional values," by which they mean intolerance and fear. A joyful gay or lesbian person messes their minds profoundly.

I don't know if AIDS has made me so brave as a writer. I don't know whether it has widened my heart the way witnessing the world at war widened Anne Frank's heart. Who would have thought that the greatest account of that war, the one that would sear the hearts of the future, would be written by a fourteen-year-old girl? And a fourteen-year-old girl who died believing people were fundamentally good. That's where I fail much of the time.

The difference between having freedom as a writer and having no freedom is as narrow as the choice that the truth is important. In Sophocles' *Antigone,* Antigone buries her brother, despite the edict of Creon, the king, that she will die if she does so. That is the great moment in classical literature between conscience and the law. "O tomb, O marriage chamber," she says, going to her death. And the play's Chorus comes out and says: "Isn't man wonderful? He longed so much to speak his heart that he taught himself language, so that what was inside him could be spoken to the world."

I was given my heart back when I came out. People say I'm too hard on myself, but if you were to read the dreary poems I wrote in my twenties, you would discover they're about nothing because they are not about me, they are not about the truth.

So I guess what I would say to my gay and lesbian brothers and sisters, especially to the gay and lesbian children of the next generation, and to all our friends and allies, is: Come out when you can. I know it's not easy for everybody. But I would not give up what the last seventeen years of being out have meant to me. It has been a joyous experience, and that even includes the decade of AIDS. I seem to be able to be as angry as I am, and as despairing, and still be a happy man, because I am glad to be out.

I have a psychologist friend who says, "It's not enough to come out." Coming out is just the first step, the outer coming out. Then we have to start the inner coming out, looking to nourish our own battered self-esteem.

And to really be a gay or lesbian citizen, you have to also give back to your community. You have to reach out and help it. Some of the people who hate us think we're out to indoctrinate their children. Frankly, we're trying to save their children from suicide. A third of all teen suicides are gay and lesbian, and they're all unnecessary, and we want those kids to have a chance.

If I believe in anything, rather than God, it's that I am part of something that goes back to Antigone and that whatever speaks the truth of our hearts can only make us stronger. We must be the last generation to live in silence.

— PAUL MONETTE

Twenty-Five Little Hurricanes—Individual Actions for Everyday Life

We've all heard and used the age-old excuse that "I'd love to do something, but I just don't have the time." *Au contraire!* Lesbians and gay men can take little steps every day to make the world a better place for us. Here are just a few suggestions for action:

1. Volunteer, volunteer, volunteer.

2. Bring something to do to a hospitalized or homebound friend with AIDS.

3. Write your local newspaper about lesbian and gay issues.

4. Write television networks in response to affirming/negative representations of lesbians and gay men.

5. Patronize lesbian- and gay-owned businesses.

6. Come out at work.

7. Take a queer friend stuck in a rut out to dinner, or if you're in the rut, ask someone to come to dinner with you.

8. Come out to a straight friend.

9. Have hot safer sex every time.

10. Take part in a local demonstration (or organize one).

11. Donate money once a month to local grass-roots AIDS and lesbian and gay organizations.

12. Stamp money as "lesbian money," "gay money," or "queer money."

13. Form a lesbian or gay social group based on your passions or hobbies.

14. Always refer to generalized professionals (doctors, lawyers, etc.) as "she."

15. Wear explicitly queer stuff.

16. Request gay- and lesbian-themed movies at your local video store.

17. Donate gay and lesbian books to your local school libraries.

18. Question your own AIDSphobia, biphobia, and transphobia.

19. If you are a man, read five books by lesbian authors. If you are a woman, read five books by gay men.

20. Talk to younger relatives about safer sex.

21. Join a lesbian/gay speakers bureau.

22. Marry your same-sex partner in your place of worship.

23. Read and listen to queer authors of color.

24. Request lesbian and gay magazines at your local supermarket, convenience store, or bookstore.

25. Be fabulous. Embarrass those around you with your flamboyance, camp, and explicit queerness.

— **DON ROMESBURG**

We Must Not Go Quietly

In a January cover story chronicling the impact of AIDS on the arts, *Newsweek* mentioned that many of us stop counting after one hundred deaths, numbed with mourning and inundated with a sense of hopelessness. Recently, I remembered this story as I wrote to Sali Ann to sympathize with the death of her brother Richard, whom I'd known for ten years. He was the ninety-third person I've known who has gone before us with AIDS.

In 1984, I began keeping a journal list of those who have gone on prematurely. Since then, every day has begun with a ritual—I read the obituaries, scanning them for names to be remembered. I felt more prepared for some deaths as a result of grappling with someone's failing health over the course of his illness. Other deaths took me by surprise; time and geography may have made communication between us infrequent, but they didn't alleviate or soften my shock and affront at the loss. I discovered still other deaths in passing conversations with mutual friends who assumed I had known of the deaths months earlier. Their grieving resolved, mine only now begun.

Once, after an extended business trip, I called my friend Lee at home to see how he was feeling. His sister answered the phone, thanked me for calling during his memorial service, and asked if I wanted to share something with the gathering. Selfishly, I felt cheated. I didn't get to say good-bye to yet another loved one. Weeks afterward I called his disconnected number, somehow hoping that he'd answer so we could talk one last time. Months later, I called his phone number again, explaining to the newly connected household how special my friend had been.

Eight years into the counting, I scan the obituaries more quickly now, decoding the terms of our invisibility —families and loved ones describe deaths as "heart failure," "lymphoma," "pneumonia," or, most fraudulently of all, "peacefully after a long illness."

However, we must not go quietly. Those who remain must witness and illuminate the lives needlessly lost. *Newsweek* may forget us and move on to other issues, but we are all living with the AIDS pandemic. There can be no shame, no separation, no distinction—no other among us.

— **JOHN R. KILLACKY**

The NAMES Project AIDS Memorial Quilt

The Quilt was conceived in November 1985 by longtime San Francisco gay rights activist Cleve Jones. As he was planning for the 1985 Harvey Milk Candlelight March, he learned that the number of San Franciscans lost to AIDS had passed the 1,000 mark. Many of them had lived and died within a few square blocks in the gay-populated Castro district, yet the neighborhood showed no physical evidence of this tremendous loss. In order to create evidence, Jones was moved to ask each of his fellow marchers to write on placards the names of friends and loved ones who had died of AIDS. At the end of the march, Jones and the others stood on ladders above the sea of candlelight, taping these placards to the walls of the San Francisco Federal Building. The wall of names looked to Jones like a patchwork quilt.

Growing from a small group in June 1987, the participants wanted to document the devastation of AIDS throughout the country. Their goal was to create a memorial for those who have died of AIDS, and to thereby help people understand the impact of the disease. The first display of twelve-foot Quilt sections was held on October 11, 1987, at the National March on Washington for Lesbian and Gay Rights. At that time, the Quilt included 1,920 individual panels.

By 1994, more than 27,000 individual three-by-six-foot memorial panels—each one commemorating the life of someone who has died of complications of AIDS—had been sewn together by friends, lovers, and family members.

The Quilt includes panels from all fifty states and twenty-nine countries, including Australia, Brazil, Cuba, Great Britain, Japan, Poland, Rwanda, Senegal, South Africa, Switzerland, and Uganda. It has been seen around

The NAMES Project AIDS Quilt was displayed in its entirety for the first time in Washington, D.C. (1987) (©JEB)

the world. Instructions are available from the NAMES Project on making a panel.

Among some of the items used in making unique panels have been Barbie dolls, car keys, champagne glasses, flags, fur, fishnet hose, photographs, tennis shoes, jockstraps, merit badges, minks, corsets, pearls, and stuffed animals.

Portions of the Quilt are displayed over a thousand times a year in locations around the country, in venues such as schools, gymnasiums, community centers, places of worship, museums, and corporate offices. The NAMES Project's thirty-eight local chapters use the Quilt to raise awareness of the epidemic and promote education in their communities. Plans are currently under way to display the entire Quilt once again in Washington, D.C., in October 1996.

No Room in the Closet for This Quilt

October 1992. I had volunteered to work on the display of the entire NAMES Project AIDS Memorial Quilt in Washington, D.C. I was overwhelmed by the magnitude of our losses when the Quilt arrived on site. In truck after rented truck the thousands of boxes came, more than 22,000 individual panels of life woven from the threads of death.

I cried unashamedly moving truckload after truckload of memories into place, as the sheer dimensions of the display washed over me like a wave. Fellow volunteers, total strangers, supported me, hugged me, held me because they understood my sadness. What most did not know was the tortured, unyielding duality of life in the closet, the jagged wounds opened by simultaneously confronting the hypocrisy of the closet and the enormity of this plague.

With every panel unfolded for the assembly, new stories, new lives were laid out before us. Men, women, children, fathers, brothers, sisters, lovers—all lost to this insidious pandemic. In the shadow of the Washington

Monument, under Lincoln's knowing gaze and within sight of the uncaring Bush White House, the numbers became names, the statistics became real, the tragedy became palpable.

Bolstered by the encouragement of four dear friends and with Quilt-strengthened resolve, I decided that day to share with my family what I had known for so many years and kept secret for so long. A new man, a free, happy, honest, gay man emerged that weekend, empowered by my loving family.

I will always remember standing in the middle of that vast Quilt, hearing name after name of the dead read aloud, blinded by the sun, surrounded by hundreds of thousands of friends, mourners, well-wishers, and volunteers. Wrapped in the enormity of this plague I felt the thought crystallize: *There is no room in the closet for this Quilt.* The closet is not where we hide, it is where the truth is, until we let it out and share it with those we love.

— STEPHEN P. BASILE

Suggestions for Action from People of Faith Against Bigotry

1. Write a letter to your friends asking them not to sign petitions for discriminatory ballot measures, and vote against these measures when they appear on the ballot.

2. Offer to make a presentation in your place of worship (or ask your leader to preach a sermon) or offer to lead an adult-education lesson that contrasts the reconciling love of God with the hateful implications of antigay ballot measures. Or ask for a speaker from local support groups for gays and lesbians belonging to faith communities.

3. Place items in church/temple bulletins that offer information regarding antigay referenda from a faith perspective.

4. Be present near a table where signatures are being gathered for antigay measures (usually near a major shopping center) and leaflet/dialogue with people who are thinking about signing.

5. Join others for scheduled events, marches, and rallies as they are announced.

6. Start an ad campaign drive in your city or community to place signature ads opposing discriminatory measures. The ads should list the names and religious affiliation of clergy and laypeople belonging to a wide variety of faith-based groups.

7. Wear buttons and display bumper stickers that proclaim both your faith in God and your belief in equality for all people. People of faith who oppose discrimination must know that they are not alone.

8. Ask your church/temple governing body to declare your place of worship a "bias-free zone" open to all people, including gay men and lesbians.

9. Organize and participate in prayer vigils.

10. Use the "bridges" theme, silent vigils holding hands across bridges, or other symbolic acts demonstrating bridges across fear and division.

11. Wear a pink triangle to show your solidarity, just as non-Jewish Danes wore yellow stars to confound the Nazi invaders.

12. Talk to friends, neighbors, and relatives. Talk about homophobic bias and the right wing to anyone who will listen. Educate them about the importance of freedom of speech and separation of church and state from your perspective as a person of faith.

13. Put together a speakers bureau among other people of faith and contact civic and religious groups and arrange to address them on the issues. Those who are heterosexual should go where gay and lesbian friends may not be able to go as easily.

14. Let your creativity run rampant with other unique ideas from your heart to fit your particular church, congregation, or group.

15. Volunteer your time.

16. Most of all, make sure you "come out" as a person of faith who opposes antigay bias in your faith group and other organizations you belong to, especially if they have not yet made resolutions to oppose right-wing bigotry.

— FROM THE NATIONAL GAY AND LESBIAN TASK FORCE 1993 FIGHT THE RIGHT HANDBOOK

Twelve Young Lesbian and Gay Individuals Making a Difference

Listed below are twelve outstanding young people who have made an impact on the national level. Any collection of names fails to acknowledge the thousands of local individuals who achieve greatness, courage, and compassion on a daily basis: the quiet leaders, the supportive friends, the young queers who refuse to remain silent, and the gay and lesbian teenagers who struggle—and choose—to survive and flourish.

- **Rick Aguirre**, twenty-three, is the publisher/creator of *insideOut*, the most widely distributed magazine for lesbian, gay, bisexual, and transgender youth.

- **Troix Bettencourt**, twenty-one, was the youngest speaker to address the hundreds of thousands of people who attended the 1993 March on Washington. He has been president of the Boston Alliance for Gay and Lesbian Youth, is a state-certified HIV educator and counselor, hosts a weekly television show, and is the recipient of numerous awards, including the Power of One Award given by the Human Rights Campaign Fund to an "individual or organization that has made a difference."

Wilson Cruz plays gay teenager Rickie Vasquez on the critically acclaimed ABC show My So-Called Life. *(Capital Cities/ABC, Inc.)*

- **Wilson Cruz**, twenty-one, is an openly gay Puerto Rican actor who is trying—and succeeding—in Hollywood. He plays bisexual Rickie on ABC's *My So-Called Life*, giving him the distinction of being the first openly gay actor to play a gay or bisexual youth on television.

- **Jennifer DiMarco**, twenty-two, is the author of ten novels, including *Escape to the Wind*, which topped the *Seattle Times* best-seller list for several weeks. She also speaks to young people in high schools and colleges in the Pacific Northwest about writing and being an out lesbian.

• **Lyn Duff**, nineteen, is the editor of *24-7: Notes from the Inside*, a publication written by and for adolescents who have survived institutionalization because of their sexuality. After her parents found out she was a lesbian, they sent her to be reprogrammed in Utah. After escaping and being recaptured, Duff escaped again and convinced a friend to contact the press, bringing unwanted national attention to Rivendell "Hospital" and the practices of places like it around the country.

• **Aaron Fricke** was eighteen in 1980 when he decided to take a same-sex date to his high school prom in Rockport, Rhode Island. When the school administration tried to stop him, he took them to court and won, paving the way for same-sex couples. He went on to write a memoir, *Confessions of a Rock Lobster*, and a book with his father.

• **Matt Marco**, twenty-two, and Steve Mathis, twenty-three, founded and publish *Y.O.U.T.H.*, a Washington, D.C.–based 'zine for lesbian and gay youth. Matt is also working to establish a sexual-minority youth advocacy group run entirely by young people.

• **Wendy O'Neil**, twenty-five, headed the Lesbian/Bisexual Alliance at Spelman College, a historically African American women's college in Atlanta. In addition, she is an activist for various lesbian and women's causes, including HIV prevention.

• **Luke Sissyfag**, twenty-one, grabbed the national spotlight when he confronted President Clinton during a press conference for the 1993 World AIDS Day and held the floor for nearly a minute on national television. His act of protest and frustration displayed how an individual can make an impact.

• **Pedro Zamora** (deceased) and **Sean Sasser**, twenty-four, became national celebrities as the two HIV-positive gay lovers on MTV's *The Real World.* Cuban-born Pedro spoke before Congressional committees, gave speeches before groups of hundreds of students both in high school and colleges, and did a great deal of education and outreach work. In November 1994, Pedro died of

AIDS-related causes. Sean works as an HIV counselor at the YES (Youth Empowerment Services) Program in San Francisco, an organization for HIV-positive and HIV-affected youth. He is also a pastry chef.

I Eat
Purple
Grass
Have A Gay Holiday!
happy gays are here again
back!
26, 27 & 28
GAY
OLYMPIC
I BOUGHT A

CHAPTER 9

Wanna Have Fun?

Lesbians and gay men have been accused more than once of taking ourselves too seriously. And while there are hundreds of ways for people to take time out from the daily grind, many of those traditional avenues require that gay men and lesbians put on "protective armor" or a second set of eyes before venturing out for an evening of activities as simple as going to the movies or dancing.

But gay people are nothing if not resourceful. And that's really what this chapter is all about: ways that lesbians and gay men have devised to put fun in our lives, to have, as the song goes, "a gay old time."

Whether it is reading the funnies, going to comedy or dance clubs, playing a sport, or going on vacation, gay men and lesbians have created a whole world of recreational activities. This chapter shows just a few of the ways we cut loose. Have fun!

"I think gay people are like blondes; there's fewer of them, but they have more fun."

RITA MAE BROWN ON THE MAURY POVICH SHOW

LAUGHING AT OURSELVES

Comedy, in the many forms it takes, is one of the strongest day-to-day sources of empowerment that lesbians and gay men possess. When we laugh, we take a little of the sting out of the homophobia we deal with every day. When we can laugh at ourselves, we remember not to always take ourselves quite so seriously. And while issues like AIDS, sexism, and racism within our communities are hardly laughing matters, there are moments of humor which unexpectedly surface because of all of them. Being able to acknowledge laughter reminds us of our humanity, and lets us celebrate our differences through humor.

Humor also has a very serious side. Because it seems less threatening than angry speeches, overtly political essays, protest marches, or confrontational art, comedy can inform people both within our communities and in the society-at-large about aspects of our culture that some might ignore or otherwise avoid. Camp, for instance, is a mainstay of our culture precisely because of its irony. It pointedly exposes and challenges gender assumptions while laughing at them. For lesbians and gay men, as for people of color and women in general, comedy is powerful.

Comedy takes different forms. Lesbians and gay men have created comic books and comic strips; we have gay funny men and women on the comedy circuit who are an integral part of our communities; and, of course, we have our own day-to-day humor. Hopefully, this section will provide you with a smile, and maybe even a little laughter.

DID YOU KNOW...

***Murphy's Manor*, by Kurt Erichson, is the longest continuously running gay comic strip in America. Started in 1982, it has run in papers around the country for the last thirteen years.**

Lesbian and Gay Comics

Lesbian and gay comic artists have long struggled to draw comics about their lives and reach people with their work. In the earliest days of the medium, depictions of gay men and lesbians were limited to lame jokes at our expense, in such publications as *Brevities*, in the 1930s and 1940s; to illegal "Tijuana Bibles" (sexually explicit chapbooks) featuring popular comic strip characters; and to sexually explicit material such as that drawn by Blade, which appeared as early as the 1940s, and circulated in the gay underground. Comics historian Maurice Horn suggests that gay people (identified mainly by their effeminacy) appeared in early comics such as "Dick Tracy" and "Terry and the Pirates" in the 1930s and 1940s. These were usually one-note jokes trading on stereotypes.

There are no overt drawings of gay people in early comic books thanks to the attitude of the times. The Comics Code Authority, set up by the comic book industry in the 1950s following Senate hearings investigating comics as a cause of juvenile delinquency, prohibited the portrayal of homosexuality and was a powerful tool of censorship for decades.

The Comics Code lost its teeth in the 1970s, and by the 1990s it was regularly circumvented via alternative distribution systems, allowing comic books to more directly address issues of homosexuality.

Since the 1980s, gay men and lesbians appeared as occasional supporting characters in mainstream comic books. "Green Arrow," "Legion of Superheroes," "Swamp Thing," "Sandman," "Blood Syndicate," and "Zot!" are just some of the mainstream titles that have featured gay characters.

But it fell to the gay community to represent itself in force. The underground comics movement, emerging as part of the counterculture of the late 1960s, opened up possibilities of gay representation. But the underground was often about shock value, and the earliest examples tended to be drawn by (presumed) heterosexuals simply for this purpose. "Captain Piss Gums" and "Ruby the Dyke" (both by the outrageous S. Clay Wilson) fit into this category. In contrast, (straight) feminist cartoonist Trina Robbins wrote and drew about effeminate boys and lesbians that were not considered authentic. Responding to the dearth of true lesbian imagery, even in the (straight) feminist "Wimmen's Comix," Roberta Gregory published the first lesbian comic book, "Dynamite Damsels," in 1976, which featured the motorcycling Doris, a self-described "tough old dyke." The first sexually explicit gay male underground comic book, Larry Fuller's "Gay Heart Throbs," also appeared in 1976. Subsequent issues appeared in 1979 and 1981. Mary Wings released "Come Out Comix" in 1977. The year 1980 saw the publication of "Gay Comix" from Kitchen Sink Press, under the editorship of Howard Cruse. Since turned over to Robert Triptow and now Andy Mangels, the recently rechristened "Gay Comics" has continued as an important source of exposure

A strip from Howard Cruse's heartfelt graphic novel Stuck Rubber Baby *(Paradox Press, 1995). (Howard Cruse)*

for cartoonists from the underground and the mainstream. From the start, "Gay Comix" eschewed gratuitous sex and strived to present political or personal narratives. Mangels has moved "Gay Comics" away from its underground roots, trying to act as a bridge to the mainstream, providing a showcase for the superhero or fantasy creators to do work with a greater gay inflection. For example, Roberta Gregory was an early portrayer of bisexuality in "Gay Comics" #2 (1981), and debuted her angry (and all-lesbian) character Bitchy Butch in "Gay Comics" #15.

Hothead Paisan, the militant, kick-butt dyke character, with her cat, Chicken. (diane dimassa)

Today, gay people are represented in all the various comics formats. There is a sense of potential from the inroads that have been made and the barrier of invisibility has been cracked. Ivan Velez, who gained prominence in the gay community for "Tales of the Closet" (1987–present), works gay characters into his more mainstream titles for Milestone and DC. Diane DiMassa ("Hothead Paisan") and Tim Barela ("Leonard and Larry") released new anthologies of their work in 1994. Alison Bechdel has taken home three Lambda Literary Awards for her "Dykes to Watch Out For" series. Andrea Natalie ("Stonewall Riots"), Eric Orner ("The Mostly Unfabulous Social Life of Ethan Green"), Jennifer Camper, Joan Hilty, and Kris Kovick all continue to produce work in various newspapers and magazines, as the distinctions between the mainstream and the recognized underground, and between the gay press and queer 'zines, continue to erode. The queer 'zine revolution has produced dozens of strips and low-circulation publications, which may launch their creators into the wider prominence of the gay mainstream. Consider that "Stuck Rubber Baby" is a personal, heartfelt chronicle of gay life, supported by DC, one of the largest comic book companies in the country. Things have never looked better for queer comics.

— **STEPHEN KENT JUSICK**

Start and Sputter—Gay Characters Who Didn't Make it

Where gay men and lesbians did appear in comics, they were often candy-coated, briefly alluded to, and quickly vanished. Here are some attempts, wholehearted and halfhearted alike, to portray gay men and lesbians in mainstream comic strips.

1950s

Brenda Starr's very butch co-worker Hank was often mistaken for a man before she was suddenly married off.

1976

Garry Trudeau introduced Andy Lippincott, a nonthreatening gay character who failed to become a "Doonsbury" fixture. He faded and reappeared in 1989, addressing the AIDS issue, only to die of the disease a year later.

1977

Hearsay has it that the artist of "Winnie Winkle" proposed a coming-out story line that the syndicate vetoed in favor of the same character's heterosexual marriage.

1980

The Incredible Hulk's alter ego, Bruce Banner, is almost raped by two sterotypically gay, lisping young men in a YMCA. Marvel was reamed so badly for their homophobia that they decided to back away from this issue. Subsequently, editor-in-chief Jim Shooter weakly declared there were no gays in the "Marvel universe."

1982

Marvel's "Captain America" #270 alluded to the homosexuality of a friend of Captain America's so cautiously that the point was probably lost on most readers.

Late 1980s

A few "Superman" comics contained some oblique references to police chief Maggie Sawyer's lesbianism, but it was all innuendo that could be denied in case of political backlash. "Superman" #15 (1988) told her coming-out story without using the words "gay" or "lesbian."

With little fanfare, a longtime DC character, the Pied Piper, casually mentioned his homosexuality to his former nemesis, the Flash. He receded into the background about a year later without much character development.

— STEPHEN KENT JUSICK

Successes — Queer Strip Characters

Not all gay characters in comics are stereotypes or one-dimensional write-offs. Here are some comic strips that have lifted veils of gay invisibility and given meaningful identities to gay and lesbian characters, by gay and straight comics alike.

Howard Cruse's character **Headrack** came out in "Barefootz Funnies" #2 (1976). This was the first phase in Cruse's personal coming-out and began his plunge into full-time gay cartooning. His strip "Wendel" ran in the *Advocate* from 1983 to 1985 and late 1986 to 1989, and has been collected into book form, as have other of his comic strips and stories. "Stuck Rubber Baby," Cruse's meditation on racism, homophobia, and individual responsibility, set against the backdrop of the civil rights movement in the 1960s South, was published in 1995 under the Paradox Press imprint of DC Comics.

"Cathartic Comics," by Rupert Kinnard, first appeared in the Cornell College newspaper in Iowa in 1977. The Brown Bomber came out in 1979 and the lesbian character Diva Flambe Touche followed in 1981, making them the oldest continuing African American gay and lesbian characters.

Jerry Mills's (1951–1993) strip **"Poppers"** ran from 1982 to 1986 in *In Touch*, and then from 1986 to 1991 in *Advocate Men*. Mills's command of humorous graphic vocabulary reflected the sexual mores of the time while staying away from the purely sexual content that is the mainstay of gay male porn.

"Dykes to Watch Out For," by Alison Bechdel, first appeared in the feminist paper *Womanews* in 1983. Now collected into books, the biweekly strip has been self-syndicated since 1985 and is now seen in over forty-five papers internationally, making it the most popular gay comic strip of all time.

Since 1986, Leyland Publications has released sixteen volumes of **"Meatmen,"** an anthology of sexually explicit gay male cartoons and comics, following in the tradition of chapbooks and Tijuana Bibles.

Jaime and Gilbert Hernandez's **"Love and Rockets"** is a bonanza for queer Latino representation. Maggie and Hopey from Jaime's "Locas" storylines have a long-standing on-again, off-again lesbian relationship. Gilbert has portrayed not only gay characters such as the lesbian couple Riri and Maricela, and activist Mike Niznick, but individuals—sometimes confused and conflicted, sometimes category-defying—willing to experiment with their sexuality.

"Hothead Paisan," by Diane DiMassa, stalked on the scene in her own series in 1991 and the "homicidal lesbian terrorist" has racked up more than fifteen issues since.

Akbar and Jeff are an unusual gay couple in Matt Groening's quirky **"Life in Hell"** series, which began in the early 1980s.

In the 1990s, DC finally admitted that some of **Wonder Woman's Amazon sisters** were indeed lesbians.

Marvel Comics published the much-ballyhooed coming-out story of its Canadian hero Northstar in **"Alpha Flight"** #106 (1992), in a storyline featuring a fight over custody rights for an infant with AIDS. There had been many subtle hints about Northstar's orientation since 1984, but this story signaled a change in Marvel's official policy of no gay characters.

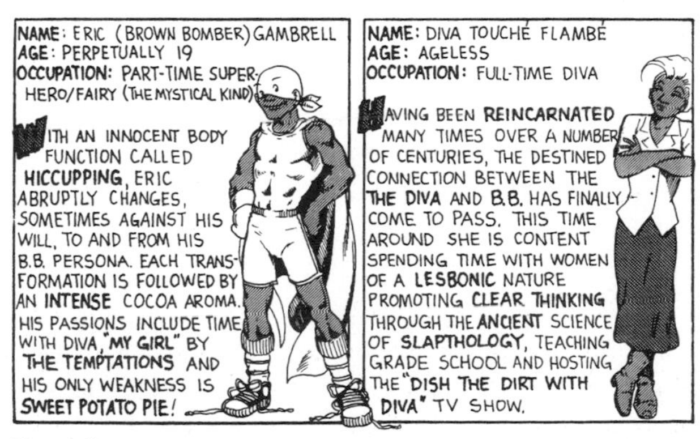

(Rupert Kinnard)

"For Better or For Worse," by Lynn Johnson, began a breakthrough five-week sequence on March 22, 1993, by revealing that Lawrence, a longtime character, was gay. He gradually came out to friends and family, and in June 1994, took his boyfriend to the high school prom.

— STEPHEN KENT JUSICK

DID YOU KNOW...

- *Lea Delaria* was the first out (and outrageous) stand-up comic on a late-night network television program when she was featured on *The Arsenio Hall Show* in March 1993.
- Comedian *Bob Smith*, one of the group Funny Gay Males, was the first openly gay comic to appear on NBC's *Tonight Show*, in July 1994.
- *Kate Clinton* was the first out lesbian/gay comedian on public TV when she was on the KQED *Comedy Tonight* program in 1991. (Kate did not identify herself as a lesbian per se; she mentioned in her routine that she had broken the Tenth Commandment: "thou shalt not covet thy neighbor's wife.")
- *Suzanne Westenhoffer* was the first openly gay person to have her own comedy special when, in July 1994, she appeared on HBO's *One Night Stand* series.

A Quick Look at AIDS in the Comics

Mainstream comics were slow to take up the representation (or mention) of AIDS. "Strip AIDS USA," a 1989 compendium of new and reprinted work that mainly served as a public service announcement, featured AIDS-related work by mainstream, underground, and newspaper strip creators. *Within Our Reach* was a benefit book for AIDS causes, published by Marvel. DC featured Death, one of its characters most popular with older readers, in a special supplement that discussed AIDS and how to use a condom. Garry Trudeau's "Doonesbury" character Andy Lippincott died of AIDS in 1990. More recently, *Image* has produced several story lines about the HIV-positive superhero Shadowhawk. "The Incredible Hulk" has made strides since 1980, with a special AIDS awareness issue in 1994, in which a former Hulk sidekick asked for a gamma ray–irradiated blood transplant from the Hulk to conquer his own HIV infection.

Queer Comics' Queer Comments

We've asked some of the lesbian and gay comics from around the country to give us some of their favorite lines on the life. Here's what they had to say:

Tom Ammiano

Homophobia: The irrational fear that three fags will break into your house and redecorate it against your will.

San Francisco is so gay, it has it's own patron saint, Saint Francis the Sissy. For his miracle, he changed breakfast into brunch.

Suzy Berger

My lover asked me if I wanted to have children. I told her I didn't know, but we should keep trying.

According to *People* magazine, 70 percent of the women in prison are lesbians . . . GET ME A GUN!

Kate Clinton

I love softball. I play third base. You would love my team. Women, who are, like, not into competition—now tell me, aren't those usually the women who come with the brand-new two-inch cleats on the first day? On my softball team, there are also some women who just can't get into the coach-player dynamic. They cannot deal with the hierarchy of that. So we do a lot of processing on our team. Velveeta should be our team sponsor.

— FROM YVONNE ZIPTER'S DIAMONDS ARE A DYKE'S BEST FRIEND

Ohio-based lesbian comedian Karen Williams. (Abigail Huller)

Lisa Geduldig

I come from a very typical Jewish family—a doctor, a lawyer, and a lesbian comic. When I decided to come out of the closet to my family, I thought I would do so where I felt most comfortable, in a Chinese restaurant . . . where I rigged the fortune cookies. I invited the whole extended family and sat my parents down at opposite ends of the table, and they got the same fortune: "Your son-in-law will be a turkey baster."

Doug Holsclaw

They say there is a gay gene. I think there are lots of gay genes. For instance, I didn't get the decorating gene or the opera gene or the neatness gene. I did, however, get the hair-obsession, multiple-sex-partner, and vicious-put-down genes. So I'm not complaining. I think I fared pretty well.

I remember when I was twenty and I had this fantasy of my ideal man who was older, maybe in his late thirties or early forties and really cute with a lot of money and a nice house, nice car, likes to travel. . . . Now *I'm* in my thirties and I find I've really changed. Now my ideal man is someone who is twenty—and really cute with a lot of money and a nice house and a nice car and likes to travel. Some things never change.

Marilyn Pittman

I was a teenage lesbian. And there was one thing we gay teenagers could do that our straight friends couldn't. I could say to my mom, "Mom, Michelle's coming over to spend the night Friday." She'd say, "Okay, honey." Johnny couldn't come over, but Michelle could!!

Ever since Milton Berle put on a dress in the fifties, people have thought fags were funny. But "lesbian comic"? Isn't that an oxymoron? Everybody knows that lesbians are mean and ugly and hate men. Well . . .

Bob Smith is a gay comedian from New York who has appeared on a number of nationally televised programs, including HBO's One Night Stand.

Karen Ripley

I tell gay and lesbian jokes because I don't ever want to be rich and famous . . . It's working. Mom wanted a girl, and Dad wanted a boy—now they're both happy.

Bob Smith

It wasn't easy telling my parents that I'm gay. I told them at Thanksgiving. I said, "Mom, would you please pass the gravy to a homosexual?" She passed it to my father. A terrible scene followed. In college, I experimented with heterosexuality. I slept with a straight guy. I was *really* drunk.

Danny Williams

If gay men and lesbians can't serve in the military, then straight men shouldn't be allowed to be florists, and straight women can't work for UPS.

In the town of Alamo, California, the residents living on a street named Gay Court were so embarrassed that they changed the name from Gay Court to High Eagle Court. I guess the name Homophobic Idiot Boulevard was already taken.

Letter From Home

I don't know if this happens to any of you, but I write a letter to my parents and talk about all kinds of thoughts, feelings, emotions, suggestions, certainties, uncertainties . . . and I get a letter back from them, addressing absolutely NOTHING that I wrote to them about. So, I decided on a new tactic. From now on, I write a letter to them and enclose a copy of the letter I'd *like* to receive from them, ask them to sign it, and send it back in the enclosed, self-addressed stamped envelope. Let me know what you think.

Dear Lisa,

We were just telling some of our friends in our P-FLAG (Parents, Family, and Friends of Lesbians and Gays) group how happy we are for you that you came out of the closet. We are just *so* proud of who you are. "My daughter is a lesbian!" I just *love* to hear myself say those words.

How are you since your recent breakup? Are you seeing any nice Jewish girls? Our neighbor has a daughter . . . we'd really like you to meet. . . . And she's a doctor!

We put a lot of thought into what you wrote in your last letter, and you have a really good point. After over thirty years of being a noncommunicative family, we're also very glad that we collectively decided to work on interpersonal relations within the immediate family. We'd *love* to come visit you in San Francisco and see your life there. We support you in *everything* you do, sister.
Love,
Mom & Dad

P.S.: What do you think about the current wave of censorship and conservatism in this country? We'd *love* to hear your opinion.

— **LISA GEDULDIG**

OUT ON THE TOWN

Sometimes you just have to get out of the house and cut loose. The work week was exhausting, your mother has been on the warpath, and your cat seems even more surly than usual. Or maybe you're just bored. In any case, lesbians and gay men have a number of gathering places to choose from for community, fun, and cruising.

Whether in small towns or large cities, lesbians and gay men are coming together in a variety of ways just for fun. Bars and social clubs are an important part of our communities. By carving out our own spaces to dance and socialize, we create communities based around more than simply our sexualities—they reflect the diversity of ways in which we shake our tail feathers and have a good time.

The Ins and Outs of Gay Bars

Unless you find yourself dead center in the Mojave Desert, you're never probably more than a few hours' drive from a gay bar. Oddly, outside of major cities they tend to be on the average larger than the typical New York or San Francisco bar. Bars in gay meccas tend to be extraordinarily specialized: leather bars, serious leather bars, dance bars, chicken/chicken hawk bars, hustler bars, yuppie bars, sing-along piano bars, bars that attract a Black or Latino or Asian American clientele. But outside of cities with very large gay populations, the bars are more like "one size fits all." In Heartland, USA, you can find bars featuring drag shows in one room, a piano player in another, and posturing leathermen in a third—a combination that attests to the diversity of the gay community throughout the country.

Though bars are a staple feature of American gay life, they aren't centers around which most gay people build their lives. For a certain percentage, the bars function as extended living rooms. For others, the bars could as well be on other planets. Most of us are somewhere in the middle—attending bars, say, once or twice weekly or monthly, or when going out with a particular group of friends.

After the thousands of hours I've spent in gay bars, it would be unseemly for me to write negatively about them. I really do think your chances of finding a lover for the rest of your life (if that's what you're looking for) are probably as good in a bar as anywhere else. And your chances for finding a trick in a bar are somewhat better than that (though in this age of AIDS, casual tricks ain't what they used to be).

In some bars it is perfectly correct to accost a complete stranger and introduce yourself with a detailed description of just what sexual activities he should participate in with you to make you happy. (In a few bars it is/was perfectly correct to accost a complete stranger and introduce yourself with a detailed description of just what sexual activities he should participate in with you *right then and there* to make you happy.)

"By heterosexuals the life after death is imagined as a world of light, where there is no parting. If there is a heaven for homosexuals, which doesn't seem very likely, it will be very poorly lit and full of people they can feel pretty confident they will never have to meet again."

QUENTIN CRISP, 1984

Since gay bar-going is a social activity, being comfortable in gay bars is not unrelated to being comfortable with one's gay identity. Most gays live their daily lives "acting straight"; even gays who are out to co-workers and family conform to varying degrees to heterosexual norms. Paradoxically, gays may therefore find it more difficult to relate to other gays than to straights. In gay bars they may feel overly intimidated, or, fueled by alcohol and/or other drugs, some gays may use bars as stages to act out new heights of obnoxiousness.

Men hanging out during an ever-popular beer bust at a gay bar. (Rink Foto)

Every primer on meeting new friends and winning lovers seems to intone "Be yourself." I'm not sure that's such good advice. Better to go to a gay bar being the person you want to be. Don't be afraid to initiate conversations; you can talk with people you have no sexual interest in. Have a positive attitude. If you keep whining about not having a lover, you'll never have a lover. Enjoy yourself. Be gay, damn it. *Gay.* Look it up.

Gay bars are not a metaphor. Though sad, self-destructive alcoholics and giddy, amoral disco bunnies are found in gay bars, these people do not epitomize the gay bar system. Neither do gay bars symbolize the decadence of society. The Jerry Falwells see gay bars as evidence of the decline of Western civilization, but gay bars are simply not *that* good. Gay bars are a phenomenon. They are there in the same way that supermarkets, laundromats, and movie theaters are there, as places to frequent if you find they fulfill a need.

— T. R. WITOMSKI

Bank Shot Cruising— The Lesbian Bar Scene

Pool playing and lesbians: genetic mandate, or socialized behavior? Maybe it's the idea of getting to knock a bunch of balls around with a stick. Maybe it's having a great excuse to watch a lot of women constantly bend over a table about the dimensions of a full-sized bed. Whatever the reasons, pool seems to be an integral part of the lesbian bar scene no matter what area of the country you're in. And every kind of lesbian you can think of participates in some aspect of the game. As a rule, the femmes tend to lend ornamentation to the contest while the b-girls and butches brandish the cues. Although I did once have the pleasure of witnessing a femme resembling Christie Brinkley knock down trick shots like the second coming in a Virginia Beach queer bar. Needless to say, my andro-butch colleagues and I were stunned out of our neochauvinist minds. Who knew a femme could play like that?

The ritual goes something like this: You and yours arrive at the joint around eight o'clock if you want a snowball's chance at the table. Sign your name on the little chalkboard provided and head to the bar for your beer or club soda. (These are props to be used for swigging to maintain cool after blown shots.) When your name is called, play like the fate of the world depends on it, so all the cute girls can see what a shark you are. And (sorry to all my fellow nonsmokers) the Marlboro dangling from the corner of the mouth greatly enhances one's pool-pro image. It gives you that added squint through the smoke so it *really* looks as though you're sizing up the shot-as-quantum physics. That's about it. . . .

What? Were you expecting some sordid insider scoop on the lesbian cruising that takes place around pool tables? Well, the sorry fact of the matter is this—lesbians don't cruise in any *practical,* get-the-damned-thing-done sense of the word. Despite the recent progressive trends in lesbian sexual behavior, in large portions we are still just a tad slow to jump on the sex-positive gravy train. If we want to achieve and maintain proper cruise control, we should take a few tips from our queer brothers (with a grain of salt):

1. Spot the trick
2. Turn around to friend and squeal, "Ohmygod!theone-intheblackvestis SOO HOT!"
3. Turn back around and make eye contact with trick.
4. Drag hapless friend around the whole place in trick's wake until you both catch her staring in ten different parts of the bar.
5. Figure out what you're going to say (quick!).
6. Move in for the kill.
7. Get phone number, or, for more efficient types, get to bed.

Lesbians make it all the way to about Step 5 and stall dead in their tracks. Mind you, Steps 5 and 6 can last the duration of one evening or continue over a weeks-long series of "next times" and near misses. It's stupid. Everyone knows clubs are meat markets. Who really goes to these places in search of friends and profound conversation? Only the clueless. So just talk to that hot honey who's been staring at you for the last half hour. You want her, go 'n' get her!

Wait a minute. It just dawned on me why lesbians take forever to talk to a chick they dig. They're deeply scrutinizing her potential for domestic partnership! In the course of one evening a lesbian must decide beyond a shadow of a doubt if the scopee is *the* woman with whom she wants to spend the rest of her natural life. Well, in that case, one cannot be too hasty.

You might want to bear in mind one variable, however—if you meet her in a bar, you'll probably spend more time staring at her than you will actually dating her.

— ARWYN MOORE

"I can think of no better place to have suspense and a real eerie feeling of decadence than a lesbian bar, because lesbians are outlaws, we've always been outlaws and I hope we always stay outlaws, and lesbian bars are our secret hiding places."

MARY WINGS, MYSTERY WRITER, IN THE FILM *LAST CALL AT MAUD'S*

SONGS THAT MOVE QUEERS

Following is a list of the songs played in mainstream gay and lesbian clubs guaranteed to get those lavender booties shakin' every time.

Gay Men
Any Village People hit
Any Madonna song
"It's Raining Men"—The Weather Girls
"Supermodel (You Better Work)"—RuPaul
"You Make Me Feel (Mighty Real)"—Sylvester

Lesbians
"Express Yourself"—Madonna
"I'm Every Woman"—Whitney Houston
"I'm Gonna Get You"—Bizarre Inc.
"Respect"—Aretha Franklin
"Bad Girls"—Donna Summer

Everybody
Any dance remix of a queer-popular song (like k.d.'s "Constant Craving")
"Don't Leave Me This Way"—Thelma Houston
"Enough is Enough"—Donna Summer and Barbra Streisand
"I Will Survive"—Gloria Gaynor
"A Deeper Love"—Aretha Franklin
"We Are Family"—Sister Sledge
"I'm Coming Out" —Diana Ross

Shake Your Groove Thing

Whether or not you know it, the club scene is as big now as it was in the seventies. Nowadays, young queers, both men and women, flock to dance clubs around the country, where lesbians and gay men can often be found dancing together. Here, two young people, Don Romesburg and Arwyn Moore, share their conversation about why they find dancing so integral to their lives.

DR: Is dancing in a gay bar revolutionary? Maybe it was a decade or two ago. But I'm a young white queer boy living in San Francisco—the Castro, no less—and I'm HIV-negative (at least according to my last test). Pretty much the only time my dancing in a gay bar is revolutionary is when I spin around.

AM: Why the fuck should everything be political? Being a Black lesbian in the queer community makes me very tired of politics! I don't do politics while I'm dancing—it's just about the only time I don't feel guilty for not being conscientious.

DR: I won't even start about my white liberal guilt. Nobody—including me—wants to hear that song anymore. But how about something by Madonna circa late 1980s? Turn that beat around. When I'm moving my body and pumping my legs until sweat drips off my face—that's what the dancing's about. The passion. The pulse.

AM: I won't even start about Madonna. That's what DJs play when the scene is beat and they need to get folks on the dance floor. I can't get behind that—I need music I can throw my whole self into without thinking about the words or who's singing them. Dancing keeps us in touch with our bodies and our instincts, which we tend to neglect in everyday life. You can't dance with your intellect.

DR: Dancing is trying to push past feeling self-conscious about what I think and what I look like. It's a crazy mixture of feeling a little uncomfortable with myself and liberating myself from feeling self-conscious. I explore the space, including the bodies in motion that surround me. When I forget myself—that's when I dance best.

AM: Your body knows what it's supposed to do; the point is whether you let it or not. It shouldn't matter what other people think your body ought to be doing. But being queer is so much about image, and that carries over to dancing. When I dance, I try to be outside myself. But if I'm with someone who makes me all paranoid 'cause she can't let go, I can't enjoy myself to the fullest.

DR: Dancing isn't really about talent or command of certain steps. It's about finding a groove that works for you. And if a person lets go of that mental control and lets their body do its thing, it's very sexy. Okay, so dancing is also about sex. Big time.

(Jill Posener)

AM: Dance and sex are synonymous because they're both about primal instinct. It's not so much about how someone moves, but what's moving them.

DR: I know. I hate to sound New Age-y, but dancing is also spiritual—it cleanses the soul. It's a kind of euphoria; that joy and invigorating exhaustion. I move in ways I wouldn't normally, using both physical and spiritual muscles I didn't know (or forgot) I had.

AM: I heard that! Don't tell me nothin' after I've just torn up the dance floor, honey. I'm so high! Sometimes I dance so damned good I embarrass myself. It's like I'm showing off. When I'm dancing, I'm immortal.

DR: It's all about that person, sexy, sweaty, and sly, who is just on top of the beat, tasting the music, and riding the energy of the room. It doesn't matter what that person's gender is. That's who I want to be when I'm dancing. I want to reach that place where it all intersects, and I'm not only dancing in a crowd, but I *am* the crowd. I am the energy. That's when dancing is love.

AM: That's the part that a lot of people will never quite get.

Two-Stepping for Beginners

Around the country, in large cities and small towns, lesbians and gay men are going to their local gay bars to two-step and line dance to country-western hits from Wynona, Garth, and Lyle Lovett. And if you've ever been out on the dance floor in a gay country bar, you know that when Billy Ray Cyrus's "Achey Breaky Heart" comes on, you'd better not be trying to two-step, because the line dancers doing the "Achey Breaky" will run you flat.

Cowboys line-dancing at the Rawhide, a gay country-western bar in San Francisco in 1985. (Rink Foto)

In *Round Up: The Gay Western and Rodeo Magazine*, Chris Hochmuth spoke to the panic that sets in when line dancers and two-steppers collide: "Imagine the chaos created on the dance floor where the 'Achey Breaky' is not taught, but almost everybody does it. The song comes on, a group of line dancers forms out in the center of the floor with couples trying to two-step shuffle around them. Break out the body bags."

Welcome to the country side of town in queer America. Country-western dancing is a fun and exciting way to get close with that cowboy or cowgirl you've had your eye on. Once you're over at the bar, you'll find that the country crowd is one of the friendliest, most open groups you've ever encountered. The ages of the patrons vary from people in their early twenties to those in their sixties and seventies, though the majority are between the ages of thirty and fifty. Most of the dancers are men, although the women hold their own, and most are white (though happily that is changing). Unlike in the thumpa-thompa-boom clubs and pickup bars, you'll notice that people are smiling, talking, and having a good time. The only attitude you might find here is on the dance floor.

If you don't know what you're doing, take a few of the lessons most bars provide before you stumble out onto the floor. Those whirling, twirling couples don't take too kindly to a slowpoke when the floor really gets moving. And wait for a few bars of a song before you get out on the floor, or you may find yourself in the middle of an "L.D.C. Express" line-dance scuff 'n' scoot without a clue whether your next move should be a grapevine, a left step forward, or to get the hell off the floor and buy yourself a stiff drink. Don't worry; nobody starts out as a pro, and you will get better. Even over the course of a single evening you'd be amazed how much better you can negotiate the footwork.

Be careful, honey, because this stuff's addictive. Ken Smith, who now teaches two-stepping at the Rawhide II in San Francisco, went the first time thinking, *This could be neat, but I hate the music.* A few months later, he had his car radio preset to the country stations. Now he can be found five nights a week dancing his heart out. Lesbian and gay country regulars always talk about the incredible sense of community that two-stepping provides, and how in nearly every state the country bar crowds are about the same: open, friendly, and fun-loving. Don't knock gay country-western bars till you've tried 'em. You may just find yourself a new family, if, that is, you can survive the dance floor.

— MISS BEVERLY HILL-BILLIE

DID YOU KNOW...

Maile and Marina are probably the hottest lesbian two-stepping duo around. They teach both two-step and country-western line dancing all across the country, using only music by female performers in their live shows and instructional videos. Their stylish dress, quick wit, and warmth have earned this longtime couple widespread fame throughout the country-western community. Devotion to each other and building community (as well as just putting on a great show) make these women both inspiring and entertaining role models to their thousands of fans.

Square Your Sets!

Square dancing offers the gay and lesbian community a unique social outlet. It is excellent exercise, and traditionally, smoking and drinking are not permitted in a square-dance hall, so it is a thoroughly healthy endeavor. Men and women meet on grounds different from the ones they are accustomed to, and find that the things that bind them are greater than the ones that divide them.

For the men, square dancing allows an opportunity to meet far from the ever-present sexual pressures in the usual bar scene. When a man asks you to be his partner in a square, you don't have to worry: "Oh, God, is he my type?" All you have to do is dance with him and say "thank you" at the end of the "tip."

The result is that prejudices such as those usually displayed in the personal ads—"Seeking: WM, age 32 to 33 1/2, Greek passive, French active, into Florsheim wingtips; no fats or fems need reply"—become immaterial. You get to know the people behind the stereotypes, and find out that—horrors!—you actually get to like some of the fats, fems, or whatever category it was you thought you wanted nothing to do with. Your square-dancing friends become the people you go out with to dinner, the movies, or the theater; the ones you call when you are blue; the ones who help lift your morale when a love affair goes sour; the ones by your bedside when you are ill.

Does gay square dancing differ from straight square dancing? Straight callers who call for gay events will tell you that there are some significant differences. Straight square dancers come, of course, in biologically identifiable couples, with each person dancing his or her biologically correct role (and don't

"We work hard to keep the club at a fifty-fifty mix. If a new class is predominantly one gender, we target our advertising to the other gender for the next class. We try very hard to make sure that the club board is evenly split. We support each other, even in small things: At the Miami convention, when the Wilde Bunch women were asked to join in the "all-woman" tip, the W.B. men came to watch and show their support. We are very sensitive to each other's needs. Our men dance gently, and our women try to learn what a red bandanna in the right back pocket with the third button of the fly open and a banana in the left ear means."

GRACE CUMMINS,
THE WILDE BUNCH
SQUARE-DANCE CLUB,
ALBUQUERQUE, NM

even think of switching!). Aside from that, straight square dancers follow a rigid dress code, which usually results in "color-coded" couples, where the man wears a shirt the same color as his partner's dress.

Among gay square dancers, the only dress code seems to be that you have to wear something while you are on the dance floor (well, even that rule is not always observed), but that "something" can be a pair of leather chaps with nothing covering your derriere. As far as the biological sex of the dancers is concerned, a gay square may be composed of five men and three women, but the three women may be dancing the men's parts! It could be a caller's nightmare, since any series of dance movements is supposed to end with original partners back together again, but callers who adjust to the challenge will tell you there is nothing like calling for a gay event.

The reason, they tell you, is the incredible energy that gay square dancers display and the way they respond to a caller's challenging choreography. Why is the dancers' reaction so different between a gay and a straight event? Some observe that straight square dancing is, for the most part, an activity of older, married couples, whereas gay square dancers are significantly younger on the average.

That does not account for Stan and Bill from the Sacramento club, however. Both are in their seventies now; they have attended all nine annual conventions since the first one in Seattle. They celebrated their fortieth anniversary together at the Vancouver convention in 1990, and were the first two people to register for the tenth anniversary convention coming this July in Seattle. Once again, you'll find them on the dance floor there with everyone else.

A well-known straight national caller, who is black himself, has a different theory about the energy of gay dancers. He says that the only place he has found a similar response from the dance floor has been when he has called for all-black square-dance events. In his opinion, the energy is that of people who have been held back their whole lives through but have finally found something they really enjoy doing. With the feeling of repression lifted in the activity, the pent-up energy just comes rushing through. Maybe he is right.

— **LUIS TORRES**

DID YOU KNOW...

Square dancing is thought to be the modern day evolution of the all-male folk dance that was popular in early Colonial America.

JOCKSTRAPS AND SPORTS BRAS

Sports in the lesbian and gay community are about far more than just the competition. We play in a variety of ways, from the butch lesbian softballer to the nellie queen who is a whiz at Ping-Pong; from the all-dyke bowling team to gay male cheerleading squads. Many of us enjoy the camaraderie, recreation, and, yes, competition that lesbian and gay athletics bring.

Queer sports are also about gender-bending and breaking stereotypes. Butches, femmes, and a variety of other dykes can and do participate in any number of sporting events. And gay men, from fey fags to gym bunnies, compete with enthusiasm on everything from wrestling mats to soccer fields across the United States. It isn't simply that lesbians (as women) and gay men (as not "real" men) shatter societal expectations of athleticism and machismo, though that in itself is revolutionary. Gay people also revitalize sports by adding to them a sense of camp, acknowledging the erotic value of athletics, and using sports as a powerful form of building gay communities.

"To play sports with women is to love women, to be passionate about women, to be intimate with women."

FORMER PRO BASKETBALL PLAYER MARIAH BURTON NELSON

Some people living with HIV and AIDS are finding empowerment through sports. Healthy living, including physical fitness, can increase both physical and emotional well-being. In addition, by excelling athletically, people with HIV and AIDS show the world that being positive doesn't have to mean being inactive. These are individuals like Rick Muñoz, a thirty-six-year-old marathon runner from Los Angeles who, after discovering he was HIV-positive in 1987, tightened up his training schedule, sharpened his focus, and reached his personal best of 2 hours 44 minutes in 1992.

Dykes, Diamonds and Double-Plays

Here's a quick question: What is the lesbian national pastime?

a) k.d. lang

b) processing

c) turkey basting

d) softball

e) commitment ceremonies

Softball is the unequivocally correct response. The girls of summer are everywhere: "Country dykes, city dykes, dykes with four-year degrees, dykes who are feminists, dykes who aren't, dykes of different races and classes, dykes who have been athletes all their lives, and dykes who are just discovering, or rediscovering after years, the value of athletic endeavors—there are softball players among all their ranks," according to Yvonne Zipter, author of *Diamonds Are a Dyke's Best Friend.*

It is a lesbian institution that began as an unofficial place to meet other lesbians. Dykes enjoy the bonding and mutual support that go with the game, but the real attraction of softball is social. It's a place to meet other women, to fall in love and have fun all at the same time.

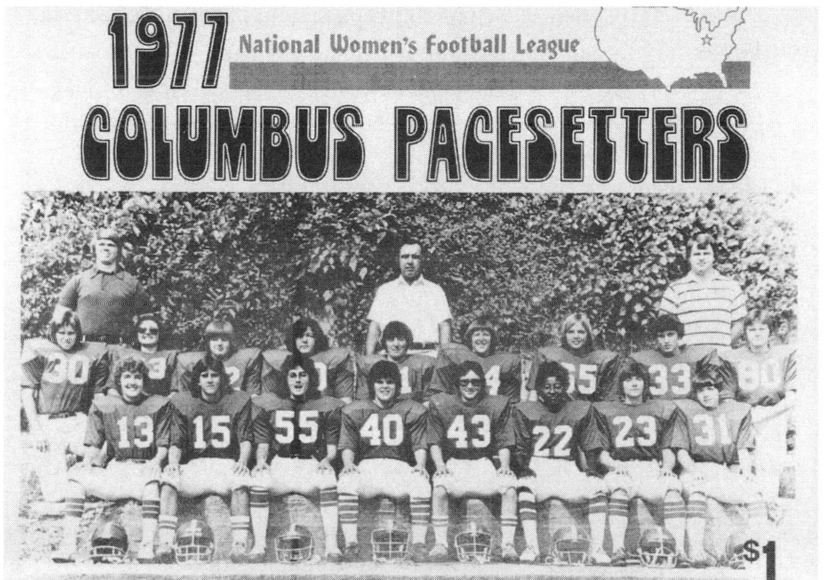

One of ten pro teams in the Women's National Football League during the seventies, the Columbus franchise was owned and operated by a a lesbian majority. Unlike their professional counterparts in golf and tennis, these women were not required to wear make-up and "dress fashionably." (Courtesy of Linda Stamps)

Several lesbians shared their experiences with Zipter. Fran found love. "I met my first lover through softball . . . I think softball is a good place to meet people and probably always will be." Valerie bypassed the bar scene, reflecting that "There are so few places for women to go and meet apart from bars. . . . It is an ideal way to get to know other people." Laurie sums it all up: "Team sports

DID YOU KNOW...

The Front Runners, a national lesbian and gay running group, began in the early 1970s when a couple of San Franciscans interested in running met at Lavender U, an experimental gay college, in a furniture restoration class. That 1974 running group became the Lavender U Joggers. In 1978, adopting the name of a popular book about a gay runner, they became the Front Runners. On July 27, 1980, the group's cosponsor, *Advocate* magazine, held the first Gay Run. The Front Runners became the first gay club to join the Amateur Athletic Union, which later became The Athletic Congress, the organization that sanctions road races across the nation.

are the main social outlets in my life. I depend on them for emotional support, physical activity, a sense of belonging, a comfortable atmosphere, and an outlet for my competitive nature."

Other players describe the pleasures of the game—the sound of a ball hitting the fat part of the bat, the feel of sweat, or the smell of a leather glove. Individual teams are as distinct as individual players. Philosophies of play vary widely. Some teams approach the game with a "winning-is-all" attitude, while others seek personal bests. Many just want to have fun. No matter what the approach, the commitment to the game is total. "As with everything else they do, lesbians are a hundred percent invested in softball," explains Alix Dobkin.

Dykes play in straight leagues, gay and lesbian leagues, lesbian-only leagues, and just about any combination imaginable. Teams are backed by businesses, players, family, and friends. In gay and lesbian leagues, bars tend to be the largest group of sponsors, fostering goodwill, supporting lesbian sports, and seeking exposure.

Softball's future in the lesbian community remains certain. It is universal, accessible, and fun. It unites the diverse elements of lesbian society unlike any other event. Diamonds *are* a girl's best friend.

— LINDA STAMPS

These Gloves Ain't Sequined, Honey: The Bay Area Boxing Club

Greg Varney first boxed when he was six years old, long before he knew he was gay. In 1976, at twenty-four, he and his lover set up a boxing ring in the attic of their San Francisco home. It was the beginning of what has become the Bay Area Boxing Club (BABC), a pugilist program for lesbians and gay men. Varney coaches and trains his team, which includes several women.

Boxing has been more than a fetish fantasy for these fighters, who are serious about the physical and emotional prizes won by being involved in the BABC. Member Scott McDonald commented in Nancy Andrew's *Family:*

Boxer Gina Guidi takes a lesson from her coach. (Jill Posener)

"I was told gay men shouldn't box or couldn't box. Some of it is that you build up confidence in everyday life. Boxing did that. I'm HIV-positive, and I have been for seven years, and I thought, 'If I want to start to do these things in my life, I better start doing them now.'" Bruno Kochis agrees, and thinks of the BABC as a community. "It creates a very good feeling between us. It makes us family; it makes us belong."

The club sponsors two lesbian and gay tournaments annually. The first, held around Memorial Day, is mostly local. The other, normally held in the winter, is the Rainbow Gloves Tournament. Boxers from around the country compete in the ring and enjoy a sense of camaraderie outside of it. But don't think that boxing is all about fun and games—the competition is stiff and vicious.

Boxing also has an additional meaning to these lesbians and gay men. In a homophobic society, the ability to physically defend oneself can provide real confidence and peace of mind. According to Varney, "Gay people, if they get hit, tend to go away, or run, or use a whistle and hope that somebody will come. You can do anything you want, but until you can stand there and say, 'Hey, I'm just as good as you, and if you try to push me, I'll knock your lights out'—until you can actually do that, we haven't got it."

— **RON WILSON**

DID YOU KNOW...

"Up in the Sky, a Bird, a Plane—a Lambda?" Touting themselves as the "world's first gay and lesbian sky-diving team," more than twenty-five gay men and lesbians have joined the TriAngels, the brainchild of Texas sky diver John Grisak. TriAngels are "dedicated to breaking stereotypes as well as creating community involvement and having fun."

"Each rodeo I entered was more fun because I got to know more and more people. We started helping each other and encouraging each other, even if we were competing against each other. It didn't seem to matter if you were a guy or a girl, or what events you were in, or if you were winning or not, we were becoming a family. We worked and competed hard, then we played hard, then we would say good-bye until the next rodeo."

JEANINE TUTTLE, LESBIAN RODEO CHAMPION, IN "A WOMAN'S POINT OF VIEW," ROUND UP: THE GAY WESTERN AND RODEO MAGAZINE

The History of Gay Rodeo

It would be difficult for a spectator seated in the arena at Dallas or Phoenix or Denver to imagine the long and colorful road down which gay rodeo has traveled. It hasn't been easy to get from there to here!

In 1975, through Reno's Imperial Court System, Emperor Phil Ragsdale chose as his cause the Muscular Dystrophy Association and proposed a gay rodeo as a means to raise funds. The Washoe County Fairgrounds was secured as a site and, despite complications imposed by livestock providers upon learning the event would be patronized by the lesbian and gay community, the National Reno Gay Rodeo was born on October 2, 1976, and later added the Mr., Ms., and Miss National Reno Gay Rodeo competition as Mr. Ragsdale's new fund-raiser.

The Colorado Gay Rodeo Association was formed in 1981. By 1982, the National Reno Gay Rodeo hosted 10,000 spectators, with Joan Rivers serving as grand marshal. The Golden State Gay Rodeo Association and Arizona Gay Rodeo Association were formed in 1984, while Texas hosted its first gay rodeo that year. This was also the ninth and final year for the National Reno Gay Rodeo.

In 1985, the International Gay Rodeo Association was formed as an umbrella organization to establish uniform rules for the state member associations and to help each work toward producing quality rodeos. IGRA had its first convention in Denver with representatives from California, Arizona, Colorado, and Texas.

By 1988, six rodeos were successfully produced annually. The IGRA Finals, scheduled for Reno, did not occur that year due to cancellation of the rodeo's contract. Two days of legal maneuvering plus a trip to the Nevada Supreme Court failed to stop the homophobic district attorney who was behind the machinations. But he could not dampen the spirit of the lesbian and gay cowpokes, and over the next several years, membership in the IGRA boomed.

By the 1990s, the momentum had proven itself to be more than a passing fancy, and corporate sponsors took notice. Miller Brewing Company in 1991 became the first sponsor of all IGRA-sanctioned rodeos. In 1992, twelve gay rodeos were held in eleven states, drawing record crowds from Seattle, Washington, to Bethesda, Maryland, with nearly 36,000 daytime spectators and more than double that number attending associated evening functions. The IGRA truly became an international organization with the Northwest Gay Rodeo Association adding British Columbia as a member. Year by year, the IGRA continues to grow in scope, vision, and participation, breaking old stereotypes about gender, sexuality, and the cowpoke way of life.

— BOB PIMENTEL, IGRA PRESIDENT

Someone's on the Fairway with Dinah

It's known as Dyke Hill. The 17th hole at the Mission Hills Country Club is a short par-three that plays uphill. For the thousands of lesbian groupies who flock to Palm Springs each spring, it is here that they get a bird's-eye view of their favorite LPGA stars—Patty Sheehan, Beth Daniels, Pat Bradley—teeing off, striding up the course for their second fairway shot, and tapping their putts into the cup.

If the 17th is Dyke Hill, the Dinah Shore Golf Tournament is Dyke Heaven. Each March, more than 5,000 lesbians pour into California's desert oasis for what has become the hottest ticket on the lesbian social calendar. With sunshine, golf, and girls, the tournament has become known as "the biggest dyke party west of the Mississippi."

Little did Dinah know when the tournament was established in 1972 by Colgate-Palmolive (and taken over by Nabisco in 1982) that it would end up as a landmark of lesbian subculture. Besides the Michigan Womyn's Music Festival, and Gay Pride parades, there may be no bigger convergence of butches, lipstick lesbians, and Long Beach blondes in the world. "I've been a half-dozen times, and I'm always amazed," says Los Angeles-based journalist Michele Kort. "I've never seen more healthy-looking lesbians in one place—ever."

GREAT NAMES IN SPORTS: GAY AND LESBIAN SPORTING GROUPS

Barnacle Busters (Los Angeles gay and lesbian scuba divers)

Bottom Dwellers (Seattle gay and lesbian scuba divers)

The Burning Butches (lesbian softball team of Bet Havarim in Atlanta)

The Chicago Smelts (gay and lesbian aquatics)

Different Spokes (gay and lesbian bicyclists)

Digging Dykes of Decatur (gardeners; yes, this is a sport)

Equus (Portland, Oregon, gay men's equestrian group)

Finny Dippers (San Diego gay and lesbian scuba divers)

Front Runners (gay and lesbian runners)

Hortophiles (gardeners and garden lovers)

Lambda Ladies of the Links (lesbian golfers in Chicago)

Lavender Winds (gay men's kite flyers)

Outriders (gay, lesbian, and bisexual bicycling group in Boston)

Rainbow Skydivers Club (gay skydivers in Dallas)

Stonewall Climbers (San Francisco gay and lesbian rockclimbers)

I called a friend who had just returned from her first trip to the Dinah Shore. She launched into an enthusiastic description of a benefit golf tournament held on the Saturday before the finals, playfully called the Lina Shore Golf Tournament, the proceeds of which go to the Susan G. Komen Breast Foundation. "You should have seen the crowd . . . very upscale, very pretty, lots of dough. They're all lawyers, doctors, psychiatrists, real estate tycoons, and their pretty girlfriends. It's not cheap, but it's worth it. And you can bid on prizes—a foursome with some famous golfer or a golf bag autographed by the girls on the tour."

Golf, of course, is secondary to many of Dinah's denizens. By early March, L.A.'s *Lesbian News* reaches fever pitch with its promotions for events featuring "gorgeous gals" and "luscious ladies." There is the Desert Palms Bra Party (guests are invited to wear their sexiest and most unusual bras) and an event called Le Moulin Rouge (which promises 3,000 *trés chic* women), as well as the French Riviera Pool Party.

By Sunday, the gals who gather at the Mission Hills clubhouse for beers are showing the strain of the sun, cruising, drinking, and golf. "It was girls as far as the eye could see," said my friend. For those few with energy left to burn, there was still the famous whipped cream wrestling night at Daddy Warbucks bar. I asked her if she'd go back next year. "In a heartbeat!"

— FROM DENEUVE, JUNE 1994

"Every big athletic competition has been essentially the Straight Games. Allegedly the Olympics are open to everyone, and there have been plenty of gay athletes who have competed. But they understood that if they were to get the publicity and the endorsements—and, in some countries, stay on the team—it was best to pretend."

ANNA QUINDLEN IN THE NEW YORK TIMES, JUNE 24, 1994

A History of the Gay Games

If the Stonewall riots is the symbolic birth of the gay rights movement, then the concept of a "Gay Olympics" in 1980 marked the measure of the gay and lesbian community's character. The brainchild of Dr. Thomas F. Waddell, the idea for the Gay Games was first introduced at a gay and lesbian community dinner in San Francisco. Waddell, an Olympic decathelete, organized a planning meeting just eighteen months before the first Gay Games opened at Kezar Stadium. The foundation upon which the Games is built reflected Waddell's belief that "to do one's personal best should be the paramount goal in any athletic endeavor."

The call to compete in the first gay olympics was answered by 1,300 athletes from 179 cities and twelve nations. At this seminal event, called "Challenge '82," competitors participated in fourteen different sports.

A second event was planned for 1986. Gay Games II, San Francisco Arts and Athletics, Inc., and the city of San Francisco welcomed 3,482 women and men representing fifty-nine cities and sixteen countries, who competed in seventeen sports. Triumph '86 was the largest international amateur sporting event held in North America in 1986. At his last closing ceremonies, Waddell presented the Games flag to representatives from the Metropolitan Vancouver, British Columbia, Athletic and Arts Association, the organizers for Gay Games III: Celebration '90. In July 1987, Waddell lost his battle with AIDS.

Gay Games III in Vancouver, British Columbia, provided the backdrop for the largest Games gathering yet. The MVAAA envisioned a grand celebration that included both athletics and the arts. More than 7,000 athletes and 1,500 cultural participants from 30 nations converged for a week in Canada. Fifty thousand spectators could choose from over twenty-six sporting events, and gorge on gay and lesbian cultural offerings. For the first time in the history of the Games, many events were officially sanctioned.

Gay Games IV: Unity '94, opened to the bustle and bright lights of New York City. Held the week before Stonewall 25, Gay Games IV and Cultural Festival hosted 11,000 athletes, along with 2,500 artists from forty-four countries. Thirty-one sports, including women's wrestling, ice hockey, and figure skating with a same-sex pairs competition, were held in twenty-eight venues. Games programs were filled with letters of support from President Clinton and Hillary Rodham Clinton, along with New York governor Mario Cuomo and mayor Rudy Giuliani. Corporate sponsors like AT&T and Hiram Walker joined with groups and individuals to help fund a $6.1 million budget. Five hundred thousand spectators enjoyed a week of fun and freedom. Olympic gold medal-

CAN YOU BELIEVE IT?

The major international athletic competition started by Tom Waddell was originally called the Gay Olympics. When the United States Olympic Committee (USOC) learned that the term "Olympics" was being associated with a gay and lesbian athletic event, they fought with the San Francisco Athletic Association, which was sponsoring the event, all the way to the Supreme Court. Unfortunately, in 1987 the Supreme Court sided with the USOC, and the Gay Olympics were renamed the Gay Games. Interestingly, the court had no problem with the Crab Cooker Olympics, the Police Olympics, the Special Olympics, or any other of the hundreds of organizations around the country that use the term "Olympics" in association with their events.

DID YOU KNOW...

In 1994, the Clinton administration through Attorney General Janet Reno issued a blanket waiver allowing HIV-positive people to enter the United States for Gay Games IV.

ist Greg Louganis thrilled diving fans with fifteen minutes of power and grace on the diving board. Closing ceremonies were held in a nearly packed Yankee Stadium, where the crowd was treated to two laser light shows, two fireworks displays, and a host of entertainers, including Patti La Belle, who left them screaming for more after she sang "Over the Rainbow."

Gay Games V will be held in Amsterdam in 1998. The Dutch government has already committed $27 million toward the event, unlike the United States, which never offered financial support to the Games. The Netherlands is home to a diverse culture that has long integrated homosexuality into its social fabric, and "Friendship '98" stands poised to be the largest and most welcoming Gay Games yet.

— LINDA STAMPS

"I was thrilled to have completed the race . . . and a more enthusiastic crowd could not have been possible. When I entered the stadium [to finish] I never heard a cheer like that. It was very exciting."

JANET WEINBERG OF NEW YORK, A WHEELCHAIR ATHLETE WHO COMPETED IN THE 10,000 METER RACE AT GAY GAMES IV

Official Sporting Events of Gay Games IV

Aerobics
Badminton
Basketball
Billiards
Bowling
Cycling
Diving
Figure Skating
Flag Football
Golf
Ice Hockey
In-Line Skating
Judo
Marathon
Martial Arts
Physique
Powerlifting
Racquetball
Soccer
Softball
Sport Climbing
Squash
Swimming
Table Tennis
Tennis
Track and Field
Triathlon
Volleyball
Water Polo
Wrestling

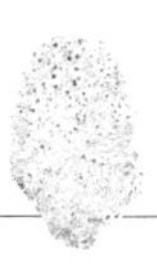

HOBBIES FOR HOMOS

For many lesbians and gay men, despite propaganda to the contrary, recreational life does not consist entirely of lesbian softball, the bar scene, and gay male sex clubs. Some of us also have hobbies, ranging from bridge clubs to kite flying, and from hiking to choral singing. Some of us, gay and lesbian alike, have even been rumored to needlepoint.

Often, when we play, we play in groups. Clubs and organizations across the country in rural, urban, and suburban America are meeting in secret and in public to stitch, gamble, gossip, and blow horns. Aside from just having fun, these clubs build community, as well as serving as an outreach to mainstream organizations with common interests. Some activities, like lesbian and gay marching bands and choruses, present a relatively nonthreatening view of gay life to heterosexuals who, because of stereotypes and assumptions, might be uncomfortable with gay people. In that way, these organizations bridge a gap that might otherwise be unbridgeable.

DID YOU KNOW...

In Seattle, the Chicken Soup Brigade, which provides everyday assistance, including transportation, home chores, and meals on wheels to people living with AIDS, has been holding monthly Gay Bingo since the fall of 1992. Because of constant sellout crowds of more than 500 people, the organization began holding biweekly games in 1994. "Buy in" for twelve games is $10, and winners are awarded cash prizes of up to $1,000 and an array of donated merchandise from local retailers. Occasionally local politicos and celebrities, including columnist Dan Savage ("Hey Faggot") and State Representative Cal Anderson, drop by to "call" a few games.

Lesbian and Gay Bands of America

Before 1982, gay men and lesbians in marching bands had no collective banner under which they could gather and march in unity. All that changed when seven independent marching bands from across the United States, uniquely identified as lesbian and gay, met one day in Chicago. The Lesbian and Gay Bands of America (LGBA) was born of a need for strong visibility and consolidation among gay marching bands. In its present form, the LGBA consists of twenty-four bands from the U.S. and Canada.

Through the LGBA, lesbians and gay men who share a love of music have the opportunity to improve their musicianship and organizational skills and bring the art of concert/marching band music to audiences from all areas of society. Member bands "band together" every year to perform in concerts and parades, as well as smaller-scale community events. The first united performance was a commemoration in 1984 of the Stonewall

The Lesbian and Gay Bands of America performed during the 1993 March on Washington. (Zoe Perry)

rebellion's fifteenth anniversary, when the LGBA presented "A Gay Night at the Hollywood Bowl."

In 1990, the LGBA debuted internationally, performing the "Beyond the Rainbow" concert in the opening and closing ceremonies of Gay Games III and Cultural Festival in Vancouver, British Columbia. In 1992, history was made when the LGBA was invited to take part as an openly gay and lesbian organization in the fifty-second presidential inaugural festivities.

The LGBA has evolved beyond the scope of its original aspirations. Associated LGBA groups are not limited to music. Under its auspices, groups such as "Band Aides" emerged—friends, family, and lovers who provide critical support at LGBA performances. Video production, baton twirlers, tap-dancing troupes, flag and rifle corps, and vocal assemblies have also come out of the larger LGBA coalition.

Why I Play in the Gay Band

I have been a member of the San Francisco Lesbian/Gay Freedom Band since August 1985. For many years, I have hardly ever taken a break from the Tuesday-night ritual. I've logged nearly 500 rehearsals, dozens of concerts, too many parades to count, and other odd performances (and I do mean odd!).

The band fills a number of needs for me. Since that day many years ago when I climbed up on my parents' piano bench and started banging away, expressing myself with music has been something I can't imagine being without. I truly feel sorry for the many people I meet who confess they played in a band or orchestra as a youngster but haven't touched their instrument in ten or twenty years. The music is within them somewhere, looking for a way to get out.

Secondly, my band is composed primarily, but not exclusively, of lesbians and gay men. All of us who share this fabulous orientation choose to "come out" in our own ways. For me, as a person not particularly interested in politics, the band has been a way to *belong* to a gay organization and make a political statement in a nonpolitical way. In the words of a dear friend, and a band member, who has since passed of AIDS, "What's more harmless than a marching band?" He likened a marching band to a teddy bear or balloon—"What's not to like?" I have witnessed this on many occasions when the band participates in its many outreach activities by performing in "straight" parades and concerts. Music is a great equalizer; almost everyone's biases or ignorance seems to melt in the face of our performances.

The third reason for my ongoing love of the band is the people. Just about all my friends these days are band members, or as we proudly call ourselves, "band geeks"! These friendships cross the normal barriers we set up in society: gender, income, religion, race, and even sexual orientation. We are one big happy family. And be careful not to mention to me that you've got a musical past, because WE RECRUIT! An important extension of the people connection is an even larger circle of band-geek friends that I have developed around the country.

Between the music, the need to express myself as a gay man, and the amazing circle of friends I have nationwide, it should be no surprise how I answer the question "Why play in a gay band?" The obvious answer: Band = Life and Life = Band!

— DOUG LITWIN

DID YOU KNOW...

The first gay and lesbian computer game was GayBlade, a fantasy role-playing game invented in 1993 by RJBest, a San Francisco–based computer game company. In the game, a gaysbian warrior combats evil lord Nanahcub (an anagram for Buchanan), using such weapons as a lethal blow dryer, a condom shield, and press-on nails for hand-to-hand combat. Soon after, Queers in History, an educational trivia computer game about lesbians and gay men in history, was developed by Quistory, Ltd.

GALA MEMBERSHIP NUMBERS BY YEAR:

1982	14 choruses
1983	39 choruses
1985	40 choruses
1986	46 choruses
1987	50 choruses
1988	55 choruses
1989	62 choruses
1990	85 choruses
1991	102 choruses
1992	116 choruses
1993	125 choruses
1994	128 and counting...

DID YOU KNOW...

On December 8, 1981, the New York City Gay Men's Chorus became the first openly gay musical group to play Carnegie Hall, with a Christmas concert featuring traditional holiday music and the world premiere of "The Chanticleer's Carol," a piece written especially for the Chorus by composer Conrad Susa.

Singing in Harmony—The History of the Lesbian and Gay Choral Movement

The beginning of the lesbian and gay choral movement is difficult to pin down precisely, just as the founding dates for some individual member choruses are difficult to determine. Men's, women's, and mixed choruses, many of them with lesbians and gay men filling their ranks, have existed for centuries. As a recent example, the Sister Singers Network includes a number of feminist and women's choruses that predate Gay and Lesbian Chorus Association (GALA) choruses by several years. They did not begin to join the GALA Choruses organization in significant numbers until the mid to late 1980s.

The founding of the San Francisco Freedom Day Marching Band and Twirling Corps in 1977, and the San Francisco Gay Men's Chorus by the late Jon Sims the following year, are cited as the beginning of the specifically gay and lesbian band and choral movements. As the first band and chorus among several in the early 1980s to proclaim their gay identities by name, the San Francisco ensembles represented openness that quickly inspired gay men and lesbians throughout the United States and Canada to establish bands and choruses.

Jay Davidson, the first general manager of the San Francisco Gay Men's Chorus, began the process of reaching out to the fledgling bands and choruses across the country. He distributed copies of the Chorus's in-house newsletter to other bands and choruses in exchange for copies of their own. It was Jay's hope that this mutual sharing would provide support for expanding the number of gay and lesbian musical organizations. This informal networking led to a casual meeting in San Francisco during 1980 with Jerry Carlson, the musical director of the Gay Men's Chorus of Los Angeles, and Nick Kelley, from Toddling Town Performing Arts in Chicago. Discussed at this meeting was the possibility of forming an organization, the Gay and Lesbian Association of Performing Arts (GALA Performing Arts), which would include both bands and choruses from around North America. Nick

Kelley agreed to host a meeting in Chicago in the spring of 1981 to which representatives from all the known bands and choruses were invited.

As of January 1, 1995, the GALA Choruses network included 128 choruses: 62 men's, 41 mixed, and 25 women's choruses. These consist of more than 6,500 individual singers and support members, and have combined annual budgets of over $5.5 million! Most choruses perform over three concerts a year, giving them an annual audience estimated at over 500,000 people.

— EXCERPTED FROM "A BRIEF HISTORY OF GALA CHORUSES," COURTESY OF KENNETH COLE

"I wonder if Socrates and Plato took a house on Crete during the summer."

WOODY ALLEN, FROM LOVE AND DEATH, 1975

GETTING AWAY

As fun as everyday lesbian and gay life can be, and as great as our friends are, sometimes we all need to take a break and get away for a while. Vacationing is always fun, exciting, and a little bit stressful. For lesbians and gay men, the stress is increased by the potential homophobia involved in traveling to unfamiliar places. Some hotels, for example, still can't fathom what it means when two men request a single room with a queen-size bed. Potential headaches abound.

Still, traveling can be an adventure, and lesbians and gay men have a variety of ways in which we spend our money and time while on vacation. Some of us like to spend our vacations in gay ghettos like West Hollywood (Los Angeles), the Castro (San Francisco), and Greenwich Village (New York). Others of us like to go to gay resort towns, like Fire Island in New York and Provincetown in Massachusetts. Still others enjoy taking lesbian and gay cruises or organized gay tours. And, of course, many gay men and lesbians travel to the same places that everybody else does, like the Grand Canyon, Disney World, and Hawaii.

DID YOU KNOW...

While gay people have been traveling to Europe from the United States for centuries, the first "official" gay tour to Europe took place in 1964. Organized by the homophile organization ONE, Inc., the tour, arranged by Michigan agent Chuck Thompson and led by Dorr Legg, took a dozen participants from all parts of the U.S. to Paris, London, and Amsterdam.

Summer Camps Making a Difference

Although many gay men and lesbians attended summer camps as children, the experiences we had were mixed, at best. Some of us felt ostracized based on the religious bent of the camp we attended. Others of us struggled with early stirrings of our sexual

DID YOU KNOW...

All around the country, there are clubs of lesbians and gay men who love to camp—and put away those heels, Mary, these folks camp with a tent and cans of Sterno! They range in size from the South Sound Outdoorsmen, a hardy band of fourteen gay and bisexual men who gather to share their mutual love for men and the outdoors in Olympia, Washington, to the Wilderness Network of the Carolinas, which has over a hundred members in North and South Carolina. The largest lesbian, gay, and bisexual outdoors group is Chiltern in New England, which boasts over 1,200 members and has a monthly newsletter detailing their hiking, skiing, biking, and canoeing adventures that are planned nearly every weekend, year-round.

awakenings and pressures to conform to heterosexual camp "romance." An entire mythology in lesbian culture, rivaled only by the gym teacher, has been constructed around the crush on a female counselor. And, of course, for the sissies, the aggressively competitive athletic bent of most boys' camps was painful, frustrating, and alienating.

But times are changing. At least three camps around the country are designed to accommodate both lesbian and gay kids, and children of gay and lesbian parents. By reinventing the idea of the traditional camp with progressive values and sensitivity to the special issues surrounding gay people, they show an exciting new trend for both gay and lesbian parents and their children, and gay and lesbian kids.

Two of these camps are in Northern California: **Camp It Up**, near Yosemite, began in 1989 and bills itself as "A Camp for All Kinds of Families." It is a summer camp with a progessive spirit and it welcomes single-parent, interracial, and lesbian and gay families. Camp It Up has swimming, arts and crafts, hiking, music, dance, theater, overnights for teens, and evening fireside sing-alongs. In addition, they have reduced registration rates for low-income people.

Camp Lavender Hill has been in operation since 1992. Camp co-director Chris Van Stone calls it an "eight-day retreat for both children of lesbian, gay, bisexual families and self-identified lesbian, gay, bisexual young people." It has traditional campfires, crafts, canoeing, and hiking, all set in a wilderness camp near Nevada City, California. But Lavender Hill also provides leadership training for their eighteen- to twenty-three-year-old counselors, who are all either lesbian, gay, and bisexual youth themselves or are children of gay parents.

In Mecklenberg, New York, there is **Mountain Meadow Summer Camp**, which since 1993 has been providing a "kids' community with a feminist conscience." Mountain Meadow is not exclusively lesbian and gay. The brochure says, "All kindsa kids come to Mountain Meadow! Kids from the city. Farm kids. Kids from Canada, Virginia, New York City, Philadelphia—all over. Biracial kids, white kids, black kids. Jewish kids.

Kids with two moms, kids with lesbian moms, kids with gay dads, kids with a mom and a dad." Through feminist approaches to leadership, cooperation, and decision making, kids have "community meetings," play volleyball, learn pottery and leathercraft, and participate in a myriad of other activities while celebrating each child's difference and uniqueness.

Summer camp doesn't have to be awkward and painful. In fact, it should be downright fun. In the words of Chris Van Stone, "Kids don't have to feel alienated; as supportive adults we *can* make a difference." These camps make that difference.

"It's all on stamps. I have it beginning with Greek mythology and bring it right up to the present time. Because my collection is on exhibit I have to be very careful about the people I put in it. I've been outing people through stamp collecting before outing became the thing to do."

PAUL HENNEFELD, GAY STAMP COLLECTOR

Top Ten Gay Destinations in the United States

San Francisco: Gay life is pervasive in our nation's number-one tourist destination. Neighborhoods like the very gay Castro and trendy South of Market are home to an unparalleled number of gay-popular restaurants, bars, and clubs.

South Beach, Miami: Buoyed by its Art Deco past and the fashion industry, South Beach is a gay destination with lots of sizzle. Trendy restaurants, electric nightlife, and a constant parade of beautiful people keep South Beach hopping.

Provincetown: Once just a summer resort, Provincetown is increasingly popular year-round, with a classic afternoon T-dance, a wide range of quality guesthouses, and a large female following.

Key West: One of the first gay resort towns, Key West has become increasingly popular with straight tourists, but it remains a top choice for gay singles and couples looking for a relaxing, warm winter getaway.

Palm Springs: Home to over twenty-five gay guesthouse resorts and the biggest lesbian party of the year, Palm Springs is a popular gay getaway offering desert scenery, year-round nightlife, and big special events.

DID YOU KNOW...

RV Women is a national organization run by and for women who like life on the road. Many members are lesbians, though there are also some married, single, and widowed straight women who join in the freewheeling fun. RV Women has its own all-women RV and trailer park just outside of Apache Junction, Arizona, which has become so popular that the organization is planning a second such community.

West Hollywood: From the day it incorporated as its own city, West Hollywood became the gayest city in the world—a full third of its population is gay or lesbian. Santa Monica Boulevard surpasses even New York's Christopher Street in its expanse of gay businesses catering to gay locals and tourists.

New York City: The city that never sleeps offers something for just about everyone. New York's gay scene is active, vibrant, and not confined to Greenwich Village. Add the city's cultural, historical, and retail opportunities, and New York's appeal is easily understood.

San Diego: No longer a distant third place to L.A. and San Francisco, San Diego's Hillcrest section is a first-rate gay destination, with a palpable concentration of gay restaurants, shopping, and nightlife.

Atlanta: The South has risen again, and Atlanta is its pinnacle. Lively nightlife, southern hospitality, and an urban sophistication are an unusual and inviting combination. Hotlanta, an annual rafting party, is one of the top events on the gay calendar.

San Juan: San Juan is the only destination in the Caribbean with a range of gay-specific accommodations and nightlife. Year-round good weather and affordable airfares draw lots of gay vacationers.

— BILLY KOLBER

Advice for Gay Travelers

1. The more information your travel agent has about your travel patterns and preferences, the better he or she will be able to help you. This may include the nature of your relationship with your "traveling companion." If you're not comfortable conversing openly with your agent, find a new one!

2. The single most important criterion for having a good vacation is the compatibility of your traveling companions. Check the demographics of the participants on a gay trip. Will the trip be all gay but mixed men and women, mixed gay-straight, mostly couples, older or younger people?

3. Make sure both names and your bedding request are clearly noted in all hotel reservations. No matter how comfortable you are, this is easier to deal with over the phone than at the front desk.

4. Don't be afraid to ask about gay-friendliness. Some easy questions to ask: Have you had gay guests stay with you before? Would you describe your hotel, guest house, yacht charter, or tour group as a friendly and welcoming place for gay singles/couples?

5. Make sure any travel insurance you buy considers your partner part of your immediate family.

Lesbian photographer Joan E. Biren took this self-portrait during her travels. (©JEB)

6. Not all frequent-flier awards are transferable to a gay spousal equivalent. If you intend to transfer an award, make sure you know who is an acceptable transferee, and how the relationship is verified. (Your lover could be your stepsister, for all TWA knows!)

7. Travel is rarely—if ever—a good cure for an ailing relationship.

— BILLY KOLBER

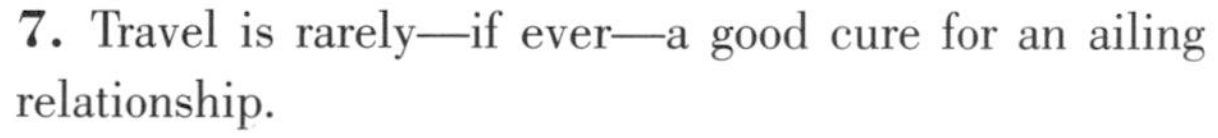

Ten Tips for Traveling Queer and Cheap

1. Road trip, road trip, road trip. There is no cheaper way to see the country, and no better way to find off-the-beaten-path places than to take a road trip. Pile into a car with a couple of friends and take off with no greater destination than "that-a-way." Make sure you've got queer friends who have cars that will be operable for over a hundred miles. If all else fails, get a bus pass and go Greyhound.

DID YOU KNOW...

Since 1990, Disney World in Florida has been taken over one day a year by dyke and faerie lovers of the Magic Kingdom. Organizers said that in 1994, nearly 15,000 gay people frolicked at the fourth annual Gay and Lesbian Day, which traditionally is held at the beginning of summer.

DID YOU KNOW...

Paul Hennefeld and his partner, Blair O'Dell, began the Gay and Lesbian History on Stamps Club in 1982. Since then, they have collected thousands of stamps and special cancelation postcards that depict gay people or related issues from all over the world. The organization, a member of the American Topical Association, the national philatelic association, in 1987 received the ATA's highest honor, the Reserved Grand Award, at the group's annual show.

2. Set daily queer goals. One sure way to make the journey through small-town America more interesting is to plan to perform at least one queer action a day. This action can be anything from wearing an "I'm Not a Lesbian but My Girlfriend Is" T-shirt to spray-painting a pink triangle on a speed limit sign. On one of our trips, we were in salt flats on Highway 89 in Nevada ("The Loneliest Road in America"), and we stopped to spell the word "QUEER" on the side of the road with large chunks of black rock. It looked fabulous against the stark white ground. Then we got the hell out of there.

3. Make cool mixed tapes. If you're going to be in the middle of nowhere, with nothing on the radio but static and Rush Limbaugh, you need some real music. And each person in the car should get an alternating turn on what gets listened to. A road trip is no place for a control queen.

4. Check out gay guides. If you have a general idea of where you're going to be on your trip in between large cities, go into the local lesbian, gay, or progressive bookstore and check out the gay travel books. Copy down any information, such as bars and information lines, for areas you'll be traveling in next.

5. Go to local queer hangouts. Nothing is better than driving into a place like Salt Lake City and, after a quick heckling trip to the Mormon Temple, driving over to the Sun Club to have a drink.

6. Ask bartenders questions. Good ones include: What do gay people do for fun in this town? How would the locals react to gold lamé? and Do you know of any gay or gay-friendly places in [the next place you're planning to go]? Especially with the third question, you might find places that are not in any gay guide.

7. Stay with friends. Friends are great. They know local stuff. They have free food. If you have to, you can also stay with relatives. Sometimes this can be fun, eye-opening, and bonding. Sometimes it might just be better to find another place to sleep (see tip #8).

8. Find a nice residential street, pull the car over, put one of those silly sun blockers over the windshield, and go to sleep. It may not be too comfortable, but it works, and it's safer than sleeping at a rest stop. Also, many states have "public land use" areas, which are like National Parks, except the land isn't as pretty, so they don't charge you to sleep there. Plus, you can often build fires on public land, and no one will bug you.

9. Treat yourselves. Nobody likes living like this all the time. Pick a night, find some great local mom-and-pop motel (try to avoid chains, so you don't give money to The Man), flip on the cable, buy a bottle of Jack Daniel's, and go crazy.

10. Practice safer sex. You may wonder why this is on the list. Safer sex is so important that it needs to be on every queer list around. Just because you're in Kansas doesn't mean you don't need to protect yourself and those you mess around with. So bring some latex.

— **TWO FAGGOTS AND A DYKE TOURS**

Gay Cruising on the Open Seas

I just knew a gay cruise would be worth trying. I thought of 800 guys in Speedos and sent the check. After three cruises (Grand Cayman, Jamaica, and the Mexican Coast) I still think of the Speedos. But there are more reasons to give a gay cruise a try:

- You really can do exactly what you want—be with people or avoid them, read inside or out, take a nap, eat wisely or not, go dancing, play cards, see a movie—and if you want to change your mind, go ahead. Sometimes I think I want a structured vacation, but when it arrives, I don't. On a cruise, that is not a problem.

- The people you want to meet will probably be there. The cruise draws those who like sun, water, travel, and can afford $900. That's

RSVP Cruises is the largest cruise company devoted solely to the travel needs of gay people. (Courtesy of RSVP Vacations)

a significant part of the community. Even if your tastes in conversation or love are narrow, the 800 passengers you have to work with should keep you busy for a week.

• With no effort on your part the scenery changes, unlike sitting on the stunning Hawaiian beach that gets duller by the day.

• If you like gay men at home, you'll like them on vacation. Same quirky humor, same good manners, same winking.

— DAVID BELL

And the Winner Is . . .

The letter arrived for Rosalinda. "Congratulations! You've won a four-night cruise to Mexico aboard Royal Caribbean Line's *Viking Serenade.* Please call to request your date of departure." What was this, another advertising gimmick? Was this one of those "buy one get one free" deals? No, Rosalinda really had won some drawing giving her passage for two aboard a 1,400-passenger ship on a cruise departing Los Angeles Harbor, sailing to Catalina Island, then on to Ensenada and back to L.A. Who would have thought that the 1,100th time she filled out an entry form in some store she'd actually win something, rather than just get her name on another mailing list?

Lucky and free! Things like this never happen to people like us, so naturally we were suspicious right up until the day we received our tickets, worrying more about whether the time we would take off from work would be wasted. We gave no thought to the potential experience of cruising with 1,398 heterosexuals. Our first clue of what this might mean came at the L.A. Harbor document check-in line. Surrounded by clusters of excited family members at various alphabetical registration stations, I stood alone in the "O's," Rosalinda a half a mile away in the "D's." Why didn't we think to use the Del Magus name merge we created and so conveniently use at our Castro district dry cleaners? The explanation of our partnership would have been their problem, not ours.

Arriving at our cabin, we find two neat little single beds in an L-shape against the walls. How will we ask the

LESBIAN AND GAY CRUISE COMPANIES

Lesbian and gay cruises now go everywhere from Alaska to the Bahamas, with packages for singles, couples, and parties. Ask your travel agent about specific trips on any of these lesbian and gay cruise lines:

Galaxsea Cruises
Journeys by Sea Yacht Charters, St. Thomas (Virgin Islands)
Olivia Women's Cruises
RSVP Travel Productions
Sailaway Cruises and Tours, Marina del Rey
Sailing Affairs, New York

– Charlie Graham of Winship Travel

handsome Latino cabin steward for a double bed? Rosalinda is Latina, so suddenly all the machismo forces from the Pope down to the Little Sisters of Mercy are conspiring against her being able to ask him. "*Una cama para dos—no hay problema* (one bed for two, no problem)," he graciously responds.

Okay, this seems workable. We dress for dinner and cheerfully trot off to the dining room. "Ladies [our subtitle for the next four days], you are at Table 38 for all your meals." We are shown to our table and share polite introductions. To my right are seated a young towheaded couple from the farmlands of Michigan, married one day. To Rosalinda's left a cute Hispanic couple from L.A.—also married one day. We're in Honeymoon Heaven. To their left a charming middle-aged couple from Hawaii. Completing the table, a blue-collar couple from Fremont, California, he with fierce-looking tattoos on both arms, celebrating their twenty-fifth wedding anniversary. Now is not the time to tell them we've just celebrated our tenth!

This, our group's first meal together, requires our earnest attention and genuine efforts to get some conversation going: "Four hundred at the wedding, how lovely" and "three grandchildren, their ages . . . how lovely." We are working our butts off. They're all answering and smiling, but obviously they haven't the foggiest notion what having two women together at their table means. Mercifully, the meal is over, the tables are cleared, and we exhaustedly stagger off to the intimate refuge of our cabin. This was work. Only eleven more meals to share at Table 38. Ain't we got fun?

Our vacation time was lovely: taking walks around deck, using the gym, getting our handwriting analyzed, watching the dolphins frolic, and, in the evenings, gambling in the casino. We read mystery novels, took aerobics classes, and let the ship's hum lull us into a restful state.

New challenges in Middle America lay ahead, however. "Captain's Night"—our photos are taken with the ship's captain standing between us and we are then released onto the dance floor. A tall, dapper fellow then takes Rosalinda's hand for a dance, and before I realize what is happening, she's gone and I'm standing in the

GAY AND LESBIAN WALKING TOURS

One way to get a feel for the gay history of a city is to check out some of the lesbian and gay walking tours offered in some localities. Most of these tours are listed with the local chamber of commerce, the gay business association, or the convention and visitor's bureau. When all else fails, read the ads in the local gay press when you get to town.

In ***San Francisco***, check out Trevor Hailey's "Cruisin' the Castro"

In ***Washington, D.C.,*** check out "Walk on Washington"

In ***New York***, see Sam Stafford's "Sidewalks of New York" tours; ask for the "Gay Olde New York" tour

In ***New Orleans***, try Roberts Batson's "The Gay Heritage Tour"

In ***London,*** take "The Pink Tour"

middle of the dance floor alone, my arms still reflexively up and ready to meet hers. She quickly returns to me after having told her amorous dance partner that her very large and jealous Puerto Rican mafioso husband was back in San Juan while she enjoyed this trip. I laughed at her inventiveness and cried inwardly at the necessity for it.

By Day Three and Meal Number Eight, Table 38 had loosened up a bit—we are still the charming inquisitors and no one has asked us a thing. In my frustration to be seen as an existence, I started using the plural pronoun and publicly recollecting many memories of our past ten years together. "Remember how much *we* enjoyed *our* trip to Italy that year?" "It was a good idea when *we* bought new luggage for *our* Greek cruise, don't you think?" "Do you remember when *we* first had the house painted?" The eavesdropping waiter asked us if we were sisters. Sure, don't we look like sisters? With Rosalinda's dark Puerto Rican complexion and African nose, and this Jewish schnozzle and my British accent, who could mistake that we must have come from the same DNA batch? I was about to burst a gut and just come out when Rosalinda kicked me hard under the table. The waiter saw this and asked what she was doing. At this point, all my years at DOB, NOW, BACW, and CSZ started to churn within me. But political and social acronyms are like military stripes—useless when you're out in the real world. At a large personal price, we restrained ourselves and did not upset Table 38's hard-earned vacation. In response to the obtrusive waiter's persistence, Rosalinda replied, "Oh, please excuse my leg, was that your foot?"

DID YOU KNOW...

Pensacola, Florida, is becoming an alternative to Provincetown and Fire Island for gay vacationers over Memorial Day weekend. A stretch of beach there known as "Gay Beach" welcomed more than 30,000 gay people for the holiday in 1994.

By the time that we approached Meal Number Ten, our group has begun to walk a very thin line of familiarity. The comfort level at Table 38 has grown. We've begun conversing, exchanging stories of our luck in the casino, laughing about our mutual overeating, marveling at the vision of the prior evening's sumptuous midnight buffet. The passage of time, the breaking of bread together, the discovery of a common ground—all have created unforeseen and unpredictable bonds among former stranger-than-strange strangers.

As our last meal together finally arrives, there's a palpable quiet at the breakfast table. The timid Michigan newlywed tells us that she'll miss our funny stories. The lovely Hawaiian husband sincerely expresses how much he's enjoyed our company. The Hispanic newlyweds ask about our home in San Francisco—sharing how much they love our home city. "We do, too" is our understated reply. We now realize that we have become a group, a unit together, and that we will miss these people as they will miss us, too. Mr. Tattoo Fremont truck driver unexpectedly reveals how much he loves San Francisco and how tolerant people are there and how he can't stand bigots. Who would have thought? There are tears all around as we hug and say good-bye. The magic of what has happened over these past four days and twelve meals does not escape any of us.

Congratulations. We've just completed our cruise in the real world. It's true that all of our future ship experiences will, no doubt, be with Olivia Women (a lesbian travel company), but, wherever we go, the love and acceptance of Table 38 will always be with us.

— **IRENE OGUS**

WORD GAYME: SIGNS OF THE TIMES

ACROSS

1. Actors Shepard and Elliot
5. Baseball bat wood
8. *Honor Bound* author Steffan
11. Kate Millett's *The Loony-Bin* ____
12. 1 or 66, e.g.
13. Fed. Express rival
14. Assistant
15. Stir up
16. Brazil or hickory
17. Gay symbols
20. "Tit for ___."
21. London weather
22. Jenifer Levin novel, ___ *of Light*
25. Computer memory type (abbr)
27. Greasy
31. Gay symbols

ACROSS (Cont'd)

35. "The French Sappho," ____ de Nouilles
36. Munched out
37. Mae West film, *Diamond* ___
38. Gun lobby
41. Rowboat tool
43. Gay symbols
49. Enemy
50. Kate Delafield and Carol Ashton, professionally
51. Kinks' hit
52. Fish eggs
53. Likely
54. Was acquainted with
55. Queers
56. Boats like 109
57. Long times

DOWN

1. Judy Garland flick, *A ____ is Born*
2. Michael Crawford solo
3. Skirt type
4. Exhausted
5. ". . . and pretty maids all in _ ___."
6. Hard
7. Hi
8. Famous psychiatrist, Karl ____
9. Great work
10. Time zone (abbr)
15. Revolving part
18. *Simpsons* brat
19. Eager
22. Healthy place
23. German article
24. *Paper, Scissors, Rock* author Decter
26. War casualty
28. Sick
29. Oahu accessory
30. Opium™ designer
32. Orson Welles' *Citizen* ____
33. Tiny particles
34. Approach
39. Sum up
40. Accept formally
42. German poet, Rainer Maria _____
43. Victuals
44. Movie critic, Rex ____
45. Chooses
46. Kiddy taboo
47. Meadow
48. Cutting tools
49. To and ___

SIGNS OF THE TIMES: ANSWERS

S	A	M	S			A	S	H		J	O	E
T	R	I	P			R	T	E		U	P	S
A	I	D	E		R	O	I	L		N	U	T
R	A	I	N	B	O	W	F	L	A	G	S	
			T	A	T		F	O	G			
S	E	A		R	O	M			O	I	L	Y
P	I	N	K	T	R	I	A	N	G	L	E	S
A	N	N	A			A	T	E		L	I	L
			N	R	A		O	A	R			
	F	R	E	E	D	O	M	R	I	N	G	S
F	O	E		C	O	P	S		L	O	L	A
R	O	E		A	P	T			K	N	E	W
O	D	D		P	T	S			E	O	N	S

The Business of DIVERSITY
Honeywell
NETWORK FOR THE
814
ON LINE
Businesses
proudly
serving
the lesbian
and gay
333-7755
NINETIES
Cocktail Lounge
Restaurant
408 Hennepin
Minnesota

CHAPTER 10

The Material World

Like our nongay counterparts, most gay men and lesbians find themselves engaged daily on the material plain: We have to work, pay the rent, and buy groceries; we have to plan and budget our money and our time; and we have to think about the future. But unlike our straight counterparts, we also have to deal with homophobia. Not all homophobia is blatant gay-bashing; much of it is subtle. Perhaps homophobia is too strong a word. But no matter how out one is, there is always the extra awareness of being "different" that travels with us in the material world.

For many gay people, this difference is most apparent at work, especially for those who are not self-employed. What do you say when a colleague asks what you did over the weekend? If your coworkers display pictures of their spouses, should you? When the company provides benefits for workers and their spouses, does this include you? If it doesn't, should you say something? Whom do you bring to the company picnic? No one? If you didn't get that promotion you were expecting, was it because of your sexuality?

While no federal law yet protects gay men and lesbians from employment discrimination, gay people at many companies have worked together with management for institutional protection against discrimination and equal benefits for domestic partners.

Some gay men (and women) have access to money. But many more gay people don't have those resources. Many of us stay in jobs that are comfortable, even if advancement opportunities aren't available. Many gay people choose to live in "gay meccas" like San Francisco and New York, not because the best paying jobs are always there, but because they want to live someplace where there is a large and active gay community.

Community is important to most of us. As gay men and lesbians have learned over the last many years of the AIDS epidemic, we have to provide the financial support necessary to sustain the groups and organizations that in turn support all of us. As a community, we are learning to give, of our time and our money, so that we can continue to grow, in our hearts and in the material world as well.

HOMO/ECONOMICS: A SURVEY OF ISSUES

From the moment we become aware of our homosexual desires and choose to act on them, we enter into a social arena that involves the use of our economic resources and that will also have an effect on our economic welfare. Going to a bar, we spend money on transportation and on drinks. Perhaps we may even buy clothes to wear at the bar. Even if we only cruise a park or a softball field we spend some money and time to get there. If we meet someone at one of these places and move in with them, it has economic results—we may save money on rent, and spend it on furniture.

Economics as a social science is devoted to understanding the individual's participation in the economy as a consumer, as an employee, and as the owner of resources. It also studies the behavior of larger economic entities, such as corporations, nonprofit institutions, markets, and governments. It organizes these studies around the problem of how economic resources are allocated to various activities—production, consumption, and leisure.

Homo/economics is a new field of economic analysis that studies the economic behavior of lesbians and gay men. It also examines the impact of other people's decisions on the economic welfare of lesbians and gay men.

Since the closet is still a significant factor in lesbian and gay life, it is impossible to measure the size of the lesbian or gay community or to estimate accurately either its income or expenditures. National polling organizations, survey research centers, marketing firms, and the U.S. Bureau of the Census are just beginning to collect the economic and demographic information we need to know in order to understand the economics of lesbian and gay life.

The Economics of the Closet

The social stigma against homosexuality has tremendous effects on the lives of lesbians, gay men, and bisexuals—its psychological devastation is now widely recognized, and socially the stigma has been a major obstacle to our pursuit of happiness, but the stigma also has had "economic" consequences that have imposed unfair burdens on the welfare of most homosexuals. The economic repercussions of the social stigma are different in different historical periods, or in different communities, or in different geographical regions, or for different characteristics like age, gender, physical traits or abilities, class, and race.

"If you removed all the homosexuals and homosexual influence from what is generally regarded as American culture, you are pretty much left with *Let's Make a Deal.*"

FRAN LEBOWITZ

Costly criminal acts. Laws against homosexual behavior still exist in twenty states in the U.S. and in many countries throughout the world. As long as those laws are enforced they not only impose severe psychological and social burdens on bisexuals, gay men, and lesbians, but also economic ones. In the 1950s, police raids of bars, tearooms, and parks not only led to arrest, legal fees, and public humiliation, but also to blackmail, the loss of jobs, and physical harm.

The high cost of double lives. Before Stonewall, living in the closet meant living a double life. Two worlds—one in which you dressed up to go to work, pretended that you dated the opposite sex and that you were planning to get married—and another world where you butched or camped it up, slipped off to the nearest gay bar, a world where people knew you only by your first name, perhaps even a false name, and no one knew where you worked. No one really knew what you did on weekends. Being in the closet was the only way of controlling the information that you were queer. It meant that you lived under a lot of stress. You lied to your family and straight friends. You didn't take your lover to the company Christmas party and people thought you were weird. Your boss was reluctant to promote you if you weren't married. The way to manage your double life was to scale back your career ambitions, segregate your social life, and live a lie that created emotional stress. Your therapy bills were huge just trying to deal with it all.

After Stonewall, the economics of the closet changed. Outside the major urban areas that had large gay populations, most homosexuals continued to lead double lives in the workplace. But it has become easier to have a social life that is somewhat more open as well as one that creates less stress.

Job Discrimination

Fear of firing. Before the growth of the lesbian and gay liberation movements, economic discrimination took the form of discouraging any closeted person from coming out. If you were arrested for some homosexual-related activity, you probably would be fired from your job or kicked out of your apartment.

The closet ceiling. Even if you stayed carefully in the closet, you might have missed cultivating important contacts in your work (so as to reduce the chances of anyone guessing that you were queer) that would have helped you get ahead. Or you might have chosen to go into a career that allowed you to express yourself more "explicitly" and where you might have found other lesbians or gay men, like becoming a male nurse, a female auto mechanic, a librarian, or a girl's gym teacher. In a survey carried out by James Woods, the author of *The Corporate Closet,* among readers of *OUT/LOOK* magazine, he found that 46 percent of those questioned said that their sexual orientation influenced their choice of career.

Worth less? If you were a woman and/or African American you were more likely to be discriminated against for being female and/or Black than for being homosexual. Economist Lee Badgett found that despite the widespread belief that gay men (especially) and lesbians had higher than average incomes, in fact by some measures they earned almost a third less than anyone else from the same social background, the same occupation, or with the same education. And if you decided not to get married, the older you got and the longer you remained single, the more likely you were to earn less than your married counterpart.

Don't ask, don't tell. Nowadays job discrimination (as well as other forms of economic discrimination) continues to exist, but it operates a little differently. It can take a bigger toll if you are out than if you are in the closet. It also is more likely to affect you if you don't conform to gender norms. One national survey in 1987 reported that one out of four Americans "strongly objects" to working with lesbians or gay men on the job—and another 27 percent said that they "would prefer not to." And Mark Fefer, writing in *Fortune* magazine, found that two-thirds of lesbian and gay employees had seen some form of overt homophobia in the workplace.

(Donelan)

Migration and the Creation of Community

You're not in Kansas anymore. Probably the most significant economic process that underlies the growth of lesbian and gay communities is the migration of homosexuals away from the suburbs, towns, and small cities that they grow up in to the anonymity of large and cosmopolitan cities—New York, San Francisco, Los Angeles, Chicago, and New Orleans have historically served as magnets for both closeted and open lesbians, gay men, and bisexuals. Overlooked Opinions, the gay marketing research firm, claims (although it is probably an overestimate) that 45 percent of lesbians and 53 percent of gay men live in urban areas, and that 32 percent of both lesbians and gay men live in the suburbs, which suggests that approximately 23 percent of lesbians and 15 percent of gay men live in rural areas.

We're here, we're queer, we're setting up house. Once some young lesbian or gay man got to the city, they often found housing in neighborhoods that housed other queer folk, such as bohemians, prostitutes, and new immigrants. That is why New York's Greenwich Village, San Francisco's North Beach, and New Orleans's French Quarter became the first gay neighborhoods after World War II. Later, other neighborhoods attracted lesbians and gay men with low rents and tolerant neighbors. As in other aspects of gay life, race and gender have a decisive effect on the residential patterns of homosexuals. By preference and in reaction to racism among white homosexuals, African American, Latino, and Asian American lesbians and gay men often live in neighborhoods traditionally inhabited by their ethnic and racial communities. Lesbians and gay men's economic differences also lead women to live in neighborhoods with lower rents.

Business comes out of the closet. If the most successful businesses serving the gay and lesbian populations before Stonewall were bars and mail-order businesses, then the growth of gay liberation spurred whole new developments—bookstores, counseling services, porn shops, newspapers and magazines, clothing boutiques, and travel agencies have emerged to satisfy gay and lesbian consumer needs that previously had not been targeted by any other businesses. Gay and lesbian businesses serve a growing and increasingly diverse population. There are now businesses that cater to the needs and interests of African Americans, Latinos, and Asian Americans, as well as bisexuals and leather folk of all identities.

The gay market boom. While the growth of lesbian and gay businesses means that more queer dollars are spent within the lesbian and gay communities than used to be the case, most queer dollars still end up in the coffers of "straight" businesses. In the last ten years, "straight" American corporations have discovered that lesbians and gay men love to shop—and they are spending more money than ever before marketing their products to queer consumers. Although studies by marketing research firms tend to overestimate the financial status of the average lesbian or gay men, their surveys do tap into lucrative market segments of the gay community. According to data from Overlooked Opinions, the average household income for lesbians in 1992 was $45,827, while for gay men it was $51,325—as a comparison, the 1990 average household income in the U.S. was $36,520. One newsletter, *Affluent Marketers Alert,* estimates that gay men spend two out of every three queer dollars. Other examples of the lifestyles of lesbians and gay men are indicated by the fact that more than 80 percent of gay men dine out more than five times in any month. Forty-three percent of lesbians own their homes, as do 48 percent of gay men. Together, lesbians and gay men took more than 162 million trips in 1991. Writing in *Dollars and Sense* magazine, Amy Gluckman and Betsey Reed have concluded that the gay marketing movment obscures the economic disparities caused by racial differences, social class, and gender that plague the gay community. Unfortunately, as Gluckman and Reed point out, the gay marketing bonanza has encouraged corporations to cultivate a narrow definition of gay identity (white, male, affluent) as a marketing tool.

CAN YOU BELIEVE IT?

Since gay and lesbian bars catered to people who were stigmatized or who engaged in "criminal acts," before the 1970s the owners of the bars in most American cities were forced to pay the police or organized crime for "protection." This made drinks more expensive, because the bar owners sought to recover the costs of "protection" by charging higher prices. Patrons had no recourse; there weren't that many other places you could take your business if you weren't happy with the decor, the price of drinks, or the clientele.

Marriage, Families, and Children

The family has become less and less an economic institution and more and more a place for the rearing and socialization of children. Legally recognized marriages and families are still a heterosexual preserve.

Domestic partners. There is, however, a strong and growing movement among lesbians and gay men for the legalization of gay marriages. Legislation for the recognition of domestic partnerships is a step in the direction of socially acknowledging the importance of homosexual relationships. Legally recognized marriages do have definite economic advantages in the form of tax breaks, health insurance coverage, and credit availability. Lesbians and gay men, whether or not they have children, do pay school taxes and their tax dollars help to support governmental social services for families and children.

A queer baby boom. Before Stonewall, of course, many lesbians and gay men were parents. Lesbians and gay men had married before they became aware of their homosexual desires, or specifically in order to raise families, as well as for the convenience of appearing straight in a hostile world. But not many of them raised children as openly gay or lesbian parents. Scientific and social innovations have made it easier and easier for a woman to get pregnant without neccessarily engaging in heterosexual intercourse. Lesbians have taken advantage of developments such as artificial insemination in order to bear children and set up families with their partners or in conjunction with their (often gay) male friends. In the last ten years, this way of having and raising children has grown tremendously. Today there are more than 10,000 children (according to *Newsweek*) being raised by lesbians who became pregnant through artificial insemination. Adoption is another important means allowing gay parents to raise children. Complicated arrangements between lovers, ex-lovers, and male friends have created new kinds of families for raising children. The economic implications of forming a queer family and raising children are quite similar to those faced by heterosexual families. The decision to raise children will often depend on the financial resources of the parents, their sense of job security, their health insurance coverage, and the availability of child care and schools. But added considerations originate in the effect of homophobia on their ability as lesbian and gay parents to provide a financially secure and stable home for their children.

"Gee, Dad, you shouldn't have." (Donelan)

Divorce bells are ringing. Breaking up is hard to do, but when those doleful divorce bells start tolling you know it will cost both of you money. Although alimony and fees for divorce lawyers are not yet common among lesbian and gay couples, they are not far off. When a couple breaks up, one partner often has to move out of their joint home, and furniture, kitchen utensils, books, and

CDs have to be divided up. Most times, each partner has to bear some additional cost—looking for a new apartment or a roommate, replacing household items and other joint purchases. Where children are involved, legal negotiations are part of the process—custody, visiting rights, and financial support are often hotly contested issues.

Human Resources and Cultural Capital

Economists often identify investments in education, migration, health care, and experience as human capital. Certainly to the extent that lesbians and gay men invest in their skills and other attributes in order to improve their economic welfare, they have invested in human capital. Discrimination, illness and death from HIV, and the limitations imposed by living inside the closet all destroy human capital.

The queering of American culture. The gay contribution to American culture is enormous—and seems to be increasing. A great deal of this queer contribution originates in the lessons that lesbians and gay men learn as outsiders, sexual rebels, and the task of inventing new ways of living their lives.

The Economics of AIDS and Health Care

The AIDS epidemic is now in its fourteenth year. In addition to the many lives it has taken, and the grief that it has spread in its wake, it has imposed a huge economic burden on the gay and lesbian communities, as well as society as a whole.

The stigma of AIDS. People with AIDS are still stigmatized in some communities and suffer discrimination in housing, employment, and health care. People of color who have AIDS experience an even greater degree of discrimination than white men with HIV. Lesbians and gay men who are IV drug users also encounter discrimination. All together, these forms of discrimination and stigmatization reduce the economic welfare of the gay men and lesbians with AIDS.

Jobs and health care. Individuals who have developed more advanced HIV-related illnesses have often lost income through the loss of full-time jobs, and even if they are able to continue working must sometimes take jobs that pay less or work fewer hours. These individuals also experience increased costs for medical care. Since most Americans receive their health insurance through their employers, many of those who have such medical coverage want to hold on to their jobs. They may often be afraid to let their employers and fellow employees know if they have AIDS—they preserve their ability to meet the medical costs of HIV, but often suffer isolation and lack of emotional support.

"The idea that open gays hit a 'lavender ceiling' is probably the biggest reason professional gays cling to the closet."

CAROL NESS IN "CORPORATE CLOSET," SAN FRANCISCO EXAMINER, OCTOBER 10, 1993

The economic impact on the community. The AIDS epidemic has drained economic resources from the gay and lesbian communities. The mobilization of the gay and lesbian communities to provide support for people with AIDS and the creation of institutions for education, care, and research about AIDS has diverted resources from other more traditional activities like education, leisure activities, investment in small businesses and careers, and improving real estate. In the last five years, probably the largest economic institutions in many gay communities have been AIDS nonprofit organizations.

Market and community. The recent discovery of a lucrative gay and lesbian market for consumer goods has provoked many reactions. Some people believe that the growth of such a market reflects an acceptance of lesbians and gay men by the broader society. Others believe that the existence of a big gay market will undermine the community that lesbians and gay men have so carefully constructed since the fifties. In truth, the existence of such a market does reflect our visibility, while at the same time creating an opportunity for non-gay-owned businesses to make money from lesbians and gay men. The tension between community and market is not new, nor is it easily resolved. The economy of the gay and lesbian community remains an arena for research and struggle over the next decade.

— JEFFREY ESCOFFIER

LESBIANS AND GAY MEN AT WORK

Lesbians and gay men are in all walks of life. We are carpenters and computer programmers, hairstylists and bookstore owners, sales reps and schoolteachers. We are self-employed and underemployed (some of us are even unemployed). But what we all share in the workplace, whether we work in a corporation or for a nonprofit firm, is the dilemma about whether or not to be out at work. Even in jobs we love, we are sometimes uncomfortable. While the decision of whether or not to be out is a personal one, the implications are public. We share, too, the struggle to be seen as equal to our nongay colleagues; the saying that a woman has to work twice as hard as a man to be seen as half as competent can be applied to gay people on the job as well.

On the other hand, many corporations, small companies, and labor unions do recognize that they have gay employees who deserve all of the rights and benefits that they provide to their straight employees. Indeed, many companies are way ahead of the laws when it comes to protecting their gay and lesbian employees. Often, we are organizing to make these changes happen. Ten years ago, there were no officially sanctioned gay and lesbian employee organizations in corporate America; today, most large companies have such groups.

In the 1990s, more and more people are going into business for themselves, and gay people are no exception. The reasons, however, are not always the same. The independence of self-employment is an added boon for gay people. Some want to earn their livelihood serving their own community. For some "obvious" gay men and lesbians, self-employment is one of the few avenues available to earn a living free of harassment; for others, being able to set a queer tone at the office is the appeal. But for whatever reasons, statistics show that lesbians and gay men are more likely to be self-employed than are the population at large.

FIVE BEST COMPANIES FOR GAY MEN AND LESBIANS

Based on employment policies, benefits, outreach, and general attitude (shown alphabetically):

Apple Computer Company (Cupertino, CA)

Federal National Mortgage Association (Fannie Mae)(Washington, D.C.)

Levi Strauss & Company (San Francisco, CA)

Silicon Graphics (Mountain View, CA)

Viacom International Inc. (New York, NY)

— ED MICKENS

"Come on! Hair and makeup! The top people who do hair are men, and the top people who do makeup are men! And each and every one of them is gay!"

KEVYN AUCOIN, GAY NEW YORK MAKEUP ARTIST, IN THE WASHINGTON POST, APRIL 25, 1993.

Is There a Lavender "Glass Ceiling"?

CAN YOU BELIEVE IT?

A 1992 survey of 1,400 gay men and lesbians in Philadelphia found that 76 percent of men and 81 percent of women conceal their orientation at work.

I've come out on the job in a big way: I became spokesperson for my company's lesbian and gay employee group. Now everybody knows. My gay colleagues say I've just committed career suicide, but I like my job, I do it well, and expected to go far in this company. Now I worry. Are they right?

This question sums up one of the biggest fears among upwardly mobile, career-minded gay men and lesbians. A company may be unlikely today to fire someone for sexual orientation, but that doesn't mean you'll get the subtle mix of credit, promotions, training, and mentoring that leads to a successful career.

The question is so important, I opened it up to a panel—and their audience—at the first National Gay and Lesbian Business Exposition held in April 1994 in New Jersey. The consensus? We just don't know yet.

The "glass ceiling" is a proven phenomenon among women, people of color, and other minorities, because we can actually count heads in middle management, upper management, boards of directors, etc., and see that they are underrepresented the further up you look in the corporate hierarchy. That doesn't work for gay people, obviously, first because we're impossible to count (and there's still the difference between those who are out and those who choose to follow a "don't ask, don't tell" approach with their employers); secondly, because we include women, people of color, and other minorities within our own numbers, and there's certain to be a complex overlap and interaction among prejudices.

A welder in the San Francisc Bay Area. (Cathy Cade)

Chicago-based career counselor Judi Lansky takes a cautious approach advising lesbian and gay clients on this issue, pointing out that there are many companies and whole industries where simply being unmarried is a career liability. A life-partner of the same gender would be beyond comprehension.

Lee Badgett, a labor economist and assistant professor at the University of Maryland School of Public Affairs, did a recent study that matched gay and straight full-time workers by many characteristics (gender, race, location, education, experience, etc.) to gauge the economic impact of antigay discrimination. Among many interesting conclusions, she found that lesbians were more likely to enter lower-paying jobs than other women, and didn't seem to experience any significant pay discrimination. Gay men, on the other hand, were more likely to go for higher-paying jobs than nongay men and tended to earn 11 to 27 percent less than their nongay peers. Badgett's data, however, did not include any information on who was out or not.

Many gay and lesbian managers who have come out, brought partners to company events, and otherwise integrated their personal and professional lives, say their careers haven't been harmed, and have even been enhanced. They observe that a glass ceiling can work in two ways: imposed by supervisors through prejudice, and self-imposed through the peculiar behavior of trying to cover up your personal life. The higher up the corporate ladder you go, the more important personal chemistry is. And if you're hiding something, it gets noticed.

Some of these out managers have already received promotions. But being out on the job is still a relatively new phenomenon, and unfortunately limited mostly to younger (I'll include up to the forties here, thank you) people still in lower and middle ranks. So we'll have to see how their careers progress over the years.

We aren't going to be short on case studies. A new study by Jay Lucas (co-author of *The Corporate Closet*) and Joe Stokes, professor of psychology at the University of Illinois at Chicago, says that a large majority of gay men and lesbians have had a good reception to their coming out at work, and most saw no negative impact on their careers. Most planned to be "more out" in the future.

— ED MICKENS, FROM THE SYNDICATED "WORKING IT OUT" COLUMN

"We believe that diversity isn't something that you should tolerate. It's something you should promote."

HARLAN LANE, PROFESSOR OF PSYCHOLOGY AT NORTHEASTERN, ON WHY THE CAMPUS HAS PROMISED TO ACTIVELY RECRUIT AND PROMOTE OPENLY GAY AND LESBIAN EMPLOYEES

DID YOU KNOW...

In 1991, Lotus Development Corporation, creator of Lotus spreadsheet software, became the first major publicly held American company to extend benefits to the domestic partners of lesbian and gay employees. Four months earlier, a similar policy was adopted by Montefiore Medical Center, a privately held company in New York (with 9,500 employees, three times as many workers as Lotus). Levi Strauss & Company followed in February 1992, becoming the largest U.S. employer, with 23,000 workers and sixty facilities nationwide, to offer health insurance to lesbian and gay domestic partners. In the years since, a number of large and highly visible companies have undertaken similar changes in their business practices.

First Statement of Lavender Labor

We are here to make a statement for the people who met last night at the lesbian/gay caucus. First, we would like to invite any other gay brothers or lesbian sisters out there who would like to do so to please stand up. Now if all the lesbians and gays here stood up, it would be the equivalent of ten tables, as at least 10 percent of the population is gay or lesbian.

The fact that so few people stood up shows how pervasive homophobia and discrimination against lesbians and gays is in our society. It just doesn't feel safe to come out even at a progressive conference such as Labor Notes. To be publicly identified as gay could cost us our jobs, our children, or our lives.

Even within our unions we are faced with ostracism, ridicule, and marginalization. We are everywhere. We are in health care, the building trades and the Teamsters, textile mills, and schools. We are all races and cultures and all countries.

We are making this statement to you because we believe that people who come to the Labor Notes Conference are people who really understand the truth of labor's slogan that "An injury to one is an injury to all." People who are involved in fighting for the rights not only of labor as a whole, but also of women workers, workers of color, workers in South Africa, Central America, or in the South. We all know that it is important to fight for all these labor movements, because the bosses capitalize on weaknesses within our ranks. Discrimination is used to divide and conquer workers.

When the union fails to defend the rights of gay and lesbian workers, the only winner is the Boss. When lesbian and gay families don't get the same benefits that other families get, the Union that bargained and worked so hard is the loser.

We offer you a challenge. There are concrete things that you can do to support your lesbian and gay sisters and brothers.

— PRESENTED AT THE LABOR NOTES CONFERENCE 1991

The Gay and Lesbian Labor Conference at Stonewall 25

It was Friday, June 24, 1994, "Stonewall 25" weekend. Roughly 250 lesbians, gay men, bisexuals, and transgendered people gathered at AFSCME District 37 headquarters, the big public employees union in New York. Hosted by the official lesbian and gay committee of the union, they came together from all over the country to found a national organization. The National Lesbian/Gay/Bi/Transgendered Labor Organization (NLGBTLO) became the first labor organization of its kind in the United States.

Some joined because union lesbians and gay men are at the cutting edge in the struggle to win equality on the job. Some joined because a relative political shift to the right by the mainstream lesbian and gay movement has encouraged the growth of anti-working-class and anti-union tendencies in lesbian and gay politics, including among self-described "progressives." This has left lesbian and gay working people feeling voiceless and frustrated. NLGBTLO strengthens the voice of working-class lesbians and gay men within our community, helping to bring class and union politics back into the lesbian and gay movement. Still others had come simply to break out of isolation and unite with other pro-union lesbians, gay men, bisexuals, and transgendered people.

DID YOU KNOW...

When studying the impacts of providing health care benefits to partners of homosexual employees, Lotus Development cited findings from a private insurance study that says committed homosexual couples are at no greater risk of catastrophic illness than are married heterosexual pairs. Moreover, with few children in gay families, there are few claims for, say, cesarean sections or routine pediatric illnesses. So much for claims by opponents of astronomic health care costs due to AIDS.

In the nation's capital, the Lesbian/Gay Labor Alliance marched with others against American involvement in Central America in 1984. (©JEB)

SUGGESTIONS FOR MAKING YOUR UNION SAFER FOR ITS LESBIAN AND GAY MEMBERS

- Participate in your city's gay pride march.
- Confront co-workers when they make anti-gay jokes.
- Include gay and lesbian issues in your local civil rights committee.
- Talk to lesbian and gay co-workers and find out what issues they think the union should take up.
- Wear a gay or lesbian button to work, just for a day, and see how people react to you.
- Start up or participate in a committee to gain domestic partner rights in your union.
- Participate in AIDS education programs.
- Support getting Lavender Labor, the newly formed International Network of Lesbian and Gay Labor Activists, which already has members from three countries, onto a plenary at the next Labor Notes Conference.
- Help distribute the *Lavender Labor Newsletter.*

While gay people have always participated in the labor movement, it was in the mid-1970s that we began to openly and boldly assert ourselves within the unions. In 1976, a crowded press conference featuring lesbian and gay activists and union leaders from more than twenty local labor unions pledged the support of the San Francisco Labor Council for gay rights in all future union contracts. As a result, 1977 demonstrated strong union opposition to the antigay Briggs Initiative, and lesbian and gay support for the Coors Beer Boycott.

Some of the activists who spearheaded these struggles on the West Coast later became the Lesbian/Gay Labor Alliance (L/GLA) in the San Francisco Bay Area. The L/GLA, together with the Gay and Lesbian Labor Activist Network (GALLAN) in Boston, the Lesbian and Gay Labor Network (LGLN) in New York, and the Lesbian and Gay Issues Committee (LAGIC) of AFSCME District 35, was the driving force behind the creation of a national labor organization for lesbians, gay men, bisexuals, and transgendered people.

Lesbian and gay unionists continue to gain a hearing within the U.S. labor movement. Nondiscrimination clauses, protection and services for people with AIDS, and domestic partnership benefits are among the rights many unions are fighting to achieve for their lesbian and gay members.

— ED HUNT

Queer Groups at Work

Gay and lesbian employees at many companies have formed official and unofficial gay networks. Here is just a sampling of groups. If your company doesn't have one, you might consider starting one informally and see where it leads.

Apple Computer: Apple Lambda

AT&T: LEAGUE (Lesbian and Gay United Employees)

Chevron: CLAGE (Chevron Lesbian and Gay Employees)

Coors Brewing: LAGER (Lesbian and Gay Employee Resource)

CoreStates Bank: Mosaic

Digital Equipment Corp.: DECplus (Digital Equipment Corp. people like us) and WICS (Women in Comfortable Shoes)

Dupont: BGLAD (Bisexual Gays and Lesbians at Dupont)

KQED TV: GALS (Gays and Lesbians)

Microsoft: GLEAM (Gay, Lesbian, and Bisexual Employees at Microsoft)

Kodak: Kodak Lambda

3M Corp.: 3MPLUS (3M people like us)

TimeWarner: LGTW (Lesbians and Gays at Time Warner)

City of Seattle: SEAGL (Seattle Employee Association of Gays and Lesbians)

Silicon Graphics: Lavender Vision

United Airlines: GLUE (Gay/Lesbian United Employees)

U.S. Government: FedGLOBE (Federal Gay and Lesbian or Bisexual Employees)

U.S. West: EAGLE (Employee Association of Gays and Lesbians)

Xerox: GALAXe (Gay and Lesbian at Xerox)

— ED MICKENS

DID YOU KNOW...

The group Gay, Lesbian, and Bisexual Employees at Microsoft (GLEAM) became the first gay employees group in the country. They received formal recognition from the company in 1991.

Subject: Coming out at the Interview

Many lesbians and gay men face the question of whether or not to be out when applying for a new job. One gay librarian posted her dilemma on the gay and lesbian librarians bulletin board. Following is her dilemma and some of the responses.

I have a job interview coming up in a couple of weeks, and I am getting very nervous. On the second page of my resume I put my involvement as co-chair of the board of directors and librarian for the local Gay and Lesbian Resource Center under "Community Service Activities." This isn't the same as saying "I'm a lesbian, y'all," but it's relatively close. Well, back then I didn't feel like I had anything to lose, but now I'm starting to want this position badly. I can feel my internalized homophobia rising—there's this nasty voice in my head that's telling me to hide, because people might not like me if they think I'm queer, and I won't get the job if they don't like me.

Some background—I live in a small, conservative city in Iowa, and currently work for a college affiliated with

DID YOU KNOW...

There has been significant lesbian and gay political activity within several major labor organizations around the country for some time. Among these organizations are the American Federation of State, County, and Municipal Employees (AFSCME), the Service Employees International Union (SEIU), the Communications Workers of America (CWA), the United Auto Workers (UAW), the Teamsters, and the United Steel Workers of America.

the Catholic Church. I am out to many of my co-workers, but not to my boss or to the campus at large. I guess what I'm looking for from my fellow librarians is some words o' wisdom from others who've been here before and found the courage to cross that line.
—A LIBRARIAN

• • • •

Does your sex life influence your work? Not usually. I have a very good job that I got just two months ago. I never said word one containing *gay* in it at the interview. I have a wedding band on, which means to me I'm married. But I'm married to another man. They didn't ask, I didn't tell. I personally don't think that not telling is bad. Really, your employers have no right to ask about your personal life. I keep my job and my personal life separate. I feel that for safety's sake, you should not tell, especially at the interview. They will hire you if they think you are the best person for the job. Your telling them could color their discussion. Heterosexuals don't tell, "Oh I'm having sex with so and so" in an interview. I've never heard that. Why should we tell?
— A.

• • • •

I work in a technical library where, aside from an occasional AIDS book purchase recommendation, my sexual orientation is irrelevant—on paper. I happen to work mostly alongside of people with less education, less experience of human diversity, and less liberal religious views than I have. Once I started work here, I dropped a few hints and mentioned a few things to avoid being presumed straight. Behind my back some of my co-workers went to the head manager and apparently tried to get me fired or disciplined. She told them to stuff it, but they can persist in their views. (Over the years they have changed, somewhat, because I'm not the green scaly monster they assumed I was.)

There was no way to predict all this from the interview. Personally, I'd go for the discreet mention on the resume (if it's relevant) and let them conjure up what they want in their own minds. You can always work to change attitudes if problems arise later.
— B.

• • • •

I agree that having something suitably clear on the resume is adequate. I keep my gay publications on my resume for just that reason. No one has ever asked me about them in an interview.

Frankly, I think there are major advantages to having the truth visible from the start. If some potential employer or co-workers are going to make a big issue of my being gay, I don't want to work for/with them. I'd rather spare myself the hassle in advance. No matter how attractive the job itself might seem, that would be more than just a fly in the ointment. (And, taking it from another angle, they don't DESERVE my efforts. I'll put them where they will be appreciated properly.)

— G.

• • • •

If your involvement with community activities is already on your resume, believe me, it *has* been duly noted. Speaking from my own experience, on both sides of the table, it is one of the first things interviewers look for, right there under the proverbial "other." If you've gotten this far in the process, then they know you can do the work. The salient question is how well you'll fit into their group. If there is a point in the interview where it seems appropriate to mention your involvement in community activities, then by all means mention it, but don't make an issue of it. Present it as part of the well-rounded professional everyone would want on their team; you are, after all, much, much more than a librarian or a lesbian.

— R.

• • • •

Because you're not in a desperate situation, you can afford to be completely yourself at your interview. I personally wouldn't want to work for an institution that didn't like something about me. No job is the center of the universe and worth compromising your life for, IMO [in my opinion]. I find that being completely out is very freeing. My spirit soars a little higher than it once did. :)

— R.

• • • •

I think there is an important question queers have to ask ourselves before we go into interviews: "Can I be happy working in an environment where I can't be 'out'?" If you can, don't include your queer stuff in your resume and don't be out at the interview.

If you can't, then be out at the interview. I always try to remember that I am interviewing the institution as much as it is interviewing me.

I have to differ with some of the opinions I have seen expressed about the relationship of our sexualities to our work and our workplace. I couldn't disagree more with the notion that heterosexuals don't tell us constantly whom they sleep with. Every family photo, mention of a husband, wife, child, every discussion of tax exemption or family tuition remission—in short, most of the daily chat of the workplace tells us that heterosexual men and women have sex.
— M.

In Our Own Words

The editors of this volume sent out a short survey to gay and lesbian workers regarding whether people were out at work, and if not, why not. We also asked for experiences, good and bad, regarding being out, as well as a subjective view of the ideal work environment. Responses came in from around the country, both on-line and in hard copy. The questions and some of the responses follow.

If you are out on the job, how does being gay or lesbian affect your relationship with co-workers and/or bosses?

It has improved personal relationships with my peers; there are people I work with that I consider friends. Being out was part of getting close. I don't think it has been to my advantage for my boss to know, although I can't prove it. I feel being out has held me back some. I've had to work harder than others for respect and recognition.
— VANESSA, MANAGER, SOFTWARE DEPARTMENT, CAMBRIDGE, MA

Surprisingly, some of the people who have been the most resentful of my being out and fighting against any bigotry have also been gay. When I began working for New York City, I had major problems with directors who could not deal with my being open. One told me that I was passed over for a title change because the person who got the position had a family. But as the gay rights movement

grew, attitudes changed drastically. Now, because of my constant fighting against discrimination, I am feared by many. My attitude is that I would rather be feared than discriminated against. At the present time, though, sexual identity rarely comes into play with employee/boss relationships unless in a positive way.
— MAX, SUPERVISOR/COMPLAINT MEDIATOR, NEW YORK

It varies—different individuals react more or less friendly, depending on where they are at. I feel safe because of many other openly gay people and an anti-discrimination policy.
— ANNETTE, AT&T CUSTOMER SERVICE REP, PROVIDENCE, RI

I am out at work and my co-workers and bosses have gotten used to it. Some don't care, some do. I have not heard any anti-gay comments at work; they know to keep their mouths shut if they feel that way. Also, I am the shop steward and this affects the work environment a lot more for me. If my co-workers have a problem or get in trouble, it's me they have to come to—the gay man.
— MARK, PARKING PATROL DEPUTY, PORTLAND, OR

When I applied for this job, it was clear on my resume and cover letter that I am gay, and I raised the issue in the job interview. I wanted us ALL to know what we were getting. When I started working here, lots of departments invited me to their staff meetings, ostensibly to talk about how we could work together, but REALLY to see what the gay guy from California was all about. That was OK with me. Now, after five years, it really isn't much of an issue. They know that I will spend some of my time working on gay/lesbian issues, but they also know that I do a good job and won't "cheat" them of hours.
— LAWRENCE, UNIVERSITY DIRECTOR OF CAREER SERVICES, MAINE

I work in a small department (five persons total, only two of us working at any given time) at the local public library. I was out to my main boss from the very beginning—came out on my application and in the interview. The others found out gradually as we got to know each other. I don't think it affects our relationships in any negative way at all now that I am completely out. Before I was completely out, I felt a need to be rather discreet in my

chatter until I realized that everyone there is okay about it. My main boss and I talk about gay things from time to time. My immediate supervisor has a similarly positive attitude toward LGBTetc persons, and we have discussed a number of different aspects of it. In all, I think it's just like any other aspect of one's personality among my boss and co-workers.
— TINA, PUBLIC LIBRARY CLERK/PAGE, KNOXVILLE, TN

I am completely "out" at work. I have my significant other's picture on my desk and have been trying to get my company to institute domestic partner's benefits. To be honest, it hasn't hurt.
— JEFF, HUMAN INTERFACE SOFTWARE ENGINEER, SAN FRANCISCO

My team leader asked and I was honest. Our working relationship has improved although she is "straight and happily married." We routinely discuss our marriage problems—and they are common. I also told her that it's not a "secret" of mine so she can share it with whoever she wishes. Hasn't been a problem, but most of us have a four-year college degree or higher and I think that makes a big difference.
— RICK, COMPUTER SPECIALIST, NORFOLK, VA

• • • •

If you're not out at work, why?

I'm not out to some folks I consider to be big time, well-rounded bigots, don't have the time to deal, what would I get out of it?
— VANESSA

For those that don't know, it's because they haven't specifically asked. Perhaps they don't want to know. I feel it's their right. On the other hand, I don't want them to think I'm drawing a focus to my relationship with my lover. That may be interpreted that I need special attention, which I don't. I wonder how many gay people do it JUST for the added attention.
— RICK P.

• • • •

What's the worst thing that's happened to you as a result of being out about your sexuality?

Feels like it's the same thing I get for being female and Puerto Rican—you know, I get 59 cents for every $1 my straight, white male co-worker gets.
— VANESSA

One man just goes out of his way to ignore me and avoid any contact whatsoever.
— CAL

Being transferred to another division after I complained to one director about comments/actions directed at me as a gay male. The director told me to stop complaining, then transferred me.
— MAX

I was fired from a previous job.
— ANNETTE

I was removed from my position as a board member of my union and strongly lobbied against for being a delegate to that same union.
— GLEN, UNION ACTIVIST/CIVIL RIGHTS WORKER, BROOKLYN

When I first started here, I got a few (three, I think) phone calls on my voice mail from a group of girls that were pretty vicious . . . in an adolescent way. A few years ago, someone shot paint pellets at my office window a few times. The campus police were great about investigating both.
— LAWRENCE

"Straight" thrill seekers are always wanting to experiment.
— EDWARD, COMPUTER NERD, UTAH

The straight boys don't talk to me very much.
— MARK

• • • •

What's the best thing that's happened to you as a result of being out about your sexuality?

"Straight" thrill seekers are always wanting to experiment.
— EDWARD

The straight boys don't talk to me very much.
— MARK

Helping teenagers that are confused by society's rules figure out that it's society's problem and not theirs and to get on with their life—their happiness is their responsibility.
— **BOB, MENTAL HEALTH WORKER, SAN FRANCISCO**

Help "educate" some people who were "borderline bigots"—people who came to like me and then discover I am a lesbian.
— **VANESSA**

Being involved in the company's and union equity committees.
— **CAL**

Being able to just be honest, not having to worry about being discovered.
— **ANNETTE**

More people come out to me and therefore we don't feel so isolated.
— **GLEN**

I will never forget when I got back from the March on Washington, and one of my co-workers held up the newspaper with a shot of the MOW crowd and asked (jokingly), "So where are you in this picture?" It just gave me such a great feeling of acceptance.
— **TINA W.**

Entrepreneurship: A Way Out? A Way In?

Entrepreneurship is one way gay men and lesbians can capitalize on our differences instead of hiding them at work. The world now seems to favor entrepreneurs with our experience and life training to master today's markets. If our experiences are different in many ways, how can the challenges we've faced count as future assets after being labeled liabilities for so long? Our survival skills often match those required for entrepreneurship; we need to mobilize these differences, not deny them. Let's look at some of the challenges, why they've often been handicaps in the past and how we can make them work to our benefit as entrepreneurs in the nineties.

1. Eliminating Isolation: Many closeted corporate gay people believe "personal factors have nothing to do with business." Yet today's emphasis on chemistry, networking, team playing, and heavy hours all push the personal into the professional. If we come out, we can network with a vengeance and position ourselves as valuable assets. In addition, we can sometimes operate outside the corporate caste system as corporate Merlins, consultants, and as entrepreneurs.

"When it comes to setting trends, queers are always at the vanguard. And the computer revolution is no different."

TOM REILLY, A FOUNDER OF DIGITAL QUEERS, A GROUP OF COMPUTER INDUSTRY GAY MEN AND LESBIANS

2. Handling Prejudice: When prejudice does show its ugly face, we need to show deep loyalties to those in whom we find tolerance, trust, acceptance, and understanding. This may be a boss, mentor, work group, employer, contact, supplier, or client. Such loyalty, rare in the nineties, is often handsomely repaid in business relationships.

3. Achieving Self-Containment: As the odd person out, perhaps we faced despair and discovered the freedom that comes from being written off. As a "society of one," an unclaimed asset, we can quickly respond not only to other gay men and lesbians but to society's "interesting" people: its movers, shakers, and leaders.

4. Taking Tax Advantage: The fact that our relationships are unrecognized and therefore defined as "arm's length" by the IRS is advantageous tax-wise. We can employ each other, sell things to each other, and in other ways take advantage of the fact that we are in reality together but legally apart.

5. Sheer Necessity: If we have fewer children and double incomes, our higher discretionary incomes may mean simply higher taxes and lower deductions as salaried employees. That alone may be a necessary reason to start our own firms. It is no accident that the wealthy have three times as many entrepreneurs in their ranks as the salaried.

6. Breaking the Glass Ceiling: When we come out and raise issues, we sometimes become stereotyped and our potential for top management can get lost under a special-interest label. Often the choice is between fighting political battles and simply building careers. When this happens the way to the top may be from the outside—from the top of our own organizations.

7. Recognizing Diversity: We are often a double or triple minority. If this translates into a desperate search for a home, we can easily get lost in a gay ghetto, nesting in a very specialized niche. But being gay *and* belonging to another minority can also be the best qualification to feel the pulse of America's developing diversity. If we've developed years of multicultural skills and style flexibility, this may translate into entrepreneurial market awareness and a client orientation.

8. Defying Homophobia: AIDS activists have shown that we can channel our anger into action; we can act up and not just act out. Many of us have capitalized on the gay experience to excel in the creative professions and launch businesses to serve our own. Perhaps we are at the point now where many of us in fact would make better entrepreneurs than employees.

A common element to successfully transforming our experiences and differences as gay men and lesbians into assets, not handicaps, may be fully coming out, which may require a willingness to take work seriously. Coming out assumes a desire to make work meaningful, as well as a willingness to shoulder entrepreneurial responsibilities and opportunities.

— PER LARSON

CAN YOU BELIEVE IT?

After watching a parody of popular beer commercials on *Saturday Night Live*, the aptly named gay attorney Michael Beery decided to produce and market his own "Pink Triangle Beer" to the gay community. Brewed in Iowa, it was launched in a half-dozen U.S. cities in 1994. What will they think of next? (There's no word yet on what happens when straight people drink it.)

Early Gay Business Associations

1962: The Tavern Guild (San Francisco): A league of gay bar owners and employees that formed after a feud between city police and state alcoholic beverage control agents had temporarily closed most gay bars in the city.

1974: The Golden Gate Business Association (San Francisco): Offshoot of the Tavern Guild.

1975: The Portland Town Council (Portland, OR).

1976: The Greater Gotham Business Council (NYC), Southern California Women for Understanding, Michigan Organization for Human Rights.

1977: The Community Business and Professional Guild (Los Angeles): Later became the Business & Professional Association of Los Angeles. Orion (Los Angeles): Set up by top young political campaign managers and businessmen.

1979: The Valley Business Alliance (Los Angeles).

1980: The National Association of Business Councils: Headed then by Jean O'Leary and Arthur Lazere, NABC held its first national convention in San Francisco in 1981, with 250 people attending. Representative Pete McClosky addressed them, and Joan Baez performed at the convention. By 1983, NABC included more than 3,000 members in twenty local groups, from Atlanta and Tampa to Milwaukee and Minneapolis–St. Paul.

DID YOU KNOW...

In 1994, the National Gay Pilots Association (NGPA), headquartered in Washington, D.C., had more than 400 members in forty-five states and five countries. According to the NGPA's executive director, Ron Swanda, "It is not unusual for us to receive letters from new members exclaiming how, before they learned of the NGPA, they believed they were the only gay or lesbian pilot in the country."

Buy Lesbian . . . Or Bye! Lesbian

While in Judith's Room bookstore in New York City recently, I glanced at their newsletter and read an excerpt from the latest newsletter of Old Wives' Tales bookstore in San Francisco. The gist of the articles was the same. Larger, mainstream bookstores are capitalizing on the trendiness of women's books and issues, thereby short-circuiting the economies of the feminist bookstores. In addition to the obvious economic repercussions, women's bookstores are experiencing a collective identity crisis and questioning their viabilty in the women's communities.

Once again, feminists and lesbians must reevaluate our politics. Even more effective would be a rehash of Economics 101: Supply and Demand, where the bookstores represent the suppliers and we, the lesbian consumers (attention: all femme shoppers!) represent the demand. Otherwise, our precious bookstores, which are more to us than mere places to make book purchases, will be forced to concede to the Barnes & Nobles of the world. Lest we forget our feminist heritage, women's bookstores were often our first experience with *free* space. An excerpt from the essay "Free Space" by Pamela Allen, 1970, recalls this development:

The group experience has helped me to synthesize and deepen my emotional and intellectual understanding of the predicaments of females in this society and of the concerns with which we must deal in building a women's movement. We have defined our group as a place in which to think: to think about our lives, our society, and our potential for being creative individuals. . . . We call this Free Space. We have had successes and failures in utilizing this space. Usually our problems stem from our failure to be completely honest with ourselves and each other. . . . Thus individual integrity—intellectual and emotional honesty—is our goal. It has been a difficult challenge.

If only that challenge had been resolved! The reality is that we face it today. Our commitment is to feminism, to lesbianism, to womanist beliefs with women's dollars. There is no other solution for the safeguarding and institutionalization of our women's culture. We must put our money where our mouths are (well, not literally, but it is a woman-to-woman thang!).

Honesty is always the best policy in the case of economic survival; we must honestly evaluate our level of commitment not only to the bookstore owners and operators but also to the many lesbian, feminist, and womanist authors, poets, storytellers, playwrights, humorists, and theoreticians who rely upon us to buy and read their work.

We may feel that because there are a few houses where women's culture is being cultivated, that the women's movement is built. While our foundation has been laid, it will take more time before the edifice is secure. That security must be financed by us, its participants. Buy Lesbian, Feminist, Womanist or be prepared to say Good-Bye to our Culture and our Heritage!

— **KAREN WILLIAMS**

OWNING OUR OWN: GAY AND LESBIAN BOOKSTORES

Bookstores have played an important role in the lives of gay men and lesbians for many years. Ever since the late sixties and early seventies, gay/lesbian and women's community-based bookstores have been in operation. During that time, in every state, many such businesses have opened their doors. Some, like the Oscar Wilde Memorial Bookstore and Amazon Bookstore, have managed to survive and thrive for decades. Others have closed due to lack of funds only to be replaced by another store nearby. In 1995, there are nearly 200 gay/lesbian and women's bookstores in the United States.

The success of many gay and women's bookstores often has more to do with serving community needs than it does with making a profit. With all gay and lesbian bookstores, but especially with the women's bookstores, the physical space of the store has been a place to gather for companionship, cultural enrichment, and political organizing. For nearly three decades, gay/lesbian and women's bookstores have been some of the most visible and enduring entrepreneurial efforts of the gay and lesbian community.

"One day two women came into Lammas [the feminist bookstore in Washington, D.C.]. They'd been travelling around in this van and looked a little forlorn. Of course, we were all hospitable then, and so when they asked if they could go upstairs for a little while, I figured they needed to take a whiz, and so I said, 'Sure.' One of them went out and got a blanket and a pillow and they went upstairs. I was running the store by myself and an hour went by, then two hours, and I thought, 'Well, hmmm.' So I went up, and the door at the top of the stairs was closed. I looked through the keyhole—and they were having sex! I thought, 'Well, okay, fine' and went back downstairs. When they were done, they said, 'Thank you,' and left. I said they were welcome. And, I don't know, I suppose that happened to other women's bookstores. . . ."

MARY FARMER

Independent Women's Bookstores

WOMEN'S BOOKSTORES

A L W A Y S

•

have books that change your life & the world

•

inspire new, diverse, and cutting-edge writing

•

guarantee the availability of books by feminists, lesbians & women of color

•

value books as cultural and intellectual expressions, not merely commodities

(Courtesy of Charis Books)

In 1971, as the second wave of feminism was getting under way, three women opened ICI, A Woman's Place bookstore, in Oakland, California. This was the first women's bookstore in the country, stocking all kinds of books by, for, and about women. (The "ICI" stood for "Information Center Incorporate.") From the beginning, A Woman's Place functioned more as an information and referral center than as a for-profit bookstore. It also shared space with the Women's Press Collective, one of the first women's print presses.

At about the same time, a few women started selling feminist and lesbian publications from their front porch in Minneapolis—a project which is now the Amazon Bookstore, the oldest existing feminist bookstore in the United States. Over the next several years, lesbians set up shops across the country in major metropolitan areas as well as smaller communities that not only sold books, but also women's music records, buttons, bumperstickers, T-shirts, and other women-made craft items. When A Woman's Place opened, there were barely enough lesbian books to fill one shelf; today, there are so many books available that the women's stores are sometimes hard pressed to stock them all.

Many of the early feminist stores were collectively run and staffed by volunteers, or owned by women who had other full-time jobs. But regardless of who legally owned the bookstores, everyone in the community often felt she had some ownership in the store. Indeed, in the early seventies and eighties, there was little separation between the lesbian community and the local feminist bookstore. The stores functioned both as cultural centers and as a place gathering places.

Charis Books in Atlanta, for example, has sponsored well-attended programs ranging from author signings to poetry readings to political discussions every Thursday night since they opened.

For many women, entering a women's bookstore was the first act of coming out. Women exploring their sexual identity could find both fiction and non-fiction books, as well as dozens of feminist periodicals and magazines. They also found themselves in safe place to hang out and be around other women in a friendly environment. All of this is just as true today. For women who are traveling, the first stop in a new city is often the women's bookstore. The bookstore staff often spends as much time answering non–book related questions (Where is the women's bar? How can I find a lesbian doctor? Do you know of any places to rent?) as they do helping customers find the right book (I need to send my parents a book about coming out—what do you recommend? I just met this woman who is a minister—what should I read?)

Over the years, as the feminist and lesbian movements have changed, the women's bookstores, too, have evolved. Today, lesbian (and gay) culture is more available through mainstream sources, as well as in the gay/lesbian bookstores. Twenty years ago, a reader could not find one book with the word "lesbian" in its title at a mainstream bookstore; today, these stores compete with both the women's and gay stores for lesbian author readings and events. If access to women's titles were the only reason for their existence, women's bookstores would not be needed in the 1990s. But the mainstream stores will never be able to recreate the sense of community and belonging that the women's stores continue to provide to a significant portion of the women's community.

— LYNN WITT AND MEV MILLER

Grand Books

In 1988, three other lesbians and I opened Grand Books, a general bookstore in Jackson, Wyoming (population 4,000, tourist population 3 million a year). We needed to employ one and a half of the four of us and decided that opening a bookstore would be a cause worthy of us—and something we would enjoy doing. Thus we began the process of starting a small business.

We didn't have enough cash of our own and so we needed a loan. We consulted with a woman who was a manager of the local savings and loan. She couldn't provide a loan, but she did spend a lot of time helping us create a business plan, mentoring us, explaining the ins and outs of banking and financing. She revealed to us how extremely difficult it is to be a woman in banking in Wyoming. At one point, she was having lunch with other women bankers from across the state, commiserating about the sexism in their industry. If they just had the right "equipment," the men would treat them equally. At the next luncheon, one of the bankers presented each of her fellow women bankers with a necklace charm—a tiny penis and balls carefully sculpted in silver! Now the women would forever know they had the right equipment.

With help from this financial adviser and many others, we formulated a dynamite business plan and went loan shopping. At the first bank, the loan officer said, "It's too bad you don't have husbands who can sign for you. We have plenty of money to loan." The second banker sat carefully behind his huge wooden desk and said, "I don't have anything against you . . . uh . . . ladies, per se . . ." as he rejected our application. By then we were disgusted. For the third and final bank, we dyked ourselves out, carrying briefcases and backpacks. We called ourselves the Lesbian Mafia. We strode into the bank as if we owned it. We got the loan!

But before we could receive the money, the loan had to be approved by the Small Business Administration. The SBA has a rule that no business borrowing money from it can support a particular ideal or philosophy. When it learned that our list of bookstore sections included Women's Studies and that half of the books in our store would be by women, it decided we were a specialty store and therefore not eligible for a loan. This ruling has been used time and time again to prevent feminists and lesbians from borrowing money. We organized a successful letter campaign (from our lawyer and our book distributors) saying that it would be *dumb* to open a "specialty" store in such a small town, and we were, after all, smarter than that. We finally got, and repaid, the loan.

We ordered bookstore fixtures that were to be trucked from "back east" and had a crowd of lesbians lined up to help unload the moving van over the Fourth of July weekend. When the Mayflower truck pulled up, we discovered that the two drivers were women and definitely "family." Their previous delivery had been to a Christian bookstore in Ohio and they were mighty pleased to be delivering to dykes.

In spite of our promises to the SBA, we did carry a wide selection of lesbian and gay books. However, we didn't want the fact that we carried "those" books to affect our sales of everything else. For this reason and our own homophobia, we decided to put the lesbian and gay section in the small back room we were using as an office and call it "The Closet." We put a sign on the door saying "The Closet" and, in our ads to the lesbian and gay community, we stated that "the books are in the closet." This made a safe place for local women to peruse the books and gave us a great conversation item with lesbians passing through. Realizing that some dykes would not be brave enough to ask us where the books were, we trained ourselves and our employees to spot and approach lesbians with questions such as "How did you find us?" and "Is there anything else we can help you find?" Our straight employee, Colleen, was sometimes better at spotting and interacting with lesbians and gays than we were.

After hiding the books in the closet for a couple of years, Colleen decided we needed a coming-out party for the books. She brought the books out of the closet and formed a great lesbian, gay, and women's studies section. Much to our surprise, sales increased and we never did receive a negative comment.

The bookstore was an oasis for locals as well as for travelers visiting conservative Wyoming and nearby states, where openly gay and lesbian organizations are few and far between, and where the spirit of appreciation for sexual diversity is not encouraged. Women coming through would stop to get a "hit" of lesbian culture/energy. This constant parade of lesbians through our doors made us feel wonderful, less isolated, more connected.

DID YOU KNOW?

Today there are more than ninety women's/feminist bookstores operating, from Alaska to Alabama. While dozens of such stores have come and gone over the years, the stores below are significant because they have been around for at least twenty years:

Amazon Bookstore
Minneapolis, MN

Charis Books & More
Atlanta, GA

Lammas Women's Books & More
Washington, DC

Mother Kali's Books
Eugene, OR

New Words Bookstore
Cambridge, MA

Old Wives' Tales
San Francisco, CA

Sisterhood Bookstore
Los Angeles, CA

Even with only a few hours' notice, we could round up audiences for lesbian happenings.

At the beginning of our second year of business, the bank changed its mind about giving us a $10,000 line of credit. As it stood, we had based our financial plan around that infusion of capital. Friends offered to loan us money to keep the store open, but after four years of Reagan and Bush we were exhausted. In February 1992, we closed Grand Books.

The most fulfilling part of owning a feminist bookstore was also the most demanding. We got to meet and interact with many wonderful people, and we were also expected to be the social service center for the lesbian and gay community. We maintain contact with lots of the great people we met through Grand Books, but it was definitely time to do something else that wasn't so emotionally taxing.

— DOROTHY HOLLAND

DID YOU KNOW...

Under One Roof, a retailing establishment on Market Street in San Francisco's Castro District, was created to assist AIDS organizations in the city to jointly market their products. Staffed and supported by volunteers, it is the nation's only gift shop for AIDS relief organizations. All of the money from sales goes to the designated organization supplying the product.

Gay/Lesbian Bookstores

In 1967, two years before the Stonewall Rebellion, a revolution of a different sort was under way. In a tiny retail storefront on New York's Mercer Street, gay activist Craig Rodwell opened the world's first gay bookstore, Oscar Wilde Memorial Bookshop.

Rodwell and his mother, Marian, stayed up all night before the grand opening, "finishing the dozen bookshelves (with about twenty-five titles total)," notes Martin Duberman in *Stonewall*. "In those years, a 'gay' bookstore had meant only one thing: pornography. But Craig had a straitlaced, proper side, and he had decided early on that the Oscar Wilde Memorial Bookshop would carry only 'the better titles' and no pornography of any kind. . . . He was determined to have a bookstore where gay people did not feel manipulated or used. There was no ADULT READING sign in the window, and no peep show in the back room. And the ad Craig later took out in the *Village Voice* was headlined 'GAY IS GOOD.'"

In addition to books, the shop carried gay buttons and cards, and it had a community bulletin board. The store also acted as a clearinghouse for information, and as a community center for several gay organizations. One of the store's earliest customers—and one of Rodwell's lovers—was Harvey Milk.

The success of Oscar Wilde inspired others to enter the risky business of selling gay and lesbian books. By the 1970s, there were gay and lesbian bookstores springing up in other major cities: Glad Day in Toronto (1970), Giovanni's Room in Philadelphia (1973), Lambda Rising in Washington, D.C. (1974), and A Different Light in Los Angeles (1979). By 1995, there were more than ninety gay and lesbian bookstores in the U.S., with combined sales of more than $30 million a year. Gay bookstores can be found even in many smaller communities today: OutRight Books in Virginia Beach, Virginia, White Rabbit Bookshop in Greensboro, North Carolina, and Phoenix Rising in Roanoke, Virginia.

Meanwhile, the growth of lesbian and gay literature did not go unnoticed by publishing houses. When Lambda Rising opened its doors in 1974, there were only about 300 titles on the shelves—all that were in print at the time. By 1994, there were nearly 15,000 gay and lesbian titles in print, with more than 300 new titles hitting the bookstore shelves in the spring 1994 season alone.

In the 1960s and earlier, it was almost impossible to find gay and lesbian literature in any bookstore. Today, even mainstream chain bookstores frequently offer a gay and lesbian section, and those living in rural or more conservative areas without nearby access to a gay and lesbian bookstore have mail order options for almost any title. The Quality Paperback Book Club made headlines in 1993 by introducing a full line of gay and lesbian titles, and many gay and lesbian bookstores now ship books anywhere in the world for customers ordering by phone, mail, fax, or even e-mail.

Gay and lesbian bookstores give authors and publishers an outlet, but, more important, they provide a valuable service for the lesbian and gay community, making the best literature, information, and resources available to all. Most such stores also serve as de facto community centers, with bulletin boards, handy guide maps, and copies of the local gay and lesbian newspapers. The bookstore staff is usually ready to answer questions about coming out, finding an attorney, or volunteering at a local health clinic, and most gay and lesbian bookstores place as much emphasis on serving the community as they do on selling a book.

— DEACON MACCUBBIN

"The real economic difference between gay and straight Americans is the daily struggle of lesbians and gay men against the psychological and economic effects of discrimination."

UNIVERSITY OF MARYLAND AT COLLEGE PARK SCHOOL OF PUBLIC AFFAIRS PROFESSOR LEE BADGETT

GAY MONEY: WHAT IS IT? WHO HAS IT?

Although it is a myth that all gay people are wealthy, it would be just as untrue to imply that all gay people are poor. Just as we cross all race and ethnic boundaries, lesbians and gay men also cross all class and economic lines. And while there are some prominent gay philanthropists, whether or not we have a lot of money individually, collectively we definitely have economic clout. The vast majority of our gay and lesbian organizations depend on that support for their economic survival, since there is not much government support, verbally or cash-wise, for queer causes. Even in the private (nongay) sector, those who would lend support to organizations such as the NAACP or the National Asian American Journalists Association, do not necessarily support similar institutions in the gay community.

Statistics show that people in the United States with the least amount of income actually give away proportionately more than the wealthier citizens. As a group, gay people are not at the top of the income pyramid. Nonetheless, most lesbians and gay men can and do donate in varying amounts to everything from the local public radio stations and environmental groups, to AIDS services organizations and national lobbying groups like the Human Rights Campaign Fund. We have learned that we must support our movement ourselves; no one is going to do that for us.

Informally, we have been supporting our community for years, from fund-raising against antigay initiatives to fund-raising in support of gay prisoners' rights projects. We have started our own foundations and gay-owned businesses, our own PACs and voter education projects. We have funded hundreds of AIDS organizations around the country. We have done all of this and more ourselves, by taking lessons from other communities, by asking each other for money, by teaching each other, and by helping each other to understand that, together, we can make a difference.

Rich and Gay?

This is a story about gay wealth, or at least the unscrutinized perception of gay wealth. This is a story about the much harped-upon $3.5 million that lesbian and gay donors gave candidate Bill Clinton. And about marketing surveys that find gays and lesbians have twice the annual income of straights. Finally, this is a story about how attempts to play up the alleged financial power of the gay and lesbian community inadvertently play right into the hands of the community's enemies.

"GAY MARKET MUSCLE" reads the banner headline in an ad that runs weekly in the Boston-area gay paper *Bay Windows.* The ad, featuring a gay white man in a banker's suit, flexing his pin-striped biceps, tells potential advertisers that *Bay Window*'s readers are "thirteen times more likely to buy thirteen or more compact discs this year," and "5.6 times more likely to have traveled to Europe in the past three years."

"According to Simmons Market Research Bureau," the small print says, "our 42,000 Gay and Lesbian readers earn an annual average income of $38,200: a 1.6 billion dollar market."

GAY MARKET MUSCLE

4.7 times more likely to buy 13 hard cover books per year.

13 times more likely to buy 13 or more compact discs this year.

4.7 times more likely to drink bottled sparkling water.

5.4 times more likely to give distilled liquor as a gift.

5.6 times more likely to have travelled to Europe in the past 3 years.

4.9 times more likely to use their American Express Card.

3.3 times more likely to purchase a suit this year.

FLEX YOUR AD DOLLARS

According to Simmons Market Research Bureau*, our 42,000 Gay and Lesbian readers earn an annual average income of $38,200: a 1.6 billion dollar market.

Advertising in mainstream media is not enough to reach this loyal consumer group. Simmons discovered that 66% of our readers don't read any other local gay newspaper. 93.9 % are likely to purchase a product or service advertised in Bay Windows.

For greater impact, target this dream market directly by advertising withBay Windows.

Bay Windows

Call to receive our media kit today.

(617) 266-6670

*compared to the average U.S. consumer.

Bay Windows, *a gay newspaper based in Boston, published this in 1993 to encourage advertisers to believe in the power of the "gay dollar."*

Ads such as these beg the question: Are lesbians and gay men richer than your garden-variety hets?

Given today's political realities, the question is essentially unanswerable, because the methods usually used to ascertain the wealth or poverty of a particular group—polling and census figures—don't work with the gay and lesbian population.

"The core problem with polling is that so many people are closeted and will not reveal their sexual orientation to interviewers, even in anonymous phone interviews," says William Schneider, professor of American politics at Boston College, who's been involved in polling for CNN and *USA Today*.

Similar problems might exist with the U.S. Census—generally considered the most reliable source of demographic information—if it were to collect statistics based on sexual orientation, something the Census does not do now.

"There are two very different homosexual populations," Schneider says. "One is the closeted population, which is unknowable, unpollable, untestable. Then there are those who live openly gay lives. Those people break down into two groups: those who don't live in a predominantly homosexual subculture, and those who do. It's only that last group you're able to poll. And it's only in some men in that last group that you find more wealth."

Schneider says that the very ability to live an openly gay life is often a function of financial security: "Once people feel financially secure, they're better able to come out—they're less afraid of losing their jobs and their homes. I think that's part of what accounts for the figures in the marketing surveys."

Also contributing to those marketing statistics, says Michael Bronski, author of *Culture Clash* and a gay activist for twenty-five years, is an attempt by gay men to purchase societal respect.

"I think people readily confuse middle-class ambition and effect with middle-class economic status. I know plenty of gay men from the bars who have low-paying jobs and buy the designer clothes and the designer sheets because it will help them fit in better and because those things are signifiers of class mobility. But what happens is that they have the signifiers without the economic status."

Bronski says that some gay publications, like *The Advocate*, have fostered the idea that gay men are high-living and free-spending. "Because we've been told that this is how gay men live," he says, "a lot of gay men try to live this way."

But less-well-to-do queers tend not to receive the high profile that has graced some of their richer fellows. "It's no different from the heterosexual community," says novelist Dorothy Allison, who grew up poor and has only recently, she says, "clawed my way into the middle class." She continues, "We don't have enough positions of authority for poor lesbians and gay men. The rich have access. They're the ones who get seen."

Indeed, gay men such as David Geffen and David Mixner—men with substantial wealth and major connections to the White House—have been all over the media in print and broadcast markets these days. As have figures about gay PAC money, and the financial support the gay community provided candidate Clinton.

Considerably less visible, though, are working-class and poor lesbians, gay men, and bisexuals, who rarely figure in coverage of the gay and lesbians movement, whether from mainstream or queer media. "I think the movement is doing a disservice by not highlighting working people," says Ginny Cutting, a member of both the Service Employees International Union and the Gay and Lesbian Labor Activists Network. "It gives the right wingers all sorts of ammunition."

In its pamphlet "What's Wrong with Gay Rights? YOU Be the Judge!", for instance, Colorado for Family Values (CFV) opines that gays are not oppressed because they're wealthier than most other Americans.

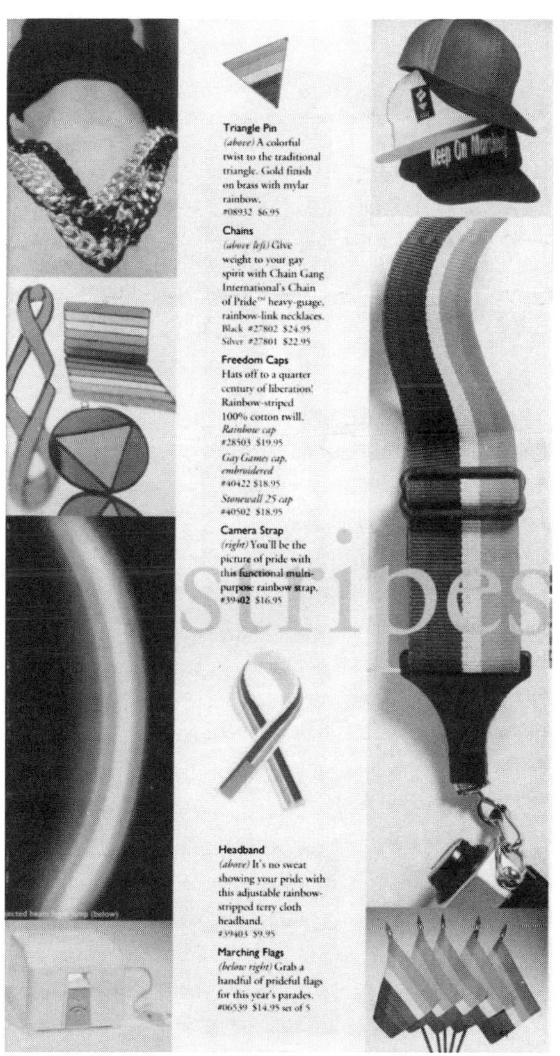

Shocking Grey, *like any number of catalogues aimed at lesbians and gay men, offers an assortment of items through which you can show your pride, including pins, chains, freedom caps, camera straps, marching flags, rainbow lamps, and stylish headbands.*

"Homosexuals are anything but disadvantaged," reads the pamphlet. "According to recent marketing studies, 'gays' have an average household income of more than $55,400—nearly $23,000 more than average American households, and a whopping $43,000 more than African Americans with 1–3 years of high school education. Gays are three times more likely to hold professional or managerial jobs. Four times more likely to be overseas travelers. Almost four times more likely to earn over $100,000 annually.

DID YOU KNOW...

This should come as no surprise: According to the Mulryan/Nash advertising agency, bars still account for most of the advertising placed in gay-oriented publications in the United States, accounting for 19.5 percent of dollars spent on print ads. Banks account for a mere 0.1 percent of the $53 million that businesses and industry spend each year placing ads in gay papers and magazines. While ads by car dealers are on the rise in 1994, phone sex lines make up roughly 12.6 percent of ad revenue dollars, followed by professional services, at 10.8 percent.

"Special civil rights protection has never been given to people who are far more economically, educationally, or culturally advantaged than others. Would it be fair for disadvantaged Americans to compete with wealthy 'gays' for minority contracts and special benefits? YOU be the judge!"

CFV twists all sorts of details in the civil rights debate, says Scott Nakagawa, "Fight the Right" organizer for the National Gay and Lesbian Task Force. First of all, the organization uses income statistics from marketing surveys—designed to impress advertisers with the wealth of a particular market—as though they were gathered from considerably more accurate sources. Secondly, they assert "that civil rights can be bestowed to people on the basis of income," says the NGLTF organizer.

But civil rights were not designed to equalize wealth. Even if you're rich, you can still be fired from your job, kicked out of your apartment, or attacked on the streets. "Pat Robertson is a multimillionaire and Pat Robertson has civil rights," Nakagawa continues. "If he were harassed or attacked because of his religion, his race, his sex, or his sexual orientation, he would have the full protection of the Constitution."

Nakagawa believes that CFV and other antigay groups use this myth of gay wealth to force a divide between the gay community and other traditional supporters of civil rights—namely, people of color. "What they're doing is purposefully putting us up against other oppressed minority groups and working people, all of whom expect to make less in this generation than their parents did. Antigay groups are suggesting that in these economic hard times, gay and lesbian rights are frivolous, and they target this information to working-class communities and communities of color. It's a way of saying we're not real minorities. . . . If you look at the African American community, for example, they on the whole make less than they did prior to the civil rights movement. So in that context, it serves to confuse people about what civil rights are. And it's particularly inflammatory and divisive."

And largely beside the point, for that matter. If, for example, you look at the seventeen cases of employment discrimination investigated since 1990 by the Gay and Lesbian Advocates and Defenders, a Boston-based legal-advocacy group, you'll find that only one or two of those complaints were brought by professionals. The others were brought by a ditch digger, two schoolteachers, a hospital orderly, an Army lieutenant, a prison guard, a mental-health worker, three retail clerks, a flight attendant, a law student, a furniture-factory worker, and a cop.

So why, then, are gay men and lesbians not fighting the perception that the community is uniformly wealthy? "Money moves PACs and money moves Congress," says Karla Jay, a longtime activist and professor of English and Women's Studies at Pace University in New York City. "I think that some politicos believe the way to push gay rights is to portray us as an affluent group which is willing to give big bucks to further our agenda. They're not seeing the kind of backlash that can happen as a result. . . . These myths of gay wealth and financial backing are very dangerous in a political sense. People see us as wanting a special payoff for our money. It's a risky strategy, I think."

— **LIZ GALST** (FROM THE BOSTON PHOENIX, **JUNE 18, 1993**)

Coming Out of the Privilege Closet

In an article titled "Living in a Double Closet" I wrote for *Gay Community News* eleven years ago, I talked about growing up in two closets, being both gay and very rich. At the time I wrote under a pseudonym, more from embarrassment about my privilege than my sexuality.

Today I write under my real name, and again admit my multiple privileges: white, male, rich, healthy, graduate-school educated, upper-class connected, etc. My father's father founded a sizable bank; my mother's grandfather founded one of the largest corporations in the country. My middle name (Pillsbury) is a well-known trademark, and I often lied about it to friends to stay in the closet. All these advantages can be difficult to work through toward an analysis of their origins and effects, particularly when awareness of their inequity produces guilt feelings, and resulting secrecy.

Growing up in a rich family is an incredibly *protected* experience. I had a very large home, 200 acres of land, private schools, servants. It is very hard work to question in such an environment. More and more I realize what a narrow escape I had from following the path laid out for me. One of the biggest stumbling blocks in that path, of course, was my sexuality; treated with almost total silence, it told me early on that in one important respect, at least, I did not belong. I think that in rich families, however, silence around money is even stronger than around sex. There are many secrets in rich families around both subjects, and any breaking of the silence is regarded as betrayal. My coming out publicly in the media (including *The New York Times* three years ago) about my sexuality and privilege did not go over too well, needless to say; often I was asked just why I felt I had to *talk* about it.

The family rule for giving money away was to be "charitable," but not extravagantly so. The cardinal money rule was "don't touch the capital," much less give it away. I've been giving away my capital for several years now. It has been a long, continuing process of study, trust, and some fear (will I be seen only as a checkbook?), but what I have realized is that privilege is a tool, and must be used for liberation.

I always wanted somehow to return my money to the communities from where it came. I also learned it was important to give the community the choice of where that money could best be used, thereby giving up the inherent power donors (especially large donors) have over organizations and agendas.

For twelve years, I have also been giving substantially to the lesbian and gay community, and still making the choice of recipients myself; this year, however, I am helping found a new, activist-controlled foundation for lesbian and gay liberation.

How do we encourage other gay men and lesbians to come out of the privilege closet? There has been considerable progress over the last decade, at least in the realm of fund-raising for gay and lesbian organizations. The most notable example, of course, is the tremendous amount of money that has come from the community in response to the AIDS crisis (for so long no money came from anywhere else). In addition, considerable funds have been raised to support electoral politics, exemplified by the success of the Human Rights Campaign Fund, now the ninth-largest PAC in the nation.

However, a good portion of this money has been given to so-called reformist groups rather than more progressive, radical efforts, particularly those in communities of color or those working toward coalition with other groups. There will be no true liberation if we fail to make such connections.

It seems so simple to realize that the gay community cuts across class lines, and that those of us with considerable class privilege should realize that AIDS strikes everyone, rich and poor; that we are all subject to harassment and physical violence; that we all are criminals if we "commit" sodomy. Therefore we *all* are in this struggle together. Indeed, we are in all struggles together. Understandably, many gay men and lesbians with money (both earned and unearned) have opted for protection from a hostile world by escaping into cultural consumption and a safe status quo (the so-called "*Advocate* lifestyle" stereotype for men), but such solutions were more understandable in the McCarthyite 1950s than they are now.

We still need gay men and lesbians with upper-class privilege to come out about it, and begin to use it for the works of the gay community and other disenfranchised communities. I know many more ridiculously underpaid activists who tithe, than I do people with a *lot* more disposable income.

"There's no gay way to brush your teeth, wash your clothes, or drive a car. Basically we live in the regular world. The difference is how you find us and how you make us feel comfortable."

JUDY RICHARD, MARKETING AND PUBLIC RELATIONS DIRECTOR AT SAN JOSE STATE UNIVERSITY, COMMENTING ON THE GROWING ADVERTISING PITCH TO GAY AND LESBIAN CONSUMERS BY MAINSTREAM BUSINESSES

Our work is not yet done. We are building the organizations that are doing it and will continue to do it, but more money will enable that work to increase and found new organizations to begin their own work.

— DAVID BECKER

Gay and Lesbian Philanthropy

My father is a good Calvinist; he is also a good man. When I was a kid he gave constant advice about working hard, making money, and saving it as part of his ongoing sales pitch to make me a businessman. I chose public service instead, but his advice on money has been invaluable to me in the philanthropic work I've done in the lesbian and gay community.

The dictionary defines "philanthropy" as increasing "human well-being, as by charitable aid." By "gay philanthropy," I mean both the money contributed to nonprofit organizations in our community, and the money contributed by lesbians and gay men to charitable causes outside the community.

While there are few statistics on "gay philanthropy," it likely mirrors giving in the rest of America, where rich foundations and corporations actually play a small role. The notion of philanthropy is supremely American; no other country in the world relies so heavily on personal giving. Socialist economies rely on the state; we rely on individuals. In America, we give at the office, we give at church, we respond to mail and phone solicitations, and so on. We support a vast array of services with our contributions.

Without gay philanthropy, we could not provide services, do political work, or foster our culture. Without it, we would have no lesbian or gay institutions, and we could not exist as a community within the American family. Gay men and lesbians give money to AIDS organizations, synagogues and churches, environmental groups, the arts, and to may other community organizations. We also give millions of dollars to political causes at all levels of government. In 1992, the Clinton presidential campaign alone acknowledged contributions of $3.5 million from our community.

There are some myths about gay philanthropy that should be quickly dispelled. Gay people do not give big bucks to charities because we have more disposable income. Despite the myth about our not having children, many of us do have children. The image is that we make fabulous salaries; the reality is a lavender ceiling. And no one ever mentions the disposable income of nongays without children, especially seniors. Disposable income is a myth.

Nor do we make charitable contributions because we are predisposed to helping other people. As an oppressed people we understand the needs of others who are hurting, so we are sometimes more sensitive, but it's doubtful that altruism comes with our genes.

Our community has faced, in rapid-fire succession, extreme prejudice from the radical right and an out-of-control epidemic. We have been forced to organize, and we have been forced to create and support our own organizations because, literally, our lives were on the line. First crisis, then invention played big roles in gay philanthropy.

As we remember Stonewall 1969 as the birth of gay resistance, we should likewise remember the 1965 dance at California Hall in San Francisco as the birth of gay philanthropy. That event was the gay community's first big-time fund-raiser. The dollars raised at the California Hall dance were the funds that made possible our community's first national civil rights effort through the Society for Individual Rights.

In the years before the epidemic changed all of our lives, inroads in philanthropy were being made, though few people appreciated the need to build and support our own nonprofit organizations. (We had, of course, been supporting gay-owned businesses, like women's bookstores and publishing companies, for years.) We understood the role of consumer, but as a community we were contribution-challenged. The biggest hindrance we faced when attempting to fund-raise was not inexperience or unworthy causes; the problem was the closet.

But persistence has paid off. Our sophistication in giving has increased faster than our incomes. The result has been that we now feed people who have AIDS, we

CAN YOU BELIEVE IT?

One early gay fund-raiser, Jim Foster, once attempted to solicit a gift from a closeted businessman. Jim got all dressed up, went to the guy's office and took his time describing the cause, and, finally, made the pitch. The businessman listened politely and said he wanted to be supportive. "But," he added, "I can't make a contribution because if I wrote you a check, my accountant would find out I'm gay." Jim looked down at his hands in his lap for a moment, then smiled and said, "Who do you think told us to ask you in the first place?"

build community centers, we play leadership roles in the fight against AIDS and in women's health issues. Our political contributions have also been crucial. Initially, we gave to nongay politicians and got to be in the room when public decisions were being made. Now we also support our own, elect them to office, and sit at the table when decisions are made. Between the two, our contributions are reshaping the face of contemporary American politics.

As mayor of New York City, David Dinkins held an annual breakfast honoring lesbians who made a significant contribution to the city. Pictured here are (from left) Dr. Marjorie Hill, Paula Ettlebrick, Phyllis Clay, Mayor Dinkins, Sandra Lowe, Lisa Winters, and Patricia Carter. (Courtesy New York City Archives)

We have learned three important lessons in our first decade of serious philanthropy in the gay community. We learned the importance of coming out. We learned that giving strengthens ties within the community. And we learned that regular giving is essential for our long-term health as a community.

With examples like the San Francisco Public Library, where the gay community raised over $2.6 million to create the nation's first Gay and Lesbian Center in the New Main Library, we are entering a new phase of philanthropy—giving to civic institutions. The test will come in cities that have treated lesbians and gay men as second-class citizens and suddenly want our money. Will they be willing to change their attitudes first? The outcome will be interesting.

Our success as a community in the future will depend, in part, upon our ability to foster and sustain philanthropy. What happens when the AIDS epidemic ends? Or when Congress passes a civil rights bill? (Both will come to pass.) Does giving end?

Bigotry will always exist, and we will always need healthy institutions to sustain the community, to foster our culture, and to maintain our hard-earned place at the political table. Beyond that, we can also become a force in shaping American culture through our participation and our philanthropy.

— CHUCK FORESTER

Advice for Giving

My father's advice on buying stock was "Avoid the flashy stocks. Find a few sound companies, invest regularly, and be prepared to weather the periodic ups and downs." With that in mind, here are a few tips on "investing" in the gay community:

1. Direct your philanthropy to the issues and services you feel good about, regardless of their tax-exempt status.

2. Find one or two groups that meet the first criterion and make a commitment to support them on a regular, sustained basis. Or select a gay foundation to regularly contribute to and let them decide whom to fund.

3. Make a monthly budget; "plan" on giving away money the same way you "plan" for paying the utility bill.

4. Break your giving into reasonable chunks. You may not be in the position to sit down and write a large check whenever the mood strikes you, but you can make a yearlong "pledge," payable monthly, to one or more organizations. Fifty dollars a month is $600 a year; to many organizations, that money will make a large impact. Even putting aside a dollar a day will make you a major donor to some organizations.

5. Think about what you spent the last time you went out to dinner. If you eat out regularly, you could go out a little less often and give that money to an AIDS organization instead. Or vow to give away at least as much as you spend eating out every month.

6. Consider a "stretch" gift; if last year you gave $1,000 to your gay community center, consider increasing it by 25 percent this year.

7. Consider tithing. While it sounds scary, tithing a portion of your gross income every year is one way to put

DID YOU KNOW...

The Horizons Foundation (orignally the Golden Gate Business Association Foundation) was founded in 1979 in San Francisco as the first specifically gay and lesbian foundation in the country. Its first funds were the excess dues of the GGBA's membership.

your money where your mouth is. And the best part of all, not only will you have done good works with your money, you will feel great, too.

— CHUCK FORESTER

Gay and Lesbian Foundations

Gay men and lesbians are actively redefining what it means to be a community. Traditionally, the label "community foundation" applies to foundations that are geographically based. But the spread-out nature of the gay community is changing that definition. While most of these foundations do not give out large grants, they do fund everything from office equipment to workshops. The gay and lesbian foundations around the country have recently begun to work together to share what they have learned with each other and to encourage philanthropy in the gay community.

Besides community foundations, there are also the progressive funders who are part of the Funding Exchange; these are progressive foundations committed to gay and lesbian issues. The Out Fund has recently joined this group. There are also private foundations, like Collin-Higgins in San Francisco and the Chicago Resource Center, that fund a variety of projects. As private foundations, they fall under different governmental regulations than the community foundations.

Today there are nine lesbian and gay community foundations:

- Astrea (New York)—funds lesbians nationally
- Cream City Foundation (Milwaukee)—serves all of Wisconsin
- Equity Foundation (Portland)—serves Oregon only; funds primarily lesbian and gay projects in nongay organizations
- Horizons Foundation (San Francisco)—serves the San Francisco Bay Area
- New Harvest Foundation (Madison)—serves Madison area only
- Philanthrofund (Minneapolis)—serves Minnesota and eastern Wisconsin

• Pride Foundation (Seattle)—serves all of Washington, Oregon, Idaho, and Montana

• The Lambda Foundation (Pittsburgh)—serves all of Pennsylvania

• The Stonewall Community Foundation (New York)—national scope

Coming Out of the Housing Closet

It all started innocently enough. My lover and I were in our apartment quietly reading the Sunday newspaper, when he said, "There's something I've always wanted to do with you, and now that we've been together for over a year, I feel I can share it with you. Let's go house shopping."

I was shocked. Oh, I knew it could happen in the best of relationships. The same people I had marched with in gay pride parades were now settling into suburbia, complete with cat and flower garden. Just the other day, someone who was fighting homophobia in the college bureaucracy was fighting wood rot in storm gutters. And I should have seen it coming sooner: how he stared when we passed a house for sale, how he ogled the fine Victorian curves, and how he seemed to undress the aluminum siding with his eyes.

He then introduced me to something called an "open house." Advertised in many respectable papers, an open house lets you make contact with several houses in one afternoon. These encounters may last only minutes, as you dart in and out, usually without even knowing the owner's name. Unsafe as this may sound, many people manage to attend several every weekend without ill effect, as long as they take certain precautions. Knowing how careless he could get when he sees an attractive facade, I insisted on coming along.

We saw several houses that afternoon, but only one stuck in my mind when we were done: a cute little Victorian on a quiet side street with a coffee shop at the end of the block that actually knew what a half-caf double latte was. It was nice, but nothing to give up my comfortable renter's lifestyle for.

Later that night, I had a dream. I was hot and sweaty, wearing nothing but my loosest pair of shorts. The sun beat down on me and the newly mown grass tickled my toes. A young man walked toward me with a smile on his face. I felt a tap on my shoulder. "The kid mowing the lawn just finished," my lover said. "You want to pay him?"

I woke up in a cold sweat. I couldn't believe I was having these feelings over nothing more than a frame of sticks and some shingles. I felt my pulse. The last time it beat that way I had spent all night watching *Frat House Fun IV* starring Blade Cox.

That at least was normal. These new feelings were an abomination.

At work the next day I tried to hide my feelings but couldn't. I heard someone call my name and say I'd been staring out the window for several minutes. I shook my head sleepily. There was a Victorian across the street with a cute little stained-glass window just like ours.

I tried to replace these thoughts with more wholesome ones. When I thought of the paneled doors, I'd think of Blade Cox's washboard stomach. When I thought of the long shapely barristers, I'd think of Blade Cox's legs. When I thought of the new long kitchen faucet, I thought of Blade's nose. But soon I got bored and started thinking of another house. I had to admit it: I had a single-track mind.

I tried aversion therapy. When I thought of the house, I pinched myself. When I thought of the neighborhood, I slapped myself. At the end of the day, it worked: I started thinking of the house less, and of getting to the doctor's more.

When I went home, I got the bad news. "The house inspector looked at the house," my lover said, "and gave it a failing report." I read it over: sagging wastepipes ready to burst, a heater that couldn't keep a broom closet toasty, and an electrical system so old the lights dimmed when you rang the doorbell. My emotions finally burst out and I broke down in tears. I should have listened to my friends, I thought. Homeownership is an unnatural lifestyle, doomed to unhappiness.

"Maybe this will cheer you up," my lover said, waving a picture of another house in front of me.

"I never want to look at another house as long as I live," I sniffed.

"This time will be different," he promised.

He carried me into the car and drove me to the house. It was beautiful. Wastepipes that could handle all the bathrooms in the city at the end of the Academy Awards broadcast. A brand-new heater that could defrost the Antarctic. And a doorbell that chimed "Ode to Joy." I was crying again, this time tears of joy, as we walked off into the sunset, hand in hand with the mortgage company representative.

— **JEFFREY MATTSON**

About the Contributors

Sandia Bear is a fifty-five-year-old Jewish lesbian crone. Her novel *The Woman Who Fell Through the Sky* begins in Santa Fe, which she still calls home, though she lives in California.

David Bell owns and operates a real estate investment company in San Francisco. He is on the board of the Human Rights Campaign Fund and loves to travel.

Andrea Bernstein is a New York–based reporter who writes frequently on politics and lesbian and gay issues.

Selisse Berry, M.Div., is a graduate of San Francisco Theological Seminary and is the national coordinator of CLOUT, an organization of out lesbians in the churches.

Joan E. Biren (JEB) has for twenty-four years been proud of her efforts to make our community visible through photographing, publishing, and producing videos that chronicle the lives of lesbian and gay people.

Wayne Blackenship is the intervention coordinator at the San Francisco AIDS Foundation.

Megan Boler, a native San Franciscan, poet, and novelist, holds a doctorate in the history of consciousness and currently teaches at the University of Auckland in New Zealand.

Michael Bronski is the author of *Culture Clash: The Making of A Gay Sensibility* (1984), as well as the forthcoming *Gay and Lesbian Culture.* He has written extensively on sexuality, culture, and politics and has been involved in the gay liberation movement for more than twenty-six years.

Richard D. Burns is the executive director of the Lesbian and Gay Community Services Center of New York City.

Stephen Capsuto lectures and writes about the history of sexual minority images in American broadcast media. Since 1991, he has served as director of the Lesbian and Gay Library/Archives of Philadelphia (a project of Penguin Place Community Center).

Quang Dang is involved in queer youth advocacy, AIDS activism, and immigrant rights, and he dreams of one day writing a cookbook of tasty eggplant dishes. He got his B.A. from Brown University and is testing his patience at the University of California's (Berkeley) law school.

Carrie Dearborn first started writing for the *New England Women's Yellow Pages* in 1976 and has a book coming out titled the *Cobblestone Sidewalk Conspiracy.*

Beth Dingman is one of the founding members of New Victoria Press. She is currently writing a book on the Women and Print Movement (1970–1990).

Jeffrey Escoffier is the author of many articles on gay and lesbian politics, economics, and scholarship. He is the author of the Chelsea House biography of John Maynard Keynes.

Alina Ever is a community builder, artist, ritualist, drummer, singer, group leader, activist, and liberation educator with a passion for fusing multicultural art/ritual and politics to heal and transform the world.

Jennifer Finlay is a graduate of Bowling Green State University. She worked with Randy Shilts on his final book, *Conduct Unbecoming*. She also worked with Eric Marcus on the upcoming *Why Suicide?*

Chuck Forester is the former co-chair of the Human Rights Campaign Fund.

Deeg Gold has been a lesbian liberation activist for twenty-four years and is currently a member of Lesbians and Gays Against Intervention (LAGAI) in San Francisco. LAGAI publishes *Ultra Violet*, a newsletter for lesbian/gay liberationists.

Michael Greer is a writer and activist living in San Francisco. He is an editor of *CrossRoads*, a monthly magazine of progressive debate and opinion, and is currently working on a book about children of gay and lesbian parents.

David Harrison is a San Francisco–based playwright/performer. His most recent work, *FTM,* is a solo performance piece exploring the classic issues of death, transformation, and enlightenment—with a twist. It's based on his own transsexual journey from female to male, as well as his personal duel with breast cancer.

Karen Hester of Scarlet Letter Management is an activist, producer, publicist, and booking agent.

Dorothy Holland, former teacher and Peace Corps Volunteer, is now a book buyer for feminist bookstores and a computer consultant for women. She also reviews books and new media for several publications.

Philip Horvitz is a performer, director, and writer who lives and works in San Francisco.

Andy Humm has been the host of *Gay USA* on the Gay Cable Network since 1985 and of WNET-TV's *Informed Sources* since 1992.

Sue Hyde is a sodomite and political activist. She has worked for the National Gay and Lesbian Task Force since 1986.

Eric Jansen is a freelance radio and print journalist living in San Francisco.

Stephen Kent Jusick is a film archivist and freelance curator who has been reading comics since 1977.

Jim Kepner is a veteran gay activist, journalist, teacher, and historian.

John R. Killacky is a curator, writer, videographer, and educator living in Minneapolis.

Dave Kinnick chronicles the small world of pornography and its denizens for magazines such as *The Advocate, Advocate Classifieds, Advocate MEN,* and *Fresh MEN* and is the editor of Adam's *Gay Video Annual Directory.* Dave's first independently published book was *Sorry I Asked: Intimate Interviews with Gay Porn's Rank and File* (Badboy Press, 1993).

Billy Kolber is the co-founder and editor of *OUT & ABOUT,* the award-winning gay/lesbian travel magazine.

David Lamble is a San Francisco-based filmmaker, writer, and host of the gay men's radio show "Fruit Punch." He is currently working on a book about gay writers called *Dead Radio Shows.*

Per Larson, a columnist for *The Advocate*, *Victory*, and *In the Life*, is an advisor to gay men and lesbians on finance and workplace issues. Based in New York, Per is on the board of the Community Lesbian and Gay Rights Institute and the Equal Opportunity Institute.

Mark Leger is a poet, gardener, and faggot witch living in Brooklyn with his lover and three cats. He is an editor, along with the luscious Aleksandra and fabulous others, of *Faerie.Gram,* the northeast Radical Faerie newsletter. Mark is currently working on a computer multimedia documentary of Anne Thompson, a longtime Brooklyn street activist.

Doug Litwin has been a member of the San Francisco Lesbian and Gay Freedom Band since 1985, and is currently president of the Lesbian and Gay Bands of America. In his other real life, he is a marketing executive.

Matthew Lore is a writer and book packager. He worked for five years at HarperSanFrancisco, the country's largest nondenominational publisher of books on religion and spirituality. He is writing the volume on spirituality for a new series, *Issues in Gay and Lesbian Life,* which will be published by Chelsea House in 1995.

Daniel Mangin started one of the nation's first courses in lesbian and gay film at City College of San Francisco. He has written about film for the *Journal of Film and Video, Culture Concrete*, *The Advocate*, and other publications and has lectured internationally on lesbian and gay film topics.

Jeff Mattson lives and writes computer documentation in Sommerville, Massachusetts.

Mev Miller is proud to say she's always been a lesbian and has NEVER been with a man, even on a date! She is currently editing an anthology of writings by fat dykes.

Arwyn Moore is a San Francisco-based writer and editor-in-chief of *insideOUT,* a magazine for queer youth. Arwyn's ultimate life goal is to train elephants for the Romanian Lesbian Circus.

Michael Nava is a lawyer and author.

Elizabeth Nonas is the author of three novels published by Naiad Press, as well as co-author with Simon LeVay of *City of Friends* (MIT Press). She teaches fiction writing at UCLA Extension and at the Institute of Gay and Lesbian Education in West Hollywood.

Naphtali Offen is a longtime community activist in the lesbian/gay, Jewish, and anti-smoking movements.

Irene Ogus is the owner of a travel magazine and directory publishing company. A native of London, England, she has lived in San Francisco for the past twenty-six delicious years.

John Paul is the owner of Spiral Studios, a graphic design firm, and Pink Triangle Adventures, a travel business for gay men and lesbians. John lives in the San Francisco Bay Area with his partner, Chip Carman. Further information on men's music can be found at John's Internet home page, http://www.spiral.com/.

Rachel Pepper envisions a life spent on Mykonos, sipping beer, gazing out at the sea, and churning out mystery novels for huge sums of money and adoring fans everywhere.

Elizabeth Pincus is the film critic for *Harper's Bazaar* and film editor of the *LA Weekly.* She is also author of the Nell Fury private eye series.

Wendell Ricketts was born on Wake Island and raised in O'ahu, Hawai'i, where he lived until moving to San Francisco in 1981. Formerly the manuscript editor of the *Journal of Homosexuality*, he writes frequently about politics, the performing arts, lesbian and gay family and legal issues, and responses to AIDS in the arts and the media.

Thomas P. Rielly is co-founder and co-chair of Digital Queers, a civil rights organizing group based in San Francisco.

Don Romesburg, the assistant editor of *Out in All Directions,* is a San Francisco-based writer and editor. His ambitions are to love well, always be a fabulous deviant in this ridiculous society, and make enough money to afford health insurance.

Cynthia Scott is a Minneapolis-based journalist. She has worked in community and neighborhood newspapers for ten years.

Anthony Slide is the author and editor of more than fifty books on the history of popular entertainment, including *Great Pretenders: A History of Female and Male Impersonation in the Performing Arts* (1986) and *Gay and Lesbian Characters and Themes in Mystery Novels* (1993).

Jakki Spicer is currently a graduate student in the comparative studies in discourse and society program at the University of Minnesota, Twin Cities, where she is pursuing the question: Queer theory, feminist theory, and postmodern/poststructuralist theory—friends, enemies, or both? An expatriate of the San Francisco Bay Area, Jakki hopes to someday be as tall as Geena Davis.

Linda Stamps is a journalist, attorney, and former professional football player. She lives in Monterey, California, with her partner, Halle, and their cat, Misha. The ex-linebacker is currently working on a book about women's football.

Victoria Starr has worked in the music industry for many years. She currently produces and hosts a regular weekly radio program, "The Motherlode," for WBAI, 99.5 fm in New York City. The former music editor, then features editor, of *Outweek*, from 1988 to 1990, she also wrote *All You Get Is Me*, a biography of k.d. lang, in 1994.

Nancy E. Stoller is a professor of community studies and sociology at the University of California, Santa Cruz, and a co-editor of *Women Resisting AIDS: Feminist Strategies of Empowerment* (1994).

Mark Thompson is a journalist and photographer and was a senior editor of *The Advocate* for twenty years. He is the author/editor of several books, including *Gay Spirit: Myth and Meaning; Leatherfolk: Radical Sex, People, Politics and Practice;* and *Gay Souls: Finding the Heart of Gay Spirit in Nature.*

Steve Vezeris currently resides in San Francisco, where he has lived for the last five years. He is still recovering from his first thirty-five years of living on the East Coast.

Greg Walker, who lives in Palo Alto, California, is active in the San Francisco Gay Men's Choral Foundation and is a closet social worker.

Karen Wickre is co-founder and co-chair of Digital Queers, a civil rights organizing group based in San Francisco.

Jim Wilke is a historian studying the American West and gay and lesbian issues.

John Wrathall is the author of the forthcoming book *Take the Young Stranger by the Hand: The YMCA and Male Homoeroticism in America, 1860-1930* (University of Chicago Press).

Reprint Information

Luis Alfaro, "Dia De Los Muertos," which originally appeared in the *Los Angeles Reader*, and "Heroes and Saints," which will be appearing in several upcoming anthologies. Both are reprinted with permission of Luis Alfaro.

Gloria Anzaldúa, "Fear of Going Home: Homophobia," from *Borderlands/La Frontera: The New Mestiza*, copyright 1987 by Gloria Anzaldúa. Reprinted with permission of Aunt Lute Books.

Tess Ayers and Paul Brown, "Seven Bad Reasons to Get Married" and "What to Answer When Your Mother Asks, 'Why in the World. . . ,'" from *The Essential Guide to Lesbian and Gay Weddings*, copyright 1994 by Tess Ayers and Paul Brown. Reprinted with permission of HarperCollins Publishers, Inc.

Stephen Basile, "No Room in the Closet for This Quilt." A longer version of this article was published in December 1992 in *On the Wilde Side*, a LesBiGay monthly magazine for the New York, New Jersey, and Connecticut gay communities. Reprinted with permission of Stephen Basile.

Susan Baumgartner, "It's Not Impossible to Be Queer in Idaho," originally appeared in the *Washington Blade* (March 18, 1994). Reprinted with permission of Susan Baumgartner.

David Becker, "Coming Out of the Privilege Closet," is excerpted from an article that originally appeared in *Gay Community News* (January 28, 1990). Reprinted by permission of *Gay Community News.*

Lisa Ben, *Vice Versa*, reprinted with permission of the June Mazer Collection.

Dorothee Benz, "It's in the Jeans: Biology, Culture, and the Struggle for Gay Liberation," first appeared in *Democratic Left*, the magazine of the Democratic Socialists of America (January 1994). Reprinted with permission of Dorothee Benz.

Kathie Berquist, "Dating: Tips on Approval," originally appeared in the "Kathie Klub" column of *Nightlines* (July 6, 1994). Reprinted by permission of Kathie Berquist.

Malcolm Boyd, "Reflections on a Birthday, a Bombshell, and a Parade," is an abridged version of the same article in *Lambda Gray* (Newcastle Publishing Co., 1993). Reprinted with permission of Newcastle Publishing Co., Inc.

Sharon Bradshaw, "Wedding Belles," originally appeared in *Outlines* (October 1993). Reprinted by permission of *Outlines.*

Randy Burns, "We Are Special," excerpted from the preface to *Living the Spirit: A Gay American Indian Anthology*, Will Roscoe, coordinating editor (St. Martin's Press, 1988). Reprinted by permission of Randy Burns.

Michael Callen, "Fighting for Our Lives," excerpted from the introduction to *Surviving AIDS* by Michael Callen (HarperCollins, 1990). Reprinted by permission of Richard Dworkin, executor of the estate of Michael Callen.

Barbara Cameron, "Gee, You Don't Seem Like an Indian from the Reservation," is an excerpt of a longer piece with the same name in *This Bridge Called My Back* (Kitchen Table: Women of Color Press, 1981). Reprinted with permission of Barbara Cameron.

Susie Day, "Stonewall 25 Radical," is an excerpt from an article that originally appeared in the *San Francisco Bay Times* (Volume 15, Number 20, July 1, 1995). Reprinted with permission of the *San Francisco Bay Times.*

Frank DeCaro, "Gays in the Fashion Industry," originally appeared in the June 1994 issue of *Newsday.* Reprinted with permission from the Times-Mirror Co.

Dallas Denny, "You're Strange and We're Wonderful," is an excerpt from a longer article of the same title that appeared in *TransSisters: The Journal of Transsexual Feminism* (Autumn 1994). Reprinted by permission of Dallas Denny.

Vashte Doublex, "Ageful Equals Rageful," first appeared in *Sinister Wisdom* (Issue 53, Summer/Fall 1994). Reprinted by permission of Vashte Doublex.

David Ehrenstein, "And I'd Like to Thank. . . ," originally appeared in *The Advocate* (June 1993). Reprinted by permission of David Ehrenstein.

FAB, "The Gift," appeared originally as part of a longer work titled "Mothers' Dreams," in *esto no tiene nombre, revista de lesbianas latinas.* Reprinted by permission of her daughter, tatiana de la tierra.

Jack Fertig, "Stonewall 25—A Celebration," originally appeared in the *San Francisco Bay Times* (Volume 15, Number 20, July 1, 1995). Reprinted by permission of the *San Francisco Bay Times.*

Liz Galst, "Rich and Gay?," originally appeared in the *Boston Phoenix* (May 18, 1993). Reprinted with permission of the *Boston Phoenix.* "A Taste of Heaven," originally appeared in *Gay Community News* (March 27, 1988). Reprinted by permission of *Gay Community News.*

Frank Golovitz, "Gay Beach, 1958," is an excerpt from a piece that appeared in *ONE Magazine* (July 1958). Reprinted by permission of Jim Kepner.

Jewelle Gomez, "I Lost It at the Movies," from *Making Face, Making Soul*, 1990. Reprinted with permission of Aunt Lute Books.

Jewelle Gomez, "When I First Saw Audre Lorde," is excerpted from "The Marches" in *Forty-Three Septembers*, copyright 1993 by Jewelle Gomez. Reprinted by permission of Firebrand Books, Ithaca, New York.

Grear Greene, "Friends of Dorothy," first appeared in *Sinister Wisdom* 53. Reprinted by permission of Grear Greene.

James Earl Hardy, "Behind the Mask," originally appeared in *The Advocate* (November 15, 1994). Reprinted by permission of *The Advocate*.

Craig Harris, "Gay, Gifted and Black, There Ain't No Turning Back," is an excerpt from an article that originally appeared in *Gay Community News* (October 18, 1994). Reprinted by permission of *Gay Community News*.

Jeffrey Hilbert, "The Politics of Drag," is an except from a longer piece that first appeared in *The Advocate* (April 23, 1991). Reprinted by permission of *The Advocate*.

Bruce Hilbok, "Notes from a Diary: A Gay Deaf Man's Concern with Communication," is an excerpt from a longer piece that originally appeared in *The Advocate* (February 7, 1984).

Mike Hippler, "Remembrances," is an excerpt from "An (A.C.) D.C. Journal," which appeared in the *Bay Area Reporter* (October 15, 1987). Reprinted by permission of the San Francisco Gay and Lesbian Historical Society.

Fenton Johnson, "Dating Again" and "Caring for Each Other," appeared as a single piece in the "About Men" column of the *New York Times Magazine* (May 9, 1993). Reprinted by permission of Fenton Johnson.

Audre Lorde, "I Am Your Sister: Black Women Organizing Across Sexualities," originally appeared in *Sister Outsider* (Firebrand Press, 1984). Reprinted by permission of Firebrand Books, Ithaca, New York.

William Macleish, "Coming Out for Love," an earlier version appeared as "About Men/The Uninvited," in the *New York Times Magazine* (November 8, 1993). Reprinted by permission of the *New York Times*.

Eric Marcus, "The Most Common Myths About Gay Men and Lesbians" and "The Most Frequently Asked Questions About Gay Men and Lesbians" are excerpted from *Is It A Choice?* (HarperCollins Publishers). An earlier version of "Greg Louganis" appeared in *Uncommon Heroes* (Fletcher Press, 1994). "Stonewall Revisited," is excerpted from a longer piece with the same name that appeared in *10 Percent* (June 1994). Reprinted with permission of Eric Marcus.

Ed Mickens, "Is There a Lavender 'Glass Ceiling'?," adapted from *The Advocate* (July 12, 1994). Reprinted by permission of Ed Mickens.

Paul Monette, "The Politics of Silence." This is an earlier version of the piece with the same name that appeared in *Last Watch of the Night* (Harcourt Brace & Co., 1994, 1993). Reprinted by permission of Harcourt Brace.

David Nava, "Why Have a Gay Pride Parade?" Copyright 1995 by David Nava. Reprinted by permission of David Nava.

Joan Nestle, "Butch-Femme Relationships," *The Encyclopedia of Homosexuality* (Garland Publications, 1990). Reprinted by permission of Garland Publications.

Niraj, "The March on Washington," excerpted from a piece that appeared in *Trikone* (July 1993). Reprinted by permission of *Trikone,* P.O. Box 21354, San Jose, CA 95151-1345.

Beryl Pears, "A Light-Hearted Look at Lesbian Novels," originally appeared in the *Lesbian Newsletter* (June 1993) in Wellington, New Zealand. Reprinted by permission of Beryl Pears and the Naiad Press.

Bob Pimentel, "The History of the Gay Rodeo," originally appeared in *Round Up: The Gay Western and Rodeo Magazine* (Spring 1993). Reprinted by permission of Bob Pimentel, International Gay Rodeo Association president.

Louise Rafkin, "Homecoming Queer" and "The Mine Field of Lesbian Fashion" originally appeared in *Queer and Pleasant Danger* (Cleis Press, 1992). Reprinted by permission of Cleis Press. "Where Do I Belong in This Parade, Anyway?" originally appeared in the *San Francisco Bay Times*. Reprinted by permission of the *San Francisco Bay Times*.

Ma Rainey, "Prove It on Me," lyrics reprinted by permission of Milestone Records.

REB, "I Was Queer When Gay Meant Happy," originally appeared in *Holy Titclamps* (Summer 1993). Reprinted by permission of Larry-bob, editor.

Colin Robinson, "You Dared Us to Dream We Were Worth Wanting Each Other," is an excerpt from a piece with the same name that appeared in *Gay Community News* (February 5, 1989). Copyright 1989 Colin Robinson. Reprinted by permission of Colin Robinson.

Andy Rose, "Yom Kippur Morning at Hehilla Community Synagogue," reprinted by permission of Andy Rose.

Catherine Saalfield, "Make DYKE TV, Not War," appeared in earlier form as "Give Me My DYKE TV," in *The Independent Film and Video Monthly* (October 1993). Reprinted by permission of Catherine Saalfield.

Mab Segrest, "Southern Reflection," is an excerpted version of a speech given by the author at the 1988 Southeastern Lesbian and Gay Conference. Another version appeared in *Memoir of a Race Traitor* by Mab Segrest (South End Press, 1994). Reprinted by permission of Mab Segrest.

Danahy Sharonrose, "Myths/Realities of Bisexuality," copyright 1989 by Danahy Sharonrose. Reprinted by permission of Danahy Sharonrose.

Terri L. Smith, "As the Twilight World Turns," originally appeared in the *LRC Community News* (September 1993). Reprinted by permission of Terri L. Smith.

Luis Torres, "Square Your Sets!" originally appeared in *Round Up: The Gay Western and Rodeo Magazine* (Spring 1993). Reprinted by permission of Luis Torres.

Vicki Torres, "Just What Is the Much Feared Gay Lifestyle?" originally appeared in the author's "Lavender Latina" column in the *Washington Blade* (January 21, 1994). Reprinted by permission of Vicki Torres.

Daniel C. Tsang, "Notes on Queer 'n' Asian Virtual Sex," originally appeared in *Amerasia Journal* (vol. 20, number 1). Reprinted by permission of the Asian American Studies Center at the University of California, Los Angeles, and Daniel C. Tsang.

Urvashi Vaid, "1993 March on Washington Speech," reprinted by permission of Urvashi Vaid.

Howard Wallace, "An Injury to One . . ." originally appeared in *Crossroads* magazine (1994). Reprinted by permission of Howard Wallace.

Eric C. Wat, "Blood, Thick and Thin," originally appeared in *Amerasia Journal* (Vol. 20, Number 1). Reprinted by permission of the Asian American Studies Center at University of California, Los Angeles, and Eric Wat.

Karen Williams, "Buy Lesbian . . . Or Bye! Lesbian" and "Festie Dyke" have appeared in a number of publications. Reprinted by permission of Karen Williams.

T. R. Witomski, "The Ins and Outs of Gay Bars," originally appeared in *Gay Life* (Doubleday, 1986). Reprinted by permission of Doubleday.

Rex Wockner, "Gay Sheep Come Out of the Closet," copyright 1989, reprinted by permission of Rex Wockner.

Kathi Wolfe, "Stonewalled? A Journal," is excerpted from *The Disability Rag and Resource* (September/October 1994). Reprinted by permission of Kathi Wolfe.

Tze-Hei Yong, "New Mexico APL," originally appeared in *The Very Inside: An Anthology of Writing by Asian and Pacific Islander Lesbian and Bisexual Women*, Sister Vision Press, 1994. Reprinted by permission of Tze-Hei Yong.

Allen Young, "Impressions of the March," excerpted from a piece with the same name in *Gay Community News* (October 27, 1979). Reprinted by permission of *Gay Community News.*

Index